Richard Martin

Dwight Martin
Garden City
June - '74

THE NEW INTERNATIONAL COMMENTARY ON
THE NEW TESTAMENT — F. F. BRUCE, *General Editor*

THE EPISTLE TO THE ROMANS

THE EPISTLE TO THE ROMANS

THE ENGLISH TEXT WITH INTRODUCTION,
EXPOSITION AND NOTES

by

JOHN MURRAY

*Professor of Systematic Theology, Westminster Theological Seminary
Philadelphia, Pennsylvania*

in two volumes

VOLUME I
Chapters 1 to 8

VOLUME II
Chapters 9 to 16

Wm. B. EERDMANS PUBLISHING CO.
GRAND RAPIDS, MICHIGAN

This one-volume edition published September **1968**

Reprinted October 1973

The Scripture text used in this commentary is that of the American Standard Version of 1901. This text is printed in full for the sake of readers who do not read Greek; the expositions are, however, based upon the Greek text.

CONTENTS

CONTENTS

EDITOR'S PREFACE

When in the early days of the development of plans for *The New International Commentary on the New Testament* Professor Murray consented to undertake the exposition of the Epistle to the Romans, the utmost encouragement was given to press forward eagerly with the entire project. And now that the present volume is about to be published, it affords me distinct pleasure to express my gratification with the finished work. If indeed full expression were to be given to my estimate of the volume, my sense of elation might easily result in the use of superlatives. A measure of restraint must be observed, however, considering especially my intimate relationships with the author over a period of nearly thirty-five years. These associations, first as a classmate in Princeton Theological Seminary and later as colleague, have led to an enthusiastic appraisal of the author as exegete and theologian as well as a warm affection for him personally.

No effort will be made here to assess in detail the scholarly character of the work, the knowledge disclosed of the problems which have emerged in the older and newer literature, the devotion of the author to the primary responsibility of expounding the text, the pervasive note of reverential devotion to the God of the Word, the elevated style which generally characterizes it. The volume must speak for itself. It will speak differently to different readers. Unless I am greatly mistaken, however, it will be recognized on all sides as a distinguished contribution to the literature on this great epistle.

Should there be a measure of disappointment that this work is confined to the first eight chapters of Romans and that a second volume on the rest of the epistle will not be immediately available, I trust that ultimately the reader will discover lasting gain in this temporary loss. Considering the intrinsic worth of this epistle and its profound significance for the understanding of Christianity, it seemed wise not to impose upon the author any rigid limitations with regard to space but rather to allow him full and free scope to deal with the text in such a way as to do the greatest possible justice to the exegetical questions. Nothing is more disconcerting to the reader of a commentary than to discover that the more thorny questions are treated in meagre fashion, if at all. Although one cannot guarantee that every reader will attach the same value as the author to the problems dealt with at considerable length, most readers, whether or not they agree with the conclusions reached, will doubtless appreciate the fullness of treatment at many points.

For those who are not otherwise familiar with the life and career of the author, a few biographical details may be of interest. Born in Scotland, John Murray received his literary education and a portion of his theological education, both undergraduate and graduate, in his native land, particularly in the Universities of Glasgow and Edinburgh. In America he studied theology in Princeton for three years, and upon graduation was awarded the Gelston-Winthrop Fellowship in Systematic Theology from that institution. His teaching career began in Princeton where he served as Instructor in Systematic Theology for one year (1929–30). Since that time he has been a member of the Faculty of Westminster Theological Seminary, serving first as Instructor and since 1937 as Professor of Systematic Theology. Besides his contributions to many journals, his major publications are *Christian Baptism* (1952), *Divorce* (1953), *Redemption, Accomplished and Applied* (1955), the Payton Lectures for 1955, *Principles of Conduct* (1957), and *The Imputation of Adam's Sin* (1959).

These lines, while written principally to introduce the volume and its author to the public, would not be complete without some reflection upon the ultimate goal of the undertaking, shared by the author with the editor, that this work may stimulate men in our times to grapple anew with the sacred text of this epistle which stands out majestically among the mountain peaks of the New Testament writings. May the devout and meticulous scholarship of the author as it finds expression in these pages contribute richly to the end that the message of the inspired apostle may come unto men "in the fulness of the blessing of Christ."

Ned B. Stonehouse
General Editor

AUTHOR'S PREFACE

In accordance with the aim of both the General Editor and the Publishers of *The New International Commentary on the New Testament* that these commentaries could be freely used by those who are not familiar with the original languages of Scripture, I have consistently refrained from the use of Greek and Hebrew terms in the text of the commentary. These have been included in the footnotes and appendixes. This practice has in many instances increased the difficulty. It is much easier for an expositor to discuss the exegesis of a particular clause, phrase, or word if the original is reproduced and the exposition proceeds on the assumption that the reader is conversant with the original text. But, when this assumption cannot be entertained, it is necessary to use other methods of acquainting the reader with the questions being discussed and considerable expansion is required. There are, however, compensations. The Editor and Publishers have shown good judgment in the design of furnishing a series of commentaries which the layman, unacquainted with the original languages, could conveniently use without the constant obstacle of being confronted with terms that are unintelligible. The Scriptures are to be translated so that "the Word of God dwelling plentifully in all, they may worship Him in an acceptable manner; and, through patience and comfort of the Scriptures, may have hope" (*The Westminster Confession of Faith*, I, viii). And commentaries, likewise, should seek to promote the interests of those who do not know the original tongues.

In terms of the policy adopted by the General Editor and Publishers of this series, the English Version reproduced in this commentary is what has commonly been known as the American Revised Version (1901). Every Version of the Scriptures places an expositor under the necessity of presenting variant renderings of particular passages. I have done this frequently in this commentary. At certain points I have taken occasion to point out the unsatisfactory renderings of the Version quoted at the head of each section. This indicates that, in my esteem, the Version concerned leaves a good deal to be desired in the matter of translation. Readers should understand, however, that no Version of the Scriptures is perfect and, no doubt, scholars will differ with me on the matter of the most accurate or appropriate renderings. Oftentimes the renderings I have given are not proposed as the most felicitous translations but as those adapted to convey the precise thought of the passage. I believe I have refrained consistently from taking undue liberties with the original text.

On the question of variant readings in the text of the original, I trust I have not posed as an authority on the highly specialised science of textual criticism. Frequently I have been indecisive and have tried to indicate what the sense would be of the respective readings. In many cases it would be presumptuous for me to be dogmatic in favour of one variant rather than another.

Every expositor has his predilections with reference to the details upon which he concentrates attention. This commentary is no exception. And this is simply to say that it reflects both the limitations and particular interests of the author. But I have attempted to set forth what I believe to have been the thought of the apostle on those questions which are central in Romans I–VIII, and I have tried to do this in a way that is oriented to the most significant contributions made by others to the exposition of this part of the epistle. The manuscript for this book had been completed and prepared for the printer before some of the most recent commentaries of the epistle to the Romans appeared or, at least, before they came to my hand. Hence I have not been able to make reference to them.

I wish to express to my esteemed colleague, Dr. Ned B. Stonehouse, the General Editor, my deep gratitude for his forbearance and encouragement and for the corrections which he supplied at several points. He is not, however, responsible to any extent for the shortcomings which this venture in the science of exposition betrays.

I gratefully acknowledge indebtedness to the following publishers for permission to quote from the copyrighted books cited: the Muhlenberg Press, Philadelphia—Anders Nygren: *Commentary on Romans* (1949); Harper & Brothers, New York—C. K. Barrett: *A Commentary on the Epistle to the Romans* (1957)—Karl Barth: *Christ and Adam* (1957); Abingdon–Cokesbury Press, New York and Nashville—*The Interpreter's Bible*, Vol. IX (1954);

B. Herder Book Co., St. Louis—Joseph Pohle, ed. Arthur Preuss: *Grace Actual and Habitual, Dogmatic Theology* VIII (1934).

It would be impossible to give adequate expression to the debt of gratitude which I owe to the unnumbered sources from which assistance and stimulus have been derived. Thought and expression are always shaped by contact with the writings of others, and it is not possible to trace the various influences which have been exerted and accord to each author the proper meed of credit. But I wish to take this occasion to express my gratitude to the authors and publishers of books in connection with which no copyright provision requires permission to quote. In the case of these, acknowledgment has been made by the appropriate identifications and citations.

To the Wm. B. Eerdmans Publishing Company for all the courtesies conferred upon me in connection with the publication of this volume I extend my warmest thanks. In this connection it is appropriate to state that the articles on "The Imputation of Adam's Sin", referred to in the footnotes and printed in four successive issues of *The Westminster Theological Journal*, are now, by the courtesy of Eerdmans, being published in book form under the title *The Imputation of Adam's Sin* and will be available in that form before the present volume comes from the press.

To Mrs. Darrell G. Harris I extend my sincere thanks for her competence in preparing the typescript.

It would be culpable beyond words to close this preface without making the acknowledgment that is supreme. The epistle to the Romans is God's Word. Its theme is the gospel of his grace, and the gospel bespeaks the marvels of his condescension and love. If we are not overwhelmed by the glory of that gospel and ushered into the holy of holies of God's presence, we have missed the grand purpose of this sacred deposit. And it is only because the God of grace has put treasure in earthen vessels that we men have been given the task and privilege of undertaking exposition. If any success has attended this effort it is only of the grace of the Holy Spirit by whose inspiration the epistle was written and by whose illumination the church has been led in the interpretation of it. Profound humility should always be ours. The excellency of the power is of God and not of us and to him alone be all praise and glory.

JOHN MURRAY

INTRODUCTION

The Author

That the apostle Paul wrote the epistle to the Romans is not a matter of dispute and for that reason, as one of the most recent commentators has said, it is "a proposition which it is unnecessary to discuss".[1] But we must not fail to appreciate the significance of Pauline authorship when we relate this fact to the contents of the epistle.

As we read the epistle we cannot escape the emphasis that falls upon the grace of God and, more specifically, upon justification by grace through faith. It was to this gospel Paul was separated (1:1). When he says "separated" he means that all bonds of interest and attachment alien to the promotion of the gospel had been rent asunder and that this gospel had made him captive. This consecration and dedication must be set against the background of what Paul had previously been. He himself testifies that "after the straitest sect of our religion I lived a Pharisee" (Acts 26:5).[2] It was his pharisaism that constrained him to think with himself that he "ought to do many things contrary to the name of Jesus of Nazareth" (Acts 26:9) and he became the arch-persecutor of the church of Christ (*cf.* Acts 26:10, 11; I Tim. 1:13). Behind this opposition was religious zeal for a way of acceptance with God that was the antithesis of grace and of justification by faith. Hence when Paul writes this greatest polemic in the exposition and defense of the gospel of grace it is as one who had known to the fullest extent in the depths of his own experience and devotion the character of that religion which now as the bondservant of Jesus Christ he must characterize as one of sin and death. Pharisaism was a religion of law. Its religious horizon was defined and circumscribed by the resources

---

[1] C. K. Barrett: *The Epistle to the Romans*, New York, 1957, p. 1.
[2] The word "Pharisees" comes from Semitic terms which convey the idea of "the separated ones". If there is any allusion to this in Paul's use of the term "separated" in Rom. 1:1, how totally different is the complexion of his separation and of the direction in which it was pointed as well as that to which he was separated.

of law and therefore by works of law. It was the spell of that religion that was decisively broken by Paul's encounter with Jesus on the road to Damascus (*cf.* Acts 9:3–6; 26:12–18). And so Paul writes: "And the commandment, which was unto life, this I found to be unto death" (Rom. 7:10); "For I through law died to law, that I might live to God" (Gal. 2:19); "From works of law no flesh will be justified" before God: "for through the law is the knowledge of sin" (Rom. 3:20). When Paul unfolds the antithesis between grace and law, faith and works, he writes of an antithesis which had been reflected in the contrast between the two periods in his own life history, periods divided by the experience of the Damascus road. And this contrast is all the more significant in his case because the zeal that marked Paul in both periods was unsurpassed in its fervour and intensity. No one knew better and perhaps none comparably the self-complacency of law-righteousness, on the one hand, and the glory of God's righteousness, on the other.

The significance of Pauline authorship is not only to be appreciated as it pertains to the central theme of the epistle—there is another conspicuous feature which must be related to the fact that Paul is the author. Readers of the epistle may sometimes wonder about the relevance of chapters IX-XI. They seem to disturb the unity and logical sequence of the argument. The intrusion of these chapters finds its explanation indeed in something far more important than the identity of Paul. But this factor must not be overlooked. Paul was a Jew. And not only so; he was a Jew who had been converted from that same perversity which at the time of Paul's writing characterized Jewry as a whole. He knew the mind of the Jew as did no other. He knew the gravity of the issues at stake in the unbelief of his kinsmen according to the flesh. He assessed the dishonour this unbelief offered to God and to his Christ. "They, being ignorant of God's righteousness, and seeking to establish their own, did not subject themselves to the righteousness of God" (Rom. 10:3). "God gave them a spirit of stupor, eyes that they should not see, and ears that they should not hear, unto this very day" (Rom. 11:8). Paul in his missionary labours had encountered much of this Jewish hostility to the gospel (*cf.* Acts 13:45–47; 14:2, 19; 17:5–9; 18:6, 12; 19:9). But this hostility and the persecution which it engendered did not quench the ardour of love for his kinsmen, a love that constrained him to utter what has scarcely a parallel in the rest of Scripture: "I could wish that I myself were anathema from Christ for my brethren's sake, my kinsmen according to the flesh" (Rom. 9:3). The extent to which the grand theme of the epistle is concerned with the characteristic sin of Jewry, a sin with which he directly charges the Jew in Rom. 2:17–29, makes it inevitable, we might say, that Paul should give expression to the burning desire of his heart for the salvation of his brethren. "My heart's desire and my supplication to God is for them, that they may be saved" (Rom. 10:1).

There is another consideration concerned with Pauline authorship that is to be noted. By way of eminence Paul was the apostle of the Gentiles (*cf.* Acts 13:47, 48; 15:12; 18:6, 7; 22:21; 26:17; Gal. 2:2, 8; Eph. 3:8; I Tim. 2:7). In this epistle we have not only express reference to this fact (11:13; *cf.* 1:13) but the writing of the epistle proceeds from the sense of commission and obligation associated with it. The apostle takes particular pains to assure the Christians at Rome that he often purposed to go there (1:11–13; 15:22–29). Prevented from fulfilling this desire he pens the epistle in pursuance of his apostolic commission. In reading the epistle we must take into account the missionary zeal and purpose by which Paul was animated as the apostle of the Gentiles, a consideration which has close bearing upon the complexion of the church at Rome and its place in that orbit which Paul regarded as preeminently the sphere of his apostolic labours.

The Occasion

When correlated with the accounts given of Paul's movements in the book of Acts there are sufficient indications given in this epistle to determine with reasonable certainty the place and time of writing. It is clear that he was on the eve of departure for Jerusalem with the contribution made in Macedonia and Achaia for the poor among the saints at Jerusalem (*cf.* Rom. 15:25–29). This would imply, to say the least, that he was near to Macedonia and Achaia. The reference to Cenchreae (Rom. 16:1), the port of Corinth, and the recommendation of Phoebe, a servant of the church there, who apparently was about to depart for Rome, are further indications of the apostle's whereabouts when he wrote the letter. Furthermore, he speaks of Gaius as his host (Rom. 16:23). In one of his letters to Corinth he speaks of

Gaius as one of those whom he baptized in Corinth (I Cor. 1:14). There is no good reason to doubt the identity of his host, when he wrote Romans, as the Gaius of Corinth.

In Acts 20:2, 3 we are informed that Paul on his third missionary journey came to Greece and spent three months there. After this he departed to go to Jerusalem and passed through Macedonia. He sailed from Philippi after the days of unleavened bread (Acts 20:6) and was hastening to be at Jerusalem on the day of Pentecost. This would mean that he had left Corinth not later than March of that year. Paul himself in his speech before Felix referred to this journey to Jerusalem and says that he came to bring alms and offerings to his nation (Acts 24:17). There is every good reason to identify this presentation of offerings with the contribution made in Macedonia and Achaia and referred to in Rom. 15:26. The evidence would indicate, therefore, that the epistle was written from Corinth or its vicinity towards the end of Paul's three months' stay in Greece at the close of his third missionary journey. The reference to the days of unleavened bread (Acts 20:6) places the departure from Philippi in late March or early April of the year concerned. This means that the epistle must have been written in the early spring of the year.

There is difference of judgment among scholars as to the precise year in which this journey to Jerusalem took place. Most recently C. K. Barrett, while admitting that "the chronology of Paul's movements cannot be settled beyond dispute", nevertheless considers that the date 55 A.D. offers fewer difficulties than any other (*op. cit.*, p. 5). And Barrett is not alone in claiming for the composition of the epistle such a comparatively early date. More common, however, is the view that the spring in question was that of 58 A.D.,[3] although W. M. Ramsay claims 57 A.D.[4] The New Testament does not mention dates and so we are dependent for calculations of this sort upon data derived from other sources respecting such events as the proconsulship of Gallio (Acts 18:12), coincident with Paul's stay in Corinth on his second missionary journey (Acts 18:1–18), and the procuratorship of Porcius Festus

---

[3] *Cf.* Theodor Zahn: *Introduction to the New Testament*, E. T., Edinburgh, 1909, Vol. I, p. 434; W. Sanday and A. C. Headlam: *The Epistle to the Romans*, New York, 1901, pp. xxxviff.; J. B. Lightfoot: *Saint Paul's Epistle to the Galatians*, London, 1905, pp. 40, 43.

[4] See his *Pauline and Other Studies*, New York, 1906, pp. 352–361

which began towards the end of Paul's captivity at Caesarea (Acts 24:27–25:12; 26:30–27:2).

The Church at Rome

It was not through Paul's own missionary activity that the church at Rome had been established. And the only reasonable inference to be drawn from Paul's own witness that he would not "build upon another man's foundation" (Rom. 15:20) is that the church there had not been founded by the labours of another apostle. How then, we may ask, did a Christian community at Rome originate? If we appreciate the strategic position of Rome in the Roman Empire and the factors which were operative in the Christian church after the day of Pentecost, the answer to the question lies at hand. One fact which must not be discounted is that there were sojourners from Rome among those who heard Peter on the day of Pentecost and witnessed its miraculous phenomena. It is hard to believe that none of these returned to Rome. We have every reason to assume that at least some, if not many, of them were converted on that occasion and returned to Rome in the faith of Jesus. Where faith is it seeks the fellowship of the saints. But even though this one consideration is sufficient of itself to explain the origin of the Christian community and of a Christian congregation, it is only one factor and we need not suppose that it was the main factor. Were we to discount it entirely, there are many other facts which point to the virtual necessity of such a development. This milieu of conditions is so well stated by Sanday and Headlam that it is enough to quote from their "Introduction". "Never in the course of previous history had there been anything like the freedom of circulation and movement which now existed in the Roman Empire. And this movement followed certain definite lines and set in certain definite directions. It was at its greatest all along the Eastern shores of the Mediterranean, and its general trend was to and from Rome. The constant coming and going of Roman officials, as one provincial governor succeeded another; the moving of troops from place to place with the sending of fresh batches of recruits and the retirement of veterans; the incessant demands of an ever-increasing trade both in necessaries and luxuries; the attraction which the huge metropolis naturally exercised on the imagination of the clever young Orientals who knew that the best openings for a career were to be sought there; a thousand motives of ambition, business, pleasure drew a constant stream from the Eastern provinces to Rome. Among the crowds there would inevitably be some Christians, and those of very varied nationality and antecedents. St. Paul himself had for the last three years been stationed at one of the greatest of the Levantine *emporia*. We may say that the three great cities at which he had spent the longest time—Antioch, Corinth, Ephesus—were just the three from which (with Alexandria) intercourse was most active. We may be sure that not a few of his own disciples would ultimately find their way to Rome. . . . That Prisca and Aquila should be at Rome is just what we might expect from one with so keen an eye for the strategy of a situation as St. Paul. When he was himself established and in full work at Ephesus with the intention of visiting Rome, it would at once occur to him what valuable work they might be doing there and what an excellent preparation they might make for his own visit, while in his immediate surroundings they were almost superfluous. So that instead of presenting any difficulty, that he should send them back to Rome where they were already known, is most natural."[5]

A question on which there is much difference of opinion is that of the complexion of the Roman church: was it preponderantly Jewish or Gentile? It scarcely needs to be shown that there were both Jews and Gentiles among those whom the apostle addresses. The direct address to the Jew in Rom. 2:17ff., the greetings conveyed, for example, to Prisca and Aquila (Rom. 16:3), of whom the latter at least was Jewish (*cf.* Acts 18:2), as well as to Andronicus, Junias, and Herodion whom Paul calls his kinsmen (Rom. 16:7, 11), the extensive treatment of questions of the deepest concern to the Jew in chapters IX-XI, not to mention other considerations bearing upon the same conclusion, are sufficient indications of the presence in the Roman church of those who were Jewish by race. That there were Gentiles is clearly shown when Paul addresses the Gentiles: "But I speak to you who are Gentiles" (Rom. 11:13; *cf.* 11:19–31). Scarcely less apparent to the same effect is Rom. 15:8–29. In this latter passage the apostle appeals to the fact that he is "a minister of Christ Jesus unto the Gentiles" as that which emboldens him

---

Op. cit., pp. xxvif.

to press upon his readers the demands of Christian love and forbearance (vss. 15, 16).

The question of the relative proportions of these two groups
the one to the other is not a matter that should be given undue
attention. We must take account of the way in which the apostle
concerns himself with the interests of both. And there is ample
evidence in the epistle of the ways in which he regarded the saving
interests of both Jews and Gentiles as mutually conditioning and
promoting one another (*cf.* especially Rom. 11:11–15, 25–28).
But the mere question of relative, numerical strength is not so
important that the interpretation of the epistle is radically affected
by the judgment we may be constrained to adopt.

No scholar who has undertaken to discuss this question is
worthy of more esteem than Theodor Zahn. He is decisive in
advocating the position that "in Rome the Gentile Christians
constituted a comparatively small minority".[6] The various arguments he advances are among the most cogent that could be
pleaded in support of this thesis. But, to the present writer, they
are not conclusive. For example, Zahn says: "It is perfectly
clear that in vii. 1–6 Paul addresses the readers as if they, like
himself, had lived under the law prior to their conversion and
new birth. No rational man could possibly say this of native
Gentiles . . . Consequently, for this reason if for no other, the
question of the nationality of the Roman Christians may be
regarded as settled, for it is equally clear that Paul is not here
addressing a part of his readers."[7] The assumption on which
this argument is based is that "under the law" refers to the
Mosaic or Old Testament economy. It is true that sometimes
the expression has that signification (*cf.* Gal. 3:23; 4:4). But
it is a fallacy that has done prejudice to the interpretation of the
Roman epistle at the hands of some of its ablest expositors to
suppose that "under law" has this restricted scope. As is shown
repeatedly in this present commentary, there is great flexibility
in Paul's use of the term "law". And the expression "under law"
cannot, on certain occasions, mean "under the Mosaic economy"
nor can its signification be limited to those who as a matter of
fact were under the Mosaic institution. This is particularly
apparent in Rom. 6:14. The "under law" of Rom. 6:14 applies

[6] *Op. cit.*, p. 422.
[7] *Op. cit.*, p. 375; *cf.* p. 421.

to all unbelievers, Jews and Gentiles. And when Paul says that "ye were put to death to the law through the body of Christ" (Rom. 7:4), he is speaking to all who have become the partakers of the virtue of Christ's death. Hence Rom. 7:1–6 cannot be pleaded in support of the thesis in question without importing an assumption which reflects erroneous exegesis of a basic datum in Paul's teaching.

Besides, when Paul says in Rom. 7:1, "I speak to them who know the law", we may not assume that this could be applied only to Jewish converts. It is true as Zahn says that "Paul does not make a distinction between those of his readers who know the law and those who do not".[8] But that these were Jewish readers and that the Roman church was therefore preponderantly Jewish is not to be inferred from this fact. Gentile Christians could likewise be credited with the knowledge of the law and more particularly of the specific ordinance to which the apostle here refers. Gentiles, when they became Christians, soon became acquainted with the Old Testament Scriptures and we may not forget that "a large proportion even of the Gentile Christians would have approached Christianity through the portals of a previous connexion with Judaism".[9] There need be little doubt that the Galatian churches were preponderantly Gentile.[10] Yet the apostle makes frequent appeal to the Old Testament in his letter to the Galatians and he surely presupposes familiarity with Old Testament history on their part.

It is true, as Zahn points out, that the term "nations"[11] is sometimes used in an inclusive sense to include both Jews and Gentiles. This is surely true in several passages in the Gospels (cf. Matt. 25:32; 28:19; Mark 11:17; Luke 24:47). It is not unreasonable to suppose that this inclusive sense appears in Rom. 1:5, 13; 15:18; 16:26. But since this term is used so frequently in this epistle of the Gentiles as distinguished from the Jews (Rom. 2:14, 24; 3:29; 9:24, 30; 11:11, 13, 25; 15:9, 10, 11, 12, 16, 27), as also in Paul's other epistles, there is a great deal to be said in favour of the view that "nations" throughout the epistle is to be understood as referring to the Gentiles. It is not

---

[8] *Op. cit.*, p. 375.
[9] Sanday and Headlam: *op. cit.*, p. xxxiv.
[10] *Cf.* Lightfoot: *op. cit.*, p. 26; Zahn: *op. cit.*, p. 421; *cf.* pp. 173–202.
[11] The term referred to is the plural ἔθνη.

to be taken for granted that the quotation from Gen. 17:5 in Rom. 4:17, 18, namely, "a father of many nations", is to be understood as including the Jewish nation as well as the Gentile nations. The promise to Abraham, as appealed to by Paul, may well be understood in the sense that the fatherhood of Abraham was to extend far beyond those of whom he was father according to the flesh. So even this passage cannot be enlisted as a clear instance of the inclusive sense of the term "nations" (*cf.* Gal. 3:8, 9). In Rom. 16:4 it is more natural to render the relevant expression as "all the churches of the Gentiles" rather than as "all the churches of the nations", "nations" being understood inclusively.

The situation in respect of usage is that in the epistles of Paul the term in question is used frequently and preponderantly in the sense of Gentiles as distinct from Jews and that although in a few instances the inclusive sense is possible and reasonable yet there is no instance in which it clearly means all nations inclusive of Jews as well as Gentiles.[12] It is quite clear that in Rom. 11:13 he is addressing Gentiles and he does so for the reason that he is the apostle of the Gentiles. It should also be clear that in Rom. 15:9–13 he is concerned with the promises of God as they concern the Gentile nations. At verse 15 he refers to the grace that had been given him by God and he reminds his readers that this grace had been given to him to the end that he might be "a minister of Christ Jesus unto the Gentiles, ministering the gospel of God, in order that the offering up of the Gentiles might be made acceptable" (vs. 16). This repeated appeal to the grace of God as it bore upon the Gentiles and to his own apostleship and ministry as preeminently directed to the Gentiles makes it difficult to interpret the purpose expressed in Rom. 1:13 as other than that he might have some fruit at Rome "even as among the rest of the Gentiles", a rendering which implies the overall Gentile character of those whom he is addressing. The immediately preceding context makes it likewise difficult to regard the obedience referred to in Rom. 15:18 as other than the "obedience of the Gentiles". Even in Rom. 16:26, though the thought is undoubtedly the ethnic universality of the revelation of the gospel mystery, yet the accent falls upon the fact that it is made

---

[12] These conclusions are concerned simply with the plural ἔθνη. Paul does speak of his Jewish people as an ἔθνος (Acts 24:17; 26:4; 28:19).

known to the Gentile nations to the end of eliciting the obedience of faith in them.

In respect of the differentiation between Jews and Gentiles it is impossible for us to determine the relative proportions within the constituency of the church at Rome. But the evidence would indicate that however important in Paul's esteem was the Jewish segment and however jealous he was to promote the highest interests of his kinsmen in their relation to God and in the unity of their fellowship in the body of Christ, yet he conceives of the church there as to a large extent, if not mainly, an example of the grace of God manifested to the Gentiles and of that which it was his aim to establish, confirm, and promote in his capacity as apostle of the Gentiles.

Summary of Contents

Paul had not yet visited Rome. It is this fact that explains the length of that section, called above, "Introduction". He is jealous to inform the church at Rome of his earnest desire and determination to go thither (1:10–15; cf. 15:22–29). But the fact that he had not visited Rome also accounts in part for the character of the salutation. In 1:3, 4 we have a summary of the gospel and we cannot overestimate the significance of this definition—the gospel is concerned with the Son of God, Jesus Christ our Lord. In like manner the theme stated in 1:16, 17 must be duly appreciated in relation to what goes before and to what follows. It is this gospel, summarily defined in 1:3, 4, that he is determined to preach at Rome (1:15); zeal for this gospel and its fruits is the only reason for his determination. And in one way or another the theme, enunciated in 1:16, 17, comprehends all that is unfolded in the rest of the epistle.

The gospel as the power of God unto salvation is meaningless apart from sin, condemnation, misery, and death. This is why Paul proceeds forthwith to demonstrate that the whole world is guilty before God and lies under his wrath and curse (1:18–3:20). We might think that the apostle would have drawn the curtain of concealment over the squalor of iniquity and degradation depicted in 1:18–32. For indeed it is a shame to speak of these religious and ethical monstrosities. But Paul was a realist and instead of drawing the curtain of concealment he draws it aside and opens to view the degeneracy of human reprobation. We ask, why? It is upon that degradation that the righteousness of God supervenes, and the glory of the gospel is that in the gospel is made manifest a righteousness of God which meets all the exigencies of our sin at the lowest depths of iniquity and misery. In assessing the exigencies arising from our sin we should come far short of appreciating their gravity if we failed to take account of the wrath of God. The apostle prefaces his description of human depravity with the declaration, "the wrath of God is revealed from heaven against all ungodliness and unrighteousness of men who hold back the truth in unrighteousness" (1:18). To be subjected to the wrath of God is the epitome of human misery. To question the reality of wrath as an "attitude of God towards us" and construe it merely as "some process or effect in the realm of objective facts"[13] is to miss the meaning of God's holiness as

---

[13] Cf. C. H. Dodd: *The Epistle of Paul to the Romans*, London, 1934, p. 22.

he reacts against that which is the contradiction of himself. God's righteousness revealed in the gospel is the provision of his grace to meet the exigency of his wrath. And nothing discloses its glory and efficacy more than this.

The righteousness contemplated is God's righteousness. It is, therefore, a righteousness with divine quality and possessed of the efficacy and virtue which divinity implies. It is not the divine attribute of justice but it is nevertheless a righteousness with divine attributes and properties, contrasted not merely with human unrighteousness but with human righteousness. The grand theme of the early part of the epistle is justification by grace through faith. And human righteousness is the essence of the religion of this world in contradiction to the gospel of God. Only a God-righteousness can measure up to the desperateness of our need and make the gospel the power of God unto salvation.

It is this theme that is unfolded in 3:21–26. Here it is made clear that this righteousness comes through the redemption which is in Christ Jesus and the propitiation in his blood. Justification with God is that which this righteousness secures and propitiation is God's own provision to show forth his justice that he may be just and the justifier of the ungodly. This thesis is brought to its focal expression in 5:15–21 where it is set forth as the free gift of righteousness and consists in the righteous action and obedience of Christ (vss. 17, 18, 19). Grace thus reigns through righteousness unto eternal life through Jesus Christ our Lord (vs. 21).

The apostle lays sustained emphasis upon faith—the gospel is "the power of God unto salvation to every one that believes" (1:16; *cf.* vs. 17; 3:22). It is not therefore a righteousness efficient unto the salvation of all unconditionally and indiscriminately. But it is one invariably efficient wherever there is faith. We must not overlook the congruity that exists here. If it is a God-righteousness, it is also a faith-righteousness—these are mutually interdependent because of their respective natures. It is faith that places us in the proper relation to this righteousness because faith is receiving and resting—it is self-renouncing, it looks away from itself and finds its all in Christ.

This doctrine of grace might seem to give licence to sin—let us continue in sin that grace may abound (*cf.* 6:1). To the refutation of this false inference chapter VI is devoted. The falsity is exposed by the simple fact that if we died to sin we can no longer live in it (6:2). And our death to sin is guaranteed by our union with Christ in his death and resurrection (6:3–5). The strength of sin is the law and if we have been put to death to the law by the body of Christ (7:4), we have died to sin. Furthermore, by union with Christ we have come under the reign of grace and sin can no longer exercise the dominion (6:14). This is the basis and assurance of sanctification. Christ died for us—this is our justification. But if he died for us, we also died with him—this is the guarantee of sanctification.

Death to sin, deliverance from the dominion of sin, newness of life after the pattern of Jesus' resurrection, the emphases so prominent in 6:1–7:6, might appear to teach that the believer is quit of sin and made perfect in holiness. Any such misapprehension is corrected by the delineation of the conflict portrayed in 7:14–25. This conflict is nothing less than a contradiction which inheres in the believer by reason of surviving and indwelling sin. But it is not the conflict of despair. "Who shall deliver me from the body of this death? I thank God through Jesus Christ our Lord" (7:24, 25). This is the note of triumph in the hope that makes not ashamed. This note of triumphant assurance does not negate the conflict; it is the reality of the conflict that gives the triumphal note its true character as the triumph of faith and hope. It is this same assurance that is expanded in chapter VIII. If the believer is not quit of conflict with sin in himself, neither is he quit of the afflictions which encompass his pilgrimage here nor of the conflict with adversaries. Chapter VIII teems with assurance that all things work together for good to them that love God and that they are more than conquerors through him that loved them. The span of God's grace for them stretches from its fountain in election before the foundation of the world to its consummation in glory with Christ—they were predestinated to be conformed to the image of the Son and they will be glorified with Christ (8:17, 28–30).

I. SALUTATION

1:1-7

1 Paul, a servant of Jesus Christ, called *to be* an apostle, separated unto the gospel of God,

2 which he promised afore through his prophets in the holy scriptures,

3 concerning his Son, who was born of the seed of David according to the flesh,

4 who was declared *to be* the Son of God with power, according to the spirit of holiness, by the resurrection from the dead; *even* Jesus Christ our Lord,

5 through whom we received grace and apostleship, unto obedience of faith among all the nations, for his name's sake;

6 among whom are ye also, called *to be* Jesus Christ's:

7 to all that are in Rome, beloved of God, called *to be* saints: Grace to you and peace from God our Father and the Lord Jesus Christ.

The salutation of this epistle is longer than that of any other of the Pauline epistles. The reason may reside in the fact that the apostle had not founded nor had he yet visited the church at Rome (*cf.* 1:10, 11, 13; 15:22). We may not overlook, however, the strongly polemic character of this epistle. Another salutation, that of the epistle to the Galatians, is likewise of considerable length and it is apparent that the polemic of this epistle prescribed the contents of the salutation. It is highly probable that both considerations, the fact that he was unknown by face to the church at Rome and the necessity of setting forth at the outset the subject matter of the gospel so as to set the points for the polemic that is to follow, dictated the character and contents of this salutation.

1, 2 In most of his epistles Paul begins with the appeal to his apostolic office (I Cor. 1:1; II Cor. 1:1; Gal. 1:1; Eph. 1:1; Col. 1:1; I Tim. 1:1; II Tim. 1:1). But in this instance (*cf.* Phil. 1:1; Tit. 1:1) he begins by identifying himself as "a servant

1

of Jesus Christ".[1] It is not to be supposed that his purpose in doing this was to place himself at the outset in the same category as those to whom he is writing (*cf.* I Cor. 7:22; Eph. 6:6; I Pet. 2:16). Paul was preeminently humble and called himself "less than the least of all saints" (Eph. 3:8). But the purpose of calling himself "a servant of Jesus Christ" is to avow at the outset the completeness of his commission by and commitment to Christ Jesus as Lord. He was not undertaking to write this epistle at his own charges; he is the servant of Christ. It is from the Old Testament that we are to derive the significance of this title "servant". Abraham (*cf.* Gen. 26:24; Ps. 105:6, 42), Moses (*cf.* Numb. 12:7, 8; Deut. 34:5; Josh. 1:1, 2, 7; Ps. 105:26), David (*cf.* II Sam. 7:5, 8; Isa. 37:35), Isaiah (*cf.* Isa. 20:3), the prophets (*cf.* Amos 3:7; Zech. 1:6) were the servants of the Lord. This high conception of dependence upon and commitment to the Lord the apostle here applies to his service of the Lord Jesus Christ and indicates that he has no hesitation in placing Christ Jesus in the position of "the Lord" in the Old Testament. It also shows the view of Christ credited to his Roman readers; he is commending himself to them as the servant of Christ Jesus.

Paul's identification of himself as an apostle in this salutation, as in all others except Philippians, I and II Thessalonians, and Philemon, indicates the importance which Paul attached to his apostolic office.[2] On occasion, when circumstances required it, he vigorously defended his apostleship (*cf.* I Cor. 9:1, 2; II Cor. 12:11–13; Gal. 1:1, 15–17). This consciousness of commission and authority as inherent in the apostolic office reflects the unique position occupied by the apostolate in the institution of Christ (*cf.* Matt. 16:17–19; 19:28; Luke 22:29, 30; John 16:12–14; 20:21–23; Acts 1:2–8, 15–26; Eph. 2:20). It is for this reason that *apostolic* teaching and preaching are invested with the authority of Christ and of the Holy Spirit.

There were certain qualifications indispensable for an apostle

---

[1] The reading Χριστοῦ Ἰησοῦ, though supported by B and a fourth century fragment of Rom. 1:1–7, can scarcely be adopted against the testimony in favour of the reading followed in the version.

[2] For an expanded study of the term ἀπόστολος *cf.* the article by Karl Heinrich Rengstorf in *Theologisches Wörterbuch zum Neuen Testament* ed. Kittel and the English translation of the same by J. R. Coates under the title *Apostleship* (London, 1952).

(*cf.* John 15:16, 27; Acts 1:21; 2:32; 3:15; 10:39–41; 26:16, 17; I Cor. 9:1, 2; 15:8; II Cor. 12:11–13; Gal. 1:1, 12). It is to the pivotal qualification that Paul refers in this instance when he says "called to be an apostle" (*cf.* I Cor. 1:1). Call and apostleship go together; it is by call that he became an apostle. And the call is the effectual appointment by which he was invested with the apostolic functions. It is the consciousness of authority derived from this appointment that alone explains and warrants the authority with which the apostle spoke and wrote (*cf.* I Cor. 5:4, 5; 7:8, 12, 17, 40; 14:37, 38; II Thess. 3:10, 12, 14).

"Separated unto the gospel of God" is parallel to "called to be an apostle". The separation here spoken of does not refer to the predestination of Paul to the office, as in Galatians 1:15, but to the effectual dedication that occurred in the actual call to apostleship and indicates what is entailed in the call. No language could be more eloquent of the decisive action of God and of the completeness of Paul's resulting commitment to the gospel. All bonds of interest and attachment alien or extraneous to the promotion of the gospel have been cut asunder and he is set apart by the investment of all his interests and ambitions in the cause of the gospel. It is, of course, implied that the gospel as a message is to be proclaimed and, if we were to understand the "gospel" as the actual proclamation, dedication to this proclamation would be an intelligible and worthy conception. However, the word "gospel" is not used in the sense of the act of proclaiming; it is the message proclaimed. And this is stated to be "the gospel of God" (*cf.* Mark 1:14). Perhaps the thought could be more aptly expressed in English by saying, "separated unto God's gospel". The stress falls upon the divine origin and character of the gospel. It is a message of glad tidings from God, and it never loses its divinity, for it ever continues to be God's message of salvation to lost men.

In verse 2 Paul shows his jealousy for the unity and continuity of the gospel dispensation with the Old Testament. The gospel unto which he had been separated is not a message which broke *de novo* upon the world with the appearing of Christ and the ministry of the apostles. It was that which God "promised afore through his prophets in holy scriptures". It was characteristic of the Lord himself in the days of his flesh to appeal to the Old

Testament and particularly significant in this connection is Luke 24:25–32, 44–47. The apostles followed the same pattern. In this epistle we shall find that a very considerable part of Paul's argument in support of his major thesis is drawn from the Old Testament. Here at the outset, when he is about to enunciate the subject matter of the gospel unto which he has been separated as a called apostle, he is careful to remind his readers that the revelation of the gospel has its roots in extant "holy scriptures".

When Paul says "promised afore" he does not mean to suggest that the disclosures given of old pertained exclusively to that which would be fulfilled and become effective in the fulness of time. This supposition would be inconsistent with what we shall find later on, especially in chapter 4. The gospel was efficacious for those who received it in the form of promise. Nevertheless, the promise feature of the Old Testament revelation must be fully appreciated and it is upon the distinction between promise and fulfilment that the accent falls in this instance. Extant Scriptures contained the gospel in promise; the subject matter with which the apostle is going to deal is the gospel in fulfilment of that promise.

It would not be feasible to limit the term "prophets" in this verse to those who were more restrictively and officially prophets. All who wrote of Christ are construed as prophets (*cf.* Luke 24:27; Acts 2:30). In this verse also it is probably more accurate to render the last clause as "in holy scriptures" rather than "in the holy scriptures". The quality of Scripture as "holy" is emphasized and the Scriptures are distinguished from all other writings by their character as holy. The stress also falls upon the fact that the promises exist as such only in the Scriptures. There are therefore two conclusions respecting the apostle's estimate of Scripture. (1) There was for Paul a body of writings possessed of unique quality and authority, distinguished from all other writings by their sacredness—they were truly sacrosanct. (2) He did not distinguish between the promise of which the prophets were the mediaries, on the one hand, and the holy Scriptures, on the other. It is in holy Scriptures that the promise is embodied. God gave promise of the gospel through his prophets; but it is in the Scriptures that this promise is given—the inscripturated Word is the word of promise. It ought to be apparent how here, as later on (*cf.* especially 3:2), Paul's conception of the relation which God's

4

revelatory Word sustains to Scripture differs radically from that of the dialectical theology. It is significant that Karl Barth in his *The Epistle to the Romans* passes over these statements of the apostle without assessing the conception of Holy Scripture implicit in them.

3, 4 These two verses inform us of that with which the promise had been concerned. But since that which had been promised is the gospel of God we must infer that these verses also define for us the subject matter of the gospel unto which the apostle had been separated; the gospel is concerned with the Son of God. When we read: "concerning his Son", it is necessary to determine that to which this title refers as it applies to him who is identified at the end of the passage as "Jesus Christ our Lord" (vs. 4). There are good reasons for thinking that in this instance the title refers to a relation which the Son sustains to the Father antecedently to and independently of his manifestation in the flesh. (1) Paul entertained the highest conception of Christ in his divine identity and eternal preexistence (*cf.* 9:5; Phil. 2:6; Col. 1:19; 2:9). The title "Son" he regarded as applicable to Christ in his eternal preexistence and as defining his eternal relation to the Father (8:3, 32; Gal. 4:4). (2) Since this is the first occasion in which the title is used in this epistle, we should expect the highest connotation to be attached to it. Furthermore, the connection in which the title is used is one that would demand no lower connotation than that which is apparent in 8:3, 32; the apostle is stating that with which the gospel as the theme of the epistle is concerned. (3) The most natural interpretation of verse 3 is that the title "Son" is not to be construed as one predicated of him in virtue of the process defined in the succeeding clauses but rather identifies him as the person who became the subject of this process and is therefore identified as the Son in the historical event of the incarnation. For these reasons we conclude that Jesus is here identified by that title which expresses his eternal relation to the Father and that when the subject matter of the gospel is defined as that which pertains to the eternal Son of God the apostle at the threshold of the epistle is commending the gospel by showing that it is concerned with him who has no lower station than that of equality with the Father. The subject matter of the gospel is the person who is on the highest plane of reality. Paul had already indicated his unreserved

5

dedication to the service of Christ Jesus (vs. 1) and to the apostolic office. In this title "Son" is the explanation why this service demands nothing less than unreserved dedication to the gospel; it is not only God's gospel but its subject matter is God's eternal Son.

The clauses which follow obviously comprise a series of parallels and contrasts. "Born" (vs. 3) corresponds to "declared" (vs. 4); "according to the flesh" (vs. 3) corresponds to "according to the Spirit of holiness" (vs. 4); "of the seed of David" (vs. 3) appears to correspond to "by the resurrection from the dead" (vs. 4.) While the correspondences, parallels, and implied contrasts cannot be overlooked, yet we may also lay overstress upon them so as to reach an artificial result.

In the history of interpretation this parallelism has been most frequently interpreted as referring to the differing aspects of or elements in the constitution of the person of the Saviour. Sometimes the distinguished aspects have been thought to be within the human nature of Christ, the physical contrasted with the spiritual.[3] By others the distinguished aspects have been regarded as the two distinct natures in the person of Christ, the human and the divine, "flesh" designating the former and "Son of God . . . according to the Spirit of holiness" the latter.[4] It cannot, of

---

[3] *Cf.* Heinrich A. W. Meyer: *Über den Brief des Paulus an die Römer* (Göttingen, 1872) *ad* Rom. 1:4. "This πνεῦμα ἅγιωσ. is, in contradistinction to the σάρξ, the other side of the being of the Son of God on earth; and, just as the σάρξ was the outward element perceptible by the senses, so is the πνεῦμα the inward mental element, the substratum of His νοῦς (1 Cor. ii. 16), *the principle and power of His* INNER life, the intellectual and moral 'Ego' which receives the communication of the divine—in short, the ἔσω ἄνθρωπος of Christ" (E. T., Edinburgh, 1876, I, p. 46). See also William Sanday and Arthur C. Headlam: *A Critical and Exegetical Commentary on the Epistle to the Romans* (New York, 1926) *ad* Rom. 1:3, 4: "κατὰ σάρκα . . . κατὰ πνεῦμα are opposed to each other, not as 'human' to 'divine,' but as 'body' to 'spirit,' both of which in Christ arhuman, though the Holiness which is the abiding property of His Spirit is something more than human" (p. 7).

[4] *Cf.* John Calvin: *Commentaries on the Epistle of Paul the Apostle to the Romans* (E. T., Grand Rapids, 1947) *ad* Rom. 1:3: "Two things must be found in Christ, in order that we may obtain salvation in him, even divinity and humane ity. . . . Hence the Apostle had expressly mentioned both in the summary he gives of the gospel, that Christ was manifested in the flesh—and that in it he declared himself to be the Son of God" (p. 44). See also J. A. Bengel: *Gnomon of the New Testament, ad* Rom. 1:4; Charles Hodge: *Commentary on the Epistle to the Romans* (Edinburgh, 1864), *ad* Rom. 1:3, 4; F. A. Philippi: *Commentary on St. Paul's Epistle to the Romans* (E. T., Edinburgh, 1878), *ad* Rom. 1:3, 4; Robert Haldane: *Exposition of the Epistle to the Romans* (Edinburgh, 1874), *ad* Rom. 1:4.

course, be doubted that "born of the seed of David according to the flesh" has reference to the incarnation of the Son of God and therefore to that which he became in respect of his human nature. But it is not at all apparent that the other expression "Son of God . . . according to the Spirit of holiness" has in view simply the other aspect of our Lord's person, namely, that which he is as divine in contrast with the human. There are good reasons for thinking that this type of interpretation whereby it is thought that reference is made to the distinguished aspects of our Lord's human nature or of our Lord's divine-human person is not the line to be followed but that the distinction drawn is that between "two successive stages" of the historical process of which the Son of God became the subject.[5] This view is in thorough agreement with the apostle's purpose in defining the subject matter of the gospel. The reasons for adopting this interpretation will become apparent as we proceed with the exposition.

(1) "Born of the seed of David." Whether we render thus or, more literally, "made of the seed of David" (*cf.* also Gal. 4:4), the clause points to an historical beginning. The subject of this beginning, it should be carefully noted, is the person who had just been identified in his divine and eternal preexistence as the Son of God; it is the Son of God, viewed in his intradivine identity as the Son, who is said to have been born of the seed of David.

---

[5] I am indebted to Geerhardus Vos for opening up this perspective in the interpretation of the passage. See his "The Eschatological Aspect of the Pauline Conception of the Spirit" in *Biblical and Theological Studies* (New York, 1912), pp. 228–230. His words are: "The reference is not to two coexisting sides in the constitution of the Saviour, but to two successive stages in his life: there was first a γενέσθαι κατὰ σάρκα, then a ὁρισθῆναι κατὰ πνεῦμα. The two prepositional phrases have adverbial force: they describe the mode of the process, yet so as to throw emphasis rather on the result than on the initial act: Christ came into being as to his sarkic existence, and he was introduced by ὁρισμός into his pneumatic existence. The ὁρίζειν is not an abstract determination, but an effectual appointment; Paul obviously avoids the repetition of γενομένου not for rhetorical reasons only, but because it might have suggested, even before the reading of the whole sentence could correct it, the misunderstanding that at the resurrection the divine sonship of Christ *as such* first originated, whereas the Apostle merely meant to affirm this late temporal origin of the divine sonship ἐν δυνάμει, the sonship as such reaching back into the state of preexistence. By the twofold κατά the mode of each state of existence is contrasted, by the twofold ἐκ the origin of each. Thus the existence κατὰ σάρκα originated 'from the seed of David', the existence κατὰ πνεῦμα originated 'out of resurrection from the dead'" (p. 229). This exegesis of Rom. 1:3, 4 is reproduced in Vos's *The Pauline Eschatology* (Princeton, 1930), pp. 155f. n.

Hence, even in verse 3, the Saviour is not viewed merely as human, though it is the assumption of human nature that is reflected on when he is said to have been born. Jealousy for the eternal sonship of Christ does not eclipse the apostle's jealousy for the historical beginning of which the Son was the subject, and neither does the emphasis upon the historical in any way prejudice the reality of the eternal sonship. Here we have unmistakable emphasis upon the coexisting aspects of our Lord's person as the incarnate Son, and of particular significance is the fact that this emphasis is already clearly enunciated in verse 3 before ever we come to the contrast expressed in verse 4.[6]

In specifying "the seed of David" there is indicated the added interest of establishing our Lord's genealogy from David. The apostle had a view to Old Testament prophecy and to its vindication in the fulfilment of its promises.

(2) "According to the flesh." In the usage of the New Testament, when applied to Christ, the denotation cannot be other than human nature in its entirety (*cf.* John 1:14: Rom. 9:5; Eph. 2:14; I Tim. 3:16; Heb. 5:7; 10:20; I Pet. 3:18; 4:1; I John 4:1; II John 7).[7] There may be particular emphasis upon the physical and sensuous, as is apparent in some of these instances cited. But it is not possible in the light of the evidence provided by such usage to regard a contrast as instituted between what was physical and what was non-physical. Hence the thought reflected upon in verse 3 is that which the Son of God became in

---

[6] There is no warrant for C. H. Dodd's allegations to the effect that the theology enunciated in verses 3 and 4 "is scarcely a statement of Paul's own theology. He held that Christ was the Son of God from all eternity, that He was 'in the fulness of time' incarnate as a man, and that by His resurrection He was invested with the full power and glory of His divine status as Lord of all. ... The present statement therefore falls short of what Paul would regard as an adequate doctrine of the Person of Christ. It recalls the primitive preaching of the Church as it is put into the mouth of Peter in Acts ii. 22–34" (*The Epistle of Paul to the Romans*, London, 1934, pp 4f.). It is quite apparent that in this passage the highest Christology is present, as also due recognition of the significance of the resurrection in the process of redemptive accomplishment, a significance likewise recognized by Peter in his Pentecost sermon, the statement of which in Acts 2:33–36 is closely akin to and elucidatory of Rom. 1:4.

[7] In this respect I am compelled to reject the interpretation of those who find in κατὰ σάρκα a reference simply to the bodily aspect of our Lord's human nature and I agree with those who regard it as designating human nature in its completeness, though I diverge from these same interpreters when they maintain that κατὰ πνεῦμα ἁγιωσύνης refers to our Lord's divine nature as contrasted with the human.

8

respect of human nature—he was born of the seed of David.
(3) "Who was declared to be the Son of God with power."
The word rendered "declared" is the word which elsewhere in
the New Testament means to "determine", "appoint", "ordain"
(Luke 22:22; Acts 2:23; 10:42; 11:29; 17:26, 31; Heb.
4:7). In none of these instances does it mean to "declare". It might
be possible to derive the meaning "declare" from its use in the
sense of "mark out" or "mark out the boundaries". In this way
Christ could be said to be marked out as the Son of God.[8] But
this process of thought by which to arrive at the meaning "declared" is unnecessary and has little to commend it. There is neither need nor warrant to resort to any other rendering than that
provided by the other New Testament instances, namely, that
Jesus was "appointed" or "constituted" Son of God with power
and points therefore to an investiture which had an historical
beginning parallel to the historical beginning mentioned in
verse 3. It might appear that this encounters an insuperable
objection; Jesus was not *appointed* Son of God; as we found, he is
conceived to be the *eternal* Son, and this sonship had no historical
beginning. But this objection has validity only as we overlook
the force of the expression "with power".[9] The apostle does not

---

[8] Frequently in the LXX ὅρια means boundaries or borders and the same
use appears in the New Testament (*cf.* Matt. 2:16; 4:13; 8:34; 15:22, 39;
19:1; Mark 5:17; 7:24, 31; 10:1; Acts 13:50). ὁρίζω is used in the LXX
in the sense of marking out or defining the boundaries (*cf.* Numb. 34:6;
Joshua 13:27; 15:12; 18:20; 23:4).
[9] Notwithstanding the weight of exegetical opinion in favour of construing
ἐν δυνάμει with ὁρισθέντος rather than with υἱοῦ Θεοῦ (*cf.*, e.g., Meyer, Sanday
and Headlam, Henry Alford, F. Godet), there appears to be no compelling
reason for this construction. II Cor. 13:4, appealed to by Sanday and Headlam
as decisive, does not present a close enough parallel to determine the question.
Since ἐν δυνάμει stands so closely with υἱοῦ Θεοῦ and since the construction
adopted fits admirably with the exegesis as a whole, there is no good reason
for adopting the other view (*cf.*, for support, Philippi: *op. cit.*, *ad loc.*; Vos:
op. cit.; J. Gresham Machen: *The Virgin Birth of Christ*, New York, 1930, p. 261;
R. C. H. Lenski: *The Interpretation of St. Paul's Epistle to the Romans*, Columbus,
1936, *ad loc.*; J. P. Lange: *The Epistle of Paul to the Romans*, E. T., New York,
1915, *ad loc.*; and, most recently, C. K. Barrett: *A Commentary on the Epistle to
the Romans*, New York, 1957, *ad loc.*). It must be said, however, that even if
construed with ὁρισθέντος this does not rule out the interpretation given above
of the verse as a whole. For, in that event, the emphasis would fall upon the
power exercised in Jesus' instatement in this new phase of his lordship rather
than upon the power possessed and exercised by Jesus as the Son of God in
his resurrection status and glory. To emphasize the power exercised and demonstrated in the resurrection and in the investiture which followed is likewise

say that Jesus was appointed "Son of God" but "Son of God in power". This addition makes all the difference. Furthermore, we may not forget that already in verse 3 the Son of God is now viewed not simply as the eternal Son but as the eternal Son incarnate, the eternal Son subject to the historical conditions introduced by his being born of the seed of David. Hence the action with which verse 4 is concerned is one that has respect to the Son of God incarnate, and it is not only proper but altogether reasonable to regard it as another phase of the historical process which provides the subject matter of the gospel. The apostle is dealing with some particular event in the history of the Son of God incarnate by which he was *instated* in a position of sovereignty and invested with power, an event which in respect of investiture with power surpassed everything that could previously be ascribed to him in his incarnate state. What this event was and in what the investiture consisted will forthwith appear. And even if we associate the expression "in power" with the verb "appointed" rather than with the title "Son of God", this does not raise an insuperable obstacle to the interpretation in question. The apostle could still say that he was appointed Son of God with express allusion to the new phase of lordship and glory upon which Jesus as the incarnate Son entered by the resurrection without in the least implying that he then began to be the Son of God. The statement would be analogous to that of Peter, that by the resurrection God made Jesus "both Lord and Christ" (Acts 2:36). Peter cannot be understood to mean that then for the first time Jesus became Lord and Christ. He is referring to the new phase of his messianic lordship.

(4) "According to the Spirit of holiness." Difficulties encompass every interpretation of this expression because it occurs nowhere else in the New Testament. Since it is parallel to "according to the flesh" in verse 3 and since the latter refers to the human nature of our Lord, it has been supposed that the term in question must have in view the divine nature. This does not follow. There are other contrasts which are relevant to the apostle's theme in these verses, and we are not shut up to this alternative. The expression "according to the Spirit of holiness" stands in the closest relation to "by the resurrection from the

consonant with that new phase upon which Jesus entered when, as the Son of God become man, he was exalted to the right hand of power.

10

dead". The latter, it must not be forgotten, concerns Christ's human nature—only in respect of his human nature was he raised from the dead. This correlation with the resurrection from the dead, moreover, provides the clearest indication of the direction in which we are to seek the meaning of the expression in question. Just as "according to the flesh" in verse 3 defines the phase which came to be through being born of the seed of David, so "according to the Spirit of holiness" characterizes the phase which came to be through the resurrection. And when we ask what that new phase was upon which the Son of God entered by his resurrection, there is copious New Testament allusion and elucidation (cf. Acts 2:36; Eph. 1:20–23; Phil. 2:9–11; I Pet. 3:21, 22). By his resurrection and ascension the Son of God incarnate entered upon a new phase of sovereignty and was endowed with new power correspondent with and unto the exercise of the mediatorial lordship which he executes as head over all things to his body, the church. It is in this same resurrection context and with allusion to Christ's resurrection endowment that the apostle says, "The last Adam was made life-giving Spirit" (I Cor. 15:45). And it is to this that he refers elsewhere when he says, "The Lord is the Spirit" (II Cor. 3:17). "Lord" in this instance, as frequently in Paul, is the Lord Christ. The only conclusion is that Christ is now by reason of the resurrection so endowed with and in control of the Holy Spirit that, without any confusion of the distinct persons, Christ is identified with the Spirit and is called "the Lord of the Spirit" (II Cor. 3:18). Thus, when we come back to the expression "according to the Spirit of holiness", our inference is that it refers to that stage of pneumatic endowment upon which Jesus entered through his resurrection. The text, furthermore, expressly relates "Son of God with power according to the Spirit of holiness" with "the resurrection from the dead" and the appointment can be none other than that which came to be by the resurrection. The thought of verse 4 would then be that the lordship in which he was instated by the resurrection is one all-pervasively conditioned by pneumatic powers. The relative weakness of his pre-resurrection state, reflected on in verse 3, is contrasted with the triumphant power exhibited in his post-resurrection lordship. What is contrasted is not a phase in which Jesus is not the Son of God and another in which he is. He is the incarnate Son of God in both states, humiliation and

11

exaltation, and to regard him as the Son of God in both states belongs to the essence of Paul's gospel as the gospel of God. But the pre-resurrection and post-resurrection states are compared and contrasted, and the contrast hinges on the investiture with power by which the latter is characterized.

The significance of historical progression in the messianic achievements of our Lord and of progressive realization of messianic investiture is hereby evinced. What signalizes this progression is the resurrection from the dead. Everything anteced-ent in the incarnate life of our Lord moves toward the resurrec-tion and everything subsequent rests upon it and is conditioned by it. This is the subject matter of the gospel of God and it is that with which prophetic promise was engaged. The apostle clinches and fixes all the points of his summation of the gospel by the combination of titles with which, at the conclusion of verse 4, he identifies the person who is himself the gospel, "Jesus Christ our Lord". Each name has its own peculiar associations and significance. "Jesus" fixes his historical identity and expresses his saviourhood. "Christ" points to his official work as the anointed. "Lord" indicates the lordship to which he is exalted at the right hand of the Father in virtue of which he exercises all authority in heaven and in earth. The historical and the official, commitment and achievement, humiliation and exaltation are all signalized in the series of titles by which the Son of God is hereby designated.

5 The mediation of Christ is something upon which the apostle will reflect again and again throughout this epistle. Here we find it for the first time. Christ is the person through whom the grace and apostleship received have been mediated. In using the plural "we received" it is not likely that he is referring to other apostles as well as to himself. Still less may we suppose that he is including other companions in labour, such as Timothy and Silvanus (cf. Phil. 1:1; I Thess. 1:1; II Thess. 1:1). These could not have been regarded as having received apostleship. The plural "we" could have been used as the "plural of category"[10] when the apostle refers simply to himself. He lays stress upon his apostleship to the Gentiles in this context, and this singularity

---

[10] The expression is that of F. Godet: *Commentary on St. Paul's Epistle to the Romans* (E. T., Edinburgh, 1880), *ad loc.*

would appear to be required at this point. "Grace and apostleship" could mean the grace of apostleship. It is more likely, however, that "grace" is here the more general unmerited favour of God. The apostle was never forgetful of the grace and mercy by which he had been saved and called into the fellowship of Christ (*cf.* I Cor. 15:10; Gal. 1:15; I Tim. 1:13-16; II Tim. 1:9; Tit. 3:5-7). The grace exemplified in salvation was not, however, in Paul's case to be conceived of apart from the apostolic office to which he had been separated. They were not separated in Paul's conversion experience on the road to Damascus (*cf.* Acts 26:12-18), a fact reflected on in his epistles (*cf.* 15:15, 16; Gal. 1:15, 16; I Tim. 1:12-16). This is an adequate reason why both the generic and the specific should be so closely conjoined in this instance (*cf.* I Cor. 15:10).[11]

The purpose for which he received grace and apostleship is stated to be "unto obedience of faith among all the nations". "Obedience of faith" could mean "obedience to faith" (*cf.* Acts 6:7; II Cor. 10:5; I Pet. 1:22). If "faith" were understood in the objective sense of the object or content of faith, the truth believed, this would provide an admirably suitable interpretation and would be equivalent to saying "obedience to the gospel" (*cf.* 10:16; II Thess. 1:8; 3:14). But it is difficult to suppose that "faith" is used here in the sense of the truth of the gospel. It is rather the subjective act of faith in response to the gospel. And though it is not impossible to think of obedience to faith as the commitment of oneself to what is involved in the act of faith, yet it is much more intelligible and suitable to take "faith" as in apposition to "obedience" and understand it as the obedience which consists in faith. Faith is regarded as an act of obedience, of commitment to the gospel of Christ. Hence the implications

---

[11] There are several expositors including, for example, Calvin and Philippi who regard "grace" in this instance as the grace of apostleship and therefore as more specific. It is true that χάρις is quite frequently used by the apostle in the sense of a particular gift, the grace given for the exercise of a particular function or office (*cf.* 12:6; I Cor. 3:10; II Cor. 1:15; 8:6, 7, 19; Gal. 2:9; Eph. 3:8; 4:7; see also I Cor. 16:3 and possibly Rom. 15:15; II Cor. 8:1). The closest parallel in construction to "grace and apostleship" here would be II Cor. 8:4 where Paul speaks of "the grace and the fellowship of the ministry which is unto the saints". Even though "grace" here is to be taken most likely, if not certainly, in the specific sense, yet it is to be distinguished from "the fellowship" and may not suitably be construed as the grace of the fellowship in ministering to the saints.

of this expression "obedience of faith" are far-reaching. For the faith which the apostleship was intended to promote was not an evanescent act of emotion but the commitment of wholehearted devotion to Christ and to the truth of his gospel. It is to such faith that all nations are called.

Whether "all the nations" is to be understood as comprising Jews and Gentiles or, more restrictively, only the Gentile nations is a question on which it is impossible to be decisive. The same difficulty appears in 16:26 and perhaps also in 15:18. Most frequently in Paul's letters "nations" is used of the Gentiles as distinguished from the Jews (cf. 2:14, 24; 3:29; 9:24, 30; 11:11; 11:25; 15:9, 10, 11, 12, 16, 27; I Cor. 1:23; 5:1). Paul is thinking here of his own apostleship and since he is the apostle of the Gentiles and glories in that fact (11:13; cf. Acts 26:17, 18; Gal. 1:16; 2:7-9) there is much more to be said in favour of the view that here the Gentile nations are in view. As the apostle of the Gentiles his office is directed specifically to the promotion of the faith of the gospel among the Gentile nations (cf. 1:13).

"For his name's sake." This should preferably be taken with the design stated in the preceding words—it is for Christ's sake that the obedience of faith is to be promoted. It is well to note the orientation provided by this addition. It is not the advantage of the nations that is paramount in the promotion of the gospel but the honour and glory of Christ. And the ambassador of Christ must have his own design in promoting the gospel oriented to this paramount concern—his subjective design must reflect God's own antecedent and objective design.

6 The believers at Rome were examples of the fruit accruing from the promotion of the gospel—"among whom are ye also the called of Jesus Christ". The use of the word "called" in this connection is significant. Paul had previously drawn attention to the fact that it was by divine call that he had been invested with the apostolic office (vs. 1). Now we are advised that it was by the same kind of action that the believers at Rome were constituted the disciples of Christ. It is not probable that "called of Jesus Christ" indicates that Jesus Christ is conceived of as the author of the call. For uniformly God the Father is represented as the author (cf. 8:30; 11:29; I Cor. 1:9; II Tim. 1:9). They are the called of Jesus Christ in the sense of belonging to Christ

14

inasmuch as they are called by the Father into the fellowship of his Son (I Cor. 1:9).

7 In verse 5, as has been noted, the apostle had in mind the promotion of the faith of the gospel among the Gentiles. In his salutation to the believers at Rome,[12] however, he allows for no racial discrimination—all at Rome, whether Jews or Gentiles, are included. The particularization is defined not in terms of race but in terms of the differentiation which arises from God's grace. Those addressed are "beloved of God, called to be saints". In this instance he does not speak expressly of the *church* in Rome (*cf. contra* I Cor. 1:2; II Cor. 1:1; Gal. 1:2; I Thess. 1:1; II Thess. 1:1). This does not mean that in Paul's esteem there was no *church* at Rome (*cf.* 12:5; 16:5); the omission of the term is merely a variation that appears in other epistles (*cf.* Eph. 1:1; Phil. 1:1; Col. 1:2). The characterization "beloved of God" Paul uses nowhere else in his salutations and only here does it occur in this precise form in the New Testament, though to the same effect is the form in Col. 3:12; I Thess. 1:4; II Thess. 2:13. The term "beloved" is a favourite one with the apostle to express the love that binds him to his brethren (*cf.* 12:19; 16:5, 8, 9, 12; I Cor. 4:14; II Cor. 7:1; II Tim. 1:2). "Beloved of God" points to the intimacy and tenderness of the love of God the Father, the embrace of his people in the bosom of his affection. It is the consciousness of this bond that binds the apostle to the saints at Rome. "Called to be saints" or "called as saints" places the emphasis upon the effectual character of the divine action by which believers became saints—it was by divine summons. They were effectually ushered into the status of saints. "Beloved of God" describes them in terms of the attitude of God to them. This is primary in the differentiation by which they are distinguished from others. "Called" describes them in terms of the determinate action of God by which his distinguishing love comes to effect. "Called *to be saints*" describes them in terms of the consecration which is the intent and effect of the effectual call. Though it is without doubt the idea of being set apart to God that is in the forefront in the word "saints", yet it is impossible to dissociate from the term the holiness of character which is the complement of such

---

[12] The evidence in support of the reading ἐν ʽΡώμῃ preponderates in favour of its retention. The same applies to vs. 15.

consecration. Believers are sanctified by the Spirit and, as will appear in the teaching of this epistle, the most characteristic feature of a believer is that he is holy in heart and manner of life.

The form of greeting adopted by the apostle is essentially Christian in character. "Grace" is, first of all, the disposition of favour on the part of God, but it would be arbitrary to exclude the concrete ways in which that disposition comes to expression in favour bestowed and enjoyed. The Pauline concept of "peace" cannot be understood except on the background of the alienation from God which sin has involved. Hence "peace" is the reconstituted favour with God based upon the reconciliation accomplished by Christ. The basic meaning is indicated in 5:1, 2. It is only as we appreciate the implications of alienation from God and the reality of the wrath which alienation evinces that we can understand the richness of the biblical notion of peace as enunciated here by the apostle. Peace means the establishment of a status of which confident and unrestrained access to the presence of God is the privilege. And peace with God cannot be dissociated from the peace of God which keeps the heart and mind in Christ Jesus (cf. Phil. 4:7). "Grace" and "peace", though necessarily distinguished, are nonetheless correlative in this salutation and sustain a close relation to each other even in respect of the concepts denoted. When taken in their mutual interdependence and relation we see the fulness of the blessing which the apostle invokes upon those addressed in his epistles (cf. I Cor. 1:3; II Cor. 1:2; Gal. 1:3; Eph. 1:2; Phil. 1:2; Col. 1:2; I Thess. 1:1; II Thess. 1:2; Tit. 1:4; Phm. 3).

"From God our Father and the Lord Jesus Christ." The following observations will indicate the rich import of this formula. (1) "God" is here the personal name of the first person of the trinity, the Father. This is characteristic of Paul's usage and will appear repeatedly throughout the epistle. This use of the title "God" must not be interpreted, however, as in any way subtracting full deity or Godhood from the other persons. "Lord" is frequently the personal name of Christ in distinction from the Father and the Spirit. But this in no way subtracts from the lordship or sovereignty of the other persons. These titles distinguish the persons from one another and as such they have great significance. But *theologically* they must not be construed as

16

predicating Godhood only of the Father or lordship only of Christ. According to Paul's own testimony Christ is "God over all blessed for ever" (9:5) and in him dwells "the fulness of Godhood" (Col. 2:9). (2) It is the Father as distinguished from the Lord Jesus Christ who is the Father of believers. This is the uniform representation of the apostle.[13] (3) The Father is not the Father of believers and of Christ conjointly. The uniqueness of Christ's sonship is jealously guarded. Christ is the Father's own Son and the distinctiveness of the relation is thereby intimated (cf. 8:3, 32). This is in accord with Jesus' own witness; never does he join with the disciples in addressing the Father as "our Father". And neither does he enjoin upon the disciples to approach the Father in the recognition of community with him in that relationship (cf. Matt. 5:45, 48; 6:9, 14; 7:11; Luke 6:36; 12:30; John 5:17, 18; 20:17). (4) The Father and the Lord Jesus Christ are conjointly the authors of the grace and peace which the apostle invokes. It is indicative of the dignity accorded to Christ that he should be represented as with the Father the source and giver of the characteristic blessings of redemption.

---

[13] For a fuller treatment of this subject, see the writer's *Redemption Accomplished and Applied* (Grand Rapids, 1955), pp. 110ff.

II. INTRODUCTION

8 First, I thank my God through Jesus Christ for you all, that your faith is proclaimed throughout the whole world.

9 For God is my witness, whom I serve in my spirit in the gospel of his Son, how unceasingly I make mention of you, always in my prayers

10 making request, if by any means now at length I may be prospered by the will of God to come unto you.

11 For I long to see you, that I may impart unto you some spiritual gift, to the end ye may be established;

12 that is, that I with you may be comforted in you, each of us by the other's faith, both yours and mine.

13 And I would not have you ignorant, brethren, that oftentimes I purposed to come unto you (and was hindered hitherto), that I might have some fruit in you also, even as in the rest of the Gentiles.

14 I am debtor both to Greeks and to Barbarians, both to the wise and to the foolish.

15 So, as much as in me is, I am ready to preach the gospel to you also that are in Rome.

In his letters to churches and individuals it is the apostle's usual pattern to pass on from salutation to thanksgiving to God for the grace bestowed upon the churches or the individuals concerned (*cf.* I Cor. 1:4; Phil. 1:3, 4; Col. 1:3; I Thess. 1:2; II Thess. 1:3; II Tim. 1:3; Phm. 4, 5). II Cor. 1:3; Eph. 1:3 are scarcely exceptions, for in these cases thanksgiving takes the form of doxology. The notable exception is Gal. 1:6 where we find "I marvel" rather than "I give thanks", and the reason is apparent.

8 In this instance the apostle draws our attention to the fact that he gives thanks "first of all". As he writes to this church which he had not yet seen, what is uppermost in his thought is the faith of the saints there. But his thanksgiving is not directed to them; it is directed to God. The faith of the saints is the evidence of God's grace and the first reaction must therefore be thanks-

18

giving to God. The form used, "I thank my God" (*cf*. Phil. 1:3; Phm. 4) brings out the strictly personal character of the relationship to God and the mutuality involved. It is as if the apostle had said, "I am his and he is mine" (*cf*. Acts 27:23). He gives thanks to God as contemplated in the intimacy of that relationship. The mediation of Christ (*cf*. vs. 5) appears in this thanksgiving. It might be that Christ is regarded simply as the one through whom the apostle is lead to give thanks[14]; he is wrought upon by Christ and Christ is therefore the causal agent of the thanksgiving. But other New Testament passages would indicate that the thanksgiving is *presented* through Christ (*cf*. Eph. 5:20; Col. 3:17; Heb. 13:15; I Pet. 2:5). Hence it is preferable to regard Jesus Christ as the mediator through whom the thanskgiving is offered to God.

It is the faith of the believers at Rome that constrains this thanksgiving—"your faith is proclaimed throughout the whole world". Undoubtedly the apostle gave thanks to God for this faith and recognized the faith they possessed as the grace of God. But it should be noted that he gives thanks *for them*, and the faith is viewed as that characteristic in virtue of which he can give thanks to God *for them*. Faith exists only in persons and has no meaning except as a relationship which persons sustain to God. The apostle betrays the intensity of his interest in persons. That he gave thanks for them *all* evinces the bond that united the apostle to *all* at Rome, even though he cannot be supposed to have known them all. The bond of Christian fellowship is not limited to the circle described by personal acquaintance. "Throughout the whole world" has been regarded as hyperbole. This is not perhaps the most felicitous way of expressing the apostle's thought. Paul did not mean, of course, that the whole world distributively, every person under heaven, had heard of the faith of the Roman believers. His terms could not be pressed into that meaning even if most literally understood. But the expression here witnesses to the extensive diffusion of the gospel throughout the known world during the apostolic age (*cf*. Col. 1:23; Acts 17:30, 31). And this passage shows that with the diffusion of the gospel went

---

[14] In Meyer's terms: "Thus Christ is the mediating *causal agent* (vermittelnde Ursächer) of the thanksgiving. To regard him as its mediating *presenter* (*Darbringer*) . . . cannot be justified from Paul's other writings, nor even by Heb. xiii. 15" (*op. cit., ad loc.*).

also the report of the faith of the believers at Rome, an evidence of the sense of fellowship existing between the various churches throughout the world and of the faithful witness borne by the Roman believers to the faith of the gospel.

9, 10 Verse 9 is confirmatory of what the apostle had asserted in verse 8 respecting his gratitude to God for the faith of the Roman believers. "For God is my witness" is a form of oath, and oath is the strongest form of asseveration. The apostle employs the oath in various forms and for various reasons (*cf.* II Cor. 1:23; 11:31; Gal. 1:20; I Thess. 2:5). This shows that oath-taking is not wrong when conducted reverently and with holy purpose. What is condemned is false and profane swearing. Why does Paul use an oath in this instance? It is for the purpose of assuring the Roman believers of his intense interest in them and concern for them and, more specifically, to certify by the most solemn kind of sanction that his failure hitherto to visit Rome was not due to any lack of desire or purpose to that effect but was due to providential interference which he later on mentions (vs. 13; 15:22–25). This shows the solicitude on Paul's part to remove all possible misunderstanding respecting the delay in visiting Rome and his concern to establish in the minds of the saints there the full assurance of the bond of affection and esteem by which he was united to them lest any contrary suspicion would interfere with the response which his apostolic epistle should receive at their hands. The appeal to God as witness is strengthened by the clause, "whom I serve in my spirit in the gospel of his Son". The depth and sincerity of his service of God is indicated by the phrase "in my spirit", and "the gospel of his Son", namely, the gospel which has God's Son as its subject matter (*cf.* vs. 3), refers to the sphere in which this service of devotion is conducted. The nature of the service as that of God in the gospel and the depth of his devotion to it, therefore, underline the seriousness of his appeal to God as the guarantor of his veracity. The truth which he enforces by appeal to God's witness is that contained in the latter part of verse 9 and in verse 10: "how unceasingly I make mention of you", *etc.* The expression "always in my prayers" could be taken with what precedes or with what follows. There are two considerations which favour the latter alternative. (1) On the former alternative there would seem to be some redundancy in using "unceasingly" and "always" with reference to the same subject. (2) If we adopt the second alternative, then "always in my prayers making request" would be an intelligible specification and explanation of what is meant by the unceasing mention made of the believers at Rome. "Unceasingly" is not to be understood in the sense of continuously constant and exclusive exercise of mind in the thing specified (*cf.* I Thess. 1:3; 2:13; II Tim. 1:3). Paul defines for us what he means by unceasing mention or, at least, he specifies one of the ways in which unceasing mention is exemplified; namely, that in his prayers he makes request to God in reference to a particular desire directly concerned with the believers at Rome.

This request is that "if by any means now at length I may be prospered by the will of God to come unto you" (vs. 10).[15] The following observations are pertinent. (1) The apostle entertained an ardent desire which he made the subject of specific request to God but concerning which he did not have certitude that it was God's decretive and providential will to fulfil. (2) The fulfilment of this desire and request had been repeatedly frustrated by the providence of God (vs. 13). (3) He did not for this reason cease to entertain the desire and make request for its fulfilment. (4) He must have been persuaded that it was consonant with the revealed will of God and, specifically, with his apostolic commission to entertain the desire and always in his prayers to make it the subject of request to God. (5) He resigns himself completely to the will of God in this matter—this is the import of "by the will of God". The emphasis rests upon the providential will of God. But it is inconceivable that he could have desired a providential ordering of the event in violation of what would have been in accord with God's preceptive good pleasure. The latter is presupposed in the desire and the request. (6) The importunity of request is not incompatible with uncertainty as to the final outcome in the ordained providence of God.

11 This verse provides the reason or explanation of the constancy of the prayer referred to in verses 9, 10. His longing desire to see the saints at Rome had in view a particular aim, namely, that he might impart to them some Spiritual gift by

---

15 Meyer has expressed the thought of εἰ πως ἤδη ποτέ by rendering "*if perhaps at length on some occasion*" (*ad loc.*).

which they might be established. Notwithstanding the confidence he entertained respecting the faith of the saints at Rome and his thanksgiving to God for the work of grace in them, the apostle here shows the extent to which his thinking and attitude had been determined by the high demands of the Christian vocation. While congratulating his readers on what have been their attainments by God's grace, yet in longing to see them he does not set his mind on congratulation but on their advancement and establishment. Phil. 3:12 expresses the sentiment that governs his thought for them as well as for himself.

A "Spiritual gift" is a gift emanating from and bestowed by the Holy Spirit. It is not so certain, however, what specific kind of gift is in view, whether a miraculous gift such as was bestowed and exercised in the apostolic churches (*cf.* I Cor. 12:9, 10, 28, 30) or a gift of grace of a more generic character (*cf.* 11:29; 15:29; 12:6–8; I Cor. 1:7; I Pet. 4:10). We are not to take for granted that the former could not be in view. Miraculous gifts were given for the confirmation and edification of the church (*cf.* I Cor. 12:9–13, 28–30; 14:3–5, 26–33; Eph. 4:11–14; Heb. 2:4). However, the indefinite character of the expression used, "some Spiritual gift", would not permit us to restrict the thought to a special or miraculous gift of the Spirit. All we can say is that the apostle longed to be the medium of conveying to the saints at Rome some gift of the Holy Spirit which would have the effect of confirmation. He does not say "that he might establish them". It would not have been unbiblical or un-Pauline for him to have said so (*cf.* Luke 22:32; Acts 18:23; I Thess. 3:2). But the reference to the Holy Spirit in this context and probably also modesty dictated the use of the passive, "to the end that ye may be established" (*cf.* 16:25; II Thess. 2:17).

12 The delicacy indicated in the passive of the preceding verse appears again more patently in verse 12. As Godet says, "Paul was too sincerely humble, and at the same time too delicate in his feelings, to allow it to be supposed that the spiritual advantage resulting from his stay among them would all be on one side".[16] And so he continues, by way of explanation or modification, "that is, that I with you may be comforted in you". The thought expressed approaches more closely to that of the preceding

---

[16] *Op. cit., ad loc.*

verse than the rendering of the version would indicate. The apostle had expressed his earnest desire for the strengthening of the saints (vs. 11). Now he indicates that he wishes to share in this strengthening and uses a term which may properly be rendered "encourage". So the thought is that he might together with them be encouraged and strengthened. The medium of this encouragement is the mutual faith of the saints and of himself. The language used is signally adapted to the thought that the same identical faith in the saints and in himself reciprocally acts and reacts to mutual strengthening and consolation [17]

13 The formula with which verse 13 begins stresses the importance of the information about to be conveyed and jealousy that believers at Rome take account of it (*cf* 11:25; I Cor. 10:1; 12:1; II Cor. 1:8; I Thess. 4:13). This information is concerned with his purpose to go to Rome. In verses 10, 11 he had expressed his earnest desire and supplication to that effect. Now he informs his readers that not only had there been the desire and prayer but also frequent purpose and that the only reason why this determination had not been carried into effect was the frustration of his plans by other circumstances or demands. This frustration of plan is alluded to again in 15:22: "Wherefore also I was hindered these many times from coming to you". But even in the latter text he does not give us any information as to the *nature* of the hindrances other than that the journey to Jerusalem (15:25-27) prevented an immediate journey to Rome. It is futile and unnecessary to speculate on the character of these hindrances. They may have been of a purely providential character and due to circumstances over which he had no control. They may have been revelatory, constraining him to action the reverse of that previously determined (*cf.* Acts 16:7). Or the hindrances may have been of both kinds. The apostle does not englighten us. The reason why he had often formed a definite purpose to go to Rome was, he tells us, "that I might have some fruit in you also, even as in the rest of the Gentiles". The humility of the apostle is again apparent in that he reflects on the fruit he was to derive from his visit to them rather than on the fruit

---

[17] "He desires to be quickened among the Romans *(ἐν ὑμῖν) at the same time with them,* and this by the faith common to both, theirs and his, which should mutually act and react in the way of the Christian sympathy that is based on specific harmony of faith" (Meyer: *op cit., ad loc.*).

they would derive from him. The idea expressed is that of gathering fruit, not that of bearing it. Underlying this figure, however, is also the progress and advantage of the saints. For if the apostle is to garner fruit it is because those at Rome were to bear fruit that would redound to their account (*cf*. Phil. 4:17). The preponderantly Gentile complexion of the church at Rome is indicated by the words, "in you also, even as in the rest of the Gentiles".

14 Verse 14 stands in close logical relation to verse 13. And since, in the latter, the stress falls upon the fruit reaped by the apostle in his ministry to the Gentiles, it might appear that the debt owing to Greeks and Barbarians, wise and foolish, is not the divine obligation under which the apostle is placed to preach the gospel to all but rather the debt of gratitude he owes to all classes for the fruit reaped among them.[18] But the term does not lend itself to the notion of indebtedness in this restricted sense. It is impossible to divorce from the term the idea of an obligation that must be met or discharged. Even in 15:27, where the idea of indebtedness arising from benefits received is certainly present, yet the emphasis rests not on the debt of gratitude but upon the *obligation* accruing from indebtedness. So in this instance (vṣ. 14), even if we are to interpret the debt in terms of the fruit which the apostle derived from his apostolic labours, yet the term "debtor" will have to be regarded as reflecting primarily upon the obligation which the apostle owes to Greeks and Barbarians, wise and foolish (*cf*. Matt. 6:12; 18:24; Luke 13:4; Rom. 8:12; Gal. 5:3). And since the stress falls upon *obligation* to be fulfilled it is more natural to take it, with the mass of commentators, as the obligation under which the apostle was placed by God to preach the gospel to all nations and classes (*cf*. I Cor. 9:16, 17). The close logical relation of verses 13 and 14 appears in this that the apostle's repeated purpose to go to Rome in order that he might garner fruit from them was in pursuance of the very terms of his apostolic commission to preach the gospel to the Gentiles without any kind of discrimination.

It is unnecessary to try to determine whether the Romans,

---

[18] So apparently Godet: "All those individuals, of whatever category, Paul regards as *his creditors*. He owes them his life, his person, in virtue of the grace bestowed on him and of the office which he has received" (*op. cit.*, *ad loc.*).

in Paul's esteem, belonged to the Greeks or to the Barbarians. It is likely that they would be classified with the wise rather than with the foolish. But even this could not be conclusively demonstrated. Since this latter distinction concerns cultural development, people of the same nationality would fall into both classifications and hence even among Romans there would be wise and unwise. The purpose of these classifications is simply that the gospel is for all without distinction of nationality or cultural development and that he as the apostle of the Gentiles is under divine obligation to preach the gospel to all.

15 Having established the fact of his obligation to preach to all, verse 15 is a statement of the necessary inference as it applies to Rome. It is not due to any reluctance to preach the gospel in Rome that he had not yet done so. To the full extent of his own desire, resolution, and purpose he is ready to do so.[19]

---

[19] How τὸ κατ᾽ ἐμὲ πρόθυμον is to be construed is a question on which expositors are divided. Some regard it as in its entirety the subject and so understand it as in effect, "my readiness is to preach the gospel to you that are at Rome also". Others regard τὸ κατ᾽ ἐμέ as the subject and πρόθυμον as the predicate. πρόθυμος can certainly be used predicatively as in Matt. 26:41; Mark 14:38. τὸ πρόθυμον could also be understood substantively (cf. LXX of III Macc. 5:26) and would mean "readiness" or "eagerness". In that event κατ᾽ ἐμέ would have possessive force and would be equivalent to "my", and so the whole phrase would mean "my readiness" (cf. this force of κατά with an accusative pronoun in Acts 17:28; 18:15; Eph. 1:15 and with Ἰουδαίους in Acts 26:3). If we adopt this view then we would have to supply in thought the verb ἐστιν and translate thus—"my readiness is to preach" etc. But τὸ κατ᾽ ἐμέ can stand by itself as subject, as τὰ κατ᾽ ἐμέ in Phil. 1:12 and the same as object of the verb in Eph. 6:21; Col. 4:7. In these instances κατ᾽ ἐμέ has still possessive force and the expression means "my affairs", "the things belonging to me". There is no reason why we should not follow the analogy of these latter instances, especially that of Phil. 1:12, and regard τὸ κατ᾽ ἐμέ as the subject and πρόθυμον as the predicate. τὸ κατ᾽ ἐμέ would then mean "that which belongs to me". The thought would be, "all that falls within my power or prerogative is ready" or "as far as I am concerned, I am ready". This is the meaning adopted by the A.V. as well as the A.S.V. as given above. Analogy as well as smoothness of construction favours it.

25

III. THEME OF THE EPISTLE

1:16, 17

16 For I am not ashamed of the gospel: for it is the power of God unto salvation to every one that believeth; to the Jew first, and also to the Greek.
17 For therein is revealed a righteousness of God from faith unto faith: as it is written, But the righteous shall live by faith.

16, 17 In the preceding verse the apostle had affirmed that to the full extent of his own resolution and purpose he was prepared to preach the gospel at Rome. In verses 16, 17 he gives the reason for this determination. We might think that the negative way of expressing his estimate of the gospel, "I am not ashamed of the gospel"[20] is scarcely consistent with the confident glorying which appears on other occasions (*cf.* 5:2, 3, 11; Gal. 6:14) or with the confidence in the efficacy of the gospel enunciated later in these same verses. But when we remember the contempt entertained for the gospel by the wise of this world (*cf.* I Cor. 1:18, 23–25) and also of the fact that Rome as the seat of world empire was the epitome of worldly power, we can discover the significance of this negative expression and the undertone of assurance which the disavowal reflects. The emotion of shame with reference to the gospel, when confronted with the pretensions of human wisdom and power, betrays unbelief in the truth of the gospel and the absence of shame is the proof of faith (*cf.* Mark 8:38; II Tim. 1:8).

There is a continuous and progressive unfolding of reasons in this text. The apostle tells us first why he is ready to preach the gospel at Rome—he is not ashamed of the gospel. Then he tells us why he is not ashamed of the gospel—it is "the power of God unto salvation". And then, finally, he tells us why it is the power of God unto salvation—therein the "righteousness of God is revealed".

---

[20] τοῦ Χριστοῦ is added to τὸ εὐαγγέλιον in D^c K L P and some other authorities. But the omission in ℵ A B C D* E G, several cursives and versions should be regarded as sufficiently weighty evidence against this reading. Moreover, it is easier to understand the addition than the omission in the course of transmission.

When we read, "it is the power of God unto salvation", the subject is undoubtedly the gospel. The gospel is the message. It is, of course, always a message proclaimed but the gospel itself is the message. We must not therefore overlook the plain import of this proposition that the message of the gospel is the power of God unto salvation; God saves through the message of the gospel (*cf.* I Cor. 1:21). And the implication is that God's power as it is operative unto salvation is through the gospel alone. It is the *gospel* that is God's power unto salvation. The message is God's word, and the word of God is living and powerful (*cf.* Heb. 4:12).

"The power of God" is the power that belongs to God and therefore the power characterized by those qualities that are specifically divine. In order to express the thought we should have to say the omnipotence of God and, consequently, the meaning is no less than this that the gospel is the omnipotence of God operative unto salvation. And "salvation" will have to be understood both negatively and positively, as salvation from sin and death unto righteousness and life. The various aspects comprised in this "salvation" are developed in the epistle.

The power of God unto salvation of which the gospel is the embodiment is not unconditionally and universally operative unto salvation. It is of this we are advised in the words "to every one that believeth". This informs us that salvation is not accomplished irrespective of faith.[21] Hence the salvation with which Paul is going to deal in this epistle has no reality, validity, or meaning apart from faith. And we are already prepared for the emphasis which is placed upon faith throughout the epistle. The concept

---

[21] The priority of effectual calling and of regeneration in the *ordo salutis* should not be allowed to prejudice this truth either in our thinking or in the preaching of the gospel. It is true that regeneration is causally prior to faith. But it is only *causally* prior and the adult person who is regenerated always exercises faith. Hence the salvation which is of the gospel is never ours apart from faith. This is true even in the case of infants, for in regeneration the germ of faith is implanted. There is order in the application of redemption, but it is order in that which constitutes an indissoluble unity comprising a variety of elements. It is salvation in its integral unity of which the apostle speaks and this is never ours without faith—we are saved by grace through faith (Eph. 2:8). The person who is *merely* regenerate is not saved, the simple reason being that there is no such person. The saved person is *also* called, justified, and adopted. It is not only pertinent to the apostle's doctrine of salvation that he should lay such emphasis upon faith but also particularly appropriate to what is the leading theme of the early part of this epistle, namely, justification. It is preeminently in connection with justification that the accent falls upon faith.

27

of salvation developed in this epistle, therefore, is *the power of God operative unto salvation through faith*. It is this salvation that is proclaimed in the gospel and the gospel as message is the embodiment of this power.

We must not discount the emphasis that the gospel is unto salvation to *every one* that believes. This is directly germane to the character of the gospel and to the meaning of faith. There is no discrimination arising from race or culture and there is no obstacle arising from the degradations of sin. Wherever there is faith, *there* the omnipotence of God is operative unto salvation. This is a law with no exceptions.

"To the Jew first, and also to the Greek." Since Paul was the apostle to the Gentiles and since the church at Rome was preponderantly Gentile (*cf.* vs. 13), it is the more significant that he should have intimated so expressly the priority of the Jew. But it was the divine economy that the gospel should have been preached first of all to the Jew (*cf.* Luke 24:49; Acts 1:4, 8; 13:46). It does not appear sufficient to regard this priority as that merely of time. In this text there is no suggestion to the effect that the priority is merely that of time. The implication appears to be rather that the power of God unto salvation through faith has primary relevance to the Jew, and the analogy of Scripture would indicate that this peculiar relevance to the Jew arises from the fact that the Jew had been chosen by God to be the recipient of the promise of the gospel and that to him were committed the oracles of God. Salvation was of the Jews (John 4:22; *cf.* Acts 2:39; Rom. 3:1, 2; 9:4, 5). The lines of preparation for the full revelation of the gospel were laid in Israel and for that reason the gospel is pre-eminently the gospel for the Jew. How totally contrary to the current attitude of Jewry that Christianity is for the Gentile but not for the Jew.

This priority that belongs to the Jew does not make the gospel less relevant to the Gentile—"and also to the Greek". The Gentile as fully as the Jew is the recipient of salvation and so, in respect of the favour enjoyed, there is no discrimination. The term "Greek" in this connection means all races other than Jews and includes the "Greeks and Barbarians" of verse 14.

In verse 17 we are given the reason why the gospel is the power of God unto salvation. And the reason is that in the gospel "is revealed a righteousness of God". It needs to be observed

28

how the concepts with which the apostle here deals are analogous to and no doubt derived from the Old Testament. Four pivotal ideas are coordinated in these verses—the power of God, salvation, revelation, and the righteousness of God. In the Old Testament we find these same ideas brought together in a way of which verses 16, 17 are plainly reminiscent. "Oh sing unto the Lord a new song; for he hath done marvellous things: his right hand, and his holy arm, hath wrought salvation for him. The Lord hath made known his salvation: his righteousness hath he openly showed in the sight of the nations" (Ps. 98:1, 2). "I will bring near my righteousness; it shall not be far off, and my salvation shall not tarry: and I will place salvation in Zion for Israel my glory" (Isa. 46:13). "My righteousness is near; my salvation is gone forth . . . my salvation shall be for ever, and my righteousness shall not be abolished . . . my righteousness shall be for ever, and my salvation from generation to generation" (Isa. 51:5–8). "My salvation is near to come, and my righteousness to be revealed" (Isa. 56:1). "For Zion's sake will I not hold my peace, and for Jerusalem's sake I will not rest, until the righteousness thereof go forth as brightness, and the salvation thereof as a lamp that burneth" (Isa. 62:1). (*Cf.* also Isa. 54:17; 61:10, 11). It is apparent that the making known of salvation and the showing forth or revelation of righteousness are parallel expressions and convey substantially the same thought. Hence in the language of the Old Testament the salvation of God and the righteousness of God in such contexts are virtually synonymous—the working of salvation and the revelation of righteousness are to the same effect. It is this same complementation that we find here. And this is why the apostle can say that the gospel is the power of God unto salvation: "for therein is revealed a righteousness of God".

In line with the force of the term "revealed" in these Old Testament passages we shall have to give to the word here (vs. 17) a dynamic meaning. When the prophet spoke of the righteousness of God as being "revealed" he meant more than that it was to be disclosed to human apprehension. He means that it was to be revealed in action and operation; the righteousness of God was to be made manifest with saving effect. So, when the apostle says, the "righteousness of God is revealed", he means that in the gospel the righteousness of God is actively and dynamically brought to bear upon man's sinful situation; it is not merely that

29

it is made known as to its character to human apprehension but that it is manifest in its saving efficacy. This is why the gospel is the power of God unto salvation—the righteousness of God is redemptively active in the sphere of human sin and ruin.

What is this "righteousness of God"? "The righteousness of God" sometimes denotes the attribute of righteousness, God's rectitude (*cf.* 3:5, 25, 26). In this instance, however (*cf.* 3:21, 22; 10:3; II Cor. 5:21; Phil. 3:9), the righteousness in view is one that is brought to bear upon us unto salvation, and it is one to which faith bears the same relation as it does to the power of God operative unto salvation. While it is true that God's attribute of justice cannot be violated in the salvation which we enjoy and while faith that is unto salvation cannot be divorced from belief in God's rectitude, yet it is not the mere attribute of justice that effects our salvation (of itself it would seal our damnation), and it is not to the mere rectitude of God that saving faith is directed. Hence the righteousness of God in this instance must be something other than the attribute of justice. Justification is the theme of this epistle, and in these two verses the apostle is giving us an introductory summary of his leading thesis. The righteousness of God is therefore the righteousness of God that is unto our justification, the righteousness which he calls later on the free gift of righteousness (5:17), the "one righteousness" (5:18), "the obedience of the one" (5:19). We must, however, inquire more closely as to the import of this designation "the righteousness of God".

Interpreters have taken it in the sense of origin, the righteousness which proceeds from God;[22] others in the sense that it is the righteousness which God approves;[23] others in the sense that it is the righteousness that avails with God and is therefore effective to the end contemplated.[24] All of these observations are in themselves true. But it is questionable if any or all of them have focused attention upon what is perhaps the most important consideration, namely, that it is a righteousness that sustains a much closer relationship to God in respect of possession and property than these other notions express. It is not the attribute of justice for the reasons given. Yet it is so intimately related to God that it is

---

[22] The genitive θεοῦ being that of origin or author; *cf.*, *e.g.*, Meyer, *ad loc.*
[23] *Cf.* Calvin, *ad loc.*
[24] *Cf.* Philippi, *ad loc.*

a righteousness of divine property and characterized by divine qualities. It is a "God-righteousness". Because it is such, God is its author; it is a righteousness that must elicit the divine approval; it is a righteousness that meets all the demands of his justice and therefore avails before God.   But the particular emphasis rests upon its divine property and is therefore contrasted not only with human unrighteousness but with human righteousness.   Man-righteousness, even though perfect and measuring up to all the demands of God's perfection, would never be adequate to the situation created by our sins.   This is the glory of the gospel; as it is God's power operative unto salvation so is it God's right-eousness supervening upon our sin and ruin.   And it is God's power operative unto salvation *because* the righteousness of God is dynamically made manifest unto our justification.   Nothing serves to point up the effectiveness, completeness, and irrevocableness of the justification which it is the apostle's purpose to establish and vindicate than this datum set forth at the outset—the right-eousness which is unto justification is one characterized by the perfection belonging to all that God is and does. It is a "God-righteousness".

The mediacy or instrumentality of faith is again brought to the forefront. "From faith unto faith" in verse 17 is to the same effect as "to every one that believeth" in verse 16.   There is much difference of opinion as to the precise intent of this formula.   It has been interpreted as referring to the advance from one degree of faith to another[25] or as equivalent to "by faith alone"[26] or as implying that the righteousness of God is by faith from beginning to end.[27]   It would appear that the clue to the interpretation is provided by Paul himself in a passage that furnishes the closest parallel, namely, 3:22 (*cf.* Gal. 3:22).[28]   There he speaks of "the righteousness of God through faith of Jesus Christ unto all who believe".   It might seem that the expression "unto all who believe" is superfluous in this instance because all that it sets

---

[25] *Cf.* Calvin, *ad loc.*
[26] *Cf.* Charles Hodge: *op cit., ad loc.:* "The sense is however perfectly clear and good, if the phrase is explained to mean, faith alone. As 'death unto death' and 'life unto life' are intensive, so 'faith unto faith' may mean, entirely of faith" (p. 32); Anders Nygren: *Commentary on Romans* (E. T., Philadelphia, 1949), pp. 78f.
[27] *Cf.* C. H. Dodd: *op. cit., ad loc.*
[28] *Cf.* Philippi, *ad loc.*

31

forth has been already stated in the expression which immediately precedes, "through faith of Jesus Christ". But the apostle must have some purpose in what seems to us repetition. And the purpose is to accent the fact that not only does the righteousness of God bear savingly upon us *through faith* but also that it bears savingly upon *every one* who believes. It is not superfluous to stress both. For the mere fact that the righteousness of God is through faith does not of itself as a proposition guarantee that faith always carries with it this effect. We found already that the apostle laid stress on this in verse 16 when he said "to *every one* that believeth". And the most reasonable view appears to be that this same emphasis is intended by the formula "from faith to faith". "From faith" points to the truth that only "by faith" are we the beneficiaries of this righteousness, and so it is a "faith-righteousness" as truly as it is a "God-righteousness". "To faith" underlines the truth that every believer is the beneficiary whatever his race or culture or the degree of his faith. Faith *always* carries with it the justifying righteousness of God.[29]

It is not unreasonable to take "from faith to faith" in construction with "a righteousness of God". For since this righteousness is operative unto salvation only through faith it can properly be designated a righteousness of faith to all who believe. It is more natural, however, to couple "from faith to faith" with the word "revealed". The dynamic force of the word "revealed" relieves this construction of an objection which might be urged against it, namely, that revelation as such is not dependent upon faith. With the dynamic import of the term "revealed" in mind, however, the thought expressed is that the righteousness of God is efficiently made known unto justification only through faith and that it is invariably operative to this end in the case of every one that believes.

The appeal to Habakkuk 2:4[30] is for the purpose of confirma-

---

[29] In more recent times the view has been presented that ἐκ πίστεως refers to God's faithfulness and εἰς πίστιν to man's faith. *Cf.* Thomas F. Torrance: "One Aspect of the Biblical Conception of Faith" in *The Expository Times*, January, 1957 (Vol. LXVIII, 4), pp. 111–114. This view is discussed in Appendix B, (pp. 363 ff.). Meyer: *op. cit., ad loc.* refers to Mehring as holding the view that εἰς πίστιν refers to the faithfulness of God and that the whole expression means faith in the faithfulness of God.

[30] For a discussion of this passage and the meaning of אמונה and πίστις *cf.* J. B. Lightfoot: *Saint Paul's Epistle to the Galatians* (London, 1905), pp. 154–158.

tion from the Old Testament.[31]   Discussion has turned on the question of the proper rendering, whether "by faith" is to be taken with the subject of the sentence or with the predicate. Are we to render the proposition, "The righteous by faith shall live"[32] or "The righteous shall live by faith"? Is the proposition to the effect that the righteous will live or to the effect of intimating how the righteous will live, namely, by faith? There are good reasons for the latter alternative. (1) Habakkuk 2:4 čannot naturally be interpreted any other way and the massoretic interpunctuation favours this view. (2) The truth being established by the apostle is that the righteousness of God is by faith—the emphasis rests upon the way in which man becomes the beneficiary of this righteousness. We should expect that the reference to "faith" in the quotation would have the same force. (3) The expression "the righteous by faith" is not one that can plead the analogy of Scripture usage.[33]

---

[31] "The apostle is so convinced of the unity which prevails between the old and new covenants, that he cannot assert one of the great truths of the gospel without quoting a passage from the Old Testament in its support" (Godet: *op. cit., ad loc.*).

[32] For a vigorous more recent defence of this construction *cf.* Anders Nygren: *op. cit.*, pp. 84ff.

[33] J. B. Lightfoot's observations in his *Notes on the Epistles of St. Paul* (London, 1895) sums up the arguments in favour of this interpretation admirably. "I cannot doubt that ἐκ πίστεως is to be taken with ζήσεται, not with ὁ δίκαιος. For (1) the original seems certainly so to intend it. . . . (2) ἐκ πίστεως here corresponds to ἐκ πίστεως in the former part of the verse, where it belongs, not to the predicate, but to the subject. It is here separated from ὁ δίκαιος as it is there separated from δικαιοσύνη. (3) ὁ δίκαιος ἐκ πίστεως is not a natural phrase, and, I think, has no parallel in St. Paul. (4) The other construction takes the emphasis off 'faith,' which the context shows to be the really emphatic word, and lays it on the verb 'live.' In Gal. iii. 11 the context is still more decisive" (pp. 250f.).

IV.
THE UNIVERSALITY OF SIN AND CONDEMNATION
(1:18—3:20)

A. THE GENTILES
(1:18–32)

1:18-23

18 For the wrath of God is revealed from heaven against
all ungodliness and unrighteousness of men, who hinder
the truth in unrighteousness;
19 because that which is known of God is manifest in them;
for God manifested it unto them.
20 For the invisible things of him since the creation of
the world are clearly seen, being perceived through
the things that are made, *even* his everlasting power
and divinity; that they may be without excuse:
21 because that, knowing God, they glorified him not as
God, neither gave thanks; but became vain in their
reasonings, and their senseless heart was darkened.
22 Professing themselves to be wise, they became fools,
23 and changed the glory of the incorruptible God for the
likeness of an image of corruptible man, and of birds,
and fourfooted beasts, and creeping things.

From 1:18 to 3:20 the theme of the apostle is the universality
of sin and condemnation. "All have sinned and come short of the
glory of God" (3:23). "There is none righteous, no, not one"
(3:10). And the consequence is that every mouth is stopped and
the whole world is made subject to the judgment of God (*cf.*
3:19). It is to the establishment of this thesis that this whole
passage is directed. The design of the apostle in establishing this
thesis appears plainly from 3:20 when he says that from works
of law no flesh will be justified in God's sight. In other words,
the design is to show that the salvation provided in the gospel is
the need of all and that the power of God is operative unto salvation only through the revelation of the righteousness of God appropriated by faith. The convergent lines of the apostle's argument all meet in a conclusive demonstration that all, both Jews

and Gentiles, are guilty before God, are utterly destitute of the good which would make them well-pleasing to God, and are therefore the subjects of his wrath. The particular section with which we are now concerned (1:18–32) deals with the sin, apostasy, and degeneration of the Gentile world.

18 The word "revealed" with which verse 18 begins in the Greek text has, for this reason, distinct emphasis. It corresponds to the same word in verse 17, but since its subject is different it is the total contrast between verse 17 and verse 18 that is thrust into prominence. "The wrath of God" stands in obvious antithesis to "the righteousness of God" in verse 17. This fact of antithesis shows unmistakably, if any confirmation were needed, that "the righteousness of God" (vs. 17) is not the attribute of justice but the righteousness provided in the gospel to meet the need of which the wrath of God is the manifestation. The justice of God being retributive in reference to sin would not be the provision for escape from wrath.

It is unnecessary, and it weakens the biblical concept of the wrath of God, to deprive it of its emotional and affective character. Wrath in God must not be conceived of in terms of the fitful passion with which anger is frequently associated in us. But to construe God's wrath as consisting simply in his purpose to punish sin or to secure the connection between sin and misery[34] is to equate wrath with its effects and virtually eliminate wrath as a movement within the mind of God. Wrath is the holy revulsion of God's being against that which is the contradiction of his holiness. The reality of God's wrath in this specific character is shown by the fact that it is "revealed from heaven against all ungodliness and unrighteousness of men". The same dynamic feature of the term "revealed", as it appears in verse 17, will have to be understood in this case also. The wrath of God is dynamically, effectively operative in the world of men and it is as proceeding from heaven, the throne of God, that it is thus

---

[34] This appears to be the conception entertained by Hodge, for example. "*The wrath of God* is his punitive justice, his determination to punish sin. . . . As anger in man leads to the infliction of evil on its object, the word is, agreeably to a principle which pervades the Scriptures, applied to the calm and unde-viating purpose of the Divine mind, which secures the connection between sin and misery, with the same general uniformity that any other law in the physical or moral government of God operates" (*op. cit., ad loc.*). To much the same effect is Calvin's comment (*op. cit., ad loc.*).

active. We must regard the penal inflictions, therefore, as due to the exercise of God's wrath upon the ungodly. There is a positive outgoing of the divine displeasure.

The contention of Philippi that the term "reveal" can refer only to "an extraordinary revelation through miraculous acts" (*ad loc.*) and therefore only to that which is supernatural has much to support it in the New Testament use of the terms "reveal" and "revelation". But to restrict the revelation of wrath spoken of to the final judgment (*cf.* 2:5) and to the extraordinary "precursory and preparatory revelations of wrath" such as the deluge, the dispersion of nations, and the division of tongues, as Philippi does, seems hardly possible. The present tense "is revealed" would seem to be parallel to the same in verse 17 and the judgments referred to in the succeeding verses, inflicted upon the Gentile nations for their sins, would require to be regarded as the penalties executed in pursuance of God's wrath. The usage of the New Testament, as Meyer points out, would likewise allow for this use of the word "reveal" (*cf.* Matt. 10:26; 16:17; Luke 2:35; II Thess. 2:3, 6, 8). In other words, these instances indicate that the term "reveal" can refer to manifestations other than those which are in the category of extraordinary and miraculous acts of God. Hence it is possible to think of God's wrath as "revealed" in respects which are not supernatural, and contextual considerations would indicate that this is necessary in this instance.

"Ungodliness" refers to perversity that is religious in character, "unrighteousness" to what is moral; the former is illustrated by idolatry, the latter by immorality. The order is, no doubt, significant. In the apostle's description of the degeneracy impiety is the precursor of immorality.

The revelation of wrath contemplated is restricted to the particular class or division of mankind with which the apostle is concerned. He is dealing, as was noted, with the Gentile nations. That restriction is intimated in verse 18 by the fact that the ungodliness and unrighteousness against which the wrath of God is revealed are specified as those "of men, who hinder the truth in unrighteousness". What is meant by this characterization? The term rendered "hinder" in the version has frequently been interpreted in the sense of "holding down" or "suppressing", and so the truth is regarded as asserting itself within the men concerned but that they hold it down or suppress it. This thought is true

enough in itself. Undoubtedly there is a witness of the truth
welling up from within which men suppress by their unrighteousness. But the version appears to have discerned the thought of
the apostle more precisely by employing the word "hinder". The
usage of the New Testament in respect of this term does not provide
any support for the notion of "holding down" or "suppressing".
Most frequently it means to "hold fast", "possess", "retain". If
this meaning is not suitable in this case[35], then the only other
meaning which the usage would warrant is that of "restraining"
or "holding back" (*cf.* II Thess. 2:6, 7 and possibly Luke 4:42;
Phm. 13). This meaning is admirably suited to the context.
For, as we shall see presently, the apostle is dealing with the truth
derived from the observable handiwork of God in the work of
creation. The notion of "holding back" is well suited to express the
reaction which men by their unrighteousness offer to the truth
thus manifested. "In unrighteousness" is instrumental and denotes
that by which this resistance of the truth takes place.

19 Verse 19 is introduced with a conjunction which specifies
a causal relation to what precedes and the question is: with what
in verse 18 is verse 19 to be taken? Does verse 19 state that on
account of which the wrath of God is revealed or does it give the
reason why it can be said that men resist the truth in unrighteousness? Contrary to much exegetical opinion the latter appears the
preferable interpretation. Verse 19 explains how it can be said
that men hinder the truth in unrighteousness; they hinder the
truth because there is a manifestation of the truth to them, and
the truth manifested to them is described as "that which is known
of God".[36] The content of this knowledge is defined in verse 20.
For the present it is stated to have been manifested *unto them* and
manifest *in them* and it is manifest *in them* because God has manifested it *unto them*. It is easy to be misled by the expression "manifest in them" into thinking that the apostle is dealing with the
same subject as he deals with later in 2:14, 15, the knowledge that
is inherent in the mind of man[37] as distinguished from the know-

---

[35] It is difficult to conceive of such a notion as that of holding fast the
truth in unrighteousness because truth is coordinate with righteousness.
Besides, the succeeding context represents the persons in view as exchanging
the truth of God for a lie (vs. 25) and refusing to have God in their knowledge
(vs. 28; *cf.* also vs. 23).

[36] Not "that which may be known", as in A.V.

[37] What has been called *notitia Dei insita* or *sensus divinitatis.*

ledge derived from revelation that is external to himself. There is no warrant for this interpretation of the terms in verse 19. It is plain that the apostle is dealing with that which God makes manifest *to men* and is known by men from the work of creation, that is to say, from his observable handiwork. And the reason why this knowledge may be said to be "manifest in them" is the simple fact that manifestation of truth to men always presupposes the mind and consciousness of man. Revelation is always to those possessed of intelligent consciousness. If it is revelation *to* us it must also be *in* us because that which makes it to us is that which is in us, namely, mind and heart.

There is a contrast instituted between "the righteousness of God is revealed" (vs. 17) and "that which is known of God" (vs. 19), a contrast as respects both mode of revelation and truth-content. The distinction is that between the manifestation that is the property of all and its corresponding effect, on the one hand, and the special revelation which is saving in its effect, on the other. Hence the holding back of the truth in unrighteousness, contemplated in this instance, does not apply to the gospel. Those in view are regarded as outside the pale of the gospel revelation and "that which is known of God" is used in a specific sense to denote the truth-content respecting God available to such.

20 The relation of verse 20 to verse 19 is well stated by E. H. Gifford: "The sentence, '*For the invisible things of him . . . are clearly seen . . .*,' is an explanation of the statement *God manifested it unto them*; and as the mode in which this manifestation *was made to them* is the mode in which it *is made* to all men, at all times, the explanation is put in the most general and abstract form (Present Tense and Passive Voice), without any limitation of time or persons . . .".[38] "The invisible things of him" are the invisible attributes specified later in the verse as "his eternal power and divinity". In characterizing them as invisible, reference is made to the fact that they are not perceived by the senses. When at the same time they are said to be "clearly seen" this is an oxymoron to indicate that what is sensuously imperceptible is nevertheless clearly apprehended in mental conception. And this sense of the term "clearly seen" is provided by the explanatory clause "being understood by the things that

---

[38] *The Epistle of St. Paul to the Romans* (London, 1886), *ad loc.*

are made"—it is the seeing of understanding, of intelligent conception. Stress is laid upon the perspicuity afforded by the things that are made in mediating to us the perception of the invisible attributes—they are "clearly seen".

"The things that are made" are obviously the created things which are observable to our senses. For this reason it appears necessary to understand the phrase "from the creation of the world" in a temporal sense, as in the version. If we were to regard it as intimating the source from which this perception of the invisible attributes is derived, there would be some tautology. "The things that are made" refer to the source from which our perception of the invisible things is derived and it is unnecessary to think of virtual repetition. Besides, "the creation of the world" does not suitably designate the visible creation, whereas, if "creation" is taken in the active sense, the temporal force is apparent and it is seen to be germane to the thought of the passage to affirm that the manifestation of God's invisible attributes has been continuously given in his visible handiwork.

"The invisible things" referred to at the beginning of the verse are now distinctly specified as God's "eternal power and divinity". It is not by any means probable that the apostle intended these terms to be a complete specification of the invisible things of God made manifest in the work of creation. The Old Testament with which the apostle was familiar had mentioned other attributes as displayed in God's visible handiwork such as his wisdom, his goodness, and even his righteousness. So the analogy of Scripture, which certainly governed Paul's thought, would demand a more extensive enumeration than he has given. But we must not fail to appreciate the significance of what the apostle does say. "Eternal power" is specific and it means that the attribute of eternity is predicated of God's power. The implication is that the eternity of God as well as the eternity of his power is in view. "Divinity" is generic as distinguished from power which is specific. This term reflects on the perfections of God and denotes, to use Meyer's words, "the totality of that which God is as a being possessed of divine attributes" (ad loc.). Hence divinity does not specify one invisible attribute but the sum of the invisible perfections which characterize God. So, after all, the statement "eternal power and divinity" is inclusive of a great many invisible attributes and reflects on the richness of the manifestation given in the visible creation of the being, majesty, and glory of God. We must not tone down the teaching of the apostle in this passage. It is a clear declaration to the effect that the visible creation as God's handiwork makes manifest the invisible perfections of God as its Creator, that from the things which are perceptible to the senses cognition of these invisible perfections is derived, and that thus a clear apprehension of God's perfections may be gained from his observable handiwork. Phenomena disclose the noumena of God's transcendent perfection and specific divinity. It is not a finite cause that the work of creation manifests but the eternal power and divinity of the Creator. This is but another way of saying that God has left the imprints of his glory upon his handiwork and this glory is manifest to all—"God manifested it unto them" (vs. 19).

The concluding clause of verse 20 may require the rendering given in the version—"that they may be without excuse", expressing purpose and not merely result. It would then be intimated that the design of God in giving so open and manifest a disclosure of his eternal power and divinity in his visible handiwork is that all men might be without excuse. If men do not glorify and worship him as God they have no excuse for their impiety, and that the *impiety* might be without excuse is the design of the manifested glory. Objection to this view fails to take account of the benignity and sufficiency of the revelation which renders men inexcusable. The giving of revelation *sufficient* to constrain men to worship and glorify the Creator and given with the design that they would be without excuse, if they failed to glorify him, cannot be unworthy of God. Besides, even if we regard the clause in question as expressing result rather than design, we cannot eliminate from the all-inclusive ordination and providence of God the design which is presupposed in the actual result. If inexcusableness is the result, it is the designed result from the aspect of decretive ordination.[39]

---

[39] The strongest argument in favour of taking the clause in question as expressing result rather than purpose is the explanatory clause at the beginning of verse 21, "because, knowing God, they glorified him not as God, neither gave thanks". This appears to give the reason why they are without excuse and can therefore be more conveniently related to result than to purpose. It does not seem decisive, however. For, as indicated above, even though the last clause in verse 20 overtly expresses purpose the thought of the result in conformity with the purpose is not suppressed and verse 21 could give the reason for the *de facto* inexcusableness without eliminating the telic force of

21   The first part of verse 21 is causally related to the last
clause in **verse** 20 and gives the reason why those concerned are
without excuse—they are without excuse "on this account that,
knowing God, they glorified him not as God, neither gave thanks".
The knowledge of God must in this context be the knowledge
derived from the manifestation given in the visible creation. It
is of this manifestation the apostle is speaking and it is this manifestation that is stated in verse 20 to leave men without excuse.
Therefore the cognitive perception elicited from the manifestation
of God's glory in the visible creation is spoken of as "knowing
God". The inexcusableness resides in the fact that being in
possession of this knowledge they did not render to God the glory
and the thanks which the knowledge they possessed ought to have
constrained. To glorify God as God is not to augment God's
glory[40] or add to it; it means simply to ascribe to God the glory
that belongs to him as God, to give to him in thought, affection,
and devotion the place that belongs to him in virtue of the perfections which the visible creation itself makes known. This
glory they failed to ascribe to him and they were destitute of that
gratitude which the knowledge possessed should have elicited and
which ought to have expressed itself in thanksgiving. Here the
apostle sets forth the origin of that degeneration and degradation
which pagan idolatry epitomizes, and we have the biblical
philosophy of false religion. "For heathenism", as Meyer says,
"is not the primeval religion, from which man might gradually
have risen to the knowledge of the true God, but is, on the contrary,
the result of a falling away from the known original revelation of
the true God in His works."[41]

Having stated that of which men were destitute, the apostle
proceeds to the positive description of their religious perversity.

---

the preceding clause. E. De Witt Burton (*Syntax of the Moods and Tenses in
New Testament Greek*, Edinburgh, 1955, § 411) maintains that εἰς with the
infinitive sometimes expresses result. Some of the instances he cites are not
conclusive, but it is difficult to find anything else than result in Heb. 11:3;
II Cor. 8:6, though Meyer contends to the contrary in connection with the
latter. For vigorous defence of the telic force of verse 20b *cf.* Meyer, *ad loc.*
and Gifford: *op. cit.*, p. 70. The instances of the telic force of εἰς with the infinitive, cited by Meyer and Gifford from the Pauline epistles, make a formidable argument in support of the telic force here. Yet we may not insist that
these instances conclusively determine the question.
[40]   See Sanday and Headlam: *op. cit.*, p. 44 for a succinct summary of the
significance of δοξάζω in its religious and biblical use.
[41]   *Op. cit., ad* 1:22.

The mind of man is never a religious vacuum; if there is the absence of the true, there is always the presence of the false—"but became vain in their reasonings, and their senseless heart was darkened". The term for "reasonings" has often an unfavourable meaning, namely, evil thoughts or imaginations.[42] This depreciatory sense very likely appears in this instance. In their evil or wicked reasonings they became destitute of any fruitful thought; reason estranged from the source of light led them into a delirium of vanity. The version may not have accurately conveyed the thought by using the word "senseless" in reference to their heart. The rendering "without understanding" is more literal and preferable.[43] The thought is that the heart as the seat of feeling, intellect, and will, already destitute of understanding, was darkened.

22, 23 These verses are a further description of this degenerate state and of the religious degradation in which it resulted. Verse 22 means not simply that they claimed to be wise when in reality they were fools but that by pretending to be wise they made themselves fools—an acute analysis of what the pretensions of those whose hearts are alienated from God really are. Verse 23 describes the religious monstrosity to which the process of degeneracy led. "They changed the glory of the incorruptible God" —this does not mean that the glory of the incorruptible God is subject to change, far less susceptible of change by men. It means simply that they *exchanged* the glory of God as the object of adoration and worship for something else. The "glory" of God is the sum of those perfections, referred to in the preceding context, as made manifest in God's visible creation (vss. 19, 20). The folly and perversity of substituting for the worship of God the worship of the likeness of created things are placed in relief by the contrast between the *glory* of God and the *likeness* of created things and between the *incorruptible* God and *corruptible* man. The monstrosity appears in the fact that not only did they worship and serve the creature rather than the Creator (vs. 25) but that for the *glory* of God they substituted "the *likeness of an image* of corruptible

---

[42] The term διαλογισμός of itself, that is to say, often refers to evil, doubtful, disputatious thought and reasoning (*cf.* especially Phil. 2:14: I Tim. 2:8 but also Luke 5:22; 24:38; Rom. 14:1; I Cor. 3:20). See διαλογισμός in *Theologisches Wörterbuch zum Neuen Testament* ed. Kittel.

[43] *Cf.* Matt. 15:16; Mark 7:18; Rom. 10:19.

man, and of birds, and four-footed beasts, and creeping things".
And the implication is clearly to the effect that they made these
likenesses the objects of worship; *these* they exchanged for the
glory of God.

24–27

> 24 Wherefore God gave them up in the lusts of their
> hearts unto uncleanness, that their bodies should be
> dishonored among themselves:
> 25 for that they exchanged the truth of God for a lie, and
> worshipped and served the creature rather than the
> Creator, who is blessed for ever.   Amen.
> 26 For this cause God gave them up unto vile passions:
> for their women changed the natural use into that
> which is against nature:
> 27 and likewise also the men, leaving the natural use of
> the woman, burned in their lust one toward another,
> men with men working unseemliness, and receiving in
> themselves that recompense of their error which was
> due.

24 In verses 21–23 we have a delineation of the apostasy of
the Gentile peoples; it is defined in religious terms and culminates
in the gross idolatry described in the latter part of verse 23. In
verse 24 the apostle deals with the divine retribution upon this
apostasy. "Wherefore" indicates that the retribution finds its
ground in the antecedent sin and is a just infliction for the sin
committed. This advises us of a principle which is invariable,
namely, that retribution is never in operation except as the
judgment of God upon sin. It is no platitude to emphasize this,
particularly in view of what we shall find presently in connection
with the specific character of the retribution involved.   The
retribution consists in giving up (*cf.* vss. 26, 28) to uncleanness.
It needs to be noted that the penalty inflicted belongs to the
moral sphere as distinguished from the *religious*—religious degeneracy is penalized by abandonment to immorality; sin in the religious realm is punished by sin in the moral sphere. It is not to be
supposed, however, that the antecedent sinfulness was exclusively
in the religious category. The phrase "in the lusts of their hearts"
describes, as Meyer says, "the moral condition in which they
were found when they were given up by God to impurity" (*ad loc.*)
and does not in this instance define that to which they were

abandoned. That to which they were given up is defined as "uncleanness" (*cf.* vss. 26, 28). But the uncleanness to which they were given up did not take its origin from the judicial act. The giving up to uncleanness presupposes the existence of the uncleanness, and the penalty consists in the fact that they were *given over* to the uncleanness which previously characterized them and is referred to as "the lusts of their hearts".

The associations of the term "uncleanness" in the usage of Paul elsewhere as well as in this context show it to be that of sexual aberration (*cf.* II Cor. 12:21; Gal. 5:19; Eph. 5:3; Col. 3:5; I Thess. 4:7). The particular form of this aberration is indicated in verse 27. The rendering of the last clause of verse 24, as given in the version, "that their bodies should be dishonored among themselves" is to be preferred to that adopted by the A.V.[44] The clause, however, need not express purpose; it may be taken as defining that in which the uncleanness consisted (*cf.* vs. 28).

The main question in this verse is that involved in the giving up. The terms "God gave them up" imply that they were consigned by God to this retribution. In assessing the character of this action some observations need to be mentioned. (1) As noted already, this consignment or giving up did not originate the moral condition—they were given up to what is conceived of as an existing condition. (2) There is undoubtedly a natural law of consequence operative in sin; it intensifies and aggravates itself when there is no restraint placed upon it. This cycle or sequence is part of sin's retribution. (3) The giving over on God's part cannot be reduced to the notion of non-interference with the natural consequences of sin. While the barely permissive or privative action of God would of itself be judicial retribution—to leave men to themselves affords a tragic prospect—yet the terms here and in verses 26 and 28 cannot be satisfied by such a construction. There is the positive infliction of handing over to that which is wholly alien to and subversive of the revealed good pleasure of God. God's displeasure is expressed in his abandonment of the persons concerned to more intensified and aggravated cultivation of the lusts of their own hearts with the result that they

---

[44] ἀτιμάζεσθαι is preferably taken as passive and the clause as a whole as defining the uncleanness (*cf.* Meyer, *ad loc.*). ἐν αὐτοῖς is the reading of ℵ B C D* *et al.;* ἐν ἑαυτοῖς that of the mass of the cursives. The sense is not changed by this variant, though the latter stresses perhaps more strongly the perversity.

reap for themselves a correspondingly greater toll of retributive vengeance.

25 Verse 25 reverts to the thought of verse 23. This virtual reiteration serves three purposes—it unfolds the character of the offence, it reaffirms the ground upon which the judicial infliction rested, and it vindicates the gravity of the infliction by emphasizing the religious perversity on account of which the penalty was imposed. The pronoun with which verse 25 is introduced can well express a causal connection and be properly rendered "for that"; it points to the kind of persons they were as those who "exchanged the truth of God for a lie", *etc.* and therefore merited the abandonment meted out to them.[45]

The expression, "the truth of God" may mean one of three things: (1) "God's truth", the truth God has made known and which belongs to him; (2) the truth that God himself is; or (3) the truth respecting God. If the clause, "and worshipped and served the creature rather than the Creator" is explanatory of the clause that precedes,[46] then "the truth of God" corresponds to "the Creator" and the worship and service of the creature corresponds to "the lie". In that event "the truth of God" would be equivalent to the true God, God in the reality of his being and glory, and the second meaning listed above could be adopted. But there does not appear to be any compelling reason to regard the two clauses as mutually explanatory. The two clauses may be coordinate and express two distinct, though closely related, ways in which the religious apostasy manifested itself. Besides, it would not be suitable, on the contrary it is rather awkward, to identify "the lie" with the worship and service of the creature. It is more acceptable to regard the first clause as pointing up the extreme iniquity of exchanging the truth which they had known for that which is the contradiction of the truth, namely, "the lie". In this way the ultimacy of the antithesis between truth and falsehood is exposed and the reason for God's judicial abandonment is made more conspicuous. "The truth of God" would then be taken in the first sense, the truth God has made known; this suits the

---

[45] οἵτινες points to the kind or class to which they belong and here emphasizes the quality by which they were characterized (*cf.* Arndt and Gingrich: *A Greek-English Lexicon of the New Testament* ad ὅστις).

[46] *Cf.*, *e.g.*, Meyer, *ad loc.*

main emphasis of the preceding context and it agrees well with the antithesis expressed in the word "lie".

The second clause may well be taken, therefore, as setting forth the way in which the exchange of the lie for the truth came to expression in the concrete acts of worship and religious devotion. "Rather than the Creator" is a proper rendering of the phrase in question. Although the Greek might be rendered "above the Creator", yet when something else is worshipped and served above the Creator, then the worship and service of the Creator is eliminated. The notion of exchange (vss. 23, 25a) applies in this case also.

The doxology with which verse 25 closes is a spontaneous outburst of adoration evoked by the mention of God as "the Creator" and in reaction against the dishonour described in the preceding clauses. Strictly speaking, this is not a doxology; it is an affirmation of the blessedness that belongs to God.. It is not a blessing of God or a thanksgiving offered to him (cf. Luke 1:68; II Cor. 1:3; Eph. 1:3; I Pet. 1:3). It is an affirmation to the effect that transcendent blessedness belongs to God and the implication is that the dishonour done by men does not detract from this intrinsic and unchangeable blessedness—God is blessed for ever. By adding "Amen" the apostle voices the assent of his heart and mind to the glory which the preceding formula attributes to God. The "Amen" is the response of worship.

26 Once again the apostle states the reason for which God delivered up the Gentile nations to this judicial infliction. The "wherefore" of verse 24, the "for that" of verse 25, and the "for this cause" of verse 26 are in this respect all to the same effect; the abandonment is the infliction for religious apostasy. In verse 26, however, the nature of the abandonment is described more intensively—"God gave them up unto vile passions", literally "unto passions of dishonour",[47] emphasizing their disgraceful character. What these disgraceful passions were are now no longer undefined—"for their women[48] changed the natural use into that which is against nature". Here we are for the first time

---

[47] ἀτιμίας is the genitive of quality or characterization.

[48] The apostle uses θήλειαι, not γυναῖκες, as also ἄρσενες, not ἄνδρες. He uses the terms "females" and "males", no doubt, because the emphasis falls upon the matter of sex—"the simple physical allusion to sex comes exclusively into view" (Philippi, ad loc.).

informed of the specific type of vice which the apostle had in
mind when he referred to "uncleanness, that their bodies should
be dishonored among themselves" (vs. 24) and to "passions of
dishonour" (vs. 26a). At least, he defines what he had in mind
as the most aggravated forms of uncleanness and vile passion.
It is apparent that what is in view here and in verse 27 is the
homosexual abomination. That he should have mentioned the
women first is undoubtedly for the purpose of accentuating the
grossness of the evil. The A.V. has drawn attention to a particle
present in the Greek which, if thus rendered, brings out this
thought: "for *even* their women". It is the delicacy which belongs
to the woman that makes more apparent the degeneracy of
homosexual indulgence in their case. While the apostle mentions
first of all the prevalence of what has been called the Lesbian
vice, he refrains from the detail of description provided in verse 27
where he deals with the homosexual practices of the men. It is
likely that delicate feeling dictated this restraint. The "natural
use" which the women are said to have exchanged for "that
which is against nature" is the same term as is used in verse 27
but which is there defined as "the natural use of the woman",
and it would be reasonable to suppose that in verse 26 it means
the natural use of the man. But there may be force in Meyer's
remark that such a thought would be unsuitable in this instance
and that what is reflected on is the natural use of their sex functions.
Although the natural use of the woman's sex functions is the
sex relation established with the man, yet the apostle may have
purposely refrained from describing it as the natural use of the man.
In any case, the stress falls upon the *unnatural* character of the
vice and in that, as also in verse 27, consists the peculiar gravity
of the abomination. The implication is that however grievous is
fornication or adultery the desecration involved in homosexuality
is on a lower plane of degeneracy; it is unnatural and therefore
evinces a perversion more basic.

27 The description of the male homosexual vice in verse 27 is
more detailed. Three expressions are worthy of special note.
(1) "Leaving the natural use of the woman." As elsewhere in the
apostle's teaching (*cf.* I Cor. 7:1–7) the honourableness of the
heterosexual act is implied and its propriety is grounded in the
natural constitution established by God. The offence of homo-

sexuality is the abandonment of the divinely constituted order in reference to sex. (2) "Burned[49] in their lust one toward another." The intensity of the passion is indicated by the word "burned". It is a mistake to equate this burning with that mentioned in I Corinthians 7:9.[50] The latter is the burning of natural sex impulse and there is no indictment of it as immoral—marriage is commended as the outlet for its satisfaction. But here it is the burning of an insatiable lust that has no natural or legitimate desire of which the lust is the perversion or distortion. It is lust directed to something that is essentially and under all circumstances illegitimate. (3) "Men with men working unseemliness." "Unseemliness" is too weak a word; the Greek should be rendered rather "the shameful thing" (cf. Eph. 5:12). This again indicates the cumulative force of the indictment levelled against the vice in question.

The concluding part of the verse harks back to the thought expressed in verses 24, 25, 26, namely, that abandonment to immorality was the judicial consequence of apostasy. Here, however, a new element is interjected—the abandonment is said to be "the recompense which was due". Arbitrariness never characterizes the divine judgment. But here the apostle expressly reflects upon the correspondence between the sin and the retribution inflicted. The "error" recompensed by abandonment to these unnatural vices is the apostasy from the worship of God described in verses 21–23, 25 and the recompense itself consists, to use Shedd's words, in "the gnawing unsatisfied lust itself, together with the dreadful physical and moral consequences of debauchery".[51] In the apostle's delineation of the moral squalor we must discover a conspicuous example of the wrath of God revealed from heaven (vs. 18). And the degeneracy evinces the degradation which follows in the wake of idolatrous worship. The proprieties which our own nature would dictate are shamefully desecrated and we "become blind at noonday".[52] We are thus

---

[49] The aorist passive in the Greek means more literally "were inflamed"; they were set on fire with the passion of lust.

[50] It is not the difference of words—ἐξεκαύθησαν here and πυροῦσθαι in I Cor. 7:9—but the total difference of assessment on the apostle's part.

[51] William G. T. Shedd: A Critical and Doctrinal Commentary upon the Epistle of St. Paul to the Romans (New York, 1879), ad loc.

[52] The expression is from Calvin, ad loc.: "ut caecutiant in meridie".

prepared for the further analysis of God's judicial abandonment
in the verse which follows.

28–32

> 28 And even as they refused to have God in *their* know-
> ledge, God gave them up unto a reprobate mind, to
> do those things which are not fitting;
> 29 being filled with all unrighteousness, wickedness,
> covetousness, maliciousness; full of envy, murder,
> strife, deceit, malignity; whisperers,
> 30 backbiters, hateful to God, insolent, haughty, boastful,
> inventors of evil things, disobedient to parents,
> 31 without understanding, covenant-breakers, without
> natural affection, unmerciful:
> 32 who, knowing the ordinance of God, that they that
> practise such things are worthy of death, not only do
> the same, but also consent with them that practise them.

28 In the preceding verses the delineation of the retribution
meted out to apostasy had been restricted to the sexual vice. The
reason is very likely that the apostle regarded the homosexual
abominations as the most overt evidences of the degeneracy to
which God in his wrath gave over the nations. In verse 28 he
shows that God's judicial abandonment was not confined to that
form of degradation and in verses 29–32 he provides us with a
summary catalogue of other vices to which the nations were
given over. The "even as" at the beginning of verse 28 expresses
substantially the same thought as we found in verse 27, namely,
the correspondence between the sin committed and the recompense
meted out. The sin in this case is described as refusing to have God
in their knowledge. The thought is that they did not deem God
fit to have in their knowledge. The godlessness of the state of
mind is apparent—they did not cherish the knowledge of God
because they did not consider God worthy of such thought and
attention. The corresponding retribution is that "God gave them
over to a reprobate mind", to a mind that is rejected because
deemed worthless (*cf.* I Cor. 9:27; II Cor. 13:5, 6, 7; II Tim. 3:8;
Tit. 1:16; Heb. 6:8). A reprobate mind is therefore one abandoned or rejected of God and therefore not fit for any activity
worthy of approbation or esteem. The judgment of God falls
upon the seat of thought and action. "To do those things which
are not fitting" is explanatory of what a reprobate mind entails

and shows that "the mind" as conceived of by the apostle is concerned with action as well as with thought.

29–31 In these verses is the catalogue of vices. It would be artificial to try to discover a system of classification in this list. The apostle's mind ranges freely over the vices which came within his own observation in his contact with the various races and conditions of men. And no doubt also his mind ranged freely among the many sources of information available to him respecting the moral state of the nations in his own generation and in those that preceded. We are impressed with the length of the list and with the variety of vice. But, after all, this is only a selection. Elsewhere he mentions other vices which are not included in this enumeration (*cf.* Gal. 5:19–21). The extent of the depravity is evident from the opening clause, "being filled with all unrighteousness". Unrighteousness is a generic term and suggests that it is the genus of which the other vices are specifications. But whether this be so or not the stress falls upon the completeness with which unrighteousness had come to exercise control over its subjects—they were filled to be the brim with all forms of unrighteousness. And the addition of the terms, "wickedness, covetousness, maliciousness" accentuates the totality of the depravity involved and the intensity with which it had been cultivated. It is a picture of the utmost degeneracy.

While we may not be warranted in discovering a system of classification in the order which the apostle follows, yet the change of construction at three points may indicate that the vices have, nevertheless, their appropriate groupings, "unrighteousness, wickedness, covetousness, maliciousness" constituting one group, "envy, murder, strife, deceit, malignity" constituting another group of kindred character, and the other characterizations to the end of verse 31 a series of vices of varied complexions. In any case as we scan the whole list we cannot but be impressed with the apostle's insight into the depravity of human nature as apostatized from God, the severity of his assessment of these moral conditions, and the breadth of his knowledge respecting the concrete ways in which human depravity came to expression.

32 This concluding verse may also be well regarded as the culminating indictment against those whom the apostle has been describing. The pronoun with which the verse begins draws attention to the character of the persons concerned—"they are of such a character that" is its force and is to be connected with the last clause of the verse. The extreme gravity of their offence consists in this that they "consent with them that practise" these vices—they offer their plaudits to the perpetrators of vice. That is the specific character which is now in view.

"The ordinance of God" in this case is the judicial ordinance of God; it is expressly defined as such in the succeeding clause, namely, "that they that practise such things are worthy of death". The knowledge of this ordinance is predicated of the people concerned. The "death" referred to cannot reasonably be restricted to temporal death. The Greeks themselves taught a doctrine of retribution for the wicked after death, and the apostle must have taken this into account in the statement of that which he credited the nations with knowing. Furthermore, he is here defining that in which the ordinance of God consists and he cannot, in terms of his own teaching elsewhere, confine it to the judgment of temporal death. Knowledge of God's penal judgment as it issues in the torments of the life to come is recognized, therefore, by the apostle as belonging to those with whom he is now concerned. The question arises, however, whether this knowledge is conceived of as belonging to them in the state of abandoned degeneracy or as knowledge which they once possessed but had now lost (cf. vs. 21). Considerations could be pleaded in support of the latter alternative. The tense used could be rendered "having known" with the implication that they no longer knew the same. Furthermore, the description given of the judicial blindness with which they had been inflicted (cf. vss. 21–23, 28) would not appear to comport with any active consciousness of the judicial ordinance of God. But there are weighty reasons for thinking that the knowledge credited is not merely that of an earlier stage of their career. (1) The tense used is quite compatible with the thought that an existing state of knowledge is in view. It can designate a state contemporaneous with the actions referred to in the latter part of the verse. (2) The knowledge of God's judicial ordinance is in this passage rather obviously intended to throw into relief the aggravated perversity of their condition. If this knowledge is relegated to the past, then the relevance of allusion to it almost disappears. Whereas, if the present fact of this knowledge is asserted, then its relevance immediately becomes apparent from the consideration that notwithstanding their knowledge of God's judgment upon these things they went on doing them and applauding the others who practised the same. (3) The apparent incompatibility of the retention of this knowledge and the degenerate state of blindness is relieved by what the apostle says in verse 21. There the knowledge of God is clearly represented as coexisting with the perversity of failing to glorify God and give him thanks. This latter knowledge of God is more comprehensive than that of the knowledge of God's judicial ordinance (vs. 32) and yet it coexisted with the perversity which constituted the essence of their apostasy. (4) To eliminate this knowledge from the consciousness of the Gentile nations would be quite contrary to the implications of 2:14, 15. Besides, as noted above, the historical evidence proves that the nations were not without that knowledge and had a keen sense of the sequence which God established in his judicial ordinance.

If this view is adopted then we have an important datum, namely, that notwithstanding all the degradation, religious, moral, and mental, delineated in the foregoing verses, the apostle recognizes these same persons to have knowledge of God's righteous ordinance to the effect that the vices perpetrated deserve the pains of hell. It is not superfluous to set forth the following inferences.

(1) The most degraded of men, degraded because judicially abandoned of God, are not destitute of the knowledge of God and of his righteous judgments. In terms of 2:14, 15, conscience asserts itself. (2) This knowledge does not of itself prevent these same persons from indulging the sins which they know merit the judgment of God and issue in death. (3) The knowledge of God's righteous judgment does not create any hatred of sin nor does it foster any disposition to repent of it.

All the preceding clauses in this verse are subordinate to the concluding—"but also consent with them that practise them". The iniquity described in the preceding verses is here shown to be consentient and concerted, and it is this mutually consentient feature of the iniquity practised that elicits the climactic indictment of Gentile degeneracy. However severe has been the apostle's delineation of the depravity of men, he has reserved for the end the characterization which is the most damning of all. It is that of the consensus of men in the pursuit of iniquity. The most damning condition is not the practice of iniquity, however much that may evidence our abandonment of God and abandonment to sin; it is that together with the practice there is also the support and encouragement of others in the practice of the same. To put it bluntly, we are not only bent on damning ourselves but we congratulate others in the doing of those things that we know have their issue in damnation. We hate others as we hate ourselves and render therefore to them the approval of what we know merits damnation. Iniquity is most aggravated when it meets with no inhibition from the disapproval of others and when there is collective, undissenting approbation.

B. THE JEWS
(2:1—16)

1-4

1 Wherefore thou art without excuse, O man, whosoever thou art that judgest: for wherein thou judgest another, thou condemnest thyself; for thou that judgest dost practise the same things.
2 And we know that the judgment of God is according to truth against them that practise such things.
3 And reckonest thou this, O man, who judgest them that practise such things, and doest the same, that thou shalt escape the judgment of God?
4 Or despisest*thou the riches of his goodness and forbearance and longsuffering, not knowing that the goodness of God leadeth thee to repentance?

Considerable difference of opinion has prevailed among interpreters respecting the identity of those addressed in the earlier part of this chapter (vss. 1–16, particularly vss. 1–8). Some maintain that the apostle, having described the condition of the Gentiles in 1:18–32, now turns to the Jew and addresses him directly, though not expressly by name until verse 17. Others hold that in these verses the apostle "advances only general propositions",[1] applicable indeed to Jews but also to others. Referring to the description of degeneracy given in the preceding chapter E. H. Gifford, for example, says: "But there were some among the heathen and many among the Jews to whom this description could not be applied in its strongest *external* features of blind idolatry and hideous vice. They had not lost all knowledge of the true nature of God; they did not practise, still less applaud, the grosser forms of vice; their moral sense was keen enough to condemn the sins of others: yet they too must be brought to feel themselves guilty before God."[2] The question is not one that

---

[1] Moses Stuart: *A Commentary on the Epistle to the Romans* (Andover, 1835), p. 95.
[2] *Op. cit.*, p. 71.

can be decisively determined. It may be that the apostle, while thinking particularly of Jews, frames his discourse in terms that are more general so as to strike not only at the Jew but also at others who did not consider themselves to be in the degraded moral and religious condition delineated in the preceding verses. In that event there would be much point to the general terms in which the address is drawn, for their more general character would not detract from the obvious relevance to the Jew and, at the same time, others worthy of the same rebuke would not be excluded. It could also be said that a rhetorical advantage could have been intended by the apostle. In bringing conviction to bear upon the Jew he established, first of all, propositions of more general application in order that he might bring them home with more telling effect in direct application to the Jew in verses 17–29.

There is, however, no conclusive reason for supposing that the address is of this more general character. On the other hand, there are weighty reasons which, if they do not decisively determine the question, point definitely in the other direction. (1) The propensity to judge the Gentiles for their religious and moral perversity was peculiarly characteristic of the Jew. He was intensely conscious of his high privilege and prerogative, a fact to which the apostle expressly refers in verses 17–20. Hence the address, "O man, whosoever thou art that judgest" identifies the Jew by means of his national characteristic. (2) The person being addressed is the participant of "the riches of his [God's] goodness and forbearance and longsuffering". While it is true that Gentiles also were partakers of God's goodness, yet the strength of the expression "the riches of his goodness" would indicate the riches of special grace such as the Jews enjoyed in the covenant privilege. (3) The argument of the apostle is to the effect that special privilege or advantage does not exempt from the judgment of God (vss. 3, 6–11). The relevance to the Jews is apparent because this was an outstanding abuse of privilege on their part that, as the children of Abraham, they expected indulgences not shared by others (cf. Matt. 3:8, 9; Luke 3:8; John 8:33, 39, 53; Gal. 2:15). Furthermore, the priority accorded to the Jew in judgment (vs. 9) and in glory (vs. 10) indicates that the special privilege is that enjoyed by the Jew. (4) The express address to the Jew in verse 17 would be rather abrupt if now for the first time the Jew is directly in view, whereas if the Jew is the person in view in the preceding verses then the more express identification in verse 17 is natural.

1 The connection indicated in verse 1 by "wherefore" is not wholly clear. It may attach itself to the whole preceding section (1:18–32),[3] or only to verse 32.[4] And one cannot dismiss the possibility that it is related not to what precedes but to what follows. On the last alternative it points to a conclusion drawn from the latter part of the verse, in other words, that the conclusion of the apostle's syllogism is stated first and the grounds are then set forth.[5] The progression of thought is as follows: (1) thou judgest another for doing certain things; (2) thou thyself doest the same things; (3) therefore thou condemnest thyself and art without excuse. If the "wherefore" is a conclusion drawn from what goes before it appears necessary to take more into account than verse 32. "Without excuse" harks back to 1:20 where the same term is applied to the Gentiles. The judging propensity of the Jew has reference to the sins catalogued in the preceding passage as a whole. The things practised by the Jew are in this same general category because he is charged with practising the same sins. It is also likely that the thought of knowing the judicial ordinance of God, that those who practise such things are worthy of death (vs. 32), is carried over to 2:1 as the premise from which the indictment of 2:1 is derived. Since thou knowest the judicial ordinance of God, as is evidenced by the fact that thou judgest others, thou art without excuse, for in that very act of judging thou hast condemned thyself.

Although, for the reasons stated above, Paul is addressing the Jew, he uses the more general term "O man", not necessarily by way of reproach (*cf.* 9:20) but simply as a more earnest and effective method of appeal. In verse 32 the climax of Gentile degeneracy was evidenced by the fact that there was no condemnation of others for the sins practised. On the contrary there was active consent and approbation. Now in the case of the Jew Paul's indictment presupposes the thing that was absent in the case of the Gentiles, namely, a condemnatory judgment of others for

---

[3] This is the view of Meyer.
[4] *Cf.* Godet, *ad loc.*
[5] *Cf.* Robert Haldane: "This particle introduces a conclusion, not from anything in the preceding chapter, but to establish a truth from what follows" (*op. cit., ad loc.*).

sins committed. It is to be noted, however, that the indictment brought against the Jew is not that he judged others for sins committed; it is rather that he judged others for the very things he practised himself. In other words, it is the blindness and hypocrisy of the Jew, hyprocrisy because he judged others for the same sins of which he himself was guilty, blindness because he failed to see his own self-condemnation in the condemnation he pronounced on others. The state of mind characterized by hypocrisy and blindness is brought home not in these express terms but in the form of the charge of inexcusableness and in this respect the Jew is placed in the same category as the Gentile.

2 Verse 1 had been concerned with the judgment which the Jew passed upon the Gentile and with the judgment which unwittingly, yet by implication, he passed upon himself. Verse 2 confronts the Jew with the judgment which God registers against those who practise such things. The "judgment" in this instance is not the act of judging but the condemnatory sentence (*cf.* vs. 3; 3:8; 5:16; 13:2; I Cor. 11:29, 34; I Tim. 3:6; 5:12; James 3:1). The expression "according to truth" means "in accordance with the facts of the case" and points to that which is stated in verse 11 that "there is no respect of persons with God". "According to truth", if it does not mean the same as equity or impartiality, is almost indistinguishable from that notion (*cf.* Ps. 96:13). This general principle is that upon which the teaching of the succeeding verses is based. God's truth and equity govern his judgments and there are special privileges for none. With reference to this principle the apostle says "we know". He means by this that it is an incontestable truth with respect to which he will not allow any hesitation. He states it as an axiom of thought apart from which we cannot speak of *God's* judgment. For God is truth (*cf.* 3:4).

3 Here the basic principle enunciated in verse 2 is applied concretely to the person whom the apostle is addressing. This is apparent because substantially the same expressions as we find in verse 1 are repeated. The form of address "O man" is again used as better adapted to summon the Jew to attention. The rhetorical question implies an emphatic negative answer. The pronoun "thou" is emphatic, confronting the Jew with the impiety of the supposition that the divine order of justice and truth would be abrogated for his benefit. The impossibility of leniency resides in the fact that the judgment of God is according to truth and therefore knows no respect of persons. "The judgment of God" is the same expression as in verse 2 and refers to his condemnatory sentence.

4 In verse 4 we have another question introduced by "or", and "despisest thou" is parallel to "reckonest thou" in verse 3. The purpose of this "or" is not that of proposing alternatives; it is rhetorical like the questions themselves. And the effect is to press home upon the Jew in *crescendo* fashion the impiety of which he is guilty. In other words, these are not alternative ways of interpreting his attitude but different ways of stating what his attitude is. And that the apostle entertains no doubt respecting the contempt offered by the Jew to the riches of God's goodness is demonstrated by verse 5. Paul is dealing with a hardened Jew and with increasing intensity of derogation points him to the perversity of which he is guilty.

"The riches" of God's goodness refer to the abundance and magnitude of the goodness bestowed upon the Jew. The strength of the expression indicates that the covenant lovingkindness of which the Jew was the partaker is contemplated (*cf.* 3:2; 9:4, 5). And the same holds true for "forbearance and longsuffering". The word "riches" governs all three terms. The abundance of God's "forbearance and longsuffering" to Israel was exemplified again and again in the history of the Old Testament but the apostle must be thinking particularly, if not exclusively, of the forbearance and longsuffering exercised to the Jew at the time of writing. For in the rejection of the grace and goodness manifested in Christ the Jew had given the utmost of ground for the execution of God's wrath and punishment to the uttermost. Only "the riches" of forbearance and longsuffering could explain the preservation accorded to him. We must not press unduly and thus artificially the distinction between "forbearance" and "longsuffering". Together they express the idea that God suspends the infliction of punishment and restrains the execution of his wrath. When he exercises forbearance and longsuffering he does not avenge sin in the instant execution of wrath. Forbearance and longsuffering, therefore, reflect upon the wrath and punishment which sin deserves and refer to the restraint exercised by

God in the infliction of sin's desert. It needs to be noted that the apostle does not think of this restraint as exercised in abstraction from the riches of God's goodness, the riches of his benignity and lovingkindness. There is a complementation that bespeaks the magnitude of God's kindness and of which the gifts of covenant privilege are the expression.[6] It is a metallic conception of God's forbearance and longsuffering that isolates them from the kindness of disposition and of benefaction which the goodness of God implies.

To "despise" is to underestimate the significance of something, to think lightly of it and thus fail to accord to it the esteem that is due. It can also take on the strength of scorning and contemning. The Jew whom Paul is addressing had indeed failed to assess the riches of goodness of which he was the beneficiary, and whenever God's gifts are underestimated they are truly despised. However, when we think of the unbelief with which the apostle is dealing as that of a Jew who had rejected the revelation of grace in Christ, we must predicate of him contempt and scorn in the most express and direct fashion. It is in these terms that we shall have to interpret Paul's question.

"Not knowing that the goodness of God leadeth thee to repentance." This must not be understood as an extenuation of guilt. The apostle is not excusing the offence by appeal to the ignorance of the person addressed; he is rather expanding the base of his indictment. He is saying in effect, "You have missed the great lesson and purpose of the goodness of God as it bears upon your responsibility". "Not knowing" has in this case the force of "not considering"[7] and implies that the purpose of God's goodness was so patent that failure to understand was totally unexcusable. "Repentance" means change of mind and refers to that transformation registered in our consciousness by which in mind, feeling, and will we turn from sin unto God. It is coordinated with faith as an activity which lies at the inception of the believer's life and is unto the remission of sins and eternal life (*cf.* Acts 20:21; Heb. 6:1; Mark 1:4; Luke 24:47; Acts 2:38; 3:19; 11:18). The assertion that the goodness of God *leads* to repentance must not be weakened to mean merely that it points

---

[6]   For passages illustrating the meaning of χρηστότης *cf.* Matt. 11:30; Luke 6:35; Rom. 11:22; Gal. 5:22; Eph. 2:7; 4:32; Col. 3:12; I Pet. 2:3.

[7]   *Cf.* Philippi, *ad loc.*

us to repentance. The word "lead" must be given its true force of conducting (*cf.* 8:14; I Cor. 12:2; I Thess. 4:14; II Tim. 3:6). The apostle is not saying that every one who is the beneficiary of God's lovingkindness is led to repentance. The presupposition of his indictment against the unbelieving Jew is quite the reverse; this Jew was the partaker of the riches of God's lovingkindness and forbearance and longsuffering and was nevertheless impenitent. Neither is the apostle dealing with that inward efficacious grace which brings forth the fruit of repentance. But he is saying that the goodness of God, including without doubt the forbearance and longsuffering, is directed to the end of constraining repentance (*cf.* II Pet. 3:9). And not only so. The presumptuous Jew interpreted the special goodness of God to him as the guarantee of immunity from the criteria by which other men would be judged and he claimed for himself indulgence on the part of God; the Gentile needed repentance but not he. What the apostle says is that the goodness of God when properly assessed leads to repentance; it is calculated to *induce* repentance, the frame of mind which the Jew considered to be the need only of the Gentile. The goodness of God has not only this as its true intent and purpose; when properly understood this is its invariable effect. And the condemnation of the Jew is that he failed to understand this simple lesson.

5–11

5 but after thy hardness and impenitent heart treasurest up for thyself wrath in the day of wrath and revelation of the righteous judgment of God;

6 who will render to every man according to his works:

7 to them that by patience in well-doing seek for glory and honor and incorruption, eternal life:

8 but unto them that are factious, and obey not the truth, but obey unrighteousness, *shall be* wrath and indignation,

9 tribulation and anguish, upon every soul of man that worketh evil, of the Jew first, and also of the Greek;

10 but glory and honor and peace to every man that worketh good, to the Jew first, and also to the Greek:

11 for there is no respect of persons with God.

5 Having stated in verse 4 what we may call the negative aspect of the Jew's account, in verse 5 the apostle proceeds to state it more positively. He does this in terms of the figure of treasure which the Jew piles up for himself. We have no longer rhetorical questions but a direct arraignment—"but after thy hardness and impenitent heart". The contrast between the melting of penitence which the goodness of God was calculated to constrain and the hardened and impenitent state of heart here predicated is to be noted. The person addressed, by reason of this hardness of heart, is represented as being himself the agent in piling up for himself wrath. The finesse of distinction involved should not be overlooked. The wrath is none other than the wrath of God (cf. 1:18 and the subsequent clauses and verses in this chapter). The wrath is therefore something of which God alone is the agent and author. But the person is said to treasure up this wrath. Again we are reminded of the principle set forth in verse 2 and applied in verse 3 that the judgment of God is according to truth. There is no wrath of God except as the reaction of his justice and truth against sin. Hence there is no increment of wrath, no addition to the pile of wrath stored up, except as sin on the part of man provokes and evokes that wrath. Hence we are said to treasure it up for ourselves.

It is better to take "in the day of wrath" with the word "wrath" which precedes rather than with "treasurest up". The sense then is that the wrath treasured up is to be executed in the day of wrath. This day, which is identified in verse 16 as "the day when God will judge the secrets of men", is also called here the day "of revelation of the righteous judgment of God".[8] The righteous judgment of God is self-explanatory. "Revelation" points to the fact that the manifestation and execution of this righteous judgment is reserved for a future day. Since it cannot be supposed that nothing of God's righteous judgment is manifest in the history of the world and since such a notion cannot be credited to the apostle, the term "revelation" in this instance must be used in the sense of the full exhibition and execution. The same dynamic import of the word "reveal", which we found in 1:17, appears here also. It is the righteous judgment of God in full operation and execution.[9] In any case the full description

---

[8] Preponderant uncial authority favours the omission of καί before δικαιοκρισίας.

[9] It could be argued, of course, that δικαιοκρισία has a restricted denotation here, namely, the last judgment. In that event it would not be necessary to stress the more pregnant sense of the term "revelation".

"the day of wrath and revelation of the righteous judgment of God" identifies the day as the day of final judgment.[10] Since the day of judgment is characterized as "the day of wrath and revelation of the righteous judgment of God" we might be disposed to regard the day spoken of here as pertaining exclusively to the judgment of the wicked. This is not the case. The twofold aspect of distributive award is in the forefront. The day of wrath for the wicked is one in which the aspirations of the righteous will be realized and they will be given glory, honour, and peace (vss. 7, 10).

6 Verse 6 enunciates three features of God's righteous judgment: (1) the universality—"to each one", a fact reiterated in verses 9, 10; (2) the criterion by which judgment is to be executed —"according to his works"; (3) the certain and effective distribution of award—"who will render". The matter of the criterion introduces the question as to whether the apostle is speaking in this passage of the judgment that will actually take place or whether he is speaking hypothetically. The latter supposition has appealed to some interpreters because, if men are to be judged according to their *works*, would this not contradict the thesis of this epistle that by *works* shall no man be justified? Could God judge any unto the reward of eternal life (*cf.* vs. 7) if *works* are the criteria? Hence it has been maintained that the apostle "speaks of law only, not of the gospel. He describes the legal position upon which man stands by creation irrespective either of apostasy or redemption, in order to exhibit the principles upon which reward and penalty are distributed under the divine government."[11] In the words of Haldane, "if these verses refer to the Gospel, they bring in upon and disturb the whole train of his reasoning, from the 18th verse of the first chapter to the 20th of the third, where he arrives at his conclusion, that by the deeds of the law there shall no flesh be justified in the sight of God".[12] But it should be noted that the principles respecting the future

---

[10] For Paul's use of the word "day" *(ἡ ἡμέρα)* as the synonym for judgment *cf.* I Cor. 4:3 and of the term "day" without further specification as an eschatological designation *cf.* 13:12; I Cor. 3:13; I Thess. 5:4 and with the simple demonstrative "that" *cf.* II Thess. 1:10; II Tim. 4:8.

[11] Shedd, *ad loc.*

[12] *Op. cit., ad* 2:7. To much the same effect is the statement of Hodge, though perhaps not so vigorously argued: "He is expounding the law, not the gospel" (*ad loc.*).

judgment set forth in this passage are not different from those set forth elsewhere in the New Testament and particularly in Paul's own epistles (*cf.* Matt. 16:27; 25:31–46; John 5:29; I Cor. 3:11–15; II Cor. 5:10; Gal. 6:7–10; Eph. 6:8; Col. 3:23, 24; *cf.* Eccl. 12:14). If the solution proposed by the interpreters quoted above were to be applied to Romans 2:6–16, then not only this passage but these others would have to be interpreted after this pattern. But examination of these other passages will show the impossibility of this procedure. Besides, we must not suppose that Paul is under the necessity of discarding the provisions of the gospel in this part of the epistle. It is true that his main purpose is to prove that all are under sin and that by the works of law shall no flesh be justified in God's sight. And it is also true that not until 3:21 does he begin to unfold in detail the theme of justification by grace through faith. But we may not forget that in 1:3, 4 he had defined that with which the gospel is concerned and in 1:16, 17 he had stated the grand theme of the epistle. Furthermore, in this passage (vs. 16) he appeals to that which is specifically the gospel doctrine of the judgment and in 2:28, 29 he establishes what has no relevance apart from the gospel. Likewise, as noted already, there is allusion in verse 4 to the special provisions of God's goodness exhibited in the gospel. Finally, the assertive way in which the apostle speaks in this passage of what will be revealed in the day of judgment constrains the conclusion of Philippi: "The apostle thus speaks, not in the way of abstract hypothesis, but of concrete assertion. . . . He says not what God would do were He to proceed in accordance with the primal rule and standard of the law, but what, proceeding according to that rule, He will actually do."[13]

In verses 7–10 the general principle stated in verse 6 is applied alternately to the two classes of men, to the just in verses 7 and 10 and to the wicked in verses 8 and 9.

7 The just are characterized first of all as those who "seek for glory and honor and incorruption". These three terms have been interpreted as meaning incorruptible glory and honour or glorious and honourable immortality. It is not necessary, however, to construe the terms thus. All three designate the distinct aspects from which the aspiration of the godly may be viewed or, pref-

---

[13] *Op. cit., ad loc.; cf.* also Sanday and Headlam, *ad loc.*

erably, the elements which are correlatively comprised in the aspiration and expectation of believers. "Glory" is frequently used by Paul in this epistle and elsewhere to describe the goal of the believer's expectation (*cf.* 5:2; 8:18, 21, 30; 9:23; I Cor. 2:7; 15:43; II Cor. 4:17; Col. 3:4) and points to the transformation that will be effected when believers will be conformed to the image of God's Son and reflect the glory of God. "Honour" is closely akin to glory (*cf.* Heb. 2:7; I Pet. 1:7; II Pet. 1:17; Rev. 4:9, 11; 5:13) and focuses attention upon the approbation God will accord to them in contrast with the reproach of men often heaped upon them and the eternal disgrace executed upon the ungodly. Always in the forefront of this use of these terms is the fact that God bestows glory and honour. "Incorruption", though correlative with glory and honour, is nevertheless a distinct ingredient in the aspiration of the godly and refers to the resurrection hope of the people of God. It is impossible to dissociate from "incorruption" as used here the connotation it has elsewhere (I Cor. 15:42, 50, 52, 53, 54; *cf.* Rom.8:23; II Cor. 5:4; I Pet. 1:4). The three terms have indisputably in the usage of Paul redemptive associations, and this consideration of itself makes it impossible to think that the eschatological aspiration referred to is anything less than that provided by redemptive revelation. The three words define aspiration in terms of the highest reaches of Christian hope. The reward of this aspiration is in like manner the eschatology of the believer, "eternal life".

"By patience in well-doing." Perhaps Meyer's comment is as close as any to the thought expressed, that this "contains the standard, the regulative principle, by which the seeking after glory . . . is guided".[14] The word rendered "patience" is perhaps better translated by "perseverance" or "endurance". We are reminded of the truth that it is he who endures to the end that will be saved (Matt. 24:13) and that "we are made partakers of Christ, if we hold fast the beginning of our confidence firm unto the end" (Heb. 3:14; *cf.* Col. 1:22, 23). The complementation of perseverance in well-doing and the aspiration of hope underlines the lesson that these may never be separated. Works without redemptive aspiration are dead works. Aspiration without good works is presumption.

---

[14] *Op. cit., ad loc.; cf.* also Philippi who adopts the same view.

8 Literally rendered, the first characterization of the ungodly given here is "those who are of contention". The form is parallel to other expressions such as "those who are of the circumcision" (Rom. 4:12; Tit. 1:10), "those who are of faith" (Gal. 3:7), "those who are of the works of the law" (Gal. 3:10), "those who are of the law" (Rom.4:14) and means simply "those who are contentious or factious", the insubjection involved being that of active insubjection to God—they are in revolt against God. This appears not only from the strength of the expression but also from the characterizations coordinated with it, "obey not the truth but obey unrighteousness". These indicate that in which the factiousness consisted.[15] Truth and unrighteousness are antithetical (*cf.* 1:18; I Cor. 13:6; II Thess. 2:12), as truth and righteousness are correlative (*cf.* Eph. 4:24). "The truth" in this instance, because of the context (*cf.* vs. 4), must be given redemptive content and in that respect is of broader scope than that referred to in 1:18. It is significant, however, that the same principle of opposition to the truth in unrighteousness appears in both cases. In 2:8 the terms used indicate the greater intensity of this opposition and the apostle concentrates upon the thought of active disobedience in unbelief. "Wrath and indignation" are the reward of this disobedience. This is the same wrath spoken of in verse 5 as the wrath stored up to be dispensed in the

---

[15] C. K. Barrett in *A Commentary on the Epistle to the Romans* (New York, 1957) says that ἐριθεία means "those who are out for quick and selfish profit on their own account" and contends that the rendering "them that are factious," assumes a false derivation of ἐριθεία, namely, that it comes from ἔρις (strife). "The word", he continues "is in fact derived from ἔριθος, a hireling; ἐριθεύειν, to act as a hireling, to work for pay, to behave, show the spirit of, a hireling. ἐριθεία should therefore mean the activity, or characteristics, or mind, of a hireling. This meaning is suitable to all the Pauline passages where the word is employed (2 Cor. xii. 20; Gal. v. 20; Phil. i. 17; ii. 3). In the first two, the word occurs in lists along with ἔρις and if the familiar translation 'faction' is employed, Paul is made to repeat himself" (p. 47). There is much to commend this interpretation of ἐριθεία and several scholars have maintained it. *Cf.*, for a careful summary treatment, Arndt and Gingrich: *A Greek-English Lexicon of the New Testament, ad* ἐριθεία. It is true that, if we interpret ἐριθεία in Rom. 2:8 in the sense of "selfish ambition", we have an appropriate characterization of the persons concerned. But the case for this meaning is not conclusive. In Phil. 1:17 the sense is surely close to, if not synonymous with, that of ἔρις in verse 15. And the fact that in lists of vices both terms occur is not a conclusive argument for sharp differentiation of meaning. For in Paul's lists of vices terms appear which are distinguished by only a slight shade of difference in meaning. And the difference between ἔρις and ἐριθεία may be that between "strife" and "faction".

day of wrath. It is the wrath of God unrestrained and unrelieved in contrast with the forbearance and longsuffering of verse 4. "Indignation", though not essentially different from wrath, reflects upon the violence of it, and the coordination serves to emphasize the reality and the intensity of the divine displeasure poured out upon the ungodly in the day of righteous judgment. Again, as we found in 1:18, we cannot interpret this wrath of God as consisting merely in the will to punish but expresses the positive displeasure of God as inflicted upon the ungodly, and this infliction implies, as Gifford observes, that "the sense of God's wrath will be a chief element" in the eternal destruction of the ungodly.

9 The thought of the apostle would have been represented much more accurately if a period or at least a colon were placed after "indignation" in verse 8. "Tribulation and anguish" (vs. 9) are not to be coordinated with "wrath and indignation" (vs. 8) as if all four, without any break in the thought, are an enumeration of the elements of the punishment inflicted. Verses 7 and 8 go together and show the consequence for godly and ungodly respectively of the revelation of the righteous judgment of God. The construction of verses 9 and 10, as Godet well expresses it, is that "the antithesis of vv. 7, 8 is reproduced in inverse order".[16] Hence there is good reason to believe that a break in the thought appears at the end of verse 8. Wrath and indignation describe the retribution of the ungodly in terms of the displeasure of God to which they are subjected whereas tribulation and anguish describe their punishment in terms of their experience. There is, of course, the closest relation, as will be noted presently. But something of the relation escapes us if we do not appreciate the break of thought. In verse 8 the characterization of the ungodly comes first and the penal consequence last. In verse 9 there is an inversion of this order; "tribulation and anguish" (vs. 9) correspond to "wrath and indignation" (vs. 8). Hence "tribulation and anguish" are to be interpreted as the consequences in human experience of God's "wrath and indignation". And, without doubt, "anguish" expresses in relation to "tribulation" the same kind of intensification that "indignation" does in reference to "wrath". It may be artificial, however, to go further and say

---

[16]   *Op. cit., ad loc.*

with Godet that tribulation corresponds to wrath and anguish to indignation. "Upon every soul of man that worketh evil" is an emphatic way of stating universality. "Soul" is not to be understood here as referring to the soul in man as the subject of tribulation and anguish. "Soul" in the usage of Scripture is often the synonym for person (*cf.* Acts 2:41, 43; 3:23; Rom. 13:1). "Of the Jew first, and also of the Greek" (*cf.* 1:16). The priority of the Jew applies to condemnation and damnation as well as to salvation. As the gospel applies to him not only with a priority of time but of relevance, so the enhancement of his privilege and responsibility magnifies correspondingly the weight of his retribution, a clear proof that the priority that belongs to the Jew by reason of the dispensation of grace will be taken into account and applied in the adjudications of the final judgment. This priority of the Jew in the execution of final punishment runs totally counter to the conceit entertained by the Jew that punitive reward is for the Gentile but not for the seed of Abraham.

10 In accord with the inverted structure referred to above the apostle now returns to the reward of the righteous (*cf.* vs. 7). He repeats two of the terms used in verse 7, "glory" and "honour". But instead of "incorruption" he now substitutes "peace". This term will have to be given its widest scope as embracing the fruits of reconciliation on the highest scale of realization, peace with God and peace of heart and mind in the full enjoyment of God to all eternity. "To the Jew first, and also to the Greek." The repetition of this formula indicates that the priority of relevance which belongs to the gospel in reference to the Jew is carried through in the final administration of reward—the Jew will have priority in the bestowal of glory itself. The final judgment will take account of the priority of the Jew not only in the dispensing of retribution (vs. 9) but also in the dispensing of bliss.

11 This verse is closely related both to what precedes and to what follows, confirmatory of what precedes and providing the transition to what follows.[17] In relation to what goes before it is a reassertion of the equity of God's judgment; he knows no

---

[17] "This remark serves as the transition to what follows, not merely as the confirmation of what went before" (Henry Alford: *The Greek Testament*, London, 1877, *ad loc.*).

partiality.[18] The criterion of judgment is not privilege or position but that affirmed repeatedly in the preceding verses, namely, the character of men's works. It might appear that the priority accorded to the Jew in verses 9, 10 is inconsistent with the principle that there is no respect of persons with God. But it is to be remembered that the priority accorded to the Jew gives him no immunity from the criterion of judgment which is applied to all indiscriminately. The determining factor in the awards of retribution or of glory is not the privileged position of the Jew but evil-doing or well-doing respectively. And the priority of the Jew applies to retributive judgment as well as to the award of bliss. As will be noted in connection with verse 12, the equity of God's judgment and the fact that there is no respect of persons with him do not interfere with the diversity of situations which are found among men. Equity of judgment on God's part takes the diversity of situation into account and hence the priority belonging to the Jew, because of his privilege, accentuates his condemnation in the event of evil-doing just as the righteous judgment of God is verified and most relevantly exemplified in the award of glory in the event of well-doing. It needs to be noted, furthermore, that no greater degree of glory, honour, and peace is represented as bestowed upon the Jew by reason of his priority.

12–16

12 For as many as have sinned without the law shall also perish without the law: and as many as have sinned under the law shall be judged by the law;
13 for not the hearers of the law are just before God, but the doers of the law shall be justified:
14 (for when Gentiles that have not the law do by nature the things of the law, these, not having the law, are the law unto themselves;
15 in that they show the work of the law written in their hearts, their conscience bearing witness therewith, and their thoughts one with another accusing or else excusing *them*;)
16 in the day when God shall judge the secrets of men, according to my gospel, by Jesus Christ.

12 As mentioned above, verse 12 sustains a close relation to

---

[18] On προσωπολημψία *cf.* I Sam. 16:7; II Chron. 19:7; Job 34:19; Acts 10:34, 35; Gal. 2:6; Eph. 6:9; Col. 3:25; James 2:1; I Pet. 1:17.

verse 11. The fact that there is no respect of persons with God is confirmed and illustrated by the consideration adduced in verse 12, namely, that in executing judgment God deals with them according to the law which they possessed. In other words, while it is true that there is no respect of *persons* with God, it is also true that he has respect to the different situations in which men are placed in reference to the knowledge of his law. And the implication is that the respect he has to these diverse situations proceeds from the equity of his judgment and corroborates the fact that there is no respect of persons with him. This diversity of situation is twofold. There are two distinct groups of mankind in terms of this type of discrimination—those "without law" and those "under the law". With the judgment of God as it concerns these two distinct groups the apostle now proceeds to deal.

It needs to be noted, however, that at this point the apostle restricts himself to the judgment of condemnation.[19] And this advises us that he is dealing now with the equity of God's judgment of *damnation* as it is brought to bear upon men who fall into these two categories. This is significant. Whatever is meant by those who are "without law" there is no suggestion to the effect that any who are "without law" attain to the reward of eternal life.

What does the apostle mean by the designation "without the law"? The adverbial form occurs only here in the New Testament. The substantive and the adjective occur more frequently. The former always means iniquity, lawlessness, transgression of the law (*cf.* 4:7; 6:19; II Cor. 6:14; Tit. 2:14; Heb. 1:9; I John 3:4) and the adjective all but uniformly means lawless, wicked (*cf.* Acts 2:23; II Thess. 2:8; I Tim. 1:9; II Pet. 2:8). The only exception is I Cor. 9:21: "To them that are without law, as without law, not being without law to God, but under law to Christ, that I might gain them that are without law". "Without law" in this instance cannot mean lawless or wicked because Paul could not have said that he became wicked or a transgressor of the law to those who were wicked. It obviously means "without law", that is to say, "not having the law". This must be the meaning of the adverbial form in Rom. 2:12.

---

[19] "Only in reference to the judgment *of condemnation*, because the idea of a Messianic bliss of unbelievers was necessarily foreign to the Apostle..." (Meyer, *ad loc.* n.).

And the two groups of men with which Paul deals and with whose condemnatory judgment he is concerned are those who had not the law and those who had. Hence the question is: Of what law is the apostle speaking? He cannot mean that those who are without the law are entirely destitute of law; in verses 14 and 15 he speaks of the same people as being a law to themselves and as showing the work of the law written in their hearts. The law they are without or which they do not have (*cf.* vs. 14) must therefore be the specially revealed law which those in the other group possess and under which they are (*cf.* vs. 12b). The contrast is therefore between those who were outside the pale of special revelation and those who were within.

With reference to the former the apostle's teaching is to the following effect. (1) Specially revealed law is not the precondition of sin—"as many as have sinned without the law". (2) Because such are sinners they will perish. The perishing referred to can be none other than that defined in the preceding verses as consisting in the infliction of God's wrath and indignation and the endurance of tribulation and anguish in contrast with the glory, honour, incorruption, and peace bestowed upon the heirs of eternal life. (3) In suffering this perdition they will not be judged according to a law which they did not have, namely, specially revealed law—they "shall also perish *without the law*". There is, therefore, an exact correspondence between the character of their sin as "without the law" and the final destruction visited upon them as also "without the law". In the context of this chapter and of Scripture in general there is undoubted allusion to the degree of its severity (*cf.* Luke 12:47, 48; Matt. 11:22, 24; Luke 10:14).

By way of contrast those who are "under the law", or more literally, "with the law", are those who have the specially revealed law. The character of their sin is determined accordingly and their final judgment will be aggravated in correspondence with the gravity of their sin. In this case the apostle does not say that they shall *perish* through the law. To say the least this would be an awkward and infelicitous expression. "Shall be judged by the law" refers to the penal judgment pronounced and implies the destruction which follows, but "the law" is properly represented as the criterion or instrument of judgment and not as the instrument of destruction.

13 This verse is directly connected with the two clauses immediately preceding and supports or confirms the proposition that the law will be the instrument of the condemnation pronounced upon those who have sinned under it. The emphasis in verse 13 falls upon the difference between "hearers of the law" and "doers of the law".[20] The mere possession of the law does not insure favorable judgment on God's part. The law is the standard of judgment but it is the law as demanding conformity. The apostle is undoubtedly guarding against that perversion so characteristic of the Jew that the possession of God's special revelation and of the corresponding privileges would afford immunity from the rigour of the judgment applied to others not thus favoured. He speaks of "the *hearers* of the law" because it was by hearing the Scriptures read that the mass of the people of Israel became acquainted with them and in that sense could be said to *have* the law (*cf.* Luke 4:16; John 12:34; Acts 15:21; II Cor. 3:14; James 1:22). It is quite unnecessary to find in this verse any doctrine of justification by works in conflict with the teaching of this epistle in later chapters. Whether any will be actually justified by works either in this life or at the final judgment is beside the apostle's interest and design at this juncture. The burden of this verse is that not the hearers or mere possessors of the law will be justified before God but that in terms of the law the criterion is *doing*, not hearing. The apostle's appeal to this principle serves that purpose truly and effectively, and there is no need to import questions that are not relevant to the universe of discourse.[21]

This is the first occasion that the word "justify" is used in this

---

[20] Following the uncials ℵ A B D G the article τοῦ is omitted before νόμου in both cases in verse 13. This does not mean that the law referred to is not definite. As is apparent in ἀνόμως and ἐν νόμῳ and διὰ νόμου in verse 12 the law contemplated is specially revealed law and is therefore specific. The omission of the definite article does not always mean indefiniteness; the definiteness can be apparent from other considerations. This is the case here, as frequently elsewhere.

[21] Philippi's statement is worthy of quotation: "Whether or not there are such perfect ποιηταὶ τοῦ νόμου the apostle does not say in this passage, but only opposes the true standard to the false standard of the Jews, that ἀκροαταὶ τοῦ νόμου are just before God. The entire reasoning of the Roman epistle tends to this conclusion, that no man is by nature such a ποιητὴς τοῦ νόμου, or can be" (*ad loc.*). *Cf.* also Godet, *ad loc.* although one cannot subscribe to his view of two justifications, "the one initial, founded exclusively on faith, the other final, founded on faith *and its fruits*".

epistle. Although it is not used here with reference to the justification which is the grand theme of the epistle, the forensic meaning of the term is evident even in this case. "Shall be justified" is synonymous with "just before God" and the latter refers to standing or status in the sight of God. To justify, therefore, would be the action whereby men would be recognized as just before God or the action whereby men are given the status of being just in God's sight. For a fuller treatment of the nature of justification and the meaning of the terms the reader is referred to the appendix on this subject (pp. 336 ff.).

14 The precise relation which this verse sustains to that which precedes is a debatable question.[22] It would seem that the most acceptable view is to relate verse 14 to verse 12[23] and regard it as providing the answer to the question arising from verse 12, namely: If the Gentiles are without the law, how can they be regarded as having sinned? For "where there is no law, neither is there transgression" (4:15; cf. 5:13). The answer is that although the Gentiles are "without the law" and "have not the law" in the sense of specially revealed law, nevertheless they are not entirely without law; the law is made known to them and is brought to bear upon them in another way. They "are the law unto themselves" and "they show the work of the law written in their hearts" (vs. 15). Therefore in reference to the law as it bears upon them in this way they are transgressors of the law and therefore have sinned. "Without the law" in one sense they are "under the law" in another. This does not mean that verse 13 would have to be regarded as a parenthesis. Verses 12 and 13 are a closely-knit unit and it is reasonable to connect verse 14 with the part of that unit that is stated first without supposing that verse 13 is made for that reason subordinate or parenthetical. The omission of the definite article before "Gentiles" may

---

[22] The view of Philippi and Godet that verse 14 is to be connected with verse 13 and particularly with 13a on the assumption that the Gentiles also are ἀκροαταὶ τοῦ νόμου is difficult to maintain for three reasons. (1) The law of 13a is quite specific; it is the written law which was heard in the synagogue every Sabbath. (2) The Gentiles could not be said to be hearers of this law because it is in reference to this law that they are said to be without law. (3) The law of nature which the Gentiles possessed could not properly be spoken of in the sense of 13a as heard by them; there would have to be a complete change of terms to express the relation to the Gentiles of the law which they possessed.

[23] Cf. Calvin, ad loc. and Hodge, ad loc.

represent Paul's thought for there is no definite article in the Greek. But we are not to suppose that the reason for its omission is that stated by Meyer that there are some Gentiles who do not have the law to whom the proposition does not apply. If the apostle meant to be restrictive and for that reason omitted the article, the reason is that there were some Gentiles who did have the law and on that account did not belong to the category of which he is speaking. The proposition is then that there are Gentiles who do not have the law and yet by nature do the things of the law. And there is no good reason to suppose that this does not apply collectively to the Gentiles who do not have the law in the sense defined above.[24]

"By nature" is contrasted with what is derived from external sources and refers to that which is engraven on our natural constitution. What is done "by nature" is done by native instinct or propension, by spontaneous impulse as distinguished from what is induced by forces extraneous to ourselves. The things done by nature are said to be "the things of the law". It is to be observed that the apostle does not say that they do or fulfil the law and he must have intentionally refrained from such an expression. "The things of the law" must mean certain things which the law prescribes and refer to those things practised by pagans which are stipulated in the law, such as the pursuit of lawful vocations, the procreation of offspring, filial and natural affection, the care of the poor and sick, and numerous other natural virtues which are required by the law.[25] In doing these things "by nature" they "are the law unto themselves". This expression should not be understood in the sense of popular current use when we say that a man is a law to himself. It means almost the opposite, that they themselves, by reason of what is implanted in their nature, confront themselves with the law of God. They themselves reveal the law of God to themselves—their persons is the medium of revelation. In the words of Meyer, "their moral nature, with

---

[24] Meyer draws attention to the distinction between μὴ νόμον ἔχ. and νόμον μὴ ἔχ. "The former negatives ... the possession of the *law* ... the latter negatives the *possession* of the law, which is *wanting* to them, whilst the Jews *have* it" (*ad loc.*).

[25] "Paul does not say simply τον νόμον; for he is thinking not of Gentiles who fulfil the law *as a whole*, but of those who *in concrete cases* by their action respond to the *particular portions* of the law *concerned*" (Meyer, *ad loc.*). *Cf.*, to the same effect, Philippi, *ad loc.* and Hodge, *ad loc.*

its voice of conscience commanding and forbidding, supplies to their own Ego the place of the revealed law possessed by the Jews".[26] Hence with respect to those without specially revealed law three things are true: (1) the law of God confronts them and registers itself in their consciousness by reason of what they natively and constitutionally are; (2) they do things which this law prescribes; (3) this doing is not by extraneous constraint but by natural impulse.[27]

15 "In that they show the work of the law written in their hearts." The pronoun with which this verse begins (*cf.* 1:25) is properly rendered "in that" or "inasmuch as", indicating a causal relation. The fact that they do the works of the law and are a law unto themselves demonstrates that the work of the law is written in their hearts. There are the following observations relevant to that which is said to be demonstrated. (1) The law referred to is definite and can be none other than the law of God specified in the preceding verses as the law which the Gentiles in view did not have, the law the Jews did have and under which they were, the law by which men will be condemned in the day of judgment. It is not therefore a different law that confronts the Gentiles who are without the law but the same law brought to bear upon them by a different method of revelation. (2) Paul does not say that the law is written upon their hearts. He refrains from this form of statement apparently for the same reason as in verse 14 he had said that the Gentiles "do the things of the law" and not that they did or fulfilled the law. Such expressions as "fulfilling the law" and "the law written upon the heart" are reserved for a state of heart and mind and will far beyond that

---

[26] *Op. cit., ad loc.*

[27] The omission of the definite article before νόμος on three occasions in verse 14 is an interesting example of the omission when the subject is specific and definite. On the first two occasions the law in mind is the specially revealed law as exemplified in Scripture. That it is definite is shown by the expression τὰ τοῦ νόμου. For this reason we should most reasonably take νόμος in the concluding clause as definite—the Gentiles are not simply *a* law to themselves but *the* law spoken of in the other clauses of the verse. This is confirmed by verse 15 where we have the expression τὸ ἔργον τοῦ νόμου. The point is that it is not an entirely different *law* with which the Gentiles are confronted; the things of the law they do are not things of an entirely different law—it is essentially the same law. The difference resides in the different method of being confronted with it and, by implication, in the less detailed and perspicuous knowledge of its content.

predicated of unbelieving Gentiles. (3) "The work of the law" is to be taken collectively and is practically equivalent to "the things of the law" (vs. 14). Things required and stipulated by the law are written upon the heart. (4) That they are written upon the heart points again to that which is called "by nature" in the preceding verse. Prescriptions of the law are inscribed upon and ingenerated with that which is deepest and most determinative in their moral and spiritual being. (5) That they are *written* in the heart alludes to the law of God as written upon the tables of stone or in the Scriptures and intimates the contrast between the way in which those who have the law are confronted with its prescriptions and the way in which these prescriptions are brought to bear upon Gentiles who are outside the pale of special revelation.

"Their conscience bearing witness therewith." Conscience must not be identified with "the work of the law written in their hearts" for these reasons: (1) Conscience is represented as giving *joint* witness. This could not be true if it were the same as that along with which it bears witness. (2) Conscience is a function; it is the person functioning in the realm of moral discrimination and judgment, the person viewed from the aspect of moral consciousness. The work of the law written in the heart is something ingenerated in our nature, is antecedent to the operations of conscience and the cause of them.[28] (3) The precise thought is that the operations of conscience bear witness to the fact that the work of the law is written in the heart. Not only does the doing of the things of the law prove the work of the law written in the heart but the witness of conscience does also. Hence the distinction between the work of the law and conscience.[29]

"And their thoughts one with another accusing or else excusing *them.*" The activity specified is to be coordinated with the witness of conscience and interpreted as another respect in which proof is given that the work of the law is written in the heart. Accusation and excusation, whether of ourselves or others, are activities which evidence moral consciousness and therefore point to our indestructible moral nature, the only rationale of which is the work

---

[28] Theologians have distinguished between *conscientia antecedens* and *conscientia consequens*. That of which Paul speaks here is the latter, and "the work of the law" would correspond to the former.

[29] Conscience is an evidence of our indestructible moral nature and is proof of the fact that God bears witness to himself in our hearts.

of the law of God in the heart. The translation given in the version appears to be ambiguous in reference to the exegetical difficulty in this place. The question is whether the expression in the original rendered "one with another" refers to the thoughts in dialogue with one another or to Gentiles with Gentiles in their mutual interchange of accusation and excusation. Both views yield a good sense appropriate to the context. Self-accusation and self-excusation are activities which evidence the ineradicable work of the law in the heart, and so do the accusation and excusation of others. There is not much in the text to show which of these thoughts the apostle intended.[30]

16 There needs to be no doubt as to what is in mind in this verse. "The day when God shall judge the secrets of men" is none other than the day defined in verse 5 as "the day of wrath and revelation of the righteous judgment of God". The only question that arises in this connection is: how is this reference to the day of judgment related to what precedes? Calvin relates it directly to the preceding clause and thinks that the apostle "refers this process of accusation and defence to the day of the Lord; not that it will then first commence, for it is now continually carried on, but that it will then also be in operation; and he says this, that no one should disregard this process, as though it were vain and evanescent".[31] It is not necessary, however, to resort to this unnatural extension and application of the accusation and defense in the preceding clause. Verse 16 can be readily connected with verse 12 or with verse 13 or with the whole passage which deals

---

[30] A.V. without warrant translated μεταξύ as an adverb, "the meanwhile". μεταξύ does have adverbial force in respect of time or place, as in John 4:31 of time. But the formula there is ἐν τῷ μεταξύ. Here in Rom. 2:15 it is a preposition with ἀλλήλων (cf. Matt. 18:15; Luke 16:26; Acts 12:6; 15:9). Hence the rendering should be "between themselves" or "between one another". The only question is whether ἀλλήλων refers to the Gentiles among themselves or their thoughts among themselves. It appears to the writer that Meyer's argument in favour of the former is the most weighty, to the effect that ἀλλήλων stands in contradistinction to αὐτῶν in the preceding clause and therefore means the Gentiles. On this view the accusations or vindications are those carried on between Gentiles and Gentiles by their moral judgments. "This view of the sense", he says, "is required by the correlation of the points αὐτῶν and μεταξὺ ἀλλήλων placed with emphasis in the foreground . . . so that thus both the *personal individual* testimony of conscience (αὐτῶν) and the *mutual* judgment of the thoughts (μεταξὺ ἀλλήλων) are adduced, as accompanying internal acts, in confirmation of the ἐνδείκνυνται" (*ad loc.*).

[31] *Op. cit., ad loc.*

with the judgment, namely, verses 5–14. The nature and consequences of the day of judgment are the burden of verses 5–16 and it is reasonable that verse 16 should be directly related to that with which it has the most apparent affinity, namely, the judgment executed by God upon all.

The two specific features of verse 16 are (1) the reference to the *secrets* of men and (2) the import of "according to my gospel". (1) It is not only the overt actions of men that are to be judged but the hidden things of the heart. We cannot overlook the fact that in this passage as a whole the apostle is concerned with the unbelieving Jew. Repeatedly he had exposed the fallacy of Jewish presumption. Now he is showing the folly of Jewish externalism. "The judgment of God is according to truth" (vs. 2) and therefore searches the thoughts and intents of the heart. "The secrets of men" are not to be restricted, however, to the thoughts and intents and dispositions of the heart but include also the deeds that are performed in secret and hid from others (*cf.* II Cor. 4:2; Eph. 5:12). (2) "According to my gospel" cannot be taken as the universal rule of judgment. This would contradict what the apostle had just said that those who "sinned without the law shall also perish without the law". If specially revealed *law* is not the criterion in such cases, how much less could specially revealed *gospel* be. We must conclude, therefore, that "according to my gospel" means either that the gospel proclaims that God will judge the secrets of men or that God will judge men *through Jesus Christ*. The latter is made known only through the gospel (*cf.* Matt. 25:31–46; Acts 17:31; I Cor. 4:5; II Cor. 5:10; II Tim. 4:1) and it is possible, as some maintain, that "according to my gospel" is to be understood as referring to that fact. But we are not required to restrict the expression to this particular datum. While it is true that knowledge of the fact of judgment is derived from other sources than the gospel, yet the proclamation of God's righteous judgment of all men and of all the secrets and deeds of men is an outstanding feature of the gospel. And when Paul says "my gospel" he is reminding his readers that the gospel committed to him, unto which he was separated (1:1), and with which he was identified, though it was truly the gospel of grace, was also one that incorporated the proclamation of judgment for all, just and unjust. Grace does not dispense with judgment. Only in the gospel does this proclamation come to full expression.

Hence it was not superfluous for the apostle to appeal to the gospel in support of the doctrine that there is a day when God will judge the secrets of men.

With reference to this passage (vss. 5–16) there is one question that demands some treatment. How can the apostle's teaching of judgment according to works be compatible with salvation by grace? Before dealing with this precise question there are two preliminary observations respecting God's judgment as it will affect those who will not be saved. (1) The judgment of those outside the pale of special revelation must be according to their works, that is to say, in accord with the criterion of the law they possessed, the law they are to themselves, the work of the law written in their hearts (vss. 14, 15), and the knowledge derived from the display of God's glory in the work of creation (1:20). This is clearly established in verse 12. Such persons could not be judged by the criterion of the gospel or by the criterion of law specially revealed to them—"they will perish without law". (2) The judgment of those inside the pale of special revelation, who rejected the gospel, will be executed in terms of three criteria, all of which were applicable to them —(a) the criterion of law naturally revealed which, of course, applies to all men, (b) the criterion of law specially revealed which did not apply to the preceding class, and (c) the criterion of the gospel which likewise did not apply to the preceding class. They will be judged by the gospel because they rejected it, that is, they will be condemned for gospel unbelief. It is a capital mistake to think, however, that unbelief of the gospel will be the only condemnation of such. It would violate all canons of truth and equity to suppose that the sins against law naturally revealed and specially revealed would be ignored. By faith in the grace of the gospel sins are blotted out but other sins are not waived by unbelief of the gospel. Hence law in the utmost of its demand and rigour will be applied to the judgment of those in this category —they will be judged according to their works. This also is expressly stated in verse 12—"as many as have sinned with the law shall be judged through the law". Judgment according to works, therefore, applies to all who will be damned.

In reference to the precise question, the judgment of believers, certain positions need to be set forth. (1) The distinction between judgment according to works and salvation on account of works needs to be fully appreciated. The latter is entirely contrary to the gospel Paul preached, is not implied in judgment according to works, and is that against which the burden of this epistle is directed. Paul does not even speak of judgment *on account of works* in reference to believers. (2) Believers are justified by faith *alone* and they are saved by grace *alone*. But two qualifications need to be added to these propositions. (a) They are never justified by a faith that is alone. (b) In salvation we must not so emphasize grace that we overlook the salvation itself. The concept of salvation involves what we are saved *to* as well as what we are saved *from*. We are saved to holiness and good works (*cf.* Eph. 2:10). And holiness manifests itself in good works. (3) The judgment of God must have respect to the person in the full extent of his relationship and must therefore take into account the fruits in which salvation issues and which constitute the saved condition. It is not to faith or justification in abstraction that God's judgment will have respect but to these in proper relationship to the sum-total of elements comprising a saved state. (4) The criterion of good works is the law of God and the law of God is not abrogated for the believer. He is not without law to God; he is under law to Christ (*cf.* I Cor. 9:21 and see comments on 6:14). The judgment of God would not be according to truth if the good works of believers were ignored. (5) Good works as the evidences of faith and of salvation by grace are therefore the criteria of judgment and to suppose that the principle, "who will render to every man according to this works" (vs. 6), has no relevance to the believer would be to exclude good works from the indispensable place which they occupy in the biblical doctrine of salvation.[32]

---

[32] It is not likely that the differing degrees of reward meted out to believers (*cf.* I Cor. 3:8–15) is in view in this passage but rather the general principle stated above.

C.
THE AGGRAVATION OF THE JEW'S CONDEMNATION
(2:17-29)

17-29

17 But if thou bearest the name of a Jew, and restest upon the law, and gloriest in God,
18 and knowest his will, and approvest the things that are excellent, being instructed out of the law,
19 and art confident that thou thyself art a guide of the blind, a light of them that are in darkness,
22 a corrector of the foolish, a teacher of babes, having in the law the form of knowledge and of the truth;
21 thou therefore that teachest another, teachest thou not thyself? thou that preachest a man should not steal, dost thou steal?
22 thou that sayest a man should not commit adultery, dost thou commit adultery? thou that abhorrest idols, dost thou rob temples?
23 thou who gloriest in the law, through thy transgression of the law dishonorest thou God?
24 For the name of God is blasphemed among the Gentiles because of you, even as it is written.
25 For circumcision indeed profiteth, if thou be a doer of the law: but if thou be a transgressor of the law, thy circumcision is become uncircumcision.
26 If therefore the uncircumcision keep the ordinances of the law, shall not his uncircumcision be reckoned for circumcision?
27 and shall not the uncircumcision which is by nature, if it fulfil the law, judge thee, who with the letter and circumcision art a transgressor of the law?
28 For he is not a Jew who is one outwardly; neither is that circumcision which is outward in the flesh:
29 but he is a Jew who is one inwardly; and circumcision is that of the heart, in the spirit not in the letter; whose praise is not of men, but of God.

The thrust of this passage flows out of the principle enunciated in verse 13 that "not the hearers of the law are just before God, but the doers of the law shall be justified". The apostle now addresses

80

the Jew directly and pointedly and shows him that all the privileges and prerogatives he enjoyed only aggravated his condemnation if he failed to carry into effect the teaching which he inculcated. This is clearly the challenge of verses 21–23. In verses 17–20 we have an enumeration of the privileges and prerogatives on which the Jew prided himself. While we cannot but detect the "latent irony"[33] and the undertones of indignation and reprobation in this enumeration, nevertheless we are not to interpret the apostle as questioning the validity of the claim of the Jew to distinctive dignity and prerogative. The peculiar advantages of the Jew are fully recognized (*cf.* vs. 25; 3:1; 9:3–5; Gal. 2:15). It is not Jewish distinctiveness or even *per se* the appreciative recognition of this distinctiveness on the part of the Jews themselves that the apostle berates. The impressive catalogue of advantages is the preface to the exposure of Jewish hypocrisy in verses 21, 22. The more enhanced the privilege the more heinous become the sins exposed. Consequently in the enumeration of prerogatives (vss. 17–20) we can anticipate the sequel and feel the rising swell of scorn and indignation which receives expression in verses 21–24. The syntax of verses 17–23 lends itself to this development of thought. Verses 17–20 are the protasis and verses 21–23 the apodosis. If certain things are true (those mentioned in vss. 17–20), then how is it that thou dost not practise the implications (vss. 21–23)?[34]

17, 18 The name "Jew" is first used in the Old Testament in II Kings 16:6. In exilic and post-exilic times it was frequently used. Paul's use of it here and in verses 28, 29 as well as other evidence (Gal. 2:15; Rev. 2:9; 3:9; *cf.* Zech. 8:23) indicates that it was a name associated in the mind of the Jew with all on which he prided himself. Hence "thou bearest the name of a Jew" is coordinate in effect with the other prerogatives which follow. "And restest upon the law" alludes to the same distortion as the apostle reproved in verse 13 that "not the hearers of the law are just before God" (*cf.* Mic. 3:11; John 5:45). "And

[33] The expression is from Gifford: *op. cit.*, *ad* 2:18.
[34] "In vv. 17–20 a supposition is made ('*if*,') in which the boasted privileges of the Jew (17, 18), and his assumed superiority over others (19, 20), are for the moment admitted; and then a series of pungent questions, founded on these admissions ('Thou *then*, v. 21), and put in startling contrast with them, brings out the flagrant inconsistency between profession and practice (21, 22)" (Gifford: *op. cit.*, p. 77).

gloriest in God"—glorying in God was in itself the epitome of true worship (*cf.* Isa. 45:25; Jer. 9:24; I Cor. 1:31). That the apostle should have referred to this in connection with what is by implication an indictment demonstrates perhaps more than any other prerogative enumerated how close lies the grossest vice to the highest privilege and how the best can be prostituted to the service of the worst. "And knowest his will." In the original it is simply "the will", indicating that such when used absolutely is self-explanatory as designating the will of God.[35] The possession of Scripture as the revealed will of God is referred to (*cf.* 3:2). "And approvest the things that are excellent." This clause is capable of a different rendering: "And provest the things that differ". If the latter is adopted then reference is made to the capacity to distinguish between right and wrong, good and bad or, preferably, to discern and reject those things that differ from the will of God. On this view there could be allusion to the casuistry in which Jews, particularly their rabbis, were adept. It is impossible to be certain of the apostle's thought. The strongest argument in favour of the rendering given in the version is that presented by Meyer, namely, that the other would be inconsistent with the climactic relation in which the two elements of verse 18 must stand to each other and would be tame and destructive of the climax after "thou knowest his will". "Being instructed out of the law" goes well with either interpretation of the preceding clause. The instruction doubtlessly refers to the public instruction received by the hearing of the law and from teaching on the part of parents, priests and Levites (*cf.* Lev. 10:11; Deut. 24:8; 33:10; Neh. 8:8).

19, 20 At verse 19 there is a transition from the enumeration of Godward privileges to the prerogatives exercised in reference to others.[36] These prerogatives flow from and are adjoined to the Godward privileges. The Jew as the possessor of the oracles of God should have been to those outside the pale of such ad-

---

[35] *Cf.* J. B. Lightfoot: *On a Fresh Revision of the English New Testament* (New York, 1873): "τὸ θέλημα is the divine will.... This word θέλημα came to be so appropriated to the divine will that it is sometimes used in this sense even without the definite article" (p. 98). He appeals to passages in Ignatius and interprets I Cor. 16:12; Rom. 15:32 in this way.

[36] The use of the enclitic particle τέ rather than the coordinating καί may indicate, however, that the first clause of vs. 19 sustains a close relation to the clause which immediately precedes.

vantages "a guide of the blind, a light of them that are in darkness, a corrector of the foolish, a teacher of babes". That he should have been convinced of this responsibility would in itself have been a virtue rather than a vice. The vice lay in the vain boast of being what he failed to bring to consistent fulfilment. "Having in the law the form of knowledge and of the truth" states the reason for which the Jew entertained the aforementioned confidence—he was assured that he possessed these teaching functions and was able to discharge them because he had in the law the embodiment of the knowledge to be imparted. "Form" in this instance does not have the same meaning as in II Timothy 3:5. There is no suggestion of semblance or unreality. In the law the Jew had in his possession the embodiment of knowledge and of the truth in well-defined and articulated form (*cf.* similar expressions in 6:17; II Tim. 1:13).

21–23 The apostle now turns to the overt rebuke for which the admissions of the three preceding verses prepared and, in Gifford's words, "a series of pungent questions, founded on these admissions . . . and put in startling contrast with them, brings out the flagrant inconsistency between profession and practice (21, 22)".[37] "Thou therefore" introduces the apodosis to the protasis that had begun at verse 17 with "but if". The fir st question "thou therefore that teachest another, teachest thou not thyself?', is in general terms and alludes not simply to "a teacher of babes" (vs. 20) but to all four of the prerogatives mentioned in verses 19' 20, the form of the question, however, being determined probably, by the prerogative that comes last in the preceding series. The other questions are concrete and specific and give illustrations of the teaching imparted to others but not practised by the Jew himself. They concern theft, adultery, and idolatry. The apostle goes to the heart of that law in which the Jew gloried (*cf.* vs. 23) and the transgressions selected are particularly well designed to expose the hypocrisy of the Jew and arouse him from the self-complacency into which his distorted conception of advantage had brought him (*cf.* Ps. 50:16–18). Nothing evoked the scorn of the Jew for his pagan neighbours more than their idolatry. And what more in the sphere of immorality than the sexual excesses

---

[37] *Op. cit.*, p. 77.

of the heathen nations? It is with these abominations that the Jew is now charged.

"Thou that abhorrest idols, dost thou rob temples?" It has been argued that this rendering is not tenable on the ground that robbing heathen temples would not provide the proper antithesis to abhorrence of idolatry and, furthermore, that the robbing of temples was not sufficiently prevalent among Jews to suit the apostle's purpose.[38] Hence the term in question, "rob temples" has been interpreted to mean the profanation of the majesty of God or the robbing of God of his honour by withholding what was due in the worship of the temple (*cf.* Mal. 1:6–14; 3:8). But since taking to oneself the objects of idolatrous worship is expressly forbidden in the law (Deut. 7:25, 26) and since the town-clerk at Ephesus defends Paul and his colleagues against any such charge as that of robbing temples (Acts 19:37), we cannot suppose that this wrong was one to which Jews were entirely immune.[39] There is no good reason for departing from the literal rendering and import. Besides, nothing would have provoked the resentment of Gentiles more than the desecration of their temples and have provided the occasion for blaspheming the name of God (vs. 24). Hence verse 24 lends some support to the propriety of the literal rendering.

Verse 23 may be taken as a question or as categorical assertion.[40] But whether taken as question or assertion it is apparent that it is a summary of all that goes before in verses 17–22. "The first clause is a summary of vv. 17–20, the last a decisive answer"[41] to the four questions of verses 21, 22. This is expressly the case if verse 23 is assertion and impliedly so if it is a question. The close relation that exists between God and his law is intimated in this charge. Transgression of the law is a dishonouring of God;

---

[38] *Cf.* Hodge, *ad loc.*: "That the Jews, subsequently to the captivity, did abhor idols, is a well known fact; that they robbed the temples of idols is not known. . . . It is something analogous to idolatry that is here charged, not the despoiling of heathen temples, which would be the natural expression of the abhorrence of idols."

[39] Josephus represents Moses as addressing the people near Jordan just before his death and as exhorting them thus among other things: "Let none blaspheme the gods which other cities revere, nor rob foreign temples, nor take treasure that has been dedicated in the name of any god" (*Antiquities of the Jews*, IV, viii, 10 as translated in Loeb Classical Library).

[40] *Cf.* Gifford: *op. cit.*, p. 77. Meyer, *ad loc.* says that "ver. 23 gives to the four questions of reproachful astonishment the decisive categorical answer".

[41] Gifford, *ad loc.*

it deprives him of the honour due to his name and offers insult to the majesty of which the law is the expression.

24 This is quotation from Isaiah 52:5 in confirmation of the preceding clause in verse 23. The form of the quotation is close to the LXX rendering, the only difference being that Paul translates into indirect speech what in Isaiah is direct. The thought in the apostle's application of the text is that the vices of the Jews give occasion to the Gentiles to blaspheme the name of God. The reasoning of the Gentiles is to the effect that a people are like their God and if the people can perpetrate such crimes their God must be of the same character and is to be execrated accordingly.[42] The tragic irony is apparent. The Jews who claimed to be the leaders of the nations for the worship of the true God had become the instruments of provoking the nations to blasphemy. With this the indictment has reached its climax.

25 The apostle now "pursues the Jew into his last retreat" (Haldane, *ad loc.*) and "proceeds to strip them [the Jews] of the last refuge to which they usually betook themselves, their illusive trust in the possession of circumcision" (Philippi, *ad loc.*). But there also appears to be an anticipation of 3:1, 2 by which the apostle is careful to indicate the advantage of circumcision—"for circumcision indeed profiteth, if thou be a doer of the law". The doing or, more accurately, the practising of the law contemplated in this case cannot have in view the perfect fulfilment of the law on the basis of legalism. Circumcision was the sign and seal of the covenant dispensed to Abraham which was a covenant of promise and of grace. Hence it had relevance only in the context of grace and not at all in the context of law and works in opposition to grace. The practising of the law, therefore, which makes circumcision profitable is the fulfilment of the conditions of faith and obedience apart from which the claim to the promises and grace and privileges of the covenant was presumption and mockery. The practising of the law is thus equivalent to the keeping of the covenant.[43] In like manner the transgression of the law which makes circumcision uncircumcision is the unfaithfulness to covenant obligations which in Old Testament terms is called the breaking of the covenant. In other words, the apostle in this

---

[42]   *Cf.* Meyer, *ad loc.*
[43]   *Cf.* φυλάσσῃ in vs. 26 and τελοῦσα in vs. 27.

passage is not enunciating the stipulations of a legalistic system but the obligations of that covenant of grace in reference to which circumcision had meaning. When these obligations are neglected and violated, circumcision has become uncircumcision and the outward sign is bereft of its significance. Implied, of course, in the light of the whole context, is the fact that circumcision is then a liability and augments condemnation. But here Paul does not reflect on that aspect.

26 "The uncircumcision" is simply those who are uncircumcised, that is to say, Gentiles. "The ordinances of the law" are the righteous requirements of the law. What then is meant by keeping the ordinances of the law on the part of the Gentiles? We cannot suppose that to "keep the ordinances of the law" is the same as to "do the things of the law" (vs. 14) and that the fulfilment of these ordinances takes place when "the Gentile obeys the moral law of nature", as Meyer maintains. The ordinances of the law are, as was noted above (vs. 25), the ordinances which belong to the context of circumcision and have therefore that covenantal complexion.[44] Neither are we to restrict the denotation to those Gentiles who were proselytes of the gate (*cf.* Acts 13:26). We are to regard the apostle as referring, in Godet's words, "to those many Gentiles converted to the gospel who, all uncircumcised as they were, nevertheless fulfil the law in virtue of the spirit of Christ, and thus become the *true* Israel, *the Israel of God*, Gal. vi. 16".[45] Keeping the ordinances of the law is therefore to be interpreted in terms of that faith and obedience which, in verse 25, we found to be the import of keeping the law. When the uncircumcised lays hold upon the covenant which circumcision represents and esteems its obligations so as to cherish the ordinances in which these obligations are expressed, then his uncircumcision is reckoned for circumcision, the reason being that the rite of circumcision is of no avail apart from that which it signifies, and if that which it signifies is present the absence of the sign does not annul this grace.

27 The version regards this verse as a question continuous with verse 26, implying the same affirmative answer. It makes no difference to the sense whether we regard it as a question or as a

---

[44] This, of course, Meyer does not deny but rather maintains.
[45] *Op. cit., ad loc.*

categorical statement. But, as in the case of verse 23, verse 27 can be taken categorically and, as an assertion, coordinated with the affirmative answer which verse 26 implies and adds another consideration which is directly aimed at the presumption and self-complacency of the Jew. "The uncircumcision which is by nature" is simply a way of characterising those who remain in their naturally uncircumcised state, appropriated here, no doubt, for the purpose of emphasizing the retention of that which to the Jew was the sign of uncleanness.[46] "If it fulfil the law" is to the same effect as "if thou be a doer of the law" (vs. 25) and "keep the ordinances of the law" (vs. 26) but each has its own significant shade of meaning.[47] "Shall judge thee" does not mean that they will sit in judgment but refers to the judgment of comparison and contrast (*cf.* Matt. 12:41, 42). "Who with the letter and circumcision art a transgressor of the law."[48] The only question here is the import of the term "letter". There is no good reason to depart from the meaning established by Paul's usage elsewhere (7:6; II Cor. 3:6, 7) where "letter" refers to the law and is so designated because the law is viewed as written on tables of stone or in the Scriptures. In this case it is the law as embodied in the Scriptures that is reflected upon and the Jew, notwithstanding his possession of the law as thus inscripturated and notwithstanding the circumcision in his flesh, is indicted as a transgressor of the law. This transgression of the law refers again to the violation of covenant obligations as they are expressed in the righteous ordinances of the law (*cf.* vss. 25, 26).

---

[46] On ἡ ἐκ φύσεως ἀκροβυστία James Denney says that "in spite of the grammatical irregularity, which in any case is not too great for a nervous writer like Paul, I prefer to connect ἐκ φύσεως, as Burton does (*Moods and Tenses*, § 427), with τελοῦσα, and to render: 'the uncircumcision which by nature fulfils the law': *cf.* ver. 14" (*St. Paul's Epistle to the Romans* in *The Expositor's Greek Testament, ad loc.*). There are three reasons for rejecting this view. (1) It is grammatically harsh to connect ἐκ φύσεως with τελοῦσα rather than with ἀκροβυστία. (2) The law the apostle has in mind here is not the law as revealed in nature (*cf.* vs. 14) but specially revealed law, for that alone consorts with the argument of the apostle here, as shown above. (3) Men do not by nature *fulfil* the law. The apostle must have in mind here the fulfilling which is by the Holy Spirit from the heart (*cf.* vs. 29) and not simply the doing by nature the things of the law attributed to Gentiles outside the pale of special revelation (vss. 14, 15).

[47] *Cf.* Sanday and Headlam, *ad vs.* 26.

[48] In the expression διὰ γράμματος καὶ περιτομῆς the διά is that of attendant circumstance and "describes the circumstances under which, or the accompaniment to which, anything is done" (Denney: *op. cit., ad loc.*).

28, 29 The apostle now proceeds to show that which truly constitutes a person a Jew and that in which circumcision truly consists; he shows who is a *true* Jew and what is *true* circumcision. This he does negatively in verse 28 and positively in verse 29. The relation to what precedes, indicated by "for" at the beginning of verse 28, is that the criteria of a *true* Jew and of *true* circumcision, set forth in verses 28, 29, support and confirm what had been affirmed in the three preceding verses. The contrast instituted is that between what is outward and what is inward.

The outward in the case of the Jew is, ostensibly, natural descent from Abraham and the possession of the privileges which that relation entailed. The outward in the case of circumcision is explained as "that which is outward in the flesh" (vs. 28), referring to that which is physically manifest. In saying that circumcision does not consist in this, the apostle is not denying the existence of the ritual act or its abiding effect in the flesh. His thought is that the outward has no spiritual significance except as the sign and seal of that which it represents, and the *true* circumcision is that work of grace in the heart which the external rite signifies.

The inward as it pertains to the Jew is not explained any further than as that which is "in the secret", that is to say, in that which is hidden from external observation (*cf.* 2:16; I Cor. 4:5; 14:25; II Cor. 4:2; I Pet. 3:4), the hidden man of the heart, and is to be understood of that which a man is in the recesses of the heart in distinction from external profession. The inward as it pertains to circumcision is defined as "that of the heart, in the spirit not in the letter". "That of the heart" is perspicuous enough and, in terms of the Old Testament, means the renewal and purification of the heart (Deut. 10:16; 30:6; Jer. 4:4; 9:25, 26). But "in the spirit not in the letter" is not immediately self-explanatory. The version has apparently interpreted "spirit" to refer to the human spirit and as therefore a further specification of the inward sphere in which the purification which circumcision signifies takes place. Since it is in the heart it is in the spirit of man. And "letter" by way of contrast would mean that which is outward, literal, physical circumcision. All of this is true in itself but there are two reasons for disputing the propriety of this interpretation. (1) It would be superfluous for the apostle to specify the sphere after he had said that "circumcision is that of *the heart*". (2) Much more cogent is the consideration that the contrast between letter and Spirit in Paul is not along this line of thought (cf. 7:6; II Cor. 3:6, 7, 8; cf. vss. 17, 18). The contrast is that between the Holy Spirit and the law as externally administered, a contrast between the life-giving power which the Holy Spirit imparts and the impotence which belongs to law as mere law. We shall have to adopt this contrast here. Hence what the apostle says is that the circumcision which is of the heart is by the Holy Spirit and not by the law.[49] He is again exposing the folly of Jewish presumption and of confidence in the mere possession of the law as embodied in the Scripture. The word "spirit" ought therefore to have been written with a capital to make plain that the reference is to the Holy Spirit. Although the doctrine of the work of the Holy Spirit is not developed until later in the epistle it is presupposed and introduced as relevant to an argument the burden of which is the universality of sin and condemnation.

Gifford has brought out the relevance of the concluding clause as well as any. "It is not at first sight apparent why St. Paul has added the clause, '*whose praise is not from men, but from God.*' But we must remember that he began his address to the Jew in *v.* 17, by an allusion to the name on which he prided himself, '*thou art called a Jew,*' and that he has just described in this verse the Jew that is worthy to be so-called. What, then, can be more natural, or more like St. Paul's style, than a renewed reference to the meaning of the name Jew? When Leah bore her fourth son she said, '*Now will I praise the Lord: therefore she called his name Judah*' (Gen. xxix. 35).

"When Jacob lay a-dying, this was the beginning of his blessing upon Judah: '*Judah, thou art he whom thy brethren shall praise*' (Gen. xlix. 8).

"St. Paul, in like manner alluding to the meaning of the name, says of the true Jew that his *praise is not from men, but from God.*"[50] There is undoubtedly, however, a combination of reasons why the apostle should have alluded to this original significance of the name "Jew". He is striking again at what lies in the back-

---

[49] This is the view of Meyer, Philippi, Hodge, Denney and others.

[50] Gifford is not, however, the first to have pointed out that there is here an evident play on the name "Jew", as Sanday and Headlam believe (*cf. op. cit., ad loc.*). This appears in Robert Haldane: *op. cit., ad loc.; cf.* also W. G. T. Shedd: *op. cit., ad loc.*

ground of his thought throughout this chapter and which forms the basis of his indictment against the Jew, namely, the iniquity of reliance upon appearance and upon what passes muster in the judgment of men. It is the application to the subject in hand of the word of the Lord himself: "How can ye believe, who receive glory one of another, and the glory that cometh from the only God ye seek not?" (John 5:44; *cf.* vss. 41–43).

D. THE FAITHFULNESS AND JUSTICE OF GOD
(3:1-8)

1-8

1 What advantage then hath the Jew? or what is the profit of circumcision?
2 Much every way: first of all, that they were intrusted with the oracles of God.
3 For what if some were without faith? shall their want of faith make of none effect the faithfulness of God?
4 God forbid: yea, let God be found true, but every man a liar; as it is written,
That thou mightest be justified in thy words,
And mightest prevail when thou comest into judgment.
5 But if our unrighteousness commendeth the righteousness of God, what shall we say? Is God unrighteous who visiteth with wrath? (I speak after the manner of men.)
6 God forbid: for then how shall God judge the world?
7 But if the truth of God through my lie abounded unto his glory, why am I also still judged as a sinner?
8 and why not (as we are slanderously reported, and as some affirm that we say), Let us do evil, that good may come? whose condemnation is just.

1, 2 Paul's foregoing argument respecting the inefficacy of circumcision in the flesh, that is, of the mere rite of circumcision divorced from the circumcision that is of the heart by the Holy Spirit, might appear to make of no avail God's institutions under the Old Testament. Especially might this be the inference drawn from Paul's statement in 2:27 that the uncircumcision by nature, when it fulfilled the law, would judge and condemn the circumcision which transgressed the law. It might seem that circumcision created disadvantage and liability rather than added privilege. It is this kind of inference that Paul anticipates and rebuts. He does so by asking and answering the pointed question: "What then is the advantage of the Jew, or what is the profit of circumcision?" His answer is "Much every way", as if he should say, much in every respect. He will not allow any depreciatory reflection to be cast upon the divine institution. In another connection, as we shall see, he insists that men's unbelief does not make void the faithfulness of God. So here his thought is that though the external rite is of no avail when it is accompanied by transgression of the law, yet this does not make void the advantage and profit accruing to the Jew as the depository of divine institution. The direction of the apostle's thought here is relevant as rebuke to much that is current in the attitude of the present day, namely, neglect of, if not contempt for, institutions which God has established in the church, on the plausible plea that in many cases those who observe these institutions do not prove faithful to their intent and purpose and that many who are indifferent and perhaps hostile to these institutions exhibit more of the evangelical faith and fervour which ought to commend these institutions. The same answer must be given and given with even greater emphasis. For if Paul could say with reference to the advantage and profit of an institution that had been discontinued as to its observance "Much every way", how much more may we esteem the institutions that are permanent in the church of Christ and which regulate its life and devotion until Christ will come again.

We should expect the apostle to specify several of the respects in which the advantage and profit of which he speaks actually obtained. He does this later in this epistle when he says that to Israel pertained "the adoption, and the glory, and the covenants, and the giving of the law, and the service of God, and the promises" (9:4). And we might all the more expect this when he begins by saying, "first of all"; we would naturally look for a second and a third. But this is not what we find. He gives us what is first and is content with that. It makes little difference whether we regard the word he uses as "first" or "chiefly". In either case what Paul appeals to is that which was preeminent in the privileges of the Jews—"they were intrusted with the oracles of God". They were the depositories of God's special revelation.

The expression "the oracles of God" is specially significant. (1) Paul is undoubtedly thinking of the Old Testament in its entirety, not simply of discrete oracular utterances given to the

Old Testament organs of revelation and embodied in the Old Testament. He speaks of that with which the Jews had been entrusted, of that which had been committed to them, and he could not be conceived of as making discrimination within the contents of that total deposit. (2) It is as Scripture that these oracles were committed to the Jews; only in this form could the *Jews* be said to have been *entrusted* with them. (3) The deposit of revelation in the Scripture of the Old Testament is called "the oracles of God". The Scripture is therefore regarded by the apostle as oracular words of God. Scripture is no less the speech or sayings of God than were the divine utterances which prophets received directly from the mouth of God. Scripture itself is a "thus saith the Lord". This is Paul's concept of the Scripture with which the Jew had been entrusted. For Paul the *written* Word is God's speech, and God's speech is conceived of as existing in the form of a "trust" to Israel; divine oracles have fixed and abiding form.

It is when viewed in this light that we can appreciate Paul's characterization of this privilege as the first or chief and we can also understand why he does not need for the present to enumerate other advantages belonging to the Jew. When we think of what, above all else, was the Jew's privilege as an abiding possession it was his entrustment with the Word of God. And Paul was not afraid of being accused of bibliolatry when he thus assessed the inscripturated Word.

3, 4 At the beginning of verse 3 Paul asks a question which may be rendered "What then?" or "For how?" It is a question provoked by the consideration that the unbelief of Israel, to whom the oracles of God had been entrusted, must not be reckoned as in any respect interfering with or prejudicing the reality of this privilege that they were in possession of the divine oracles. For it might seem that, if what Paul says in the latter part of chapter 2 is correct, then Israel had forfeited this privilege. This is what Paul denies. For he proceeds with a question which is intended to offset in the most emphatic terms any such insinuation or allegation: "If some did not believe, shall their unbelief make the faith of God of none effect?" We expect a negative answer and Paul supplies it in a form which indicates his abhorrence of the suggestion. The formula he uses could be rendered more

93

literally as "far from it", but it really needs the force of the expression given in our version "God forbid".[1]

The most reasonable view of the unbelief in view in the foregoing question is the unbelief of the Jews in Paul's day, exhibited in the rejection of Jesus as the Messiah and therefore the unbelief of the oracles of God referred to in verse 2. By implication he charges the unbelieving Jews with the rejection of those very oracles on which they prided themselves. This indicates the apostle's estimate of the relation that the rejection of the gospel sustained to the Old Testament institution as a whole but particularly to that institution as it was focused in the messianic promises, an estimate which comes to expression more fully in his epistle to the Galatians. The reason why the unbelief of the Jews of his own day should be considered as that in view here is not only the terms he uses but also the fact that in the context he is addressing the unbelieving and disobedient Jews (cf. 2:17ff.). He is careful, however, not to include all Jews in this category; he says, "if some did not believe".

The argument, therefore, is that the unbelief of some Jews does not invalidate the privilege of Israel in the possession of the oracles of God nor does it negate the advantage of the Jew over the Gentile in this respect. But of even greater moment as implicit in the argument is the fact that the unbelief of Jews does not disestablish the truth and abiding validity of God's oracles. The unbelief of some does not bring to nought "the faith of God". This expression "the faith of God" does not mean our faith in God but God's faithfulness. This is apparent from verse 4; the latter is in such close juxtaposition to verse 3 that it explains for us that which is intended by "the faith of God". It is God's faith-keeping in contrast with man's faithlessness, and this is simply God's truth or trothfulness.

"Let God be found true, but every man a liar" is an arresting

---

[1] There is Old Testament warrant for the rendering "God forbid". μὴ γένοιτο corresponds to the Hebrew חָלִילָה and occurs as the rendering of the same in the LXX (cf. Gen. 44:7, 17; Josh. 22:29; 24:16; I Kings 20:3). And חָלִילָה is sometimes used with the names for God יהוה and אלהים and אל (I Sam. 24:6; 26:11; I Kings 21:3; I Chron. 11:19; Job 34:10; cf. I Sam. 2:30) and with the pronoun when the same refers to God (Gen. 18:25). Hence our English expression "God forbid" has biblical precedent. The Greek μὴ γένοιτο, indicating the recoil of abhorrence, needs the strength of this English rendering derived from the Hebrew Cf. J. B. Lightfoot: Comm., ad Gal. 2:17.

way of placing in the forefront the indefectible faithfulness of God to his Word. It illustrates the conception which governs this epistle, that God is not determined in his purposes or in his promises by what is extraneous to himself or to his will. What could advertise this truth more than the consideration that the oracles which are concerned with the gospel of God's grace to men are not annuled even in their promissory design by that unbelief which offers contradiction to their truth and purport. God's truthfulness is inviolate even though *all* men be liars.[2]

The appeal to Scripture (Psalm 51:4) in this connection presents some difficulty because of the difference between the relationship in which David spoke these words and that in which Paul adduces them. David said: "Against thee, thee only, have I sinned and done the evil in thy sight, that thou mayest be justified when thou speakest, and be clear when thou judgest". The thought would appear to be as follows. Sin is directed against God and sin even against fellow men (as was David's) is sin against them because it is first of all and ultimately sin against God; therefore God in his judgments upon men for sin is always just. And not only so. The character of sin as directed against God, and for the reason that it is directed against God, subserves the purpose of vindicating the justness of God's condemnatory judgment. So far from detracting from the justice of God, sin as against God promotes the vindication and exhibition of his justice in the judgment he pronounces with reference to it. While this may appear to be harsh reasoning yet it is consonant with the subject the apostle has in hand. He has been making emphatic protestation to the effect that the unbelief of men does not bring to nought the faithfulness of God. The appeal to David's confession provides him with the strongest kind of confirmation. For David had said that sin, since it is against God, vindicates and establishes God's justice. If sin does not disestablish the *justice* of God, neither can man's faithlessness and untruth make void the *faithfulness* and *truth* of God. God must be true though every man be a liar. That this is the apostle's use and interpretation of Psalm 51:4 the succeeding context indicates. For he proceeds forthwith to deal with the false inferences which opponents would derive

---

[2] There is eloquent progression here. It is not simply in the face of the fact that some do not believe (vs. 3) that God's faithfulness is inviolate. Even if all men were liars God's truth remains unmoved (*cf.* Psalm 100:5).

from the proposition that sin vindicates the justice and judgment of God—"but if our unrighteousness commendeth the righteousness of God, what shall we say?" (vs. 5).[3]

5–8 In verse 5 two questions are asked which may most properly be regarded as contemplating an abuse of the doctrine set forth in the preceding verses[4], an abuse to the effect that if our unbelief of the promises does not make void God's faithfulness but renders it more conspicuous or, in terms of verse 5, if the unrighteousness of man serves to exhibit more clearly the righteousness of God, then God would be unrighteous in executing his wrath upon the ungodly. For it is plausible and apparently inevitable logic to say that God cannot justly inflict punishment upon the action which is instrumental in the more illustrious display of the truth and righteousness which are his glory. The precise terms which Paul uses in verse 5 accentuate the seeming cogency of the argument. How can God manifest his displeasure and inflict wrath upon that which sets off his glory in more conspicuous relief, especially when we consider that the exhibition

---

[3] The difficulty arising from the rendering of the LXX, which Paul quotes, is not as great from the standpoint of interpretation as it might appear to be. In the Hebrew the two parts quoted by Paul should reasonably be taken as parallel and therefore as substantially to the same effect—God is justified when he speaks; he is clear (quit) when he judges. The LXX, as quoted by Paul, would appear to introduce a distinct change of thought in the second part. For it renders the Hebrew יזכה by νικήσεις and שפטך by κρίνεσθαι and so the rendering could be "thou mayest overcome (prevail) when thou art judged", κρίνεσθαι being taken as passive. Thus God is represented as being subjected to judgment but as, nevertheless, coming out clear or quit in the lawsuit. It should be appreciated, however, that this rendering does not disturb the thought which the apostle is interested in adducing, namely, that sin does not in the least derogate from the justice of God but rather subserves the purpose of vindicating and establishing it. However, we are not shut up to the view that κρίνεσθαι is passive; it may be middle (*cf.* Matt. 5:40; I Cor. 6:6 and possibly I Cor. 6:1). In that event there is no substantial change in the LXX rendering and the meaning is the same as in the Hebrew with the exception that νικήσεις has a different shade of meaning from that of יזכה in Hebrew.

[4] Hodge maintains (*ad loc.*) that Paul is answering the objections of the Jews to his doctrine and not false inferences. I have taken the position that Paul is dealing with an inference that could readily be drawn from the doctrine he had just stated. That Paul was charged with this false inference either by opponents or by those who professed to espouse his doctrine is apparent from vs. 8—"some affirm that we say". It may be that the Jews urged this as an objection to his teaching. But in any case that with which he deals is a false inference from or an erroneous application of the teaching of the preceding verses.

of his glory must gratify himself? "Let us do evil that good may come" appears to be the unavoidable moral lesson.

There does not appear to be good reason for thinking that there is any substantial difference between the false inference or abuse contemplated in the two questions of verse 5 and the two questions of verses 7 and 8. The inference proposed in verse 8 is that if the truth of God, that is to say, his faithfulness in fulfilling his promises, has been more abundantly exemplified by man's unbelief and contradiction and God thereby glorified, then the agent of this unbelief cannot any longer be regarded as a sinner. When Paul identifies himself with the lie that is given to the promises of God and says "by my lie", this is but a rhetorical way of expressing the thought; he is not reflecting on his former unbelief and on the way in which the grace of God abounded in his own case. This would be extraneous to the subject in hand; he is not now dealing with the truth that "where sin abounded grace did much more abound" (5:20).

The matter dealt with in verse 7[5] is carried on in verse 8 and the question of the latter is closely attached to the interrogative part of verse 7, "why am I also still judged as a sinner?" The essence of verse 8 could then be paraphrased thus: "Instead of being judged as a sinner for the lie that we give to God's promises, why not rather let us do evil that good may come?" The immorality implicit in this latter slogan appears to be the necessary inference to be drawn from the fact stated expressly in the preceding verses and implied throughout, namely, that the glory of God is made more conspicuous by man's unbelief and sin. The slogan pointedly sets forth the underlying assumption with which Paul is dealing from verse 5 onwards.

The construction of verse 8 may be somewhat irregular but the thought is not obscure if we recognize that the two clauses, "as we are slanderously reported and as some affirm that we say" are parenthetical to the leading drift of the thought, as has been indicated by the paraphrase given above. This parenthesis,

---

[5] The variant in verse 7 between δέ and γάρ is one in connection with which it is difficult to be decisive. Both readings yield good sense and have substantial ms. support. I would venture the suggestion that if we adopt the reading δέ, vs. 7 is the reiterated objection to what is the implied emphatic denial in μὴ γένοιτο (vs. 6). If we adopt the reading γάρ, then vs. 7 is an explanation or expansion of the objection urged in vs. 6—vs. 7 would be another form of the same objection urged in support of its apparent cogency.

however, throws much light on the passage. The apostle is not dealing with a hypothetical situation in these four verses. The antinomian perversion had been laid to Paul's account. His teaching had been interpreted as giving scope to licentiousness, indeed as placing a premium upon it.

Those who pleaded that this was Paul's position, or at least the practical effect of his teaching, could have been those who espoused his doctrine and added to their espousal this distortion —they might have been his alleged friends. Paul had occasion to deal with this distortion of the doctrine of grace later in his epistle (*cf.* especially chap. 6). But it is far more likely that those in view were his legalistic opponents who sought to calumniate his teaching by imputing to him this abuse. It is of little consequence for the interpretation of the passage whether they alleged that this was the apostle's express teaching or that it was the practical effect of his teaching; the terms, "some affirm that we say" would more probably imply the former.

The concluding statement, "whose condemnation is just" should not be restricted to those who "slanderously reported" but includes all who are conceived of as giving way to the abuse in question or who regarded it as an inference to be drawn from the apostle's teaching. The clauses, "as we are slanderously reported, and as some affirm that we say", we must not forget are parenthetical and the concluding clause is not immediately attached to them but to the false reasoning dealt with in the whole passage and summed up in the slogan, "let us do evil, that good may come". The just condemnation is, therefore, that executed upon those who turn the truth and faithfulness of God into lasciviousness or who consider that the doctrine Paul is propounding leads to that immoral result. The distortion the apostle is exposing is therefore condemned in the most emphatic terms by this concluding statement.

What then is Paul's answer to the distortion with which he is dealing in verses 5–8? We might expect a lengthy argument after the pattern of Paul's rebuttal of the antinomian bias in chapter 6. This we do not find. We must bear in mind that the distortions in view in the respective passages are not identical, though they are similar. In chapter 6 Paul is dealing with the abuse applied to the doctrine of grace, whereas in 3:5–8 he is dealing with an assault upon the justice or rectitude of God. "The righteousness of God" (vs. 5) is the attribute of righteousness, not "the righteousness of God" revealed from faith to faith in the grace of justification (*cf.* 1:17; 3:21, 22; 10:3). It is the inherent equity of God and is to be coordinated with the truth or truthfulness of God (vss. 5, 7). The abuse with which verses 5–8 deal is, therefore, of a different cast, and it is significant that Paul has no lengthy refutation. The consideration he pits against the distortion is simply: "God forbid: in that event how will God judge the world?" (vs. 6).

It might seem that this consideration begs the question. For of what avail is it to affirm that God will judge the world if the question is: how can God be just in executing judgment if his righteousness is commended by our unrighteousness? Categorical assertion of the thing to be proved is no argument! This, however, is what we discover in this instance. Paul appeals to the fact of universal judgment and he does not proceed to prove it. He accepts it as an ultimate datum of revelation, and he confronts the objection of verse 5 with this fact. About the certainty of God's judgment there can be no dispute. Once the judgment is accepted as a certainty, then all such objection as is implied in verses 5, 7, 8 falls to the ground. The apostle's answer in this case illustrates what must always be true when we are dealing with the ultimate facts of revelation. These facts are ultimate and argument must be content with categorical affirmation. The answer to objections is proclamation.

There is one further expression in this passage that needs explication—"I speak as a man" (vs. 5). Paul is not to be interpreted as contrasting what he says now as a mere man with what on other occasions he says as an apostle or Christian.[6] He is writing as an apostle. The thought is that in asking the foregoing questions he is accommodating himself to the human mode of interrogation and reasoning. In reality the questions are impertinent and out of place. For God's justice is not something that may be called in question. And we may only utter these questions as voicing those that arise in the human mind and then only for the purpose of intimating the recoil of abhorrence from the very suggestion that God might be unjust. This is exactly what Paul does; he adds immediately the formula (*cf.* vs. 4 and note

---

[6] *Cf. contra* Hodge who says that here Paul declares that "he is not speaking in his character of an apostle or Christian, but speaking as others speak, expressing their thoughts, not his own" (*ad loc.*).

thereon) of emphatic negation, "God forbid". The holiness and righteousness of God do not allow for calling his rectitude into question or for any suggestion of his inequity. It is that fundamental datum that Paul's apologetic expression, "I speak as a man" underlines. It is for the purpose of repudiating the suggestion that he voices the questions.

E. CONCLUSION
(3:9–20)

9 What then? are we better than they? No, in no wise:
for we before laid to the charge both of Jews and
Greeks, that they are all under sin;
10 as it is written,
There is none righteous, no, not one;
11 There is none that understandeth,
There is none that seeketh after God;
12 They have all turned aside, they are together become
unprofitable;
There is none that doeth good, no, not so much as one:
13 Their throat is an open sepulchre;
With their tongues they have used deceit:
The poison of asps is under their lips:
14 Whose mouth is full of cursing and bitterness:
15 Their feet are swift to shed blood;
16 Destruction and misery are in their ways;
17 And the way of peace have they not known:
18 There is no fear of God before their eyes.

9 At the beginning of verse 9 there are two brief questions.
The first is adequately rendered "What then?" meaning "What
then follows?" or, "What is the case?" Respecting the second
question there is difficulty in determining its exact force and there
is much difference of opinion among expositors. It is not likely
that the rendering "are we better than they?" is correct.[7] It is

---

7 Although there are variant readings there is not sufficient support for
the other variants to depart from the reading προεχόμεθα. The difficulty in
determining the import resides largely in the fact that only here in the New
Testament does this verb occur and the usage elsewhere does not decisively
indicate the sense here. "Unfortunately we have as yet no such new light as
F. B. Westcott . . . hoped for from 'some fortunate exhumed sherd, or strip
of papyrus' to help to explain the difficult προεχόμεθα of Rom. 3:9" (Moulton
and Milligan: *The Vocabulary of the Greek Testament ad προέχω*). J. B. Lightfoot
regards the form as passive and adopts the rendering, "are we excelled?"
and continues in elucidation of this rendering: " 'What then,' argues the Jew,
'do you mean to tell me that others have the advantage over us?' St Paul's
answer is, 'Not at all. We said before that Jews and Gentiles all were under
sin. But if we do not give them any advantage over you, neither do we give
you any advantage over them. Your Scriptures show that you are not ex-

more likely that the thought is, "Are we excelled?" or, in Meyer's words, "*Do we put forward* (anything) *in our defence?*" But, in any case, whether the question is that of the superiority of the Jew over the Gentile, or of the Gentile over the Jew, or of the advantage which the Jew might be conceived of as enjoying in reference to the judgment of God by reason of the privilege which he possessed (*cf.* vss. 1, 2), the succeeding context shows that the question is introductory to the demonstration that there is no difference in respect of sin and condemnation. Whatever the precise import of the question, the answer is a sweeping denial—"not by any means", "not in any respect", "altogether no".[8] "For we have before laid to the charge of both Jews and Greeks that they are all under sin." This indictment[9] must be that comprised in 1:18–2:24. What is intended by the expression "under sin" is explicated in the quotations from the Old Testament which follow, mostly derived from the book of Psalms. To be "under sin" is to be under the dominion of sin, and the pervasiveness of the resulting perversity is demonstrated by the manifold ways in which it is manifested. The apostle has selected a series of indictments drawn from the Old Testament and covering the wide range of human character and activity to show that, from whatever aspect men may be viewed, the verdict of Scripture is one of universal and total depravity. The quotation in verses 10–18 is not derived from any one place in the Old Testament. The apostle places together various passages which when thus combined provide a unified summary of the witness of the Old Testament to the pervasive sinfulness of mankind.

10 This verse is not a verbation quotation of any one passage but it may be Paul's summary rendering of the sense of Psalm 14:3 which in both the Hebrew and LXX reads: "there is none that doeth good, no, not even one" and which he quotes verbatim

---

empted'" (*Notes on the Epistles of St. Paul*, London, 1895, p. 267). Likewise Frederick Field says that the passive sense "Are we excelled?" is "the best if not the only solution of the difficulty" and against the meaning "*to make use of anything as a pretext or excuse*" he pleads that "when προέχεσθαι is thus used, it is never *absolute positum*, as in the text" (*Notes on the Translation of the New Testament*, Cambridge, 1899, p. 153).

[8] οὐ πάντως is not to be understood as in I Cor. 5:10 but as πάντως οὐκ in I Cor. 16:12.

[9] προαιτιάομαι is ἅπαξ λεγόμενον in the New Testament and is not to be rendered "we have before proved" (*cf.* Lightfoot: *idem*).

at the end of verse 12. There need be no question as to the propriety or the purpose of this initial summary statement. It is the precipitate of the Biblical teaching and it is particularly relevant to the charge made in verse 9 that all are under sin. The most direct biblical support is that "there is none righteous, no, not one". Righteousness is the criterion by which sin is judged and the absence of righteousness means the presence of sin.

11 This verse is clearly derived from Psalms 14:2; 53:3. But again it is not verbatim quotation of either the Hebrew or the LXX. These Psalms read: "The Lord (God in 53:3) looked down from heaven upon the children of men, to see if there were any that did understand, that did seek after God". The implication is that there were none. Paul quotes in the form of this implication and uses the same terms in the form of direct negation—"there is none that understandeth, there is none that seeketh after God". Verse 10 had been a statement in general terms; this verse is more specific and particularizes respects in which universal sinfulness appears. In the noetic sphere there is no understanding; in the conative there is no movement towards God. With reference to God all men are noetically blind and in respect of Godward aspiration they are dead.

12 This is verbatim quotation from the LXX of Psalms 14:3; 53:4 which quite accurately reflect the Hebrew.[10] The turning aside is that of backsliding and apostasy and we can scarcely dissociate the thought from that of 1:21 where apostasy is first mentioned and described—"knowing God, they glorified him not as God, neither gave thanks". Declension is, therefore, an indictment which the apostle brings against all men. In one way or another all are guilty of turning aside from the way of godliness. "They are together become unprofitable." The Greek in this case reflects on the uselessness, the Hebrew on the corruption. Like salt that has lost its savour or as fruit that is rotten no longer serves any useful purpose, so all men are viewed as having "gone bad"; that there is no exception is expressed by the word "to-gether"—to a man they are corrupted. The terms in which the concluding clause is expressed leave no loophole for exception—

---

[10] The slight variation in the Hebrew of Psalm 53:4, especially that from סר of 14:3 to סג of 53:4, makes no difference to the meaning. Both verbs are well rendered by ἐξέκλιναν of the Greek.

there is not even one who does good. To state the thought of verse 12 both negatively and positively it is that as respects well-doing there is not one, as respects evil-doing there is no exception.

13–17 The first two clauses of verse 13 are a verbatim quotation from the Hebrew and Greek of Psalm 5:10 and the last clause is similarly from the LXX of Psalm 139:4 with which the Hebrew of Psalm 140:4 is practically identical. Verse 14 corresponds rather closely to the Hebrew of Psalm 10:7 (*cf.* LXX of Psalm 9:28). Verse 15 is taken from Isaiah 59:7 but is an abbreviated form of what we find in both Hebrew and Greek, an abbreviation, however, which conveys the substantial thought. Verse 16 is also from Isaiah 59:7 and is verbatim as in the LXX with only slight, if any, divergence from the Hebrew. Verse 17 is from Isaiah 59:8 and is an exact rendering with the exception that a different verb and tense are used in the LXX for the word "know".

In these verses (13–17) the apostle becomes more concrete in his indictment. This is apparent from the mention of five distinct bodily organs in the five clauses of verses 13–15, the first four being organs of speech and the fifth the feet. The concentration upon organs of speech in verses 13, 14 shows how, in the apostle's esteem, the depravity of man is exemplified in his words and how diverse are the ways in which speech betrays the wickedness of the heart. In the words of Godet, "the *throat* (*larynx*) is compared to a sepulchre; this refers to the language of the gross and brutal man, of whom it is said in common parlance: it seems as if he would like to eat you. The characteristic which follows contrasts with the former; it is the sugared *tongue*, which charms you like a melodious instrument."[11] Or it may well be that the throat as an open sepulchre simply reflects quite generally upon the corruption of which vile speech is the expression.

18 This is verbatim quotation from the Hebrew of Psalm 36:2 (LXX 35:2) with the exception that the apostle uses the plural pronoun for the sake of uniformity with the plural in the preceding quotations. In the teaching of Scripture the fear of God is the soul of godliness and its absence the epitome of impiety. To be destitute of the fear of God is to be godless, and no indictment

---

[11] *Op. cit., ad loc.*

could be more inclusive and decisive than the charge here made. As the throat, the tongue, the lip, the mouth, the feet had been used in the preceding verses in their appropriate relationships in each case, so here the eyes. The eyes are the organs of vision and the fear of God is appropriately expressed as before our eyes because the fear of God means that God is constantly in the centre of our thought and apprehension, and life is characterized by the all-pervasive consciousness of dependence upon him and responsibility to him. The absence of this fear means that God is excluded not only from the centre of thought and calculation but from the whole horizon of our reckoning; God is not in all our thoughts. Figuratively, he is not before our eyes. And this is unqualified godlessness.

> 19 Now we know that what things soever the law saith, it speaketh to them that are under the law; that every mouth may be stopped, and all the world may be brought under the judgment of God:
> 20 because by the works of the law shall no flesh be justified in his sight; for through the law *cometh* the knowledge of sin.

19 Having quoted these testimonies from the Old Testament to support what he had established in the earlier part of the epistle that all, both Jews and Greeks, were under sin, the apostle in verses 19, 20 draws his conclusions from this witness of Scripture to the effect that all without exception lie under the judgment of God. When in verse 19 he says, "we know that whatsoever things the law says it speaks to those who are in the law", there are some things to be noted. (1) Having quoted from the Psalms and the prophet Isaiah he must be using the word "law" in an inclusive sense as synonymous with the Old Testament. Here "law" is not restricted to the specifically legislative contents of the Old Testament nor to the books of Moses. Paul can designate the whole of the Old Testament as "the law" when this designation is consonant with the thought in hand, and, though the quotations are not drawn from what is specifically the law, they have nevertheless the force and relevance that belong to law in its more specific denotation. It is not Pauline, therefore, to regard the law that is epitomized in the ten commandments as a law that can be segregated; the Old Testament in its entirety is permeated with the requirements and judgments which are summed up in the ten commandments. (2) He regards the law which is deposited in the Old Testament as speaking—"whatsoever things the law says it speaks to those who are in the law". The Scripture is not a dead word; it is living speech. (3) It is living speech with relevance to the present. The apostle was not dealing merely with the past; he was writing of what was true in his day and in ours. (4) The law speaks to those who are in the law.

This expression "in the law" is not to be equated with "under law" (6:14). In this latter case "under law" is the antithesis of "under grace" and Paul at this juncture in his epistle is not suggesting that all those "in the law" were thereby excluded from the operations of grace. "In the law" means the sphere of the law, the sphere in which the law of which he had spoken and of which he had given samples was applicable by way of demand and judgment. The question arises: how extensive is this sphere of the law's application? Does its relevance apply only to those who had the Old Testament, namely, the Jews to whom these oracles had been committed (vs. 2)? This is what we might be led to expect and hence conclude that in this verse Paul is showing the judgment that falls upon the Jews. It would not be unreasonable to infer such limitation in this instance because his main interest is to show the Jews that they were no better than the Gentiles in reference to the judgment concerned. The sinnership and hence condemnation of the Gentiles could be taken for granted as not in dispute among the Jews. But it is a significant fact that this limitation is not borne out by the terms of the passage. For Paul says that "what things soever the law says it speaks to them who are in the law, *in order that every mouth may be stopped and the whole world may become liable to God*". There can be no question but here is the note of all-inclusive universality, especially in the words "the whole world". Paul includes the Gentiles who did not have the law in the sense of the Old Testament or of specially revealed law (*cf.* 2:14). The Gentiles are therefore regarded as "in the law", that is to say, in the sphere within which the law of which Paul had quoted samples had relevance. This establishes the all-important consideration that although the Gentiles did not have the Old Testament law and in that sense were without law, yet they were not outside the sphere of the judgment which the Old Testament pronounced. This is saying that the descriptions given in those passages quoted were characteristic of the Gentiles as well as of the Jews and the corresponding judgment rested upon them to the end that they all might be without excuse and be condemned in the sight of God.[12]

20 The term by which verse 20 is introduced is not properly rendered by "therefore" (as in A.V.) but by "because". This verse gives the reason why every mouth is stopped and the whole world is condemned, to wit, that "from the works of the law no flesh will be justified" before God. This does not overthrow the principle stated in 2:13 that "the doers of the law will be justified". This holds true as a principle of equity but, existentially, it never comes into operation in the human race for the reason that there are no doers of the law, no doing of the law that will ground or elicit justification—"there is none righteous, no, not one" (vs. 10). For this reason that there is actually no justification by the works of the law the function of the law is to convince of sin (vs. 20b). The law does perform this necessary and contributory service in connection with justification; it imparts the knowledge of sin and enables us to perceive that from the works of the law no flesh will be justified and therefore every mouth is stopped and the whole world rests under God's judgment.

The future tense in "will be justified" and the "becoming" intimated in "become liable to God" do not refer to the future judgment. These expressions point rather to the certainty and the universality of the propositions with which they are concerned.

---

[12] ὑπόδικος occurs only here in the New Testament. In classical Greek it means to be liable to or brought under the cognizance of. *Cf.* Moulton and Milligan: *op. cit.;* J. B. Lightfoot: *Notes, ad loc.*

V. THE RIGHTEOUSNESS OF GOD
(3:21-31)

21-26

21 But now apart from the law a righteousness of God
hath been manifested, being witnessed by the law and
the prophets;

22 even the righteousness of God through faith in Jesus
Christ unto all them that believe; for there is no
distinction;

23 for all have sinned, and fall short of the glory of God;

24 being justified freely by his grace through the redemption that is in Christ Jesus:

25 whom God set forth *to be* a propitiation, through faith,
in his blood, to show his righteousness because of the
passing over of the sins done aforetime, in the forbearance of God;

26 for the showing, *I say*, of his righteousness at this present
season: that he might himself be just, and the justifier
of him that hath faith in Jesus.

21-23   Meyer contends that the "now" at the beginning of
verse 21 is not an adverb of time expressing "the contrast between
two *periods*", but that it expresses the contrast "between two
relations", namely, "the relation of dependence on the law and
the relation of independence on the law" (*ad loc.*).   He does
draw attention to the pivotal contrast instituted here between
justification "through law" (which is nonexistent) and justification
"without law" or "apart from law" which is the provision of
the gospel and with which Paul proceeds to deal forthwith.   But
it is not apparent that the "now" in question should be deprived
of its temporal force.   Paul is emphasizing not only the contrast
between justification through the works of law and justification
without the law, that is, without works of law, but he is also
emphasizing the *manifestation* of the latter which came with the
revelation of Jesus Christ.   *Now*, in contrast with the past, this
righteousness of God is manifested; it has come to lie open to full
view, as Meyer so admirably shows later on in his exposition.
This does not mean for Paul that justification without the law

108

was now for the first time revealed and that in the earlier period all that men knew was justification by works of law.[13] It is far otherwise. To obviate any such discrepancy between the past and the present Paul expressly reminds us that this righteousness of God now manifested was witnessed by the law and the prophets.[14] He is jealous to maintain in this matter as in other respects the continuity between the two Testaments. But consistently with this continuity there can still be distinct emphasis upon the momentous change in the New Testament in respect of *manifestation*. The temporal force of the "now" can therefore be recognized without impairing either the contrast of relations or the continuity of the two periods contrasted.

When Paul says "without the law" the absoluteness of this negation must not be toned down. He means this without any reservation or equivocation in reference to the justifying righteousness which is the theme of this part of the epistle. This implies that in justification there is no contribution, preparatory, accessory, or subsidiary, that is given by works of law. This fact is set forth here both by the expression itself and by its emphatic position in the sentence. And it is borne out by the sustained polemic of the epistle as a whole. To overlook this accent is to miss the central message of the epistle. To equivocate here is to distort what could not be more plainly and consistently stated.[15]

The expression, "without the law" is not to be understood in the canonical sense nor in the sense of dispensation. It is not said that the righteousness of God now manifested was apart from

---

[13] Sanday and Headlam, in controverting Meyer's view, do not, however, state the case accurately when they say, "But here the two states or relations correspond to two periods succeeding each other in order of time" (*op. cit., ad loc.*). The parallels which they quote (Rom. 16:25, 26; Eph. 2:12, 13; Col. 1:26, 27; II Tim. 1:9, 10; Heb. 9:26), though directly pertinent to Paul's thought here, do not bear out the position that the two relations correspond with the two periods. It is the difference in respect of manifestation that is emphasized by the temporal νυνὶ δέ, as is also attested by the parallels cited. Still, Sanday and Headlam are explicit to the effect that, according to Paul, "the new order of things is in no way contrary to the old, but rather a development which was duly foreseen and provided for" (*ad loc.* on μαρτυρουμένη κ.τ.λ.).

[14] "The law and the prophets" as a formula is no doubt inclusive, comprising the whole of the Old Testament.

[15] The Romish doctrine of justification as consisting in sanctifying grace by which sins are remitted and we are made just conceives of justification as a process and hence justification is increased by good works. For the refutation of the Romish position the reader is referred to the appendix on "Justification" (pp. 336 ff.).

the Old Testament viewed either as canon or as period. Paul says the opposite—"it was witnessed by the law and the prophets" in the sense that the law and the prophets bore witness to it. In the expression "apart from the law" the term "law" is used in the sense of "works of law" (vs. 20) and the thought is simply that law as commandment or as constraining to and producing works contributes nothing to our justification. We have here an instructive example of the ease with which the apostle can turn from one denotation of the word "law" to another. The righteousness that is unreservedly without law in one sense of the word "law" is, nevertheless, witnessed to and therefore proclaimed by the law in another sense of that term. Law in one sense pronounces the opposite of justification, the law in another sense preaches justification. This illustrates the necessity in each case of determining the precise sense in which the term "law" is used by the apostle and we must not suppose that the term has always the same denotation and connotation. Exposition has suffered from failure to recognize this variation. Here the variation is exemplified in two consecutive clauses.

It is possible that "apart from the law" in verse 21 is to be construed directly with "is manifest" rather than with "the righteousness of God". In this event the emphasis falls upon the manifestation without law rather than upon the fact that it is a righteousness without law (cf. Meyer, ad loc.). Even if, syntactically, this construction were favoured, it would still follow by inference that it is a righteousness without law. It is possible, however, that "without law" should be construed with "the righteousness of God" and in that event the righteousness is directly characterized as one without law.

"The righteousness of God" that is said to be manifested is that which we have already found in 1:17. The reader is referred to the exposition at that point.

"The righteousness of God" of verse 22 is the same as that of verse 21 and 1:17 and the words "through faith of Jesus Christ unto all who believe" have the same force as "from faith to faith" of 1:17. To the exposition at that point the reader is again referred. It is necessary, however, to note the additional elements, implied in 1:17, but set forth here overtly. The apostle is careful to define this faith as faith in Jesus Christ. It is hardly necessary to show that Jesus Christ is the object and not the subject of the

faith spoken of. It would be alien to the whole teaching of the
apostle to suppose that what he has in mind is a faith that is
patterned after the faith which Jesus himself exemplified, far less
that we are justified by Jesus' own faith, that is to say, by the
faith which he exercised. Although the notion that the faithfulness of Christ is in view would not be contrary to the analogy
of Scripture in general, yet there is not good warrant for this
interpretation here any more than in 1:17. The reader is again
referred to the appendix on this subject (pp. 363 ff.).

In representing Jesus Christ as the object of faith the apostle
brings to the forefront a consideration which had not been
expressly stated so far in this epistle. The faith that is brought into
relation to justification is not a general faith in God; far less is it
faith without well-defined and intelligible content. It is faith
directed to Christ, and when he is denominated "Jesus Christ"
these titles are redolent of all that Jesus was and is personally,
historically, and officially. It is Jesus Christ in terms of Romans
1:3, 4 who is the object of justifying faith. In terms of verses 21,
22, it is this faith that places us in effectual relation to the righteousness of God. In the succeeding verses the apostle defines the
accomplishment of Christ by which he is constituted the appropriate object of this faith, an accomplishment defined as redemption, propitiation, and the vindication of justice. It is Jesus Christ
in the efficacy that belongs to him as redeemer and propitiator
who is the proper object of faith. Faith is focused upon him in
the specific character that is his as Saviour, Redeemer, and Lord.

In view of these implications of the expression "through the
faith of Jesus Christ" we may wonder why there is the addition,
"unto all who believe". It is admitted that it is difficult to arrive
at certainty respecting the precise thought intended. But the
most reasonable interpretation would appear to be (*cf.* comments
on 1:17) that not only is the righteousness of God brought into
effectual relation to men through faith in Christ but it is brought
into this effectual relation to *all* believers.[16] Faith is not only
effectual to this end; it is invariably effective whoever the person
believing is. It was not superfluous for the apostle to emphasize

---

[16] This would be strengthened if we were to adopt the reading of D G,
the mass of the cursives, and some versions, namely, εἰς πάντας καὶ ἐπὶ πάντας
τοὺς πιστεύοντας. But the shorter reading of ℵ* A B C and some other versions,
namely, εἰς πάντας τοὺς πιστεύοντας bears out unmistakably the same thought.
The variant readings in no way affect the thought.

111

this truth. He had proved that all, both Jews and Gentiles, were under sin. In respect of the penal judgment of God there is no difference. The glory of the gospel is that there is no discrimination in the favourable judgment of God when faith comes into operation. There is no discrimination among believers—the righteousness of God comes upon them *all* without distinction.

This interpretation receives confirmation from the immediately succeeding clauses: "for there is no difference: for all have sinned and come short of the glory of God". As all are sinners, so all believers are justified freely by God's grace. There are thus two distinct shades of thought in the two elements of the clause. "Through faith of Jesus Christ" stresses the fact that it is only through faith in Christ that this righteousness of God is operative unto justification. "Unto all who believe" stresses the fact that this righteousness is always operative when there is faith.

The clause, "all have sinned" (vs. 23), views the sin of every man "as a historical fact of the past" (Meyer, *ad loc.*). The tense used is one that can do service for every aspect from which the sinfulness of the human race may be viewed, and it would not be defensible to restrict the reference to the sin of Adam and the involvement of posterity therein (*cf.* 5:12). The interest of the apostle here is to affirm that, whatever differences may obtain among members of the race in respect of the aggravations by which sinfulness is intensified, all without exception or discrimination are in the category of sinners (*cf.* vss. 9, 10).

The import of the coordinate clause, "and come short of the glory of God" is not immediately apparent; there are several possibilities. The verb means "to lack", "to want", "to be destitute of" (*cf.* Matt. 19:20; Luke 15:14; I Cor. 1:7; 8:8; 12:24; Phil. 4:12). It refers to a condition, not to an action, though, of course, the condition may arise from the absence of action which would have remedied or prevented the condition. The question that raises some difficulty and on which commentators differ is: what is the glory of God of which we come short and are destitute? There are four possibilities: (1) to fail to render to God the glory, to fail to glorify him or do what is to the praise of his glory (*cf.* for this use of the word "glory" Luke 17:18; Acts 12:23; Rom. 4:20; I Cor. 10:31; II Cor. 4:15; 8:19; Phil. 1:11; 2:11; I Thess. 2:6; Rev. 4:9, 11; 11:13; 14:7; 16:9); (2) to fail of receiving the glory, honour, or approba-

112

tion which God bestows (*cf.* John 5:41, 44; 8:50; 12:43; Rom. 2:7, 10; Heb. 3:3; I Pet. 1:7; II Pet. 1:17); (3) to come short of reflecting the glory of God, that is, of conformity to his image (*cf.* I Cor. 11:7; II Cor. 3:18; 8:23); (4) to fail of the consummated glory that will be dispensed to the people of God at the coming of Christ (*cf.* Rom. 5:2; 8:18, 21; I Cor. 2:7; 15:43; II Cor. 4:17; Col. 1:27; 3:4; II Thess. 2:14; II Tim. 2:10; Heb. 2:10; I Pet. 5:1, 4).

The difficulty is not a little accentuated by the fact that there is no precise parallel to this expression in the New Testament and a good case might be made for each of the four interpretations. One can only indicate a slight balance of considerations in favour of interpretation (3).

(a) Paul uses the present tense of a verb which is descriptive of a state or condition. We should infer therefore that he is reflecting on a present condition of all men arising from the fact of sin; it is coordinate with the fact that all have sinned. This consideration would tend to make (4) less tenable. (b) If (1) were intended by the apostle it is reasonable to suppose that he would have inserted some other term such as that of "giving" glory to God after the pattern of the usage of the New Testament in general and of himself in particular, or he would have used the preposition "unto" and have adapted the whole expression so as to read "unto the glory of God", as in passages cited above under (1). (c) Although the phrase "the glory of God" could, in terms of New Testament usage, be applied to the praise that comes from God (*cf.* John 12:43), yet the more perspicuous in this regard would be "glory from God".[17] (d) It is quite Pauline to represent that which redemption secures, in contrast with that which sin has brought, as transformation into the image of God (*cf.* II Cor. 3:18). In describing our present condition nothing would be more pertinent or descriptive than to define it in terms of our destitution in this regard. We are destitute of that perfection which is the reflection of the divine perfection and therefore of the glory of God.

24 Commentators have encountered difficulty with the construction at the beginning of verse 24. The participle "being justified" does not appear to stand in relation to what precedes

---

[17] That is παρὰ θεοῦ, as in John 5:44; II Pet. 1:17.

in a way that is easily intelligible. The most tenable view is that of those interpreters who regard what immediately precedes in verses 22b, 23, "for there is no difference: for all have sinned and come short of the glory of God", as parenthetical to that which is the main subject of this paragraph. As regards construction and intent, therefore, "being justified" is to be construed in direct sequence with "a righteousness of God through faith of Jesus Christ, unto all who believe" (vs. 22a). It is perhaps not irrelevant to observe that this is the first time in this epistle that Paul uses this *verb* directly and positively in reference to what is the leading theme of this epistle.[18] He had just defined his theme in terms of the righteousness of God operative through faith in Christ and now he is giving explication in express terms of justification freely by the grace of God. These two thoughts, namely, that this righteousness of God is our justification in contrast with the impossibility of the works of the law (vs. 20) and that this justification is the free gift of God by grace are sufficient ground for the defining participle, "being justified". And there is no reason for hesitating at what may appear to us as unusual construction. Even if we do not allow that the immediately preceding clauses are parenthetical to the main thought of this passage—a position that has much to commend it—there should be no difficulty with the construction. For the fact that there is no difference and that all have sinned and come short of the glory of God has close bearing upon the thought expressed in the participle "being justified". As we have found already, the fact of universal sinfulness bears directly upon the other fact that there is no discrimination among believers—they all are beneficiaries of the righteousness of God. So now in defining this theme in the express terms of justification the universality of sin is equally pertinent to the freeness and graciousness of justification as well as to that which justification itself connotes. In other words, verses 22b, 23 stand in the most significant relation both to what precedes and to what follows and verse 24 resumes the theme of verse 22a in terms that define and expand the latter.

---

[18] The verb δικαιόω is used on three occasions previously. In 2:13 it is used in reference to the principle of equity that doers of the law would be justified, in 3:4 in reference to the vindication of God, and in 3:20 the use is negative to the effect that no flesh will be justified by the works of the law. In these instances the same forensic meaning is apparent.

The combination of the terms "freely" and "by his grace" has the effect of emphasizing the completely unmerited character of God's justifying act. The free and sovereign graciousness of the act is the positive complement to that which had been asserted in verse 20 that "from the works of the law no flesh will be justified" in God's sight. No element in Paul's doctrine of justification is more central than this—God's justifying act is not constrained to any extent or degree by anything that we are or do which could be esteemed as predisposing God to this act. And not only is it the case that nothing in us or done by us constrains to this act but all that is ours compels the opposite judgment—the whole world is brought in guilty before God (cf. vss. 9, 19). This action on God's part derives its whole motivation, explanation, and determination from what God himself is and does in the exercise of free and sovereign grace. Merit of any kind on the part of man, when brought into relation to justification, contradicts the first article of the Pauline doctrine and therefore of his gospel. It is the glory of the gospel of Christ that it is one of free grace.

The accent placed here on the freeness and graciousness of the justifying act must be noted on its own account. But a contextual consideration and the lessons derived from it must not be overlooked. The accent upon free grace does not eliminate the medium through which this free grace has come into operation. That is the lesson of what Paul immediately adds: "through the redemption which is in Christ Jesus". This mediation shows two things in reference to the grace of justification: (1) the costly price at which this justification was procured; (2) the price at which it was procured does not negative but enhances the gracious character of the act. How eloquent is this collocation of justification by grace and justification through redemption in the correction of all argument to the effect that if justification is free it cannot be through price and if through price it cannot be free. It is both, and the price magnifies the marvel of the free grace. Justification is through the redemption that is in Christ Jesus; it is not through any price of ours; it is the costly price that Christ paid in order that free grace might flow unto the justification of the ungodly.

The root meaning of "redemption" is to ransom by the payment of a price. It is impossible to reduce the New Testament concept

115

of redemption to the mere notion of liberation. Our Lord's saying (Matt. 20:28; Mark 10:45) is expressly in terms of substitutive ransom and the giving of his life, which in the New Testament is the same as the shedding of his blood, the price of this redemption. It is this same concept that appears in the term Paul uses here as also elsewhere in other epistles (*cf.* Eph. 1:7; Titus 2:14 and in an eschatological sense in Rom. 8:23; I Cor. 1:30; Eph. 1:14; 4:30; see also in other New Testament writers Luke 1:68; 2:38; 24:21; Heb. 9:12, 15; I Pet. 1:18). Another term used by Paul (Gal. 3:13; 4:5; *cf.* also I Cor. 6:20; II Pet. 2:1; Rev. 5:9; 14:3, 4) conveys the same thought. Hence "the redemption that is in Christ Jesus" cannot be reduced to lower terms than the ransom secured by Christ in the shedding of his blood and the giving of his life.[19] It should be noted in addition that the apostle conceives of this redemption as something that has its permanent and abiding tenancy in Christ; it is "the redemption that is in Christ Jesus". The redemption is not simply that which we have in Christ (Eph. 1:7) but it is the redemption of which Christ is the embodiment. Redemption has not only been wrought by Christ but in the Redeemer this redemption resides in its unabbreviated virtue and efficacy. And it is redemption thus conceived that provides the mediacy through which justification by God's free grace is applied.

25, 26 In verse 25 we have another category in terms of which the provision which God has made for our justification is viewed. It is that of propitiation. Redemption contemplates our bondage and is the provision of grace to release us from that bondage. Propitiation contemplates our liability to the wrath of God and is the provision of grace whereby we may be freed from that wrath. It is wholly consonant with Paul's teaching in this epistle that he should enunciate the provision of God's grace unto our justification in this way. For he had begun his demonstration that the whole human race is under sin with the affirmation that "the wrath of God is revealed from heaven upon all ungodliness and unrighteousness of men" (1:18). And instead of stumbling

---

[19] The terms referred to above as expressing redemption are: λύτρον, ἀντίλυτρον, λύτρωσις, λυτροῦσθαι, ἀπολύτρωσις, ἐξαγοράζω, ἀγοράζω, and περιποιεῖσθαι. For a full treatment *cf.* "The New Testament Terminology of 'Redemption'" by B. B. Warfield in *Biblical Doctrines* (New York, 1929), pp. 327-372.

at this concept of propitiation we should rather anticipate that the precise category suited to the need and liability created by the wrath of God would be enlisted to describe or define the provision of God's grace.

Although the word used here by the apostle occurs only twice in the New Testament and in the other instance (Heb. 9:5) plainly means the mercy-seat, the covering of the ark of the covenant in the most holy place, yet there is good reason for believing that in this case it means "propitiatory offering" and is to be interpreted after the analogy of I John 2:2; 4:10; Heb. 2:17 (*cf.* Luke 18:13; Heb. 8:12).[20] Christ is therefore said to have been a propitiatory sacrifice.

The precise language of the text is to be carefully observed. It is not said here that Christ gave himself a propitiatory sacrifice, though such language would have been in accord with the teaching of Scripture. Our attention is drawn to the fact that *God set him forth*[21] a propitiatory sacrifice, and since the person in view is thus distinguished from Christ it is God the Father who is represented as setting him forth (*cf.* 5:8, 10; 8:3; I Cor. 8:6; II Cor. 5:18, 19; Eph. 4:4-6; Heb. 2:10-13). It is quite alien to biblical thought to overlook the agency of God the Father in the provisions of redemption and it is perversion to represent the Father as won over to the exercise of grace and mercy by the intervention of

---

[20] ἱλαστήριον in Rom. 3:25; Heb. 9:5, ἱλασμός in I John 2:2; 4:10, and ἱλάσκεσθαι in Heb. 2:17. For a thorough study of the concept of propitiation *cf.* Roger R. Nicole: "C. H. Dodd and the Doctrine of Propitiation" in *The Westminster Theological Journal*, XVII, 2, pp. 117-157; Leon Morris: "The Use of ἱλάσκεσθαι etc. in Biblical Greek" in *The Expository Times*, LXII, 8, pp. 227-233: *The Apostolic Preaching of the Cross* (London, 1955), pp. 125-185. For the view that ἱλαστήριον means propitiatory offering in Rom. 3:25 *cf.* Meyer: *op. cit., ad loc.*; J. B. Lightfoot: *Notes, ad loc.* For the contrary view that it refers to the mercy-seat *cf.* Philippi: *op. cit., ad loc.*; Gifford: *op. cit.*, pp. 96-98; Nygren: *op. cit.*, pp. 156ff.

[21] προέθετο is aorist middle and in the New Testament is used only here and in 1:13; Eph. 1:9. In the two other instances it is used in the sense of "purpose" as the substantive πρόθεσις (*cf.* 8:28: 9:11; Eph. 1:11; 3:11; II Tim. 1:9). The meaning "purpose" is not impossible in 3:25 and is adopted by J. B. Lightfoot: *Notes, ad loc.; cf.* also *ibid., ad* Eph. 1:9. Moulton and Milligan give examples to show that frequently in the papyri προτίθημι means "to set forth publicly". As Sanday and Headlam point out, the context is full of terms denoting publicity and this consideration as well as the usage elsewhere would strongly favour this rendering. J. H. Moulton suggests, on the basis of analogy from an inscription, that the meaning "offer" is possible (*cf.* Moulton and Milligan: *op. cit., ad* προτίθημι). The middle of προτίθημι. in the sense of setting forth appears in the LXX in Psalms 53:5; 85:14; 100:3ι

117

Christ's propitiatory accomplishment. Paul here represents the Father as taking the initiative in this action and as making the provision by which propitiation was wrought.

The term rendered "set forth" may most properly bear this signification. It could mean "purposed" as in 1:13; Ephesians 1:9. But the context and the usage in other Greek sources would indicate that the thought is that of public setting forth. The form suggests that there may be the reflexive idea and in that event some emphasis would fall upon the fact that God set forth for himself a propitiation. This thought is admirably in accord with the total purport of the passage and of the apostle's teaching elsewhere; it would be a reminder to us that divine interests or exigencies are fulfilled by the propitiatory provision. While, however, we may not press this significance of the verb itself, the same thought is conveyed by the fact that God the Father set forth Christ a propitiation to show forth his righteousness. The propitiation has a Godward reference. The interests of men are, of course, promoted to the highest degree, but in realizing these interests exigencies of divine import are conserved. We are not left to surmise what these are—the setting forth was to the end of demonstrating God's righteousness.

It would not be incongruous with the thought of this passage if we regarded "the righteousness of God" referred to here in verse 25 as the righteousness of God that is constitutive of our justification, as in verses 21, 22 and 1:17. For it is true that this righteousness is openly set forth in the propitiation and the propitiation could be viewed as directed to that end. The propitiation effects our justifying righteousness and therefore may be construed as our righteousness exhibited. But there are compelling reasons for thinking that the righteousness of God in this case is the attribute of justice, as in verse 5. (1) In verse 26 Paul returns to this same consideration and informs us specifically of the end to which this demonstration of righteousness is directed; it is to the end "that he may be just and the justifier of him who is of the faith of Jesus". This intimates that the exigency in view is the justice of God in the justification of sinners. In the provisions of propitiation two things cohere and coalesce, the justice of God and the justification of the ungodly. This justice of God implied in the expression, "that he might be just" cannot be the righteousness of God that is operative unto and constitutive of our jus-

118

tification. The form of the expression shows that it is the inherent righteousness of God that cannot be violated on any account and must be vindicated and conserved in the justification of sinners. This shows that the righteousness contemplated in the demonstration in verse 25, as well as in verse 26, is the inherent justice of God. (2) We are not only informed in verse 26 of the end to which this demonstration of righteousness was directed but also in verse 25 of a reason for which the demonstration was necessary. It is "on account of the passing over of the sins committed beforehand in the forbearance of God". Two passages in Paul's speeches as reported in Acts (14:16; 17:30) illumine for us what he means by "the forbearance of God"; he is referring to the generations gone by when God "suffered all the nations to walk in their own ways", "the times of ignorance" in contrast with the change which occurred in God's economy of grace when "now he commands men that they should all everywhere repent" (Acts 17:30). In these generations gone by God did not visit men with wrath commensurate with their sins. In this sense there was a by-passing or overlooking of their sins. This by-passing is not to be equated with remission. Suspension is not equivalent to forgiveness. It is this consideration—in the ages gone by God did not execute upon men the full measure of his displeasure but exercised forbearance—that the apostle adduces here as one reason why God exhibited his righteousness in Christ as the propitiation. The forbearance exercised in past ages tended to obscure in the apprehension of men the inviolability of God's justice. Forbearance was liable to be interpreted as indifference to the claims of justice and suspension of judgment as revocation and remission of the same. Hence now in Christ and in his propitiation God gave open demonstration that in order to the revocation of his wrath and punitive judgment it was necessary to provide a propitiation. "Passing over"[22] is not justification and

---

[22] πάρεσις occurs only here in the New Testament but from other Greek sources the meaning is shown to be "letting go unpunished", "passing over". *Cf.* Arndt and Gingrich: *op. cit.;* Moulton and Milligan: *op. cit.* In J. B. Lightfoot's words, "The distinction between ἄφεσις the revocation of punishment and πάρεσις the suspension of punishment ... is borne out by classical usage. ... The best commentary on the passage is St. Paul's own language in Acts xvii. 30, where the term ὑπεριδών expresses the idea exactly (comp. Acts xiv. 16). To substitute ἄφεσιν for πάρεσιν here would entirely destroy the sense. It was because the sins had been passed over and had not been

justification requires a propitiation that fully satisfies and vindicates God's justice. It can readily be seen therefore that the passing over of sins in the forbearance of God did not make it necessary for God to demonstrate his justifying righteousness, but that the passing over did make it necessary for him to demonstrate his inherent justice and that by showing (to all men in the worldwide proclamation of the gospel) that justification demands nothing less than the propitiation made in Jesus' blood.

We conclude therefore that the righteousness of God, referred to in verses 25, 26 as demonstrated, is the inherent justice of God. This is of basic relevance in our interpretation of Paul's teaching. It indicates that the vindication and satisfaction of the dictates of justice lie at the heart of his doctrine of redemption and propitiation as the provisions of God's grace in order to the justification of sinners. We may say, if we will, that the *demonstration* is governmental or rectoral. The demonstration is necessary to that government of God that is concerned with and is registered in the justification of sinners. But we cannot say that the *justice* demonstrated in the propitiation is merely governmental; it is the inherent justice of God that is demonstrated in a propitiation which meets and removes the judgment of his wrath. It is this complex of thought that is to be elicited from Romans 3:24–26. And this passage exemplifies how the apostle can interweave such categories as redemption, propitiation, and the vindication of justice because they are but different aspects from which the provisions of his grace for the salvation of men may be viewed and different facets of that process by which he is just when he justifies those who have faith in Jesus.

There are a few additional questions pertinent to verses 25 and 26 that call for comment.

How are we to construe the relation to one another of the component parts of "a propitiation through faith in his blood"? It is difficult to be dogmatic. Some construe "in his blood" as the object of faith; others connect "in his blood" directly with the propitiation, and faith is regarded as sufficiently defined by the context to be faith in Christ. If we are guided by the analogy of the expression in verse 22, "a righteousness of God through faith of Jesus Christ", this latter alternative seems preferable.

forgiven, that the exhibition of God's righteousness in the Incarnation and Passion of Christ was necessary" (*Notes, ad loc.*).

The propitiation is undoubtedly that which is made in the blood of Christ Jesus and it is in accord with Paul's thought both to regard the blood of Christ as defining that in which the propitiatory sacrifice consisted and as that which served to set forth openly the propitiation (*cf.* Gal. 3:1). Furthermore, it is in accord with Paul's pattern to refer to faith in such connections, without necessarily defining its object (*cf.* vs. 22b; 1:17), as the instrumentality by which we become the actual partakers of the objective gift in view, in this case propitiation in Jesus' blood. Finally, it might be a deviation from the precision of Paul's usage in representing Christ himself as the object of faith, especially in this context (*cf.* vss. 22a, 26b), to take the blood of Christ here as that on which faith terminates.

The definite specification of time in the expression "at this present time" (vs. 26) is another example of the significance attached to the historical epoch in which God gave this demonstration of his justice. It is contrasted with the generations of the past when God's forbearance was in exercise, and it shows that location in history belongs to those accomplishments which have a Godward reference at their centre. We are not to relegate to the realm of the superhistorical that which meets divine interests and exigencies.

The formula at the end of verse 26, "of the faith of Jesus", though it has close parallels (Gal. 2:16; 3:22; Phil. 3:9), is not used anywhere else in this precise form. In view of what we have found above (vs. 22 and footnote thereon) it would be totally indefensible to suppose that it is to be interpreted after the analogy of an expression which Paul uses and which in form is identical, namely, "of the faith of Abraham" (4:16). This latter formula undoubtedly means faith patterned after the faith of Abraham. But the formula "of the faith of Jesus" must be interpreted in accord with the analogy of Paul's usage elsewhere in which Jesus Christ or Christ Jesus or Christ is the object of the faith referred to. There is, however, in this unique formula the touch of tenderness, on the one hand, and of majesty, on the other. The name Jesus suggests the intimacy of personal relationship to the Saviour in that character evinced in his historical manifestation in the days of his flesh. But when Paul conceives of him as the object of this faith there is intimated the majesty with which he regarded the same historical Jesus as invested.

27-31

27 Where then is the glorying? It is excluded. By what manner of law? of works? Nay: but by a law of faith.
28 We reckon therefore that a man is justified by faith apart from the works of the law.
29 Or is God *the God* of Jews only? is he not *the God* of Gentiles also? Yea, of Gentiles also:
30 if so be that God is one, and he shall justify the circumcision by faith, and the uncircumcision through faith.
31 Do we then make the law of none effect through faith? God forbid: nay, we establish the law.

27-31 Verses 27–31 may properly be regarded as a concluding peroration setting forth the results to be drawn from the gospel of grace delineated in verses 21–26. The note of decisive inference and confidence is apparent. "Where then is boasting? It is excluded." The boasting in mind is that of active exultation and self-gratulation. It is uncertain whether the apostle has in mind the Jew specifically, as one given to boasting in his peculiar privileges and good works which afforded, in his esteem, acceptance with God, in contrast with the Gentiles, or whether Paul is thinking in more general terms of all self-gratulation on the part of men. But even on the latter alternative there is marked pertinence to the Jew (*cf.* 2:17–25, esp. vs. 23). The answer to the question is decisive. The tense used has the force, as Sanday and Headlam point out, "it is shut out once for all" (*ad loc.*) and is expressed sufficiently by the rendering, "It is excluded".

"Through what law? of works? Nay, but through the law of faith." These questions and the answer show that the word "law" is used in a different sense from that used hitherto in this epistle. But it is used later on in this same sense (7:21, 23; 8:2). It is obvious that when Paul speaks of "the law of faith" he cannot mean the law in the sense in which it is opposed to faith (*cf.* vss. 19, 20, 21, 28). For in that event there would be contradiction in the expression, "the law of faith". This again evinces the flexibility of the word "law" in the usage of the epistle and how easily the apostle may pass from one denotation or connotation to another. Here therefore "law" in both instances when applied to "works" and "faith" must mean "system", "principle", "method", "order", or "rule". The contrast instituted is that between the order of things in which works are the medium of justification and that in which justification is exclusively by faith. The latter is the principle which the apostle triumphantly asserts as the inference to be drawn from the gospel set forth in verses 21–26. In verse 28 he gives the reason (rather than a conclusion) for this assertion of the law of faith: "For we reckon that by faith a man is justified without the deeds of the law". There are two elements in this statement that are particularly germane to the thought: first, that it is by *faith* we are justified and, second, that it is by faith *any man* is justified, whether he is Jew or Gentile.

We are required to ask how the principle of faith is so rigidly exclusive of and antithetical to works of law in the matter of justification. The only answer is the specific quality of faith as opposed to that of works. Justification by works always finds its ground in that which the person is and does; it is always oriented to that consideration of virtue attaching to the person justified. The specific quality of faith is trust and commitment to another; it is essentially extraspective and in that respect is the diametric opposite of works. Faith is *self*-renouncing; works are *self*-congratulatory. Faith looks to what God does; works have respect to what we are. It is this antithesis of principle that enables the apostle to base the complete exclusion of works upon the principle of faith. Only faith has relevance within that gospel delineated in verses 21–26. And, if faith, then it is "without works of law". It follows therefore that "by faith *alone*" is implicit in the apostle's argument. Luther added nothing to the *sense* of the passage when he said "by faith alone".

In verses 29, 30 the appeal is to the fact that God is one. The oneness of God was the first article of Jewish faith (Deut. 6:4; *cf.* Isa. 45:5). Paul brings this article to bear upon the unity of principle that obtains in the matter of justification—if God is one he is God of both Jews and Gentiles (vs. 29) and there can be no diversity in the *modus operandi* of his justifying judgment. Identity of principle in his saving operations follows from the unity of his relationship to all as the one God of all (*cf.* Isa. 43:11; 45:21, 22). Hence he "will justify the circumcision by faith and the uncircumcision through faith" (vs. 30). The future tense "will justify" is used not with reference to the final judgment but, in

Meyer's words, "is to be understood as in ver. 20 *of every case of justification* to be accomplished" (*ad loc.*). The variation of prepositions "by faith" and "through faith" are not to be interpreted as indicating any difference respecting the faith intended or its relationships. This would prejudice the contention of the passage that there is no discrimination (*cf.* also vss. 22–24). Paul uses both forms though he has a decided preference for the former. The variation of preposition only serves to underline the identity of method.

The interest of the apostle in arguing for the absence of all difference between Jews and Gentiles in justification is liable to be taken for granted by us and, as Dr. Hodge says, "these sublime truths are so familiar to our minds that they have, in a measure, lost their power" (*ad loc.*). But if we bear in mind what Meyer calls "the degenerate theocratic exclusiveness" of the Jew or what Hodge calls "his narrow national and religious prejudices" we discover the necessity of this insistence. And upon believing Jews this truth must have dawned "with unwonted emotions of wonder, gratitude, and joy" (Hodge). But we must not suppose that Paul has merely in view the correction of Jewish prejudices. He has the interest of the Gentile at heart also. And this ethnic universalism of the gospel must have dawned also upon Gentiles with emotions of joy and wonderment.

The exact relation to the context and the interpretation of verse 31 have been questions on which considerable difference of opinion has arisen among expositors. Does verse 31 go with chapter 3 or does it belong to the next chapter? If we adopt the latter alternative then the law referred to in this verse would have to be taken in the sense of the Pentateuch or the Old Testament in general, a denotation which is not without warrant in Pauline usage (*cf.* 2:18, 20; 5:13; 7:1; I Cor. 9:8, 20; Gal. 3:19, 21, 23; 4:4). For, in this event, by appeal to Abraham and David (4:1–8) the apostle would be showing that the doctrine of justification by faith was imbedded in the Old Testament itself, that it was at the centre of the revelation which had been entrusted to the Jews and in the possession of which they boasted. On this view of the denotation of the word "law" in verse 31 Paul would be saying that the Old Testament (whether considered as the books of Moses specifically or as a whole), so far from being overthrown by the gospel of grace, was confirmed and established. This interpretation is in accord with Paul's view of the Old Testament and of the relation of its doctrine to the gospel he is defending (cf. 4:1-25; Gal. 3:17-22). Verse 31 would then be a vigorous repudiation of the suggestion that the Old Testament was made void and an emphatic assertion of its confirmation, a fitting introduction to chapter 4. This view would obviate the criticism sometimes offered that verse 31 is abrupt, too summary to be an adequate answer to the question asked, and therefore out of place.[23]

However appealing this view is and though tenable because consonant with Paul's view of the Old Testament, there are reasons for another interpretation of its contextual relationships and of the denotation of the word "law". (1) This verse stands in logical relation to what precedes. It raises a question which naturally and inevitably issues. Paul had argued that "from works of law" no flesh could be justified (vs. 20), that a righteousness of God had been manifested "without the law" (vs. 21), that the principle of the gospel is that of faith, not that of works (vs. 27), that a man is justified by faith "without works of law" (vs. 28). This reiterated negation of works of law makes irresistible the question: what then of the law? Is it useless? Is it abrogated? Indeed, is it a liability to be cast off? These very questions are implicit in the question: "do we then make void the law through faith?" (2) As regards construction verse 31 stands in more intimate relation to what precedes than to what follows. The "therefore" at the beginning suggests that the inference supposed follows from what had been said. Furthermore, if verse 31 is attached to 4:1 the question of the latter does not appear to be in suitable relation to the categorical declaration of verse 31b. And chapter 4 can stand perfectly well without any such introduction as verse 31 would supply.

For these reasons we may regard verse 31 as the conclusion to the argument of chapter 3. What, on this construction, is the

---

[23] "The new chapter should have begun with ver. 31, since that verse contains the theme of the following discussion. If we should, with Augustine, Beza, Calvin, Melancthon, Bengel, and many others ... assume that at iv. 1 there is again introduced something new, and that Paul does not carry further the νόμον ἱστῶμεν ... we should then have the extraordinary phenomenon of Paul as it were dictatorially dismissing]an objection so extremely important ... merely by an opposite assertion, and then immediately, like one who has not a clear case, leaping away to something else" (Meyer: *op. cit., ad loc.*).

force of Paul's question and answer and what is the denotation of the word "law"? This question has been virtually answered above. In the sustained argument of the preceding verses the negation of works of law as having any instrumentality or efficiency in justification has in view works performed in obedience to divine commandment and therefore the law contemplated is the law of commandment from whatever aspect it may be regarded. What is in view is law as commanding to compliance and performance. And the insistence of the apostle is that *any* works in performance of *any* such commandment are of no avail in justification. The question is then: does this abrogate the law of commandment and make it irrelevant and inoperative in every respect? Paul's answer is in terms of his most emphatic formula of denial. He recoils with abhorrence from the suggestion and says: "God forbid". Having thus rejected the supposition he says apodictically the affirmative opposite: "Yea, we establish the law".

Paul is well aware of the danger of the antinomian inference from the doctrines of grace. He deals with it in detail in chapter 6 and offers the arguments which not only refute it but reduce it to absurdity. But here he anticipates the objection and he answers it summarily. The summariness is eloquent. He is guarding against a distortion which cannot be granted a moment's toleration. In the words of Philippi, "The present verse then contains merely a passing thought interposed by way of anticipation, an abrupt setting aside of a natural objection . . . Here the apostle glances, so to speak, merely by anticipation, at the more complete argument which follows later on" (*op. cit.*, *ad loc.*).[24]

---

[24] *Cf.* also Gifford: *op. cit.*, *ad loc.* and the excellent footnote by John Owen, the translator of Calvin's commentary on Romans, *ad loc.*

VI. CORROBORATION FROM THE OLD TESTAMENT
(4:1–25)

1–5

> 1 What then shall we say that Abraham, our forefather, hath found according to the flesh?
> 2 For if Abraham was justified by works, he hath whereof to glory; but not toward God.
> 3 For what saith the scripture? And Abraham believed God, and it was reckoned unto him for righteousness.
> 4 Now to him that worketh, the reward is not reckoned as of grace, but as of debt.
> 5 But to him that worketh not, but believeth on him that justifieth the ungodly, his faith is reckoned for righteousness.

In chapter 4 Paul proceeds to prove from the Scripture of the Old Testament the pivotal element of the doctrine which he had unfolded in the preceding chapter. It cannot be doubted that the cardinal interest of the apostle in the argument which he had presented is the antithesis between justification by works and justification by faith (cf. 3:20, 22, 25, 26, 27, 28, 30). It is this interest that is in the forefront in the series of demonstrations which he derives from the Old Testament. He appeals first of all to the case of Abraham. The appropriateness of appeal to Abraham is conspicuous for, as has been well said, "the case of Abraham was the centre and stronghold of the whole Jewish position".[1]

1 It is preferable to regard the conjunction at the beginning of verse 1 as transitional rather than inferential.[2] It does not draw a conclusion from what precedes (the view held by those who regard 3:31 as belonging to chapter 4) but intimates advance to the consideration of what the example of Abraham establishes —"What then shall we say that Abraham, our forefather, hath

---

[1] Sanday and Headlam: *op. cit., ad loc.*
[2] *Cf.* Hodge: *op. cit., ad loc.*

found according to the flesh?"[3] Several of the ablest commentators maintain that "according to the flesh" must be taken with the verb "hath found".[4] It is questionable, however, if we can be so decisive. It may well be taken with "Abraham our forefather"[5]. Paul has almost a monopoly of this precise expression and he quite frequently uses it in the depreciative sense of our English term "carnally", that is, "according to the sinful impulses and principles", "flesh" being synonymous with human nature as dominated by sin (cf. Rom. 8:4, 5, 12, 13; I Cor. 1:26; II Cor. 1:17; 10:2; 11:18). He also uses it in a sense less depreciatory but still with depreciatory reflection (II Cor. 5:16). But he also uses the expression without any depreciatory implications: in respect of our Lord in his human identity (Rom. 1:3; 9:5) and also with reference to men (Rom. 9:3; I Cor. 10:18; Eph. 6:5; Col. 3:22; cf. Heb. 12:9).[6] It is clear therefore that Paul

---

[3] The interpretation of verse 1 is perplexed by the textual variants in respect of the position or presence of εὑρηκέναι. In ℵ A C D E F G, supported by several versions and some patristic authority, it occurs before 'Αβραάμ. In the mass of the cursives it occurs after ἡμῶν and this reading is also supported by some patristic authority. In B 1739 1908* it is omitted entirely. One cannot dismiss offhand the judgment of J. B. Lightfoot that "εὑρηκέναι must be regarded as at least suspicious" in view of its varying positions in the other mss. and from the tendency of scribes to supply an elliptical expression, as well as from its omission by B (Notes, p. 276). It should be understood that if εὑρηκέναι is omitted the sense of the verse is not perplexed. If this verb is retained and we follow the mass of the cursives and place it after ἡμῶν, then it would be difficult to understand κατὰ σάρκα in any other sense than the ethical, namely, in the power of the flesh. If we adopt the reading of ℵ A et al., then there is no reason why κατὰ σάρκα should be interpreted in any other sense than that of natural paternity; if we omit εὑρηκέναι, then the same holds true. Thus only if we follow the mass of the cursives may we interpret κατὰ σάρκα ethically. With respect to this reading there are two things to be said. (1) With such external authority against this reading we may not assume its genuineness. (2) On exegetical grounds there is weighty objection to the supposition that the apostle would suggest even by way of question that Abraham would have attained to anything in the power of the flesh, that is to say, to anything relevant to the subject with which Paul is dealing. Every consideration would favour the view that here we have a question which is simply to the effect: what is the case as it concerns Abraham our forefather after the flesh?

[4] Meyer, Godet, Philippi, Hodge, et al. If we were to adopt the reading in which εὑρηκέναι immediately precedes κατὰ σάρκα (see preceding note), then this interpretation would be the most natural.

[5] προπάτορα is supported by ℵ* A B C* et al. Since this term is used only here in the New Testament, this is a strong argument in its favour from the viewpoint of transcriptional probability. The usual expression is 'Αβραὰμ ὁ πατὴρ ἡμῶν.

[6] The precise force of the expression in Gal. 4:23, 29 is to me doubtful.

could have used it in Romans 4:1 of the paternity of Abraham in terms of natural generation and it is gratuitous to suppose it unnecessary for Paul, in calling Abraham "our forefather", to add the further qualification that he is forefather by natural generation. The conjunction of "according to the flesh" with "Abraham our forefather" makes this tenable, if not more acceptable, and there is no obvious consideration that requires us to take the expression in question as modifying or defining "hath found". The question of the verse as a whole can remain general in its express terms—what are we to say that Abraham found in reference to the matter being discussed? What was the case as far as Abraham was concerned?

If we adopt the other construction that "according to the flesh" is to be taken with "hath found", then the thought is: did Abraham attain to justification with God by the energy of his own natural powers? "The flesh" would be parallel to "from works" (vs. 2), works done in the energy of the flesh. Perhaps the strongest argument in support of this interpretation is that the first clause of verse 2 appears to require an express allusion to justification by works in what precedes. Otherwise the hypothetical supposition expressed in verse 2 would be abrupt and the conjunction "for" would be without the antecedent we might expect. However, this is not conclusive. The apostle had reflected sufficiently in the preceding chapter on the antithesis between works and faith so that the reference to justification by works in verse 2 is thoroughly relevant and pointed without any express allusion to the same in verse 1. No more than the open question: what was true in the case of Abraham? is needed to make verse 2 appropriate as the introduction to what the apostle proceeds to demonstrate from the Scripture respecting Abraham. Hence there is no decisive argument arising from the context in support of the view that "according to the flesh" goes with "hath found".

2, 3 The thought of verse 2—"for if Abraham was justified by works he hath whereof to glory"—implies a certain supposition. If we were to grant that "according to the flesh" in verse 1 is to be construed with "hath found", then this supposition carries on the suggestion of verse 1 to the effect that Abraham might perchance have attained to justification by works and draws the inference that, if this were true, then Abraham would have had ground for glorying.[7] On the supposition the inference is inevitable—Abraham could then have boasted in his self-achieved attainment. It is apparent, however, that the apostle is not making a suggestion or supposition that has any reality in fact and he is not making a suggestion that allows for the entertainment of the possibility that Abraham might have been justified by works. It is simply an hypothesis for the sake of argument, an argument which is immediately directed to the refutation of the hypothesis. In short the "if" is that of an hypothesis wholly contrary to fact. The answer of the apostle to the inevitable consequence of the hypothesis is contained in the latter part of verse 2—"But not with God". This answer is that as a matter of fact there is no glorying or any ground for glorying in reference to God or, as we should say, Godwards. The condensation of the apostle's expression here is liable to obscure for us his argument. It is to the effect of the following syllogism. (1) If a man is justified by works he has ground for glorying. (2) Abraham was justified by works. (3) Therefore Abraham had ground for glorying. Paul emphatically challenges and denies the conclusion. He is saying in effect: though the syllogism is formally correct, it does not apply to Abraham. How does he disprove the conclusion? By showing that the minor premise is not true. He proves that Abraham was *not* justified by works and, by proving this, he refutes the conclusion. This is the import of the statement, "But not toward God". And how does he disprove the minor premise? Simply by appeal to Scripture; he quotes Genesis 15:6 which must on all accounts be regarded as the most relevant to the case in hand. Genesis 15:6 says nothing of works. "For what saith the Scripture? Abraham believed God and it was reckoned to him for righteousness" (vs. 3). In appealing to this text it should be apparent that Paul is basing his argument mainly upon the fact that it is the *faith* of Abraham that is in the foreground. That this is Paul's main interest in this text is shown by verses 4 and 5. For in these the argument again turns on the antithesis faith and works.

In the Hebrew Genesis 15:6 is as follows: "And he [Abraham]

---

[7] "Ground for boasting" is required in thought whether, with Meyer, we regard καύχημα as expressly denoting *materies gloriandi* or as the synonym of *gloriatio*. *Cf.* Lightfoot: *Notes, ad loc.*

believed in the Lord, and he reckoned it to him righteousness". The formula is similar to that used in the case of Phinehas in reference to his zeal for the Lord: "And it was reckoned to him for righteousness to all generations for ever" (Psalm 106:31). There need be no question but it was the zealous act of Phinehas that was reckoned to him for righteousness, and the formula in Genesis 15:6 both from its own terms and from the analogy of Psalm 106:31 is to be interpreted similarly, namely, that God reckoned Abraham's faith to him for righteousness. Paul's quotation here (*cf.* also vss. 9, 22, 23; Gal. 3:6) is to be interpreted likewise. Verse 9 is explicit to the effect that "faith" was reckoned for righteousness. And the word "reckoned" here, as in the Hebrew, means that it was placed to his account, it was imputed to him. And the implication is that the corresponding results followed upon this imputation.

We must, however, recognize the difference between the two cases (Gen. 15:6 and Psalm 106:31). In the case of Phinehas it is an act of righteous zeal on his part; it is a deed. He was credited with the devotion which his faith in God produced —righteousness in the ethical and religious sense. But that which was reckoned to Abraham is of a very different sort. In Paul's interpretation and application of Genesis 15:6 this becomes quite patent. Paul could not have appealed to Psalm 106:31 in this connection without violating his whole argument. For if he had appealed to Psalm 106:31 in the matter of *justification*, the justification of the ungodly (*cf.* vs. 5), then the case of Phinehas would have provided an inherent contradiction and would have demonstrated *justification* by a righteous and zealous act. Though then the formula in Genesis 15:6 is similar to that of Psalm 106:31, the subjects with which they deal are diverse. Genesis 15:6 is dealing with *justification*, as Paul shows; Psalm 106:31 is dealing with the good works which were the fruit of faith. This distinction must be kept in view in the interpretation of Genesis 15:6, particularly as applied by Paul in this chapter.

It is with justification by *faith* as opposed to *works* that Paul is concerned in this passage. That is why he appeals to Genesis 15:6; it is the *faith* of Abraham that is accented in that passage. And the precise formula to the effect that faith was imputed to him draws our attention simply to the fact that it was the faith of Abraham that was taken into account. Paul focuses his attention

131

on that one consideration and frames his argument accordingly, to wit, that it was faith in contrast with works that entered into God's accounting with Abraham in the matter of his justification. In terms of the formula, it was faith that was reckoned to him for the righteousness with which justification is concerned. In each case of appeal to Genesis 15:6, therefore, we must not, for dogmatic reasons, fail to recognize that it is faith that is imputed (vss. 5, 9, 10, 11, 22, 23). How this comports with the truth attested so clearly elsewhere in this epistle that the righteousness of Christ is the ground of justification, the righteousness by which we are justified, is a question that must be dealt with in its proper place.[8] It is not in the interests of exegesis to evade the force of the apostle's terms here or fail to take account of the emphasis, so germane to the whole doctrine, that *faith* is reckoned for righteousness in justification.

4, 5 By showing from Genesis 15:6 that by *faith* Abraham was justified Paul has proved the point of verse 2 that not by works was Abraham justified and therefore that Abraham had no occasion to glory. In verses 4 and 5 the thought implicit in verse 2 is expanded in express terms of the antithesis between reward in accordance with debt accruing from work performed and the method of grace. It is questionable if the apostle in dealing with this subject could have spoken of "reward according to grace". He does not actually do so; his reference to grace in verse 4 is to deny that the reward of the worker is "according to grace". The antithesis is therefore between the idea of compensation and that of grace—the worker has compensation in view, he who does not work must have regard to grace. In verse 5 we do not read therefore by way of contrast, "but to him that worketh not the reward is not reckoned of debt but of grace". On that side of the antithesis the terms are carefully chosen to suit the main interest at this point. The antithesis is not simply between the worker and the non-worker but between the worker and the person who does not work *but believes*. And it is not only believing but believing with a specific quality and direction—"believing upon him who justifies the ungodly". The issue is then stated in the language of the formula on which everything turns, namely, that "his faith is reckoned for righteousness".

---

[8] See the discussion in Appendix A (pp. 336 ff.)

The description given in verse 5, "him who justifies the ungodly" is intended to set off the munificence of the gospel of grace. The word "ungodly" is a strong one and shows the magnitude and extent of God's grace; his justifying judgment is exercised not simply upon the unrighteous but upon the ungodly. Verse 5 is a general statement of the method of grace and is not intended to describe Abraham specifically. We have here, rather, the governing principle of grace; it is exemplified in the case of Abraham because he believed in accordance with that principle.

6–8

> 6 Even as David also pronounceth blessing upon the man, unto whom God reckoneth righteousness apart from works,
> 7 *saying*,
> Blessed are they whose iniquities are forgiven,
> And whose sins are covered.
> 8 Blessed is the man to whom the Lord will not reckon sin.

In verses 6–8 the second example from the Old Testament is adduced to prove that justification by faith is imbedded in the Scriptures of the old covenant. It is the instance of David. The appeal to David and to the psalm which is here attributed to him is not, however, independent of that demonstration drawn from the case of Abraham. It is confirmatory or, to use Meyer's expression, "accessory". This is shown by the way in which the appeal to David is introduced, "even as David also", and by the fact that Paul returns to the demonstration provided by Abraham's faith at verse 9 and continues the same to the end of the chapter. It is clear, therefore, that David's pronouncement regarding the man who is blessed, in addition to its being confirmatory of what precedes, leads the apostle on to the enunciation of another aspect of the history of Abraham which bears with equal conclusiveness upon the subject of his polemic.

David pronounced blessed "those whose iniquities are forgiven, and whose sins are covered" (vs. 7), and this is parallel to the pronouncement of blessedness upon "the man to whom the Lord will not reckon sin" (vs. 8). It is this pronouncement of blessedness that is in view in verse 6 when Paul refers to the utterance of David respecting "the blessedness of the man to whom God reckoneth righteousness apart from works". What David spoke of in terms of the non-imputation and forgiveness of sin Paul interprets more positively as the imputation of righteousness. Several observations need to be noted.

(1) The appeal to David's declaration is particularly pertinent to the apostle's theme. He is dealing with justification by faith in opposition to works. Nothing could be more illustrative of this thesis than the pronouncement that the blessed man is the man whose iniquities are forgiven and to whom the Lord does not impute sin. For what is contemplated in this pronouncement is not good works but the opposite, iniquities and sins. And the blessed man is not the man who has good works laid to his account but whose *sins* are *not* laid to his account. David's religion, therefore, was not one determined by the concept of good works but by that of the gracious remission of sin, and the blessedness, regarded as the epitome of divine favour, had no affinity with that secured by works of merit. The relevance to Paul's argument is unmistakable.

(2) When Paul speaks of God as "imputing righteousness" (vs. 6), he must be using this expression as synonymous with justification. Otherwise his argument would be invalid. For his thesis is justification by faith without works. Hence to "impute righteousness without works" is equivalent to justification without works. This advises us that in the esteem of the apostle the formula derived from Genesis 15:6, namely, "to impute for righteousness" or, as it is rendered in verse 6, "to impute righteousness" has the same force as "to justify" and the formula that "faith was imputed for righteousness" must be tantamount to the other that a man "is justified by faith" (*cf.* 3:26, 28, 30; 5:1).

(3) When Paul derives his positive doctrine of justification, in terms of the imputation of righteousness (vs. 6), from a declaration of David that is in terms of the remission and non-imputation of sin (vss. 6, 7) and therefore formally negative, he must have regarded justification as correlative with, if not as defined in terms of, remission of sin. This inference is conclusive against the Romish view that justification consists in the infusion of grace. Justification must be forensic, as remission itself is.

(4) We may not say that Paul intended to define the whole nature of justification as consisting in remission of sin. Where justification is, remission must be and *vice versa*. That is why he makes virtual equation in these verses. But as Paul has shown

134

already (*cf.* 1:17; 3:21–26) and as he will show later (*cf.* 5:17–21; 10:3–6), remission does not *define* justification, though justification must embrace remission. The more restricted interest of the apostle at this point must be appreciated. He is jealous to establish from the Scriptures, particularly from the Scriptures as they are concerned with Abraham, the antithesis between justification by works and that by faith. The appeal to David and to Psalm 32:1, 2, in addition to that said of Abraham, is for the purpose of demonstrating that what the Scripture conceives of as the epitome of blessing and felicity is not the reward of works but the bestowment of grace through faith. Blessedness consists in that which is illustrated by the remission of sins and not by that which falls into the category of reward according to merit. In this passage the correlation of remission and justification and the virtual identification of the one with the other must therefore be understood in the light of the particular interest and emphasis of the apostle at this point and must not be enlisted as proof that justification and remission are synonymous and reciprocally define each other. Justification embraces remission, and, in respect of the antithesis between works and faith, the specific character of justification is of that sort which remission exemplifies.

9–12

> 9 Is this blessing then pronounced upon the circumcision, or upon the uncircumcision also? for we say, To Abraham his faith was reckoned for righteousness.
> 10 How then was it reckoned? when he was in circumcision, or in uncircumcision? Not in circumcision, but in uncircumcision:
> 11 and he received the sign of circumcision, a seal of the righteousness of the faith which he had while he was in uncircumcision: that he might be the father of all them that believe, though they be in uncircumcision, that righteousness might be reckoned unto them;
> 12 and the father of circumcision to them who not only are of the circumcision, but who also walk in the steps of that faith of our father Abraham which he had in uncircumcision.

Verses 9–12 develop the argument derived from the consideration that Abraham had been justified before he was circumcised. Paul appeals to this fact to show that circumcision could have

135

had no instrumentality in Abraham's justification and therefore that justification by faith is as relevant to those who are uncircumcised as to those who are circumcised. The historical fact that Abraham was justified long before he was circumcised lies on the face of the book of Genesis. The institution of circumcision we find in Genesis 17:10–13, but the reference to Abraham's justification by faith is in Genesis 15:6 and at least fourteen years elapsed between the events associated with the former and the time of the latter. It may seem to us so obvious a lesson to be drawn from the history of Abraham that we deem it unnecessary to devote so much argumentation to it. But it was an obvious lesson that the Jews had failed to learn. When we consider that Jewish tradition had interpreted the preeminence of Abraham, and the distinctive privilege of the Jewish people as the descendants of Abraham, to such an extent in terms of circumcision and had associated blessedness in the present life and in that to come with circumcision, we discover the pertinence of this argument to the demonstration which the apostle is presenting. He shows from the record that the blessedness declared by David, contemplated as the epitome of felicity and divine favour, belongs to the uncircumcised as well as to the circumcised. It is when presented in this light that the obvious lesson of the history is perceived to counter Jewish distortion. Hence the relevance and the necessity of the argument.

9, 10 When we read in verse 9, "For we say, faith was reckoned to Abraham for righteousness", Paul is referring again to Genesis 15:6 and the word "we say" is to be regarded as implying an assertion that will not of itself be questioned—it is an admitted fact. The emphasis rests upon the *faith* of Abraham and, as we found already, the whole statement, "faith was reckoned to Abraham for righteousness" is equivalent to "Abraham was justified by faith". Having laid down this admitted premise, Paul proceeds to the question which is pivotal at this point, "How then was it reckoned?" (vs. 10). The subject implied is faith. And the thought is: how was faith reckoned unto Abraham's justification? The form of the question by means of "how" rather than "when" appears to have significance. He is asking, as Meyer observes, "under what *circumstances* as *to status*"[9] was

---

[9] *Op. cit., ad loc.*

Abraham justified by faith. Was it in the circumcision-status or in the uncircumcision-status? "When he was in circumcision, or in uncircumcision?" (vs. 10). He is putting the question in its most pointed form. For if it was in the state of circumcision, then the mere fact that Abraham was justified by faith would not have the same cogency in the present argument; it might still be objected that circumcision was a determining factor. To say the least, it would be a circumstance, and the legalist could still plead the necessity of this accompanying condition. It is in this light that the precise form of the question and of the answer adds cogency to the argument. "Not in circumcision, but in uncircumcision" is the apostle's answer. Hence in the matter of justification and of the faith that was unto justification circumcision was no factor at all, not even in the sense of a conditioning circumstance. This is the force of the lesson which is derived from the sequence in the history of Abraham. It is more than the question of temporal sequence; it is that circumcision had nothing whatsoever to do with Abraham's faith or justification.

11, 12 At verse 11 Paul does define for us, however, the relation of circumcision to Abraham's faith. Although circumcision contributed in no way to the exercise of faith nor to the justification through faith, for the simple reason that it did not yet exist, yet circumcision did sustain a relationship to faith. Circumcision, he insists, was not a purely secular rite nor merely a mark of racial identity. The meaning it possessed was one related to faith. Paul did not make the capital mistake of thinking that, because it had no efficiency in creating faith or the blessedness attendant upon faith, it had therefore no religious significance or value. Its significance, he shows, was derived from its relation to faith and the righteousness of faith. "And he [Abraham] received the sign of circumcision, a seal of the righteousness of the faith which he had in uncircumcision" (vs. 11). In a word, it signified and sealed his faith.

This relationship of circumcision to faith adds to the argument of the apostle. For if circumcision signified faith, the faith must be conceived of as existing prior to the signification given and, in a way still more apparent, a seal or authentication presupposes the existence of the thing sealed and the seal does not add to the content of the thing sealed.

137

It is usual to discover a distinction between a sign and a seal; a sign points to the existence of that which it signifies, whereas a seal authenticates, confirms, and guarantees the genuineness of that which is signified. This distinction was no doubt intended by the apostle. The seal is more than definitive of that in which the sign consisted; it adds the thought of authentication. And the seal is that which God himself appended to assure Abraham that the faith he exercised in God's promise was accepted by God to the end of fulfilling to Abraham the promise which he believed. In Genesis 17:10–14 circumcision is clearly stated to be the sign of the covenant. There is no incompatibility. As the sign and seal of the covenant it was also the seal of that faith and of the justification by faith apart from which the covenant is meaningless. The promises of Genesis 15:4, 5, to which the faith of Abraham, mentioned in Genesis 15:6, was directed and for the fulfilment of which Abraham trusted in the Lord, were essentially the same promises as were embodied in and confirmed by the covenant of Genesis 17:2–14 (*cf.* Gen. 15:4, 5 with Gen. 17:2, 4). We must regard Genesis 12:1–3; 15:4–6, 18–21; 17:1–21 as the unified though progressive unfolding to Abraham of God's covenant grace and purpose, and the faith of Abraham registered in all these instances is the same faith responding with enlarged understanding and devotion to the progressive disclosures of God's purpose. We cannot think of these covenant disclosures in abstraction from the faith elicited by them nor can we think of the faith in abstraction from the disclosures of promise and purpose to which the faith of Abraham was directed. It is the impossibility of abstraction that renders harmonious the two facts that circumcision was both the seal of the covenant and the seal of faith.

The latter part of verse 11 and verse 12 are a unit defining the purpose served by the two salient facts mentioned in the first part of verse 11. These two facts are (1) that Abraham *did* receive the sign of circumcision and (2) that this was a seal of the faith he had before he was circumcised. Both considerations are relevant. The significance of circumcision as the seal of faith is not to be discounted. And yet the other fact that the faith it sealed was exercised in his uncircumcised status must also be appreciated. What then is the purpose contemplated? The apostle first reflects on the purpose served by the second fact, and this is stated in the latter part of verse 11. The purpose is that Abraham might be the father of all who believe though uncircumcised, that is, of all uncircumcised believers, and that since Abraham is the father of all such the righteousness which was imputed to Abraham will be imputed to them also. All such believers, irrespective of circumcision, will enjoy the same justification before God that Abraham enjoyed. In verse 12 Paul defines the purpose of the other fact, that Abraham received the seal of circumcision, and it is to the effect that Abraham might be the father of circumcised persons also as well as of uncircumcised. While, on the one hand, the fact of being uncircumcised is no obstacle to faith and to the justification that is by faith, no hindrance to our being the children of Abraham, yet, on the other hand, we must not suppose that circumcision is a liability. The apostle is jealous to guard against any such inference; the case of Jews is not prejudiced by the fact of circumcision. Hence he says, "the father of circumcision" (vs. 12). But it is equally necessary to insist that it is not the fact of circumcision that makes children of Abraham and so he adds: "to those who are not of the circumcision only but who also walk in the steps of the faith in uncircumcision of our father Abraham" (vs. 12). Circumcision is no obstacle. Yet it is not the determining factor; it is the other feature that must be coordinated with it, namely, to follow the example of Abraham's *faith*. The expressions used to describe this factor are to be noted. To "walk in the steps" is to march in file. Abraham is conceived of as the leader of the band and we walk, not abreast, but in file, following in the footprints left by Abraham. And it is the steps of Abraham's "uncircumcision-faith", a faith that receives no conditioning or efficacy from the fact of circumcision. Circumcision is not an excluding factor and neither is it a contributing factor to that by which we become the children of Abraham. All who are of faith "these are the sons of Abraham" (Gal. 3:7). It is the identity of faith that is in view when believers are said to be the sons of Abraham, just as identity of mode of dwelling when Jabal is called the father of all such as dwell in tents (Gen. 4:20) and identity of occupation when Jubal is called the father of all such as handle the harp and organ (Gen. 4:21).[10]

---

[10] *Cf.* Hodge: *op. cit., ad loc.*

13-18

13 For not through the law was the promise to Abraham or to his seed that he should be heir of the world, but through the righteousness of faith.
14 For if they that are of the law are heirs, faith is made void, and the promise is made of none effect:
15 for the law worketh wrath; but where there is no law, neither is there transgression.
16 For this cause *it is* of faith, that *it may be* according to grace; to the end that the promise may be sure to all the seed; not to that only which is of the law, but to that also which is of the faith of Abraham, who is the father of us all
17 (as it is written, A father of many nations have I made thee) before him whom he believed, *even* God, who giveth life to the dead, and calleth the things that are not, as though they were.
18 Who in hope believed against hope, to the end that he might become a father of many nations, according to that which had been spoken, So shall thy seed be.

13 At verse 13 there is no break in the argument. There is *transition to another consideration* pertinent to the proof derived from Old Testament data that justification is by faith and that Abraham is the father of all who believe whether they be of the circumcision or of uncircumcision. But that the ruling interest is the same is shown by the apostle's sustained appeal to the antithesis between faith and works of law (*cf.* vss. 13, 14, 16, 22, 23, 24) and to the fact that Abraham is the father of all who believe (*cf.* vss. 16–18). The *new* element introduced at verse 13, however, is the antithesis between *law* and *promise*, and considerations incident to promise are now developed with the same degree of cogency as was manifest in the preceding verses in the argument derived from Abraham's faith in uncircumcision.

When we read that "not through law was the promise to Abraham or to his seed",[11] there are particularly two questions. What is meant by "law"? And what is the seed of Abraham in this instance? In reference to the first there is no good reason

---

[11] There is good reason for the marginal rendering "not through law". The omission of the article here serves to emphasize that what is in view is not the Mosaic law as an economy but simply law as law demanding obedience.

for taking "law" in any other sense than that argued for above (3:31). The word "law" should be regarded as referring to law as commandment demanding obedience and applies to all law which falls into this category. It is true, of course, that the Mosaic law gave the most articulate and impressive revelation of the law of God in this respect and the ten commandments were the most summary and concentrated expression of what law as commandment is. But it does not provide us with the antithesis between "law" and "promise" in terms of the argument here to suppose that what Paul means is the contrast between the Abrahamic dispensation of promise and the Mosaic dispensation. The Mosaic administration (as Paul shows in Galatians 3:17–22) did not abrogate or suspend the promise given to Abraham—the promise was valid and fully in operation when the Mosaic covenant was given 430 years after; and it remained in operation. Hence it is misleading and indefensible to say summarily that the "law", referred to here in verse 13, means the law of Moses and interpret it in the sense of the Mosaic economy. Far less may we regard the "law" as the Old Testament in the canonical sense. That would be still further removed from the terms of the antithesis. Hence we shall have to regard Paul as meaning by "law" law of commandment with allusion to the works of law which the law of commandment demands. And what the apostle is asserting is the complete contrast between "law" and "promise". Law commands and it produces wrath when it is violated (*cf.* vs. 15); it knows no grace. Promise is the assurance of gracious bestowment; it is a free gift. Assuming this antithesis between the provisions of law and the provisions of promise, Paul asserts categorically that not through law was the promise to Abraham. That it was a promise was an unquestionable fact. Therefore, by reason of the implied contrast, it was not through law. This is in line with the whole development of Paul's argument from 3:20 onwards.[12]

The question in reference to Abraham's seed is readily answered. In Galatians 3:16 the "seed" is obviously Christ. But in this instance the seed must be the collective seed of Abraham since in verses 16 and 17 Paul speaks of the promise as being sure "to all the seed, not to that which is of the law only but to that

---

[12] The affirmative opposite of "not through law" is "through the righteousness of faith".

also which is of the faith of Abraham, who is the father of us all, as it is written, A father of many nations have I made thee". He is referring to the "many" of whom Abraham is the father (*cf.* vss. 11, 12). And these verses also establish the denotation as being not the natural descendants of Abraham, but all, both of the circumcision and the uncircumcision, who are "of the faith of Abraham" (vs. 16). The "promise" is therefore that given to all who believe and all who believe are Abraham's seed.

The clause, "that he should be heir of the world" is explanatory of the promise given to Abraham and his seed; it tells us what the promise was. We do not find any promise in the Old Testament in these express terms. What is it? We naturally think of the promise to Abraham that in him all the families of the earth would be blessed (Gen. 12:3) and the correlative promises given later (*cf.* Gen. 13:14–17; 15:4, 5, 18–21; 17:2–21; 22:15–18). In the light of Pauline teaching as a whole, however, we cannot exclude from the scope of this promise, as defined by the apostle, the most inclusive messianic purport. It is defined as the promise to Abraham that *he* should be heir of the world, but it is also a promise to his seed and, therefore, can hardly involve anything less than the worldwide dominion promised to Christ and to the spiritual seed of Abraham in him. It is a promise that receives its ultimate fulfilment in the consummated order of the new heavens and the new earth.

14, 15 In verse 14 the thought of the negation that "not through law is the promise" (vs. 13) is resumed and the necessity of the negation is demonstrated by showing the consequence that would follow if it were assumed—"for if those who are of the law are heirs, faith is made void, and the promise is made of none effect". The expression "of law" is contrasted with "of faith" and "law" must mean, as found repeatedly, the law of commandment demanding obedience and performance. "Those who are of law" are those who are governed by law as the guiding and determining principle of their religion in contrast with those of whose religion faith is the basic principle. "Those who are of law" are simply those who are "of the works of law". Law here is no more the Mosaic economy viewed as an administration than in verse 13. And the inference to the effect that, if those of the works of the law are heirs, faith is made void and the promise brought to nought

142

is one drawn from the acknowledged contradiction between faith
and works; the one is exclusive of the other. And the same
is true of law and promise, for promise is correlative with faith.

Another reason, however, is given here why the foregoing inference respecting the voiding of faith and promise, on the
hypothesis being refuted, follows. It is given in verse 15: "For
the law works wrath: and where no law is, neither is there
transgression". In other words, this is the particular reason
urged in this instance why law makes both faith and promise void.
What is this wrath which the law works? It has been proposed
that it is the wrath or enmity provoked in the human breast
by the law, a truth on which Paul lays much stress later on (cf.
7:8, 11, 13). And it would not be irrelevant to the subject at
this point. For it does fit in with the refutation of legalism to
be reminded that law of itself only provokes to greater transgression and not to obedience and performance. But there is
reason to believe that this is not the thought here but rather that
the wrath is the wrath of God. Although Paul does use the word
"wrath" in reference to the unholy wrath of which man is subject
(Eph. 4:31; Col. 3:8; I Tim. 2:8; cf. James 1:19, 20), yet most
frequently in Paul's epistles and generally in the New Testament
the term is used of the wrath of God, and in this epistle, with the
possible exception of 13:4, 5 (where even then it is not the
unholy wrath of man), it is always the wrath of God. There would
have to be compelling reasons for departure from this meaning
in this instance. And Paul, when dealing with the enmity aroused
in the human heart, as sin takes occasion by the commandment
(Rom. 7:8, 11, 13), does not use this term. Besides, the term
"wrath" is not the most suitable to convey the thought of this
latter reaction in the human breast. After the analogy of the usage
in this epistle, therefore, we should regard the wrath which the law
works as the wrath of God. And when we ask the question how the
law works the wrath of God, the succeeding clause provides the
answer—"where no law is, neither is there transgression".
Without law there would be no sin, for sin consists in the transgression of the law. In our sinful situation, therefore, there is
always transgression of the law and it is this transgression that
evokes the wrath of God. The sequence of the thought is: law
existing, sinful man transgressing law, the wrath of God provoked
to exercise by transgression. Paul's enunciation of this is condensed;

that is why he says "the law works wrath"; it works wrath only, however, because of the transgression.

This consideration that the law works wrath is pertinent to the hypothesis which Paul had stated in the preceding verse. For if it is the *wrath* of God that the law works, then there cannot be *by law* the favour which faith and the promise presuppose; by law the context of faith and promise is eliminated, the opposite comes into operation, and faith and promise are thus made void.

16 This interpretation of verse 15 lays the proper basis for verse 16: "Therefore it is of faith in order that it may be according to grace". Since law works wrath in view of transgression, law knows no grace. Therefore the inheritance cannot be of law and those who are of law cannot be the heirs. The only alternative is the principle of faith and so the inheritance is of faith in order that it might be by grace. Faith and grace cohere; law and the promised inheritance are contradictory.

The latter part of verse 16 expresses the design that is promoted by the fact that the inheritance is of faith and therefore by grace—"to the end that the promise might be sure to all the seed, not to that only which is of the law, but also to that which is of the faith of Abraham". The parallelism to the design stated in the second half of verse 11 and in verse 12 is too clear to be called in question. But here in verse 16 this design is stated in relation to the promise, whereas in verses 11, 12 it is stated in reference to the import and purpose of circumcision. Here (vs. 16) the principle of faith and grace is said to be the guarantee that the promise comprises all the seed, that is to say, all who believe, whether they be Jews or Gentiles (*cf.* vs. 13).

The designation "of the law" in verse 16 must have a different reference here from the expressions "through law" in verse 13 and "of law" in verse 14. For in these latter instances "through law" and "of law" are antithetical to and exclusive of faith; the promise is not "through law" (vs. 13) and those who are "of law" are not heirs (vs. 14); faith and promise are negated if law is in operation. But in verse 16 the seed which is "of the law" is not excluded; the promise is said to be sure to them provided they have faith. Consequently, their being "of the law" does not place them outside the category of faith, whereas in verses 13, 14 "through law" and "of law" are in the sharpest opposition to faith. We shall have to conclude that "of the law" (vs. 16) is equivalent in meaning to "of the circumcision" in verse 12. The parallelism and identical purport of "the father of the circumcision to those who are not of the circumcision only but who also walk in the steps of the faith of our father Abraham which he had in uncircumcision" (vs. 12), on the one hand, and "not to that which is of the law only but also to that which is of the faith of Abraham" (vs. 16), on the other, are apparent. So "of the law" (vs. 16) must mean "of the Mosaic law" and refers to those who had the advantage of being under the Mosaic economy. This illustrates again the flexibility there is in Paul's use of this word "law" and the different shades of meaning that must be discovered if we are to do justice to his thought. Those who are "of law" are excluded from the seed; those who are of the Mosaic law, considered as an economy, are not excluded. But Paul is insistent that the latter must also be "of the faith of Abraham" if they are to be his seed.

17 The appeal to Scripture at the beginning of verse 17—"as it is written, a father of many nations have I made thee"—must be regarded in the syntax of the sentence as parenthetical. But we may not think that it is an aside in the apostle's argument. This appeal to Scripture is in corroboration of the preceding clause, "who is the father of us all", and both clauses taken together reiterate the thought of verses 11 and 12. Here, however, the stress is laid upon the community of right and privilege in the fatherhood of Abraham on the part of *all* believers—"who is the father of us all"—and upon the ethnic universality of this relationship—"a father of many nations have I made thee"—in a way that surpasses the forms of expression in verses 11 and 12. In the earlier instance the terms of the argument required Paul to say, "the father of all who believe through uncircumcision" and "the father of circumcision", thus indicating this kind of distinction. But now he dispenses with even that distinction and says expressly without any discrimination, "who is the father of us all" and "a father of many nations I have made thee".

The parenthetical nature of the clauses pertaining to the appeal to Scripture (vs. 17a) helps us to understand the connection of the latter part of verse 17, "before him whom he believed" *etc.* This is to be taken with the clause, "who is the father of us all",

145

and means that Abraham is the father of us all before God. The fatherhood of Abraham partakes of all the validity and sanction derived from divine recognition and institution. Or it may reflect on the fact that the faith of Abraham in which his fatherhood resides was a faith exercised and maintained in the presence of God (*cf.* Gen. 17:1; II Cor. 2:17).

The clauses which follow, "who giveth life to the dead, and calleth the things that are not, as though they were", are descriptive of the aspects of God's character which are peculiarly appropriate to the faith exercised; they point to those attributes of God which are the specific bases of Abraham's faith or, at least, to the attributes which were in the forefront of Abraham's apprehension when he believed the promises and put his trust in the Lord. The first of these, "who giveth life to the dead", has in view the life-giving power of God by which he can raise the dead to life. In Scripture this is regarded as the peculiar index to God's omnipotence, and Paul elsewhere indicates this (*cf.* Eph. 1:19, 20). It is only as Abraham had respect to such an attribute of God as is exemplified in raising the dead that he could have believed the promise that he would be the father of many nations. And the reason for this (as shown later in the subsequent verses) is that the fulfilment was as naturally and humanly impossible as raising the dead. The second clause, "who calleth the things that are not, as though they were", presents more difficulty. It has been variously interpreted. It has been regarded as referring to the creative activity of God by which he calls into being things which had no existence prior to his fiat, an aspect of God's character appropriate to the faith of Abraham but hardly that expressed by the formula Paul uses. He does not say "who calleth into being things that are not" but "calleth the things that are not *as* being". And the things in view are things that are not rather than things which are brought into being. A view that has received wide acceptance is that the formula has reference to God's disposing decree and control over all things actual and possible, that "the things which are not" are the possible and "the things which are" are the actual. But again the formula is not adapted to such an interpretation. It is gratuitous to assume that "the things which are not" are the things *possible*. And, besides, the things possible, and merely possible, cannot be regarded even by God as being. But this is the import of the formula that the non-existing things are regarded as being. The interpretation which appears to do justice to the formula and which is eminently appropriate to the faith of Abraham is that which regards "the things which are not" as referring to the things determined by God to come to pass but which have not yet been fulfilled. These things do not yet exist, but since determined by God they are "called" by him as having existence. The certainty of their futurition is just as secure as if they had come to pass. And the word "call" is used of God's effectual word and determination. The promises given to Abraham were in that category; the things promised had not yet come into being, they were non-existent as respects realization. But, because God promised them and therefore determined that they should come to pass, the certainty of their realization was secure. It was to this truth, namely, that what God has determined and promised, though not yet fulfilled, is spoken of as if it had been fulfilled and therefore *as being* in his determinate purpose, that Abraham's faith was directed, and it was in God as possessing this character that Abraham rested. God's promise was for Abraham as good as fulfilment. The things that were not yet did not belong to the category of the possible but to that of determinate certainty, and Abraham possessed the promises in God (*cf.* Heb. 11:1).

18 Verse 18 is a further amplification of the character of Abraham's faith and of the design that his faith subserved. The relative pronoun at the beginning refers to Abraham (*cf.* vs. 17b). "Against hope" and "in hope" point in opposite directions. The former envisions the circumstances mentioned in verse 19 which would be calculated of themselves to destroy all hope. In terms of human resources there was no possibility of fulfilment. This, however, places in relief the other expression "in hope" and the calculation of faith which it bespeaks. In face of the calculations which appearances might induce, Abraham entertained hope because he believed, and the calculations of faith were with the omnipotence and faithfulness of God (*cf.* vs. 17). It is difficult to ascertain the precise relations and interrelations of faith and hope in this text. "Believed in hope" does not mean that he had faith in his own hope. The object of faith is clearly God in the omnipotence of his character, the determinateness of his purpose, and the security of his promises. Apparently what is meant by "believed in hope" is that Abraham's faith was exercised in the confident hope which the promise of God engendered. Faith and hope were mutually interactive and complementary. They both rested upon the same foundation, the promises of God, the specific quality of faith being unreserved commitment to God and his promises and the specific quality of hope being the outreach of expectation in reference to fulfilment.

The second part of verse 18 states the design of Abraham's faith; it was "to the end that he might become the father of many nations, according to that which is spoken, So shall thy seed be". It is possible that this is intended to define the aim consciously entertained by Abraham and therefore that his faith was directed to the fulfilment of the promises mentioned in this part of the text. That is to say, Abraham confidently believed in the assurance of hope lest the promises that he would be the father of many nations and his seed as the stars of heaven should fail of fulfilment. Both promises stated in the text, "a father of many nations" and "so shall thy seed be", were promises given to Abraham (Gen. 15:5; 17:5) and they therefore came within the compass of his faith. Hence to dismiss summarily the view that this defines the design of Abraham in believing is without warrant.[13] But, in any case, the design is that embraced in the ordination of God. The strongest consideration in favour of restricting the design to the ordination and intention of God is the parallel in verse 11 where, without question, God's design is in view.[14] But the argument drawn from verse 11 is not conclusive to this effect. In the latter the design stated is clearly that of God's own action, whereas in verse 18 the design is related directly to the act of Abraham in believing. Of course, God's ordination is indicated even if what is expressly stated is the design of Abraham. There appears to be no good reason for excluding the latter.

19-25

> 19 And without being weakened in faith he considered his own body now as good as dead (he being about a hundred years old), and the deadness of Sarah's womb;
> 20 yet, looking unto the promise of God, he wavered not

---

[13] *Cf.* Meyer: *op. cit., ad loc.*
[14] *Cf.* Meyer: *idem.*

> through unbelief, but waxed strong through faith, giving glory to God,
>
> 21 and being fully assured that what he had promised, he was able also to perform.
>
> 22 Wherefore also it was reckoned unto him for righteousness.
>
> 23 Now it was not written for his sake alone, that it was reckoned unto him;
>
> 24 but for our sake also, unto whom it shall be reckoned, who believe on him that raised Jesus our Lord from the dead,
>
> 25 who was delivered up for our trespasses, and was raised for our justification.

19 In verse 19 there is a question as to the correct Greek text. There is a significant variant in the manuscripts.[15] Are we to read: "he did *not* consider his own body dead" or "he did consider his own body dead"? The negative appears in some manuscripts and not in others. This might seem to offer entirely different interpretations. But in this context, strange as it may seem, the difference of thought is not so great and both readings are compatible with the context and with what we know of Abraham.

On the former reading the thought would be that he did not consider his own dead body and the deadness of Sarah's womb. That is to say, he did not set his mind upon, he did not become so absorbed with, the procreative impotency of his own body nor the fact that Sarah was past age for the conception and bearing of children (*cf.* Gen. 18:11) so as to become weak in faith. This implies that his body was procreatively impotent and the reason is given, namely, that he was about a hundred years old. And it implies that Sarah also was past the age of bearing, as Genesis 18:11 attests. Abraham was cognizant of these facts (*cf.* Gen. 17:17). But he did not allow them to loom up in his thought to such an extent that his faith in the promise of God was undermined. As verse 20 says, "he did not waver at the promise of God in unbelief". While he did not close his eyes to the facts of his own age and Sarah's, yet he was so absorbed with the promise of God that faith did not waver.[16]

---

[15] The affirmative κατενόησεν is the reading of ℵ A B C 424** 1739, several versions and some fathers, whereas the negative οὐ κατενόησεν is the reading of D, G, the mass of the cursives, some versions, and several fathers. The discussion above shows that either reading is agreeable to the thought.

[16] It may not be out of place to suggest that on the reading οὐ κατενόησεν

On the latter reading the thought is that Abraham did consider his own body dead and the deadness of Sarah's womb. In this case there is express emphasis upon what is *implied* on the other reading but the word "consider" would have a different shade of meaning. In the former case it would mean "become absorbed with", "fix attention upon", whereas now it means "take into account", "reckon with". And the thought would be that although he was fully aware of his own procreative decrepitude and the deadness of Sarah's womb (*cf.* Gen. 17:17; 18:11), nevertheless he was not weak in faith. And the reason why he was not weak in faith is that he fixed his attention upon the promise of God and did not waver in unbelief. Hence the difference of meaning on the two readings is one of emphasis and both readings are quite in accord with the facts of the case and with the construction of the passage. The latter reading, however, appears to have the stronger support and may therefore be followed.

20, 21 Verse 20 is explanatory of the clause at the beginning of verse 19, "and not being weak in faith" and describes Abraham's faith both negatively and positively. This is the force of the adversative at the middle of the verse. Abraham did not stagger, he did not entertain doubting thoughts, with reference to *the promise of God*. The promise of God occupies the position of emphasis in the sentence in order to set off in bolder relief that upon which Abraham's faith was focused. If Abraham had wavered at the promise it would have been through *unbelief*. Doubt of the promise of God has no affinity with faith and the apostle accords it no credit. The positive characterization of Abraham's faith is that "he was strengthened in faith". It is usual to take "the faith" referred to here as meaning *in respect of* his faith after the analogy of verse 19a which is to the effect that Abraham did not become weakened in respect of his faith. And so the meaning is taken to be that Abraham was strengthened in respect of his faith. It is not unreasonable, however, to regard the faith referred to here as instrumental after the pattern of the

the thought could be that, though on all natural calculations, Abraham would have considered his own body and the womb of Sarah procreatively dead, yet, because of the promise of God, he refused to reckon this to be the case and so resisted the calculation which, apart from God's promise, would have been inevitable. This would in no way cast any reflection upon the faith of Abraham. He did actually beget and Sarah did actually conceive and bear Isaac.

150

unbelief in the preceding clause and thus understand the clause to mean that Abraham was strengthened, that is, empowered, *by* his faith. The sense would then be that the strength by which Abraham was able to perform the procreative act in begetting Isaac was ministered through the instrumentality of faith. Faith would thus be brought into direct relation to the procreative act.[17] We must not forget that Isaac was begotten by Abraham and conceived by Sarah. And this view of "strengthened in faith" would indicate that it was by the strength ministered by faith and exercised in faith that Abraham begat Isaac (*cf.* Heb. 11:11 in the case of Sarah—"by faith ... she received strength to conceive seed"). It is a strange prejudice that leads Meyer to say that this "can hardly fail to convey a very indelicate idea" (*ad loc.*).

There are two reasons, however, why this interpretation should not be adopted. (1) There is no evidence that Paul has in view simply the later period in Abraham's life of faith when he actually begat Isaac. The promises quoted in this chapter have reference to an earlier period (*cf.* vs. 22). (2) The idea that the strength by which Abraham begat Isaac is in the forefront here does not so well accord with the clauses which follow. "Giving glory to God" and "being fully persuaded", *etc.* define for us that in which the strengthening of faith consisted or, at least, the ways in which the strengthening of faith was expressed; they indicate what was simultaneous with the strengthening of faith and, very likely, what was involved in the strengthening of faith. The content of his full persuasion is stated to be that what had been promised God was able to perform.

"Giving glory to God" and "being fully persuaded that what he has promised he is able also to perform" are coordinate and describe the exercises or states of mind which were involved in Abraham's faith. To give glory to God is to reckon God to be what he is and to rely upon his power and faithfulness. To be fully persuaded denotes the full assurance and efflorescence of conviction (*cf.* 14:5; Col. 4:12). The object of this conviction is stated to be "that what he [God] has promised he is able also to perform". Both clauses in coordination mark a fulness of expression indicative of the strength and vigour of Abraham's faith.

---

[17] This would be consonant with the interpretation suggested in the preceding footnote.

22 In verse 22 we have another appeal to Genesis 15:6 (*cf.* vss. 3, 9): "wherefore also it was reckoned to him for righteousness". As in these other instances and as is required by the foregoing context the emphasis in this case is placed upon *faith*. The formula of Genesis 15:6, as was noted already, refers to justification but the leading lesson which the apostle elicits from it is that by faith Abraham was justified. Hence there is good reason why he should have concluded his elaboration of the true character of Abraham's faith with the appeal to this text. It is this analysis of the faith of Abraham, given in the preceding verses, that explains the "wherefore also" with which this verse begins. The grandeur of Abraham's faith makes all the more apparent why it was imputed for righteousness. And, from the standpoint of the reader of the epistle, he is now in a better position to assess the true character of this faith and more intelligently to appreciate the fact that it was imputed for righteousness. But if we fail to discern a correlative emphasis in this context we miss what is central in our assessment and definition of faith. Paul had just said that Abraham was "strengthened in faith, giving glory to God", *etc.* The "wherefore also" is in immediate conjunction with these clauses. The grandeur of faith consists in this that it gives all the glory to God and rests in God's power and faithfulness. The efficacy of faith's instrumentality resides in the fact that it gives God the glory and rests upon him in the fulness of that perfection which demands the ascription of glory.[18]

23–25 These concluding verses of this chapter deal with the relevance to us of this faith of Abraham. Paul is now applying to the subject of justification the principle enunciated elsewhere, "Now these things happened to them by way of example, and they were written for our instruction, upon whom the ends of the ages have come" (I Cor. 10:11). In this passage he says: "Now it was not written on his account only that it was imputed to him, but on our account also" (vss. 23, 24a). In terms of doctrine, the truth elicited from the example of Abraham is

[18] Although Paul in vss. 19–21 is bringing within the scope of his thought the faith of Abraham as it was exemplified in a much later period than that to which Gen. 15:6 first of all refers, yet there is no discrepancy. The faith of Gen. 15:6 is directed specifically to the promise of a seed (*cf.* Gen. 15:2–5) and the faith exemplified in the later period was the same faith directed to the same promise. Gen. 15:6 can therefore be appealed to as that which is illustrated at all stages of the history of Abraham and of his faith.

applied to the subject with which Paul is dealing, justification by faith. Faith was not only imputed to Abraham for righteousness but will also be imputed to all who believe. This is to say that not only was Abraham justified by faith but all who believe after the pattern of Abraham will also be justified by faith. And then the apostle proceeds to state specifically to whom and to what *our* faith is to be directed.

If we are to be justified by faith, obviously the circumstances of our faith cannot be identical with those of Abraham's. We are not now in the same historical context and our faith cannot be exemplified in the same ways (*cf.* esp. vss. 19–21). May we go farther and say that our faith has different content and different objects? It is precisely in relation to these considerations that verses 24 and 25 are significant. The object of faith is carefully specified by the apostle—faith is imputed "to those who believe upon him who raised Jesus our Lord from the dead" (vs. 24). Certain observations will show the implications of this statement. (1) It is God who raised Jesus from the dead. Therefore there is this identity between the faith of Abraham and our faith. We believe upon God and the pivotal consideration in all that Paul had said respecting Abraham is that he believed God. (2) The God in whom we believe is identified as the one who raised Jesus our Lord from the dead; it is in that specific character that he is viewed. This establishes another point of connection between our faith and that of Abraham. Paul is careful to inform us that Abraham's faith was directed to God as the one who quickens the dead (vs. 17). As noted above, Abraham's faith was focused upon God in his character as omnipotent, an omnipotence exemplified in his making alive the dead. Our faith likewise is focused upon God in the character that is exemplified by the miracle of the resurrection of Jesus from the dead. The sameness as respects essential feature is apparent. (3) Our faith in God as the one who raised Jesus from the dead is, for this reason, Christologically conditioned; it cannot be abstracted from that which God has done in reference to the fulfilment of the promise. Here again is a principle of identity. Abraham's faith was concerned with the promise, as Paul had demonstrated in the preceding verses. His faith, as it became occupied with the promise, was one that did not waver because it rested upon God as the one who "calls the things that be not as being" (vs. 17;

153

cf. exposition at that point). Abraham possessed the promise in the security of God's determinate purpose and faithfulness. We do the same in the fulfilment that has been registered in the resurrection of Jesus.

Other features of similarity and identity could readily be discovered but these are sufficient to demonstrate the essential unity of Abraham's faith and ours and the continuity implicit in Paul's statement, "Now it was not written on his account alone that it was imputed to him, but on our account also" (vs. 23). We must not, however, discount the differences created by progressive revelation and the historic events of redemptive accomplishment. This passage is also eloquent of that distinction. And Paul does not suppress the significance for our faith of the actual fulfilment of the promise. It was promise that loomed on Abraham's horizon; it is accomplishment that is focal in our purview. The full panorama of redemptive realization stretches before us to give that specific content to our faith. Hence the apostle provides us with a statement, unsurpassed in its succinctness, of what is comprised in the gospel and of what comes within the compass of our faith—"to those who believe upon him who raised Jesus our Lord from the dead, who was delivered up on account of our offences and was raised on account of our justification" (vss. 24, 25). He is not forgetful that upon us "the ends of the ages have come" (I Cor. 10:11) and that "now once in the consummation of the ages he [Christ] hath been manifested to put away sin by the sacrifice of himself" (Heb. 9:26).

Verse 25 offers two possibilities as to interpretation. The question turns on the exact force of the two expressions which are parallel to each other and are identical in the form of construction, "on account of our trespasses" and "on account of our justification". The former is related to the delivering up of Christ, his crucifixion, and gives the reason for it. The latter is related to the resurrection of Christ and gives the reason for it. Since the clauses are parallel we shall have to regard "our trespasses" as sustaining to the crucifixion of Christ the same kind of relationship as "our justification" sustains to his resurrection. If the one is retrospective so must be the other or if the one is prospective so must be the other.

On the former alternative the thought would be that Jesus was delivered up because our trespasses were placed upon him and that he was raised from the dead because we had been justified. On this view the resurrection of Jesus is regarded as the consequence of our justification and justification is conceived of as complete prior to the resurrection. This interpretation would require us to construe the justification in this instance as equivalent to reconciliation and propitiation, belonging to the sphere of objective, historical, once-for-all accomplishment. It is not impossible to take justification in this sense. It may be used in this sense in 5:9—there is a certain parallelism between verses 9 and 10 and in verse 10 it is objective reconciliation that is in view. And if justification is thus interpreted it is quite compatible with New Testament thought to regard the resurrection of Jesus as the inevitable sequel to the work perfected by his death and as the seal upon this perfection. Furthermore, the parallel clause that Jesus "was delivered up on account of our offences" can well mean that Jesus was delivered up because our sins were laid to his account and that the death of Jesus was the inevitable consequence of the imputation to him of our sins. This interpretation, then, does not violate biblical teaching as such nor Pauline doctrine in general.

The other alternative is that Jesus was delivered up in order to atone for our sins and was raised in order that we might be justified. The two expressions, "on account of our trespasses" and "on account of our justification" have thus prospective reference. And the resurrection is viewed as that which lays the basis for our justification. There is reason for adopting this alternative. In the preceding context Paul had been dealing with actual justification, that is to say, with our actual acceptance with God as righteous. The formula, "it was imputed for righteousness", which is the pivot of the argument in the whole of this chapter, refers to our acceptance with God, in other words, that which falls within the application of redemption. It is the justification which is inseparable from faith. And since in all the earlier instances in this epistle the term "to justify" is used in this sense (2:13; 3:20, 24, 26, 28, 30; 4:2, 5) and Paul is dealing with the same in the immediately preceding context, we must conclude that it would be a deviation from his theme to use the word justification here in a sense different from that of the context. Justification, we may infer therefore, refers to actual justification by faith and the resurrection of Jesus is viewed as that which lays the basis for this justification. We shall have to interpret the other clause in uniformity with this and say that Jesus was delivered up in order to atone for our sins.

The *efficacy* of the death of Christ and of his resurrection lies on the face of the text. As Jesus rose again in order to guarantee our justification, so he was delivered up in order to deal effectively with our trespasses. We are not, of course, to interpret the text artificially and think of the death of Christ as sustaining no relation to our justification and the resurrection as having no relation to our sins. Justification is related directly to the blood of Christ (3:24; *cf.* Eph. 1:7; Rom. 5:9; 6:7; 8:33, 34) and the atonement therefore lays the basis for our justification. But the apostle, in the way most appropriate to his theme and, particularly, to his foregoing argument respecting Abraham's faith, concentrates attention upon the most salient and pertinent relationships of the two central and indivisible facts of redemptive action, the death and resurrection of Christ.

The turn of expression used in this verse is to be noted. Jesus was "delivered up" and he "was raised". The redemptive action is viewed from the aspect of that to which Jesus was subjected and so thought is focused on the action of God in reference to Jesus. Since distinction is drawn between God as acting and Jesus our Lord as acted upon, the person acting must be God the Father. He delivered up Jesus (*cf.* 8:32) and he raised Jesus from the dead (Acts 3:15; 4:10; 10:40; 13:30, 37; Rom. 6:4; 8:11; Gal. 1:1; Eph. 1:19, 20; Col. 2:12; I Thess. 1:10; I Pet. 1:21). This does no prejudice to the action of Jesus himself in his death and resurrection. But it is important to observe here as elsewhere how the apostle brings into distinct prominence the actions of God the Father in the acts of redemption. And in relation to the main interest of the apostle in this chapter it is noteworthy that faith as resting upon him who raised Jesus from the dead (vs. 24) is faith directed to God the Father himself.

The respects in which the resurrection of Christ may be conceived of as serving the end of justification are manifold. In terms of Paul's own teaching a few may be mentioned. (1) We are justified by faith, and this faith must be directed to Jesus (3:22, 26). But only as the living Lord can he be the object of faith. (2) It is in union with Christ that we are justified (*cf.* 8:1; II Cor. 5:21). Only as active through resurrection can any virtue proceed from Christ to us and only with a living Christ can union have efficacy. (3) The righteousness of Christ by which we are justified (5:17, 18, 19) has its abiding embodiment in Christ; it can never be thought of in abstraction from him as a reservoir of merit stored up. Only as the living one can Christ be the embodiment of righteousness and be made to us righteousness from God (I Cor. 1:30). (4) The death and resurrection of Christ are inseparable. Hence even the death or blood of Christ as related to our justification (3:24, 25; 5:9; 8:33, 34) could have no efficacy to that end in isolation from the resurrection. (5) It is through the mediation of Christ that we come to stand in the grace of justification (5:2). But the mediation of Christ could not be operative if he were still under the power of death.

VII. FRUITS OF JUSTIFICATION
(5:1-11)

1-5

1 Being therefore justified by faith, we have peace with God through our Lord Jesus Christ;
2 through whom also we have had our access by faith into this grace wherein we stand; and we rejoice in hope of the glory of God.
3 And not only so, but we also rejoice in our tribulations: knowing that tribulation worketh stedfastness;
4 and stedfastness, approvedness; and approvedness, hope:
5 and hope putteth not to shame; because the love of God hath been shed abroad in our hearts through the Holy Spirit which was given unto us.

At the beginning of this chapter we have the intimations of climactic and triumphant conclusion. The "therefore" indicates that an inference is being drawn from the doctrine that had been unfolded and demonstrated in the preceding chapters (3:21–4:25). In verses 1–11 the apostle exhibits the privileges which emanate from justification and belong to the justified. We cannot escape the notes of assurance and exultation—"we exult in hope of the glory of God" (vs. 2); "we glory in the tribulations" (vs. 3); "hope does not make ashamed, because the love of God is shed abroad in our hearts" (vs. 5); "much more therefore, having been justified now in his blood, shall we be saved through him from the wrath" (vs. 9); "we glory in God through our Lord Jesus Christ" (vs. 11). What are the consequences flowing from justification which evoke such unrestrained rejoicing and assurance? Examination of the text will show.

1 The apostle places in the forefront "peace with God through our Lord Jesus Christ" (vs. 1).[1] Peace with God is a blessing

---

[1] The reading ἔχωμεν is supported by א* A B* C D E K L and other uncials as well as by several versions and fathers. The external authority for

coordinate with justification. The background of the latter is condemnation and subjection to the wrath of God and it contemplates our acceptance with God as righteous. The background of the former is our alienation from God and it contemplates our instatement in the favour of God and in the light of his countenance. That peace with God should be given preeminence in the blessings accruing from justification is consonant with the status which justification secures. "Peace with God" denotes relationship to God. It is not the composure and tranquillity of our minds and hearts; it is the status of peace flowing from the reconciliation (vss. 10, 11) and reflects primarily upon God's alienation from us and our instatement in his favour. Peace of heart and mind proceeds from "peace with God" and is the reflection in our consciousness of the relation established by justification. But it is the objective relation that is in view here when Paul speaks of "peace with God". It is "through our Lord Jesus Christ" that we have this peace. The mediation of Christ is not dispensed with in the bestowment of the privileges which proceed from justification, and this reminds us that our dependence upon the mediation of Christ is never suspended. All spiritual blessings are *in* Christ. But they are also enjoyed *through* Christ's continued mediatory activity.

2 The emphasis placed upon the mediation of Christ in verse 1 is continued in verse 2—"through whom also we have access by faith[2] into this grace wherein we stand". Whatever difficulties

---

this reading is, therefore, so formidable that it cannot be summarily rejected, even though on internal grounds ἔχομεν seems much more consonant with the context. The latter reading is found in אᶜ Bᶜ F G P, most cursives, some versions, and a few fathers. The case for ἔχομεν on internal grounds has been stated perhaps most strongly by Meyer who says that "the writer now enters on a new and important *doctrinal topic*, and an exhortation at the very outset, especially regarding a subject not yet expressly spoken of, would at this stage be *out of place*" (*op. cit., ad loc.*). However, if we were to adopt the hortatory reading, we need not suppose that the indicative, expressed by the other reading ἔχομεν, is thereby ruled out. May not the exhortation here, as in other cases, presuppose the indicative (*cf.* 6:12 with 6:14)? And the thought would be: "since we have peace with God, let us take full advantage of this status". Paradoxically stated, it would mean: "since we have it, let us have it". "Peace with God" is a gift of grace flowing from justification and inseparable from it, but exhortation is relevant and necessary to the cultivation of the privilege.

[2] τῇ πίστει is omitted in B D G and a few versions. External authority preponderates in favour of its retention and it is much easier to understand how it could be omitted rather than added in the course of transcription.

belong to the interpretation of this verse they do not obscure the fact that the primary thought is the mediation of Christ. The words "through whom also" make this clear. The first question that arises is that of the grace referred to. There needs to be little doubt but the grace in view is some grace referred to in the preceding verse. Since the emphasis falls upon the mediation of Christ and since the specification "this grace" should naturally be taken to refer to that which had been specified, we should not look for some other privilege above and beyond that which had been already stated. To which then of the graces specified in verse 1 does verse 2 refer? If it were "peace with God", then there would be unnecessary repetition. In verse 1 "peace with God" is stated expressly to be through Christ, and in reference to this mediation it would not be good sense to say "through whom also" if the same grace or benefit is in view. The expression "through whom also" compels us, therefore, to think of the other grace mentioned in verse 1, namely, justification. And the main thought of verse 2 is, therefore, to stress the fact that it is through the mediation of Christ that we have been instated in the grace of justification, a grace represented as one in which we have come to stand—it is an abiding and immovable status arising from a past action.

A question arises as to the precise import of the word "access". Does it mean introduction or access? If the former, then the accent falls upon the action of Christ as mediator in bringing us nigh to God and instating us in this grace.[3] If the latter, then the accent falls upon our approach to God in drawing nigh. Paul's use of this same term elsewhere (Eph. 2:18; 3:12) favours the latter interpretation and in that event the privilege afforded believers of free access to God is placed in the foreground. Hence, while the mediation of Christ in the bestowment of justification is the leading thought of the verse, yet in connection with this grace of justification the particular emphasis falls upon the fact

---

[3] προσαγωγή has the meaning of "bringing nigh" or "leading towards" in Greek writers. This meaning appears in the New Testament in the verb προσάγω (cf. Matt. 18:24; Luke 9:41; I Pet. 3:18). In Eph. 2:18 it is not certain that the thought is that of access rather than of introduction. As far as Rom. 5:2 is concerned it does not appear possible to be decisive on the exact nuance of thought conveyed by the term. Either shade of meaning is in thorough accord with the thrust of the context and dogmatism in favour of one against the other is scarcely warranted.

that the free access or approach to God, which the grace of justification imparts, is itself mediated through Christ. Even in our drawing nigh to God with confidence we are dependent upon Christ's mediation—it is through him that we have come to have access and this access is an abiding privilege resultant upon the action which justification involves.[4] The element of acceptance with God, as an implicate of justification, is no doubt in the forefront, since that aspect of justification is particularly appropriate to the thought of access.

It is difficult to ascertain with which of the preceding clauses the last clause of verse 2 is to be taken. The most tenable view is that it is to be coordinated with the leading thought of the preceding verses, namely, "we have peace with God". All that intervenes is subordinate to that consideration and, furthermore, verse 3 must be coordinated with the last clause of verse 2 as an additional aspect of the glorying which the last clause of verse 2 specifies. The clause in question, "we exult in hope of the glory of God"[5] refers to rejoicing and boasting on the highest level. It is exultant rejoicing and confident glorying (*cf.* vss. 3, 11; I Cor. 1:31; Phil. 3:3). The object of this glorying is stated to be "the hope of the glory of God". The glorying is a state of mind in the present but that which evokes it is something to be realized in the future; this future attainment is brought into relation to the present by hope. We project ourselves into the future in hope. This expectation is called "the glory of God." Undoubtedly this denotes that of which Paul speaks later in this epistle as "the glory to be revealed" (8:18) and "the liberty of the glory of the children of God" (8:21; *cf.* vss. 23, 24). But why does he call it "the glory of God"? It will not suffice to say that it is called the glory of God because God is the author of

---

[4] In order to bring out the force of the tenses in vs. 2 the following rendering helps: "through whom also we have come to have access by faith into this grace in which we have come to stand".

[5] καὶ καυχώμεθα etc. could be taken as coordinate with ἐσχήκαμεν (*cf.*, *e.g.*, Lightfoot: *Notes, ad loc.*). On this supposition it is indicative, as rendered in the version. If it is coordinated with ἔχομεν or ἔχωμεν (vs. 1), then it can be taken as hortatory, "let us rejoice", as in the margin of the version. If we adopt ἔχωμεν as the genuine reading in vs. 1 and connect καυχώμεθα with vs. 1, then undoubtedly καυχώμεθα would have to be taken as hortatory in agreement with ἔχωμεν. On this construction there would be no radical interference with the note of exultation which the indicative expressly conveys. For the exhortation implies the right to exult in hope of the glory of God and therefore the possession of hope.

the glory bestowed upon his children. We should miss an important element of New Testament and Pauline teaching if we did not bring this expression into direct relation to the glory which is God's own. The consummation of redemption, in the teaching of the New Testament, is coincident with the manifestation of the glory of God (*cf.* Matt. 16:27; 25:31; 24:30; Tit. 2:13; I Pet. 4:13; Jude 24). And this is more than mere coincidence; it is because the glory of God will be made manifest that redemption will be consummated and the hope of the saints realized. Hence "the glory of God" here must be taken as reflecting upon the manifestation of the glory which is God's own. When we ask how the goal of the believer's hope can be called "the glory of God" another strand of New Testament teaching has to be taken into account, namely, that the believer is to be conformed into the image of that glory that will be revealed—"we shall be like him for we shall see him as he is" (I John 3:2). Most frequently this conformity is set forth in the terms of likeness to Christ in the image of his glory (*cf.* John 17:22, 24; Rom. 8:29; II Cor. 3:18; Phil. 3:21; Col. 3:4; II Thess. 2:14). "The glory of God" then is, first of all, the manifestation of God's own glory. This is entertained as the glory of the children of God because in that manifestation the glory of God will be reflected in them and it is this reflection that will constitute their glory (*cf.* 8:17; 9:23; I Cor. 2:7; II Cor. 4:17; Col. 1:27; I Thess. 2:12; II Tim. 2:10; Heb. 2:10; I Pet. 5:1, 4, 10). The revelation of God's glory at the coming of Christ will be epitomized in the consummation of redemption for the children of God. The soul of redemptive blessing consists in the assurance "I will be your God", and eschatological expectation is summed up in the fact that believers are "heirs of God and joint-heirs with Christ" (8:17). When the glory of God will be revealed, this possession will attain the full fruition of its meaning. The revelation of the glory of God at the consummation has also another interest for believers as the goal of hope. They are interested in the manifestation of the glory of God for its own sake. The glory of God is their chief end and they long for and hasten unto that day when with undimmed vision they will behold the glory of God in its fullest exhibition and vindication.

3, 4 Paul continues the subject of the exultant rejoicing or glorying that had been introduced at the end of verse 2. "And not only so, but we also glory in the tribulations" (vs. 3).[6] We not only glory in our hope; we even glory in the present. Paul was a realist; he was not so absorbed in the glory of the future that he closed his eyes to the realities of the present. He was aware of the tribulations which encompassed his own life as well as the life of other believers, and the exultant joy evoked by hope could not discount the realism of the distresses and afflictions in which the pilgrimage to the attainment of that hope was cast. The remarkable feature of the attitude to tribulation is that the exultant rejoicing entertained with reference to future glory is also entertained in reference to the tribulations. Paul did not commiserate himself or other believers in the sufferings endured. Nor did he passively submit to these tribulations as trials which he recognized to be necessities of the span that separated the present from the future glory. He *gloried* in these tribulations and he assumed that other believers participated with him in this glorying. We find here an entirely different attitude from that which we are too liable to entertain with reference to the tribulations of the church of Christ. We pity ourselves and we pity others. Not so the apostle.

We are not left in doubt as to what these tribulations were (*cf.* 8:35-39; I Cor. 4:9-13; II Cor. 1:4-10; 11:23-30; 12:7-10; Phil. 4:12; II Tim. 3:11, 12; 4:14-16). Paramount in his thought was the consideration that these afflictions were for Christ's sake (II Cor. 12:10), that they gave occasion for the exhibition of the power and grace of Christ (II Cor. 12:9), and that thereby the interests of the church as the body of Christ were promoted (II Cor. 1:4-6; Col. 1:24; *cf.* I Pet. 4:13). In this passage, however, there is delineated for us the ministry which tribulation performs in the development of the Christian graces and the progression which flows from this ministration —"tribulation worketh patience, and patience approvedness, and

---

[6] For καυχώμεθα in vs. 3 B C read καυχώμενοι and this is supported by some patristic authority. There is a good deal to be said in favour of this reading from transcriptional considerations (*cf.* Lightfoot: *Notes, ad loc.*). But it is difficult to adopt it in face of the external authority supporting καυχώμεθα. If the latter is correct then it can be regarded as hortative here likewise: "And not only so, but let us also rejoice in the tribulations". The clauses which follow provide the reasons why we may thus rejoice. As mentioned above, in connection with ἔχωμεν and καυχώμεθα (vs. 2), this interpretation does not disturb the exultant confidence reflected in the passage.

approvedness hope" (vs. 4). When Paul says that tribulation works patience, he has in mind the tribulation which belongs to the context of the Christian profession; he is not making a general statement that this is the effect of all the troubles that visit men. "The tribulations" are specific—they are those in Christ and for Christ's sake. All the afflictions of the godly are in that category. These tribulations bear the fruit of patience. Patience is not the passive quality which we often associate with this word; it is endurance and constancy (cf. Matt. 10:22; Rom. 2:7; II Cor. 1:6; II Thess. 1:4; Heb. 10:36; James 1:3; II Pet. 1:6). This constancy works approvedness, the triedness which is proven by testing (cf. II Cor. 2:9; 8:2; 13:3; Phil. 2:22). And this approvedness works hope.

In delineating the progression, it is represented as having its inception in tribulation and its terminus in hope. We glory, he says, in hope (vs. 2), and we glory in the tribulations because they initiate a sanctifying process which ends in hope (vss. 3, 4). He has described a circle, beginning with hope and *therefore* ending with hope. This drives home the lesson that the glorying in tribulations is not something dissociated from rejoicing in hope of the glory of God; it is not even coordinate or complementary. Glorying in tribulations is subordinate. We glory in tribulations because they have an eschatological orientation—they subserve the interests of hope. We are reminded of I Cor. 15:19 and advised that the complexion imparted to the perplexities of this life as in themselves the opposite of the glory to be revealed is a complexion determined by the eschatological destination of the people of God. The present of the believer's pilgrimage must never be abstracted from its relation to the ultimate sequel, the glory of God.

5 Here we are told the reason why this hope is well grounded and secure. It is not a hope that will put us to shame and not one with respect to which we need to entertain any shame. On the contrary it is one in which we may boast, one which we may confidently protest against all adversaries; it will not disappoint us or prove illusory. Why? "Because the love of God is shed abroad in our hearts through the Holy Spirit who was given unto us" (vs. 5). This is one of the most condensed statements in the epistle. It is a striking example of the combination in few words of the objective grounds and the subjective certainty of the believer's hope.

"The love of God" is not our love to God but God's love to us (*cf*. vs. 8; 8:35, 39). If we should suppose the former, the foundation of the assurance and of the security which this verse bespeaks would be destroyed. What is it that gives solidity to this hope and guarantees its validity? It is the love of God to believers, a love that suffers no fluctuation or reverse. Hence the hope which it promises is as irreversible as the love itself. This love of God must, however, come within our apprehension and appropriation if it is to be the ground of assurance and evoke this confident glorying (vs. 2). This is the significance of the shedding abroad in our hearts. The expression "shed abroad" indicates the abundant diffusion of this love. The hearts of believers are regarded as being suffused with the love of God; it controls and captivates their hearts. And the Holy Spirit as the Spirit of God and of Christ (*cf*. 8:9), the Spirit who "searches all things, yea, the deep things of God" (I Cor. 2:10), is the person who sheds abroad this love, and he is the seal of its efficacy and genuineness. It is the Holy Spirit as given to us, and for that reason indwelling and governing, who imparts the assurance of this love. He bears witness to the spirit of believers that they are the children of God (8:16). All the elements of this verse conspire with and converge upon one another to guarantee the certitude of which the text is redolent—the unchangeable love of God, the effectual agency of the Holy Spirit as donated to us, and the heart, the determining centre of thought and life, as the sphere of the Spirit's operation. This confluence would make anything other than exultant rejoicing incongruous. To impugn such confidence is to impugn God's veracity.

6–11

6 For while we were yet weak, in due season Christ died for the ungodly.

7 For scarcely for a righteous man will one die; for peradventure for the good man some one would even dare to die.

8 But God commendeth his own love toward us, in that, while we were yet sinners, Christ died for us.

9 Much more then, being now justified by his blood, shall we be saved from the wrath *of* God through him.

165

10 For if, while we were enemies, we were reconciled to God through the death of his Son, much more, being reconciled, shall we be saved by his life;

11 and not only so, but we also rejoice in God through our Lord Jesus Christ, through whom we have now received the reconciliation.

6 By what considerations do we know of this love of God, referred to in verse 5 as shed abroad in our hearts by the Holy Spirit? This is not an irrelevant or irreverent question. It is the question of the process of revelation and of redemptive accomplishment by which this love of God has been demonstrated. It is the answer to this question that is provided by verse 6. The demonstration required is furnished by the death of Christ—"for while we were yet weak, in due season Christ died for the ungodly". This is the force of the conjunction "for" with which the verse begins; it is explanatory or confirmatory.[7]

If we take the love of God for granted we shall not appreciate the sequence of the apostle's thought. But when we assess our weakness and particularly our ungodliness, then we discover both the need and the marvel of the proof God has given. What looms up in our conviction when our ungodliness is properly weighed is our detestability and the wrath of God, and it is impossible to take God's love for granted. That God could love the ungodly, far less that he did love them, would never have entered into the heart of man (*cf.* I Cor. 2:9, 10). On that background the text must be understood. The marvel of God's love is that it was love to the ungodly. And here is the proof—"Christ died for the ungodly". And not only so. When Christ died for them they were still weak, that is to say, they were still ungodly and contemplated as ungodly. Hence the love of which the death of Christ is the expression and provision is a love exercised to them as

---

[7] The variants in verse 6 require some attention. In view of the weight of the external authority in its favour ἔτι after ἀσθενῶν will have to be retained. The other variants at the beginning of the verse cause more difficulty. ℵ A C D* and some other uncials read ἔτι γάρ, Dᶜ and the mass of the cursives read ἔτι alone, Dᵇ G read εἰς τί γάρ, and B reads εἴ γε. There are other variants which are weakly supported. The external authority in favour of ἔτι γάρ constrains to the conclusion that it is the correct reading, and it is not difficult to see how this reading could have been corrupted in the course of transmission in order to avoid the repetition of ἔτι. The two occurrences of ἔτι in such close proximity favour the retention of both and in that event the most strongly attested reading at the beginning of the verse is ἔτι γάρ.

ungodly. It is not a love constrained by commendable qualities in them, not even by the qualities which they would one day exhibit by the power of God's grace. It is an antecedent love because it is the love presupposed in the death of Christ for them while they were still in misery and sin. It is not the love of complacency but love that finds its whole urge and incentive in the goodness of God. That is the kind of love the death of Christ demonstrates and it is a love efficient to a saving purpose because the death of Christ is on behalf of the ungodly and therefore to the end of securing the high destiny which the context has in view.

This death was "in due season". This cannot mean less than the appointed time. But it is likely that it is intended to express more, namely, the proper time. It was the proper and fitting time because it was the time of our helplessness. There may be in this notification of time a strengthening of the idea expressed in "died for the ungodly", namely, that of efficacy. The time of man's extremity was the time for God's efficacious work in the accomplishments wrought by the death of his Son. It is, however, difficult to exclude from the apostle's use of this expression here a reference to the fulness of the time (Gal. 4:4) as that in which God sent forth his Son to die for the ungodly. The fulness of the time is consummating time, "the crowning dispensation"[8], "the consummation of the ages" (Heb. 9:26), the time upon which all other times converge and in which God's purpose of the ages reaches its fulfilment (cf. Acts 2:17; I Cor. 10:11; I Tim. 2:6; Tit. 1:3; Heb. 1:2). The death of Christ belongs to the consummating era of this world's history. Appropriateness for us, exhibition of God's wisdom and love, efficacy of accomplishment are all bound up with this fact.

7, 8 Verses 7 and 8 expand what is implicit in verse 6; verse 7 shows the unheard-of-ness of one dying for the ungodly and verse 8 the commendation given to the love of God by the fact that Christ died for sinners. Verse 7 is frequently, if not usually, interpreted as drawing a distinction between a "righteous" man and the "good" man, the righteous man being the man who has regard for justice and will not deviate from the right and who for that reason commands our admiration and

---

[8] The expression is Lightfoot's (*Notes, ad* Eph.: 1: 10, p. 321).

respect; the good man, on the other hand, being the man who is not only just but also benevolent and kind and for that reason commands affection. The thought then would be that "scarcely for a righteous man will one die" but, by way of contrast, perhaps one might be prepared to die for a good man.[9] The constraint of respect for justice will scarcely cause us to die for a just man but the constraint of affection may cause us to die for a good man. It is difficult to elicit such an interpretation from the text, and it is scarcely defensible to plead this distinction between the righteous man and the good man. The terms of the text would appear rather to support the view that no such sharp contrast is drawn between the righteous and the good but that these two epithets are used to designate the same individual as both righteous and good.[10] And the thought of the text would be that among men it is *scarcely* true that one will die even for a righteous and good man, far less for a godless, wicked person. But perchance it may happen that for such a good man one will die. The constraint of respect and esteem may cause one to die on behalf of another. It is on this background of concession that the complete contrast between the human and the divine appears, and that is the force of verse 8: "But God commendeth his own love toward us, in that, while we were yet sinners, Christ died for us". In the human sphere scarcely for a *righteous* and *good* man will one die but God exhibits and commends *his* love in that it was for *sinners* Christ died.

There is particular emphasis on the fact that this is God's own love. Literally it means the love "of himself", not as love borne to himself, of which he himself is the object, but as the love that is peculiar to himself and commended (*cf.* 3:5) by the fact that it was for sinners Christ died. The love of God is here brought into direct relationship to the death of Christ. In verse 6 this relationship is implied because of the close connection between verse 6 and verse 5. But now it is expressly stated. And the relationship is that the death of Christ is the manifestation and expression of the love of God. The death of Christ does not

---

[9] *Cf.* Alford, Philippi, Gifford, Hodge, Sanday and Headlam, *ad loc.*

[10] The point here is not that, connotatively speaking, there is no distinction between the epithets δίκαιος and ἀγαθός. Of course, as indicated above, they reflect upon distinct characteristics (*cf.* Lightfoot: *Notes, ad loc.*). The point is simply that, denotatively, two distinct persons are not here contemplated so as to contrast what one may not do for a *righteous* man with what he may perchance do for a *good* man. *Cf.*, for this interpretation, Calvin, Meyer, *ad loc.*

constrain or elicit the love of God but the love of God constrained
to the death of Christ as the only adequate provision of this love.
The love of God is the impulsive force and its distinctive character
is demonstrated in that which emanates from it. The clause
"while we were yet sinners" is parallel to "while we were yet
weak" in verse 6; they are mutually definitive of one another. As
in verse 6, our attention is drawn to the fact that the love of God is
exercised to men as sinners and while they are sinners; it is not
constrained by qualities in men which would evoke the divine
complacency. And, in like manner, the design of the death of
Christ has respect to men as sinners and contemplates a benefit
of which men as *sinners* are to be the beneficiaries.

9, 10   Verses 9 and 10 are *a fortiori* arguments, to the effect
that if one thing is true how much more must something else be
true. In verse 9 the premise posited is that we have now "been
justified in his [Jesus'] blood" and the inference drawn is that we
shall therefore with all the greater certainty be saved through
him from the wrath. The premise in verse 10 is that we have been
reconciled to God through the death of Christ, while we were
still enemies, and the inference drawn is, with how much greater
certainty shall we be saved by the life of Christ. The two verses
are parallel in construction and they both enunciate the same
substantial truth. But this parallelism and substantial identity
as regards the truth unfolded must not obscure the distinctive
features of the thought in each verse.

In verses 6 and 8 the apostle had not defined specifically the
nature of the death of Christ on our behalf. He stated simply
that it was death on behalf of the ungodly (vs. 6) and on our
behalf (vs. 8). There is an intimation of the intent and the kind of
benefit contemplated in the consideration that it was for the
ungodly and for sinners, but there is no further amplification of
the specific character of the work accomplished in Jesus' death
or of the kind of benefit accruing to the ungodly from that
accomplishment. The apostle had done that earlier in 3:21-26;
4:25. And that delineation was to be assumed in verses 6 and 8.
But now in verses 9 and 10 we are provided with additional
definition of the specific character of the death of Christ and of
the benefits secured by it. It is not to be overlooked, of course,
that he introduces these specifications of the character and intent

of Jesus' death in the premises of *a fortiori* arguments and they are in that respect assumptions on which he bases other conclusions as his main interest. But as premises they are eloquent of what the death of Christ is conceived of as being and accomplishing.

In verse 9 the death of Christ, spoken of in this instance as his blood, is viewed from the aspect of what it accomplished in reference to justification—"having now been justified in his blood". We have been frequently confronted with the subject of justification in the earlier parts of the epistle. And it had been used uniformly of that forensic act of God by which we are declared to be righteous and accepted as such with God, the justification inseparable from faith on the part of the subject. It is possible, however, that in this instance the term is used in a sense coordinate with the reconciliation of verses 10 and 11 and in that event applies not to actual justification by faith but to the objective ground established by the death of Christ. Paul uses the substantive derived from this same term in that sense in verse 18 of this chapter, as will be shown at that point. In Isaiah 53:11 it is distinctly possible that the word "justify" is used in this sense (*cf.* the appendix on Isa. 53:11, pp. 375 ff.). And the parallelism in verses 9 and 10 would create some presumption in favour of regarding justification in verse 9 as similar to reconciliation in verse 10. On this interpretation the blood of Christ would be construed as having in itself, objectively, a justifying effect and the justification in view would consist in the obedience and righteousness of Christ which is the ground of actual justification through faith. If, on the other hand, justification in this instance is interpreted in the sense which is all but uniform in Paul, then what the apostle has in mind is our actual justification viewed as taking place through the blood of Christ; it comes to us in Jesus' blood, and the latter is the ground of our justification. It is Jesus' blood that secures our justification and it comes to us in the sprinkling of his blood. On either alternative the blood of Christ is stated to have efficacy and virtue in reference to that which is the cardinal doctrine of this epistle. Justification is strictly forensic in its nature and therefore the blood of Christ, whether viewed as constituting justification or as laying the ground for our justification, must be interpreted as having forensic efficacy. Thus it is impossible not to define the efficacy and virtue of Jesus' blood in forensic categories. For here it is directly

170

related to what is specifically and only forensic. This is not a category suddenly thrust forward by the apostle; it was already implicit in 3:25, 26.

The main thought of verse 9 is, however, in the conclusion that is to be drawn from the foregoing—"how much more . . . shall we be saved through him from the wrath". This refers to what will be true in the future as compared with what is true now in the present. *Now* we are justified—accepted with God as righteous and therefore at peace with God. And this guarantees future salvation. What is the salvation in view? "The wrath" spoken of indicates the answer. The wrath is the wrath that will be dispensed to the ungodly at the day of judgment, the eschatological wrath (2:5, 8; I Thess. 1:10; 5:9; *cf.* Matt. 3:7; Rev. 6:16, 17; 11:18). And the assurance to be derived from a present justification—whether viewed as the justification which consists in the blood of Christ or as the justification secured by that blood—is that no wrath is reserved for the justified at the judgment seat. Justification is the opposite of condemnation and since justification is complete and irrevocable there is no condemnation reserved for those who are in Christ Jesus (*cf.* 8:1). It is symptomatic of the confidence expressed in verses 2 and 5 in reference to the hope of the glory of God that the apostle should now explicate another aspect of that hope, namely, the assurance of deliverance from that which epitomizes the displeasure of God and alienation from him. It was not irrelevant for the apostle to speak in terms of negation as well as affirmation. The hope of glory is negative as well as positive. In order to be positive it must be negative of all that sin entails. In order to be salvation *to* it must be salvation *from*. And nothing sums up this "*from*" more significantly than the concept of the wrath of God. It was a virile conception of God that the apostle entertained and, because so, it was one that took account of the terror of God's wrath. Salvation from the future exhibition of that terror was an ingredient of the hope of glory.

Verse 10 introduces new elements of truth to reinforce this confidence or at least new aspects of the same truth to inform and establish this confidence. "For if, while we were enemies, we were reconciled to God through the death of his Son, how much more, being reconciled, shall we be saved by his life." The analysis of this text requires us to take note of the import of the various expressions.

171

(1) "While we were enemies"—the word "enemies" should be understood passively, not actively.[11] That is to say, it does not refer to our active enmity against God but to God's holy hostility to and alienation from us. The word is used in this sense in 11:28 to denote the alienation from the favour of God to which Israel had been subjected. It is contrasted in this latter instance with "beloved", and "beloved" means, obviously, beloved of God, not the love of Israel to God. Hence "enemies" refers to an hostility of which God is the agent and means the alienation to which Israel had been subjected in God's judgment. Furthermore, in 11:28 the sense of active hostility to God is not appropriate to the context. The context is dealing with the dispensations of God to Israel. Likewise in 5:10 it is this meaning that is appropriate to the context. What is in view is the alienation from God and the fact that the reconciliation took place when we were in a state of alienation.

(2) "We were reconciled to God." This might suggest to us that what is contemplated in the reconciliation is the removal of our enmity against God. This is not so; it is rather the removal of God's alienation from us. If we dissociate from the word "enmity" in this case all that is malignant and malicious, it means the removal of God's holy enmity against us. Only such an interpretation will satisfy the thought. (a) "Reconciled to God through the death of his Son" is parallel to "being justified now in his blood" in verse 9. The latter, as was noted above, is strictly forensic. Hence "reconciled" must also be forensic in character. But the removal of our enmity, whether viewed as an act of God or an act of ours, is not forensic in its nature; it is ethical in contrast

---

[11] Lightfoot's remark that the active meaning of ἐχθρός "is the universal use in the New Testament" (*Notes, ad loc.*) is surely off the mark. *Cf.*, for correction of Lightfoot, Sanday and Headlam: *op. cit.*, pp. 129f.; Meyer: *op. cit., ad loc.;* Denney: *op. cit., ad loc.;* Gerhard Kittel: *Theologisches Wörterbuch zum Neuen Testament,* II, p. 814; Arndt and Gingrich: *op. cit., ad ἐχθρός.* Lightfoot's contention is in line with his failure to appreciate the import of the New Testament teaching respecting the reconciliation (*cf.* his remarks *ad* Col. 1:21 in his commentary on this epistle). He is right in observing that in the language of the New Testament God is not spoken of as being reconciled to us but rather that we are reconciled to God. But when the teaching of the New Testament is properly weighed it will be seen that what is in the forefront in the reconciliation is not our active enmity against God and its removal but God's alienation from us and the means God has provided for the removal of the same. *Cf.*, by the writer, *Redemption Accomplished and Applied* (Grand Rapids, 1955), pp. 39ff.

with what is forensic. This consideration of itself is sufficient to show that the reconciliation must be interpreted in forensic terms. Otherwise the parallel would break down. (b) Reconciliation is viewed as something accomplished once for all in the death of the Son of God. But the removal of our enmity to God cannot be regarded as something accomplished once for all in the historic past. (c) In verse 11 we are said to receive the reconciliation. This form of statement is not suited to the notion of the removal of our enmity. The removal of our enmity, however it is construed, refers to a subjective transformation, whereas receiving the reconciliation implies, as Sanday and Headlam observe, "that the reconciliation comes to man from the side of God".[12] It is a gift received and this concept is entirely appropriate to the thought that reconciliation is a status established, a standing secured by gracious bestowment on God's part. (d) This concept of reconciliation is in agreement with what stands in the forefront at the beginning of this passage, namely, peace with God as the grace into which we have been introduced and in which we stand. Peace with God is the status of favour resultant upon the removal of our alienation from God. The reconciliation, viewed as the removal of God's alienation from us, is correlative with peace with God; it is the ground upon which the latter rests. (e) The emphasis of the more immediate context upon the love of God and the proof afforded by the death of Christ gives the whole passage an orientation which reconciliation, interpreted as above, carries on and climaxes, whereas a subjective interpretation interferes with this direction of thought and is not in agreement with the governing thought of the passage.

(3) "The death of his Son"—the title "Son", appearing now for the first time since the introduction (1:3, 9), draws our attention to some highly relevant considerations. (a) The person of the Godhead specifically in view as the one to whom we are reconciled is the Father. This follows from the fact that the title "God" in this verse refers to the person with respect to whom Christ can be called "his Son", and only of the Father can Christ be called the Son. (b) The title "God" therefore in verse 8 must also have the Father specifically in mind. Hence it is the Father who commends his love towards us. And the same holds true

---

[12] *Op. cit.*, p. 130.

for verse 5—it is specifically the love of the Father that is shed abroad in our hearts. (c) That we are reconciled to the Father and that it is the love of the Father that is commended to us guards against any supposition to the effect that the Father's love is constrained by the reconciliation, as also against the thought of incompatibility between love as antecedent and reconciliation as consequent. The simple lesson is that the Father loves and is also reconciled. And the reconciliation is one of the ways in which the intent and effect of the death of Christ, as the supreme proof of the Father's love, are to be interpreted—reconciliation demonstrates the love of the Father. (d) That the death of Christ is the death of God's own Son shows how the death in question can be the demonstration of God's love—the intimacy of relation expressed in the title "Son" exhibits the marvel of the Father's love to sinners. How unspeakable must this love be when it was "the Son" who died to make good its urge and aim! And what exigencies were involved when the Father gave his Son to die!

(4) "Reconciled . . . through the death of his Son"—it is the death of Christ that is set forth as the reconciling action and therefore as that which removed the alienation and secured instatement in the favour of God. The death of Christ is synonymous with the blood of Christ. Hence the apostle has provided us with a new category in terms of which we are to interpret the significance of Jesus' shed blood. These various categories have their own distinguishing features because they take into account the multiform aspects of our need and the manifoldness of the divine provision to meet these needs. Reconciliation has as its background our alienation from God and it must be interpreted in the perspective of that exigency.

(5) "We shall be saved by his life." The life of Christ referred to here is not what we often speak of as the life of Christ, his sojourn in this world in the days of his flesh. It is the resurrection life of Christ. There lies back of the expression an implied contrast between the death of Christ and his resurrection (cf. 4:25). It is not simply the resurrection as an event that is in view, however. Paul does not say, we shall be saved by his resurrection, but "by his life", and therefore it is the exalted life of the Redeemer that is intended. The resurrection is in the background as conditioning the exaltation life. Since the clause in question is parallel to that in verse 9—" we shall be saved through him from the wrath"—

and since the latter has eschatological reference, it is likely that the salvation here envisaged is also eschatological. On that assumption the guarantee of the final and consummated salvation is the exaltation life of Christ. This is a more embracive way of expressing the truth that the guarantee of the believer's resurrection is the resurrection of Christ (*cf.* I Cor. 15:20-24).

The *a fortiori* argument of the apostle is thus apparent. It is to the effect that if, when we were in a state of alienation from God, God showed his love to such an extent that he reconciled us to himself and instated us in his favour through the death of his own Son, how much more, when this alienation is removed and we are instated in his favour, shall the exaltation life of Christ insure our being saved to the uttermost. It would be a violation of the wisdom, goodness, and faithfulness of God to suppose that he would have done the greater and fail in the lesser. This argument also shows the indissoluble connection that there is between the death and resurrection of Christ and that since these may never be dissociated so the benefits accruing from the one may never be severed from those accruing from the other. It is a frequent emphasis of Paul (*cf.* 6:3-5; II Cor. 5:14, 15; Eph. 2:4-7; Col. 3:3, 4). Hence those who are the beneficiaries of Jesus' death must also be the beneficiaries of all that is entailed in his resurrection life. In this passage this is viewed from the aspect of reconciliation by Jesus' death and the corresponding guarantee for the future.

11 There is some question as to the connection between verse 10 and verse 11. This will appear to the English reader if we give a literal rendering of verse 11: "And not only so but also rejoicing in God through our Lord Jesus Christ, through whom now we have received the reconciliation".[13] And the question revolves around the participle "rejoicing". With what in the preceding verse or context is it to be connected? It could be taken with another participle in the preceding verse, namely, "being reconciled".[14] And the thought would be that not only

---

[13] καυχώμενοι is supported by preponderant external authority, א B C D and the mass of the cursives. καυχώμεθα has arisen, no doubt, from assimilation to the same in vss. 2, 3.

[14] *Cf.* Meyer, *ad loc.* who thinks that the participle καταλλάγεντες is to be supplied in the elliptical οὐ μόνον δέ. Thus the sense would be "and not only being reconciled but also rejoicing".

does the fact of reconciliation assure us of the future salvation but also the fact that we now glory in God through our Lord Jesus Christ—our present rejoicing in God is an additional guarantee of our future salvation. Or the participle could be taken with the clause, "we shall be saved by his life", and the thought would be that not only do we derive from our reconciliation the assurance that we shall have salvation in the future but also exultant glorying in the present.[15]

In any case it appears necessary to regard the exultant rejoicing referred to as rejoicing in the present. The last clause in the verse emphasizes the present status of reconciliation, "through whom now we have received the reconciliation". As in verses 1 and 2 the mediation of Christ is stressed in connection with the bestowment of peace and justification, so now the reception of reconciliation is represented as through the same mediation. But particular stress rests upon the enjoyment of this privilege in the present; reconciliation is a status once for all received and since it has been received we are to recognize the implications of this standing before God. It is this consideration of present privilege that explains the exultant joy in God referred to in the preceding clause and it is scarcely possible to relegate it to the future. If we bear in mind that exultant glorying is a prominent feature of this passage—"we exult in hope of the glory of God" (vs. 2); "we glory in the tribulations" (vs. 3)—we should expect that, after unfolding the relationship to God constituted by reconciliation and when the note of exultant joy is resumed, the apostle should give expression to the confident rejoicing in God which the privilege now possessed must constrain. Glorying knows no restraint and cannot be too exaggerated when it is in God through our Lord Jesus Christ (cf. I Cor. 1:30, 31). It is not only that God is the object of this glorying; it is not only that he is the ground of it; it is in union and fellowship with him as our own God that the glorying is conducted.

When Paul says, "through whom now we have received the reconciliation", he is surely reflecting on the actual application to us of the reconciliation as distinguished from its objective

---

[15] The exultant glorying (καυχώμενοι) might be taken as a characterization of the salvation that will be enjoyed in the future; it is the kind of salvation that will carry with it the most joyful exultation in God. But this projection of the rejoicing into the future hardly comports with the glorying in the present with which the passage as a whole is replete.

accomplishment. It is characteristic that he should have represented our entrance upon the *possession* and *enjoyment* of this status as mediated through Christ. The mediation of Christ is not suspended at the point of application any more than at the point of accomplishment. And the glorying that is the fruit of reception into God's favour and fellowship is likewise "through our Lord Jesus Christ". Our experiential exultation may never be dissociated from our consciousness of the ever-active and efficient mediation of our Lord and Saviour.

VIII. THE ANALOGY
(5:12–21)

12 Therefore, as through one man sin entered into the
world, and death through sin; and so death passed
unto all men, for that all sinned:—

13 for until the law sin was in the world; but sin is not
imputed when there is no law.

14 Nevertheless death reigned from Adam until Moses,
even over them that had not sinned after the likeness
of Adam's transgression, who is a figure of him that
was to come.

15 But not as the trespass, so also *is* the free gift. For if
by the trespass of the one the many died, much more
did the grace of God, and the gift by the grace of the
one man, Jesus Christ, abound unto the many.

16 And not as through one that sinned, so is the gift:
for the judgment *came* of one unto condemnation, but
the free gift *came* of many trespasses unto justification.

17 For if, by the trespass of the one, death reigned through
the one; much more shall they that receive the abundance of grace and of the gift of righteousness reign in
life through the one, *even* Jesus Christ.

18 So then as through one trespass *the judgment came* unto
all men to condemnation; even so through one act of
righteousness *the free gift came* unto all men to justification of life.

19 For as through the one man's disobedience the many
were made sinners, even so through the obedience of
the one shall the many be made righteous.

20 And the law came in besides, that the trespass might
abound; but where sin abounded, grace did abound
more exceedingly:

21 that, as sin reigned in death, even so might grace reign
through righteousness unto eternal life through Jesus
Christ our Lord.

In verses 12–21 the apostle develops the parallel between
Adam and Christ, Adam as the head of the whole human race,

Christ as the head of the new humanity.[16] That there is analogy
is shown by the statement in verse 14 that Adam is "the type of
the one to come". But it is also shown by the sustained comparisons that are instituted throughout the passage, whether expressly
or by implication (vss. 12, 15-19). When we say that there are
parallels and comparisons we must not overlook the fact that
from the outset there is a sustained contrast between the process
that was set in operation by Adam and that set in operation by
Christ. There is analogy but analogy in respect of what is completely antithetical. We cannot grasp the truths of world-wide
significance set forth in this passage unless we recognize that two
antithetical complexes are contrasted. The first is the complex
of sin-condemnation-death and the second is that of righteousness-
justification-life. These are invariable combinations. Sin sets in
operation the inevitable consequents of condemnation and death,
righteousness the consequents of justification and life, and, as is
obvious, these are antithetical at each point of the parallel.

The fact of paramount importance, however, in this passage is
that the operation of these complexes in the human race is not
to be viewed atomistically. Solidarity comes into effect. Sin does
not set in operation the sequence associated with it apart from
the corporate relationship which Adam sustains to the race and
the race to Adam. And righteousness is not brought to bear upon
the sin-condemnation-death complex, which Adam inaugurated,
apart from the solidaric relationship which Christ sustains to
lost men and lost men to Christ. This passage is eviscerated of
its governing principle if these two solidaric relationships are not
appreciated, and it is futile to try to interpret the passage except
in these terms.

We may not forget that the apostle is still dealing with his
grand theme, justification by faith. In verses 1-11 he had dealt
with some of the consequences emanating from justification and
with the assurances toward God which these fruits evoked. What
is the purpose of this passage (vss. 12-21) in relation to his theme?
Various answers could properly be given. But perhaps none is
more relevant than that the apostle is now demonstrating that
the divine method of justifying the ungodly proceeds from and is
necessitated by the principles in terms of which God governs

---

[16]   On Karl Barth's view of this passage see the appendix on this subject
(pp. 384 ff.).

the human race. God governs men and relates himself to men in terms of solidaric relationship. And just as the sin, condemnation, and death in which all members of the race are involved can never be construed or estimated in purely individualistic terms, so we never find righteousness, justification, and life in operation except as the solidarity constituted by God's grace is brought to bear upon our human situation. There is an identity of *modus operandi* and this *modus operandi* in God's dealings with men belongs to the integrity of his established government. It is the broad perspective of the divine philosophy of divine-human relationships that comes before us in this passage. And to aver that this passage is extraneous to the doctrine of the apostle or a digression in the style of rabbinical allegorizing is to miss what is pivotal in the central thesis of this epistle.[17]

12 The close logical connection between this passage and that which precedes is shown by the "therefore" with which verse 12 begins. There is considerable difference of opinion as to how much of the preceding context is to be regarded as supplying the basis of the conclusion which verses 12ff. enunciate, whether verse 11 merely or verses 1–11 or 3:21–5:11 or the whole of the preceding part of the epistle from 1:18 onwards. It is impossible to be dogmatic, and this is not a question of great moment. Suffice it to know that we have here a conclusion intimately germane to the doctrine unfolded earlier.

Verse 12 clearly begins a comparison but does not complete it. At the middle of the verse we have the words "and so" which must not be rendered "even so". The latter closes a comparison but the former, as here, carries on what had been affirmed and is coordinative or continuative. Most interpreters recognize this and do not argue the question. Verse 12 is an unfinished comparison; it has a protasis but not apodosis. Therefore it is an unfinished sentence. Why so? It is not difficult to find the reason. In verse 12, particularly at the end, the apostle had stated something which needed a parenthesis and this parenthesis we have in verses 13, 14. In other words, the facts stated in verse 12 dictated the necessity of adding without delay the data given in verses

---

[17] For a fuller treatment of this passage from the theological point of view see the series, "The Imputation of Adam's Sin" in *The Westminster Theological Journal*, XVIII, 2, XIX, 1 and 2, XX, 1 by the writer.

13 and 14. Hence the particular thought of verse 12 is broken off at the end of the verse, and it so happens that the apostle did not come back again to complete his comparison in the terms of verse 12. This should not perplex us. Paul did not follow stereotyped stylistic patterns and, as we shall see, the parenthesis which broke off the comparison is a very eloquent one. The comparison is incomplete but the thought is not broken off. The development of thought dictated the construction which we find here.

"Through one man sin entered into the world." The one man is without question Adam (vs. 14). The account given in Genesis 3 is the basis of this statement and the apostle places his imprimatur upon the authenticity of this account. The importance he attached to this incident of Genesis 3 is attested by the fact that the subsequent development of his argument turns on it.[18] That sin entered through one man is an integral element of the comparison or parallel upon which is to be built Paul's doctrine of justification. This attests the crucial place it occupied in his esteem. It is to evacuate exegesis to suppose that it is only incidental. When he says "entered into the world" he refers to the beginning of sin in the human race and "the world" means the sphere of human existence. Paul does not reflect here upon the inception of sin as such.[19]

"And through sin death"—again there is allusion to Genesis 2:17; 3:19. The juxtaposition of sin and death bears the emphasis. On the question as to whether the moral and spiritual aspects of death and their eternal consequences are comprised in the word "death", one thing must be appreciated that in the usage of Scripture and in the conception of Paul the dissolution which consists in the separation of body and spirit and the return to dust of the former had far more significance as the epitome of the wages of sin than we are disposed to attach to it. The catastrophe of misery which befell mankind by sin is summed up in this

---

[18] It is exegetically monstrous to say with C. H. Dodd, "Thus Paul' doctrine of Christ as the 'second Adam' is not so bound up with the story of the Fall as a literal happening that it ceases to have meaning when we no longer accept the story as such. Indeed, we should not too readily assume that Paul did so accept it" (*op. cit.*, p. 80). So basic to Paul's doctrine is the one trespass of the one man Adam that any interference with this datum wrecks Paul's whole argument. We cease to be exegetes when we try to pour Paul's teaching into moulds other than his own.
[19] Elsewhere, Paul's statements bear upon the activity of Satan (*cf.* II Cor. 11:3; I Tim. 2:14).

dissolution and it exemplifies the principle of separation which comes to expression in all aspects of death. In verse 14 it is this death that is in view and there is no need to introduce other aspects of death in the subsequent references to the universal reign of death (vss. 15, 17). It is this aspect of death that is in the forefront in Genesis 2:17; 3:19, and although it is true that death in all its aspects is the wages of sin, yet there is not sufficient evidence to show that the apostle is comprehending all these aspects in his purview when he says "and death through sin".

In the second half of verse 12 we have a continuative comparison introduced by "and so". In order to grasp the force of this we must note the specific thought of the two parts of the verse. In the first half the accent falls upon the *entrance* of sin and death through *one man*. In the second part the accent falls upon the universal *penetration* of death and the sin of *all*. And a correspondence is intimated as obtaining between the way in which death *entered* the world and the way in which it *permeated* to the whole human race. It *entered* through the sin of the *one man*; it permeated through the sin of *all*. To state the matter more fully: just as sin and death *entered* the world through the sin of the one man, so death *permeated* to all men because all sinned. So although verse 12 is an unfinished comparison, containing the protasis but not the apodosis, yet the comparison that is implicit in the two parts of the protasis may be stated in the form of the protasis and apodosis stated in the foregoing sentence. Hence the thought of the apostle is plainly that the entrance of sin and death is caused by the sin of Adam and the universal reign of death by the sin of all. And we must not suppose that the Pelagian interpretation of this verse, whereby the sin of all is construed as the actual sins of all men, is refuted by the consideration that verse12 is an unfinished comparison. Verse 12 of itself is compatible with a Pelagian interpretation, and if Paul had entertained the Pelagian view he could have stated it admirably well in these terms. The whole question revolves on the meaning of the last clause in verse 12, "in that all sinned". There can be no question but the fact that "all sinned" is stated in the most explicit fashion to be the ground upon which death penetrated to all men, just as the sin of Adam is the reason why death entered the world.

The crucial question is: What is meant by "in that all sinned"? It is quite unnecessary to argue the propriety of this translation.

The clause should not be rendered "in whom all sinned". The terms used have the force of the conjunction "because" or "on the ground of the fact that" and clearly specify the reason why death went through to all men. If Paul meant that death passed upon all because all men were guilty of actual transgression, this is the way he would have said it. At least no more suitable way could be considered. Is this what the apostle meant? Pelagians say so.[20] There are conclusive objections to this view on factual, exegetical, and theological grounds.

(1) It is not historically true. Not all die because they actually and voluntarily sin. Infants die and they do not voluntarily sin.

(2) In verses 13 and 14 Paul says the opposite—death reigned over those who did not sin after the similitude of Adam's transgression. It is futile to try to evade the direct bearing of this fact upon the view in question. If all die because they are guilty of actual transgression, then they die because they sin just as Adam did. But Paul says the reverse; some died even though they did not sin after the pattern of Adam.

(3) The most conclusive refutation of the view in question is the explicit and repeated affirmations of the context to the effect that condemnation and death reign over all because of the *one sin* of the *one man* Adam. On at least five occasions in verses 15-19 this is asserted—"by the trespass of the one the many died" (vs. 15); "the judgment was from one unto comdemnation" (vs. 16); "by the trespass of the one death reigned through the one" (vs. 17); "through one trespass judgment came upon all men unto condemnation" (vs. 18); "through the disobedience of

---

[20] In referring to Pelagians we have in mind not only the view of Pelagius himself but of all who interpret πάντες ἥμαρτον as having reference to the personal voluntary sins of men. More recently in *The Interpreter's Bible* (New York, 1954) both John Knox and Gerald R. Cragg in their exegesis and exposition of this passage show a distinct tendency to this interpretation, if, indeed, they do not adopt it. To quote the latter: "*All men sinned*, he says tersely; and he is but repeating what he has previously said, 'all have sinned, and come short of the glory of God'. . . . From his own experience he knew how it stood with a sensitive Jew; observation showed him how urgently the Gentile world needed moral regeneration. He states his conclusion from facts which he regards as incontestable" (vol. IX, p. 463). In like manner James Denney says: "Because all men were, in point of fact, sinners, the death which is inseparable from sin extended over all. To drag in the case of infants to refute this . . . is to misconceive the situation: to Paul's mind the world consists of sinners capable of sinning and being saved" (*op. cit., ad loc.*). Most recently *cf.* C. K. Barrett: *A Commentary on the Epistle to the Romans* (New York, 1957), p. 111.

the one man the many were constituted sinners" (vs. 19). This reiteration establishes beyond doubt that the apostle regarded condemnation and death as having passed on to all men by the one trespass of the one man Adam. This sustained appeal to the one sin of the one man rules out the possibility of construing it as equivalent to the actual personal transgressions of countless individuals.

(4) This view is inconsistent with the analogy which supplies the framework of this passage as a whole. The polemic of this epistle is directed against the thesis that we are justified by works, and the doctrine being established is that men are justified and attain to life by the righteousness of the one, Jesus Christ. How contradictory would be the appeal to the parallel obtaining on the side of condemnation and death if Paul finds the basis of the condemnation and death of all in the actual transgression of each individual. If this latter were Paul's teaching here the parallel that would be necessary on the other side would be justification by works, that each individual would be justified by his own actions and attain to life on that basis. But we know that this is the reverse of Paul's teaching.

On these grounds we must reject the supposition that when Paul says, "in that all sinned" he means the actual voluntary sins of all men.

In the Augustinian tradition it has often been maintained that the clause in question refers to original sin, to wit, that all posterity became depraved in Adam.[21] Hence the thought would be that death penetrated to all because all derived from Adam a corrupt nature and the ground upon which condemnation and death wield their universal sway is that all, even infants, are afflicted with this hereditary taint. This view stands on more biblical ground than the foregoing. It is true that all are by nature defiled and depraved by sin and this of itself does entail universal condemnation and death. But there are also good reasons for thinking that this is not the sin the apostle has in mind when he says, "in that all sinned". There are two conclusive objections.

(1) It is inconsistent with the repeated affirmations of verses 15–19 to the effect that condemnation and death came to reign over all by reason of the one sin of the one man Adam. This

---

[21] For more detailed exposition and refutation see the series referred to in note 17, particularly XVIII, 2, pp. 153–159.

sustained emphasis upon the one trespass of the one man does not comport with the notion of original sin or hereditary depravity. The latter cannot by any means be characterized as the one sin of the one man.

(2) It is inconsistent with the parallel which is drawn in this passage as a whole. We are not justified on the ground that we are made inherently righteous. But if we are condemned and suffer death because we are depraved and inherently sinful the only analogy or parallel to this would be that we are justified because we become inherently holy. And that is plainly not Paul's doctrine. We are justified and attain to life by the obedience and righteousness of the one, namely, Jesus Christ.

If neither the actual transgressions of men nor the depravity with which all are inflicted will comport with the teaching of this passage, the question still remains: what sin is in view when Paul says, "in that all sinned"? The following considerations lead to one conclusion, that for some reason the one sin of the one man Adam is accounted to be the sin of all.

(1) It is unquestionable that the universal sway of death is represented in verse 12 as based upon the fact that "all sinned" —"death passed on to all men on the ground of the fact that all sinned".

(2) In verses 15–19 it is asserted with equal clearness that the universal reign of death is based on the one trespass of the one man Adam and, in like manner, universal condemnation is based on the same fact of the one sin of the one man.

(3) We cannot suppose that the apostle is dealing with two different facts when in verse 12 the death of all is grounded upon the sin of all and when in the subsequent verses the death of all is grounded upon the one sin of the one man. The whole passage is a unit. The central strand is the analogy that exists between the passing of condemnation and death to all by the sin of the one and the passing of justification and life to the justified by the righteousness of Christ. Furthermore, verse 12 is an unfinished comparison. It would be out of the question to suppose that the apostle, dealing as he is with the universal reign of death, should so explicitly and repeatedly affirm in the succeeding verses something quite different from that which he affirms in the unfinished introduction to his argument. If verse 12 were in a context of its own and if there were an obvious transition from

185

one subject to another, then we might say that in verse 12 he deals with one fact and in verses 15–19 with another. We cannot posit any such transition for the simple reason that verse 12 relies upon the succeeding verses to complete the subject which it had introduced. And finally, as noted earlier, verse 14 makes it impossible to interpret the "all sinned" of verse 12 as we might be disposed to interpret it if it stood apart from what follows. "All sinned" cannot mean the actual voluntary transgressions of men because if this were the case Paul would have contradicted himself.

For these reasons we must conclude that the "all sinned" of verse 12 and the one trespass of the one man of verses 15–19 must refer to the same fact or event, that the one fact can be expressed in terms of both singularity and plurality, as the sin of one and the sin of all. And the only solution is that there must be some kind of solidarity existing between the "one" and "the all" with the result that the sin of the one may at the same time and with equal relevance be regarded as the sin of all. What this solidarity is it is not our purpose at present to determine. But once the fact of solidarity is appreciated, then we understand why the apostle can speak of the one sin and the sin of all. We must not tone down either the singularity or the universality.

We are now in a position to grasp the force of the comparison or correspondence implied in the continuative "and so" in verse 12. A comparison is instituted between the way in which sin and death *entered* and the way in which they became universal. Adam sinned and with sin came death. There is an inevitable sequence. But the same sequence applies to all. Since the sin of Adam is the sin of all, death spreads to all as inevitably as it fell to the lot of Adam and thus entered the world. The immediate sequence exemplified in Adam and in the entrance of death applies also to the universal reign of death. The solidarity existing between Adam and posterity establishes a correspondence between that which is exemplified in the case of Adam himself and that which happens to the whole human race. Adam sinned and death entered; in Adam all sinned and therefore death passed through to all. This is the force of "and so". There is an exact parallel between what occurred in the case of Adam himself and that which occurred in the case of all. And the parallel in this case can only be properly understood when we appreciate the solidarity in sin. Paul says elsewhere, "In Adam all die"

(I Cor. 15:22). The only adequate explanation is that provided by Romans 5:12 that in Adam all sin.

13, 14 At verse 13 begins the parenthesis which interrupts the completion of the comparison of verse 12. As an interruption it must have close bearing upon something stated in the preceding verse and this is indicated by the conjunction "for". "For until the law sin was in the world, but sin is not imputed when there is no law". This verse stands in close relation to verse 14 and the strong adversative with which the latter begins indicates that the thought of verse 13 is preparatory to that of verse 14 and moves on to verse 14 as expressing what is of particular relevance to the subject. We must not allow our minds to be diverted from this emphasis and thus permit the primary purpose of these two verses to escape us. The main thought is that "death reigned . . . over those who did not sin after the similitude of Adam's transgression" (vs. 14). If this is once recognized, then we may ask at the outset: what bearing does that observation have upon the thought of verse 12? The question should not be considered difficult. In verse 12 the doctrine of particular significance to the argument being developed is that death came to all men, not by reason of their own actual transgression or individual sin but because of their involvement in the sin of Adam, in other words, by reason of solidaric sin. This thesis required in the esteem of the apostle some demonstration or at least some exemplification to make it apparent. Hence he inserted a parenthesis which would make obvious the necessity of this construction of the reason for the universality of death. And what could be more pertinent than appeal to the fact that death reigned over those who did not sin after the similitude of Adam's transgression, that is to say, over those who did not voluntarily and overtly violate an expressly revealed ordinance of God? Apparently there was in the background of the apostle's thought the other alternative which would be the only plausible one as a rival to the doctrine he had propounded, namely, the alternative that all men die because they transgress as Adam did. It was sufficient for the apostle's purpose to appeal to the fact that many died who did not sin as Adam did and rest the case for the rejection of that other alternative on that fact. We discover therefore the direct relevance of the proposition in verse 14 to the main point of

187

verse 12 as the point upon which his whole argument is going to turn.

There is one further observation to be made regarding verse 14 before we turn to the other features of this parenthesis. It is the force of the concluding clause of verse 14: "who is the type of the one to come". The reference is plainly to Adam as the type of Christ. The connection of this with what immediately precedes should not be overlooked. The apostle had just referred to Adam's transgression. That he should in this connection have adduced the fact of Adam's typical significance and relationship suggests that Adam's transgression provided a parallel or analogy in terms of which the reverse on the part of Christ is to be interpreted. The reverse in the case of Christ is his obedience and, as we shall see later, this is placed in antithesis to the transgression or trespass of Adam. That Paul should have introduced allusion to this fact here throws into relief the relevance of the preceding part of verse 14 to the subject which had been introduced at verse 12; it is eminently germane to the whole argument of this passage that death reigned over those who did not sin after the similitude of Adam's transgression. For the apostle is chiefly interested in demonstrating that men are justified who do not act righteously after the similitude of Christ's obedience. Hence the appeal to this fact that death reigned over those who did not sin after the similitude of Adam's transgression has the greatest significance in the total argument of the apostle; it contributes to the proof of the assertion in verse 12 that death penetrated to all because they were involved in Adam's sin and sinned in him and with him. The concluding clause of verse 14 is therefore corroborative and shows how germane this doctrine is to the doctrine of justification—Adam is the type of the one to come.

Having thus discovered the main interest of verses 13, 14, the other features of this parenthesis may now be considered.

(1) The statement, "sin is not imputed when there is no law" (vs. 13) enunciates a general principle on which Paul is insistent. "Where no law is, neither is there transgression" (4:15). Since sin is transgression of law, it is apparent that there can be no sin if there is not law. It is not consonant with Paul's teaching nor with the Scripture in general to suppose that what Paul means here is that although there may be sin yet it is not *imputed*

as sin when there is not a law.²² This would contradict 4:15. Apart from the provisions of justifying grace, which are not in view in this verse, when sin is *not imputed* it is because sin does not exist.

(2) "Until the law" (vs. 13) means until the giving of the law by Moses. This is shown by verse 14 where the period concerned is stated to be "from Adam to Moses" (*cf.* Gal. 3:19). In this period, the apostle says, "sin was in the world" (vs. 13). In accord with the principle stated above, this implies that there must also have been law. And the thought is that, even though the law had not been promulgated as it was by Moses at Sinai, nevertheless there was law and this is shown by the fact that there was sin—if there had been no law there would have been no sin. There is no difficulty in discovering the respects in which law was in effect during this period, and neither is there difficulty in discovering examples of the sin to which the apostle refers.

(3) These foregoing observations elicited from verse 13 do not of themselves lend any support to the thesis that death penetrated to all because of the sin of Adam. In fact, they might seem to point in the opposite direction. It is for this reason that we must appreciate the strength of the adversative at the beginning of verse 14 and the emphasis which falls upon the consideration that death reigned over those who did not sin after the similitude of Adam's transgression. The thought may be paraphrased thus: although it is true that from Adam to Moses sin was in the world and therefore law, though thus there was sin such as would explain the presence of death, yet in that period death reigned

---

²² This is the view held by many of the ablest commentators. The thought of such interpreters is that although there is sin yet, in the absence of law, there is no imputation, at least it is not imputed as transgression such as would warrant the infliction of death (*cf.* Philippi, Meyer, Godet, Gifford, *ad loc.*, and Lightfoot: *Notes, ad loc.*). The view adopted by Calvin and others that the imputation refers to self-imputation is quite untenable. The imputation refers plainly to the divine judgment. If the interpretation of Meyer and others were adopted it fits in perfectly well with the thought of the passage. For in that event the period before Sinai would be a conclusive demonstration that it was for the sin of Adam that men died in that period. If sin was not imputed during that period, then the sentence of death could not be inflicted. But the sentence of death was inflicted. Therefore it must have been inflicted on the ground of the sin that was imputed, namely, the sin of Adam, a sin that could be *imputed* because it was the violation of expressly revealed law. The reason why I am not able to adopt this view is that, in terms of 4:15, sin exists only as transgression of law and where sin exists it must be imputed for what it is.

not only over those who were violators of expressly revealed law, as was Adam, but also over those who did not sin in that manner, that is, after the pattern of Adam. It is this datum that bears upon the apostle's thesis.

(4) Why did Paul select this segment of history—from Adam to Moses—to support his thesis? For is not this same truth exemplified in every era of human history, namely, that death reigns over those who do not sin after the similitude of Adam's transgression? This is true. But there was an appropriateness in selecting this period. The period after Moses, because of the more abundant revelation of law and ordinance, did not provide the apostle with as suitable an example of what was now his particular interest, namely, that death reigned over those who did not sin after the pattern of Adam. This would have been more especially the case when he had in mind his Jewish readers. They appreciated the significance of the Mosaic revelation and in respect of its concreteness and definiteness would compare it with the revelation given to Adam. The pre-Mosaic period furnished a better example of those who did not sin as Adam did. In selecting this period, however, Paul does not say nor does he allow that it was one in which law was not operative nor one in which there was no sin nor one in which sin was not imputed.

(5) In terms of the foregoing interpretation of verses 13, 14 the clause, "even over them who did not sin after the likeness of Adam's transgression", would have to be understood restrictively, that is to say, not of all mankind from Adam to Moses but of a certain division of mankind, namely, those who did not violate an expressly revealed commandment. Many commentators have understood this class to be infants who died in infancy. Undoubtedly they fall into this category and they are the most obvious example of such a division of the human race. If the apostle had infants exclusively in mind, the relevance and cogency of the appeal to their death in support of his thesis must be fully appreciated. For nothing evinces the sin of all and the death of all in the sin of Adam more than the death of little infants. It is not so certain, however, that only infants are in view. Those who were outside the pale of special revelation could be regarded as belonging to this category—they did not transgress an expressly and specially revealed commandment as Adam did. And although adults in this category sinned against the law of nature (*cf.* 2:14,

190

15), yet the *reign* of death over all such could be adduced by the apostle as pointing to the sin of Adam and as requiring the premise on which his interest is now focused, namely, the sin of all in the sin of Adam. In other words, when all the facts of the pre-Mosaic period are taken into account the only explanation of the *universal reign* is solidarity in the sin of Adam.[23]

15 At verse 15 the kind of construction which had been introduced at verse 12 but had been interrupted by the parenthesis of verses 13 and 14 is resumed. That is to say, we now have the two elements of a completed comparison indicated by "as" and "so also"—"but not as the trespass, so also the free gift". It is noteworthy, however, that the form is negative, not positive; it is upon the difference rather then the similarity that attention is focused. We might have expected the apostle to continue the parallel which he had begun to institute in verse 12 and to which he does revert in verses 18 and 19. All the more so might we have anticipated this since at the end of verse 14 he had said that Adam was the type of the one to come. But he does not do this

---

[23] I am quite aware of the objection that could be urged against the interpretation presented above. On the principles followed it could be objected that the violation of the law of nature (*cf.* 2:14, 15) would be sufficient to ground the infliction of death upon those who were outside the pale of special revelation. Consequently the only class left that would provide an example relevant to the apostle's thesis would be infants and imbeciles. If this is cogent, so it might well be that infants are in view. But, it may be objected, if infants are in mind, why did the apostle select this period. For, as respects infants, the same holds true in every period and no one period is a better example than another.

The answer to this objection or series of objections is that the apostle is thinking of the universal reign of death and of the solidarity of the whole race in this infliction. He is not thinking of the members of the race atomistically and, consequently, he is placed under the necessity of finding an explanation of this universality. He adduces the case of those who had not sinned after the pattern of Adam as peculiarly relevant to his interest. We may not be able to determine the precise scope of this classification. But the relevance of appeal to such is apparent. For the underlying assumption of his thought is that the *universal* reign of death cannot be explained except in terms of violation of an expressly revealed commandment of God, a violation that cannot be predicated of each and every member of the race in his own individuality and particularity. The only sin that provides the explanation is the sin of Adam and the participation of all in that sin.

If we were to omit μή before ἁμαρτήσαντες with some cursives and some fathers going back as far as Origen, then the exegesis of vs. 14 would have to be radically modified. But the preponderant external authority in support of μή would not favour this reading. For the retention of μή *cf.* Lightfoot: *Notes, ad loc.*

and hence we have negation rather than affirmation. This fact bespeaks an interest for which Paul must be jealous. The negation at the beginning of verse 15 is the introduction to a theme which is continued and unfolded to the end of verse 17. The keynotes of this theme are readily discovered; they appear in the latter part of verse 15—"how much more" and "hath abounded".

We must not suppose that this negation with which verse 15 begins and which appears again in verse 16 is a negation of the parallel between Christ and Adam nor of the similitude that obtains between these two representative heads of humanity. This would contradict the implication of verse 12, the express statement of the last clause in verse 14, and the construction of verses 18 and 19. And not only so but the negations and contrasts of verses 15–17 are built upon the assumption of the parallel. It is because there is similitude that the superabundance of grace can be exhibited. This thought of super-abounding grace explicates for us the intended force of the negation with which verse 15 opens. The latter part of verse 15 establishes this to be the case; it expresses the reason why the free gift is not as the trespass —"for if by the trespass of the one the many died, much more the grace of God and the free gift by grace which is of the one man Jesus Christ hath abounded unto the many".

We have here an *a fortiori* argument, illustrated earlier in verses 9 and 10. The premise from which the conclusion is drawn is, however, very different. In the earlier instances the argument is from one manifestation of grace to another. Here it is from the operation of judicial judgment to the bestowments of God's grace.

"The trespass of the one" can refer to nothing else but the fall of Adam, that by which sin entered into the world (vs. 12; *cf.* the reference to Adam and his transgression in vs. 14). It is expressly and specifically identified as the trespass of the one, and just as definitely it is stated to be the ground upon which the many died. No doubt can reasonably be entertained respecting this causal relationship between the sin of Adam and the death of the many when we take into account the parallel expressions in verses 16 and 17, to wit, "the judgment was from one unto condemnation" and "by the trespass of the one death reigned through the one". The one sin of Adam is the judicial ground or reason for the death of the many. When Paul uses the expression "the many", he is not intending to delimit the denotation. The scope of "the many" must be the same as the "all men" of verses 12 and 18. He uses "the many" here, as in verse 19, for the purpose of contrasting more effectively "the one" and "the many", singularity and plurality—it was the trespass of "the one", indeed "the one trespass" (vs. 18) of the one, but "the many" died as a result. And, furthermore, he is going to institute another contrast, as we shall see presently, through the use of the same expression, "the many". If he had simply said "all", the thought would not have been so forcefully expressed, even though in the same context the thought demands express reference to the fact that "all" died.

What is then the effect of the argument derived from the foregoing? "How much more the grace of God." The thought is not simply the greater assurance[24] we may entertain respecting the gifts of grace. Admittedly this follows. But the apostle is dealing with the objective ground of subjective assurance, the abundant plus which emanates from the grace of God. It would also be gratuitous to assume that the abundance of grace reflected on is that God takes more pleasure in bestowing grace than in executing judgment.[25] The abounding of grace, which is asserted here, is simply that which the apostle finds to be the case in accordance with what is stated later on, that "where sin abounded grace has superabounded" (vs. 20). He recognizes the fact of judgment and there is no suggestion to the effect that it is ineffective; it works relentlessly—"by the trespass of the one the many died". But Paul recognizes also that grace comes into operation and the abounding plus is evident because the grace of God not only negates the operation of judgment but abounds unto the opposite, unto justification and life. Sin has reigned unto death but grace has reigned through righteousness unto eternal life (vs. 21). There is no depreciation of the efficacy of judgment. But the emphasis is placed on the greater achievements of grace.

We cannot but observe the piling up of expressions to throw into relief the free grace of God. "The grace of God" is the disposition of gratuitous favour; "the free gift" is the bestowment which issues to us and is to be identified with "the free gift of

---

[24] Cf. Sanday and Headlam (op. cit., ad loc.) who interpret πολλῷ μᾶλλον thus.
[25] Cf. Ezek. 18:23; 33:11.

righteousness" (vs. 17); "the free gift by grace" indicates that what is bestowed upon us is altogether of grace. This reiteration of emphasis upon grace is not redundancy but, in a manner characteristic of the apostle, an eloquent fulness and variety of expression to advertise the freeness from every angle of thought. Besides, there is a distinguishing feature to each expression used. This becomes particularly apparent in the expression "the grace of the one man, Jesus Christ", more properly rendered, "the grace which is of the one man, Jesus Christ". The grace by which we receive the free gift of righteousness is defined as that which is of Jesus Christ. The construction here would indicate that the grace is that *exercised* by Jesus Christ and not, in this case, the grace of God mediated or issuing to us through Jesus Christ. The grace of Christ himself is operative in our justification (*cf.* Acts 15:11; II Cor. 8:9; I Tim. 1:14). But what particular manifestation of the grace exercised by Christ is in view here, whether that by which he secured our justification or that continuously displayed in the actual bestowment of justification, is not apparent. The context and the general teaching of the apostle would favour the former.[26] But the most significant lesson is that the grace of Christ as the one man is exhibited in that free gift of grace and righteousness that abounds unto the many.

16 The introductory clause in verse 16 is of similar import to the same in verse 15. Literally rendered, "And not as one having sinned the free gift", it is a compressed statement, indicating that the parallel between Adam and Christ does not imply uniformity. This is the sustained emphasis of verses 15–17 and Paul does not consider it superfluous to reiterate. But the reiteration is not mere repetition. There are distinguishing features to this reiteration. First, the expression "through one having sinned" brings Adam and his sin into close conjunction; in Meyer's words it "indicates the unity of the person and the accomplished sinful act" (*ad loc.*). Second, this clause is introductory and the form is adapted to the distinctive features of the superabundance of the operations of grace on which verse 16 reflects. The latter part of verse 16 informs us of the respects in which the free gift is dissimilar. "For the judgment was from one unto condemnation, but the

---

[26] Meyer, Gifford *et al.* construe ἐν χάριτι τῇ τοῦ ἑνὸς ἀνθρώπου Ἰησοῦ Χριστοῦ with the verb ἐπερίσσευσεν rather than with δωρεά. *Cf. contra* Godet, Sanday and Headlam, *et al.*

free gift is of many trespasses unto justification". There are several
details that demand treatment before we can appreciate the
contrast here enunciated.

(1) "The judgment" is the judicial sentence, and the character
of this sentence is defined as "condemnation". Hitherto the
judgment issuing from Adam's sin had been spoken of in terms of
death (vss. 12, 14, 15). Now a new concept is introduced, namely,
condemnation. Hence there is progression in the thought. How
appropriate and necessary the introduction of this concept is
lies open before us—condemnation is the opposite of justification
and sets the points for our interpretation of the character of
justification. Condemnation is a judicial sentence, as noted above,
and it is the judicial sentence which pronounces us to be unrighteous. Death is the penal consequence of sin but condemnation
is the divine sentence which is pronounced upon it.

(2) This sentence was "from one". It is difficult to ascertain
whether he means the one trespass or the one man. In the earlier
part of the verse the similar expression "through one" means the
one man, but that which is set in contrast with "of one" in this
part of the verse is "from many trespasses". If we are influenced
in our thinking by what precedes we should say the intent is
"from one man", if by what follows we should say "from one
trespass". And there seems to be no conclusive consideration in
favour of one view rather than the other. But if we keep in mind
what was noted above, namely, the unity of the person and the
sinful act, the question is of no consequence. In either event it is
the one trespass (*cf.* vs. 18) of the one man. What is affirmed here,
therefore, is that the divine sentence of condemnation (by implication upon all men; *cf.* vss. 12, 15, 18) proceeded from the one
sin of the one man. What we found already respecting the
relation of this trespass to the death of all (vss. 12, 15) holds true
also in the condemnation of all. All men are under the condemnation of God because of the one sin of the one man.

(3) "The free gift", as twice in verse 15, as in the earlier part
of this verse and in verse 17, refers to the gift *bestowed* in distinction
from the disposition of grace from which the gift bestowed
proceeds.[27] "The free gift" is antithetical to "the judgment"—the

---

[27] Any distinction which may be drawn between χάρισμα, δωρεά, and
δώρημα does not affect the conclusion that in each case there is reference to
the gift bestowed.

judgment is unto condemnation, the free gift is unto justification. As condemnation defines the character of the sentence of judgment, so justification defines the character of the free gift.

(4) "From many trespasses" is antithetical to "from one", namely, the one trespass of Adam. A striking parallel is hereby intimated. It is clear that the judgment of condemnation proceeded from the one trespass—the latter is the ground of the former. But may we say that the free gift of justification proceeds from the many trespasses and is grounded upon them? The parallel underlying the contrast requires a certain identity of operation. It would scarcely be feasible, however, to insist that the free gift is grounded upon the many trespasses. What then is the similarity of relation? It can be stated thus. What the judgment unto condemnation took into account was simply the one trespass; the sentence needed only the one trespass to give it validity and sanction; in fact, the one trespass demanded nothing less than the condemnation of all. But the free gift unto justification is of such a character that it must take the many trespasses into its reckoning; it could not be the free gift of justification unless it blotted out the many trespasses. Consequently, the free gift is conditioned as to its nature and effect by the many trespasses just as the judgment was conditioned as to its nature and effect by the one trespass alone. In this way we can perceive the identity which the apostle has in view and we can see how the magnitude of grace is exhibited by the manifold trespasses with which grace reckons.

(5) "Unto justification" is contrasted with condemnation and must mean the sentence of justification; it is the justifying act.

With these details in mind we can see that the introductory clause of verse 16 points to the distinguishing emphasis of this verse; it is the *contrast* between "the one" and "the many". In verse 15 the thought is that in *both judgment and grace* the movement proceeds from "the one" to "the many"—in *judgment* the many died by the trespass of the one, in *grace* the free gift abounds unto the many by the one man Jesus Christ. But in verse 16 it is upon the antithesis between the one and the many that the thought turns. Judgment and condemnation take into account only one sin of one man and the whole race is condemned. But the free gift and justification take into account the many sins, the multitudinous sins of a great multitude. How aggravated must sin be and how unspeakable grace must be!

17 This verse is similar in construction and sentiment to verse 15. It is in the form of an *a fortiori* argument, and the provisions of grace are set in contrast with the depredations of death. The particular emphasis of verse 17 is, however, the contrast between the *reign* of death by and through the one trespass of the one man and the *reign* of life through the one, Jesus Christ. In verse 15 it is the abounding of grace that is accented, in verse 16 it is the embracive and definitive character of the justifying act, in verse 17 it is the abounding rule of life as provided by grace and established by justification. "For if by the trespass of the one death reigned through the one, how much more those receiving the abundance of grace and of the free gift of righteousness shall reign in life through the one, Jesus Christ."

(1) "Death reigned through the one". The expression "through the one", because of the parallel to "through the one, Jesus Christ" at the end of the verse, must be taken to refer to Adam.[28] And so the apostle asserts that not only did death reign by reason of "the trespass of the one" but also through the mediacy of the one. Adam sustained such a relationship to the human race that *through* him death exercised its universal sway over men. The relationship explains the reason why Adam's one trespass carries such a result for all posterity. And the consequence is indicated by the power which death is represented as exercising—"death reigned", it wielded its undisputed sway.

(2) The *a fortiori*, "how much more" is applied in this case to the more abundant reign of life which emanates from grace.

(3) "Those receiving the abundance of grace and of the free gift of righteousness shall reign in life." The contrasted modes of expression are no doubt significant. *Death* reigned; it is not said that the subjects of death reigned in death. Death exercises its sway over them. But on the other side it is not said expressly that life reigns. This would not necessarily be inappropriate. But the form used is that the subjects of life "reign in life"; they are represented as exercising dominion in life. The reason why they reign in life is that they receive "the abundance of grace and of the free gift of righteousness". The distinction between "grace" and "the free gift" has been noted already.

---

[28] Likewise τοῦ ἑνός in the preceding clause refers to Adam, as also the same in the first clause of vs. 15, δι' ἑνός in the first clause of vs. 16, and τοῦ ἑνός again in the first clause of vs. 19.

It should be observed that "the abundance" governs both the grace and the free gift; it is the abundance, the overteeming plenty of grace both as disposition and bestowment. The word "receiving" enhances the thought expressed in "the free gift"; it does not refer to our believing acceptance[29] of the free gift but to our being made the recipients, and we are regarded as the passive beneficiaries of both the grace and the free gift in their overflowing fulness.

"The free gift" is in this instance defined for us; it is the free gift of righteousness and therefore the free gift which consists in righteousness. What is this righteousness? It would not be beside the drift of the passage to say that it is justification, the justifying act of God. But there is good reason for thinking that it is not, specifically, the justifying act but the righteousness which is bestowed upon us in the justifying act. It is "the righteousness of God" (1:17; 3:21, 22; 10:3; Phil. 3:9) which becomes ours, and, although it is this righteousness bestowed upon us and of which we become the recipients that constitutes our justification, yet much more is intimated than the justifying act. As we shall see later in connection with verses 18, 19, and 21 we are here introduced to the justifying righteousness. And we are apprised of the fact that justification consists in the donation to us of a righteousness which is more expressly defined for us in the verses which follow. Suffice it at present to observe that in justification there is the bestowment upon us of the gift of righteousness.

(4) "Shall reign in life through the one, Jesus Christ"—this shows that the same type of relationship to Christ for those reigning in life is assumed as obtains between Adam and those over whom death reigns. The permanency of the mediation of Christ in virtue of a certain relationship is stated to be the condition of the reign in life. It is likely that the reign in life has in its purview the consummated order. But the future tense "will reign" need not confine the reign to the future. It can be interpreted as expressing the certainty and security of the reign in life rather than its futurity. But the implication of the certainty and security is that it will continue for ever and, in accord with the apostle's teaching, come to its fullest realization in the future.

---

[29] "οἱ λαμβάνοντες not those who believingly *accept* ... but simply the *recipients*" (Meyer, *ad loc.*).

18 Whether we regard verse 18 as resumptive or recapitulatory[30] it is undoubtedly a summation of the doctrine set forth in the whole passage from verse 12 onwards. Examination will show that every element of verse 18 is already present either implicitly or explicitly in the preceding verses. This explains the "therefore" or "consequently then" with which verse 18 begins. The parallel between Adam and Christ is now stated in the clearest terms and the comparison is completed in the terms of positive construction. "Consequently then as through one trespass judgment came upon all men unto condemnation, even so through one righteous act judgment came upon all men unto justification of life."[31] The syntactical construction which had been begun in verse 12 but had been broken off by the insertion of a parenthesis is now taken up again and carried on in regular fashion to its conclusion. We are thus left in no doubt as to what verse 12 would have been if the comparison had been completed. It would have been as follows: "Therefore as through one man sin entered into the world and death through sin, and so death passed on to all men, in that all sinned, even so through one man righteousness entered into the world and life through righteousness, and so life passed on to all men, in that all were accounted righteous". Verse 18, however, states the parallel more succinctly and does not confront us with the difficulties of interpretation or, for that matter, of construction encountered in verse 12. The details of verse 18, nevertheless, call for comment.

(1) "Through one trespass"—this rendering is more natural than "through the trespass of one". This is the first time that

---

[30] If it is resumptive, it takes up again the thought that had been broken off at verse 12. If it is recapitulatory, then the parallel begun in verse 12 but not completed is developed in vss. 15–17 though not precisely in the form begun in verse 12 or carried to completion in vss. 18, 19. It is not feasible to regard the parallel as absent from vss. 15–17, for, as we found, the parallel underlies the contrasts of these verses. Hence it is not proper to regard the parallel as postponed from vs. 12 until vs. 18. The word "resumptive" could rightly be used, however, if it refers to the resumption of the precise kind of construction which was begun in vs. 12 but had not been completed. In terms of content vs. 18 is really recapitulatory of what we find in the preceding verses.

[31] The ellipsis in this verse cannot be more relevantly supplied than by the insertion of "judgment came". Or, if we adopt the terminology of vs. 16, we can quite properly supply "judgment (κρῖμα) came" in the protasis and "the free gift (χάρισμα) came" in the apodosis. In support of the latter Lightfoot (*Notes, ad loc.*) appeals to 10:17; Gal. 2:9; I Cor. 6:13; Rev. 6:6 as examples of this elliptical form in two antithetical clauses.

199

the sin of Adam is expressly called the "one trespass" although it was implied earlier (vs. 16). Our attention is therefore drawn to the fact that the sin in view as that by which all men died and fell under condemnation is the one sin of Adam. We can be in no doubt that it was the first sin, that of eating the forbidden fruit. This sin Paul could not think of in abstraction from the dispositional complex from which it proceeded and which it registered. But, like Genesis 3 itself, he focuses attention upon the particular sin to which the dispositional complex was directed and in which it was expressed. The eating of the fruit interprets the whole movement of defection and gives it unity as sin. Here again is affirmed what we have found repeatedly that this one trespass of Adam is the reason for the condemnation of all; it is the medium of God's judgment of condemnation upon all.

(2) "Through one righteous act." What is the righteous act? It is readily assumed by many commentators that this is the act of justification,[32] and it is easy to appeal to verse 16 in support of this view. In the latter it undoubtedly refers to justification because it is contrasted with condemnation and there is no reason for any other notion at that point. There are, however, decisive objections to this interpretation here. (a) It is gratuitous to assume that the apostle must have used the same word in the same sense in these two verses. We have already noted how quickly Paul may pass from one meaning of a word to another. To appreciate this flexibility is indispensable to exegesis. (b) The sense in which a word is used is determined, first of all, by the immediate context. In verse 16 the sense is determined by the contrast with condemnation. But in verse 18 there is a different contrast, and this term is placed in antithesis to trespass, not to condemnation. It is this contrast that fixes the sense here. (c) In verse 18 the word condemnation appears again and its contrast is

[32] Cf. Calvin, Meyer, Godet, Gifford, Shedd, Sanday and Headlam and contra Philippi, Haldane, Hodge, and apparently Lightfoot. Lightfoot (Notes, ad 5:16) adduces Rev. 15:4; 19:8 as examples of δικαίωμα in the sense of "righteous deed". It is pointless for Godet to argue in favour of the meaning, "sentence of justification", that "in Paul's terminology it is God and not Jesus Christ who is the justifier" (op. cit., ad loc.). "The righteous act" of Christ does not refer to the sentence which, as Godet rightly observes, is the act of God as distinguished from Christ but to the righteousness of Christ's obedience and is parallel to ὑπακοή in vs. 19. On the meaning of δικαίωμα cf. the fine treatment by G. Schrenk in Theologisches Wörterbuch zum Neuen Testament, ad loc.

instituted but not through the term in question but the other, namely, "justification of life" which undoubtedly means justification. (d) If the term in question means justification, then the thought of verse 18 is perplexed by a redundancy. For, in that event, the apodosis would read: "even so through one justification judgment came upon all men unto justification of life". (e) In this passage, throughout, the expression "the one" always refers either to Adam or Christ and "one" without the article either to Adam or to his transgression. This sustained use of the term would lead us to expect that when "*one* righteous act" is mentioned it is the righteous act which is peculiarly Christ's in contradistinction from the one trespass which is peculiarly Adam's. For these reasons we conclude that the "one righteous act" in this verse is contrasted with the "one trespass" of Adam, as is apparent from the construction. And just as the trespass of Adam is the ground of condemnation upon all so the "one righteous act" is the ground upon which justification comes upon all. And since, in terms of the passage, this must be the righteous act of the one man Jesus Christ as that alone which provides the parallel and the contrast, the reference must be to the righteousness of Christ as that on the basis of which judgment passes upon all men unto justification of life.[33] If the question be asked how the righteousness of Christ could be defined as "one righteous act", the answer is that the righteousness of Christ is regarded in its compact unity in parallelism with the one trespass, and there is good reason for speaking of it as the one righteous act because,

---

[33] If it is objected that, if δικαίωμα here means the righteousness of Christ, the apostle would have used δικαιοσύνη, the answer is that δικαίωμα suited his thought as a more apparent contrast to παράπτωμα.

It has been maintained that since ἑνός in the other instances in this passage is personal, referring either to Adam or to Christ, so in this verse ἑνός in both protasis and apodosis must be personal, "the trespass of the one" and "the righteous act of the one". This argument is not conclusive. In every instance where ἑνός is clearly personal the definite article is used (vss. 15, 17, 19) except in vss. 12a, 16a. In these two instances, for obvious reasons, there is no need of the article to demonstrate the personal reference. In vs. 16b ἐξ ἑνός, because of the contrast with ἐκ πολλῶν παραπτωμάτων, is much more reasonably taken as "from one trespass" rather as "from one man". There is no good reason, therefore, why ἑνός in both instances in vs. 18 should not be taken as qualifying παράπτωμα and δικαίωμα. If Paul intended ἑνός to be personal we should expect him to insert the article after the pattern of the construction in vss. 15, 17, or after the pattern of vs. 19, although in the former case the ambiguity would not be entirely removed because of the genitive in both ἑνός and the substantives.

as the one trespass is the trespass of the one, so the one righteousness is the righteousness of the one and the unity of the person and of his accomplishment must always be assumed.

(3) "Justification of life." This cannot mean that the justification consists in life. In verse 17 we have this same kind of construction, "the free gift of righteousness" and righteousness defines the free gift, the free gift that consists in righteousness. But in this instance justification could not be defined as consisting in life. It is rather the justification which is unto life and issues in life. In this verse, therefore, we have clearly set before us the combination, righteousness, justification, life.

(4) Perhaps the most crucial question that arises in connection with this verse is the extent of the apodosis—"through one righteous act judgment came upon all men unto justification of life". Is this to be interpreted as embracively as the terms appear to imply? In the protasis we must conclude that the extent is universal. For the judgment of condemnation did pass upon all without exception (cf. vss. 12, 14, 15, 17). Must we assume that the same applies to the apodosis? There is no possibility of escaping the conclusion that, if the apostle meant the apodosis to be as embracive in its scope as the protasis, then the whole human race must eventually attain to eternal life. There is no escape from this conclusion by distinguishing between the objective provision and subjective appropriation.[34] Nor is it possible to evade this inference by placing upon the justification of life an attenuated interpretation such as would be compatible with everlasting perdition. The justification with which the apostle deals in this verse is that with which he is dealing in this particular passage and in the epistle as a whole. It is the justification that takes account of the multitudinous trespasses of those who are its recipients (vs. 16); it is the justification in which grace abounds (vs. 15), in which the recipients reign in life through Jesus Christ (vs. 17); it is the justification by which the justified are constituted righteous (vs. 19); it is the justification that issues in the permanent standing of peace with God (vss. 1, 2). To put the issue of this justification beyond all dispute it is sufficient to appeal to verse 21. This is surely the apostle's summation of the entire argument—"as sin hath reigned in death, even so might grace reign through

---

[34] This is Meyer's supposition. Yet he is insistent that nothing can be deduced from this passage in favour of a final ἀποκατάστασις (op. cit., ad loc.).

righteousness unto eternal life through Jesus Christ our Lord". The righteousness and the justification with which verse 18 deals can be nothing less than those which issue in everlasting life, and the expression "justification of life" is itself capable of no other interpretation.

When we ask the question: Is it Pauline to posit universal salvation? the answer must be decisively negative (*cf.* II Thess. 1:8, 9). Hence we cannot interpret the apodosis in verse 18 in the sense of inclusive universalism, and it is consistent with sound canons of interpretation to assume a restrictive implication. In I Cor. 15:22 Paul says, "As in Adam all die, even so in Christ shall all be made alive". As the context will demonstrate the apostle is here dealing with the resurrection to life, with those who are Christ's and will be raised at his coming. The "all" of the second clause is therefore restrictive in a way that the "all" in the first clause is not. In like manner in Rom. 5:18 we may and must recognize a restriction in the "all men" of the apodosis that is not present in the "all men" of the protasis. What the apostle is interested in showing is not the numerical extent of those who are justified as identical with the numerical extent of those condemned but the parallel that obtains between the way of condemnation and the way of justification. It is the *modus operandi* that is in view. All who are condemned, and this includes the whole human race, are condemned because of the one trespass of Adam; all who are justified are justified because of the righteousness of Christ. But we are not to give to justification the denotative extent of condemnation, and the parallel does not demand this.

19 Verse 19 is confirmatory and explicatory of verse 18. This is apparent not only from the construction and content of verse 19 but also from the way in which they are related; verse 19 begins with "for". "For as through the disobedience of the one man the many were constituted sinners, even so through the obedience of the one the many will be constituted righteous." We have here again a completed comparison after the pattern of verse 18. Though the doctrine is substantially the same, new facets of this doctrine are set forth.

(1) "The disobedience of the one man." The sin of Adam is characterized as transgression (vs. 14), as trespass (vss. 15, 17, 18), now as disobedience. Each term possesses its own emphasis and

203

indicates that the fall of Adam was regarded by the apostle as sin in all the respects in which sin may be defined.

(2) "The many were constituted sinners." In the preceding verses we found that death passed on to all men by reason of the sin of Adam (vss. 12, 14, 15, 17). We found also that condemnation was pronounced upon all men through the sin of Adam (vss. 16, 18). Implicit in these reiterated declarations is the solidarity that existed between Adam and posterity. It would have been a necessary inference from the solidarity in death and condemnation to posit a solidarity in sin also, because death and condemnation presuppose sin. But we are not left to inference. The apostle is now explicit to the effect that the solidarity extended to sin itself. We discovered earlier that the only feasible way of interpreting the clause in verse 12, "in that all sinned" is that this refers to the involvement of all in the sin of Adam. But again the propriety of that interpretation is demonstrated by what is now said expressly in verse 19, "through the disobedience of the one man the many were constituted sinners". The expression used here "constituted sinners" is definitely to the effect that the many were made to be sinners, they were placed in the category of sinners. Not only did death rule over them, not only did they come under the sentence of condemnation, but sinnership itself became theirs by reason of the sin of Adam. It is here again that the variety of terms which the apostle uses to characterize sin becomes eloquent of what is meant by being constituted sinners. Sin is transgression, trespass, disobedience, and therefore solidarity in *sin* is involvement in the disobedience, transgression, trespass of Adam. The last clause of verse 12 likewise can mean nothing less, for it says "all *sinned*". By a confluence of considerations inherent in this passage we are informed that the sin of Adam was the sin of all and the solidarity in condemnation and death is traced to its source and ground, solidarity in sin. To attempt to escape from this conclusion is to waive exegesis.

(3) "Through the obedience of the one." This is parallel to "through one righteous act" in verse 18 and there can be no doubt but it refers to the obedience of Christ. Even if doubt should persist as to the import of the "righteous act" in verse 18 there can be no doubt in verse 19. The obedience of Christ is stated to be that through which the many are constituted righteous. The

concept of obedience as applied to the work of Christ on behalf of believers is more embracive than any other (*cf.* Isa. 42:1; 52:13-53:12; John 6:38, 39; 10:17, 18; 17:4, 5; Gal. 4:4; Phil. 2:7, 8; Heb. 2:10; 5:8, 9). It is significant that it should be used here. It indicates the broad perspective from which we must view that accomplishment of Christ which constitutes the basis of God's justifying act. Undoubtedly it was in the cross of Christ and the shedding of his blood that this obedience came to its climactic expression, but obedience comprehends the totality of the Father's will as fulfilled by Christ. And this brings into the clearest focus what was implied in "the grace of the one man Jesus Christ" (vs. 15), "through the one, Jesus Christ" (vs. 17), and "through the one righteous act" (vs. 18).

(4) "The many will be constituted righteous." The notion of being constituted righteous cannot be in a different category from the "justification" of verse 16 or "the free gift of righteousness" of verse 17 (*cf.* vss. 15, 16) or the "justification of life" of verse 18. We could not suppose that at this climactic point in his argument the apostle had introduced a category extraneous to the foregoing context or to his main thesis up to this point. This is to say that "constituted righteous" has the same forensic character as justification and must be a variant mode of expression. This consideration gives us the direction in which we are to interpret the antithetic expression, "constituted sinners". While we must not tone down the latter so as to eliminate our involvement in the sin, transgression, trespass, disobedience of Adam, yet this involvement must be interpreted in forensic terms. Our involvement cannot be that of personal voluntary transgression on our part. It can only be that of imputation, that by reason of representative unity the sin of Adam is reckoned to our account and therefore reckoned as ours with all the entail of implication and consequence which sin carries with it. In the judicial judgment of God the sin of Adam is the sin of all.

Though the expression "constituted righteous" belongs strictly to the forensic sphere, yet we must not overlook the distinctive aspect from which justification is viewed in the use of this formula. Justification is a constitutive act, not barely declarative. And this constitutive act consists in our being placed in the category of righteous persons by reason of our relation to Christ. The same principle of solidarity that appears in our relation to Adam, and by reason of which we are involved in his sin, obtains in our relation to Christ. And just as the relation to Adam means the imputation to us of his disobedience, so the relation to Christ means the imputation to us of his obedience. Justification means our involvement in the obedience of Christ in terms of the same principle by which we are involved in Adam's sin. Nothing less is demanded by the analogy instituted in this verse. Again, the involvement in the obedience of Christ is not that of our personal voluntary obedience nor that of our subjective holiness. This would violate the forensic character of the justification with which the apostle is dealing. But we must not tone down the formula "constituted righteous" to any lower terms than the gracious judgment on God's part whereby the obedience of Christ is reckoned to our account and therefore reckoned as ours with all the entail of consequence which righteousness carries with it. This interprets for us "the free gift of righteousness" (vs. 17) of which believers become the recipients and also how "through the one righteous act" judgment comes upon them "unto justification of life" (vs. 18).

The future tense in "will be constituted righteous" must not be taken as referring to an act that is reserved for the consummation.[35] This would violate the nature of justification as a free gift received by believers here and now in its completeness and perfection. The future tense can well be used to indicate that this act of God's grace is being continually exercised and will continue to be exercised throughout future generations of mankind.[36] In this respect it differs from the judgment by which men were constituted sinners; the latter was a judgment that passed upon all men once for all in the identification of the whole race with Adam in his sin. The change of tense intimates the progressive realization of the fruits of Christ's obedience through the ever-continuing acts of grace in justifying the ungodly.

20, 21 In verses 12–19 the apostle had dealt with the analogy obtaining between Adam and Christ. These sustain unique relations to the human race. Nothing bears this out more force-

---

[35] Meyer has a decided tendency to interpret these future tenses in this passage eschatologically (*cf. ad.* vs. 17 as well as here). In this instance he says: "The *future* refers to the future revelation of glory after the resurrection" and corresponds, he says, to the βασιλεύουσι in vs. 17.

[36] *Cf.* Sanday and Headlam: *op. cit., ad loc.*

fully than the fact stated in verse 14 that Adam is the type of the one to come. With Adam is bound up the entrance of sin into the world and the reign of sin, condemnation, and death. With Christ is bound up the entrance of righteousness and the reign of grace, righteousness, justification, life. These two heads of humanity and the two parallel yet opposing complexes bound up with them are the pivots on which the history of humanity turns. God's government of the race can be interpreted only in terms of these two headships and of the respective complexes which the heads set in operation. These are the pivots of redemptive revelation, the first as making redemption necessary, the second as accomplishing and securing redemption.

The fact that the giving of the law by Moses should have been so expressly referred to by the apostle in the heart of his development of this subject (vss. 13, 14) shows the epochal significance of the Mosaic revelation. It is in this light that we must understand verse 20: "And the law came in besides, that the trespass might abound". The "law" cannot reasonably be taken in any other way than the law as revealed by Moses. The Mosaic economy was not legal as opposed to grace. But the promulgation of the law and of its sanctions was an outstanding feature of the Mosaic revelation and it is upon that feature that stress is laid. What is said is that the law "came in alongside".[37] It is true it came in "between"[38] Adam and the manifestation of Christ and this must be understood as implied. But the precise thought is that it came alongside; it was complementary (cf. Gal. 3:19), not for the purpose of displacing or suspending but for the purpose of subserving an end coordinate with both sin and grace. What is this purpose? It is that the trespass might abound, namely, that sin might be multiplied. We might have expected the opposite, that sin might be restrained and diminished. But the language is explicit.

There is some question as to "the trespass" in this instance. In the preceding verses this term refers to the trespass of Adam (vss. 15, 17, 18; cf. vss. 14, 16, 19). And it might seem necessary to adopt this specification here. It is difficult, however, to see how the one trespass of Adam was made to abound by the entrance of the law. The solution would appear to be that there is allusion

---

[37] This is Meyer's rendering.
[38] Cf. Calvin and others.

to the trespass of Adam as supplying the pattern of that which is made to abound by the entrance of the law. Adam's trespass was disobedience to expressly revealed commandment. When the law came in through Moses, there was henceforth a multiplication of the kind of transgression exemplified in Adam's trespass, that is to say, transgression of clearly revealed commandment. The more explicit the revelation of law the more heinous and aggravated are the violations of it. And there is little question that the apostle is here reflecting upon an effect on which he elaborates more fully in 7:8, 11, 13, to wit, that the more law is brought to bear upon the heart of sinful man the more the enmity of the heart is aroused to transgression. This multiplication of trespass is stated clearly to be the purpose for which the law came in alongside. This is not a definition of the whole purpose of the giving of the law by Moses. Other purposes are stated elsewhere[39] but this is the purpose most relevant to the doctrine which the apostle proceeds to unfold.

The second part of verse 20, "but where sin abounded, grace superabounded", advises us that we must never abstract the foregoing purpose served by the law from the more abundant provisions of grace. The apostle construes the multiplying of trespass which the giving of the law promoted as magnifying and demonstrating the superabounding riches of divine grace. The more transgression is multiplied and aggravated the greater is the grace that abounds unto justification and the more the lustre of that grace is made manifest. The surpassing efficacy and glory of God's grace are stressed by the superlative, "superabounded".

The latter part of verse 20 should be taken in close connection with verse 21. The latter defines the purpose why grace has superabounded. It is stated to be: "in order that as sin reigned in death, even so might grace reign through righteousness unto eternal life through Jesus Christ our Lord". This is the apostle's concluding summation of both the parallel and the antithesis instituted in the preceding verses. There is analogy between the reign of sin and death, on the one hand, and the reign of righteousness and life, on the other. But the analogy is for the purpose of exhibiting the total contrast at every point of the parallelism.

---

[39] *Cf.* Gal. 3:17–25; II Cor. 3:6–11; I Tim. 1:8–11.

Grace has superabounded to the end that it might *reign* through righteousness unto eternal life.

The similarity of verse 21 to verse 17 is apparent; the governing thought in both is the *reign* contemplated. But the differences are worthy of note. In verse 17 it is the reign of death, in verse 21 it is the reign of sin in death; in verse 17 the recipients of the gift of grace reign in life, in verse 21 grace reigns unto eternal life. "Sin reigned in death." That sin is conceived of as reigning is prepared for by the fact mentioned in the preceding verse that the trespass and sin have come to abound. Hence it is the reigning of sin itself that is emphasized and it reigns "in death". One trespass was enough to cause death to reign (vs. 17), but when the trespass abounds how much more accentuated becomes the death that follows in its train. And this in turn accentuates the reign of grace which comes into operation through righteousness unto eternal life.

The "righteousness" contemplated in this case can be none other than the "righteousness" donated and of which the justified become the recipients (vs. 17), the "one righteousness" through which judgment passes upon them unto justification (vs. 18), "the obedience of the one" through which they are constituted righteous (vs. 19), "the righteousness of God" revealed (1:17; 3:21, 22; 10:3). This verse is still unfolding the antithesis between the complex originating from the trespass of Adam and intensified by the abounding of the trespass, namely, sin-condemnation-death, and the complex proceeding from the grace of God and brought into operation by the righteousness of Christ, namely, righteousness-justification-life. And what provides the antithesis to sin is the righteousness and obedience of Christ. Hence the whole development of the apostle's thought as well as the express intimations given in the immediately preceding context point definitely to the conclusion that the "righteousness" is that contemplated in the justifying act rather than the justifying act itself.

The superabundance of grace is exemplified in the result which issues from this righteousness or the end towards which it is directed, to wit, "eternal life". This is, of course, in antithesis to death but it is life that death cannot invade and life that cannot be forfeited; it is life eternal.

We have noted already that the mediation of Christ is implicit in the concept of "righteousness" through which grace reigns unto eternal life. But the apostle is jealous to make that mediation explicit. He cannot allow the thought of grace reigning through righteousness unto eternal life to be divorced for a moment from the mediacy and mediatorship of "Jesus Christ our Lord". And Paul is, without doubt, thinking of the exalted and glorified Lord, so that not only is the grace conceived of as reigning through Christ's righteousness but the eternal life in which this reign of grace issues is not capable of being defined or contemplated except in terms of the mediation of the glorified Lord.

IX.   THE SANCTIFYING EFFECTS
(6:1–23)

A.   THE ABUSE OF GRACE EXPOSED
(6:1–11)

1–4

> 1 What shall we say then? Shall we continue in sin, that grace may abound?
> 2 God forbid. We who died to sin, how shall we any longer live therein?
> 3 Or are ye ignorant that all we who were baptized into Christ Jesus were baptized into his death?
> 4 We were buried therefore with him through baptism into death: that like as Christ was raised from the dead through the glory of the Father, so we also might walk in newness of life.

The transition from one phase of teaching to another at the beginning of this chapter is quite conspicuous. In verses 12–21 of the preceding chapter the argument bearing upon justification had been brought to a climactic conclusion by instituting the parallel between Adam and Christ and on the basis of that parallel demonstrating the contrasts which the superabundance of grace brings into effective and regnant operation. The invariable combinations of sin, condemnation, and death introduced by the sin of Adam, on the one hand, and of righteousness, justification, and life emanating from the grace of God and realized through the mediation of Christ, on the other, have been set forth by way of analogy and contrast as the ruling conceptions in terms of which we are to interpret God's dealings with men. Having brought the basic thesis of the epistle to this climactic conclusion the apostle is now prepared to unfold other elements of that gospel which is the power of God unto salvation. To speak in general terms, chapter 6 deals with sanctification as the preceding chapters had dealt with justification. We are not

211

to suppose, however, that this transition means that sanctification can be divorced either in fact or in the development of its meaning from the justification on which it rests and with which it is inseparably connected. This is evident from the reiterated references to justification in the subsequent chapters and from the way in which sanctification no less than justification springs from the efficacy of Christ's death and the virtue of his resurrection. If the mediation of Christ is always in the forefront in justification it is likewise in sanctification.

The intimacy of the relations between justification and sanctification is made evident by the way in which chapters 5 and 6 are connected. There is no abruptness of transition. The question with which chapter 6 begins arises from the emphasis at the close of chapter 5. If grace superabounds where sin abounds, if the multiplication of transgression serves to exhibit the lustre of grace, and if the law administered by Moses came in alongside in order that the trespass might abound, the logical inference would seem to be, let us sin all the more in order that God may be glorified in the magnifying of his grace. This is the antinomian distortion of the doctrine of grace and it is also the objection of the legalist to the doctrine of justification apart from works by free grace through faith. It is both the distortion and the objection that the apostle answers in this chapter, and in his answer he develops the implications of the death and resurrection of Christ.

1, 2 "What shall we say then? Shall we continue in sin that grace may abound? God forbid."[1] The apostle puts the inference in the form of a question and then by his characteristic formula indicates the recoil of abhorrence from the suggestion. In verse 2 he states the reason why the question should be answered with such decisive and emphatic negation. The reason is not in the form of elaborate argument but in the form of a question to show the inherent contradiction, indeed absurdity, of the supposed inference. "We who died to sin, how shall we still live in it?"

---

[1] ἐπιμένωμεν is supported by A B C D G and others, ἐπιμένομεν by ℵ, and ἐπιμενοῦμεν by the mass of the cursives. The meaning is not affected by these variants. Only the first, as subjunctive, lends strength to the implied objection that there is some obligation to continue in sin because it magnifies grace. This is the reading favoured by the editors of the text. It is the strongest form in which the question could be asked and the rejoinder "God forbid" takes on the greater vehemence.

(vs. 2).[2] The relative pronoun in this instance at the beginning is that of quality and means "we who are of the sort" or "as many of us who". It is the appropriate relative in this connection because it points to a particular kind of relationship or character, namely, those who are such that they died to sin. The first clause in this verse is in that position for emphasis; it throws into prominence the consideration which contains within itself the answer to the false inference. If we died to sin how can we any longer live in it? Death and life cannot coexist; we cannot be dead and living with respect to the same thing at the same time.

It needs to be stressed at the outset in the exposition of this chapter that the fact of having died to sin is the fundamental premise of the apostle's thought. This is the identity of the believer—he died to sin. It is not strictly proper to render the clause concerned "we that are dead to sin" (A. V.). While true that the person who has died is dead, yet the tense used in this instance is one that points to a definitive act in the past and no translation which suggests a state of being does justice to the thought. What the apostle has in view is the once-for-all definitive breach with sin which constitutes the identity of the believer. A believer cannot therefore live in sin; if a man lives in sin he is not a believer. If we view sin as a realm or sphere then the believer no longer lives in that realm or sphere. And just as it is true with reference to life in the sphere of this world that the person who has died "passed away, and, lo, he was not: yea, I sought him, but he could not be found" (Psalm 37:36; cf. 103:16), so is it with the sphere of sin; the believer is no longer there because he has died to sin. Failure to appreciate this premise upon which the subsequent argument rests and of which it is an expansion will distort our understanding of this chapter. The believer died to sin once and he has been translated to another realm.

3 At verse 3 the apostle proceeds to *vindicate* and *explicate* this premise. Obviously, the apodictic statement that the believer died to sin must be validated and explained. How did he die to sin? What are its implications? What is the new sphere of life into which he has been translated?

---

[2] In this verse ζήσομεν, being supported by ℵ A B D and the mass of the cursives, is certainly to be adopted rather than ζήσωμεν which is not strongly attested.

213

The vindication of the premise consists in the appeal to the *import* of baptism: "Or do ye not know that as many as were baptized into Christ Jesus were baptized into his death?" (vs. 3). The appeal is to their knowledge of the identification involved in baptism. Even if we suppose that the apostle is castigating them for failure to recognize and appreciate the implications of baptism the intent of his appeal is not altered. It is clear that he is eliciting from baptism the argument particularly relevant to the proposition that the believer died to sin and is to the effect that the ordinance of baptism signifies union with Christ in his death. Several observations are necessary. (1) The appeal to baptism certifies that the readers of the epistle were aware of the place and importance of baptism in the Christian profession. It was the sign and seal of membership in the body of Christ, and the apostle assumes that the believers at Rome did not call in question the necessity and privilege of this seal of their status as Christians, an index of the fact that baptism was reckoned to be a note of the Christian church. This was a tenet beyond controversy. (2) Baptism "into Christ Jesus" means baptism into union with Christ. To be baptized "into Moses" (I Cor. 10:2) is to be baptized into the discipleship of Moses or into the participation of the privileges which the Mosaic economy entailed. To be baptized "into the name of Paul" (I Cor. 1:13) is to be baptized into the discipleship of Paul, a suggestion which Paul violently rejects. To be baptized "into the name of the Father and of the Son and of the Holy Ghost" (Matt. 28:19) is to be baptized into the fellowship of the three persons of the Godhead. Hence baptism into Christ signifies simply union with him and participation of all the privileges which he as Christ Jesus embodies. (3) If baptism signifies union with Christ, it must mean union with him in all that he is and in all phases of his work as the Mediator. Christ Jesus cannot be contemplated apart from his work nor his work apart from him. Neither can one phase of his redemptive accomplishment be separated from another. Therefore union with Christ, which baptism signifies, means union with him in his death. This is the force of what the apostle says that "as many as were baptized into Christ Jesus were baptized into his death"; baptism into Christ must carry this implication. Hereby is vindicated the apostle's premise, and it is vindicated by drawing out the implications of that baptism which believers at Rome prized and cherished. For if baptism means union with Christ Jesus in his death, then believers died with Christ in his death. This is not only vindication; it is also elucidation of the proposition that believers died to sin. It is, however, only the first step in that elucidation; the succeeding verses are relied on for fuller explication. (4) We are not to impute to the apostle a sacerdotalist view of the efficacy of baptism. It is sufficient that in an appeal of this kind he should have elicited from the import of baptism as sign and seal the significance which pointed to the vindication and elucidation of his thesis that believers died to sin. This holds true as truly on an evangelical view of the efficacy of baptism as on the sacerdotalist, and what the apostle's view was would have to be elicited from other data.

4 Verse 4 has the form of a consequence drawn from what precedes: "Therefore we were buried with him through baptism into death". The sequence of inference seems to be that if we were united with Christ Jesus in his death we must therefore have been buried with him.[3] The inseparable conjunction of death and burial in the case of Jesus himself carries of necessity a similar conjunction in the case of those who are united with him in his death. The purpose of bringing this aspect of union with Christ into focus is apparently twofold. It stresses the completeness of identification with Christ in his death—the burial of Jesus was the proof of the reality of his death—and it prepares for that which is to follow in the latter part of this verse, namely, union with Christ in his resurrection—it is burial that gives meaning to resurrection.

While it would not be impossible to take "into death" along with

---

[3] The assumption of so many commentators, non-baptist as well as baptist, to the effect that the apostle has in view the mode of immersion as vividly portraying our burial with Christ and emergence with him in his resurrection is without warrant. *Cf.* most recently for the presentation of this interpretation *A Catholic Commentary on Holy Scripture* (London, 1953), pp. 1058f. For a treatment of this question by the writer see *Christian Baptism* (Philadelphia, 1952), pp. 9–33 and particularly pp. 29–33. Suffice it at present to be reminded that we have no more warrant to find a reference to the mode of baptism in συνετάφημεν here in vs. 4 than in σύμφυτοι in vs. 5, συνεσταυρώθη in vs. 6, ἐνεδύσασθε in Gal. 3:27, all of which bear no analogy to the mode of immersion. It is rather lame for Lightfoot to suggest that Χριστὸν ἐνεδύσασθε in Gal. 3:27 "may be an image taken from another part of the baptismal ceremony" (*Notes, ad loc.*), just as it is without any cogency for him to cite Col. 2:12; Eph. 5:14; I Cor. 10:2 as bringing out more clearly the idea of immersion.

"we were buried with him" (*cf.* 3:25) and so think of our being buried into death, death thus strengthening what is involved in burial or burial confirming what is involved in death, yet it is more natural to take "into death" with baptism and read "we were buried with him through baptism into death". This is the precise thought of the preceding clause in verse 3, "we were baptized into his death" and the repetition is not superfluous because what is enunciated in verse 4 is that in being baptized into Jesus' death we are also baptized into burial with him, burial carrying with it the emphases mentioned above.

The latter part of verse 4 states the purpose contemplated in our burial with Christ—"in order that as Christ was raised from the dead through the glory of the Father, even so we should walk in newness of life". Of necessity the apostle's thought moves on to the newness of life which follows upon death to sin, and that for two reasons. Death to sin is not of itself an adequate characterization of the believer's identity; it is basic and it is the fundamental premise of the argument. But death to sin is but the precondition of that life which is the final issue of grace (*cf.* 5:15, 17, 18, 21). And baptism as signifying union with Christ (vs. 3) must mean also union with Christ in his resurrection and therefore in his resurrection life. This explains the purpose which burial with Christ is represented as fulfilling. We cannot be partakers of Christ's resurrection life unless we are partakers of his death, and death is certified and confirmed in burial.

The purpose clauses are in the form of a comparison in which the newness of life in which the believer comes to walk is compared with the resurrection of Christ. It is, however, much more than bare comparison. Christ rose from the dead and, since his resurrection is the analogue of the believer's, newness of life for the believer is the inevitable outcome. As surely as Christ rose from the dead so surely shall we walk in newness of life. That this certainty is implicit in the parallel is confirmed by verse 5, for the latter is closely connected with verse 4 and has confirmatory force.

Christ is said to have been raised from the dead "through the glory of the Father". Already the apostle had represented the Father as the active agent in Christ's resurrection (4:24, 25). But here we have a unique expression. It is possible that "the glory" refers to the glory *in* which Christ was raised from the dead.

But it is more in accord with usage to think of the glory as that *through* which Christ was raised. The glory of God is the majesty of God, the sum of his perfections. If this meaning holds in this instance, then the Father's majesty or perfection in its fulness is conceived of as operative in the resurrection of Christ and, in that event, this expression more than any other in the New Testament would signalize the redemptive, vindicatory, and revelatory significance of the Father's act in raising Christ from the dead—the plenitude of the Father's glory is manifest in the resurrection of his own Son. It may well be, however, that the Father's power is specifically in view (*cf.* II Cor. 13:4; Eph. 1:19) and in that event it is the glory of his omnipotence that is stressed. In either case the use of the term "glory" is intended to place in marked relief the agency of the Father and the certification which that agency implies.

"Newness of life" is the newness which consists in life. We can scarcely suppress the thought that "the glory of the Father", as registered in the resurrection of Christ, is brought to bear upon the newness of life as the guarantee of its certainty and the dynamic in its realization.

That believers "walk" in newness of life indicates that the life is not conceived of as otiose possession but as engaging the activity of the believer.

5-11

> 5 For if we have become united with *him* in the likeness of his death, we shall be also *in the likeness* of his resurrection;
> 6 knowing this, that our old man was crucified with *him*, that the body of sin might be done away, that so we should no longer be in bondage to sin;
> 7 for he that hath died is justified from sin.
> 8 But if we died with Christ, we believe that we shall also live with him;
> 9 knowing that Christ being raised from the dead dieth no more; death no more hath dominion over him.
> 10 For the death that he died, he died unto sin once: but the life that he liveth, he liveth unto God.
> 11 Even so reckon ye also yourselves to be dead unto sin, but alive unto God in Christ Jesus.

5 Verse 5 is confirmatory of verse 4, the thought being that we

217

shall walk in newness of life *for the reason* that, having become identified with Christ in the likeness of his death, we shall be also in the likeness of his resurrection. (1) The underlying thought is again the inseparable conjunction of Christ's death and resurrection, and the inference drawn from this conjunction is that if we are united with Christ in his death we must be also in his resurrection. Disjunction in our case is as impossible as disjunction in his. (2) The word used to express our union with Christ in his death and resurrection means, strictly, "grown together"[4]—"if we have become grown together in the likeness of his death". No term could more adequately convey the intimacy of the union involved. It is not that this relationship is conceived of as a process of growth progressively realized. The terms of the clause in question and the context do not allow for this notion. The death of Christ was not a process and neither is our conformity to his death a process. We are in the condition of having become conformed to his death. But "grown together" points to the *closeness* of our relation to him in his death. (3) It is not to be overlooked that it is in the "likeness" of Christ's death we are "grown together".[5] If "grown together" points to the closeness of the relation to Christ's death, "likeness" enunciates an important distinction. Likeness is not identity. The apostle is not dealing here with *our* physical death and resurrection; he is dealing with our death to sin and our resurrection to Spiritual life, as is apparent from the preceding context and will become even more apparent in the verses that follow. Hence it is necessary to introduce the principle of analogy. Our union with Christ in his death and resurrection must not be bereft of its intimacy, but with equal jealousy it must be interpreted in terms of Spiritual and mystical relationship. And the death and resurrection of Christ in their bearing upon us must likewise be construed in such terms. It is to this that "likeness of his death" refers. (4) Although the words "grown together in the likeness" are not repeated in the

---

[4] σύμφυτος occurs only here in the New Testament but *cf.* συνφύομαι in Luke 8:7.

[5] In reference to this point of taking σύμφυτοι with τῷ ὁμοιώματι Lightfoot says that the latter "is to be taken closely with σύμφυτοι 'connate with the likeness'; for the connection is at once suggested by the συν—, and is required by the ellipse" (*Notes, ad loc.*). *Cf.* also Field (*op. cit., ad loc.*) who says that "σύμφυτος has a natural affinity with a dative case; and . . . if no such connexion were intended, St. Paul would, probably, have guarded against misconstruction by writing ἐν ὁμοιώματι, as he has done in Rom. viii. 3, Phil. ii. 7".

second clause, we shall have to assume that they are implied and read "we shall be also in the likeness of the resurrection", the resurrection being the resurrection of Christ.[6] (5) The future tense, "we shall be" is indicative of certainty (*cf.* 5:17, 19).[7]

The sum of verse 5 is, therefore, that if we have become identified with Christ in his death and if the ethical and Spiritual efficacy accruing from his death pertains to us, then we must also derive from his resurrection the ethical and Spiritual virtue which our being identified with him in his resurrection implies. These implications for us of union with Christ make impossible the inference that we may continue in sin that grace may abound. Grace reigns only through the mediation of Christ and this mediation is operative for us through union with him in the efficacy of his death and the virtue of his resurrection.

6 Here appeal is made to the transformation wrought by the believer's relation to Christ in order to show that what had been stated in the preceding verse is the only explanation of this radical change. Commentators interpret the "knowing this", with which verse 6 begins, as an appeal to the confirmation derived from the experience of the believer.[8] It is questionable if this is the precise intent. It seems rather that it is Paul's way of introducing another element of truth (*cf.* vs. 9) directly relevant to his argument and which his readers ought to know and acknowledge to be truth, even though the implications were not perspicuous to them and therefore needed explication. The truth in question is that "our old man has been crucified with Christ in order that the body of sin might be destroyed, to the end that no longer should we serve sin"—this defines for us the content of that which is said to be known.

(1) "Our old man" is the old self or ego, the unregenerate man in his entirety in contrast with the new man as the regenerate man in his entirety. It is a mistake to think of the believer as both an old man and new man or as having in him both the

---

[6] On ἀλλὰ καί *cf.* Lightfoot: *Notes, ad loc.* The clause is *a fortiori;* in Lightfoot's terms ἀλλά "is used to show that there is a distinction in favour of the proposition stated in the apodosis" or, as Alford says (*op. cit., ad loc.*) "ἀλλά after a hypothetical clause serves to strengthen the inference".

[7] *Cf.* Gifford: *op. cit., ad loc.*

[8] *Cf.* Meyer who says that "the *objective* relation is confirmed by the corresponding experimental *conscious knowledge*" (*op. cit., ad loc.*); Hodge: *op. cit., ad loc.*

old man and the new man, the latter in view of regeneration and the former because of remaining corruption. That this is not Paul's concept is made apparent here by the fact that the "old man" is represented as having been crucified with Christ and the tense indicates a once-for-all definitive act after the pattern of Christ's crucifixion. The "old man" can no more be regarded as in the process of being crucified than Christ in his sphere could he thus regarded. Furthermore, as was noted already, Paul is insisting in this context upon the definitive breach with sin which occurs through union with Christ in his death, and the appeal to the crucifixion of the old man is coordinate with this insistence and particularly illustrative or probative of it. Eph. 4:22–24; Col. 3:9, 10 do not support the other view but confirm the conception stated above.[9]

(2) "The body of sin" has been interpreted figuratively by many commentators and sin is viewed as an organism with many members. Substantially the same view is represented by those who take body in the sense of "mass" and interpret Paul as referring to the mass of sin and corruption.[10] There is no need, however, to resort to any such figurative interpretation. "Body" can well refer in this case to the physical organism. "Body" is certainly used in this sense in verse 12 in the expression "your mortal body". The same is true in 8:10, 11, 13, 23; 12:1 (cf. I Cor. 6:13, 15, 16, 20; II Cor. 4:10; Phil. 1:20; 3:21; Col. 2:11; I Thess. 5:23). These references suffice to show the extent to which the apostle thought of sin and sanctification as associated with the body. The expression "the body of sin" would mean the body as conditioned and controlled by sin, the sinful body. If this is the meaning how can he speak of "the body of sin" as being brought to n ought? It is altogether in accord with the

---

[9] For a fuller treatment of this question by the writer see *Principles of Conduct* (London and Grand Rapids, 1957), pp. 211–219.

[10] "Plainly, as the expression in the preceding clause, the *old man*, is figurative, so is this other, the *body of sin*, and doth not mean the human body, but that whole system of corrupt principles, propensities, lusts, and passions, which have, since the fall, possessed man's nature, and is co-extended and commensurate to all the human powers and faculties" (James Fraser: *A Treatise on Sanctification*, London, 1897, p. 61). To the same effect is Calvin who says that it does not mean "flesh and bones, but the corrupted mass; for man, left to his own nature, is a mass made up of sin" (*op. cit., ad loc.*). Hodge favours the view that sin is personified and is represented as an organism with members. *Cf.* also Philippi who regards the expression as figurative.

thought of this passage, as a whole and in its discrete elements, that the definitive breach with sin should be conceived of as drawing within its scope the body as well as the spirit of the believer. The body is an integral part of personality and since the old man has been crucified the destruction of the body of sin is an indispensable aspect of that radical transformation of the entire person which the crucifixion of the old man connotes. The body of the believer is no longer a body conditioned and controlled by sin. The body that is his now is one conditioned and controlled by what has come to be the ruling principle of the believer in his totality, namely, "obedience unto righteousness" (vs. 16). In this verse the destruction of the body of sin is stated to be the *purpose* of the crucifixion of the old man; the clause in question is one of purpose. This does not require or warrant the narrowing of the concept expressed by the "old man" nor does it require a broadening of the denotation of "the body of sin". That the purpose served by the crucifixion of the old man should in this instance be defined to be the destruction of the sinful body indicates the extent to which sinfulness as associated with the body loomed on the horizon of the apostle. The subsequent parts of this epistle and his other epistles will corroborate this practical concern.[11]

(3) The concluding clause of verse 6 also expresses purpose, "to the end that no longer should we serve sin". It is uncertain whether this should be taken with the preceding clause alone or with the two preceding clauses. But the sense is not materially affected by this uncertainty. In any case the purpose served by what precedes is that the bondservice to sin might be terminated. This notion of bondservice to sin and release from it is one that pervades the succeeding verses. Here we are introduced to it for the first time. The definitive cleavage with sin, which is the fundamental premise of this chapter, is here defined in terms of

---

[11] Any allegation to the effect that this interpretation would tend to represent the body as the source or seat of sinfulness is without any warrant. That Paul did not regard the body as the source or seat of sin lies on the face of his epistles. But the apostle was concrete and practical and he knew only too well from experience and observation (as the references given above indicate) the extent to which sin is associated with and registered through the body. There is no under-estimation of the sins of the human spirit but there is an honest assessment of the sinfulness that characterizes the body and of the sins particularly associated with the body. It is this concrete interest that comes to expression here in the emphasis placed upon the *body* as sinful.

deliverance from the bondservice to sin which characterized the pre-Christian state. This bondservice, it should be noted, is conceived of as one that we voluntarily render—we serve sin. It is not a service to which we are involuntarily and compulsorily consigned. This appears throughout the passage and must be taken into account.

7 Many commentators regard verse 7 as a general proposition.[12] While it is not possible to be decisively dogmatic, yet the context would rather favour the view that the apostle is here again referring to the death of the believer with Christ through baptism into Jesus' death. At least this thought had been sufficiently stressed in the preceding verses (*cf.* vss. 2, 3, 5) that there is no necessity to consider verse 7 as other than a succinct statement of what had been developed in the preceding verses and introduced here by way of confirmation in support of the doctrine stated in verse 6. Furthermore, the first clause in verse 8, "But if we died with Christ" would suggest that verse 7 is to be interpreted in that sense. "Justified from sin" will have to bear the forensic meaning in view of the forensic import of the word "justify". But since the context deals with deliverance from the power of sin the thought is, no doubt, that of being "quit "of sin. The decisive breach with the reigning power of sin is viewed after the analogy of the kind of dismissal which a judge gives when an arraigned person is justified. Sin has no further claim upon the person who is thus vindicated. This judicial aspect from which deliverance from the power of sin is to be viewed needs to be appreciated. It shows that the forensic is present not only in justification but also in that which lies at the basis of sanctification. A judgment is executed upon the power of sin in the death of Christ (*cf.* John 12:31) and deliverance from this power on the part of the believer arises from the efficacy of this judgment. This also prepares us for the interpretation of the forensic terms which Paul uses later in 8:1, 3, namely, "condemnation" and "condemned", and shows that these terms may likewise point to that which Christ once for all wrought in reference to the *power* of sin (8:3) and to our deliverance from this *power* in virtue of the judgment executed upon it in Jesus' cross (8:1).

[12] For example, the criminal who died is no longer liable to the penalty of his capital crime—he has fulfilled the demands of justice.

8 The teaching of verse 8 is essentially that of verses 3 and 5. The pivotal thought of this passage is that believers "died to sin" (vs. 2) and the succeeding verses are the explication. Now in verse 8 the reason why believers have died to sin is given expressly in terms of having died with Christ, and the verses which follow show why dying with Christ entails death to sin. It is not, however, the fact of having died with Christ that bears the emphasis in this instance but living together with him. Dying with Christ is assumed and the inference is drawn that we shall also live with him. Two features of this inference are worthy of note. (1) The certitude of faith in this result is indicated in "we believe". It is an article of faith, not of conjecture, that the life of Jesus' resurrection belongs to those who have been united with Christ in his death. (2) The future tense, "we shall live" does not refer exclusively to the future resurrection state but, as found above (*cf.* vs. 5), points to the certainty of participation in the resurrection life of Christ here and now; it is the life of Spiritual, mystical union. No doubt the resurrection of the body is the ultimate fruition of this union. But we may not restrict the thought to that hope.

9 This verse expresses the ground upon which the assurance of living together with Christ is entertained. There can be suspension or interruption of participation in Christ's resurrection life or reversion to death in sin no more than can the fact of Jesus' resurrection be negated or repeated. "Christ being raised from the dead dies no more". And because of union with Christ in his resurrection the newness of life which this union involves for the believer is as definitively abiding as is the resurrection of Christ. The irreversibility of Jesus' resurrection is interpreted in the concluding clause of verse 9 as meaning that "death no longer rules over him". This implies that death did at one time rule over him. Because he was vicariously identified with sin, he was likewise identified with the wages of sin which is death. And so he was subject to the power of death. The resurrection from the dead is the guarantee that he vanquished the power of death and this victory over death is an irrevocable finality. Death can never again lord it over him. The finality of the resurrection of Christ, emphasized here in the strongest terms, certifies again the decisiveness of the breach with the power of sin which is the burden of this passage. The believer is not regarded as dying and rising with Christ again and again. Undoubtedly there is process and progression in the believer's life and this may properly be understood as progressive realization of the implications and claims of having died and risen with Christ. But the dying and rising with Christ are not viewed as process but as definitive and decisive event and can no more be construed as continuous process than can the death and resurrection of Christ himself.

10 Verse 10[13] is confirmatory and the accent falls upon the once-for-allness of the death of Christ. The apostle does not weary of reiterating the finality and decisiveness of that event, for, as we have seen, it is the implication of this once-for-allness that is his paramount interest in this part of the epistle. We are not served, however, with monotonous repetition. We are now introduced to one of the most significant statements regarding the meaning of the death of Christ—it is that Christ "died to sin". Admittedly it is difficult to determine the force of this expression. In verse 2 the same formula is used with reference to our death to sin and in verse 11 we are said "to be dead to sin". Is it possible to apply the same meaning to the death of Christ? It would appear to be arbitrary to interpret the formula as it applies to Christ in a way entirely different from the meaning in verses 2 and 11. Furthermore, there is a parallelism between verses 10 and 11, Christ's dying to sin once (vs. 10) being parallel to our being dead to sin (vs. 11), and Christ's living to God (vs. 10) being parallel to our living to God in Christ Jesus (vs. 11). The parallels indicate similitude, and if Christ's dying to sin bears no analogy to our death to sin the similitude would break down. So we shall have to proceed on the assumption that the formula as it applies to us provides the direction in which we are to seek the meaning as it applies to Christ.[14]

---

[13] The neuter ὅ is most probably to be taken in the sense of "as regards". "The Neut. ὅ before a whole clause, in the sense of *as to* etc. (like *quod* in Latin), occurs in Rom. vi. 10 . . . Gal. ii. 20. . . . In both passages, however, ὅ may also be taken for an objective case: *quod vivit, vita, quam vivit*" (G. B. Winer: *A Grammar of the Idiom of the New Testament*, Andover, 1892, § 24, 4, note 3).

[14] *Cf.*, for this interpretation, Meyer, Philippi, Gifford, *et al.* The interpretation insisted upon by Haldane (*op. cit., ad loc.*) that it refers exclusively to dying to the guilt of sin fails to take account of the leading thought of vss.

As applied to believers in verses 2 and 11 the thought is that they died to the power of sin. May the same be said of Christ? It cannot be said of Christ that sin exercised its power over him in the same sense in which it ruled over us. We were the bond-slaves of sin in its defilement and power; sin did not thus rule over him. Nevertheless, Christ was identified in such a way with the sin which he vicariously bore that he dealt not only with its guilt but also with its power. Death ruled over him until he broke its power (vs. 9). So sin may be said to have ruled over him in that his humiliation state was conditioned by the sin with which he was vicariously identified. He was made sin (II Cor. 5:21), and sin as power must be taken into account in this relationship. It was by his own dying that he destroyed the power of sin, and in his resurrection he entered upon a state that was not conditioned by sin. There is good reason to believe that it is this victory over sin as power that the apostle has in view when he says that Christ "died to sin once". And it is because Christ triumphed over the power of sin in his death that those united to him in his death die to the power of sin and become dead to sin (vss. 2, 11).

The latter part of verse 10 refers to Christ's own resurrection life and is described as living to God. This does not reflect prejudicially upon the completeness of Christ's devotion to the Father in his state of humiliation. The meaning is to be derived from the contrast between his pre-resurrection and post-resurrection states. The former was conditioned by the sin which he vicariously bore, and sin is the contradiction of what God is. But since he made an end of sin in his death, his resurrection life is in no way conditioned by what is antithetical to God—no factor enters into that life that is alien to the perfection and glory of God.

11 This verse is hortatory. "Reckon yourselves" is imperative rather than indicative.[15] What is commanded needs to be carefully noted. We are not commanded to become dead to sin and

---

1-11. And it also misses an all-important aspect of our Lord's vicarious identification with sin and of the efficacy accruing to us from his victory over sin's power.

[15] λογίζεσθε is preferably taken as imperative. The hortatory flows more naturally from what precedes and also agrees with the imperatives which follow in vss. 12, 13.

alive to God; these are presupposed. And it is not by reckoning these to be facts that they become facts. The force of the imperative is that we are to reckon with and appreciate the facts which already obtain by virtue of union with Christ. The expression "dead unto sin" implies an abiding state or condition resultant upon the once-for-all decisive event of having died to sin by union with Christ in the efficacy of his death. And the complementation of "dead unto sin" and "alive unto God," as parallel to Christ's death to sin and life to God (vs. 10), implies that the life to God is of abiding continuance just as being dead to sin is. The security and permanence of this life to God are insured by the fact that it is "in Christ Jesus" the life is maintained.[16]

B. THE IMPERATIVES FOR THE SANCTIFIED
(6:12–23)

12–14

12 Let not sin therefore reign in your mortal body, that ye should obey the lusts thereof:
13 neither present your members unto sin *as* instruments of unrighteousness; but present yourselves unto God, as alive from the dead, and your members *as* instruments of righteousness unto God.
14 For sin shall not have dominion over you: for ye are not under law, but under grace.

12 At verse 12 we have again the language of exhortation, introduced in the form of inference to be drawn from what precedes: "Let not sin therefore reign in your mortal body, to the end that ye should obey its lusts". It is not to be supposed that sin is conceived of as reigning in the believer and that now he is exhorted to terminate that reign of sin. This would run counter to all that has been set forth in the preceding verses regarding the status of the believer as dead to sin and alive to God. And, furthermore, we have in this passage the assurance

---

[16] The addition at the end of vs. 11 τῷ κυρίῳ ἡμῶν cannot be lightly excluded as not genuine, since it is supported by ℵ C and the mass of the cursives as well as by some ancient versions. Von Soden adopts this reading. It would be rather gratuitous to argue that the insertion arose from assimilation to vs. 23.

that sin will not have dominion because the believer is not under law but under grace (vs. 14). The force of the imperative can be understood only in the light of the relation of the indicative to the imperative. Sin does not have the dominion—this is the indicative. This indicative is not only expressly asserted in verse 14, it is implicit in all that the apostle has argued in the verses that precede verse 12. Let not sin reign—this is the imperative. And it flows from the indicative. It is only because sin does not reign that it can be said, "Therefore let not sin reign". In other words, the presupposition of the exhortation is not that sin reigns but the opposite, that it does not reign, and it is for that reason that the exhortation can have validity and appeal. To say to the slave who has not been emancipated, "Do not behave as a slave" is to mock his enslavement. But to say the same to the slave who has been set free is the necessary appeal to put into effect the privileges and rights of his liberation. So in this case the sequence is: sin does not have the dominion; therefore do not allow it to reign. Deliverance from the dominion of sin is both the basis of and the incentive to the fulfilment of the exhortation, "Let not sin reign".

The mortal body is without question the physical organism as subject to dissolution (*cf.* vs. 6; 8:10, 11), and the lusts are those particularly associated with the body. The concrete and practical interest of the apostle is evinced in the prominence given here, as in verse 6, to the lust associated with and registered through the body. The lusts of the body are conceived of as demanding obedience. It is a spurious spirituality that can be indifferent to the claims of holiness as they bear upon the sanctification of our physical being. Death to sin and life to God, deliverance from the dominion of sin, will demonstrate their reality in the tangible and visible by denying to the lusts of the body the gratification they demand. And the mortality of the body underlines the folly of yielding to its lust; the life of the believer is incorruptible and immortal.

13 The interpretation of verse 13 must be governed by the interpretation given above of verse 12. If "mortal body" means the physical organism, then the "members" referred to in this verse must mean the members of the body, such as eye, hand, and foot. Sin is conceived of as a master at whose disposal we place these members in order that they may be instruments[17] to promote unrighteousness. The exhortation is to the effect that we are not to go on placing our physical organs at the disposal of sin for the furtherance of such an end. The positive counterpart is that we are to present ourselves to God as those alive from the dead and our members as instruments of righteousness to God. This fuller statement shows that although the thought had been concentrated upon the bodily (vss. 12, 13a), yet the apostle does not regard the physical as comprehending the sum-total of devotion. Believers are to present *themselves* to God as those alive from the dead. Here the whole personality is in view. In the last clause the members of the body are mentioned again. The tense that is used in this instance indicates the once-for-allness of the dedication involved in the presentation of ourselves and of our members. We are regarded as presenting ourselves and our members once for all to God for his service and the promotion of righteousness.[18]

14 The first clause in verse 14, "For sin will not have dominion over you" is a statement of assured fact and should not be interpreted as imperative nor as pointing to a blessing reserved for the future. As in instances noted already, the future tense here also expresses the certainty of that which is affirmed. As indicative rather than imperative the assurance affirmed makes valid and relevant the exhortations in verses 12 and 13 and provides the encouragement and incentive to the fulfilment of these imperatives. Obedience to the latter is supported by the assurance that God's grace insures the realization of what is contemplated in the exhortations.

The second clause in verse 14, "For ye are not under law but under grace" gives the reason why sin will not exercise the dominion. "Law" in this case must be understood in the general sense of law as law. That it is not to be understood in the sense of the Mosaic law as an economy appears plainly from the fact that many who were under the Mosaic economy were the recip-

---

[17] The term in Greek is "weapons"; *cf.* 13:12; II Cor. 6:7; 10:4. Lightfoot's note is to the point: "Sin is regarded as a sovereign (μὴ βασιλευέτω ver. 12), who demands the military service of subjects (εἰς τὸ ὑπακούειν ver. 12), levies their quota of arms (ὅπλα ἀδικίας ver. 13), and gives them their soldier's pay of death (ὀψώνια ver. 23)" (*Notes, ad loc.*).

[18] *Cf.* Winer: *op. cit.*, § 43, 3a, b; Philippi, Meyer, Gifford, *ad loc.*

ients of grace and in that regard were under grace, and also from the fact that relief from the Mosaic law as an economy does not of itself place persons in the category of being under grace. Law must be understood, therefore, in much more general terms of law as commandment. In order to understand the force of the clause in question it is necessary to state what law *can* do and what it *cannot* do, and it is in the light of what it cannot do that the meaning of "under grace" will become apparent. (1) Law commands and demands. (2) Law pronounces approval and blessing upon conformity to its demands (*cf.* 7:10; Gal. 3:12). (3) Law pronounces condemnation upon every infraction of its demand (*cf.* Gal. 3:10). (4) Law exposes and convicts of sin (*cf.* 7:7, 14; Heb. 4:12). (5) Law excites and incites sin to more aggravated transgression (*cf.* 7:8, 9, 11, 13). What law *cannot* do is implicit in these limits of its potency. (1) Law can do nothing to justify the person who has violated it. (2) Law can do nothing to relieve the bondage of sin; it accentuates and confirms that bondage.

It is this last feature of the impotency of the law that is particularly in view in the clause in question. The person who is "under law", upon whom only law has been brought to bear, whose life is being determined by the resources of law, is the bondservant of sin. Hence to be "under law" is to be the bondservant of sin. It is in this light that "under grace" becomes significant; the word "grace" sums up everything that by way of contrast with law is embraced in the provisions of redemption. Believers have come *under* all the resources of redeeming and renewing grace which find their epitome in the death and resurrection of Christ. The virtue which ever continues to emanate from the death and resurrection of Christ is operative in them through union with him. All of this the expression "under grace" implies. And, in terms of this passage and of the subject with which it is concerned, there is an absolute antithesis between the potency and provisions of law and the potency and provisions of grace. Grace is the sovereign will and power of God coming to expression for the deliverance of men from the servitude of sin. Because this is so, to be "under grace" is the guarantee that sin will not exercise the dominion—"sin will not lord it over you, for ye are not under law but under grace".

15–23

15 What then? shall we sin, because we are not under law, but under grace? God forbid.

16 Know ye not, that to whom ye present yourselves *as* servants unto obedience, his servants ye are whom ye obey; whether of sin unto death, or of obedience unto righteousness?

17 But thanks be to God, that, whereas ye were servants of sin, ye became obedient from the heart to that form of teaching whereunto ye were delivered;

18 and being made free from sin, ye became servants of righteousness.

19 I speak after the manner of men because of the infirmity of your flesh: for as ye presented your members *as* servants to uncleanness and to iniquity unto iniquity, even so now present your members *as* servants to righteousness unto sanctification.

20 For when ye were servants of sin, ye were free in regard of righteousness.

21 What fruit then had ye at that time in the things whereof ye are now ashamed? for the end of those things is death.

22 But now being made free from sin and become servants to God, ye have your fruit unto sanctification, and the end eternal life.

23 For the wages of sin is death; but the free gift of God is eternal life in Christ Jesus our Lord.

15 At verse 15 the apostle takes up again essentially the same question as that with which the chapter opened. The question, however, assumes a new form because the precise consideration which provokes the question is different. At verse 1 the question is oriented to the consideration that where sin abounded grace did much more abound and to the fallacy of inferring from this fact that we may continue in sin so that grace may abound all the more. At verse 15 the question is oriented to the consideration that we are not under law and to the fallacy of the inference that we may, for that reason, transgress the law, that the law ceases to have relevance to us and that therefore we may sin. "What then? are we to sin, because we are not under law, but under grace?" The answer is the usual formula of emphatic denial which again is properly rendered by "God forbid". This indicates that not being "under law", in the sense of the preceding verse, in no way releases us from the obligation to conformity with the law and gives no license to sin as the transgression of the law. In one sense the believer is not "under law", in another sense he is (*cf.* I Cor. 9:21). In the verses which follow verse 15 Paul proceeds to show how intolerable is the inference that we may sin because we are not under law but under grace.

16 Here we have the same appeal to what his readers know, or at least should know, as we found at verse 3. The principle established by the question is that we are the bondslaves of that to which we present ourselves for obedience. It is that expressed by the Lord himself: "Every one that committeth sin is the bondservant of sin" (John 8:34); "No servant can serve two masters: for either he will hate the one, and love the other; or else he will hold to the one, and despise the other. Ye cannot serve God and mammon" (Luke 16:13). In like manner the apostle shows in this verse that there are only two alignments in the ethico-religious realm and that the criterion of our alignment is that to which we render obedience, whether it be "sin unto death" or "obedience unto righteousness".

What is meant by "death" in this instance is difficult to determine. Most probably it is used inclusively to refer to death in all its aspects, culminating in that eternal death of "everlasting destruction from the presence of the Lord and the glory of his power" (II Thess. 1:9). Sin is deathly and death in every respect follows in its wake. Similarly the righteousness which obedience promotes should also be interpreted inclusively to refer to righteousness in all its aspects, culminating, indeed, in the consummated righteousness of the new heavens and the new earth.

The emphasis upon obedience shows that obedience to God is the criterion of our devotion to him and that the principle of righteousness is to present ourselves to God as servants unto obedience.

17 In the thanksgiving that the believers at Rome "were servants of sin", the emphasis rests upon the past tense and in order to express the thought in English we have to use some such conjunction as "whereas" or "although"—"whereas ye were servants of sin". The emphasis rests upon the change that took place when they came to obey the form of teaching unto which they were delivered. There are three questions to be considered in connection with the latter part of this text. (1) What is the "form of teaching"? There can be no reasonable question but it means the pattern or standard of teaching and there is no warrant for supposing that it was a specifically Pauline pattern as distinguished from other forms of apostolic teaching.[19] It is "the form of sound words" (II Tim. 1:13; *cf.* I Tim. 1:10; II Tim. 4:3; Tit. 1:9; 2:1), and in this instance there is stress upon the ethical implications of gospel teaching. (2) This pattern of gospel teaching is represented as that to which obedience was rendered, and the change from the service of sin is registered in and characterized by obedience to a well-defined and articulated doctrinal pattern. The supposition that Christianity has no fixed pattern of teaching regulative of thought and practice is entirely alien to the apostle's conception of the Christian ethic. The pattern prescribed in the gospel in no way interferes with the true liberty and spontaneity of the believer—he obeys "from the heart". Objective prescription, presupposed in obedience, is not incompatible with the voluntariness indispensable to obedience. (3) We might have expected the apostle to say that this form of teaching had been delivered to the believers, but, instead, he says that *they* were delivered to it—they were handed over to the gospel pattern. This indicates that their devotion to the gospel was one of total commitment and that this commitment is not one of their option but is that to which they are subjected. This again underlines the objectivity of the pattern as well as our passivity in being committed to it, an objectivity and passivity which in no way militate against the wholehearted voluntariness of the result, namely, the commitment of obedience from the heart.

18 These observations regarding verse 17 are confirmed by verse 18, which must be taken in close connection with verse 17. The first clause of verse 18, "and being made free from sin", corresponds to "ye *were* servants of sin" in verse 17, and the last clause corresponds to "ye obeyed from the heart the form of teaching unto which ye were delivered". However, the passivity of this change in both its negative and positive aspects is now expressed. They were the subjects of deliverance from sin and

---

[19] *Cf.* the fine statement of F. J. A. Hort: *Prolegomena to St. Paul's Epistles to the Romans and the Ephesians* (London, 1895), pp. 32f.

they were made the bondservants of righteousness. The force of the passive in both cases must not be overlooked. This brings to the forefront the implications of the passive in verse 17, namely, that they were delivered up to the gospel pattern of teaching. And the commitment involved is to the same effect. Commitment to the gospel pattern is equivalent to bondservice to righteousness.

19 When the apostle says, "I speak after the manner of men" he is referring to the *form* of his teaching in the preceding and succeeding verses. He describes the condition of unbelievers as slavery to sin and he also describes the state of believers as bondservice to righteousness. The institution of slavery, well known to his readers, is the medium through which he expresses the truth. In using this analogy drawn from the sphere of human relations he speaks after the manner of men. After all, the new life in Christ is not "slavery" as it exists among men; it is the highest and only freedom. But the institution of slavery does service to set forth the totality of our commitment to God in that emancipation from the bondage of sin which union with Christ involves. It is on account of the infirmity of their flesh that he speaks thus to his readers. The dulness of our understanding makes it necessary that we be taught the truth in figures drawn from the sphere of our human relations.[20]

The thought of the latter part of verse 19 is similar to that of verse 13. Here, however, the past state in which our members were presented in the bondservice of sin enforces, by way of parallel and contrast, the necessity of presenting our members

---

[20] The question on which interpreters are divided in reference to this statement is whether the infirmity of the flesh to which the apostle refers is to be taken intellectually or morally. If the former, then it is to meet the frailty of understanding that he speaks after the manner of men. If the latter, then he speaks thus in order to meet the moral weakness of his readers so as not to lay too great a burden upon their moral resources—ethical demands are accommodated to our infirmity. This latter view is not compatible with the emphasis of the context—it is the totality of commitment to the service of God and of righteousness that is being urged. In Meyer's words, this view "would be inappropriate to the morally ideal character of the whole hortatory discourse, which is not injured by the concrete figurative form" (*op. cit., ad loc.*). *Cf.* also Bengel, Gifford, Sanday and Headlam, Hodge, *ad loc.* This does not mean, however, that the infirmity of the flesh does not reflect on our moral weakness. Undoubtedly weakness of understanding is bound up with our moral weakness. The only point is that "speaking after the manner of men" is not to be understood as an adjustment of demands to our weakness but as an accommodation of the form of speech to the weakness of our understanding.

THE EPISTLE TO THE ROMANS

now in the bondservice of righteousness. And the terms in which
the past state is described are peculiarly adapted to set forth
the intensity of dedication to the service of sin—"ye presented
your members as servants to uncleanness and to iniquity unto
iniquity". "Uncleanness" reflects upon the corruption and
defilement to which we were dedicated, "iniquity" upon sin as
violation of law (*cf.* I John 3:4). The end to which the service
of iniquity (lawlessness) was directed is nothing less than the
aggravation and confirmation of that iniquity—it was "unto
iniquity".

The exhortation is in the terms of both *parallel* and *contrast* to
the definition of the sinful state. The *parallel* appears in the
construction of the sentence; there is protasis and apodosis—as
one thing was true so let something else now be true. It also
appears in the repetition of the language of dedication, "present
your members as servants"—there is to be no relaxation in
respect of the *bondservice* involved. On the other hand, the *contrast*
appears in the kind of bondservice rendered and the end to
which it is directed. In the former state it was bondservice to
"uncleanness and iniquity"; now it is bondservice to "righteousness". Formerly the bondservice was directed to "iniquity";
now it is to be directed unto "sanctification"[21]. The bondservice
of righteousness, which defines the dedication of the believer,
and the end to which this dedication is directed have in view the
holiness of heart and of life without which no man shall see the
Lord (*cf.* Heb. 12:14; I Cor. 1:20; I Thess. 4:3, 4, 7). The
concrete and practical interest is evinced again, as in verse 13,
by focusing attention upon our physical organs. This concen-

---

[21] "Sanctification" in English can denote a process or a state. Notwithstanding the opinion of some able commentators (e.g., Gifford, Sanday and
Headlam) ἁγιασμός here, as well as in vs. 22, does not most suitably refer to
a process but to the state of holiness or consecration. It is not by any means
apparent that in other instances ἁγιασμός contemplates process rather than
state (I Cor. 1:30; I Thess. 4:3, 4, 7; II Thess. 2:13; I Tim. 2:15; Heb.
12:14; I Pet. 1:2). In several of these the meaning holiness or consecration
is far more suitable, and it is questionable if the thought of process is in the
forefront in any. Furthermore, in this context, as we have found, the emphasis
falls upon the once-for-all breach with sin and commitment to righteousness.
Hence the rendering "holiness" of the A.V. is more suitable than the ambiguous
word "sanctification". And "consecration", though not felicitous as translation, may convey the thought most effectively. Arndt and Gingrich (*op. cit.*,
ad loc.) do not appear to be on good ground when, of I Cor. 1:30, they say that
the abstract is used for the concrete, namely, the author of holiness. Surely
this misses something that is central in the relation of Christ to the believer.

234

tration of thought upon our bodily members does not detract from the dedication that must characterize the whole person, as becomes apparent in the next verse. It only underlines the concreteness of the demands of holiness and of the ways in which it is exemplified.

20 It is not easy to determine the precise relation that verse 20 sustains to the preceding verse. But the most tenable view, it would appear, is that it must be taken in close conjunction with the question which follows in verse 21 and, when thus interpreted, both verses (20, 21) are intended to enforce the necessity of compliance with the exhortation in the latter part of verse 19. In paraphrase the thought would be as follows: "Present your members servants to righteousness unto holiness (vs. 19). For consider that in your former state of service to sin you had no concern at all for righteousness and no good fruit whatsoever accrued from abandonment to the service of sin, nothing indeed but that of which you are now ashamed and the end of which is death. How urgent, therefore, is the claim of righteousness and the necessity of commitment to its bondservice."

"For when ye were servants of sin, ye were free in regard of righteousness"—this is simply to say that they were not the bondservants of righteousness and righteousness. therefore, did not exercise its authority and mastery over them. They were carefree in respect of the demands of righteousness; with undivided heart and a single eye they were the bondservants of sin, and that was the only mastery they knew.

21 The question of verse 21, as rendered in the version, implies a decisive negative as the answer. "What fruit then had ye at that time in the things whereof ye are now ashamed?" The implied answer is "none". "Fruit", on this construction, would have the meaning which it has uniformly in Paul's letters, namely, good fruit (*cf.* 1:13; 15:28; Gal. 5:22; Eph. 5:9; Phil. 1:11, 22; 4:17). It is possible, however, to punctuate verse 21 so that the question is: "What fruit then had ye at that time?"[22] And the answer would be: "In the things whereof ye are now ashamed". The only fruit accruing from the service of sin was the things which now fill with shame. Both constructions

---

[22] See Meyer (*op. cit., ad loc.*) for a list of those holding this view which he himself for good reasons rejects.

are possible and yield a good sense. While there is no decisive reason for rejecting the second construction, there is more to be said in favour of the former. (1) The second view would require departure from the usual meaning of "fruit" as that which is good unless qualified as evil.[23] (2) The first view accords more suitably with the last clause of verse 21; if the answer to the question is that no fruit (in the sense of good fruit) has accrued from the life of sin, then the clause, "for the end of those things is death", supplies the reason for or adds confirmation to the negative answer which the question implies—there is no good fruit, for the end of these things is death. (3) On the second construction the concluding clause would give the reason why the fruits of the sinful way of life cause shame. It would scarcely be proper to restrict the reason for shame to the fact that the end of these things is death. The thought is not merely that the things of the life of sin will put to shame and disappoint but that believers are ashamed of them.[24] (4) The sharp contrast between "at that time" and "now" does not require, as has been alleged,[25] the second construction. The contrast retains its full force on the other view, the implication being that even *at that time*, before they came to realize the shame, there was no fruit in the service of sin.

On either construction, however, the following observations are necessary. (1) Believers are ashamed of their past life—"so far are they from endeavouring to excuse it, that, on the contrary, they feel ashamed of themselves. Yea, further, they call to mind the remembrance of their own disgrace, that being thus ashamed, they may more truly and more readily be humbled before God".[26] (2) Death, which is the end of these things, can be nothing less than death in its most ultimate expression and, though not restricted to everlasting perdition, must nevertheless include it. Emancipation from the service of sin interrupts this sequence only because there is deliverance from sin itself (*cf.* vs. 22), and this

---

[23] *Cf.* the references given above and Meyer's discussion of the point in question; also Lightfoot (*Notes, ad loc.*) who says, "St. Paul never uses καρπός of the results of evil-doing, but always substitutes ἔργα: see Gal. v. 19, 22, Eph. v. 9, 11".

[24] "He only then is imbued with the principles of Christian philosophy, who has well learnt to be really displeased with himself, and to be confounded with shame for his own wretchedness" (Calvin: *op. cit., ad loc.*).

[25] *Cf.* Godet and Denney, *ad loc.*

[26] Calvin: *op. cit., ad loc.*

interruption does not disestablish the fact that death is the inevitable issue of sin. The sequence is obviated and deliverance from it obtains only where there is the removal of sin itself.

22 Verses 21, 22 stand in conspicuous contrast with each other. Verse 21 shows the fruitlessness, the shame, and the death which follow in the wake of sin. Verse 22 shows the fruit and the issue of deliverance from sin. The same passivity in respect of the subjects of this deliverance appears here as in verse 18; they have been delivered and they have been made bondservants. The only significant difference from verse 18 in the first part of verse 22 is that instead of saying bondservants "to righteousness" (vs. 18) the apostle now speaks of being made bondservants "to God". This shows that the one presupposes the other. Bondservice to righteousness is not to an abstract quality; it is to the righteousness which God's perfection demands, and the personal relationship to God is never suppressed. Bondservice to God, on the other hand, must exemplify itself in obedience to the concrete and practical demands of righteousness. The leading feature of the contrast in verse 22, however, is the emphasis upon the fruit enjoyed and the issue resulting—"ye have your fruit unto holiness, and the end eternal life". In the service of sin there was no fruit; now they bear fruit that is unto holiness.[27] And this fruit-bearing has its final issue in eternal life. Just as death, the issue of sin (vs. 21), should be taken inclusively, so should eternal life. While not restricted to the consummated life of the world to come this must, nevertheless, be included. The final issue of deliverance from sin, of bondservice to God, and of the fruit-bearing that is unto holiness is the *possession* of life incorruptible in the age to come.

23 This is the triumphant conclusion to chapter 6 and should be compared in this respect to 5:21 as the triumphant conclusion to chapter 5. The contrast between sin and grace is maintained and there is summation of what had been set forth in more detail in the preceding verses. But there are also new elements of thought, at least of emphasis. These concern principally the contrast between "wages" and "free gift". Remuneration is the principle by which we become heirs of death; unmerited favour

---

[27] See note 21 for the rendering "holiness".

is that by which we receive eternal life. Death is earned,[28] eternal life is purely gratuitous. In the clause, "the wages of sin is death", there are two thoughts: (1) that the death with which we are inflicted is no more and no less than what we have earned; (2) that death is the inevitable consequence of sin. Rectitude governs the payment of wages and we therefore receive exactly and inevitably what we owe. In the clause, "but the free gift of God is eternal life in Christ Jesus our Lord" the governing idea is that of God's free grace in contrast with the notion of remuneration, and the magnitude of this free grace is emphasized by the nature of the gift bestowed. The thought is not that the free grace of God issues in eternal life for us, though this is in itself true. But the precise thought is that the free gift *consists* in eternal life. When wages are in operation our lot is death, inescapably and in its ultimate expression. When the free gift of God is in operation our lot is life, eternal and indestructible. How totally alien to such contrasts is the importation of merit in any form or degree into the method of salvation.

In 5:21 the apostle had said that grace reigns through righteousness unto eternal life *through* Jesus Christ our Lord. Here in 6:23 he speaks of eternal life *in* Christ Jesus our Lord. The distinction is to be noted. In this instance the accent falls upon the truth that it is in Christ Jesus eternal life exists for believers. They are never conceived of, even in the highest reaches of the Father's free gift to them, as severed from Christ. And none of the blessings bestowed by the Father, however much the gratuitousness appears, are apart from Christ nor are they enjoyed except in union with him.

---

[28] "The word ὀψώνιον strictly denotes *payment in kind*, then the payment in money which a general gives his soldiers. And so it is obvious that the complement τῆς ἁμαρτίας, *of sin*, is not here the genitive of the object: the wages paid *for* sin, but the genitive of the subject: the wages paid *by* sin" (Godet: *op. cit., ad loc.*). Cf. also quotation from Lightfoot in note 17.

X. DEATH TO THE LAW
(7:1-6)

1-4

1 Or are ye ignorant, brethren (for I speak to men who know the law), that the law hath dominion over a man for so long time as he liveth?
2 For the woman that hath a husband is bound by law to the husband while he liveth; but if the husband die, she is discharged from the law of the husband.
3 So then if, while the husband liveth, she be joined to another man, she shall be called an adulteress: but if the husband die, she is free from the law, so that she is no adulteress, though she be joined to another man.
4 Wherefore, my brethren, ye also were made dead to the law through the body of Christ; that ye should be joined to another, *even* to him who was raised from the dead, that we might bring forth fruit unto God.

Romans 7:1-6 is to be connected with what the apostle had stated in 6:14, "Ye are not under law, but under grace". In this earlier context the statement gives the reason or ground of the assurance that sin will not have dominion over the believer. There is, however, at that point no expansion or validation of the proposition that the believer is not under law. For, immediately, the apostle turns to the refutation of the false inference that might be drawn from the proposition. In the verses intervening between 6:14 and 7:1 he had developed the answer to this abuse and now at 7:1 he returns to the question of release from the law and shows how this discharge has come to be. It is preferable, therefore, to relate the question, "Or are ye ignorant?" (7:1) directly with 6:14 rather than with 6:23.[1]

1 The question "Or are ye ignorant?" is an appeal to what the apostle assumes his readers to know, as is evident from the parenthesis which follows, "for I speak to them who know the

---

[1] *Cf.* Lightfoot: *Notes, ad loc.;* Meyer: *op. cit., ad loc.*

law". We are not to regard this as in any way restrictive—he is not distinguishing between those who know and those who do not. All are credited with this knowledge.

What is this law, with the knowledge of which Paul credits his readers? It cannot reasonably be confined to the general principle which he is just about to state, namely, that "the law has dominion over a man for so long a time as he lives". The law they are assumed to know must be more embracive and the principle, that the law has dominion over a man, is one assumed to be readily granted by his readers because of their knowledge of the law in some broader sense. The law assumed to be known is surely the written law of the Old Testament, particularly the Mosaic law. Paul uses "law" in this sense (3:19; 5:13; I Cor. 9:8, 9; 14:21, 24; Gal. 3:10, 19) and there is no need to look for any other denotation here. Gentiles as well as Jews in the church at Rome could be credited with the knowledge of the Old Testament.

The proposition that "the law has dominion over a man for so long a time as he lives" we may properly regard as intended to state a general principle and that the apostle is not referring specifically to the marriage law which in verses 2 and 3 is adduced as an example and application of the general principle. The law binds a man as long as he lives, and the implication is that when he dies that dominion is dissolved.

2, 3 In verses 2 and 3 we have the application of this general principle to the case of marriage. There is no reason to suppose that these verses are anything more than a statement of what holds true in the marital relation of man and wife, and it is quite arbitrary to subject them to allegorical interpretation. It is at verse 4 that the apostle begins to apply the analogy of ordinary marriage to the spiritual sphere of our relations to the law and to Christ. Verses 2 and 3 are illustration and there is nothing in the text to suggest allegorical intent. The facts stated need no exposition, for they are simply to the effect that a wife is bound to her husband as long as he lives, that if, while he lives, she is married to another she thereby commits adultery and will be called an adulteress,[2] but that when the husband dies the

---

[2] On the interpretation of this passage as it bears on the question of divorce for adultery see *Divorce* (Philadelphia, 1953), pp. 78–95, by the writer.

marriage with him is dissolved and she is then free to marry another man. The main point of the illustration is that the death of the husband releases the *woman* from the bond of that marriage. Attention is focused upon the woman as bound and as released, bound as long as the husband lives, released on the event of his death. Nothing is said respecting the man as released from the bond of marriage by the death of his wife, not because this is not in itself true but because this was not germane to the subject being illustrated.

4 It is at verse 4 that the analogy of the marital relation is applied to the subject the apostle has in view. It is the severely restricted feature of the illustration, as we have just noted, that has occasioned much difficulty for expositors. For in the application we (believers) are represented as dying with Christ and by that event released from the bond of the law in order that we might be united to him (Jesus Christ) as raised from the dead. And there seems to be some inversion, if not dislocation, in the application. The husband in the illustration must correspond to the law in the application. The woman in the illustration must correspond to the believer in the application. In other words, we are married to the law as the woman is to the husband and we cannot be released from the law until death occurs, just as the woman is not released until the husband dies. Now, if the parallel were carried through, we should expect the apostle to say that the law had died and that through this death of the law we are released, as the woman in the illustration. But this is not what Paul says. He says rather that "*we* have been put to death to the law". And this does not correspond to the terms of the illustration; in the latter Paul says nothing of the death of the woman but only of the husband. How is this failure to carry out the precise terms of the parallel to be explained?

It has been maintained that although Paul did not expressly say that the law is put to death, nevertheless this is the meaning, and the law is conceived of as put to death through the body of Christ.[3] On this view there is no inversion but only a contraction of thought and expression. It is noteworthy, however,

---

[3] In Philippi's words: "Moreover, since the σῶμα τοῦ Χριστοῦ is to be conceived of as θανατωθέν the law is at the same time slain . . ., we can scarcely speak of an inversion of the simile" (*op. cit., ad loc.*).

that nowhere in this epistle or in the epistle to the Galatians, in both of which he is most intimately concerned with the believer's relation to the law, does the apostle speak of the law as being put to death. His terms are express to the effect that "we have been put to death to the law" (7:4), that "we have been discharged from the law, having died to that wherein we were held fast" (7:6). And he also says: "I through law died to law, in order that I might live to God" (Gal. 2:19). Since he could easily have used the other expression that the law died or was put to death in respect of us, we are constrained to infer that his abstaining from this mode of expression reflects a jealous interest.[4] Consequently the difficulty cannot be resolved by supposing that the parallel is carried out strictly in the thought of verse 4.

The most tenable solution would appear to be that we are not expected to find in verse 4 something that exactly corresponds to the death of the husband in the illustration of verses 2 and 3. The main point of the illustration is that only by the death of her husband is the woman released from the law of her husband. And the main point in the application (vs. 4) is how we may be released from the law. In this latter case there cannot be release by a method that literally follows the pattern of the analogy drawn from marital relations. But, nevertheless, there is a death which releases the bond just as decisively as the death of the husband in the other case. And that death is our death to the law in the death of Christ. This is the definitive dissolution corresponding to the death of the husband in the marital similitude. It should be quite obvious why the apostle did not think or write in terms of a literal parallel. To speak of the death of the woman as dissolving the bond of marriage in verses 2 and 3 would have radically interfered with the analogy because, in this sphere of human relations, when the woman dies she cannot then marry another, and remarriage is something indispensable to the illustration. The only alternative, therefore, in this case of ordinary marriage is to posit the death of the husband. And yet to speak of the death of the law in the spiritual application

---

[4] Philippi's appeal to Eph. 2:15; Col. 2:14, in support of his view that the law is slain, is not cogent. These passages are not really parallel to Rom. 7:4. Besides, Paul's refraining here from the terms used in Eph. 2:15; Col. 2:14 or from terms which would have similar effect only serves to underline the avoidance in this instance of such a notion as that the law was put to death.

would have introduced an erroneous concept. Hence we can speak only of our death to the law. This is entirely feasible in the spiritual sphere because this is precisely what occurs—we die and rise again with Christ, a combination of events entirely irrelevant in the ordinary marital relationship.

Verse 4, therefore, is the unfolding of the way in which grace in contrast with law takes effect unto our deliverance from the dominion of sin. Law, as we found (6:14), confirms and seals our bondage to sin. As long as law governs us there is no possibility of release from the bondage of sin. The only alternative is discharge from the law. This occurs in our union with Christ in his death, because all the virtue of Christ's death in meeting the claims of the law becomes ours and we are free from the bond-service and power of sin to which the law had consigned us.

The expression used in verse 4, "we have been put to death to the law" has been interpreted as signifying the violence perpetrated in the death of Christ.[5] Be this as it may, our passivity and the effectiveness of the action are clearly indicated. "The body of Christ" refers to the crucifixion of our Lord in the body and places in relief the concreteness of that event by which we have been discharged from the law. The purpose designed in our being put to death to the law is stated to be, "that ye should be joined to another, even to him who was raised from the dead, that we might bring forth fruit unto God". Discharge from the law is not an end in itself; it is directed to a *positive* end. This is another way of setting forth what has been repeatedly noted in this part of the epistle, that union with Christ in his death must never be severed from union with him in his resurrection. Here, however, the stress falls not merely on union with Christ in his resurrection but upon union with him as the one who has been raised from the dead. It is union with him, therefore, not only in the virtue and power of that historical event but union with him now and for ever in that identity that belongs to him as the resurrected Lord. We can hardly suppress the application at this point of the permanency of the bond after the analogy of the marriage bond. "Christ being raised from the dead dies no more" (6:9) and this immortality seals the indissolubility of this marital bond (*cf.* Eph. 5:22-32). The end served by this

---

[5] *Cf.* Gifford: *op. cit., ad loc.*

union is that we may bring forth fruit to God (*cf.* 6:22), fruit that is acceptable to God and redounds to his glory, a consideration directed against all licentious abuse of the doctrine that we are not under law but under grace.[6] It may be that the figure of marriage is here continued so that the fruit is viewed as the fruitfulness of a marriage relation that knows no frustration.[7] But the continuance of the figure is not necessary nor is it clearly evident.

5, 6

> 5 For when we were in the flesh, the sinful passions, which were through the law, wrought in our members to bring forth fruit unto death.
>
> 6 But now we have been discharged from the law, having died to that wherein we were held; so that we serve in newness of the spirit, and not in oldness of the letter.

Verses 5 and 6 are in obvious contrast, the one describing the past estate having its fruit in death, the other the transformed estate arising from our discharge from the law.

5 "When we were in the flesh"—with the possible exception of 6:19 in which there may be some reflection upon "flesh" as used here, this is the first occasion in this epistle in which the word "flesh" is used in its fully depreciatory ethical sense, a sense which appears later on in this epistle and frequently in other epistles of Paul. It is all important that its signification should be determined at the outset. "Flesh" in this ethically depreciatory sense means "human nature as controlled and directed by sin". It is not because the word "flesh" of itself denotes what is bad or connotes badness. It is often used without any evil reflection

---

[6] "He even annexes the final cause, lest any should indulge the liberty of their flesh and their own lusts, under the pretense that Christ has delivered them from the bondage of the law" (Calvin: *op. cit.*, *ad loc.*).

[7] "The opinion of Reiche and Fritzsche that καρποφ. taken in the sense of the *fruit of marriage* yields an *undignified* allegory . . . is untenable, seeing that the union with Christ, if regarded as a *marriage* at all, must also necessarily, in accordance with its moral design, be conceived of as a *fruitful marriage*" (Meyer: *op. cit.*, *ad loc.*). Perhaps Lightfoot's remark is safer: "This seems hardly to be a continuation of the same metaphor, 'bear offspring.' Otherwise some more definite word would have been preferred" (*Notes*, *ad loc.*). The idea of fruitbearing in 6:22 and again in vs. 5 is not suggestive of the specific metaphor which applies to marriage. But Meyer is surely right in opposing the notion that it would be an *undignified* metaphor.

or association (*cf.* John 1:14; 6:51, 53; Acts 2:26; Rom. 1:3; 9:3, 5; Eph. 2:14; 5:29; 6:5; Col. 1:22; 2:1, 5; I Tim. 3:16; Heb. 5:7; 10:20; 12:9; I Pet. 3:18; I John 4:2). The frequency with which the word is used of our Lord is sufficient to show that "flesh" is not intrinsically evil. And neither are we to suppose that "flesh", when conceived of as sinful, derives this character from the physical. Sin does not arise from our bodily or physical being, and flesh when used simply of the physical as distinguished from the psychical has no evil connotation. It is when "flesh" is used in an ethical sense that it takes on this sinful quality. With that meaning it is used frequently, especially by Paul (8:4, 5, 6, 7, 8, 9, 12, 13; 13:14; I Cor. 5:5; II Cor. 10:2; Gal. 5:13, 17, 19, 24; 6:8; Eph. 2:3; Col. 2:11, 18, 23; II Pet. 2:10, 18; Jude 23). "Flesh" when used in this sense has no good or even neutral associations; it is unqualifiedly evil. Hence when Paul speaks of having been "in the flesh" he is referring to that period when sin exercised the dominion and is equivalent to saying "when we were in sin".

"The passions of sins", rendered "the sinful passions", are usually interpreted to mean the passions which lead to sin and express themselves in sins.[8] There is no good reason why they should not be interpreted as "sinful passions" (*cf.* 6:6; Col. 2:11).[9] These sinful passions are said to be through the law. This is explained for us in verses 8, 11, 13. The clause, "which were through the law", is not a restrictive relative clause as if a distinction were made between the sinful passions which were through the law and those which were not. These sinful passions were working in our members to bring forth fruit to death. This is in contrast with bringing forth fruit to God (vs. 4). Death is personified and viewed as a master to whom we bring forth fruit, that is to say, to whom we render service. And death is to be construed as in 6:21, 23.

6 "But now"—in contrast with "when we were in the flesh"— "we have been discharged from the law, having died to that wherein we were held".[10] The last clause defines the way in

---

[8] *Cf.* Meyer, Philippi, Gifford, *et al.*, *ad loc.*

[9] Only here and in Gal. 5:24 does πάθημα occur in this sense. Elsewhere it refers to afflictions or sufferings (*cf.* 8:18).

[10] ἀποθανόντες is undoubtedly the correct reading. ἀποθανόντος, followed by A. V., is not supported by manuscript authority. The reading τοῦ θανάτου,

which we have been discharged from the law; it is by our having died to the law. This death to the law had been accomplished in the death of Christ and our union with him in his death, as stated explicitly in verse 4. The version renders the latter part of verse 6, "so that we serve", *etc.* This form of words in English leaves some ambiguity. They might be interpreted to denote purpose or aim But the Greek clearly implies result. The thought, therefore, is that we have died to that wherein we were held with the result that we serve in newness of the Spirit.[11]

"Newness of the Spirit" as contrasted with "oldness of the letter" is not the contrast which we often draw between the "letter" and the "spirit", as when we distinguish between the letter of the law and the spirit of the law. Neither is it a contrast between the "literal" sense and the "spiritual" sense. "Newness of the Spirit" is a reference to the Holy Spirit and the newness is that which the Holy Spirit effects. Grammatically, it may be the newness which consists in the Holy Spirit. "The oldness of the letter" refers to the law, and the law is called the letter because it was written. The writing may refer to the two tables of stone on which the ten commandments were written or to the fact of the law as contained in Scripture. It is law simply as written that is characterized as oldness and the oldness consists in the law. This is apparent not only from the context where the apostle has been dealing with the powerlessness of the law to deliver from sin and the confirmation it adds to our servitude but also from the parallel passage in II Cor. 3:6. The contrast there between the letter and the Spirit is the contrast between the law and the gospel, and when Paul says "the letter kills, but the Spirit makes alive", the letter is shown by the context to refer to that which was engraven on stones, the law delivered by Moses, and the Spirit is the Spirit of the Lord (vs. 17). The

---

instead of ἀποθανόντες, though yielding a good sense, cannot be accepted in face of the external authority supporting ἀποθανόντες.

[11] Sanday and Headlam is insistent that there is a true distinction between ὥστε with the infinitive and ὥστε with the indicative, the latter stating "the definite result which as a matter of fact *does* follow", the former "the contemplated result which in the natural course *ought* to follow" (*op. cit., ad loc.*). It is not, however, by any means apparent that the ὥστε with the infinitive in this instance can mean anything less than actual and assured result. The preceding clauses would carry this implication and, as Gifford observes, the clause in question has the same force as the corresponding clauses in 6:22, particularly "ye have your fruit unto holiness".

thought is, therefore, that, having died to the law and having been thus discharged from it, believers no longer serve in the servitude which law ministers but in the newness of the liberty of which the Holy Spirit is the author (cf. Gal. 3:3).[12]

---

[12] Cf. 2:29 where the same contrast between γράμμα and πνεῦμα occurs. The genitives πνεύματος and γράμματος can be taken as genitives of apposition, indicating that in which the newness and oldness consists (cf. Sanday and Headlam: op. cit., ad loc.) or they may be taken as genitives of source.

XI. TRANSITIONAL EXPERIENCE
(7:7–13)

7–13

7 What shall we say then? Is the law sin? God forbid. Howbeit, I had not known sin, except through the law: for I had not known coveting, except the law had said, Thou shalt not covet:
8 but sin, finding occasion, wrought in me through the commandment all manner of coveting: for apart from the law sin *is* dead.
9 And I was alive apart from the law once: but when the commandment came, sin revived, and I died;
10 and the commandment, which *was* unto life, this I found *to be* unto death:
11 for sin, finding occasion, through the commandment beguiled me, and through it slew me.
12 So that the law is holy, and the commandment holy, and righteous, and good.
13 Did then that which is good become death unto me? God forbid. But sin, that it might be shown to be sin, by working death to me through that which is good;—that through the commandment sin might become exceeding sinful.

7 The sustained polemic of the apostle in 6:14; 7:1–6 respecting the impotency of the law to deliver from sin, the aggravation and confirmation which law adds to our bondage to sin, the antithesis between law and grace, and the exordium accorded to grace as insuring that sin will not have dominion over us might appear to imply a depreciation of law as in itself bad. This is the reason for the questions of verse 7: "What shall we say then? Is the law sin?" The answer is the usual negative which expresses the recoil of abhorrence from the suggestion contained in the questions, "God forbid". In the verses which follow the apostle provides us with an assessment of the law and an analysis of its functions. He does this by setting forth his own experience. What phase of his experience is here delineated can be discussed more profitably at the end of the exposition of this section.

"Is the law sin?" "Sin" in this question may most naturally be interpreted as meaning "sinful". Only, the form used intensifies the thought (*cf.* II Cor. 5:21) and would make the question equivalent to: "Is the law wholly bad?" To use E. H. Gifford's words, "Is the sin, of which it is the occasion, inherent in its own nature?" (*ad loc.*).

The version renders the second part of verse 7: "Howbeit, I had not known sin, except through the law". This rendering is based upon the interpretation that this part of the verse is restrictive, "abating the completeness of the negation involved in the protest".[13] The objection to this view is that it does not accord with the other passages that are closely parallel in construction (3:31; 7:13; 11:11).[14] Hence the thought is "On the contrary" and is expressed well in the A. V. by "Nay". "I had not known sin" could well be rendered, "I did not come to know sin". Paul is here referring to the principle that "through the law is the knowledge of sin" (3:20) as verified in his own experience, and the knowledge is not the merely theoretical knowledge respecting the nature and fact of sin but the practical experiential conviction that he himself was sinful. The law convicted him of his own sin and sinfulness.

"For I had not known coveting, except the law had said, Thou shalt not covet." The way in which this is connected with what precedes would indicate that in the experience of the apostle this is the particular respect in which the law came home to him and exposed his sinfulness. The law is particularized in commandments, and its convicting operations in our consciousness are focused in the exposure of particular aspects of our sinfulness through the instrumentality of those commandments against which these aspects of sin are directed. Conviction was first aroused in the apostle's breast by the agency of the tenth commandment. Apparently covetousness was the last vice of which he suspected himself; it was the first to be exposed. This appeal to the tenth commandment of the decalogue indicates what the apostle meant by "the law" in this context. It is the law exem-

---

13 Denney: *op. cit., ad loc.*

14 "To the false notion just rejected, St. Paul now opposes his own experience of the real effect of the law, which is to expose sin in its true nature.... Compare iii, 31, vii, 13, xi, 11, in all which passages, as here, ἀλλά introduces the contrary notion to that which is rejected in μὴ γένοιτο" (Gifford: *op. cit., ad loc.*).

plified by the ten commandments. These are the precepts through which, preeminently, comes the knowledge of sin.

8 Here is described for us the process by which the apostle had come to the knowledge that covetous lust was operative in his own heart. It is difficult to ascertain whether "finding occasion" is a better rendering than "taking occasion". The former indicates that a situation exists of which sin takes advantage; the latter expresses more active agency on the part of sin. It is more likely that the latter is to be preferred because in the passage sin is represented as active, and the idea of laying hold of the opportunity is in agreement with the character depicted. "Through the commandment" is to be taken with "wrought" (*cf.* vs. 13 where sin is said to work death *through that which is good*, namely, the law or commandment).[15] Sin through this means wrought "all manner of coveting". It is the last clause of verse 8 that clarifies and validates what precedes: "for apart from the law sin is dead". There is no verb in the Greek. The translators in this case have inserted "is" and have construed Paul as enunciating a general principle. The propriety of this interpretation is disputable. It would seem that the verb to be inserted should be "was". Paul is describing his experience. His experience is indeed representative and in that respect the clause in question states what is the common feature of the experience which the apostle here describes and analyses. It must not be assumed, however, that what the apostle is dealing with here is the principle stated elsewhere that "where no law is, there is no transgression" (4:15; *cf.* 5:13; I Cor. 15:56). Paul here in verse 8 is not speaking about the non-existence of sin but of sin as existing, yet as dead. And what he is referring to is the inertness, inactivity, in that sense deadness, of sin, in contrast with the coming to life of sin to which he will presently refer. Hence "apart from the law sin was dead" is the preferable rendering and is to be interpreted as that which is true in the realm of psychology and consciousness.[16] We are now in a position to understand the whole verse. Prior to the process here delineated the sinful principle in the apostle was inactive. Then the commandment "Thou shalt not covet" entered into his consciousness—it came home with power and

---

[15] *Cf.* Alford: *op. cit., ad loc.*
[16] *Cf.* Hodge: *op. cit., ad loc.*

authority. Sin then was aroused to activity. It was no longer dead. And it took occasion to stir up all manner of covetous lust. It did this through the instrumentality of the commandment; the sinful principle was aroused to all manner of desire contrary to the commandment through the commandment itself. Later on the apostle provides us with further analysis and description of this process.

9 Verse 9 is a graphic description of what took place in the transition referred to in verse 8. When the apostle says, "I was alive apart from the law", the word "alive" cannot be used here in the sense of life eternal or life unto God. He is speaking of the unperturbed, self-complacent, self-righteous life which he once lived before the turbulent motions and conviction of sin, described in the two preceding verses, overtook him. We are not able to determine the time in the apostle's career when the commandment began to arouse the sinful passions (vs. 5). But there is no need or warrant to restrict what he describes as being "alive apart from the law" to the years of unreflecting childhood (*cf.* Phil. 3:4-6).[17] "But when the commandment came, sin revived, and I died." The commandment is that mentioned in verse 7, "Thou shalt not covet", and the coming of the commandment is undoubtedly the coming home to his consciousness and the registration in consciousness by which sin took occasion to work in him all manner of covetous lust. This latter is the reviving of sin. "I died" is placed in contrast with "I was alive apart from the law" and must, therefore, be interpreted as the death of the complacent self-assurance and calm which the former "being alive" denotes. He was no longer at rest in his self-complacency. This dying cannot be equated with the dying to sin by union with Christ in his death (6:2) for two reasons. (1) The dying of verse 9 is a dying wrought through the instrumentality of the law, the commandment. It is not so with *death to sin*; the latter is through the gospel and union with Christ. (2) It is not *death to sin* that is in view here but the revival of sin, the arousing of the inherent depravity to overt and more virulent activity. "Sin revived" is the opposite of "we died to sin".

10 In this verse it is necessary to preserve the more literal

---

[17] "Paul means the *death-free* (ver. 10) *life of childlike innocence* . . . resembling the condition of our first parents in Paradise" (Meyer: *op. cit., ad loc.*).

251

rendering, "And the commandment, which was unto life, this was found by me to be unto death". The reference is to the original purpose of the law. The purpose of law in man's original estate was not to give occasion to sin but to direct and regulate man's life in the path of righteousness and, therefore, to guard and promote life. By reason of sin, however, that same law promotes death, in that it gives occasion to sin. And the wages of sin is death. The more law is registered in our consciousness the more sin is aroused to action, and law, merely as law, can exercise no restraining or remedial effect. That the law "was found" to be unto death reflects on the tragedy of Paul's own experience and the disappointment, the disillusionment, which overtook him.

11 Verse 11 again reverts to the notion of sin as taking hold of the occasion. But in this instance the action of sin is categorized as deception in distinction from working all manner of lust (vs. 8). The deception consisted in this that, since the commandment was originally and intrinsically unto life, his conception of its efficacy had been framed accordingly and he had expected the commandment to yield that result. But, instead, the commandment became the occasion for the opposite. The more cognizant he became of its demands, the more he relied upon it as the way of life, the more the opposite fruit was borne. This is the deception —it yielded the opposite of what he had anticipated.[18] Sin, however, is the perpetrator of this deception and the law is but the instrumentality. Because sin deceived him it also "slew" him. This slaying, though viewed here as the action of sin through the instrumentality of the commandment and therefore viewed as the action to which the apostle was subjected, is, however, the same as respects result as "I died" (vs. 9).

12 "So that the law is holy." "So that" intimates a conclusion drawn from what precedes. We might have expected, "Nevertheless the law is holy", in view of the function performed by the law as providing the occasion for sin. But, instead, we have a deduction drawn from verses 7–11 to the effect that the

---

[18] "He expected life, and found death. He expected happiness, and found misery; he looked for holiness, and found increased corruption. He fancied that by the law all these desirable ends could be secured, when its operation was discovered to produce the directly opposite effect. Sin therefore deceived by the commandment, and by it slew him, instead of its being to him the source of holiness and blessedness" (Hodge: *op. cit., ad loc.*).

law is holy. What is it that warrants this inference? It is surely the fact that the law intrinsically and originally was unto life and therefore directed to the promotion of what is holy, just, and good. It becomes the occasion of sin only because of the contradiction which inheres in sin both as principle and as principle incited to action. The law is not sinful (vs. 7). "The law is holy, and the commandment holy, and righteous, and good." The law itself and in its concrete stipulations is holy. The "commandment", no doubt, reflects specifically on that mentioned in verse 7, "thou shalt not covet". But the proposition that it is holy, just, and good applies to every commandment. As holy, just, and good it reflects the character of God and is the transcript of his perfection. It bears the imprint of its author. This, as we shall see, is stated expressly in different terms in verse 14. As "holy" the commandment reflects the transcendence and purity of God and demands of us the correspondent consecration and purity; as "righteous" it reflects the equity of God and exacts of us in its demand and sanction nothing but that which is equitable; as "good" it promotes man's highest well-being and thus expresses the goodness of God.

13, 14a As the question of verse 7 was provoked by the consideration that the sinful passions were operative through the law (vs. 5), so the question of verse 13, "Did then that which is good become death to me?" is necessitated by what the apostle had just said, namely, that the commandment was found by him to be unto death (vs. 10; *cf.* vs. 11). The reply is his vigorous denial, "God forbid". On the contrary, he immediately adds, it is *sin* that works death. Respecting the latter part of verse 13, "But sin, that it might be shown to be sin" *etc.*, the following observations are to be noted. (1) Sin worked death through that which is good, that is, through the commandment. This is a reiteration of what had been stated in different terms in verse 11. The resumption of this thought here, however, is for the purpose of showing the end promoted. (2) This end is that sin "might be shown to be sin", that its true character might be exposed. Its true character as sin is exposed by the fact that it works death *through the thing that is good*; its perversity is demonstrated because it turns that which is holy, and just, and good, that which was ordained to life, into an instrument of death. (3) The wickedness

253

of sin is not only demonstrated when it uses the thing that is good as an instrument of death; sin is for the same reason aggravated in its intensity—"in order that through the commandment sin might become exceeding sinful". This is not merely the *demonstration* of sin's exceeding sinfulness. The abuse of the commandment aggravates beyond measure the gravity of sin itself and, in Meyer's words, the "solemnly painful, tragic effect" (*ad loc.*) is hereby emphasized. And all this is adduced by the apostle to vindicate the law as holy, and just, and good and from any aspersion to the effect that it is the minister of sin or of death. It is the perversity of sin, as the contradiction of the law and as using the law for the aggravation of that contradiction, that vindicates the law as holy.

The law exposes sin and convicts of it. The law becomes the occasion of sin in that the depravity residing in us is thereby aroused to activity. The law aggravates sin—it is the instrumentality through which sin is aggravated in its expression. But the law is not sinful.

The first part of verse 14 is confirmatory of this vindication and is an appeal to the knowledge "that the law is Spiritual". The word "Spiritual" is not derived from the human spirit. It does not mean that the law has relevance to or affinity with the human spirit as distinguished from the human body. The emphasis which the apostle places upon the human body in these chapters is sufficient to refute any such notion. If the body is sinful (6:6) and is the subject of the renewing influences of grace (6:12, 13, 19), the law as holy, just, and good must have relevance to the body as well as to the spirit. Paul's usage will show that the word "Spiritual" is derived from the Holy Spirit. "Spiritual words" (I Cor. 2:13) are words taught of the Holy Spirit. The "Spiritual man" (I Cor. 2:15) is the man indwelt and controlled by the Holy Spirit. "Spiritual songs" (Eph. 5:19; Col. 3:16) are songs indited by the Holy Spirit. "Spiritual understanding" (Col. 1:9) is the understanding imparted by the Holy Spirit (*cf.* also Rom. 1:11; I Cor. 3:1; 10:3, 4; 12:1; 15:44, 46; I Pet. 2:5). Hence the statement, "the law is Spiritual" refers to its divine origin and character. Since it is Spiritual it is possessed of those qualities which are divine—holy, just, and good.

In verses 7–13 the apostle has delineated for us some phase of his experience. Since his experience as thus portrayed arose from his own sinfulness and from the operations and effects of the law of God as it was registered in his consciousness, he is aware that his experience cannot be unique. Other men are likewise sinful and the law of God must evoke and occasion similar experiences in the hearts of others. He is writing thus as representative of what must occur in the experience of others. And his main interest is, without doubt, not to put on record a chapter in human biography but to set forth the relations of the law of God to our sin and, particularly, while, on the one hand, demonstrating the impotency of the law to deliver from sin, yet, on the other, vindicating the law from any aspersion as the author of sin. But the question is: what phase of his experience is here portrayed? Is it his experience as a regenerate or as an unregenerate man? It is quite clear that it is not his experience as an unregenerate man in a state of self-complacency and spiritual torpor. He is convicted of sin (vs. 7). He is no longer alive in the sense of verse 9. The commandment had come home and had aroused the covetous lust of his heart. But is he regenerate? There is no indication in this passage that the experience is that of one who had become dead to sin by the body of Christ. Perhaps most conclusive of all to this effect is the fact that the passions of sins which were through the law, referred to in verse 5, are precisely the passions described in this passage—"sin taking occasion wrought in me through the commandment all manner of lust" (vs. 8). But in verse 5 this state is located as the time "when we were in the flesh" and this is none other than the pre-regenerate state. We must conclude, therefore, that this passage is an account of pre-regenerate experience. It is not, however, the period of pre-regenerate self-complacency but his experience after he had been aroused from his spiritual torpor and awakened to a sense of his sin. It is the preparatory and transitional phase of his spiritual pilgrimage when, shaken by the conviction which the law of God ministers, his state of mind was no longer one of unperturbed calm and self-esteem.

XII. THE CONTRADICTION IN THE BELIEVER
(7:14–25)

The main question in the interpretation of verses 14–25 is one on which there has been deep-seated difference of judgment in the history of interpretation. Does Paul continue to delineate for us his pre-regenerate experience as in verses 7–13? Or does the present tense of verse 14 indicate that he has made a transition to the description of his present experience in the state of grace? There are features which would seem to be quite incompatible with the latter alternative and these have appeared to many interpreters to settle the question beyond reasonable dispute in favour of the view that there is no transition from one phase of experience to another but that verses 7–25 constitute in this respect a unit. The chief support for this view and the main obstacle to the other view is the strength of the expressions Paul uses to describe himself. "I am carnal." Does this not mean that he is the opposite of "Spiritual" and therefore still "in the flesh" (vs. 5) and under the dominion of sin? "Sold under sin"—is this not to the same effect as being the bondslave of sin and therefore under its dominion, the opposite of being under grace (*cf.* 6:14)? Or, when he says, "To will is present with me, but to do that which is good is not" (vs. 18), are we to suppose that the man in whom the powers of grace are operative is destitute of the good works which are the fruit of the Spirit? Again, surely the complaint of verse 24, "Wretched man that I am!" is far from being the state of mind of one who has entered into the joy and liberty of the gospel (*cf.* 7:6). Besides, the relation to the law of God, assumed in this passage (*cf.* vss. 21–23), would hardly appear to be different from that in verses 7–13. It should not surprise us therefore that for these considerations as well as others notable expositors should insist that the Paul of Romans 7:14–25 is the same as that of 7:7–13 and a different Paul from the exultant and triumphant Paul of Romans 8.[19]

---

[19] The Greek Fathers generally adopted this position. For a brief survey of the history of interpretation of this passage and for a searching examination of the view, as propounded by W. Kümmel, R. Bultmann, and P. Althaus,

There are, however, considerations on the other side which, in my judgment, turn the scales decisively in favour of the view that there is transition at verse 14[20] or at least at verse 15.[21] And it is disappointing that some of the more modern expositors have dealt so inadequately with these considerations.[22] (1) Paul says, "I delight in the law of God after the inward man" (7:22). It is not our concern now to determine what he means by "the inward man". Whatever its precise import, it must refer to that which is most determinative in his personality. In his inmost being, in what is central in will and affection, he delights in the law of God. This cannot be said of the unregenerate man still under law and in the flesh. It would be totally contrary to Paul's own teaching. "The mind of the flesh", he says, "is enmity against God; for it is not subject to the law of God, neither indeed can it be" (8:7). The mind of the flesh is the mind of those

---

that Paul is here discussing the unregenerate man under the law as faith sees him, *cf.* Anders Nygren: *op cit.*, pp. 284–296. Nygren subjects this interpretation to most effective criticism. There is, however, in the judgment of the writer, much more of internal soul discordance in the delineation of Rom. 7:14–25 than Nygren is prepared to acknowledge.

There are interpreters who take the position that Paul is not here giving a description of normal or actual Christian life but of what follows for any man, whether regenerate or unregenerate, who relies upon the law and his own efforts for sanctification. "The one point of the passage is that it describes a man who is trying to be good and holy by his own efforts and is beaten back every time by the power of indwelling sin. This is the experience of any man who tries the experiment, whether he be regenerate or unregenerate. The experiences here described are certainly not those of the Christian life as it ought to be, and as it may be, the normal Christianity, that is, of ch. vi. 17, 18; vii. 4, 6; viii. 1, 2; 1 Peter i. 8, 9" (W. H. Griffith Thomas: *St. Paul's Epistle to the Romans*, Grand Rapids, 1946, p. 191).

[20] The view that the passage refers to the regenerate man and to the conflict ensuing in the Christian life was set forth by Augustine and had been, to a large extent, adopted in the Western church. Some of the ablest commentators, however, in more recent times have abandoned what may be called, the Augustinian interpretation (*e. g.*, Bengel, Meyer, Godet, Moses Stuart, Sanday and Headlam, Denney).

[21] Calvin regards the transition as taking place at vs. 15, that here Paul comes to deal with a man already regenerated. If this view were adopted then the difficulties of applying the expressions "carnal" and "sold under sin" to a regenerate person disappear. As will be shown, there is no need to regard these difficulties as insurmountable and vs. 14b can readily be conjoined with vs. 15 as descriptive of the same state.

[22] One of the ablest and most thorough treatments of the question and of the considerations in support of the view that Paul is describing his experience in a state of grace is that by James Fraser: *A Treatise on Sanctification*, London, 1898, pp. 254–356. *Cf.* also Philippi: *op. cit., ad loc.;* Hodge: *op. cit.*, pp. 239–245; Calvin: *op. cit., ad* 7:15–25.

who are "in the flesh" (8:8). Nothing could be stronger than to say that the mind is "enmity" against God and, by implication, against the law of God; enmity is the opposite of delight in the law. Hence the Paul of 7:22 is not "in the flesh" and his mind is not "the mind of the flesh"; his mind must be that of the Spirit (8:6). (2) The foregoing (vs. 22) is similar to the import of verse 25: "Consequently then I myself with the mind serve the law of God". This is service which means subjection of heart and will, something impossible for the unregenerate man. He is not subject to the law of God and he cannot be because he is "in the flesh", he is "after the flesh," and he has "the mind of the flesh" (8:5–8). (3) The person portrayed in 7:14–25 is one whose will is toward that which is good (vss. 15, 18, 19, 21) and the evil that he does is in violation of that which he wills and loves (vss. 16, 19, 20). This means, without doubt, that his most characteristic will, the prevailing bent and propension of his will, is the good. And this again is totally unlike the unregenerate man of 8:5–8. The man of 7:14–25 does bad things but he hates them and they violate the prevailing bent of his will to the good. The unregenerate man hates the good; the man of 7:14–25 hates the evil. (4) The tension which appears in 7:14–25 between that which Paul delights in, loves, approves, and wills and that which he is and does in contravention is inevitable in a regenerate man as long as sin remains in him. These two complexes in him—righteousness, on the one hand, sin, on the other—are contradictory and the more sensitive he is to the demands of holiness, the more sensitive to that pattern after which his most characteristic self is formed, the more will the contradiction which still exists in him be focused in his consciousness. And the more sanctified he becomes the more painful to him must be the presence in himself of that which contradicts the perfect standard of holiness. The complaint, "Wretched man that I am!", is the honest expression of this painful experience of internal conflict and contradiction. The complaint of verse 24 is the mark of candour and the proof of sensitivity. Once we admit that sin persists in the believer, the tension of 7:14–25 is inevitable and it is not the way of truth to ignore it. (5) We are not to suppose that 7:14–25 is destitute of the triumphant note which is so conspicuous in chapter 8. "I thank God through Jesus Christ our Lord" (vs. 25). This is Paul's answer to the complaint of verse 24.

It is not the answer of defeat; it is the answer of assured confidence and hope. It breathes the same triumphant note of I Corinthians 15:57: "But thanks be to God who giveth us the victory through our Lord Jesus Christ". The thanksgiving of verse 25 is not the language of the unregenerate man under the bondage of sin. And the conclusion of verse 25 stands in the closest logical connection with the exultant faith and assurance of the introductory thanksgiving.

For these reasons we are compelled to conclude that 7:14–25 is the delineation of Paul's experience in the state of grace. This conclusion will necessarily affect the interpretation of the details of the passage.

14–20

14 For we know that the law is spiritual: but I am carnal, sold under sin.

15 For that which I do I know not: for not what I would, that do I practise; but what I hate, that I do.

16 But if what I would not, that I do, I consent unto the law that it is good.

17 So now it is no more I that do it, but sin which dwelleth in me.

18 For I know that in me, that is, in my flesh, dwelleth no good thing: for to will is present with me, but to do that which is good *is* not.

19 For the good which I would I do not: but the evil which I would not, that I practise.

20 But if what I would not, that I do, it is no more I that do it, but sin which dwelleth in me.

14 "But I am carnal, sold under sin." Both predicates stand in sharp contrast to "Spiritual" in the preceding clause. "Carnal" because of its contrast with "Spiritual" and because it is coordinated with, if not interpreted in terms of, "sold under sin" must reflect on moral quality and means, therefore, fleshly.[23]

---

[23]   σάρκινος, supported by ℵ* A B C D E F G, is surely to be preferred to σαρκικός which is supported by ℵᶜ L P and the mass of the cursives. σάρκινος means "fleshy", "made of flesh", and occurs in this sense in II Cor. 3:3 where it is contrasted with λίθινος, "made of stone". σαρκικός means "fleshly". It is not to be supposed, however, that σάρκινος is destitute of the ethical quality which belongs to σαρκικός quite plainly in I Cor. 3:3; II Cor. 1;12; I Pet. 2:11 and possibly in II Cor. 10:4. It is quite impossible to divest σάρκινος in I Cor. 3:1 of the depreciatory ethical quality belonging to σαρκικός in vs. 3. Just as σαρκικός can be used without any depreciatory ethical reflection,

The "flesh" (*cf.* vs. 5) is used in a wholly depreciatory sense, and when Paul says that he is "fleshly" he is applying to himself that ethical indictment which the word "flesh" in this connection carries with it. The question is then: how can he do this if he is a regenerate man and therefore no longer "in the flesh"? Are we to suppose that to be called "fleshly" is the same as to be "in the flesh" (vs. 5; 8:8) and to be "after the flesh" (8:5)? This does not follow and that for two reasons. (1) In I Cor. 3:1, 3 Paul charges the Corinthians with being carnal because of their envy and strife. He does not mean that they were unregenerate; the assumption is that they were believers, that they were at least babes in Christ. Hence to be called carnal is not necessarily equivalent to being categorized as "in the flesh". (2) Paul recognizes that the flesh still resides in him (vss. 18, 25). This is closely associated if not synonymous with the fact that sin dwells in him (vss. 17, 20). If the flesh still dwells in him, it is inevitable that in respect of the "flesh" in him he should be called "fleshly", and it is not inconsistent with his being regenerate that he should so characterize himself because of the flesh which is still his.

The other indictment brought against himself, "sold under sin", seems to offer more difficulty. This is a strong expression and because of its similarity to an Old Testament expression it has been contended that it could not characterize a regenerate person. It is not used in this ethical sense elsewhere in the New Testament. But in the Old Testament it is said of Ahab that he sold himself to do evil in the sight of the Lord (I Kings 21:20, 25; *cf.* II Kings 17:17).[24] It is assumed by some expositors that the terms used here by Paul must have the same force as this Old Testament expression.[25] If this were the case the question would be settled. For, as applied to Ahab, it means that he abandoned himself to iniquity, a characterization which cannot belong to a regenerate man and, most obviously, not to Paul after his conversion. It is strange, however, that expositors would so easily have taken for

---

as in Rom. 15:27; I Cor. 9:11, so σάρκινος can be used with depreciatory reflection and therefore in the sense of fleshly or carnal. *Cf.* Lightfoot: *Notes*, pp. 184f.

[24] In the LXX the references are III Kings 20:20, 25; *cf.* IV Kings 17:17. In the LXX the same verb is used as in Rom. 7:14. The Hebrew is the Hithpael התמכר.

[25] *Cf.* Bengel, Meyer, Gifford.

granted that the two forms of expression have the same force. It is one thing to sell oneself to do iniquity; it is another to be sold under the power of sin. In the former case the person is the active agent, in the latter he is subjected to a power that is alien to his own will. It is the latter that appears here. And since the flesh and sin still inhered in the apostle and exercised a power over him, it is the necessary reaction of his sanctified sensibility to deplore the captivity to which, in the nature of the case, he was subjected by reason of indwelling sin. That the captivity to sin of which Paul here speaks is alien to his most characteristic self and will is abundantly attested by the verses which follow. It becomes clear how different are the two states, that of one man who with resolute and abandoned will sells himself to iniquity and that of the other who reproaches himself for the sin he commits and bemoans his being carried away captive by it. To such an extent is the distinction perspicuous that it is surprising that expositors would even have appealed to the instance of Ahab as offering any analogy.[26]

Though these two predicates which the apostle applied to himself seemed at first to offer the most cogent objection to the view being maintained, on closer examination they are found to fall into accord with the data which establish the necessity of this interpretation.

15 This verse is closely connected with verse 14. It can be regarded as confirmatory or explanatory of the indictment which he registered against himself in the preceding verse. As such it focuses attention upon the discrepancy between that which his will and affection dictated, on the one hand, and what he was able to bring to effective fruition, on the other. What he did he did not know; what he willed he did not practise. It is difficult to ascertain the precise force of the word "know" in the first part of the verse, "For that which I do I know not". The simplest solution is that he uses the word "know" in the sense of loving or delighting in, as frequently in Scripture[27] and as the opposite of "hate" which appears in the latter part of the verse. In this event we must not suppress the cognitive element so as to exclude it.

---

[26] Cf. the discussion by James Fraser: op. cit., pp. 271–274; G. C. Berkouwer: *Faith and Sanctification*, Grand Rapids, 1952, pp. 59f.

[27] Cf. the exposition of 8:29 for the evidence in support of this import of the word "know"

There is still emphasis upon the intelligence and understanding with which the apostle set his heart upon that in which he was frustrated by a contrary power. And there may be reflection upon the confusion and bewilderment which overtook the apostle in his failure to bring to effective fruition the ideals on which he had set his heart.

In the apostle's word, occurring here in verse 15 and substantially with variation of terms in verses 18, 19, 21, "For not what I would, that do I practise", we have posed for us the question of the psychological quality of "I would". The version has adopted this rendering and thereby suggests that the apostle distinguishes between his determined wish and that which is executively willed and effected. This interpretation of the Greek term finds support in Paul's usage (*cf.* 1:13; I Cor. 7:7, 32; II Cor. 5:4; 12:20; Gal. 4:21). On this interpretation it has much the same quality as our word "wish" or "desire". It is doubtful, however, if this is strong enough to express the thought. There appears to be the determined resolution and volition, that is to say, will to the fullest extent of volition, though not of executive volition, for in that event it would pass into the sphere of practice which in this instance is excluded. What passes into execution is what he hates, the opposite of his delight and characteristic volition. Therefore that which comes to fruition in practice is that which he does not will in the sense of the determinate volition contemplated.

16 Verse 16 corroborates what has just been said. Paul proceeds, "But if that which I do not will, that I do", implying that what comes to fruition in practice is not what was willed but what was not willed in terms of the will spoken of in verse 15. His chief interest in verse 16, however, is not to corroborate verse 15 but, on the assumption of what is stated in verse 15, to show his agreement with the law of God in what, as we should say, is the most characteristic and fundamental propension of his will: "I consent to the law that it is good". The term used for "good" is that which predicates of the law the highest quality of goodness. The law, therefore, defines for us that which is called unreservedly the "good" in the succeeding context. This reference to the law proves that, in the ethical assessment which Paul is making and in this judgment which he passes upon himself, the law is the norm, indicating, as will appear in verses 22 and 25 with even greater emphasis, the relevance of the law of God to the believer's obligation. However much the apostle bemoans his condition, there is consolation in his whole-souled endorsement of the law and of his alignment with it in the most determinative bent of his will.

17, 18 Verse 17 may most properly be regarded as inference drawn from the statement of the case in the preceding verses and thus rendered as in the version: "So now it is no more I that do it, but sin which dwelleth in me". Here the apostle identifies his ego, his person, with that determinate will which is in agreement with the law of God, and he appears to dissociate his own self from the sin committed. He distinguishes between his self and the sin that dwells in him and places the responsibility for the sin committed upon the indwelling sin. Verse 18 provides the confirmation and elucidation of what had been stated in verse 17: "For I know that in me, that is, in my flesh, dwelleth no good thing". The following propositions are clearly implied. (1) The flesh is wholly sinful—no good thing dwells in it. (2) The flesh is still associated with his person—the flesh is *his* flesh and it is *in him*. (3) Sin is also associated with his person, for it is in his flesh that sin inheres. Hence verse 17 cannot be interpreted as a disavowal of responsibility for the sin that dwells in him or for the sin committed in frustration of his determinate will. The latter part of verse 18 is to the same effect as verse 15, though the terms are different.[28]

19, 20 Verse 19, likewise, reiterates the thought of verse 15 with the difference that the thing willed is now defined as the "good" and the thing not willed but practised is defined as the "evil".[29]

Verse 20 is a reiteration of the thought of verse 17 with the exception that in verse 20 it is explicitly stated why the conclusion is drawn that no longer does *he* commit the sin but rather the sin

---

[28] The variants at the end of vs. 18 do not change the meaning. If we read simply οὐ with ℵ A B C and several cursives, then we should have to supply in thought παράκειταί μοι from the preceding clause. If we read οὐχ εὑρίσκω with D G and the mass of the cursives, then the verb is supplied and the apostle gives an added emphasis to his lament.

[29] The contrast in vs. 19 would perhaps be more effectively expressed by the rendering, "For not that which I will, namely the good, do I do, but that which I do not will, namely the evil, this I practise". He wills the good, he does not will the evil. He performs the evil, he does not perform the good.

that dwells in him—the reason is that what he does *he* does not will.[30]

21–25

> 21 I find then the law, that, to me who would do good, evil is present.
> 22 For I delight in the law of God after the inward man:
> 23 but I see a different law in my members, warring against the law of my mind, and bringing me into captivity under the law of sin which is in my members.
> 24 Wretched man that I am! who shall deliver me out of the body of this death?
> 25 I thank God through Jesus Christ our Lord. So then I of myself with the mind, indeed, serve the law of God; but with the flesh the law of sin.

21 The question on which interpreters are greatly divided is the denotation of "the law" in this verse,[31] whether it refers to the law of God (vs. 22) or to the "other law", "the law of sin" in our members (vs. 23). Either interpretation makes good sense and is both grammatically and syntactically acceptable. On the former view, namely, that "the law" refers to the law of God, the thought would be as follows: "For me willing conformity to the law in order to do the good I find that the evil is present with me". Hence what he finds is that evil is present notwithstanding his determinate will to the good which the law of God requires. This fits in well with verse 22 in which he defines this determinate will to the good as delight in the law of God after the inward man. And it is also in accord with verse 23 where the opposing law of sin in his members is called "another law" in contrast with the law of God which, up to this point it is maintained, is the only law referred to in the passage. There is, however, no conclusive objection to the other interpretation, namely, that "the law of sin" (vss. 23, 25) is in view here and that it is defined in terms of the presence of evil in opposition to the determinate will to good.[32] This is the view adopted in

---

[30] ἐγώ is inserted after θέλω in vs. 20 by ℵ A and the mass of the cursives.
[31] For a summary and discussion of the various views *cf.* Meyer: *op. cit., ad loc.*
[32] For a defence of this view *cf.* Philippi: *op. cit., ad loc.;* Hodge: *op. cit., ad loc.* It is not necessary to assume a trajection of the ὅτι in the last clause and place it before τῷ θέλοντι. The last clause defines what "the law" is and although in translation it is more felicitous to insert "that" before "to me who

the version and, if followed, means that "law" in this instance is used in the sense of rule or principle of action. The usual significa-tion of law, however, as that which propounds and demands action need not be suppressed. "The law of sin" may be conceived of as not only impelling to action that is antithetical to the law of God but also as dictating such action.

22, 23 Whether "the law" of verse 21 is taken as the law of God or as the law of sin, verses 22 and 23 must be taken together as explanatory of the antithesis enunciated in verse 21. When we ask how the evil can be present when there is the determinate will to the good, the answer resides in the fact that there are two antithetical laws, the law of God and the law of sin, both of which bear upon our persons and are therefore registered in us in a way that reflects the antithesis in which they stand to each other.

The interpretation of verse 22 is bound up to a large extent with the meaning we attach to "the inward man". It would appear reasonable to assume that "the inward man" is contrasted with "the outward man" and, as Paul uses that contrast expressly elsewhere (II Cor. 4:16), it is proper to interpret the expression in the light of this latter passage. In the words of E. H. Gifford: "it indicates the '*mind*' (. . . v. 23 and v. 25), '*the spirit of man*' (1 Cor. ii. 11) as contrasted with '*the outward man*,' the body or flesh (2 Cor. iv. 16)".[33] In any case there can be no question but "the inward man" of verse 22 refers to what Paul was in his inmost spirit, in the centre of his personality, and it is also true that "the inward man" approximates to, if it is not to be identified with, the "mind" of verses 23, 25. There is, however, no warrant for supposing that the contrast between the "mind" and the "flesh" in verse 25 is that between "mind" and "body". "Flesh" in Paul's usage, when used with ethical purport (as obviously here), applies to the operations of what we call the mind as well as to those of the body. "Flesh", ethically conceived, does not have its seat in the body and does not take its origin from the

---

would do the good", yet the thought is that "the law" referred to is the pres-ence of the evil. In correlation with vs. 22, "to me willing to do the good" (vs. 21) corresponds to "I delight in the law of God" (vs. 22) and "the evil is present" (vs. 21) corresponds to "another law in my members, warring against the law of my mind" (vs. 23).
[33] *Op. cit., ad loc.*

body as contrasted with the mind or spirit of man. We may not, therefore, try to find the meaning of "the inward man" of verse 22 in any metaphysical distinction between body and spirit, mind and matter. "The inward man" in this case must be interpreted in terms of this context, a context ethically complexioned from beginning to end. If we follow the train of the apostle's thought in the preceding verses we shall be in a position to understand what he means by "the inward man" better than by simple appeal to II Cor. 4:16.

Paul had been contrasting that which he willed with that which he did not will, the former being the good and the latter the bad. He had identified himself with that which he willed (vss. 17, 20) and therefore with the good; he had associated that which he did not will, the evil, with the sin and the flesh still inhering in him. In a word, he identifies himself in his deepest and most determinate will with the law of God which is the good. What is more reasonable than to infer that he calls this determinate will to the good (with which he identifies his self) "the inward man"? As he makes moral assessment of himself, as he analyses himself and his conduct in the light of ethical criteria, he finds that that which represents his deepest and truest self is the determinate will to the good and it is that deepest and truest self he calls "the inward man". It is "inward" because it is deepest and inmost. And there is no reason or warrant to go further afield to discover the denotation of "the inward man". Furthermore, we are hereby furnished with the solution of the difficulty we encounter in the apparent dissociation of his personality from the sin which dwelt in him and from the flesh which he called his own.[34] Paul's affirmation is that, notwithstanding all the frustration of his determinate will to the good, he delights in the law of the Lord. And this delight is not peripheral but belongs to that which is deepest and inmost in his moral and spiritual being.

The antithesis which is evident in verse 21 needs, however, the presence of another law than the law of God. It is with this that Paul deals in verse 23: "but I see a different law in my members". This different law is not to be interpreted as something other than "the law of sin". Both are said to be in our members and it would scarcely be possible to distinguish them. "The law of sin" should

---

[34] The apparent dissociation of himself from the indwelling sin and the flesh is discussed at the end of the exposition of this chapter.

be taken, therefore, as defining for us that in which this other law consists. The law of sin is the law that proceeds from sin and which sin propounds. It is contrasted with the law of God and must be antithetical to it in every particular. Hence the apostle says, "warring against the law of my mind". The law of the mind is not strictly parallel to the other law, "the law of sin"; the law of the mind is not the law that proceeds from and is propounded by the mind. It is rather the law of God as the law that regulates the mind and which the mind serves (*cf.* vs. 25). The antithesis between the law of sin and the law of God is registered in our persons in the warfare that is carried on in the realm of our consciousness between the dictates of sin and the law of God as that which is consented to, approved, and delighted in by our minds. The military figure of warfare is carried on and is expressed also in the clause, "bringing me into captivity under the law of sin".[35] The apostle represents himself as led captive to the law of sin. The strength of the expression is analogous to "sold under sin" in verse 14 and should be interpreted in the same way. At this stage of the portrayal of the conflict we should not find undue difficulty with such strong language. Since the determinate will of the apostle is not brought to successful execution (vss. 15–21) and he does that which he does not will, the figure of being led captive is an appropriate description of the moral situation delineated. He is not his own master for he does that which contravenes the inmost and deepest self-determination. It is this subjection to a will other than his deepest and most characteristic will that is appropriately described as being brought into captivity.

The "members" in which the law of sin is said to reside will have to be taken in the sense of the same term in 6:13, 19. If the thought is focused on our physical members, as appeared necessary in the earlier instances, we are not to suppose that "the law of sin" springs from or has its seat in the physical. It would merely indicate, as has been maintained already, that the apostle brings to the forefront the concrete and overt ways in which the law of sin expresses itself and that our physical members cannot be divorced from the operation of the law of sin. Our captivity to the law of sin is evidenced by the fact that our physical

<hr>

[35] The preposition ἐν before τῷ νόμῳ is so strongly supported by the external authorities that it must be retained.

members are the agents and instruments of the power which sin wields over us. But again we are reminded, as in 6:13, that, however significant may be our physical members, the captivity resulting is not that merely of our members but that of our persons —"bringing *me* into captivity to the law of sin which is in my members".

24 "Wretched man that I am!" The sense of misery underlying this exclamation will cause us surprise only if we have failed to appreciate the contradiction and frustration set forth in the preceding verses. A sense of wretchedness is the inevitable reaction to the conflict and to its issue. Only if the sensitivity and discernment which the apostle exemplifies are absent shall we be lacking in understanding. The apostle does not abstract himself from the captivity which the law of sin is successful in accomplishing; it is reflected in his consciousness in what Gifford calls the "wail of anguish". The difficulty which does arise in this verse concerns the meaning of the question: "who shall deliver me from the body of this death?"

"The body of this death" could be rendered "this body of death". In that event the emphasis would fall upon the body as characterized by death. The context would suggest, however, that the emphasis falls upon "death", that is to say, upon the death which is intrinsic to or flows from captivity to the law of sin. It is the death belonging to this captivity, and therefore it is much more feasible to take the demonstrative pronoun "this" as referring to death rather than to the body. The question then is: what is "the body of this death"? "Body" has been taken to mean "mass" and body of death "the whole mass of sin".[36] Hence what Paul longs to be delivered from is sin in all its aspects and consequences. *Undoubtedly* this was the apostle's earnest longing and is implied in his question as well as in the complaint which precedes. But there does not appear to be warrant for interpreting the expression in this fashion. "Body" in Paul's usage, as was noted at 6:6, refers to the physical body and there is not evidence to support the view that it is used figuratively. Hence we are constrained to think in this instance of the physical body. How then is it conceived of as the body of this death?

---

[36] Calvin: *op. cit., ad loc.; cf.* also those commentators referred to at 6:6 who regard "the body of sin" in the same way.

The death, we have just found, should be taken as referring to the death which issues from captivity to the law of sin (vs. 23). But this law of sin is operative in our physical members. It is in this way that the body can be regarded as the body of this death —the bodily members are the sphere in which the law of sin is operative unto that death which is the wages of sin.

"Who shall deliver me?" This deliverance longed for and, as we shall see presently, confidently assured of is deliverance from the captivity of the preceding verse. Here is a cry for deliverance from the body of this death because the body is the instrument and sphere of operation of the law of sin to the captivity of which the apostle was consigned. It is this orientation that prepares us for the thanksgiving of the next verse.

25 "I thank God through Jesus Christ our Lord."[37] This is the answer to the question of vs. 24, and it expresses triumphant assurance of ultimate deliverance from the body of this death and from the captivity to the law of sin which elicits the anguish of his complaint. The "heart-rending cry"[38] cannot therefore be construed as one of despair; it must never be dissociated from the sequel of confident hope. What is in view in this thanksgiving? If "the body of this death" refers to the body through which the law of sin carries on its warfare, then no other interpretation suits the terms of the thanksgiving itself or the analogy of Paul's teaching more adequately or relevantly than the assurance of the resurrection. That it parallels I Cor. 15:57, where the hope of the resurrection is beyond question, is not by any means an unreasonable supposition. And what could be more relevant to the anguish which the exclamation expresses and to the consideration that the body is the body of the death alluded to than the assurance of the deliverance that will be wrought when the body of our humiliation will be transformed into the likeness of the body of Christ's glory (Phil. 3:21) as that which believers groan and wait for (8:23)? It was not death that Paul longed for as the blessed hope but the deliverance bestowed when the corruptible

---

[37] The variant readings in the formula of thanksgiving have all the same force. In the matter of external authority choice would appear to rest between εὐχαριστῶ τῷ θεῷ and χάρις τῷ θεῷ, the former supported by ℵ* A and the mass of the cursives, the latter by B.

[38] The expression is from Sanday and Headlam: *op. cit., ad* 7:24. But it is far from being "from the depths of despair" as they allege.

269

will put on incorruption and the mortal immortality (I Cor. 15:54; II Cor. 5:4). The terseness of the thanksgiving in no way unsuits it as the formula of eschatological hope. It brings to the forefront the power and grace of God and the mediation of Christ, the elements which make up the essence of the hope to come. And it is confirmatory of this interpretation that in the latter part of verse 25 the apostle gives us in summary a reiteration of the life of conflict and contradiction which had been unfolded in detail in verses 14–24. This repetition would indicate that the triumphant thanksgiving in the early part of the verse does not itself bring to an end the conflict delineated. Hope is embraced, and that hope is exultant and breaks out in thanksgiving. But realization is not yet, for what a man seeth why doth he yet hope for? In patience he waits for it (*cf.* 8:24, 25). "Consequently then", Paul continues, "I myself with the mind serve the law of God, but with the flesh the law of sin". The warfare continues, but he is upheld in the conflict by the assurance that finally there will be complete deliverance.

In this latter part of the verse the elements of the antithesis are stated in the terms of the preceding context, the law of God (*cf.* vss. 14, 16, 22) versus the law of sin (*cf.* vs. 23)[39] and the mind (*cf.* vs. 23) versus the flesh (*cf.* vs. 18). The mind will have to be regarded as synonymous with the inward man (vs. 22) and therefore with that which he most deeply and centrally is. In view of his consent to the law (vs. 16) and his delight in the law of God (vs. 22) the service of the law of God implies that the commitment involved in the bondservice rendered is one of wholehearted spontaneous obedience. This thought of service indicates that the devotion given is not merely that of determinate will but also of fruitful action—the determinate will issues in service on the apostle's part. The "flesh", on the other hand, must be identified with the indwelling sin (vss. 17, 20) which in verse 18 he calls "my flesh" and in which no good resides. As the mind renders service to the law of God, the flesh serves the law of sin. The most significant aspect of this concluding description is the way in which the apostle emphatically identifies

---

[39] "'*The law of God*' and '*the law of sin*' have both been mentioned above in *vv.* 22, 23, each with its article: here the articles are omitted in order to bring out more clearly *what each law* is in its nature and quality, the one '*a law of God*,' the other '*a law of sin*'" (Gifford: *op. cit.*, *ad loc.*).

himself as the agent in both cases. He does not say that the mind serves the law of God and the flesh the law of sin but rather "I myself" with the mind and with the flesh. This is conclusive to the effect that the apostle did not disavow his own personal responsibility and agency in the service of the law of sin and corrects the impression that we might have derived from verses 17 and 20.[40] Apart altogether from verse 25 we should have been compelled to judge that the apostle had not isolated himself from the sin committed, as verses 17 and 20 might appear to imply. In verse 14 he says "*I* am carnal" and thus in the clearest terms brings an indictment against *himself* on the ground of the flesh which he later calls his own (vs. 18). Furthermore, even when he characterizes himself as doing that which he does not will, he nevertheless represents himself to be the agent (vss. 15, 16, 19). But the most conclusive evidence that he identifies himself with the sin committed and does not disavow responsibility is the "I myself" as the subject of both kinds of service in verse 25. The exclamation of wretchedness itself cannot be devoid of ethical evaluation—it likewise is self-denunciatory.

There is one question which calls for further treatment before we leave this passage (vss. 14–25). It is what we may call the psychological question. It is quite apparent that what the apostle refers to repeatedly as "that which he wills" (vss. 15, 19; *cf.* vss. 18, 21) is the determinate will to the good. It is this will to the good that is frustrated, with the result that "what he does not will" is the thing done and practised (vss. 16, 19, 20). The question is whether the evil done and practised in contravention of his determinate will to the good was done and practised without any will or volition on his part to that effect. If this were the case he would be the involuntary and helpless victim of some alien power wholly extrinsic to his responsible and voluntary agency and he would be relieved of all moral responsibility to that effect; the action would be outside the realm of his own moral, responsible agency. This is an impossible supposition.

---

[40] Gifford is surely off the track when he says: "If Christ is my deliverer, it is implied that '*I myself*' without Christ cannot get beyond the state of distraction and self-contradiction already described in *vv.* 14–23" (*op. cit.*, *ad loc.*). It is only *in Christ* that the experience described can be a reality, and it must not be overlooked that "I myself" is the subject of "with the mind serve the law of God", a condition that cannot obtain apart from union with Christ.

As we have found, the apostle does not abstract his own personal agency from the evil that he did and practised. He upbraided himself for it; he characterized himself as carnal; he says that he did this evil; and finally he says without equivocation, "I myself . . . with the flesh serve the law of sin" (vs. 25). Hence the *sine qua non* of responsible action, namely, volition must have been present in the actions concerned, actions for which he condemned himself and on account of which he gave expression to the wail of anguish, "Wretched man that I am!" (vs. 24). How then are we to interpret the repeated expressions that it was not what he willed that he practised but rather what he did not will (vss. 15, 16, 19, 20)? It might be a solution to say that the word we have rendered "will" has the force merely of desire or wish and that the evil that he performed was contrary to his wish or desire. But from the psychological point of view this does not, in the last analysis, solve the question. Some pleasure or gratification must have been derived from the performance; otherwise there would be no volition. Besides, I am not satisfied that the word "will" in question can be allowed to remain on the level of mere wish or desire. We shall have to suppose the stronger force of determinate will. What then is the solution? It would appear to be that the apostle is using the word "will" throughout this passage, when he speaks both of what he does will and of what he does not will, in the highly restricted sense of that determinate will to the good, in accordance with the will of God, which is characteristic of his deepest and inmost self, the will of "the inward man" (vs. 22). It is that will that is frustrated by the flesh and indwelling sin. And when he does the evil he does what is not the will of his deepest and truest self, the inward man. This explains both types of expression, namely, that what *he wills* he does not do and what *he does not will* he does. If we appreciate this restricted, specialized use of the word "will", then it does not mean and the apostle is not to be understood as meaning that will in our psychological sense of the term was not present in that practice and performance which he upbraids as evil and which was in contravention of his determinate will in the more specialized sense.

One other aspect of the question merits a word of reservation. When the apostle says that he did not perform what he willed (*cf.* vs. 15), we are not to suppose that his determinate will to the good came to no effective fruition in practice. This would be universalizing the apostle's language beyond all reasonable limits. It is surely sufficient that in this particular case, where the apostle is dealing with the contradiction which arises from the presence of sin and of the flesh, that he should declare and deplore the frustration of his determinate will to the good without giving us a *statistical* history of the outcome.

XIII. LIFE IN THE SPIRIT
(8:1–39)

1–4

1 There is therefore now no condemnation to them that are in Christ Jesus.
2 For the law of the Spirit of life in Christ Jesus made me free from the law of sin and of death.
3 For what the law could not do, in that it was weak through the flesh, God, sending his own Son in the likeness of sinful flesh and for sin, condemned sin in the flesh:
4 that the ordinance of the law might be fulfilled in us, who walk not after the flesh, but after the Spirit.

1 "Condemnation" is the opposite of justification (*cf.* 5:16; 8:34) and justification implies the absence of condemnation. Since the justification which is the theme of this epistle is the complete and irreversible justification of the ungodly, it carries with it the annulment of all condemnation. This is the thought of verse 1—the negative bears the emphasis. The "therefore" means that this complete absence of condemnation is an inference drawn from what precedes. What part of the preceding context is the basis of this inference? This is a difficult question on which interpreters greatly differ. In order to discover the answer it is necessary to examine more closely the scope of the condemnation which the apostle has in view in this passage. If the apostle is thinking merely of freedom from the guilt of sin and from the condemnation which guilt entails, then we should have to find the basis of the inference in that part of the epistle which deals particularly with that subject (3:21–5:21). But if there is included in freedom from condemnation not only deliverance from the guilt of sin but also from its power, then the "therefore" could be related quite properly to what immediately precedes (6:1–7:25) as well as to the more remote context. It is this latter alternative which the evidence would appear to demand. The word "condemnation" here can scarcely be interpreted apart from the immediately succeeding context in which it appears and so we must look for the specific complexion given to the word by this context to which it is so closely related. In this context, as will be shown later, the apostle is not dealing with justification and the expiatory aspect of Christ's work but with sanctification and with what God has done in Christ to deliver us from the power of sin. Hence what is thrust into the foreground in the terms "no condemnation" is not only freedom from the guilt but also freedom from the enslaving power of sin. If this appears to be a strange notion in connection with "condemnation" we shall have to wait for a vindication of this concept in the exposition of the verses which follow. If, however, this view of "condemnation" is adopted, then this verse, as inference, can be connected with what immediately precedes, either restrictedly (7:25) or more inclusively (6:1–7:25). The latter alternative is preferable, as will appear later on.

"In Christ Jesus"—this harks back to 6:3–11 where the theme of union with Christ in the virtue of his death and the power of his resurrection is developed as the pivot on which turns the argument of the apostle respecting death to sin and newness of life in Christ. To be reminded of union with Christ in this connection is no less pertinent than to be assured of freedom from condemnation, because the potency of sin and of the flesh, evident in the conflict of 7:14–25, makes it all the more necessary to appreciate the victory which belongs to the believer in the bonds of Christ Jesus. It is a succinct way of alluding to all the grace implied in the argument of the earlier passage.[1]

2 Verse 2 supplies the reason for the assurance given in verse 1: "For the law of the Spirit of life in Christ Jesus made me free from the law of sin and of death".[2] The two verses are not

---

[1] In 𝕂* B C D* F G, several cursives and some versions there is no addition after Ἰησοῦ in vs. 1. If we were to follow A D^b 263 and several versions and add μὴ κατὰ σάρκα περιπατοῦσιν or with 𝕂^c D^e and the mass of the cursives add also ἀλλὰ κατὰ πνεῦμα, this addition in whole or in part would provide some additional support for the inclusive meaning of the term "condemnation", for, in that event, our attention would be drawn immediately to the character and behaviour which the breach with the dominion of sin produces. But the external evidence is such that we cannot assume the genuineness of this addition in whole or in part. It is most likely that it was inserted from the end of vs. 4 in the course of transcription. In the latter case there is no textual question.

[2] It is difficult to decide between the readings με and σε in vs. 2. The

only bound together by the particle "for" but also by the repetition in verse 2 of "in Christ Jesus". Verse 2 unfolds the implication of the union with Christ emphasized at the close of verse 1. The main question is: what is "the law of the Spirit of life"? "The Spirit of life" must, in accord with Pauline and New Testament usage, refer to the Holy Spirit (*cf.* vss. 6, 10, 11; John 6:63; I Cor. 15:45; especially II Cor. 3:6, 17, 18; Gal. 6:8). The Holy Spirit is the Spirit of life because he is the author of life and also because he is life (*cf.* vs. 10). The question then becomes: what is "the law" in this connection? We can only arrive at the answer by determining what is "the law" with which it is contrasted, namely, "the law of sin and of death". The context should be regarded as decisive in this case. In 7:23, 25 the apostle had spoken of "the law of sin". As we found, it is most probably this same law that is spoken of in 7:21. And it is not without significance that, by reason of the activity of the law of sin in his members, he should call his body "the body of this death". Since the wages of sin is death "the law of sin" must also be the "law of death". The word "law" is used in this connection as a regulating and actuating power as well as a legislating authority. In view, therefore, of this contrast "the law of the Spirit of life" should be understood as the regulating and actuating power of the Holy Spirit as the Spirit of life. It is eminently appropriate that the Holy Spirit should be designated as the Spirit of life because the power he exercises is unto life as distinguished from the power of sin which is unto death. "The law of the Spirit of life" is, therefore, the power of the Holy Spirit operative in us to make us free from the power of sin which is unto death. This deliverance from the power of sin is correlative with that enunciated by the apostle in 6:2-14. The Holy Spirit is the Spirit of Christ (*cf.* vs. 9) and it is only in Christ Jesus that the Spirit's power is operative unto life.

It is not certain whether "in Christ Jesus" in this verse is to be taken with "the law of the Spirit of life" or with "made me free". In the former case the stress falls upon the fact that it is in Christ Jesus the actuating, life-giving power of the Holy Spirit is operative, in the latter case that it was in Christ Jesus the power of the Spirit made us free. The one views this life-

---

latter is supported by ℵ B F G, the former by A C D E K L P and several versions. Editors are interestingly divided. The sense is not affected.

giving law as being in Christ, the other views the action as wrought in Christ.

These considerations indicate that verse 2 is to be interpreted in terms of a power that is operative in us and that the ruling thought has respect to our deliverance from the power of sin —"the law of sin and death"—rather than to deliverance from the guilt of sin. The thought moves in the realm of internal operation and not in that of objective accomplishment. We must not assume, however, that the basis upon which this internal operation rests and from which it derives its power is far from the apostle's thought. This is clearly in the forefront in the verse that follows.

3 "What the law could not do",[3] as conceived of in this case, is to be interpreted in the light of what God did; he condemned sin in the flesh, something which the law could not do. What then is this action on God's part? There does not appear to be good warrant for supposing, as has been done by many interpreters, that the reference is to the expiatory action of God in the sacrifice of Christ.[4] While it is true that the work of Christ in reference to sin was expiatory and in that respect involved for him the vicarious endurance of the condemnation due to sin, yet that expiatory accomplishment is not defined in terms of the *condemnation* of sin. Furthermore, as we found already, the governing thought of this passage is concerned with deliverance from the law of sin and death and, therefore, from sin as a ruling and regulating power. Hence we are compelled to look in some other direction to see if there is any respect in which we might conceive of God as condemning sin in a way that is relevant to the governing thought of the passage. Did Christ in the work once for all accomplished do something decisively in reference to the power of sin which can be construed as God's condemning sin in the flesh? The answer will have to be in the affirmative.[5]

---

[3] τὸ ἀδύνατον τοῦ νόμου is commonly regarded as a nominative absolute in the sense that the impotence of the law is premised and set in contrast with that which God did, namely, "condemned sin in the flesh". It has also been taken as an accusative (*cf.* Sanday and Headlam: *op. cit., ad loc.*) in apposition to that which is the principal clause, "God ... condemned sin in the flesh". On the question whether ἀδύνατον is active or passive *cf.* the discussions by Gifford, Sanday and Headlam *et al., ad loc.*

[4] *Cf.* Calvin, Philippi, Hodge, Haldane, Shedd, *ad loc.*

[5] *Cf.* Alford: *op. cit., ad loc.* where there is a very helpful discussion. Meyer's words are likewise to the same effect and are worthy of recital. "This condemnation of sin (the latter conceived as principle and power) is that which was

We found that this aspect of Christ's once-for-all accomplishment comes to clear expression in 6:2–14. And this is clearly the teaching of our Lord himself and of the Scriptures elsewhere. Jesus said with reference to his death: "Now is the judgment of this world: now shall the prince of this world be cast out" (John 12:31). Here the victory over the world and Satan is represented as a judgment executed, and judicial language is used to express it. The victory over the powers of darkness is, according to Paul, a work wrought by the cross of Christ (Col. 2:15). The word "condemn" is used in the New Testament in the sense of consigning to destruction as well as of pronouncing the sentence of condemnation (cf. I Cor. 11:32; II Pet. 2:6). That is to say, condemnation may be viewed as not only the sentence but the putting of the sentence into execution. This would be an eminently appropriate use of the term when the action of God is contemplated because his pronouncement of judgment is efficient to the end of putting into execution the judgment pronounced. Since then judicial language is applied to the destruction of the power of the world and of the prince of darkness and since the term "condemnation" is used here respecting the work of Christ, there is warrant for the conclusion that the condemning of sin in the flesh refers to the judicial judgment which was executed upon the power of sin in the cross of Christ. God executed this judgment and overthrew the power of sin; he not only declared sin to be what it was but pronounced and executed judgment upon it. Furthermore, it is this constitutive meaning of condemnation that provides the proper contrast to what the law could not do. In the barely declarative sense the law could condemn sin; this is one of its chief functions. But the law cannot execute judgment upon sin so as to destroy its power. As the apostle had shown repeatedly in the preceding chapter, the law, rather than depriving sin of its power, only provides the occasion for the more violent exercise of its power. To execute judgment upon sin to the destruction of its power the law is impotent. This is exactly what God did by sending his

---

impossible on the part of the law, owing to the hindrance of the flesh. It is erroneous, therefore, to take it as: 'He exhibited sin as worthy of condemnation' . . . and: 'He punished sin'. . . . Impossible to the law was only such a condemnation of sin, as should depose the latter from the sway which it had hitherto maintained; consequently: He made sin forfeit its dominion. This de facto judicial condemnation . . . is designated by κατέκρινε" (op. cit., ad loc.).

own Son in the likeness of sinful flesh and for sin. Hence when both the negative and the positive elements of the text are analyzed they mutually support each other in pointing to the interpretation presented.

Corroboration of this view of the expression "condemned sin in the flesh" is derived from the expression "is justified from sin" in 6:7, as was noted in the exposition at that point. In that context the apostle is undoubtedly dealing with deliverance from the power of sin. "We died to sin" (6:2) is the thesis unfolded in that chapter, and the forensic term "justify" is used with reference to the judgment executed upon the power of sin in the death of Christ. The result is that all who have died with Christ are the beneficiaries of this judgment executed and are therefore quit of sin's dominion. This is the force of the expression "justified from sin". In like manner the forensic term "condemn" can be used in this instance to express the judicial judgment executed upon the power of sin in the flesh of Christ.

The law could not overcome the power of sin "in that it was weak through the flesh". The flesh is sinful human nature. The impotence of the law reflects upon the fact that it has no redemptive quality or efficiency. Therefore, as it is confronted with sin, it can do nothing to meet the exigency created by the flesh.

"God, sending his own Son in the likeness of sinful flesh and for sin, condemned sin in the flesh." (1) "God" here refers to the Father, as frequently in the usage of the apostle. Only of the Father is the second person the Son. (2) The Father sent the Son. The initiative in the whole process of redemptive accomplishment must be traced to the love and grace of the Father. (3) " His own Son"—this indicates the uniqueness of the sonship belonging to Christ and the uniqueness of the fatherhood belonging to the Father in relation to the Son. The same thought appears in verse 32. In the language of Paul this corresponds to the title "only-begotten" as it appears in John (John 1:14, 18; 3:16, 18; I John 4:9). It is the eternal sonship that is in view and to this sonship there is no approximation in the adoptive sonship that belongs to redeemed men. The same applies to the fatherhood of the first person. In the sense in which he is the eternal Father in relation to the Son he is not the Father of his adopted children. (4) "In the likeness of sinful flesh"—this mode of expression occurs nowhere else. Why did Paul use it

279

here? He speaks elsewhere of Christ as "made of the seed of David according to the flesh" (1:3; *cf.* 9:5), of his being "manifested in the flesh" (I Tim. 3:16; *cf.* John 1:14; I John 4:2), of his being "made in the likeness of men" (Phil. 2:7). The unique combination of terms in this instance must serve some special purpose. He is using the word "likeness" not for the purpose of suggesting any unreality in respect of our Lord's human nature. That would contradict Paul's express language elsewhere in this epistle and in his other epistles. He is under the necessity of using this word here because he uses the term "sinful flesh" and he could not have said that Christ was sent in "sinful flesh". That would have contradicted the sinlessness of Jesus for which the New Testament is jealous throughout. So the question is: why did Paul use the term "sinful flesh" when it is necessary to guard so jealously the sinlessness of the Lord's flesh? He is concerned to show that when the Father sent the Son into this world of sin, of misery, and of death, he sent him in a manner that brought him into the closest relation to sinful humanity that it was possible for him to come without becoming himself sinful. He himself was holy and undefiled—the word "likeness" guards this truth. But he came in the same human nature. And that is the purpose of saying "sinful flesh". No other combination of terms could have fulfilled these purposes so perfectly. There is emblazoned on the apostle's language the great truth that when the Father sent the Son he sent him for the deepest humiliation conceivable for him who was the Son of God and who, in his human nature, was "holy, harmless, undefiled, separate from sinners" (Heb. 7:26). (5) "And for sin"—this is to be construed as the purpose for which the Son was sent. It would be in accord with Scripture to regard "sin" as meaning sin-offering. But there is no good reason to inject any other thought than that when the Father sent the Son it was for the purpose of dealing with sin. Nothing should be allowed to detract from the eloquence of that simple but profound truth. For by it we are advised that the coming of the Son of God into the world had no relevance apart from the fact of sin. It was to deal with sin that he came and, in view of the preceding clause, there is distinctly suggested to us that not only did he come in a way that brought him into the closest possible relation to sinful humanity without becoming himself sinful but he also came into the closest relation to *sin* that was possible without becoming himself sinful. This definition of the purpose of his coming is sufficiently inclusive to comprehend the restricted result particularly in view in the principal clause, namely, "condemned sin in the flesh". (6) "Condemned sin in the flesh". It must not be overlooked that the Father is the subject in this clause and is therefore viewed as the agent. Our conception of the work of Christ is truncated unless we take into account the action of God the Father in those events which lie at the centre of redemption (cf. 4:24, 25; 8:32; II Cor. 5:18-21). It has been intimated already how we should interpret this action of condemning sin. But the following observations are now in order. (a) It is not sufficient to think merely of the condemnation of sin which the unblemished life of Jesus in the flesh offered. This is undoubtedly true in itself—the spotless holiness and purity of Jesus was the most signal and potent condemnation of the sin of the world.[6] But the two preceding phrases, "in the likeness of sinful flesh" and "for sin", particularly the latter, militate against the view that this is the ruling conception. Since the Son was sent to deal with sin, we must construe the action of condemning sin in redemptive terms. And, as maintained above, this action in this context will have to be regarded as the judicial judgment executed upon sin, after the analogy of John 12:31, unfolded for us in greater detail and in different terms in 6:2-14. It is the damnatory judgment by which sin has been deprived of its power and by reason of which the beneficiaries are delivered from the law of sin and of death and walk not after the flesh but after the Spirit. God the Father executed this judgment. And we are thereby reminded that the agency of the Father is present in that accomplishment which is preeminently the undertaking of the Son in his incarnate mission and commitment. (b) "In the flesh"—we cannot escape the eloquent contrasts which the use here of the word "flesh" throws into relief. The law "was weak through the flesh" and here "flesh" means sinful human nature. God sent his own Son in the likeness of sinful flesh and again "flesh", because it is the flesh of sin, is used in the depreciatory sense. But now sin was condemned in the "flesh". It is not that sin in the flesh was

---

[6] Godet is emphatic in restricting the thought to this notion. "Paul has in view neither the *destruction* of sin by the Holy Spirit (ver. 4), nor its *condemnation* on the cross; he is regarding *Christ's holy life* as a living condemnation of sin" (*op. cit., ad loc.*).

condemned[7] but that sin was condemned through the flesh. In that same nature which in all others was sinful, in that very nature which in all others was dominated and directed by sin, in that nature assumed by the Son of God but free from sin, God condemned sin and overthrew its power. Jesus not only blotted out sin's guilt and brought us nigh to God. He also vanquished sin as power and set us free from its enslaving dominion. And this could not have been done except in the "flesh". The battle was joined and the triumph secured in that same flesh which in us is the seat and agent of sin.

Before closing our discussion of verses 1–3 it is necessary to return to the condemnation referred to in verse 1. It will have become apparent why it was maintained at the outset that "condemnation" should be interpreted more inclusively than freedom from the guilt of sin. There is no need to suppose that this means departure from the strictly forensic import of condemnation. As has been shown, it is the judicial aspect that is in view in God's condemnation of sin in the flesh. And it is this same judicial aspect of our enslavement to the power of sin that comes into view in verse 1. Our enslavement to sin is properly viewed as the judgment to which we are consigned and there can be no release from this bondage, contemplated in its judicial character, until sin as power receives its judicial condemnation in the cross of Christ and until the effectual application to us takes effect. Hence freedom from condemnation must embrace freedom from the judgment of sin's power as well as the judgment of sin's guilt. The emphasis placed upon *no* condemnation would in itself suggest that every aspect from which condemnation can be viewed is included in this negation. And, in relation to the preceding context, what comfort is more appropriate and necessary for the believer engaged in the conflict described, a conflict in which the power of sin and of the flesh is so patent, than the assurance that the power of sin has been once for all decisively judged and that the ruling power in the believer is the law of the Spirit of life in Christ Jesus?

4 Since it is deliverance from the power of sin that is in the forefront and since "the law of the Spirit of life" (vs. 2) is the

---

[7] ἐν τῇ σάρκι is to be construed with κατέκρινε. There would be a redundancy in speaking of "sin in the flesh", whereas to intimate that it was "in the flesh" that sin was condemned is altogether apposite in this context.

regulating and controlling power of the Holy Spirit, verse 4 will have to be regarded as the designed effect in us of the judgment executed upon the power of sin in the cross of Christ and of the inwardly operative power of the Holy Spirit based upon and emanating from the once-for-all accomplishment in the cross of Christ. "The ordinance of the law" is the righteous requirement of the law (2:26; cf. Luke 1:6).[8] It is eloquent of the apostle's view of the place of the law of God in the life of the believer that he should conceive of the holiness, which is the end promoted by the redemptive work of Christ, as the fulfilment of the ordinance of God's law. It is all the more significant in this context because he had represented deliverance from the power of sin in 6:14 as proceeding from the fact that we are not "under law" but "under grace". In chapter 7 he had returned to that theme and showed that we are not "under law" because "we have been put to death to the law through the body of Christ" and "have been discharged from the law" (7:4, 6). He had also demonstrated that the law was unto death because sin took occasion from the law to work all manner of lust (7:8–13). And, finally, in this chapter he had just spoken of the impotence of the law (8:3). How then can he construe the holiness of the Christian state as the fulfilment of the law's requirement? The fact, however, cannot be disputed, and it is conclusive proof that the law of God has the fullest normative relevance in that state which is the product of grace. To construe the relations of law and grace otherwise is to go counter to the plain import of this text. We had been prepared for this, however, in earlier notifications to this same effect (cf. 3:31; 6:15; 7:12, 14, 16, 22, 25). And in the subsequent development of the subject of sanctification there is abundant corroboration (cf. 13:8–10).

The term "fulfilled" expresses the plenary character of the fulfilment which the law receives and it indicates that the goal contemplated in the sanctifying process is nothing short of the perfection which the law of God requires. The description given of those who are the partakers of this grace is one consonant with the tenor of the passage—they "walk not after the flesh

---

[8] δικαίωμα has a variety of meanings in this epistle. In 1:32 it is judicial sentence; in 5:16 it is the justifying sentence, justification; in 5:18 it is the justifying righteousness; here, as in 2:26, it is the righteous demand or requirement; cf. the exposition at these other points.

but after the Spirit". The Spirit is the Holy Spirit (vs. 2) and the contrast means that the directing power in their lives is not the flesh but the Holy Spirit. It is by the indwelling and direction of the Holy Spirit that the ordinance of the law comes to its fulfilment in the believer, and by the operations of grace there is no antinomy between the law as demanding and the Holy Spirit as energizing—"the law is Spiritual" (7:14).[9]

5–8

> 5 For they that are after the flesh mind the things of the flesh; but they that are after the Spirit the things of the Spirit.
> 6 For the mind of the flesh is death; but the mind of the Spirit is life and peace:
> 7 because the mind of the flesh is enmity against God; for it is not subject to the law of God, neither indeed can it be:
> 8 and they that are in the flesh cannot please God.

5–8 As is apparent from the sustained use of connecting conjunctions these verses are a closely knit unit and are intimately related to verse 4. "After the flesh" in verse 5 continues the thought of the same expression in verse 4, and the same holds true of "after the Spirit". Verse 5 is, therefore, confirmatory, or perhaps explanatory, of the contrast at the end of verse 4. Verse 6 is confirmatory, preferably explanatory, of verse 5. And verse 7 gives the reason for what is stated in verse 6. Verse 8 expands the impossibility stated at the end of verse 7. The whole passage is an expansion of the contrast between the flesh and the Spirit and an elucidation of what is involved in each of these contrasted elements. The emphasis of verse 4 is not, however, to be overlooked, namely, "*not* after the flesh, but after the Spirit". In other words, the interest is not simply to contrast these opposing elements but to show why the persons in view do *not* walk after the flesh but after the Spirit.

The two expressions "after the flesh" (vss. 4, 5) and "in the flesh" (vss. 8, 9) have the same effect, with this difference that in the former the flesh is viewed as the determining pattern and in the latter as the conditioning sphere—the persons concerned are conditioned by and patterned after the flesh. "The flesh"

---

[9] *Cf.* "Law and Grace" in *Principles of Conduct* (Grand Rapids, 1957), pp. 181–201, by the writer.

is human nature as corrupted, directed, and controlled by sin. "After the Spirit" (vss. 4, 5) and "in the Spirit" (vs. 9) are also to the same effect, with a similar distinction as to the angle from which the relationship to the Holy Spirit is viewed. Those concerned are conditioned by and patterned after the Holy Spirit. To "mind the things of the flesh" (vs. 5) is to have the things of the flesh as the absorbing objects of thought, interest, affection, and purpose. And "the mind of the flesh" (vs. 6) is the dispositional complex, including not simply the activities of reason but also those of feeling and will, patterned after and controlled by the flesh. In like manner to mind "the things of the Spirit" (vs. 5) is to have the things of the Holy Spirit as the absorbing objects of thought, interest, affection, and purpose, and "the mind of the Spirit" is the dispositional complex, including the exercises of reason, feeling, and will, patterned after and controlled by the Holy Spirit.

The expressions, "after the flesh" ("in the flesh"), "mind the things of the flesh" ("the mind of the flesh"), "walk after the flesh" stand in causal relationship to one another and are also, most probably, to be understood as causally related in the order stated. The first defines the basic moral condition, the second the inward frame of heart and mind resulting from that condition, and the third the practice emanating from both but more particularly from the first through the second. The same principles in the opposite direction hold with reference to "after the Spirit" ("in the Spirit"), to mind "the things of the Spirit" ("the mind of the Spirit"), and walk "after the Spirit".

"The mind of the flesh is death" (vs. 6) does not mean that the mind of the flesh causes or leads to death. There is an equation, and the predicate specifies that in which the mind of the flesh consists. The principle of death is separation, and here the most accentuated expression of that principle is in view, namely, separation from God (cf. Isa. 59:2). This separation is thought of in terms of our estrangement from God whereby we are dead in trespasses and sins (cf. Eph. 2:1). The mind of the flesh is therefore that kind of death.

"The mind of the Spirit is life and peace" (vs. 6). The same kind of identification appears here. "Life" is contrasted with "death" and in its highest expression, which must be in view here, it means the knowledge and fellowship of God (cf. John 17:3;

I John 1:3), the communion which is the apex of true religion. "Peace" can readily be seen to be the correlate of life. In this case it is no doubt the subjective effect of peace with God (5:1) that is contemplated, the sense of being at one with God and the tranquillity of heart and mind which the sense of reconciliation evokes (*cf*. Phil. 4:7). Peace is the antithesis of the alienation and misery which sin creates.

Verse 7 gives the reason *why* the mind of the flesh is death. It is "enmity against God". We have the same kind of equation. The essence of sin is to be against God; it is the contradiction of God. This predication is much stronger than to say that we are enemies of God, for it defines the mind of the flesh, the mind characterizing those who are "after the flesh" and "in the flesh", as one that is conditioned and governed by "enmity", enmity of which God is the object. Enmity towards God is the actuating principle and governing propension of the mind of the flesh. And when we keep in view what is meant by "mind" in this connection the implication is that the disposition underlying all activity is one of opposition to and hatred of God. The latter part of verse 7 is confirmatory of the first part. The law of God reflects the divine character and will and the attitude to the law is the index of the relation to God. Insubjection to the law is therefore construed as the concrete way in which enmity against God manifests itself, and the strength of the expression "enmity against God" shows the gravity with which insubjection to the law is viewed. This reference to the law of God in such a context evinces that same estimate of its sanctity and majesty which we found repeatedly in the earlier parts of the epistle. The last clause, "neither indeed can it be", points to the impossibility that resides in the mind of the flesh and means nothing less than that it is a moral and psychological impossibility for those who are "in the flesh" to have any disposition of obedience with respect to the law of God.

Verse 8[10] continues the thought of the last clause in verse 7, namely, the impossibility belonging to those who are "in the flesh". But a directly personal complexion is given to the thought by speaking of what is *well-pleasing to God*. And the extent of the impossibility is accentuated by the broader scope which is implicit

---

[10] The δέ in verse 8 is continuative and may best be rendered by "and", as in the version.

in the expression "please God". It is implied, of course, that "the law of God" enunciates what is well-pleasing to God. But what is pleasing to God comprehends more than is included in the term "law". Hence by saying that "they that are in the flesh *cannot please God*" the extent of the impossibility is expanded to cover the whole range of what is pleasing to God. This is an inference necessarily drawn from the first clause in verse 7, that the mind of the flesh is enmity against God. But the apostle does not leave his readers to inference; he expressly states what is to the effect that it is a moral and psychological impossibility for those who are in the flesh to do anything that elicits the divine approval and good pleasure. Here we have nothing less than the doctrine of the total inability of the natural man, that is to say, total inability to be well-pleasing to God or to do what is well-pleasing in his sight.

In the whole passage we have the biblical basis for the doctrines of total depravity and total inability. It should be recognized, therefore, that resistance to these doctrines must come to terms not simply with the present-day proponents of these doctrines but with the apostle himself. "Enmity against God" is nothing other than total depravity and "cannot please God" nothing less than total inability.

9–11

> 9 But ye are not in the flesh but in the Spirit, if so be that the Spirit of God dwelleth in you. But if any man hath not the Spirit of Christ, he is none of his.
> 10 And if Christ is in you, the body is dead because of sin; but the spirit is life because of righteousness.
> 11 But if the Spirit of him that raised up Jesus from the dead dwelleth in you, he that raised up Christ Jesus from the dead shall give life also to your mortal bodies through his Spirit that dwelleth in you.

9 The contrast between the flesh and the Spirit is as noted above. The apostle is careful to impart to believers the assurance and consolation which belong to them as those who are "in the Spirit" and are therefore under the direction and control of the Holy Spirit. Nevertheless he is likewise careful to lay down the condition upon which this assurance may be entertained—"if so

287

be that the Spirit of God dwelleth in you".[11] This refers to the abiding indwelling of the Holy Spirit in believers (cf. Eph. 2:22) and, as the latter part of verse 9 indicates, this indwelling is the *sine qua non* of being "in the Spirit". Both ways of expressing the relation of the Holy Spirit to the believer and *vice versa* are to be noted—the believer is in the Spirit and the Spirit is in the believer. These are distinguishable relationships but they are inseparable.

"But if any man hath not the Spirit of Christ, he is none of his." This is an emphatic negative way of stating what was implied in the preceding clause. "The Spirit of Christ" is none other than "the Spirit of God" of the preceding clause and indicates that the Holy Spirit sustains to Christ a relation similar to that which he sustains to the Father (cf. II Cor. 3:17, 18; Gal. 4:6; Phil. 1:19; I Pet. 1:11).[12] The force of the criterion which the apostle here establishes needs to be appreciated. If a person does not have the Holy Spirit he is not a believer. *Every* believer is indwelt by the Holy Spirit and is, therefore, as observed above, in the Spirit. This is to say, in terms of the apostle's teaching elsewhere (cf. ad 7:14), that *every* believer is "Spiritual" and there is no such discrimination among Christians as the distinction between those who are "in the Spirit" and those who are not "in the Spirit". The strength of the expression "he is none of his" leaves no room for doubt that the person not having the Spirit (cf. Jude 19) is outside the fold of Christ's called ones (cf. 1:6).

10 "And if Christ is in you"—this variation of terms shows that the indwelling of the Spirit of God, having the Spirit of Christ, and Christ in us are all to the same effect. This does not mean, however, that there is any blurring of the distinction between Christ and the Holy Spirit. Neither does it eliminate the distinctive modes of indwelling or the distinctive operations of the respective persons of the Godhead. But it does underline the intimacy of the relationship that exists between Christ and

---

[11] εἴπερ could be interpreted in the sense of "since" or "seeing that" (cf. II Thess. 1:6). But it is more usual for εἴπερ to specify a condition (cf. vs. 17; I Cor. 8:5; 15:15; II Cor. 5:3). Here it specifies the condition or ground upon which the assurance of the preceding clauses is based (cf. Col. 1:23). In the latter part of vs. 9 the warning is expressly stated in negative form.

[12] This is one of the strongest supports for the *filioque* clause.

the Holy Spirit in that union by which the believer becomes the habitation of both.

"The body is dead because of sin." There is no warrant for the view that this clause refers to the death to sin effected by union with Christ (cf. 6:2). This would not comport with the words "because of sin", and in view of reference to the resurrection of our "mortal bodies" in verse 11 there is every reason to regard the "body" here as the physical body and the death predicated of it as the dissolution that takes place when body and spirit are separated. The apostle can say that the body "is dead" because the principle of death is present and the body, to use Meyer's expression, is "the prey of death". "Because of sin" points back to 5:12 and 6:23 and reasserts the truth so often emphasized that the reason why death has invaded the physical aspect of our being is the fact of sin. Bodily death is the wages of sin.

"But the Spirit is life because of righteousness." Contrary to the interpretation adopted by the version and to all but uniform exegetical opinion[13], "the Spirit" in this clause I take to be the Holy Spirit. The contrast between the body as dead and the Spirit as life does not require that the elements contrasted must be man's body and man's spirit, as many exegetes categorically affirm. The following considerations are to be taken into account in support of the view that the Holy Spirit is contemplated. (1) In the preceding context and in verse 11 the Holy Spirit is unquestionably in view in each use of the term "Spirit"—"in the Spirit", "the Spirit of God" (vs. 9), "the Spirit of Christ" (vs. 10), "the Spirit of him that raised up Jesus from the dead", "his Spirit that dwelleth in you" (vs. 11). It would require much more evidence than is available to depart from this denotation at the end of verse 10. (2) Reference to the Holy Spirit as life is highly consonant with the thought introduced at the beginning of verse 11. For nothing is more pertinent to the certainty of the resurrection, which is the theme of verse 11, than that the Spirit who dwells in believers should be conceived

---

[13] The common view may be stated in the terms of Sanday and Headlam: "Clearly the πνεῦμα here meant is the human πνεῦμα which has the properties of life infused into it by the presence of the Divine πνεῦμα" (op. cit., ad loc.). Calvin adopts the view propounded above that it is the Holy Spirit. "Readers have been already reminded, that by the word Spirit they are not to understand the soul, but the Spirit of regeneration" (op. cit., ad loc.). Some others before and after Calvin adopted the same view.

of as *life*. (3) It is a mistake to think of the death referred to in this verse as merely *physical*; death is the separation of body and spirit and the latter, though not undergoing the corruption which affects the body, is nevertheless the subject of this separation. It would be strange, therefore, if the apostle would set up the human spirit of the believer as that which stands in antithesis to the death which is overtly predicated of the body. Something much more antithetical, something antithetical by way of the redemptive annulment of death, is demanded. The Holy Spirit as life supplies this antithesis, whereas the human spirit, however much it may be conceived of as imbued with life, does not. (4) The ruling thought of the verse is that although believers die and this fact is conspicuously exhibited in the dissolution of the body, yet, since Christ dwells in believers, life-giving forces are brought to bear upon death and this life is placed in sharp contrast with the disintegrating power which is exemplified in the return to dust on the part of the body. Reference to the Holy Spirit as life is signally congruous with this thought.

If the clause in question refers to the Holy Spirit, then the proposition that "the Spirit is life" is to be understood without reservation as identifying the Holy Spirit with that life which guarantees the annulment of death in the resurrection. The apostle had prepared us for this predication. Christ himself is the resurrection and the life (*cf.* John 11:25). But, as noted above, the apostle had shown the intimacy of the relationship between Christ and the Holy Spirit when he had called the Spirit "the Spirit of Christ" and had equated the indwelling of the Spirit with the indwelling of Christ (vss. 9, 10a). It must be observed, however, that when the Spirit is said to be "life" it is life as overcoming and delivering from death that is in view, the Holy Spirit as life in the consummating act of redemption, namely, the resurrection. This explains what is meant when it is said that "the Spirit is life *because of righteousness*". The Holy Spirit is not life in the redemptive sphere apart from the accomplishment of redemption by Christ. Here again we have the same intimacy of interdependence. This is just saying that the Holy Spirit is not the life spoken of here apart from the righteousness which is the grand theme of this epistle. It is *on account of* the righteousness which the apostle calls "the righteousness of God" and which is the righteousness and obedience of Christ that the

290

Holy Spirit is life in relation to and annulment of that death which conditions our sinful situation.

11 The Spirit referred to is none other than the Holy Spirit. He that "raised up Jesus from the dead" is without question the Father (*cf.* 4:25, 26; 6:4; Gal. 1:1; Eph. 1:17, 20). The Father is the specific agent in the resurrection of Christ. Since the Holy Spirit is called "the Spirit of him that raised up Jesus from the dead", this means that the Holy Spirit sustains a close relationship to the Father in that specific action which belongs *par excellence* to the Father in the economy of redemption. Just as the Holy Spirit is the Spirit of Christ because of the intimacy of relation he sustains to Christ in the messianic office which the name "Christ" denotes, so he is the Spirit of the Father because of the intimacy of relation he sustains to the Father in the raising up of Jesus. This relation supplies the basis for the proposition at the close of verse 10, namely, that "the Spirit is life"—the life he is, is resurrection life, life with resurrection power and virtue. Furthermore, the indwelling of the Holy Spirit, which is the main thought of the first part of verse 11, is viewed from the aspect of the character imparted to this indwelling in virtue of the fact that it is as the Spirit of him who raised up Jesus that he dwells in believers. And this stands in close relation to the inference drawn from the fact of his indwelling, to wit, "he that raised up Christ Jesus from the dead shall give life also to your mortal bodies through his Spirit that dwelleth in you".

"He that raised up Christ Jesus" is again the Father. He is represented, therefore, as the specific agent in the resurrection of believers. And this resurrection is defined in terms of "making alive your mortal bodies". Since this refers to the resurrection from the dead we might have expected the apostle to say "dead bodies" rather than "mortal bodies" (*cf.* vs. 10). But the language is significant. The term "mortal" describes the bodies of believers from the aspect of the mortality that belongs to them in this life prior to the event of death. And, although it is as dead bodies they will be made alive at the resurrection, yet the identification of them as "mortal bodies" shows that it is the same bodies which believers now possess that will be made alive at the resurrection. The identity and continuity are intimated in the description which the apostle here adopts, identity and continuity in no way interfering with the newness of quality by which these same bodies will be fitted for the resurrection state (*cf.* I Cor. 15:35-54).

The text followed by the version expressly indicates that the Holy Spirit will be active in the resurrection—"through his Spirit that dwelleth in you".[14] Though the Father is the specific agent in the resurrection of believers as in that of Christ, this does not exclude the agency of the Holy Spirit. The persons of the Godhead are co-active in the acts of redemption and will be also in the consummating act. If we follow this textual variant, there is the further implication that the Holy Spirit was also active in the resurrection of Christ from the dead. The Father's raising up of Christ is represented in this text as the guarantee that believers will be raised up, too. There is also the suggestion that the pattern provided by the resurrection of Christ is followed in the resurrection of believers (*cf.* Eph. 1:17ff.). Hence if the Holy Spirit is active in the resurrection of believers, it would follow that he was also active in the resurrection of Christ. For the latter supplies the basis and the pattern for the former.

The leading thought of the whole verse may be set forth thus. (1) The Father raised up Christ. (2) The Holy Spirit is the Spirit of the Father when the Father is contemplated in this specific capacity as the one who raised up Jesus. (3) The Holy Spirit dwells in believers and dwells in them as the Spirit of the Father. (4) This indwelling of the Spirit, since it is an indwelling of the Spirit of him who raised up Jesus, guarantees the resurrection from the dead of those thus indwelt.

12-17

12 So then, brethren, we are debtors, not to the flesh, to live after the flesh:
13 for if ye live after the flesh, ye must die; but if by the Spirit ye put to death the deeds of the body, ye shall live.

---

[14] The variant is that between διά with the genitive and διά with the accusative. The former — τοῦ ἐνοικοῦντος αὐτοῦ πνεύματος — is supported by ℵ A C P² and several versions, the latter—τὸ ἐνοικοῦν αὐτοῦ πνεῦμα—by B D G and the mass of the cursives with a few versions. The former indicates the direct agency of the Holy Spirit. The latter, however, does not exclude this agency and indeed suggests the same. Only, if the latter reading were adopted, it would be possible to suppress the thought of the Holy Spirit's agency in the resurrection. If, however, the indwelling of the Spirit is given as the reason for the resurrection (διά with the acc.), it is difficult to eliminate the causality of the Spirit.

14 For as many as are led by the Spirit of God, these are sons of God.

15 For ye received not the spirit of bondage again unto fear; but ye received the spirit of adoption, whereby we cry, Abba, Father.

16 The Spirit himself beareth witness with our spirit, that we are children of God:

17 and if children, then heirs; heirs of God, and joint-heirs with Christ; if so be that we suffer with *him*, that we may be also glorified with *him*.

12 Verse 12 is an inference drawn from the preceding verses and probably all of the earlier part of the chapter is to be understood as the basis of this conclusion. The inference has hortatory implications, though not expressly in the language of exhortation. More generally we think of the sacrificial work of Christ as that which places us under debt to the life of holiness. But here it is the work and particularly the indwelling of the Holy Spirit that are pleaded as the reason for consecration. The form in which the obligation devolving upon us is stated is negative—"debtors, not to the flesh, to live after the flesh". It is implied, of course, that we are debtors to the Spirit to live after the Spirit, but this is allowed to be inferred from its negative opposite. The "flesh" is the complex of sinful desire, motive, affection, propension, principle, and purpose, and "to live after the flesh" is to be governed and directed by that complex. The force of the inference is apparent. How contradictory for us, having been delivered by the Spirit from the law of sin and death and being indwelt by the Holy Spirit, to yield our obedience and service to that from which the Holy Spirit has emancipated us!

13 Verse 13 gives the reason for both the expressed negation and the implied affirmation of verse 12 and it does so by setting forth the antithetical issues of life after the flesh and life after the Spirit. "If ye live after the flesh, ye shall die." Here is an inevitable and invariable sequence, a sequence which God himself does not and cannot violate. To make life the issue of life after the flesh would be an inherent contradiction. God saves from the flesh but not in it. Paul is speaking here to believers and to them he says, "if ye live after the flesh, ye shall die". The death referred to must be understood in its broadest scope and does not stop short of death in its ultimate manifestation, eternal separation from God. The doctrine of the security of the believer does not obviate this sequence. The only way of avoiding the issue of death is to be delivered and desist from the life of the flesh. "But if by the Spirit ye put to death the deeds of the body, ye shall live." The sequence in this case is as inevitable and invariable as in the other. It is noteworthy that in this case the apostle does not use a parallel mode of expression, "if ye live after the Spirit". He becomes much more concrete and reverts to a negative formula, indicating again the practical bent of the apostle's thinking and the fact that consecration must be negative as well as positive—"if by the Spirit ye put to death the deeds of the body ye shall live". Several observations are necessary in regard to this statement. (1) "Put to death" refers to activity on our part. In 7:4 believers are represented as having been put to death and as having died to that wherein they were held (7:6). In these verses the passivity of the believer is in view. Now his responsible activity is enlisted. The latter is based on the former. The believer's once-for-all death to the law and to sin does not free him from the necessity of mortifying sin in his members; it makes it *necessary* and *possible* for him to do so. (2) "The deeds of the body." The physical entity which we call the body is undoubtedly intended (*cf.* vss. 10, 11) and implies, therefore, that the apostle is thinking of those sins associated with and registered by the body. As was noted in connection with 6:6, the thought is not that the body is the source of sin nor that the sins to be put to death are merely those of which the body is the executive organ. It is rather the pointed concreteness and practicalness of the demands placed upon the believer that are made apparent. "The deeds of the body" are those practices characteristic of the body of sin (*cf.* 6:6), practices which the believer must put to death if he is to live (*cf.* Col. 3:5). (3) This activity is not apart from the Holy Spirit—it is "by the Spirit". The believer is not endowed with a reservoir of strength from which he draws. It is always "by the Spirit" that each sanctified and sanctifying activity is exercised. (4) The life which is the sequel, just as death in the opposing parallel, is life in its broadest reference and does not fall short of that eternal life which the saints will enjoy eternally in the presence and fellowship of God.

14 The connection between this verse and the preceding is as follows. Those who by the Spirit put to death the deeds of the body are led by the Spirit of God. But those who are led by the Spirit of God are the sons of God. And, if they are the sons of God, that status is the guarantee of eternal life. Verse 14 is, therefore, to be interpreted as providing the basis for the assurance given in verse 13, namely, "ye shall live", the specific consideration being that eternal life is the invariable issue of sonship. It is taken for granted that those who by the Spirit put to death the deeds of the body are led by the Spirit of God and it is categorically asserted that as many as are led by the Spirit *these* are the sons of God.[15] "Led by the Spirit" implies that they are governed by the Spirit and the emphasis is placed upon the activity of the Spirit and the passivity of the subjects. "Put to death the deeds of the body" (vs. 13) emphasizes the activity of the believer. These are complementary. The activity of the believer is the evidence of the Spirit's activity and the activity of the Spirit is the cause of the believer's activity.

15 This verse adds further confirmation to the thought expressed in verses 13, 14, namely, that sonship is the guarantee of eternal life. The implications of sonship are now unfolded. Much difference of opinion exists as to the meaning of "spirit of bondage" and "spirit of adoption". A common view, if not the most prevalent, is that the "spirit of bondage" is the slavish spirit or temper of mind which controls us prior to liberation by the gospel, a disposition which arouses or is accompanied by fear and dread. In like manner, the "spirit of adoption" is the filial disposition of confidence which expresses itself in the address "Abba, Father".[16] The term "spirit" can be used in this sense of disposition, frame of mind (*cf.* 11:8; I Cor. 4:21; Gal. 6:1; I Pet. 3:4; possibly II Tim. 1:7) in both a good and bad sense. Furthermore, it would appear impossible to interpret "spirit of bondage" in any other sense; the Holy Spirit is not the Spirit of bondage but of liberty (*cf.* II Cor. 3:17). And since it would

---

[15] οὗτοι has the emphasis and has the force of "these and no other".

[16] *Cf., e.g.,* Luther, Philippi, Meyer, Gifford, Sanday and Headlam, Denney, Dodd, *ad loc.* It may be that Sanday and Headlam take "Spirit of adoption" in a different sense from that of "spirit of bondage" and regard the former as referring to the Holy Spirit. This is the case with Haldane, *e.g.,* who takes "spirit of bondage" in the sense of servile spirit but "Spirit of adoption" as of the Holy Spirit.

be harsh to take the word "spirit" in one sense in "spirit of bondage" and in another in "spirit of adoption", it is not surprising that expositors have adopted the foregoing interpretation. There is, however, good reason for rejecting this interpretation. Gal. 4:6 is closely parallel to this verse: "And because ye are sons, God sent forth the Spirit of his Son into our hearts, crying, Abba, Father". Here, without question, the Holy Spirit is in view and it is by him that we cry, "Abba, Father". The parallelism of the thought constrains the conclusion that in Rom. 8:15 "the Spirit of adoption, whereby we cry, Abba, Father" is the Holy Spirit.[17] He is called "the Spirit of adoption", not because he is the agent of adoption but because it is he who creates in the children of God the filial love and confidence by which they are able to cry, "Abba, Father" and exercise the rights and privileges of God's children.[18] With reference to the address "Abba, Father" (cf. Mark 14:36; Gal 4:6) the most tenable view is that both the Aramaic and the Greek words were used by our Lord himself and that his disciples, or at least some of them, followed his example with the result that both terms were combined in the form of address adopted.[19] The repetition indicates the warmth as well as the confidence with which the Holy Spirit emboldens the people of God to draw nigh as children to a father able and ready to help them.[20] The hesitation to entertain this confidence of approach to God the Father is not a mark of true humility. It is to be noted that it is by or in the Holy Spirit that this approach is made. Without the filial reverence and tenderness fostered by the Spirit the address is presumption and arrogance.

If "the Spirit of adoption" is the Holy Spirit, what is the "spirit of bondage"? It would seem arbitrary to take "Spirit" in the one case as a proper name and not in the other. The Holy Spirit, however, cannot be called "the Spirit of bondage" for, as noted above, where he is, *there* is liberty. The solution resides

---

[17] *Cf.* Calvin, Alford, Hodge, Haldane, Godet, *ad loc.*
[18] It is not necessary or strictly correct to say with Hodge that "the Spirit is so called because he adopts. It is by him we are made the sons of God" (*op. cit., ad loc.*). It is the Father who, by way of eminence, is the agent in adoption. The evidence, particularly in the Pauline epistles, indicates that it is to the Father believers sustain the relation of sons by adoption and it is therefore the Father who adopts.
[19] *Cf.* Philippi, Meyer, Godet, Sanday and Headlam, *ad loc.*
[20] *Cf. Westminster Shorter Catechism*, Q. 100.

in the consideration that the proposition respecting the "Spirit
of bondage" is negative and there is no reason why we should
not interpret the thought to be, "Ye did not receive the Holy
Spirit as a Spirit of bondage but as the Spirit of adoption".
The expression "again unto fear" is to be understood in the
sense that the reception of the Holy Spirit does not have the
effect of a relapse into that slavish fear which characterized the
pre-Christian state, and the reason for this is that the Holy Spirit
is not the Spirit of bondage but of adoption, the Spirit whose
activities are promotive of what is consonant with adoption, not
with what is symptomatic of bondage.

16 To understand the thought of this verse it is necessary to
revert to the preceding. In verse 15 reference is made to the filial
response registered in the heart of the believer himself—"*We* cry,
Abba, Father". To use the language of verse 16, it is the witness
borne *by* the believer's own consciousness in virtue of the Holy
Spirit's indwelling as the Spirit of adoption. Now in verse 16
it is the witness borne by the Holy Spirit *himself*. And this latter
witness is conceived of as working conjointly with the witness
borne by the believer's own consciousness. The Spirit's witness
must, therefore, be distinguished from the witness of our filial
consciousness. It is a witness given *to* us as distinct from the witness
given *by* us. The witness thus given is to the effect that "we are
children of God".[21] We are not to construe this witness of the
Spirit as consisting in a direct propositional revelation to the
effect, "Thou art a child of God". It is to us indeed the witness
is given and it is "to our spirit", but there are many respects in
which this witness is borne. Particularly is it made manifest in

---

[21] In the New Testament Paul has a monopoly of the word υἱοθεσία (8:15,
23; 9:4; Gal. 4:5; Eph. 1:5). It is noteworthy that he does not restrict himself
to the term υἱός to designate the adopted. In this chapter we have an interesting
example of the flexibility of usage; in vss. 16, 17, 21 he uses τέκνα and in vss.
14, 19 he uses υἱοί. We find the same variation elsewhere, τέκνα in 9:7, 8;
Eph. 5:1; Phil. 2:15 and υἱοί in 9:26; II Cor. 6:18; Gal. 3:26; 4:6, 7. It
would be artificial to find a different concept. There is no evidence that,
in terms of the derivation of τέκνον, Paul conceived of this sonship as constituted
by regeneration. John's usage is different. He does not use υἱός with reference
to this relationship except in Rev. 21:7 and possibly in John 12:36. He uses
τέκνα in John 1:12; I John 3:1, 2, 10; 5:2; cf. John 11:52; II John 1, 4, 13;
III John 4. It may be that John relates sonship more closely to regeneration
(cf. John 1:12, 13; I John 2:29; 3:9; 4:7; 5:1, 4, 18). But even in John the
distinct act of bestowment of privilege is also apparent (cf. John 1:12; I John
3:1).

sealing to the hearts of believers the promises which are theirs as heirs of God and joint-heirs with Christ and the generating in them of the assurance of the great love the Father has bestowed upon them that they should be called children of God (*cf.* I John 3:1).[22]

17 This verse obviously states the inference drawn from the fact of sonship respecting the glory that awaits the people of God and is to be related to verse 14. There the fact of sonship was adduced as the guarantee of eternal life. Here this is expanded and the life that awaits the people of God is defined—"heirs of God, and joint-heirs with Christ" (*cf.* Gal. 4:7 where the same logical sequence is expressed even more succinctly). "Heirs of God" can involve nothing less than that the sons of God are heirs of the inheritance which God himself has laid up for them. But it is difficult to suppress the richer and deeper thought that God himself is the inheritance of his children (*cf.* Psalm 73:25, 26; Lam. 3:24). Support is given to this notion when we consider that they are "joint-heirs with Christ". The reward of Christ was preeminently that he was glorified with the Father; and the Lord was the portion of his inheritance (*cf.* John 17:5; Psalm 16:5). "Joint-heirs with Christ" means that the children of God enter in jointly with Christ into the possession of the inheritance which was bestowed upon him. This is the aspect from which union and communion with Christ (which the apostle had emphasized in other connections in earlier portions of this epistle) are to be viewed in the state of glory. Just as Christ in his sufferings, death, and resurrection cannot be contemplated apart from those on whose behalf he suffered, died, and rose again, so in the glory bestowed upon him as the reward of his finished work he cannot be contemplated apart from them. And they in the state of glory cannot be contemplated apart from him. Therefore the glory of their inheritance can be none other than the glory which is Christ's in the reward of his exaltation. This is expressly stated in the final clause of the verse, "that we may be also glorified with him". It is well to be reminded that this is what Jesus prayed for on behalf of his own: "Father, I will that they also whom thou hast given me be with me where I am, that they may behold

---

[22] *Cf.* for helpful exposition Robert Haldane: *op cit., ad loc.;* Thomas Chalmers: *Lectures on the Epistle of Paul the Apostle to the Romans,* Lecture LIV.

my glory, which thou hast given me" (John 17:24). "Joint-heirs with Christ" is not a loftier conception than "heirs of God" but it gives concrete expression and elucidation to what is involved in being "heirs of God".

"If so be that we suffer with him, that we may be also glorified with him" is the condition upon which the attainment of the inheritance is contingent (cf. vs. 9). There is no sharing in Christ's glory unless there is sharing in his sufferings. Sufferings and then glory was the order appointed for Christ himself. It could not have been otherwise in terms of his messianic undertaking and design (cf. Luke 24:26; Phil. 2:6–11; I Pet. 1:11). The same order applies to those who are heirs with him. It is not only, however, that they must suffer and then enter glory; it is more than a parallelism of order. It needs to be noted that they suffer *with* him and this *joint* participation is emphasized in the case of suffering as it is in the case of glorification. This is both the reason for and the import of the emphasis which is placed in the New Testament and particularly in Paul upon the sufferings of the people of God as the sufferings of Christ (cf. II Cor. 1:5; Phil. 3:10; Col. 1:24; II Tim. 2:11; I Pet. 4:13; cf. Mark 10:39). Believers do not contribute to the accomplishment of expiation, propitiation, reconciliation, and redemption. Nowhere are their sufferings represented as having such virtue or efficacy. The Lord laid his people's iniquities upon Christ alone and in him alone did God reconcile the world to himself. Christ alone redeemed us by his blood. Nevertheless there are other aspects from which the sufferings of the children of God are to be classified with the sufferings of Christ himself. They partake of the sufferings which Christ endured and they are regarded as filling up the total quota of sufferings requisite to the consummation of redemption and the glorification of the whole body of Christ (cf. Col. 1:24). Again union and communion with Christ are the explanation and validation of this participation.

18–25

> 18 For I reckon that the sufferings of this present time are not worthy to be compared with the glory which shall be revealed to us-ward.
> 19 For the earnest expectation of the creation waiteth for the revealing of the sons of God.

20 For the creation was subjected to vanity, not of its own will, but by reason of him who subjected it, in hope

21 that the creation itself also shall be delivered from the bondage of corruption into the liberty of the glory of the children of God.

22 For we know that the whole creation groaneth and travaileth in pain together until now.

23 And not only so, but ourselves also, who have the first-fruits of the Spirit, even we ourselves groan within ourselves, waiting for *our* adoption, *to wit*, the redemption of our body.

24 For in hope were we saved: but hope that is seen is not hope: for who hopeth for that which he seeth?

25 But if we hope for that which we see not, *then* do we with patience wait for it.

There are three grounds of encouragement which the apostle adduces for the support and consolation of the children of God in the sufferings they are called upon to endure for Christ's sake and as the necessary precondition of their glorification with Christ. These verses comprise the considerations which constitute the first of these grounds.

18 This verse is an appeal to the great disproportion between the sufferings endured in this life and the weight of glory reserved for the children of God—the present sufferings fade into insignificance when compared with the glory to be revealed in the future. The apostle appeals to this consideration as an inducement to patient endurance of the sufferings. When he says "I reckon" (*cf.* 3:28; Phil. 3:13), he is giving by way of understatement his judgment respecting a truth of which there is no gainsaying (*cf.* II Cor. 4:17). The "present time" is stated to be the period within which these sufferings fall. This is a technical expression and is not to be equated with our common phrase, "the time being". The present time is "this age" or "present age" in contrast with "the age to come" (*cf.* Matt. 12:32; Mark 10:30; Luke 16:8; 20:34, 35; Rom. 12:2; Gal. 1:4; Eph. 1:21). The age to come is the age of the resurrection and of the glory to be revealed. The contrast is not between the sufferings endured by a believer in this life prior to death and the bliss upon which he enters at death (*cf.* II Cor. 5:8; Phil. 1:23). The glory contemplated is that of the resurrection and of the age to come. It is said to be "the glory which shall be revealed to us-ward". The expression bespeaks the certainty of the revelation in the future. It would be inviting to stress the concealment presupposed in the word "reveal" to the extent of supposing that the glory to be revealed is conceived of as already existing in concealment and needing only to be made manifest. The glory would then be the glory that belongs to Christ now and which will be bestowed upon believers in the future. The term "reveal", however, does not necessarily have this implication (cf. Gal. 3:23). And the glory to be revealed is so bound up with the resurrection (vs. 23) that we cannot conceive of it as existing now except in the design and purpose of God. This glory is to be revealed "unto us", that is to say, it is to reach unto us, is to be bestowed upon us, so that we become the actual partakers; it is not a glory of which we are to be mere spectators.

19 Considerable difference of opinion reasonably exists as to the precise element in verse 18 with which this verse is to be connected.[23] When there is good reason for doubt, one can only express his judgment and the reason for it. It seems that verse 19 is intended to lend confirmation and support to the patient and confident expectation to which, by implication, believers are urged in verse 18 and that this is done by instancing the "earnest expectation" of the creation. If "the creation" entertains persistent expectation, believers should do likewise —let us be astride the creation itself. The word "creation" denotes the creative act in 1:20. Here it must refer to the product. The question is: How much of created reality does it include? It must be observed that it is delimited by verses 20–23. And the best way to arrive at the denotation is to proceed by way of exclusion in terms of this delimitation.[24] *Angels* are not included because they were not subjected to vanity and to the bondage of corruption. *Satan* and

---

[23] Meyer thinks that it is the *certainty* of the future glory that is being witnessed to in vs. 19 and he lays stress upon "the emphatic prominence of μέλλουσαν" (*op. cit., ad loc.*). Philippi thinks that it is not so much the *certainty* as the *futurity* of the glory, to the effect that the futurity is shown by the waiting and sighing of both believers and the creation. Others find in verse 19 the confirmation of the *greatness* of the future glory.

[24] In Hodge's words, "the words πᾶσα ἡ κτίσις, *the whole creation*, are so comprehensive, that nothing should be excluded which the nature of the subject and the context do not show cannot be embraced within their scope" (*op. cit., ad loc.*).

the *demons* are not included because they cannot be regarded as longing for the manifestation of the sons of God and they will not share in the liberty of the glory of the children of God. The *children of God* themselves are not included because they are distinguished from "the creation" (vss. 19, 21, 23)—there would be no purpose, for example, in saying "and not only so, but ourselves also" (vs. 23) if believers were included in the groaning predicated of creation in the preceding verse. *Mankind in general* must be excluded because it could not be said of mankind that it "was subjected to vanity, not of its own will"—mankind was subjected to all the evil it is called upon to endure because of the voluntary act of transgression. The *unbelieving* of mankind cannot be included because the earnest expectation does not characterize them. Even those who are at present unbelieving but will be converted are excluded because they will be comprised in the children of God who, as the partakers of the glory to be revealed, are distinguished from "the creation" (vss. 19, 21). We thus see that all of *rational* creation is excluded by the terms of verses 20–23. We are restricted, therefore, to non-rational creation, animate and inanimate. Since in verse 22 the apostle speaks of "the *whole* creation", we are compelled, in the restricted sphere of the non-rational, to give the term comprehensive scope and we are prevented from positing any further limitation. Speculation, however, would be indefensible.[25]

Of the material heavens and earth, therefore, the apostle speaks when he says "the earnest expectation of the creation waiteth for the revelation of the sons of God." There is, no doubt, personification here. But this is quite common in Scripture (*cf.* Psalm 98:8; Isa. 55:12; Ezek. 31:15). The truth set forth is not obscured by personifying what is not personal; non-rational creation is reserved for a regeneration that is correlative with "the revelation of the sons of God".[26] This "revelation" is but

---

[25] For a more detailed refutation of opposing views and defence of this one *cf.* Hodge: *op. cit., ad loc.* and Meyer: *op. cit., ad loc.* This view is the one most widely maintained by the commentators.

[26] It is most reasonable to regard the ἀποκατάστασις πάντων of Acts 3:21 as referring to this same regeneration. In Matt. 19:28 παλιγγενεσία has frequently been interpreted in the same way. There need be no doubt that the new heavens and the new earth of II Pet. 3:13 refer to this regeneration. In this latter passage we have ultimate eschatology, and the description given in Rom. 8:19–23 of the nature of the deliverance which the creation will enjoy at the revelation of the sons of God is one that leaves room for no higher

another aspect from which the glory to be revealed unto them is viewed. Not till then will the children of God be made manifest to themselves and others in the plenitude of their status and privilege as sons, and not until they are all glorified together with Christ will the body of Christ be *manifested* in its integrity and unity (*cf.* Col. 3:3, 4).

20 This verse gives the reason why "the creation" is imbued with earnest expectation and is waiting for the revelation of the sons of God. There are three considerations mentioned: (1) it was subjected to vanity; (2) it was subjected not of its own will; (3) it was subjected in hope. The "vanity" to which creation was subjected would appear to refer to the lack of vitality which inhibits the order of nature and the frustration which the forces of nature meet with in achieving their proper ends. In relation to this earth this is surely Paul's commentary on Gen. 3:17, 18. But we may not restrict the term "creation" to this earth; the apostle's horizon is much wider. While it is possible for us to derive from Gen. 3:17, 18 (*cf.* Psalm 107:34; Isa 24:5–13) some notion of this vanity as it has affected our earth, we are not able to understand the implications for creation as a whole. But that the whole creation is affected is apparent from verse 22. "Not of its own will" does not imply that "the creation" possesses will or that it could have willed its own subjection to vanity. This is simply a statement to emphasize the fact that it was wholly on account of the will of another that the subjection took place. "By reason of him who subjected it"—this can be none other than God, not Satan, nor man. Neither Satan nor man could have subjected it *in hope*; only God could have subjected it with such a design. Besides, the context indicates that the hope will one day be realized and, since only by God's action can this be, in like manner God alone could have established the necessity or ground for hope. "In hope" shows that the non-rational creation, when subjected to vanity,[27] was not consigned to this evil condition apart from God's design of ultimate deliverance, and its present

---

or more ultimate glory—it is defined as deliverance "into the liberty of the glory of the children of God". This liberty for the sons of God is consummate; the liberty enjoyed by the creation in its own sphere must also be consummate.

[27] It does not make much difference whether ἐπ᾿ ἐλπίδι is taken with ὑπετάγη or with ὑποτάξαντα. But it is preferably taken with the former as the main verb rather than with the participle.

state, therefore, is not a finality. In other words, hope conditioned the act of subjection and continues to condition the vanity and corruption imposed upon it. This fact anticipates and confirms the thought of deliverance and restoration so explicitly set forth in the following verses and it explains the "earnest expectation" of verse 19.[28]

21 In the version the conjunction at the beginning is rendered by "that". In this event verse 21 defines the object of the hope—it is a hope that the creation will be delivered. This conjunction may also be rendered "because"[29] and in that event tells the reason why the creation was subjected to vanity in hope. Both renderings and interpretations are true and in accord with the context. It is difficult to ascertain which is correct. But uncertainty does not obscure the main thought that the creation "will be delivered from the bondage of corruption into the liberty of the glory of the children of God". "The bondage of corruption" is the bondage which consists in corruption and, since it is not ethical in character, must be taken in the sense of the decay and death apparent even in non-rational creation.[30] "The liberty of the glory of the children of God" is the liberty that consists in the glory of God's children and, as *liberty*, stands in overt contrast with the *bondage* of corruption. The "glory" is that referred to in verses 17, 18. The creation is to share, therefore, in the glory that will be bestowed upon the children of God. It can only participate in that glory, however, in a way that is compatible with its nature as non-rational. Yet the glory of the children of

---

[28] This representation is not consistent with the notion sometimes entertained that the material creation is to be annihilated, for such a notion is alien to all that *hope* implies. Hope involves the expectation of something of which the hoping subject is to be the recipient. In this case it is emancipation into the liberty of the glory of the children of God. Annihilation could not supply this positive ingredient—annihilation is ultimate negation.

[29] This would be necessary if, instead of ὅτι with A B C Dᶜ E K L P, we were to read διότι with ℵ D* F G. Notable editors follow the latter reading.

[30] If φθορά has here ethical connotation (*cf.* Gal. 6:8; II Pet. 1:4; 2:19), then the bondage would be the bondage proceeding from man's ethical depravity, the bondage to which the creation is subjected as a result of man's sin, and φθορά itself would not be predicated of the creation. It is more natural to take τῆς φθορᾶς as in apposition, the bondage which consists in corruption, just as the opposite, τὴν ἐλευθερίαν τῆς δόξης, should be interpreted. φθορά is used in this non-ethical sense in Col. 2:22; II Pet. 2:12a. In I Cor. 15:42, 50 this same non-ethical force is most probable—it is the mortality of the body that is in view.

God is one that comprises the creation also and must not be conceived of apart from the cosmic regeneration—the glory of the people of God will be in the context of the restitution of all things (cf. Acts. 3:21). The liberty reserved for the creation is the goal of its "earnest expectation" and the terminus of its groaning and travailing.

22 Here the apostle appeals to an incontestable fact in confirmation of what had been affirmed respecting *the hope* of the creation. Whether it is intended to be directly confirmatory of the vanity and corruption to which the creation has been subjected it is difficult to say. In any case it is confirmation of the liberation for which the creation is destined. This import of verse 22 becomes apparent only when we appreciate the force of the terms used, "groaneth and travaileth in pain". These groans and travails are not death pangs but birth pangs. In the words of Calvin, "as creatures . . . have a hope of being hereafter freed from corruption, it hence follows, that they groan like a woman in travail until they shall be delivered. But it is a most suitable similitude; it shows that the groaning of which he speaks will not be in vain and without effect; for it will at length bring forth a joyful and blessed fruit."[31] "Until now" indicates that the birth of the new order has not yet taken place, but it also is a token that the birth pangs have not ceased and that hope has not been quenched. "Together" is better regarded as referring to creation in its entirety and all its parts as uniting in this travail rather than as uniting with believers. The emphasis upon the *whole* creation and the fact that believers' participation with creation is so expressly intimated in the next verse militate against the latter view. In Philippi's words, "The entire creation, as it were, sets up a grand symphony of sighs".[32]

23 "And not only so"—here the conjoint groaning of the children of God is reflected on; not only does the whole creation groan but we also. The distinction, however, is to be observed. The thought is not that since the creation groans it is to be expected that we also should groan. Nor is the thought that since creation groans for its liberation how much more should we

---

[31] *Op. cit., ad loc.; cf.* Meyer: *op. cit., ad loc., et al.*
[32] *Op. cit., ad loc.*

305

who have the firstfruits of the Spirit.[33] The groaning of the children of God is introduced as something surprising.[34] But, though surprising, yet for that reason it is all the more confirmatory of the hope which is set before both the creation and the children of God. The rendering of the version, "who have the firstfruits of the Spirit", is possible and does not necessarily disturb the sense.[35] This clause may also be rendered, "having the firstfruits of the Spirit" and is to be understood in the sense of since or though we have the firstfruits of the Spirit.[36] Expositors seem to have a preference for the rendering, "though we have the firstfruits of the Spirit" and understand the passage to mean that notwithstanding the grace and privilege bestowed upon us we still groan within ourselves.[37] Thereby is certified all the more forcefully the place that hope occupies in the outlook of the believer. "The firstfruits of the Spirit", in accord with the analogy of Scripture usage (cf. 11:16; 16:5; I Cor. 15:20; 16:15; James 1:18; Rev. 14:4), should preferably be taken as the token gift of the Spirit given to believers now as the pledge of the plenitude of the Spirit to be bestowed at the resurrec-

---

[33] This is Calvin's view. ". . . how much more it behoves us, who have been illuminated by the Spirit of God, to aspire and strive with firmness of hope and with ardour of desire, after the attainment of so great a benefit" (*op. cit., ad loc.*).

[34] *Cf.* Philippi who says, "we should naturally expect no στενάζειν any longer to have place in us" (*op. cit., ad loc.*).

[35] ἔχοντες may be attributive. But even as such, as Burton says, it "may like a relative clause convey a subsidiary idea of cause, purpose, condition, or concession" (*op. cit.*, § 428).

[36] In this case ἔχοντες is taken as adverbial. Of course, in this event, the subject is well understood as those who have the firstfruits of the Spirit. But if ἔχοντες is regarded as adverbial, then the causal, or conditional, or concessive idea is more patently expressed.

[37] *Cf.* Philippi, Meyer, Gifford, Alford, Godet, *ad loc.* Grammatically, on the supposition that ἔχοντες is adverbial, there is no reason why the clause in question should not be rendered, "since we have the firstfruits of the Spirit". This would give the reason why we groan within ourselves and the accent would fall upon the fact that it is only the firstfruits we now have in contrast with the full harvest—the firstfruits whet the appetite for the fulness which the adoption will administer. This causes us to yearn for the adoption and therefore groaning is the result. The textual variants in this verse do not materially change the sense. ἡμεῖς καὶ αὐτοί is supported by p[46] ℵ C 1908, καὶ ἡμεῖς αὐτοί by the mass of the cursives, καὶ αὐτοί by B 104 and the Latin Vulgate, and αὐτοί by D G. If we adopt the first of these, then ἡμεῖς can be taken with ἔχοντες (*cf.* A. Souter: *Novum Testamentum Graece*), if the second, ἡμεῖς must be taken with στενάζομεν; it is simply the question with which verb we are to take the pronoun. But even if ἡμεῖς is omitted altogether, it is understood as the subject of both ἔχοντες and στενάζομεν.

tion.[38] Although the hope is not defined in terms of the plenitude of the Spirit but rather as "the adoption, the redemption of our body", yet this does not militate against the propriety of the concept of the plenitude of the Spirit in the consummation. In I Cor. 15:44 this concept is applied to the resurrection body —the resurrection body is fully conditioned by the Holy Spirit and is therefore adapted for the eschatological kingdom of God and bears the image of the heavenly (cf. I Cor. 15:48–50). The resurrection body is therefore "a Spiritual body". There is no reason why the apostle should not allude to this concept in the expression, "the firstfruits of the Spirit".[39] "Groan within ourselves" must refer to the inward groaning in the hearts of believers, not to groaning among believers as if they groaned to one another and joined together in a "symphony of sighs". "Waiting for the adoption, the redemption of our body". The groaning is complemented by the expectation of that which will bring the process of redemption to its completion. It is not then mere groaning under the burden of the imperfection of the present but groaning for the glory to be revealed (cf. II Cor. 5:4). Though the idea of travailing in birth is not here used of believers, yet the coordination of groaning and waiting shows that hope, oriented to the adoption, conditions the groaning so as to make the groaning itself the portent of liberation. "Adoption" is used here of grace to be bestowed in the future. This does not interfere with the reality and privilege of the adoption enjoyed now (cf. vs. 15;

[38] This is to say that the Genitive is partitive. It is maintained by some that it is a Genitive of apposition as in the expression "the earnest of the Spirit" (II Cor. 1:22; 5:5; cf. Eph. 1:14). In this case the Spirit himself is the firstfruits and the firstfruits is not that which he imparts as a token of the plenitude to be bestowed at the consummation. Although the expression ἀπαρχὴ τοῦ Πνεύματος is ἅπαξ λεγόμενον in the New Testament, yet it is difficult to adopt another view of the Genitive than that which prevails elsewhere in connection with ἀπαρχή. It must be said, however, that if the Genitive is that of apposition, this does not detract from the place the Holy Spirit occupies in the consummation, and such an interpretation would only serve to strengthen the concessive idea conveyed by the rendering, "though we have the firstfruits of the Spirit". For if the Spirit is the firstfruits in possession, this fact would appear all the more to rule out the necessity of the pain and travail implied in groaning.

[39] Cf. contra Meyer who says that "a merely provisional reception of the Spirit ... in contrast to the future full effusion in the kingdom of heaven ... is not contained in ἀπ. τ. πν., because Paul, had he wished to speak here of a preliminary reception in contrast to the future plenitude, must necessarily, in accordance with the connection, have so spoken of the υἱοθεσία or δόξα" (op. cit., ad loc.).

Gal. 4:4–6). It means simply that the term is used both of a present privilege and of a future bestowment and that the latter brings to the fullest realization the status and privilege enjoyed in this life as sons of God. In this respect "adoption" is used as are the terms "salvation" and "redemption". Sometimes they refer to what is in the possession of the believer now (*cf.* 1:16; 11:11; 3:24; Eph. 1:7), at other times to the consummation of salvation and redemption at the coming of Christ (*cf.* 13:11; Phil. 2:12; Luke 21:28; Eph. 1:14; 4:30). "Adoption" is peculiarly appropriate to designate the glory that awaits God's people because it denotes the acme of privilege bestowed; nothing serves more to enhance the lustre of the glory reserved than to represent it as sonship come to its full fruition and enjoyment. "The redemption of our body"[40] specifies that in which the "adoption" consists—it is the resurrection when the sons of God will be clothed with the immortal and incorruptible body (*cf.* vs. 11; I Cor. 15:50–55; II Cor. 5:2, 3; Phil. 3:21). That adoption should be identified thus with the resurrection of the body and that the resurrection should be called the *redemption* of the body draw attention again to the place accorded to the body in the apostle's thinking. The consummation of the redemptive process is waiting for the transformation by which the body of our humiliation will be conformed to the likeness of the body of Christ's glory (*cf.* Phil. 3:21) and it is for that consummation that the sons of God wait.

24 "For in hope were we saved". This rendering conveys the thought of the original as well as can be in English. The tense of the verb indicates that what is in view is the salvation which the believer has already come to possess, not the future salvation reserved for him. The thought is not that he will attain to the future salvation by the instrumentality of hope. And neither is the thought that the salvation in the believer's possession came to be his by the instrumentality of hope.[41] The uniform teaching of the apostle, as of Scripture in general, is that we were saved by *faith* (*cf.* 1:16, 17; Eph. 2:8). "In hope" refers to the fact that the salvation bestowed in the past, the salvation now in possession, is characterized by hope.[42] Hope is an ingredient

---

[40] τοῦ σώματος is genitive of the subject.

[41] Hope, in this respect, cannot be used in the place of faith. Paul distinguishes the functions of faith and hope (*cf.* 5:1–5; I Cor. 13:13; Col. 1:5–7).

[42] ἐλπίδι is a modal dative. *Cf.* Winer: *op. cit.*, § 31, 7d, p. 216 and the

inseparable from the salvation possessed; in that sense it is salvation conditioned by and oriented to hope. This is simply to say that salvation can never be divorced from the outlook and outreach which hope implies. The salvation now in possession is incomplete, and this is reflected in the consciousness of the believer in the expectancy of hope directed to the adoption, the redemption of the body. We must see the connection between verse 24 and the preceding. Since hope conditions the salvation possessed, "we groan within ourselves waiting for the adoption". "Hope", as used in this clause, is hope as exercised by the believer, not the object of hope as in the next clause.

"But hope that is seen is not hope: for who hopeth for that which he seeth?"[43] These clauses scarcely need comment; they express the obvious truth that hope is no longer in exercise when the thing hoped for is realized. They provide, however, a patent example of the two uses of the term hope. In the first clause, "hope" refers to the thing hoped for, the object of hope; in the second, hope denotes the state of mind entertained in reference to the thing hoped for. The obvious facts mentioned also accentuate the necessity of giving full scope to the exercise of hope and they prepare for the emphasis of verse 25.

25 Hope is imbued with that same confidence which characterizes faith (*cf.* Heb. 11:1). As faith is contrasted with sight (II Cor. 5:7), so is hope, and hope is not dimmed although its object is not present to sense or attained in experience. "With patience we wait for it."[44] "Patience" is endurance and constancy; it describes the attitude which hope constrains. In Calvin's words, "Hope then ever draws patience with it. Thus it is a most

---

examples provided by him, namely, I Cor. 11:5; 10:30; Col. 2:11; Phil. 1:18; II Pet. 2:4. The sense may be expressed by the word "hopewise".

[43] The version has apparently adopted the reading τίς ἐλπίζει at the end of verse 24, a reading supported by p⁴⁶ B* 1908 ᵐᵍ. There are several variants in competition with the simple τίς as τίς καί in ℵ* 1739 1908; τις, τί in D G and the Latin versions; τις, τί καί in A C and the mass of the cursives. If τις, τί or τις, τί καί were adopted then the translation differs because τίς goes with the preceding verb βλέπει and the rendering would be "For what one sees, why does he hope for?" or "For what one sees, why does he also hope for?" respectively. The sense is not materially affected.
If instead of ἐλπίζει we should read ὑπομένει, again the sense is the same. ℵ* A 1908ᵐᵍ support this latter reading.

[44] δι' ὑπομόνης is the genitive of attendant circumstance. *Cf.* Winer: *op. cit.*, pp. 379f. and the instances cited by him: Rom. 2:27; 4:11; 14:20; I John 5:6.

apt conclusion—that whatever the gospel promises respecting the glory of the resurrection, vanishes away, except we spend our present life in patiently bearing the cross and tribulations."[45] The stress upon patience is a fitting finale to the whole passage (vss. 18–25). It is with the consummation of redemption that the passage is concerned. But the consummating act of redemption will bring to completion the process of redemption, and process means history. It is in that history that the sons of God now find themselves. Patient waiting is the correlative in them of the history which God has designed. Impatience spells dispute and dissatisfaction with God's design. Attempts to claim for the present life elements which belong to consummated perfection, whether it be in the individual sphere or in the collective, are but symptoms of that impatience which would disrupt divine order. Expectancy and hope must not cross the bounds of history; they must wait for *the end*, "the liberty of the glory of the children of God".

26, 27

> 26 And in like manner the Spirit also helpeth our infirmity: for we know not how to pray as we ought; but the Spirit himself maketh intercession for *us* with groanings which cannot be uttered;
> 27 and he that searcheth the hearts knoweth what is the mind of the Spirit, because he maketh intercession for the saints according to *the will of* God.

This is the second ground for encouragement extended to the children of God to support them in the sufferings which are the precondition of being glorified together with Christ (vs. 17).

26 "In like manner" points to something in the preceding context to which what follows in these two verses is likened. It would appear that the thought is as follows. The hope and expectation of the glory to be revealed sustain the people of God in the *sufferings* and *groanings* of this present time (vss. 18–25). In like manner the Holy Spirit helps our *infirmity*. In the preceding verses the accent falls upon the *sufferings* and the *support* afforded in these; in verses 26, 27 the accent falls upon our *infirmity* and the

---

[45] *Op. cit., ad loc.*

help given for its relief. As hope sustains us in suffering, so the Holy Spirit helps our infirmity.

"Infirmity" is a comprehensive term in itself and can cover the whole range of the weakness which characterizes us in this life. We need not suppose that the infirmity in view is restricted to the matter of prayer. But that "we know not what to pray for as we ought"[46] brings to the forefront how helpless we are in our infirmity and lays the basis for the particular kind of help afforded by the Spirit. Prayer covers every aspect of our need, and our weakness is exemplified and laid bare by the fact that we know not what to pray for as is meet and proper.[47] It is not our ignorance of the right manner of prayer that is reflected on, as the rendering of the version might suggest. It is rather our ignorance respecting the proper content—we know not what to pray as the exigencies of our situations demand.[48] It is at the point of this destitution on our part that the Holy Spirit comes to our help, and upon this particular aspect of the Spirit's activity the apostle concentrates attention as peculiarly and by way of eminence the grace of the Spirit in reference to our infirmity, the grace which consists in the fact that he "himself maketh intercession for us with groanings which cannot be uttered". Several observations are necessary.

(1) The children of God have two divine intercessors. Christ is their intercessor in the court of heaven (*cf.* vs. 34; Heb. 7:25; I John 2:1). The Holy Spirit is their intercessor in the theatre of their own hearts (*cf.* John 14:16, 17).[49] Too seldom has the

---

[46] The article τό goes with the whole clause τί προσευξώμεθα καθὸ δεῖ and specifies what it is that we do not know; *cf.* examples cited by Gifford: *op. cit., ad loc.*—Luke 1:62; 9:46; 19:48; 22:2, 4, 23, 24, 37; Acts 22:30; Rom. 13:9; Eph. 4:9; I Thess. 4:1.

[47] It may not be possible to determine whether καθὸ δεῖ should be rendered "as we ought" or "as is meet". I Cor. 8:2 would suggest the former. However, the thought may be simply that we do not know what to pray as is suited to the occasion, i.e., as our necessities require. There is always, of course, ethical and spiritual failure on our part so that we come short of what we *ought* to be, and think, and do. But it is not so certain that the emphasis falls upon the violation of duty.

[48] This is illustrated in the apostle's own case by II Cor. 12:7-10. Our specific petitions, though they may appear to be in accord with what the exigencies dictate, are not the measure of God's wisdom, love, and grace, and the latter often demand the denial of our petitions. This the apostle came to recognize in this instance (*cf.* vss. 9, 10).

[49] "It does not take place in the heavenly sanctuary, like that of the glorified Christ (Heb. vii. 25). It has for its theatre the believer's own heart" (Godet: *op. cit., ad loc.*).

311

intercessory activity of the Holy Spirit been taken into account. The glory of Christ's intercession should not be allowed to place the Spirit's intercession in eclipse. (2) The Spirit intercedes "with groanings which cannot be uttered". Whatever view we may adopt respecting these groanings, we may not overlook or suppress the truth that they are the groanings of which the Holy Spirit is the author. They are the concrete ways in which the intercession of the Spirit comes to expression; they define the content of his intercession. It is not sufficient to say that they are created and indited by the Holy Spirit; they are the intercessions of the Spirit and the groanings are but the way in which these intercessions are registered in the hearts of God's children. (3) Whether we render the Greek term by the word "unutterable" or "unuttered", we must note that the groanings are not expressed in articulate speech; they are not requests or petitions or supplications which are formulated in intelligible utterance. While far from being devoid of content, meaning, and intent, they nevertheless transcend articulated formulation. (4) The groanings will have to be understood as the groanings which are registered in the hearts of the children of God. We cannot reasonably think of the Holy Spirit himself, apart from the agency and instrumentality of those on whose behalf he intercedes, as presenting his intercessions to the Father in the form of his own groanings. The reference to the hearts in verse 27 clearly implies that the hearts are those of the children of God. It must be, therefore, in their hearts that the groanings take place and the groanings are those of the saints. They are, however, the *media* of the Holy Spirit's intercession and they ascend to the throne of grace in the form of groanings.

27 Only as we appreciate the leading thought of verse 26, to the effect that the groanings register the intercession of the Holy Spirit, are we able to interpret this verse. "He that searcheth the hearts" is none other than God and specifically the Father (*cf.* I Chron. 28:9; Psalm 139:1, 23; Jer. 17:10; I Cor. 4:5; Heb. 4:13). "The mind of the Spirit" is not in this instance the mind created and fostered in us by the Holy Spirit (*cf.* vs. 6); it is the mind of the Holy Spirit himself as is made apparent by the emphasis upon the intercession of the Spirit in verse 26 and particularly by what follows in this verse—"because he maketh

intercession for the saints according to the will of God". It is
the Holy Spirit who makes intercession. Since his intercession
must be in accordance with the mind and will of God, this is
the guarantee that the searcher of the hearts knows the content
and intent of the intercession. This knowledge is stated to be
knowing "the mind of the Spirit" and, therefore, the latter can
be none other than that of the Holy Spirit himself. The thought
of the passage is, therefore, as follows. As God searches the heart
of the children of God he finds unuttered and unutterable groanings. Though they are thus inarticulate, there is a meaning
and intent that cannot escape the omniscient eye of God—they
are wholly intelligible to him. And, furthermore, they are found
to be in accordance with his will. They are consonant with his
will because, though surpassing our understanding and utterance,
they are indited by the Holy Spirit and are the ways in which his
intercessions come to expression in our consciousness. Since they
are the intercessions of the Holy Spirit, they always meet with
the understanding and approval of God. They are agreeable
to his will as are the intercessions of Christ at the right hand of
God. The encouragement extended to the people of God is that
the unuttered groans are the index to the fact that God does
"exceeding abundantly above all that we ask or think" (Eph.
3:20) and that not our infirmity of understanding and request
is the measure of God's grace but the knowledge, wisdom, and
love of the Holy Spirit.

28–30

28 And we know that to them that love God all things
work together for good, *even* to them that are called
according to *his* purpose.
29 For whom he foreknew, he also foreordained *to be*
conformed to the image of his Son, that he might be
the firstborn among many brethren:
30 and whom he foreordained, them he also called: and
whom he called, them he also justified: and whom he
justified, them he also glorified.

This is the third ground of encouragement for the support of
the children of God in the sufferings they are called upon to
endure in this life. It consists in the consolation and assurance
to be derived from the fact that all things work together for
their good.

313

28 The version is probably correct in introducing these verses by the conjunction "and" rather than by "but". The thought is not apparently adversative but transitional. When the apostle says "we know", he is again intimating that the truth asserted is not one to be gainsaid. "To them that love God" is placed in the position of emphasis and characterizes those to whom the assurance belongs. They are described in terms of their subjective attitude. In such terms no criterion could be more discriminating, for love to God is both the most elementary and the highest mark of being in the favour of God. "All things" may not be restricted, though undoubtedly the things contemplated are particularly those that fall within the compass of believers' experience, especially suffering and adversity. Some of the ablest expositors maintain that "work together" does not mean that all things work in concert and cooperation with one another but that all things work in concert with the believer or with God.[50] But it is unnecessary and perhaps arbitrary to depart from the more natural sense, namely, that in the benign and all-embracing plan of God the discrete elements all work together for good to them that love God. It is not to be supposed that they have any virtue or efficacy in themselves to work in concert for this end. Though not expressed, the ruling thought is that in the sovereign love and wisdom of God they are all made to converge upon and contribute to that goal. Many of the things comprised are evil in themselves and it is the marvel of God's wisdom and grace that they, when taken in concert with the whole, are made to work for good. Not one detail works ultimately for evil to the people of God; in the end only good will be their lot. "To them that are called according to purpose" is a further definition of those to whom this assurance belongs. But the difference is significant. The former characterized them in terms of their subjective attitude, the latter in terms of God's action exclusively. In the latter, therefore, there is an intimation of

---

[50] *Cf.* Philippi, Meyer, Godet, *ad loc.* If after συνεργεῖ we read ὁ θεός with p⁴⁶ A B and Origen on two or three occasions, this would not establish the view that "work together" refers to concert with God. On that reading συνεργεῖ would have to be understood transitively in the sense of "cause to work together" and πάντα would be accusative. But it would still be true that God makes all things to work together. As indicated above, it is by God's providence that all things work together for good. This is expressly stated when ὁ θεός is added; it is implied if ὁ θεός is omitted.

the reason why all things work for good—the action of God
involved in their call is the guarantee that such will be the
result.[51] The call is the effectual call (cf. 1:7; vs. 30) which ushers
into the fellowship of Christ (I Cor. 1:9) and is indissolubly
linked with predestination, on the one hand, and glorification,
on the other. "According to purpose" refers without question
to God's determinate and eternal purpose (cf. 9:11; Eph. 1:11;
3:11; II Tim. 1:9). The last cited text is Paul's own expansion
of the thought summed up in the word "purpose": "who saved us,
and called us with a holy calling, not according to our works,
but according to his own purpose and grace, which was given us
in Christ Jesus before times eternal". Determinate efficacy
characterizes the call because it is given in accordance with
eternal purpose.

29 This verse unfolds in greater detail the elements included
in the "purpose" of verse 28, and verses 29, 30 are a "continued
confirmation"[52] of the truth that all things work for good to those
who are the called of God. There is no question but the apostle
here introduces us to the eternal counsel of God as it pertains to
the people of God and delineates for us its various aspects.

"Whom he foreknew"—few questions have provoked more
difference of interpretation than that concerned with the meaning
of God's foreknowledge as referred to here. It is, of course,
true that the word is used in the sense of "to know beforehand"
(cf. Acts 26:5; II Pet. 3:17). As applied to God it could, therefore,
refer to his eternal prevision, his foresight of all that would come
to pass. It has been maintained by many expositors that this
sense will have to be adopted here. Since, however, those whom
God is said to have foreknown are distinguished from others and
identified with those whom God also predestinated to be conformed to the image of his Son, and since the expression "whom
he foreknew" does not, on this view of its meaning, intimate any
distinction by which the people of God could be differentiated,
various ways of supplying this distinguishing element have been

---

[51] "Respecting the idea itself, there is causally involved in the relation
of being *the called* according to His purpose (for the emphasis rests upon κλητοῖς),
the certainty that to them all things, etc." (Meyer: *op. cit., ad loc.*). "Sufferings, of
course, can only tend to our benefit upon the assumption that we love God;
but the ground of their salutary operation lies not in our love, but in our
calling according to the divine purpose" (Philippi: *op. cit., ad loc.*).
[52] The phrase is Meyer's.

proposed. The most common is to suppose that what is in view is God's foresight of faith.[53] God foreknew who would believe; he foreknew them as his *by faith*. On this interpretation predestination is conceived of as conditioned upon this prevision of faith. Frequently, though not necessarily in all instances, this view of foreknowledge is considered to obviate the doctrine of unconditional election, and so dogmatic interest is often apparent in those who espouse it.

It needs to be emphasized that the rejection of this interpretation is not dictated by a predestinarian interest. Even if it were granted that "foreknew" means the foresight of faith, the biblical doctrine of sovereign election is not thereby eliminated or disproven. For it is certainly true that God foresees faith; he foresees all that comes to pass. The question would then simply be: whence proceeds this faith which God foresees? And the only biblical answer is that the faith which God foresees is the faith he himself creates (*cf.* John 3:3–8; 6:44, 45, 65; Eph. 2:8; Phil. 1:29; II Pet. 1:2). Hence his eternal foresight of faith is preconditioned by his decree to generate this faith in those whom he foresees as believing, and we are thrown back upon the differentiation which proceeds from God's own eternal and sovereign election to faith and its consequents. The interest, therefore, is simply one of interpretation as it should be applied to this passage. On exegetical grounds we shall have to reject the view that "foreknew" refers to the foresight of faith.

It should be observed that the text says *"whom he foreknew"*; *whom* is the object of the verb and there is no qualifying addition. This, of itself, shows that, unless there is some other compelling

---

[53] "The meaning to which we are brought seems to me to be this: those on whom His eye fixed from all eternity with love; whom He eternally contemplated and discerned *as His*. In what respect did God thus *foreknow* them?.... There is but one answer: foreknown as sure to fulfil the condition of salvation, viz. *faith;* so: foreknown as His *by faith*" (Godet: *op. cit., ad loc.*). "The right view, since faith is the subjective ground of salvation, is that held by Calovius and our older dogmatists: 'quos *credituros* praevidit vel *suscepturos vocationem'*" (Meyer: *op. cit., ad loc.; cf.* also *ad* vs. 30). *Cf.* also Philippi (*op. cit., ad loc.*) who regards the meaning to know beforehand as the only reasonable one and that the implied qualification is that of faith. However, Philippi regards the faith which God foresees as nothing but his own creation. And so he finds in this passage "a *dictum probans* for the doctrine of *praedestinatio*, not absolute, but based upon *praevisio*". On John Wesley's interpretation, as representative of the Arminian view, *cf. The Works of the Rev. John Wesley*, London, 1878, vol. VI, pp. 226f.

reason, the expression "whom he foreknew" contains within itself the differentiation which is presupposed. If the apostle had in mind some "qualifying adjunct"[54] it would have been simple to supply it. Since he adds none we are forced to inquire if the actual terms he uses can express the differentiation implied. The usage of Scripture provides an affirmative answer. Although the term "foreknow" is used seldom in the New Testament, it is altogether indefensible to ignore the meaning so frequently given to the word "know" in the usage of Scripture; "foreknow" merely adds the thought of "beforehand" to the word "know". Many times in Scripture "know" has a pregnant meaning which goes beyond that of mere cognition.[55] It is used in a sense practically synonymous with "love", to set regard upon, to know with peculiar interest, delight, affection, and action (cf. Gen. 18:19; Exod. 2:25; Psalm 1:6; 144:3; Jer. 1:5; Amos 3:2; Hosea 13:5; Matt. 7:23; I Cor. 8:3; Gal. 4:9; II Tim. 2:19; I John 3:1). There is no reason why this import of the word "know" should not be applied to "foreknow" in this passage, as also in 11:2 where it also occurs in the same kind of construction and where the thought of election is patently present (cf. 11:5, 6.)[56] When this import is appreciated, then there is no reason for adding any qualifying notion and "whom he foreknew" is seen to contain within itself the differentiating element required. It means "whom he set regard upon" or "whom he knew from eternity with distinguishing affection and delight" and is virtually equivalent to "whom he foreloved". This interpretation, furthermore, is in agreement with the efficient and determining action which is so conspicuous in every other link of the chain—it is God who

---

[54]   The expression is Shedd's.

[55]   It is instructive to note how even Daniel Whitby takes account of this import and adopts it in his exposition of this passage; cf. A Paraphrase and Commentary on the New Testament, London, 1744, ad Rom. 8:29; 11:2.

[56]   It is gratuitous for Meyer to argue that προγινώσκω "never in the N.T. (not even in xi. 2, i Pet. 1.20) means anything else than to know beforehand" (op. cit., ad loc.). Undoubtedly it has this meaning in Acts 26:5; II Pet. 3:17, where it is applied to men. The only other instance in the New Testament besides Rom. 8:29; 11:2 is I Pet. 1:20, in all three of which God is the subject (cf. πρόγνωσις in Acts 2:23; I Pet. 1:2). In these five instances of the idea as applied to God the one consideration that weighs more than any other in determining the precise import is the frequent use of ידע in Hebrew and γινώσκω in Greek in the pregnant sense defined above. It is likewise significant that in this use of γινώσκω the accusative occurs without any qualifying adjunct to specify the differentiation necessarily involved (cf. Matt. 7:23; II Tim. 2:19; I John 3:1).

predestinates, it is God who calls, it is God who justifies, and it is he who glorifies. Foresight of faith would be out of accord with the determinative action which is predicated of God in these other instances and would constitute a weakening of the total emphasis at the point where we should least expect it. Foresight has too little of the active to do justice to the divine monergism upon which so much of the emphasis falls. It is not the foresight of difference but the foreknowledge that makes difference to exist, not a foresight that recognizes existence but the foreknowledge that determines existence. It is sovereign distinguishing love.

"He also foreordained." One of the main objections urged against the foregoing view of "whom he foreknew" is that it would obliterate the distinction between foreknowledge and predestination.[57] There is ostensible progression of thought expressed in "he also foreordained". But there is no need to suppose that this progression is disturbed if "foreknew" is interpreted in the way propounded. "Foreknew" focuses attention upon the distinguishing love of God whereby the sons of God were elected. But it does not inform us of the destination to which those thus chosen are appointed. It is precisely that information that "he also foreordained" supplies, and it is by no means superfluous. When we consider the high destiny defined, "to be conformed to the image of his Son", there is exhibited not only the dignity of this ordination but also the greatness of the love from which the appointment flows. God's love is not passive emotion; it is active volition and it moves determinatively to nothing less than the highest goal conceivable for his adopted children, conformity to the image of the only-begotten Son. To allege that the pregnant force of "foreknew" does not leave room for the distinct enunciation of this high destiny is palpably without warrant or reason.[58]

"Conformed to the image of his Son" defines the destination

---

[57] Meyer says that this view of προέγνω "would necessarily include the προορισμός, and consequently exclude the latter as a special and accessory act" (idem).

[58] In this respect the relation of προέγνω to προώρισε is parallel to that of ἀγάπη to προορίσας in Eph. 1:5. Meyer argues for the reading ἐν ἀγάπη προορίσας at that point and must therefore recognize the love as causally antecedent—it was out of love that God predestinated the elect unto adoption. Why then should there be any difficulty in discovering the antecedence of electing love in Rom. 8:29 together with the distinction and the progression of thought which the two terms in question express?

to which the elect of God are appointed. The apostle has in view the conformity to Christ that will be realized when they will be glorified with Christ (vs. 17; *cf.* vss. 18, 19, 21, 23, 30), the final and complete conformity of resurrection glory (*cf.* I Cor. 15:49; II Cor. 3:18; Phil. 3:21; I John 3:2). It is noteworthy that this should be described as conformity to the image of the *Son*; it enhances the marvel of the destination. The title "Son" has reference to Christ as the only-begotten (*cf.* vss. 3, 32) and therefore the unique and eternal Sonship is contemplated. The conformity cannot, of course, have in view conformity to him in that relation or capacity; the conformity embraces the transformation of the body of our humiliation to the likeness of the body of Christ's glory (Phil. 3:21) and must therefore be conceived of as conformity to the image of the incarnate Son as glorified by his exaltation. Nevertheless, the glorified Christ does not cease to be the eternal Son and it is the eternal Son who is the glorified incarnate Son. Conformity to his image as incarnate and glorified, therefore, is conformity to the image of him who is the eternal and only-begotten Son.

"That he might be the firstborn among many brethren." This specifies the final aim of the conformity just spoken of. We might well ask: What can be more final than the complete conformity of the sons of God to the image of Christ? It is this question that brings to the forefront the significance of this concluding clause. There is a final end that is more ultimate than the glorification of the people of God; it is that which is concerned with the preeminence of Christ. As Meyer correctly notes: "Paul contemplates *Christ* as the One, to whom the divine decree referred *as to its final aim*".[59] The term "firstborn" reflects on the *priority* and the *supremacy* of Christ (*cf.* Col. 1:15, 18; Heb. 1:6; Rev. 1:5).[60] It is all the more striking that, when the unique and eternal Sonship is contemplated in the title "Son" and the priority and supremacy of Christ in the designation "firstborn", the people of God should be classified with Christ as "brethren" (*cf.* Heb. 2:11, 12). His unique sonship and the fact that he is the firstborn guard Christ's distinctiveness and preeminence, but

---

[59] *Op. cit., ad loc.* In Philippi's words also, "Thus not so much to glorify us as to glorify Christ has God ordained for us such glory" (*op. cit., ad loc.*).

[60] On the meaning of πρωτότοκος *cf.* J. B. Lightfoot: *St. Paul's Epistles to the Colossians and Philemon,* ad Col. 1:15.

it is among many brethren that his preeminence appears. This is another example of the intimacy of the relation existing between Christ and the people of God. The union means also community and this community is here expressed as that of "brethren". The fraternal relationship is subsumed under the ultimate end of the predestinating decree, and this means that the preeminence of Christ carries with it the eminence that belongs to the children of God. In other words, the unique dignity of the Son in his essential relation to the Father and in his messianic investiture enhances the marvel of the dignity bestowed upon the people of God. The Son is not ashamed to call them brethren (Heb. 2:11).

30 The two preceding verses deal with the eternal and pre-temporal counsel of God; the "purpose" of verse 28 is explicated in verse 29 in terms of foreknowledge and predestination, the latter defining the ultimate goal of the counsel of salvation. Verse 30 introduces us to the realm of the temporal and indicates the actions by which the eternal counsel is brought to actual fruition in the children of God. Three actions are mentioned, calling, justification, and glorification. There is an unbreakable bond between these three actions themselves, on the one hand, and the two elements of the eternal counsel, on the other. All five elements are co-extensive. The sustained use of "also" and the repetition of the terms "foreordained", "called", "justified" in the three relative clauses in verse 30 signalize the denotative equation. Thus it is made abundantly evident that there cannot be one element without the others and that the three elements which are temporal flow by way of consequence from the eternal counsel, particularly from predestination because it stands in the closest logical relation to calling as the first in the sequence of temporal events.[61]

It is to be observed that calling, justification, and glorification are set forth as acts of God—"he called", "he justified", "he glorified". The same divine monergism appears as in "he foreknew" and "he foreordained". It is contrary to this emphasis to define any of these elements of the application of redemption in any other terms than those of *divine action*. It is true that all three affect us men, they draw our persons within their scope,

---

[61] On the priority of calling in the *ordo salutis* cf. *Redemption—Accomplished and Applied*, pp. 100ff.; 114f., by the writer.

and are of the deepest practical moment to us in the actual experience of salvation. But God alone is active in those events which are here mentioned and no activity on the part of men supplies any ingredient of their definition or contributes to their efficacy.[62] For reasons which are rather obvious but which need not be developed we should infer that the sequence which the apostle follows represents the order in the application of redemption. The apostle enumerates only three elements. These, however, as the pivotal events in our actual salvation, serve the apostle's purpose in delineating the divine plan of salvation from its fount in the love of God to its consummation in the glorification of the sons of God. Glorification, unlike calling and justification, belongs to the future. It would not be feasible in this context (*cf.* 5:2; vss. 17, 18, 21, 24, 25, 29) to regard it as other than the completion of the process of salvation and, though "glorified" is in the past tense, this is proleptic, intimating the certainty of its accomplishment.[63]

In extending encouragement and support to the people of God in their sufferings and adversities, groanings and infirmities, the apostle has reached this triumphant conclusion. He has shown how the present pilgrimage of the people of God falls into its place in that determinate and undefeatable plan of God that is bounded by two foci, the sovereign love of God in his eternal counsel and glorification with Christ in the age to come. It is when they apprehend by faith this panorama that stretches from the love of God before times eternal to the grand finale of the redemptive process that the sufferings of this present time are viewed in their true perspective and are seen, *sub specie aeternitatis*, to be but the circumstances of pilgrimage to, and preconditions of, a glory to be revealed so great in its weight that the tribulations are not worthy of comparison.

---

[62] It is true that calling elicits the appropriate response, and justification is through the instrumentality of faith. Therefore these acts of God do not occur irrespective of faith, in the former case as result, in the latter as precondition. But these acts of God are not to be defined in terms of human activity. Calling is therefore effectual, and it would be as sensible to speak of resisting the divine act of justification as of resisting this call.

[63] Surely a proleptic aorist representing, as Meyer says, "the *de facto* certainly future glorification as so necessary and certain, that it appears as if already given and completed with the ἐδικαίωσεν " (*op. cit., ad loc.*).

31–39

31 What then shall we say to these things? If God *is* for us, who *is* against us?

32 He that spared not his own Son, but delivered him up for us all, how shall he not also with him freely give us all things?

33 Who shall lay anything to the charge of God's elect? It is God that justifieth;

34 who is he that condemneth? It is Christ Jesus that died, yea rather, that was raised from the dead, who is at the right hand of God, who also maketh intercession for us.

35 Who shall separate us from the love of Christ? shall tribulation, or anguish, or persecution, or famine, or nakedness, or peril, or sword?

36 Even as it is written,
For thy sake we are killed all the day long;
We were accounted as sheep for the slaughter.

37 Nay, in all these things we are more than conquerors through him that loved us.

38 For I am persuaded, that neither death, nor life, nor angels, nor principalities, nor things present, nor things to come, nor powers,

39 nor height, nor depth, nor any other creature, shall be able to separate us from the love of God, which is in Christ Jesus our Lord.

This is the triumphant conclusion to the consolation which had been unfolded in the preceding verses, especially from verse 18. In Philippi's words it is "the highest rung in the ladder of comfort which, from ver. 18 onward, writer, like reader, has been mounting".[64]

31 "What then shall we say to these things?" has the force of "what is the inference to be drawn from these things?" What is to be our response? The answer is in the form of another question, a question obviously rhetorical, to the effect that, if God is for us, all opposition from others is of no account. When it is said "if God is for us", there is no suggestion of doubt;[65] this clause simply states the basis of the confident assurance implied in the

---

[64] *Op. cit., ad loc.*
[65] Not the "if" of uncertainty but of presupposition.

succeeding question. "Who is against us?" does not mean that there are no adversaries. Verses 35, 36 refer to the most violent kinds of opposition. The thought is simply that no adversary is of any account when God is for us. In reality, in terms of verse 28, nothing is *against us* so as to work ultimately for evil: if God is for us, all things work together for our good. In the last analysis there is no *against* within the orbit of the interests of the people of God. It is this truth that is enunciated in verse 31 in respect of all personal adversaries, satanic, demonic, and human.

32 Here is adduced the most conclusive proof of God's grace; it is in the form of an argument from the greater to the less. If God has done for our good the greatest that is conceivable, will not all other blessings follow by necessity? "He that spared not his own Son." Several observations are to be noted. (1) The person of the Godhead in view is God the Father, for of the Father alone is the Son the Son. (2) "His own Son" means that there is no other who stands in this same relation to the Father (*cf.* 8:3).[66] Jesus called God "his own Father" (John 5:18) and this means that the Father alone stood in that precise relation to him. God has many sons by adoption. But the Scripture allows no confusion to exist between the sonship of the only-begotten and the sonship of the adopted. No other but the only-begotten is the Father's own Son and this is so because there is an eternal, incomparable, and ineffable sonship. (3) The Father did not spare his own Son. Sparing refers to suffering inflicted. Parents spare their children when they do not inflict the full measure of chastisement due. Judges spare criminals when they do not pronounce a sentence commensurate with the crime committed. By way of contrast, this is not what God the Father did. He did not withhold or lighten one whit of the full toll of judgment executed upon his own well-beloved and only-begotten Son. There was no alleviation of the stroke, for "it pleased the Lord to bruise him; he hath put him to grief" (Isa. 53:10). There was no mitigation; judgment was dispensed upon the Son in its unrelieved intensity. "Spared not" expresses nothing less. (4) In the endurance of what was involved in the non-sparing there was no suspension of the relation intimated

---

[66] *Cf.* for examples of the individuality and particularity implied in ἴδιος Rom. 14:5; I Cor. 3:8; 4:12; 7:2, 4, 7, 37; Gal. 6:5; Eph. 5:22; I Tim. 3:4.

by the words "his own Son" and therefore no suspension of the love the relation bespeaks. (5) It is this conjunction of incomparable relationship and love, on the one hand, and non-sparing, on the other, that exhibits the incomprehensible marvel of this fact from which the apostle draws his argument.

"But delivered him up for us all." The preceding clause is negative in form—"he spared not". This clause is positive—"he delivered him up". This reflects on what the apostle elsewhere declares, that Christ was made sin (II Cor. 5:21) and a curse (Gal. 3:13). The Father delivered over his own Son to the damnation and abandonment which sin merited. There was no amelioration of the condemnation executed upon him; Gethsemane and Calvary are the proofs. We may not overlook the conjunction which is exemplified here again. It was only because the Son was the subject of unique relationship and the object of incomparable love that he could be thus delivered over to the damnation which he endured and ended. There may be also within the apostle's purview another aspect of this delivering up, namely, the giving up to all that the arch-enemy and his instruments could do against him. Jesus said to his adversaries on the eve of the crucifixion, "This is your hour, and the power of darkness" (Luke 22:53). And the descriptions of inspired prophecy must be taken into account in this connection (Psalm 22:12, 13, 16; 69:26). Jesus was delivered up by "the determinate counsel and foreknowledge of God" and by the hands of wicked men he was crucified and slain. If restraint had been placed upon the power of the enemy, he would not have despoiled the forces of darkness and made a show openly of the principalities and the powers. He would not have triumphed over them and bound them effectively to the triumphal chariot of his cross. Is this not further proof of the Father's grace, that he should have given over his own Son to the malignity and hate, the ingenuity and power of the prince of darkness and his hosts? It was the Father who delivered him up, not the hosts of darkness. "Who delivered up Jesus to die? Not Judas, for money; not Pilate, for fear; not the Jews, for envy;—but the Father, for love!"[67]

It is only as the ordeal of Gethsemane and Calvary is viewed in the perspective of damnation vicariously borne, damnation

[67] Octavius Winslow: *No Condemnation in Christ Jesus* (London, 1857), p. 358.

324

executed with the sanctions of unrelenting justice, and damnation
endured when the hosts of darkness were released to wreak the
utmost of their vengeance that we shall be able to apprehend the
wonder and taste the sweetness of love that passes knowledge,
love eternally to be explored but eternally inexhaustible.

"For us all." (1) The spectacle of Gethsemane and Calvary is
intelligible only when it is viewed vicariously—it was for us Jesus
was delivered up. (2) The extent of "us all" is defined by the
context. The denotation is the same as that of verse 31 and
"us all" of verse 32 cannot be more inclusive than the "us" of
verse 31. The "us" of verse 31 are those spoken of in the preceding
verses, expressly identified as the foreknown, predestinated, called,
justified, glorified. And, furthermore, the succeeding context
specifies just as distinctly those of whom the apostle is speaking
—they are God's elect (vs. 33), those on behalf of whom Christ
makes intercession (vs. 34), those who can never be separated
from the love of Christ (vss. 35, 39). The sustained identification
of the persons in these terms shows that this passage offers no
support to the notion of universal atonement. It is "for all
of us" who belong to the category defined in the context that
Christ was delivered up. (3) Though "us all" does not denote all
mankind, yet we must not overlook the indiscriminateness
expressed. Within the scope of those embraced there is no
restriction and exclusion. Each person has his own individuality,
and this is also true in respect of sin, misery, and liability. God does
not save men in the mass. He deals with each individual in his
particularity. And this is to be taken into account in the Father's
giving up of his own Son. The Father contemplated all on behalf
of whom he delivered up the Son in the distinctiveness of the sin,
misery, liability, and need of each. If we had been submerged
in the mass, if we had not been contemplated in the particularity that belongs to each of us, there would be no salvation. The
Father had respect to all of us when he delivered up the Son.

"How shall he not also with him freely give us all things?"[68]
All that precedes in verse 32 leads on to this rhetorical question.

· · [68] *καί* has been taken with *πῶς οὐχί* (Philippi), with *σὺν αὐτῷ* (Meyer),
and with *χαρίσεται* (Godet). It makes no material difference to the main
thought. But it would appear more natural and more in accord with the
argument *a majori ad minus* to take it with *σὺν αὐτῷ*. A great deal turns on the
σὺν αὐτῷ; it is the pivotal consideration, and it is, exegetically speaking, more
feasible to connect the *καί* with it.

The conclusion is put in the form of a question in order to set off more forcibly the unthinkableness of the opposite. Its purpose is to drive home the incontestable assurance that all things requisite to, yea all things securing and furthering, the glorification of the people of God will be freely and unfailingly bestowed. If the Father did not spare his own Son but delivered him up to the agony and shame of Calvary, how could he possibly fail to bring to fruition the end contemplated in such sacrifice. The greatest gift of the Father, the most precious donation given to us, was not things. It was not calling, nor justification, nor even glorification. It is not even the security with which the apostle concludes his peroration (vs. 39). These are favours dispensed in the fulfilment of God's gracious design. But the unspeakable and incomparable gift is the giving up of his own Son. So great is that gift, so marvellous are its implications, so far-reaching its consequences that all graces of lesser proportion are certain of free bestowment. Whether the word "also" is tied to "with him" or to the term "freely give", the significance of "with him" must be appreciated. Christ is represented as given *to us*— the giving up *for us* is to be construed as a gift *to us*. Since he is the supreme expression and embodiment of free gift and since his being given over by the Father is the supreme demonstration of the Father's love, every other grace must follow upon and with the possession of Christ. It is not likely that "all things", in this instance made definite by the presence of the article, refers to all things as working together for good (vs. 28).[69] The things contemplated are the gifts and blessings of grace ·bestowed upon believers and are, therefore, all of the things which the context, as one dealing with salvation in its whole expanse, would be expected to indicate. In any case "all things" is an obvious example of an expression in universal terms used in a restrictive sense.

33, 34a The questions which appear in verses 33–35 have been related to one another and to their immediate context in different ways. The difference of opinion is related particularly to the question, "who is he that condemneth?" (vs. 34). Is this to be taken directly with what precedes, namely, "It is God that

---

[69] Though all things embraced in the experience of the believer work together for good (see *ad* vs. 28), it would be harsh to conceive of *all* these things as "freely given" (χαρίσεται).

justifieth" or is it to be taken as the question to which the remainder of verse 34 is the answer? On the former alternative the latter part of verse 34 ("it is Christ Jesus that died", *etc.*) is not the answer to "Who is he that condemneth?" but supplies the basis for the question and challenge of verse 35, namely, "Who shall separate us from the love of Christ?" It is not reasonable to be dogmatic in deciding which of these views is correct. But there do appear to be some considerations in favour of the former view. (1) "Who is he that condemneth?" goes naturally with the protestation that it is God who justifies. The challenge flows inevitably from the categorical proposition. (2) If the clause, "Who is he that condemneth?" finds its answer in the latter part of the same verse, then Christ Jesus would, by implication, be represented as the justifier. This is not Pauline usage. Christ indeed lays the ground for justification and we are justified through his righteousness (5:18, 19). But God, that is God the Father as distinguished from Christ, is the justifier, and in the statement, "It is God that justifieth" this is clearly intimated. (3) The question of verse 35a goes appropriately with what immediately precedes in verse 34—verse 34b is concerned with what Christ has done and is doing, verse 35a is the appropriate challenge proceeding from the facts stated in reference to Christ. Just as the challenge of verse 34a is the confidence arising from what God does as the justifier, so the challenge of verse 35a is the confidence produced by what Christ has done and continues to do. On the assumption that this is the preferable construction the interpretation presented will be in accordance with the same.

"Who shall lay anything to the charge of God's elect?" The same line of thought is to be applied here as was applied to the question in verse 31, "Who is against us?" Many accusers are envisaged, but their accusations are of no account since God has pronounced his justifying sentence. There is no appeal from his tribunal. The charges of all others are worthy only of contempt. The designation "God's elect" reflects on the category to which they belong—they are *such* as are elect of God. And not only are they conceived of as having been elected by God but they stand in that relationship to him as his elected ones. The election can be none other than that specified in different terms in verse 29, and in Ephesians 1:4 as election in Christ before the foundation of the world (*cf.* Acts 9:15; Rom. 9:11; 11:5, 7; 16:13; Col.

3:12; I Thess. 1:4; II Tim. 2:10; Tit. 1:1; Matt. 24:22, 24; Mark 13:20, 22; Luke 18:7; I Pet. 1:1; II Pet. 1:10).

"It is God that justifieth; who is he that condemneth?" As indicated already, these are to be taken together. Again the challenge in the question is to be interpreted along the lines applied to the questions, "who is against us?" (vs. 31) and "who shall lay anything to the charge of God's elect?" (vs. 33). In this case, however, the vindication has reached its zenith. In the appeal to God's verdict of justification every tongue that rises in judgment is silenced (cf. Isa. 54:17). The parallel between this passage and the protestation of the Servant in Isa. 50:8, 9 is too close to be disputed: "He is near that justifieth me; who will contend with me? let us stand up together: who is mine adversary? ... Behold, the Lord Jehovah will help me; who is he that shall condemn me?"

34b The apostle now turns our thought to the security which belongs to God's elect by reason of what Christ has done and continues to do. In Gifford's words, "as if bounding on from one rock to another, he passes from the Father's love to that of the Son".[70] Four pivotal elements in Christ's redemptive work are adduced as the guarantee that nothing can separate from the love of Christ.

"It is Christ Jesus that died."[71] Here there is no express reference to the purpose for which Jesus died nor to the persons on whose behalf he died. The apostle had sufficiently dwelt on these aspects (cf. 3:21–26; 4:25; 5:8–11; 6:4–10; 8:3, 4). The terseness at this point draws attention to the stupendous significance of the death of Christ in the series of redemptive facts instanced in this verse. That Christ Jesus should have died is in itself so arresting a fact that the simple statement summons us to reflection on the implications.

"Yea, rather, that was raised from the dead." "Yea, rather", formally, indicates amendment or correction. But it is not for the purpose of retracting in any way the foregoing proposition nor to tone down the reality of Jesus' death. It is to stress the fact that Jesus' death would have been of no avail in fulfilling the ends in

---

[70] *Op. cit., ad loc.*
[71] Χριστὸς Ἰησοῦς is the reading of p[46] ℵ A C G L and several ancient versions including the Latin Vulgate. Χριστός alone is the reading of B D and the mass of the cursives.

view apart from the resurrection. It is as the living Lord he insures the security of his own. As noted above (4:25; 6:5) the death and resurrection of Christ are inseparable in the accomplishment of redemption.[72] "Who is at the right hand of God." There is figurative or anthropomorphic language here. But the import is apparent. Christ is highly exalted and "the right hand of God" indicates the sovereignty and dominion with which he is invested, the glory with which he is crowned (cf. Matt. 26:64; Mark 14:62; Acts 2:33; 5:31; 7:55, 56; Eph. 1:20; Col. 3:1; Heb. 1:3; 8:1; 10:12; 12:2; I Pet. 3:22). Neither does the figurative expression provide any warrant for denying the reality of Christ's location in heaven. Since he is exalted as the God-man, his human nature must be located. Otherwise he would not be truly human in his exalted state. The apostle's appeal to the exalted glory, authority, and dominion is related directly to the assurance of the security belonging to the elect of God. Since he has all authority in heaven and in earth, no adverse circumstance or hostile power can wrench his people from his hand or separate from his love.

"Who also maketh intercession for us." As the preceding clause affirms the authority and dominion with which Christ is endowed and, by implication, the lordship he exercises in his exalted glory, so the present clause appeals to his continued high priestly activity. Only here and in Hebrews 7:25 is the heavenly intercession of Christ expressly mentioned. But it is implied in other passages (cf. John 14:16; I John 2:1; possibly Isa. 53:12). That "intercession" is referred to in this verse is beyond reasonable question —the same term is used with reference to the Holy Spirit in verses 26, 27.[73] The reality of heavenly intercession on the part of Christ is, therefore, beyond question. While the high priestly activity of Christ must not be restricted to intercession (cf. Heb. 2:18; 4:14–16), yet the latter is a clearly established phase of the heavenly ministry of Jesus. And the evidence will demonstrate that every need of the believer and every grace requisite to consummate his redemption are brought within the scope of

---

[72] ἐγερθείς is aorist passive and may thus reflect upon the action of the Father in raising up Jesus (cf. 4:25; 6:4; 8:11). But the *rising* of Jesus from the dead may be in view and thus be coordinate with ἀποθανών and ἐντυγχάνει. Cf., by the writer, "Who Raised Up Jesus?" in *The Westminster Theological Journal*, vol. III, pp. 113–123, especially pp. 115–117.

[73] ὑπερεντυγχάνω in vs. 26, ἐντυγχάνω, as in this instance, in vs. 27.

Christ's intercession (*cf.* Heb. 7:24, 25). We may not regard this as mythical any more than may we regard as mythical the resurrection and exalted glory of our Redeemer. It is difficult to suppress a sense of the climactic when we arrive at this fourth and final element in the series. For nothing serves to verify the intimacy and constancy of the Redeemer's preoccupation with the security of his people, nothing assures us of his unchanging love more than the tenderness which his heavenly priesthood bespeaks and particularly as it comes to expression in intercession for us. That he makes intercession "for us" is the reminder that the particularity of concern and provision which we noted already in the "for us all" of verse 32 is exemplified here also. Intercession must have regard to the distinctive situation of each individual. The apostle has now prepared us for the triumphant challenge which the question of verse 35 enunciates.

35 "Who shall separate us from the love of Christ?" This question is coordinate with the three preceding—"who is against us?" (vs. 31), "who shall bring a charge against God's elect?" (vs. 33), "who is he that condemneth?" (vs. 34). Since the words tribulation, anguish, persecution, famine, nakedness, peril, and sword are specifications of the things which might of themselves be considered as calculated to separate us from the love of Christ, they are necessarily to be taken as amplifications of the same question. Obviously the thought is, shall tribulation or anguish, *etc.* separate us from the love of Christ? This is, therefore, the last in the series of questions which in each case imply the most assured and triumphant denial. Not only the fact that it is the last in the series but the expansion of the question and the continuation of the same theme to the end of the chapter make it evident that the question is climactic. The notes of victory and assurance are now to reach their highest pitch.

"The love of Christ" is clearly Christ's love to his people, not their love to him. This is shown by the clause, "through him who loved us" (vs. 37) and by the expression, "the love of God, which is in Christ Jesus our Lord" (vs. 39). Besides, the idea of being separated from our love to Christ does not make good sense. It is the impossibility of being cut loose from the embrace of Christ's love that is affirmed, and the ground of this confidence is the character and constancy of Christ's love as certified by the facts mentioned in verse 34. The things cited in verse 35 are those which signalize the adverse circumstances in which the earthly pilgrimage of the saints of God is cast, so conspicuously exemplified in the earthly warfare of the apostle himself (*cf.* II Cor. 11:23–33), and which would appear to belie the love of Christ to them. The more accentuated is the kind of adversity denoted by these terms, the more decisive is the assurance given of the immutability of Christ's love.

36 This is a verbatim quotation of Psalm 44:22 (Heb. 44:23) as rendered by the LXX (43:23). The adversity of which the apostle had given examples (vs. 35) was the lot of the people of God in all generations (*cf.* Acts 14:22; Heb. 11:35–38). It is noteworthy that by adducing this quotation attention should have been drawn to the fact that it was for the Lord's sake the people of God were downtrodden and regarded as fit only for slaughter. This injects an eloquent, though easily overlooked, ingredient into the assurance which the apostle is unfolding. It is the reproach of Christ that persecution betokens. "All the day long" expresses well the thought of the original. It is not simply "every day". Violence unto death at the hands of persecutors is always present.

37 There are three observations. (1) "More than conquerors" is a felicitous rendering. What is stressed is the superlative of victory. Appearance to the contrary places the reality and completeness of the victory in bolder relief. Martyrdom seems to be defeat; so it is regarded by the perpetrators. Too often we look upon the outcome of conflict with the forces of iniquity as mere escape, perhaps by the skin of our teeth. In truth it is victory and that not merely but completely and gloriously. The designs of adversaries are wholly overthrown and we come off as conquerors with all the laurels of conquest. (2) This victory is always the case—"in all these things". In every encounter with adversity, even with the hostility that is unto death, the victory is unqualified. Unbelievable! Yes, indeed, were it not for the transcendent factors perceived only by faith. (3) "Through him that loved us"—this must refer to Christ specifically, in view of verse 34 and the reference to the love of Christ in verse 35. The tense of the verb "loved" points to the love exercised in and exhibited by the death upon the cross. This is not to suggest in the least that the love of Christ is in the past. Verse 35 conceives of this love as abiding and, as such, insuring the security of the believer. But it is the love exercised towards us when we were alienated from God, sinners and without strength (*cf.* 5:6–10), that certifies the reality and intensity of Christ's love. We may well have staggered at the superlative terms in which the victory had been described. Here we have the explanation and validation—it is only "through him that loved us". This is the transcendent factor which contradicts all appearance and turns apparent defeat into victory. Without question the constant activity of Christ as risen and at the right hand of God (vs. 34) is contemplated in the mediation reflected on here. But we cannot but think also of the conquest secured once for all by Christ himself in that cross which exhibited his love. It was then that he "despoiled the principalities and the powers and made a show of them openly, triumphing over them in it" (Col. 2:15).

38, 39 "For I am persuaded" is an express declaration of the confidence entertained respecting the impossibility of separation from the love of Christ. It is the reflex in the apostle's consciousness of the facts which demonstrate the invincible character of that love. The expressions which follow are quite plainly intended to universalize in the most emphatic way the negation with which these two verses are concerned. To a considerable extent these expressions occur in pairs and in these instances the one expression is the opposite of the other. This is apparent in death and life, things present and things to come, height and depth. But there is sufficient variation to show that no uniform pattern is followed in the catalogue adduced.

"Neither death, nor life"—these opposites comprise the two possibilities which lie before men. It may not be proper to try to particularize the respects in which death or life might have been conceived of by the apostle as offering temptation to the people of God or as in themselves calculated to separate from Christ's love. It is sufficient to say that whichever of these eventualities falls to our lot the embrace of Christ's love is the same (*cf.* 14:7, 8).

"Nor angels, nor principalities." If we were to regard these as expressing a certain antithesis, then the evidence would require that "angels" are the good and "principalities" the evil. That preternatural beings are in view need not be questioned. The word "angels" can be used of evil spirits, angels that kept not their first estate (*cf.* Matt. 25:41; II Pet. 2:4: Jude 6). But it is questionable if the term "angel" without any further qualification is ever used in the New Testament of evil spirits.[74] Hence the evidence would favour the view that "angels" are the good spirits. "Principalities" is used in the New Testament of both good (Col. 1:16; 2:10) and evil (I Cor. 15:24; Eph. 6:12; Col. 2:15).[75] Hence "principalities" could readily, according to Paul's usage, refer to the principalities of wickedness. It would be in accord with the antithetical pattern which the apostle follows to find the same in this instance. But we cannot be certain. Both terms may have good spirits in view and in that event the hierarchy among angelic beings would be reflected on. To aver that angelic beings could not be conceived of as tending to separate us from the love of Christ is not a valid objection. Hypothetically, Paul can speak of an angel from heaven as preaching another gospel (Gal. 1:8).[76] He might speak similarly in this text. The mere hypothesis strengthens the force of the *anathema* in Gal. 1:8. In this instance the negation would be strengthened. Besides, the purpose of the apostle is to cover the wide range of created things and the inclusion of good angels is germane to the thought.

"Nor things present, nor things to come, nor powers, nor height, nor depth."[77] In the first antithesis we have a linear dimension, in the last a vertical or, as it has been stated, "no dimensions of time . . . no dimensions of space".[78] These expressions clearly emphasize the universality which, as the leading idea of the whole passage, the apostle brings within the scope of his negation. It is more difficult to understand the import of "powers" inserted between these two pairs. Commentators frequently associate this term

---

[74] Meyer is dogmatic that ἄγγελοι is to be "understood of *good* angels, because the wicked are *never* termed ἄγγελοι without some defining adjunct" (*op. cit., ad loc.*). It is not apparent that the instances cited by Gifford to controvert Meyer's contention show the opposite. It is too strong to say that Meyer's inference is "quite inadmissible in I Cor. vi. 3; Heb. ii. 16", as Gifford says (*op. cit., ad loc.*).

[75] Eph. 1:21 is uncertain; perhaps both good and evil are in view in this instance.

[76] *Cf.* Meyer, *ad loc.*, on this point.

[77] The reading οὔτε ἐνεστῶτα οὔτε μέλλοντα οὔτε δυνάμεις, being supported by p⁴⁶ ℵ A B C D G and several ancient versions, is surely to be preferred in view of the diversity of the evidence in its favour. It is also the more difficult reading.

[78] Gifford: *op. cit., ad loc.*

with "angels" and "principalities" and regard it as referring to preternatural beings. This interpretation can appeal to I Pet. 3:22 and also to Paul's own usage in I Cor. 15:24; Eph. 1:21 where "power" in the singular is coordinated with principality and authority. "Powers" (plural), however, in New Testament usage, including Paul's epistles, most frequently denotes "mighty works" or "miracles" (cf. Matt. 11:21; Luke 13:58; Acts 2:22; 8:13; I Cor. 12:10, 28, 29; II Cor. 12:12; Gal. 3:5; Heb. 2:4). It is possible that this meaning could apply here—no mighty work or miracle (cf. especially II Thess. 2:9) can be effective in separating from Christ. But probably personal agents are contemplated, as in the passages cited above.

"Nor any other creature." It has been proposed that this should be rendered "any other creation" in the sense of "different creation". There is not sufficient warrant for this.[79] The apostle has been comprehensive in the catalogue he gives, and the reason is to establish universality. But this concluding negation is for the purpose of leaving no loophole—no being or thing in the whole realm of created reality is excluded.[80]

"The love of God, which is in Christ Jesus our Lord." In verse 35 the apostle had spoken of "the love of Christ" as that from which the people of God cannot be separated. Now he expands the scope of the love contemplated or at least characterizes it with a broader reference. It is not only the love of Christ but the love of the Father (cf. 5:8; 8:29, 32, 33). The love of the Father has its distinctive features. Preeminently it is the love that gave the Son. And the love of Christ is preeminently that he gave himself. But there is always correlation and conjunction, and it is characteristic of the apostle to set forth the conjoint operations of the persons of the Godhead in the economy of redemption. It is God's own love that is commended (5:8); it is commended by the fact that Christ died; it is the Holy Spirit who sheds abroad this love in our hearts (5:5). In binding together the love of the Father and of Christ the apostle brings together the two subjects on which his protestations from verse 31 onwards had been based, the love and action of God the Father (vss. 31–34a) and the love and action of Christ (vss. 34b–38). However,

---

[79] Cf. Godet.
[80] Cf. 13:9 where, in reference to the commandments, Paul says εἴ τις ἑτέρα ἐντολή.

it is not merely the conjunction of the love of the Father and of Christ that is indicated by this concluding expression; there is also the note of exclusiveness. The love of God from which we cannot be separated is the love of God *which is in Christ Jesus our Lord.* It is only in Christ Jesus it exists, only in him has it been manifest, only in him is it operative, and only in Christ Jesus as our Lord can *we* know the embrace and bond of this love of God.

APPENDIX A

JUSTIFICATION

THE OLD TESTAMENT

I. The Usage

In the usage of the Old Testament the root with which we are mainly concerned is that of צדק in its various forms as substantive, adjective, and verb. As a substantive it is frequently used in the Old Testament to denote the quality of righteousness or justice and is preeminently predicated of God. As applied to God it refers to his attribute of righteousness or justice. It is also predicated of men and describes their character or conduct or both as upright or just or righteous. In this study, however, we are particularly concerned with the verbal form in its various stems and parts.

The evidence will show that the verb has a variety of significations.

1. *Stative.* By this is meant that a state of being is referred to. When with the use of the Qal stem Jacob is reported to have said of Tamar "she hath been more righteous than I" (Gen. 38:26) or when we read in Job 4:17, "shall man be more just than God?" this stative force is apparent (*cf.* also Job 9:15; 33:12; 34:5; Psalm 19:10; Ezek. 16:52). It is possible that some instances in the Old Testament which are generally rendered forensically in the sense of declared or pronounced to be righteous fall into this category. In Psalm 143:2, for example, the clause, "in thy sight shall no man living be justified", could be rendered "in thy sight no man living is righteous" (*cf.* Ezek. 16:52). This stative use reflects on character or behaviour and does not deal with the question how this condition came to be when it is predicated of men.

2. *Causative.* The thought here is that of causing to be righteous or making righteous. In Dan. 8:14, where the Imperfect Niphal is used of the holy place, it would be difficult to maintain the rendering, "the holy place will be justified" whereas "the holy

336

place will be made righteous", in the sense that it will be purified or cleansed and thus put right, is the appropriate rendering. If there should be any doubt in the case of Daniel 8:14 there can be none in the case of Dan. 12:3. Here we have the Hiphil Participle and the literal rendering would be, "those who make the many righteous". The thought is that the persons in view are the instruments of turning many to righteousness. In this sense they make them to be righteous. Even if Daniel 12:3 were the only instance of this causative sense it is evidence that צדק can be used in this sense and there is no good reason why, when the action of God upon men is in view, the Hiphil should not be used with reference to the internal operative action of God in making men upright. And this use we should all the more expect since the root in its substantival and adjectival forms and in the Qal stem of the verb is frequently used to denote righteousness of character and behaviour. It is a striking fact, however, that what we might expect is actually not the case. With the exception of Daniel 8:14 where the Niphal occurs, Dan. 12:3 is the only clear instance of this causative sense of "making righteous". It is indeed abstractly possible in Isa. 50:8; 53:11 where God and the righteous servant respectively are in view. But the contexts will indicate in these two instances that another meaning applies. The reason for the infrequency of this causative meaning probably proceeds from considerations which will presently be mentioned.

3. *Demonstrative.* The meaning in this case is to show to be righteous. Ezek. 16:51, 52 provides an interesting example of this use of the Piel. In reproof of the abominations of Jerusalem she is said to have justified her sisters Sodom and Samaria. The thought is that Jerusalem had surpassed Sodom and Samaria in iniquity and in that sense, comparatively speaking, had placed her sisters in more favourable light. Thus she is said to have justified them—a rhetorical way of expressing her aggravated sin. The sense is not, however, quite that of the forensic. It is not that Jerusalem pronounced Samaria and Sodom to be righteous but that she made her sisters to appear to be more righteous—she had shown them to be righteous in that they were more righteous than she. Jer. 3:11 is to a similar effect. The Piel is again used and if the term "justify" were adopted as translation the rendering would be, "Backsliding Israel hath justified herself more than

treacherous Judah". But a more felicitous rendering would be, "Backsliding Israel hath shown herself to be more righteous than treacherous Judah". The demonstrative force is obvious. This meaning has close affinity with the forensic. In this respect the import is distinctly removed from both the stative and the causative and comes so close to the forensic that the term "justify" might properly be used to convey the idea.

4. *Forensic.* This meaning corresponds to that of our English term "justify". It is the declarative force that appears in sharp distinction from the causative. In the Hiphil this is explicit in Exod. 23:7; Deut. 25:1; I Kings 8:32; II Chron. 6:23; Job 27:5; Prov. 17:15; Isa. 5:23. In the Piel this meaning is not less apparent in Job 32:2; 33:32 and, in the Hithpael, Gen. 44:16 may not be essentially different. The instances in the Hiphil and Piel are so clear that there is no need to discuss them; no other connotation would be feasible. Although, as was observed above, Isa. 50:8; 53:11 could abstractly bear the causative sense, yet the contexts decidedly turn the scales in favour of the forensic. The protestations that follow in the case of 50:8 place it beyond reasonable doubt that the situation contemplated is that of judicial process and vindication. "Who will contend with me? . . . who is mine adversary? . . . who is he that shall condemn me" (vss. 8, 9). These are terms of confident challenge and the premise of this confidence is the affirmation, "He is near that justifieth me". No other rendering fits the thought of the context so suitably. And even if we give to the term in question vindicatory force, it is within the forensic that such a notion falls and would have to be rendered as "declare righteous". The expiatory character of the context of Isa. 53:11 would point definitely in the same direction and, as will be observed later on, the forensic signification in the Hiphil and Piel stems is so pervasive that no other force suggests itself unless there is an obvious consideration to the contrary.

In the Qal there are several instances, as noted above, where the stative signification is present. There are some instances where it is difficult to be decisive. They may be stative or forensic—Job 13:18; 25:4; Psalm 51:4(6); 143:2; Isa. 45:25. In Job 40:8, however, the contrast with "condemn" makes it more natural to take the Imperfect Qal in the forensic sense of "justified". It is more natural to take Job 9:20 in the same way. In Isa.

43:9, 26 no other idea than the forensic is appropriate. The context of verse 26 will readily be seen to require this meaning. If we find this forensic notion in a few instances of the Imperfect Qal this creates a presumption in favour of the forensic meaning in other instances where the context is not decisive but where there is even slight ground for this preference, as, for example, in Job 9:20; Psalm 51:4(6); 143:2; Isa. 45:25.

We see, therefore, that there is a pervasive use of the forensic signification of the root צדק in the Qal, Hiphil, and Piel stems and the one instance of the Hithpael (Gen. 44:16) is not essentially different. With respect to the Hiphil and Piel the usage is such that no other signification would suggest itself unless there were some obvious considerations requiring another.

The Septuagint usage is of importance because this version is the link between the Old Testament Hebrew usage and the New Testament. In those instances cited above where in the Hiphil the forensic meaning is explicit the LXX uses the verb δικαιόω except in Job 27:5; Prov. 17:15, and in the latter the rendering (δίκαιος κρίνειν) makes the forensic idea equally explicit. In the Piel where we deemed the forensic no less apparent (Job 32:2; 33:32), Job 32:2 is rendered ἀπέφηνεν ἑαυτὸν δίκαιος which clearly conveys declarative force and in Job 33:32 we have δικαιόω. And the only instance of the Hithpael (Gen. 44:16) is rendered by δικαιόω. It is also significant that instances of the Imperfect Qal which figured in our discussion (Psalm 51:4(6); 143:2; Isa. 45:25; Ezek. 16:52; cf. also Isa. 43:9, 26) are rendered by δικαιόω and likewise Isa. 50:8; 53:11. It is also interesting that in Daniel 8:14; 12:3, where the causative sense appears, the LXX refrains from the use of δικαιόω. In Psalm 73:13, where in Hebrew we have the Piel of זכה, the LXX (72:13) renders the clause in question by ματαίως ἐδικαίωσα τὴν καρδίαν μου. The causative sense of δικαιόω is distinctly possible in this instance. But this cannot be insisted upon. The sense may be that of "clearing oneself". The clause which follows, "I have washed my hands in innocency", does not appear to mean that he cleansed his hands from defilement but rather washed his hands in testimony of his innocence. So the justifying of his heart may well be the clearing of himself of blame rather than that of cleansing his heart from impurity. So even Psalm 73:13 (LXX 72:13) cannot be appealed to as an instance of δικαιόω in the causative sense. It is also of interest that in some cases where we might properly be in doubt as to whether the stative or the forensic is the precise sense in the Hebrew the LXX uses δικαιόω (*cf.* Psalm 51:4(6); 143:2) and in Ezek. 16:51, 52; Jer. 3:11, where a demonstrative shade of thought appears, δικαιόω is used in both instances.

We found repeated instances of the stative use of צדק in Hebrew, particularly in the Qal stem. In some instances this is rendered by the verb δικαιόω in the LXX (Gen. 38:26; Psalm 19:10; LXX 18:10). It is not so certain, however, that the translators intended the stative idea to be expressed. The reason for doubt is that in numerous other instances where the stative idea appears in the Hebrew with the use of the Perfect or Imperfect Qal the LXX does not use δικαιόω but εἶναι δίκαιος or εἶναι καθαρός or δίκαιος ἀναφαίνομαι (Job 4:17; 9:2, 15, 20; 10:15; 11:2; 13:18; 15:14; 25:4; 34:5; 35:7; 40:8). This shows that δικαιόω was not considered appropriate in these instances. However, the use of the Perfect Passive in Gen. 38:26; Psalm 19:10 may indicate that the thought expressed by the Perfect tense was suitable to convey the stative idea. This same phenomenon may be present in the New Testament as we shall see later on.

II. *God's Justification of Men*

In I Kings 8:32 God is said to justify the righteous and in Exod. 23:7 it is denied that he will justify the wicked. When he is said to justify the righteous this act of judgment is a declaring to be that which is conceived of as antecedently and actually the case. The person is of righteous character and conduct and the act of justifying is simply a judgment in accordance with the antecedent facts. This use of the term "justify" as applied to God is precisely the same as that which is applied to men in Deut. 25:1 when it is required of judges that they "justify the righteous, and condemn the wicked" and, by implication, the same as we find in Prov. 17:15 when it is said that "he that justifieth the wicked, and he that condemneth the just, both of them alike are an abomination to the Lord". In each case what is stressed is the necessity of equity in judgment and, since God's judgment is always according to truth, he will justify the righteous and he will not justify the wicked. Since his judgment is of this character we must recognize that in Old Testament usage there is a righteousness conceived of as predicable of men of which God himself takes account and on the basis of which he is said to justify them, that is to say, he declares and pronounces them to be what they are. In the case of God, preeminently, he renders judgment in accordance with the facts as they are.

This immediately raises the question provoked by the protestation appearing in various forms in the Old Testament that in God's sight no man living is justified. "How can man be just with God?" asks Job, and Bildad reiterates the same (Job 9:2; 25:4). The psalmist states the matter affirmatively, "Enter not into judgment with thy servant; for in thy sight no man living is justified" (Psalm 143:2). Again, "If thou, Lord, shouldest mark iniquities, O Lord, who shall stand" (Psalm 130:3). And that Job's question, as also Bildad's, implies a negative answer is apparent, for Job continues, "If he be pleased to contend with him, he cannot answer him one of a thousand" (Job 9:3) and Bildad, "How shall he be clean that is born of a woman?" (Job 25:4). Perhaps the most sweeping indictment of all is, "there is none that doeth good, no, not one" (Psalm 14:3; 53:3).

When we find in the Old Testament protestations of integrity on the part of the faithful, we are not to regard these as necessarily the pleadings of self-righteousness inconsistent with the recognition of utter sinfulness and plealessness before God. We find in Job himself repeated protestations to this effect (cf. Job 6:29; 12:4; 13:18, 19; 16:19–21; 17:9; 27:5, 6; 29:14; 31:1–40). An upright man may properly plead his integrity against false accusations of both friends and enemies. In Job 9:2 it is speechlessness before God, when we are weighed in the balances of his spotless judgment, that is in view. The thought is identical with that of Psalm 143:2 that in God's sight no man living is righteous or of Psalm 130:3, "If thou Lord shouldest mark iniquities, O Lord, who shall stand?" It is the same judgment that comes to its deepest expression later on in Job's own case, "Behold, I am vile; what shall I answer thee? I will lay my hand upon my mouth. Once have I spoken, and I will not answer; yea, twice, but I will proceed no further" (Job 40:4, 5); "I have heard of thee by the hearing of the ear; but now mine eye seeth thee: wherefore I abhor myself, and repent in dust and ashes" (Job 42:5, 6). Apparently the error of Bildad and his friends (cf. Job 25:4) was that they pleaded this truth in reference to Job's

341

claim to integrity against false charges. The fact that no man can stand justified in the balances of God's absolute and ultimate judgment is not incompatible with self-defence and self-vindication against unjust allegations by men. It is what we find in the psalmist, too. "Judge me, O Lord, for I have walked in my integrity" (Psalm 26:1) is not contradictory of Psalm 130:3; 143:2, as if the former were the language of self-righteous boasting and the latter by way of contrast that of humble contrition. Both attitudes are proper in their respective viewpoints.

This truth that in God's sight no man is justified and that there is none righteous, no, not one, a truth embedded in the piety of the Old Testament, lays the basis for two other features with which the piety of the Old Testament is pervaded, the plea of mercy and the plea for forgiveness (*cf.* Psalm 32:1, 2; 51:1, 2; 130:4; Dan. 9:9, 18, 19). The plea of mercy can be valid only where it is recognized that there is no plea in justice. And the plea of forgiveness is that of the person condemned and imbued with the sense of that condemnation. That the faith of forgiveness should occupy so central a place in Old Testament piety flows from the centrality of this promise in the covenants of grace (*cf.* Exod. 34:6, 7; Isa. 43:25; 44:22; Micah 7:18, 19).

All of these considerations show, therefore, that embedded in the Old Testament is the truth that before God's tribunal no one can stand and plead the claims of justice in support of his justification. There is none righteous, no, not one.

This leads us, however, to another strand of Old Testament teaching. It is to the effect that God does justify and he justifies those of whom it is also said that in God's sight they are not justified. This appears contradictory. According to the criteria and standards which obtain among men these data are contradictory. Among men, to justify the wicked is an abomination to the Lord. But this is what God does. Hence we read: "Declare thou that thou mayest be justified" (Isa. 43:26); "In the Lord shall all the seed of Israel be justified, and shall glory" (Isa. 45:25); "By his knowledge shall my servant, the righteous one, justify many" (Isa. 53:11).

In connection with this justifying act of God we must reckon with the possibility that the justifying act, though strictly forensic in character, might still have respect to a righteousness of character and behaviour predicable of the persons justified, after the analogy of I Kings 8:32. We must remember that the declarative act itself denoted by the term justify does not lose its forensic force when the righteousness contemplated as the ground is that of subjective character and behaviour. The case in this event would be as follows. All men are sinfully corrupt; they rest under the condemnation of God. But God in his grace renews men and gives them new character and behaviour. On the basis of this change he gives judgment accordingly; he declares the person to be what he has come to be by transforming grace. The process which supplies the ground for the justifying act is operative or causative but the justifying act itself is strictly and only forensic. The question is inescapable: Does the Old Testament teaching follow this pattern?

In answering the question we cannot overlook the first explicit reference to God's justification in the history of revelation, namely, Genesis 15:6: Abraham "believed in the Lord; and he reckoned it to him for righteousness". The term "justify" does not occur but that the text bears upon the question cannot be disputed; it concerns God's judgment in the matter of righteousness. Four considerations are to be noted.

1. The decisive feature of Abraham that is thrust into the forefront is faith, faith as reliance upon and trust in the Lord. Faith focuses attention upon the character of God and in this case specifically upon his power and faithfulness

2. The judgment of God with reference to Abraham was that of reckoning something to his account; it was an imputation.

3. What was reckoned was righteousness.

4. It was the faith of Abraham that was reckoned as righteousness. It was not his righteousness of character or behaviour that was brought into account in this instance but something which derived all of its significance and efficacy from the character of God.

From these considerations we derive no presumption in favour of the notion that here we have a justifying act of God based upon the recognition of Abraham's righteous character and behaviour. We are pointed in the opposite direction by the stress which falls upon the fact that it was faith that was imputed for righteousness, faith as magnifying the power and truth of God and therefore faith in contrast with personal performance in the realm of behaviour. In other words, we have here a milieu of thought quite diverse from that of I Kings 8:32. In the latter text God justifies the righteous and gives him according to his righteousness. In Genesis 15:6 it is the contrast with this procedure that strikes our attention.

With this orientation provided by Genesis 15:6 we must now turn to the consideration of other evidence bearing upon the question of the justification that is placed against the background of condemnation. This evidence is concerned with one of the most striking features of the Old Testament, namely, that it is in the Lord that God's people are justified. There are at least three distinct respects in which this truth is expressed. (1) It is in the Lord that Israel is justified. (2) It is in the Lord that their righteousness resides. (3) The Lord himself is the righteousness of his people. It is particularly in the prophets Isaiah and Jeremiah and in the Psalms that this truth comes to expression.

In Isa. 45:25 it is expressed, "In the Lord shall all the seed of Israel be righteous and shall glory". It makes no difference to the question before us now whether the verb is rendered statively or forensically, "be righteous" or "will be justified". The point of interest is the fact that in either case it is "in the Lord". It is more feasible to adopt the rendering "in the Lord" rather than "by the Lord". In the preceding verse the same expression surely means "in the Lord" and this rendering is ostensibly more suitable with the other verb "shall glory" than would be the rendering "by the Lord". The preceding verse (45:24) states the other respect in which the truth is expressed, that it is in the Lord righteousness resides: "Only in the Lord, it is said of me, is righteousness and strength." The idea of "righteousness" is in this case enforced by the use of the plural, the plural of magnitude or fulness. There need be no question but Israel is represented as righteous or justified in the Lord because the righteousness that resides in the Lord is brought to bear upon Israel. And if confirmation is required it is provided by Isa. 54:17: "No weapon that is formed against thee shall prosper, and every tongue that shall rise against thee in judgment thou shalt condemn. This is the heritage of the servants of the Lord, and their righteousness is of me, saith the Lord." These observations drawn from these two passages must be coordinated with a series of passages in which the Lord's righteousness is represented as near to come

344

or as about to be revealed unto the salvation of his people (Isa. 46:13; 51:5, 6, 8; 56:1; 61:10, 11; 62:1). The parallelism between salvation as near to come and righteousness to be revealed, between clothing with the garments of salvation and covering with the robe of righteousness, between righteousness as near and salvation as gone forth indicates that the righteousness contemplated is righteousness unto salvation. At least it is righteousness correlative with salvation and therefore righteousness brought to bear upon the children of men. It is righteousness operative unto the end of that judgment which righteousness elicits, a judgment of justification. It is the righteousness of God himself that is thus revealed in saving action. Hence we see how it could be said that in the Lord's righteousness Israel is justified and that Israel's righteousness is of him (*cf.* Psalm 24:5; 89:16(17); 103:17; Isa. 32:17; 63:1).

Jer. 23:6 is no doubt a messianic prophecy. In verse 5 this is made plain: "Behold, the days come, saith the Lord, and I will raise up to David a righteous branch, and a king shall reign and act wisely and do judgment and righteousness in the earth". The feature of verse 6 in which we are now particularly interested is the name by which the "righteous branch" will be called. Whatever may be the proper rendering of the clauses in question, the name indicates the specific identity of the person in view. There are two possible renderings: "This is his name which the Lord will call him, our righteousness" or "This is his name which he will be called (one will call him), the Lord our righteousness". On the former alternative it is apparent that we are said to have property in his righteousness—he is our righteousness. He is brought into such relation to us as the righteous branch that his righteousness in some way or other is our righteousness. This points definitely to the conclusion that in one respect at least the righteousness predicated of those contemplated is not a righteousness of their own but a righteousness which they have in the righteous branch. This rendering would not, of itself, say that the Lord is the righteousness of his people. But when coordinated with the other two respects established above that it is in the Lord Israel is justified and that their righteousness resides in the Lord, we are brought, to say the least, to the threshold of identifying the righteous branch with the Lord, in which case the righteous branch would be the Lord in whom Israel is justified and the

345

righteousness which resides in the Lord would be the righteousness of the righteous branch.

There are, however, considerations which may be pleaded in favour of the other construction in which "the Lord" is joined with "our righteousness" as the name by which the righteous branch is called. (1) The massoretic interpunctuation undoubtedly indicates that this was the interpretation of the massoretes. (2) There are other instances in the Old Testament where the tetragram must be joined with that which follows. Of course, these instances are not precisely parallel; they do not admit of another construction. Nevertheless they do create a presumption in favour of following, in the case of Jer. 23:6, the construction which is so apparent in these other cases. That is to say, the conjunction found in these others would provide a pattern for the interpretation of Jer. 23:6. The other passages are Gen. 22:14; Exod. 17:15; Judges 6:24; Ezek. 48:35. (3) While it is freely admitted that the tetragram may be the subject of "will call him" (*cf.* Gen. 26:18), yet if the tetragram is the subject we should expect a different construction after the pattern of numerous Old Testament passages. That is, we should expect first the verb "will call", then the tetragram as the subject, then "his name" as the object with "our righteousness" in apposition to "his name" (*cf.* Gen. 3:20; 4:25; 5:3; 16:11; 19:22; 25:30; 29:34; 35:18; Josh. 7:26; I Chron. 4:9; Isa. 7:14; Jer. 11:16; 20:3). (4) Jer. 33:16 is a close parallel to 23:6 and the same denomination occurs with the same construction. Referring in this case to Jerusalem we read, "And this is that which she shall be called, the Lord our righteousness". On exegetical grounds we should have to reject as untenable the rendering, "This is that which the Lord will call her, our righteousness". The reason is apparent. Neither analogy of Old Testament teaching nor good sense would allow that Jerusalem could be represented in any way as the righteousness of Israel. Consequently we must conjoin the tetragram with "our righteousness" in this case and interpret the clause as meaning that Jerusalem was to be identified by the motto, "The Lord our righteousness". The pattern provided by Jer. 33:16 is all but conclusive for understanding the construction in 23:6 in the same way. When all of these considerations are taken into account, they preponderate in favour of the conjunction of the tetragram and "our righteousness" as the name by which the Messiah is called. The question would still remain whether the thought is that the righteous branch is "the Lord our righteousness" or whether his name is "The Lord is our righteousness". In the former case he would be called "the Lord", in the latter case he would not necessarily be. In Jer. 33:16 the title ascribed to Jerusalem cannot be understood as identifying Jerusalem with the Lord, and the meaning of the title would then be "the Lord is our righteousness". In the other instances cited above (Gen. 22:14; Exod. 17:15; Judg. 6:24; Ezek. 48:35) we should have to adopt the same rendering. These facts make the case to be such that we cannot be dogmatic as to the rendering "the Lord our righteousness" in 23:6. In other words, all that can be insisted on is "the Lord is our righteousness". But this plainly establishes the thesis that, in the thought of the Old Testament, we do arrive at the point where the Lord himself is set forth as the righteousness of his people. Hence we have the threefold respect in which the justification of men is grounded and validated—it is in the Lord that men are justified, it is in the Lord their righteousness resides, the Lord himself is their righteousness. This is the answer to the question, how can man be just with God? And it meets the dilemma of the contradiction between condemnation and justification. Here we have the high point of revelation in the Old Testament respecting our topic. It is in the light of the New Testament that we can understand how the Lord himself is our righteousness. But it is also true that it is on the background of this Old Testament witness that the high point of New Testament disclosure is to be understood. The Pauline doctrine of the righteousness of God from faith to faith (cf. Rom. 1:17; 3:21, 22; 10:3; II Cor. 5:21; Phil. 3:9) can only be understood in the light of its Old Testament counterpart.

THE NEW TESTAMENT

I. The Terms

In the New Testament the term that expresses the concept of justification more than any other is δικαιόω. The question arises: Do we find in the New Testament the various meanings in the use of this term which we found in the Old Testament in the

347

usc of the corresponding Hebrew root, namely, the stative, the causative, the demonstrative, and the forensic?

Examination of the instances will show rather clearly that δικαιόω never has stative force in the active voice; it is a verb of action and does not denote a state. Luke 7:29 shows how patent the *active* force is—"all the people when they heard and the publicans justified God". The same is true in Luke 10:29 when it says of the lawyer, "but he willing to justify himself", and in Luke 16:15—"ye are they who justify yourselves in the sight of men" (*cf.* also Rom. 3:26, 30; 4:5; 8:30, 33; Gal. 3:8). In most cases it takes a direct object but this is not uniform (*cf.* Rom. 8:33). This fact would create the presumption that the passive would mean, "being subjected to the action denoted by the active voice". There is the possibility that, as in the LXX (Gen. 38:26; Psalm 19:10), the perfect passive could be used in the stative sense. With reference to the publican in Luke 18:14 the clause in question could be rendered, "this one went down to his house righteous", that is to say, in a righteous state. And, though the perfect passive lends itself more readily to this meaning (*cf.* I Cor. 4:4), other tenses could yield a similar sense. In Acts 13:39 the relevant clause with the present passive could be, "In this one every one who believes is righteous". In Rom. 3:4, as we found with the Hebrew, the clause could be rendered, "in order that thou mightest be righteous in thy words", even though the tense is aorist. In Rom. 2:13; 3:20 the future passive could be thus interpreted and in Rom. 3:28; Gal. 2:16; 3:11; 5:4; James 2:24 the present passive.

There are, however, reasons which favour the strictly passive sense.

1. In several of these instances where the stative is possible the passive rendering is more natural; there is an element of harshness to the stative rendering (*cf.* Rom. 3:20; I Cor. 4:4), especially when related to the immediate context.
2. There does not appear to be one instance where this stative rendering and force are required and thus proven.
3. Since δικαιόω is a verb of action it would require the strongest evidence to show that the natural force of the passive is not intended. This evidence is not available.
4. The aorist passive which appears in many instances does not well accord with the stative idea.

5. In many instances this stative force is ruled out (*cf.* Matt. 11:19; 12:37; Luke 7:35; Rom. 3:24; 6:7; I Cor. 6:11; I Tim. 3:16). It needs no argument to see this in these cases. For these reasons we cannot reckon with the stative use of δικαιόω in the New Testament except, as will be observed later, there is a stative idea which approximates to the forensic notion. As respects the causative sense, we found that the LXX refrained from the use of δικαιόω in those cases where the Hebrew root was used in that sense (Dan. 8:14; 12:3). Only in Psalm 73:13 (LXX 72:13) may this causative sense appear and even then it is doubtful if this is the correct signification. This LXX background creates a strong presumption against interpreting any instance of δικαιόω in the New Testament in the causative sense unless there is a compelling reason for doing so. The question then is: do we find in the New Testament any instances where the causative sense of making righteous or pure, that is to say, the meaning "purify", appears. We must not prejudge the question on the basis of what is the preponderant meaning. In the New Testament, terms are flexible in their precise connotation and only the context will determine in which of alternative senses a term is used. This is true of the apostle Paul in whose epistles most instances of δικαιόω appear. There is one case where it is contended that ἐδικαιώθητε, because of the context, means "you have become pure" (I Cor. 6:11). This is the view of Walter Bauer (*Griechisch-Deutsches Wörterbuch ad* δικαιόω; *cf.* also Arndt and Gingrich: *op. cit., ad loc.*) and of some commentators. The context in this case does deal with purification—"but ye have been washed, but ye have been sanctified"—and the clause in question is continuous with these preceding clauses. There is, therefore, presumption in favour of an interpretation which belongs to the same category as washing and sanctification. Furthermore, the phrase at the end of the verse "by the Spirit of our God", whether construed with all three preceding verbs or not, cannot be dissociated from ἐδικαιώθητε. If the latter term is interpreted forensically as referring to justification, then it would be difficult to find any analogy in Paul's teaching for this representation that the Holy Spirit is the agent in justification or the person "in whom" we are justified. There are, therefore, weighty considerations in favour of the non-forensic interpretation here. There is the reservation, however, that the case is not a

349

closed one, and that for the following reasons. (1) In Titus 3:5-7 δικαιόω (again in the aorist passive) occurs in close conjunction with terms which are in the same category as those in I Cor. 6:11—"through the washing of regeneration and renewal of the Holy Spirit, which he shed on us abundantly through Jesus Christ our Saviour, in order that being justified by his grace we might be made heirs according to the hope of eternal life". It is true that we do not have the same coordination as we have in I Cor. 6:11 but there is sufficiently close correlation and subordination to caution us against a too easy assumption regarding the effect of the coordination in I Cor. 6:11. (2) There is no good reason why δικαιόω in Titus 3:7 should not be taken as the forensic use. That with which it is related, "by his [God's] grace", and that to which it is directed, "made heirs according to the hope of eternal life", are, in Paul's teaching elsewhere, thus associated with justification. Our conclusion must be that in I Cor. 6:11 we may have an instance of the causative sense but that this cannot be established beyond question. If, however, the sense of being made pure appears here, then the unfrequency of this signification only certifies how exceptional it is, and we have in the New Testament a situation practically identical with that of the LXX.

In the New Testament there are other instances in which the causative sense would not make obvious nonsense—it is abstractly possible. But, on the other hand, there are so many instances where the causative sense is out of the question, so many other considerations arising from correlative and antithetical expressions indicating the forensic meaning, and the suitability of the forensic meaning in those cases where there is the abstract possibility of the causative sense that to impose an abstract possibility, contrary to the pervasive usage in the New Testament, in such cases would be wholly arbitrary and indefensible.

With the possible exception of I Cor. 6:11 in the causative sense and with the exception of a stative use that assimilates itself to the forensic, we are restricted to the demonstrative and forensic meanings. In respect of the distinction between these two senses it is clear enough that "show to be righteous" may be distinguished from "declare to be righteous". Yet when we examine instances of δικαιόω in the New Testament, where the former might be judged to convey the more precise shade of thought, it is to be admitted that the propriety of maintaining this demonstrative sense might be challenged. In Matt. 11:19; Luke 7:35, where wisdom is said to be justified from her works or from her children, there would appear to be some reason for interpreting this to mean that wisdom is shown to be righteous or vindicated from her works or from her children. At least it would seem that the term "justify" takes on more of the demonstrative force than it does of the declarative. In Luke 16:15 the thought is apparently "ye are they who show yourselves off as righteous in the sight of men" and may not have the strength of "pronouncing" themselves righteous. In Rom. 3:4 this sense expresses well what may be thought of God—he is vindicated in his judgments. The same meaning may well appear in I Cor. 4:4; I Tim. 3:16. If this import commends itself, then it is possible to interpret James 2:21, 24, 25 in this way and the apparent discrepancy between the teaching of Paul and that of James would be considerably relieved. In any case, if we once admit that in some instances the accent falls upon the demonstrative notion as distinguished from the judicially declarative, then we have gone a long way in resolving what might appear at first to be open contradiction. For in James the accent would fall upon the *probative* character of good works, whereas in the Pauline polemic the accent falls without question upon the judicially constitutive and declarative.

With few exceptions, therefore, the only meanings that appear in the New Testament are the demonstrative and the forensic and these shades of thought are so close that in some instances the balance in favour of the demonstrative is so slight that we can scarcely insist on that meaning as distinguished from the forensic. The evidence supporting the distinctly forensic signification is so abundant that it is unnecessary to adduce the same in detail. The prevalence of this import in the LXX is itself one of the most determinative data for the understanding of the same term in the New Testament. In Luke 7:29, only the sense of "declare righteous" could obtain and any causative idea of the sense of "making righteous" is entirely excluded. In reference to Paul's polemic for justification by faith the contrast in Rom. 8:33 between "condemn" and "justify" establishes the forensic signification of the latter. This fixes the import of the same term in verse 30. And if this is the meaning in the passage where justification is given its locus among the pivotal elements in the chain of salvation, then this same precise signification must apply throughout the earlier part of the epistle in which justification is the theme. Confirmatory is the equivalent expression which is employed to such an extent in Rom. 4, namely, that faith was reckoned to Abraham for righteousness (4:3, 5, 6, 11, 22, 23). Whatever may be the difficulties arising from this expression derived from Gen. 15:6, the formula clearly points in an imputative direction and has no affinity with the subjectively operative idea which the causative signification implies. Reckoning righteousness to our account falls clearly into the forensic sphere.

While it is apparent that the forensic meaning governs New Testament usage it does not follow that our English term "declare righteous" or "pronounce righteous" is thoroughly adequate to express all that is involved in the forensic connotation. We may readily suspect that in some instances more is involved than our English expressions are competent to convey. In Luke 18:14 —"this one went down to his house justified"—we may rightly sense that "declared to be righteous" is too attenuated to express the thought. We may not by any means remove the concept from the realm of the judicial or forensic. But there is surely reflection here upon the status constituted as well as upon the status declared to be—the publican went down to his house in a righteous state. And the term "justified" indicates the righteous state effected as well as the righteous state declared to be. If the forensic import is duly maintained, the thought could be expressed by saying that he went down to his house "righteous". Here the stative idea, as indicated above, approximates, if it does not assimilate itself, to the forensic meaning. Likewise in Rom. 3:24—"being justified freely by his grace"—we can readily sense that the bare notion of pronouncement or declaration does not measure up to the richness of that which is embraced in the justifying act. In other words, there is an action of God implied in the justification of the ungodly that is not fully expressed by the declarative formula. The other formula which Paul uses helps us to discover what this additional ingredient is—it is to reckon righteousness to the account of a person. Without prejudging at this stage what this precise formula means, it is at least apparent that in the act of justifying there is an *imputative* act as well as a declarative. If we will, we may say that it is declarative in such a way that it is also imputative. It is this imputative notion that fills up the deficiency which we may properly sense in the term "declare righteous". And that this more positive action is involved is borne out still further by the expression "constituted righteous" (Rom. 5:19) which in the context must have the same force as justification. The justifying act is constitutive. But since this cannot negate the forensic meaning, it must be within the forensic sphere that it is constitutive. Hence we may sum up by saying that justification of the ungodly is constitutively and imputatively declarative.

II. *The Righteousness Contemplated*

If we think of justification declaratively as declaring or pronouncing to be righteous, the righteous status or relationship must be contemplated as existing or at least as having come to exist by the declaration in view. If we focus thought on the forensic signification, then the judgment conceived and registered must have righteousness in view as the basis of the judgment. If we think in terms of the constitutive act after the pattern of Rom. 5:19, then the righteousness by which this status is constituted is presupposed. And, finally, if the imputative notion is brought into view, then, explicitly, righteousness is contemplated as the thing imputed because the formula is expressly that "God imputes righteousness" (Rom. 4:6). The question is therefore: What is the righteousness by which God justifies the ungodly?

The formula derived from Gen. 15:6 is to the effect that faith was reckoned for righteousness (Rom. 4:3, 5, 9, 10, 22, 23; Gal. 3:6; James 2:23). This would appear to mean that faith itself is the righteousness imputed. If faith itself is the righteousness contemplated and is that *on account of which* God justifies the ungodly, then the question poses itself: how is this to be reconciled with what is the burden of New Testament teaching in this connection, namely, that the redemption which is in Christ, the propitiation and reconciliation through his blood, and his obedience unto death constitute that on the basis of which sinners are justified? If faith is itself the righteousness, how does the redemptive work of Christ come into direct relation to our justification, as the teaching of Paul in particular indicates? Various attempts have been made in the history of theology to resolve this difficulty and in many instances these proposed solutions have been to

353

the effect that, in Gen. 15:6 and the corresponding passages from the New Testament, faith itself is not to be construed as the righteousness referred to in these passages. If we were to resort to this type of solution, then probably the most acceptable interpretation would be that the expression "impute for righteousness" or "impute righteousness" is but a synonym, derived from the Old Testament, for the verb "justify", and so the whole formula "faith is imputed for righteousness" means simply that "faith justifies" or, preferably, that a person "is justified by faith". Lest, however, we should be subjecting the formula to arbitrary interpretation it is more feasible to take it to mean that it was the faith of Abraham that was reckoned as righteousness. It is this signification that the same kind of formula has in Psalm 106:31, even though in the latter there is slight variation of terms. The thought then would be that God reckoned to Abraham the faith which he exercised and that it was reckoned as righteousness. Faith is well-pleasing to God and in that respect it is reckoned or imputed for what it is.

If this interpretation is adopted there are two considerations which would appear to support the thesis that faith is itself the righteousness unto justification. (1) The formula is set in contrast with justification by works of law (cf. Rom. 4:2–6, 13, 14, 16; Gal. 3:5, 6; cf. Rom. 10:5, 6). In the case of justification by works it is clear that the works themselves would be the ground upon which the justification would rest (Rom. 2:13). If faith is contrasted with works, then we should expect that faith would occupy the same position as works in the event of justification by works. (2) The expression "righteousness of faith" (cf. Rom. 4:11, 13) could be interpreted in the sense that it is the righteousness which consists in faith, faith being an appositional or definitive genitive.

If the formula is to be interpreted as indicated, may we thus dismiss our question and say that faith is the righteousness contemplated in justification and that no further exposition of the biblical data is necessary? There are various reasons for a decisive negative. We cannot allow one formula to determine our whole doctrine of the ground of justification, however significant that formula may be in itself.

1. In the context in which Paul makes sustained use of this formula our suspicion is aroused that more is involved in the

imputation of righteousness than the imputation of faith. In Rom. 4:6–8 Paul appeals to David and specifically to Psalm 32:1, 2. Here Paul interprets the blessedness of which David speaks as "the blessedness of the man to whom God imputes righteousness without works" (vs. 6). There can be no question, therefore, but he has in mind the imputation of righteousness referred to in the formula of Gen. 15:6 which he quotes repeatedly in this context. Consequently the quotation from Psalm 32:1, 2 throws some light on what Paul considered to be embraced in the imputation of righteousness. It is significant that David speaks simply of the forgiveness of iniquities, the covering of sins, and the non-imputation of sin. These are negative in form and David does not speak positively in terms of the imputation of righteousness. But Paul does speak positively and he must conceive of the imputation of righteousness as embracing the non-imputation and forgiveness of sin. Exegetically we may not be justified at this point in importing into the imputation of righteousness anything more than this non-imputation and forgiveness. But it is quite apparent that if, in Paul's esteem, the righteousness imputed consisted simply in faith, it would not be compatible with such a restricted conception to include the non-imputation and forgiveness of sin. Thus from the context in which Paul makes the greatest use of Gen. 15:6 we derive at least one consideration which gives to the righteousness imputed a broader connotation than faith itself would indicate, and we are pointed in the direction of seeking within Paul's own teaching something correlative with the non-imputation of sin that will supply the positive complement which the expression "impute righteousness" appears to demand.

2. In Rom. 10:10 we have the expression "it is believed unto righteousness". The righteousness in this instance can be none other than "the righteousness of faith", referred to in verse 6, which, in turn, must be identified with "the righteousness of God" in verse 3. Any indication given in verse 10 of the character of this righteousness must be taken into account in our interpretation of verse 6. And anything derived from verse 10, relevant to the relation of faith to this righteousness, will bear upon the expression "the righteousness of faith" in verse 6. It must be noted that the clause in verse 10 is parallel to the other clause in the same verse, namely, "it is confessed unto salvation". And this

355

latter clause helps us to understand the relation of believing to righteousness in the preceding clause. Just as salvation does not consist in confession nor is it to be defined in terms of confession, so righteousness does not consist in faith nor is it to be defined in terms of faith itself. The conclusion must be that faith is *unto* righteousness and hence the expression in verse 6, "the righteousness of faith" cannot mean the righteousness that consists in faith but "of faith" must be given the instrumental force which it has frequently elsewhere in the New Testament.

Furthermore, in connection with this same passage, the expression in verse 3, that "they did not subject themselves to the righteousness of God", would yield, to say the least, an awkward idea if faith itself is the righteousness contemplated. Faith is itself that by which we subject ourselves to the righteousness of God and cannot therefore be that to which we subject ourselves.

3. It cannot be reasonably questioned that in Paul's teaching the righteousness contemplated in justification is "the righteousness of God". Rom. 1:17 puts this beyond dispute, for it is there called "the righteousness of God revealed from faith to faith". And whatever may be the signification of "the righteousness of God" in this connection or of the phrase "from faith to faith", what is in view must be that which the apostle elsewhere calls "the righteousness of faith" (Rom. 4:11, 13; 9:30; 10:6), the righteousness which on all accounts is that contemplated in justification. Hence the expression "the righteousness of God" in Rom. 1:17 and in other passages (Rom. 3:21, 22; 10:3; II Cor. 5:21; Phil. 3:9; *cf.* II Pet. 1:1) must be the righteousness with which we are now concerned. But if faith itself is the righteousness, how could it be called the righteousness of God when, as we shall see later, this righteousness is a righteousness with divine property, a God-righteousness as distinct from human righteousness? We know not by what stretch of imagination faith could be called the righteousness of God.

Moreover, the righteousness of God is said to be revealed or manifested (Rom. 1:17; 3:21). In that respect it constitutes the gospel message—it is the provision of God's grace in the gospel revealed by God and proclaimed by men. But it is impossible to conceive of faith itself as fitting such a description or as filling such conditions.

4. Christ himself is said to be made unto us righteousness

and we are said to be made the righteousness of God in him (I Cor.
1:30; II Cor. 5:21). The underlying assumption of these passages
is that Christ himself is the righteousness and that, by union with
him or by some kind of relationship which we come to sustain
to him, we gain property in that righteousness which he is, a
righteousness which is expressly called, after the pattern of these
other passages, the righteousness of God. How then could our
faith be equated with the righteousness which Christ himself is
and which we become in him?

5. The righteousness unto justification is a free gift received
(Rom. 5:17). It is true that faith is the gift of God. But it is so
only in the sense of being generated in the heart by God's grace.
The language of Rom. 5:17 is the language of objective bestowment, not that of subjective renewal.

6. We are in the most express fashion pointed to the obedience
of Christ as that through which we are justified (Rom. 5:19).
"Constituted righteous" must in this context have the same import
as "justified" and that the constituting righteousness is the
obedience of Christ is put beyond question.

7. The way in which faith is related to this justifying righteousness is far from indicating that faith itself is the righteousness.
In Rom. 3:22 the righteousness of God made manifest is defined
to be "a righteousness of God through faith of Jesus Christ unto
all who believe". "Through faith of Jesus Christ" indicates
the means through which this righteousness is brought to bear
upon us and is far from suggesting that it is definitive of the
righteousness itself. But the difficulty would become insuperable
when we take into account the concluding clause. For, if faith
is the righteousness, then we would have to think that "faith"
is unto all who believe, an impossible concept. Again in Phil.
3:9 the righteousness is described as "the righteousness of God by
faith", and the construction ill befits any such notion as we are
controverting. Besides, if faith is the righteousness, we would
expect the construction "on account of faith" *(διὰ πίστιν)* which
never occurs in the New Testament.

8. The righteousness contemplated in justification is introduced in other passages in such connections that it is impossible to
substitute "faith" for righteousness in these cases. In Rom. 5:21
we have the summation of Paul's argument from verse 12. And
when we ask: What is the righteousness through which grace

reigns unto eternal life? the answer must be that it is the righteousness bestowed as a free gift (vs. 17), the one righteous act (vs. 18), and the obedience of the one (vs. 19), none of which can be equated with faith. In II Cor. 3:9 "the ministration of righteousness" of which the apostle speaks can be none other than the righteousness on which the gospel of justification turns, and we can hardly equate it with the ministration of faith. Or, to take another example, Heb. 11:7 speaks of Noah as having become heir of the righteousness by faith (κατὰ πίστιν). Here an inheritance is conceived of and it is defined as "righteousness". Faith cannot be regarded as an inheritance and, besides, the righteousness is characterized as "according to faith", a characterization which well defines the relation of faith to the inheritance but cannot define the inheritance itself.

9. The prepositions used in connection with justification —διά and ἐκ with the genitive, ἐπί and ἐν with the dative, κατά and εἰς with the accusative—are far from indicating any such view of the meaning of faith. And even in the expressions "the righteousness of faith" (Rom. 10:6), "the righteousness which is of faith" (Rom. 9:30), and "the righteousness according to faith" (Heb. 11:7), the prepositional phrases rather clearly indicate that faith is not the righteousness but stands in some instrumental relation to it.

For these reasons we are compelled to say that in New Testament teaching the righteousness contemplated in justification is not faith itself but something that comes into our possession by faith. The question then remains why, in the formula of Gen. 15:6 as quoted by Paul, is faith represented as reckoned for righteousness? It may not be possible to answer this question with any decisiveness. But the consideration that appears more relevant than any other is that the righteousness contemplated in justification is righteousness by faith in contrast with righteousness by works and the emphasis falls to such an extent upon this fact that although it is a God-righteousness yet it is also and with equal emphasis a faith-righteousness. In reality these two features are correlative: it is the righteousness of God brought to bear upon us because it is by faith, and it is by faith that we become the beneficiaries of this righteousness because it is a God-righteousness. So indispensable is this complementation in the justification of the ungodly that the righteousness may be called "the righteousness of God" or "the righteousness of faith" without in the least implying that faith sustains the same relation to this righteousness as God does. In like manner in the formula of Gen. 15:6 faith can be regarded as that which is reckoned for righteousness without thereby implying that it sustains the same relation to justification as does the righteousness of God. The righteousness is a God-righteousness and it is a faith-righteousness. But it is a God-righteousness because it is of divine property; it is a faith-righteousness because it is brought to bear upon us *by faith*. When faith is said to be imputed for righteousness this variation of formula is warranted by the correlativity of righteousness and faith, and it is in terms of this correlativity that the formula is to be interpreted rather than in terms of equation.

The doctrine of Paul respecting the nature of the righteousness by which God justifies the ungodly is sufficiently dealt with in the exposition, particularly at Rom. 1:17; 3:21-26; 4:25; 5:12-21, and it is unnecessary to deal with the subject in any further detail in this appendix.

The Romish Doctrine of Justification

The Romish doctrine is set forth in the canons and decrees of the Council of Trent (Session VI, "Decree Concerning Justification") and is summed up in Chapters VI and VII. The doctrine is set forth in terms of the various *causes*. The *final* cause is the glory of God and of Christ; the *efficient* cause is the merciful God who washes and sanctifies; the *meritorious* cause is the Lord Jesus Christ who merited justification by his passion and made satisfaction to the Father for us; the *instrumental* cause is the sacrament of baptism; the *formal* cause is the justice of God by which we are made just and consists in the infusion of sanctifying grace. Though the canons do not speak expressly of the *predisposing* or *preparatory* cause, yet the teaching of the two chapters referred to imply the same and define this cause in terms of faith, fear, hope, love, and contrition.

With reference to what is called the *meritorious* cause, Rome is insistent that Christ by his merits and satisfaction has procured for us the grace of justification. But this is not to be construed as meaning that it is by the righteousness and obedience of Christ that we are justified. Canon X while, on the one hand, insisting that Christ by his righteousness merited for us to be justified, yet, on the other hand, pronounces its anathema upon anyone who says that it is by that righteousness we are formally just. This distinction becomes clear when we bear in mind that, for Rome, justification is not a forensic or declarative act but consists in the sanctification and renewal of the inward man. Negatively, justification consists in the remission of sin and, positively, in the renewal of the soul. But the causal relation of these two elements in justification is that by the renewal of the soul, that is by regeneration, "a man's sins are blotted out and he becomes truly just" (Joseph Pohle ed. Arthur Preuss: *Dogmatic Theology*, VII, St. Louis, 1934, p. 303).

It is on this doctrine of justification as consisting in sanctification and renewal, the infusion of righteousness and sanctifying grace, that the polemic of Rome turns, and it is preeminently at this point that the issue between the Romish and Protestant positions must be joined. If anything has been demonstrated by the foregoing study of the usage both in the Old Testament and in the New it is that justification is a term of forensic import and refers to the judgment conceived and registered with reference to judicial status. It is strange that Rome should be so reluctant to recognize this. For even if Rome admitted that justification as to its *nature* is forensic, she could still retain what belongs to the essence of her position, namely, that the ground upon which this favourable judgment of God rests is not the righteousness and obedience of Christ but righteousness infused, inwrought, and outwrought in the works which are the fruit of *fides formata*, namely, faith informed with charity. This admission would reorient, of course, the terms of Rome's polemic as also of the anti-Romish Protestant polemic. But the crux of the controversy would still be the question of infused righteousness versus the vicarious and imputed righteousness of Christ. However, Rome is adamant in her insistence that justification is to be defined as *consisting* in sanctification and renewal, the impartation of sanctifying grace, after the pattern of the decrees of Trent. Hence it is necessary to join issue with Rome on both questions, namely, the *nature* and the *ground* of justification.

Rome's polemic is directed most vigorously against the tenet that we are justified by faith alone. This is necessitated by her conception of the nature of justification and, more particularly, by her view of the progressive character of justification and of the merits accruing to the believer from the works of faith. Here again the divergence of Rome from the sustained witness of Scripture to the effect that we are justified by faith apart from works is most patent. If anything is apparent from the evidence with which we have dealt in the commentary and in the foregoing pages of this appendix it is that "faith" is accorded the instrumental agency in connection with justification. Nothing should serve to expose the fallacy of Rome's doctrine more effectively than the incompatibility of this sustained emphasis upon faith with the Romish emphasis upon works and the merit accruing therefrom. It is symptomatic of the total discrepancy between Rome's position and the teaching of Scripture that baptism should be conceived of as the instrumental cause. The efficiency that Scripture accords to faith Rome accords to baptism. Is it not sufficient to make suspect any such formulation of the doctrine of justification to ask the question: where is baptism brought into such relation to that act of God denoted by the terms of which the term "justify" is the proper rendering? In contrast, how frequently is faith, to the express exclusion of works, brought into this relation to justification!

Rome errs in its failure to recognize the precise character of justification as an act of God in the sphere of putative and declarative judgment. In this respect the Romish doctrine is directly counter to the pervasive import of the term "justify" and its cognates in the usage of Scripture. Justification is thus confused with regeneration, renovation, and sanctification. The effect is that the distinctiveness of the grand article of justification by grace through faith is eliminated from the gospel. From this failure to reckon with justification in its true and distinguishing character arises a series of correlative deviations and distortions. The righteousness of Christ's obedience, in the nature of the case, cannot sustain to justification any other relation than that which it sustains to regeneration and sanctification—it is not the righteousness by which we are justified. And this is a denial that impinges directly upon the teaching of Paul in Rom. 5:17, 18, 19; II Cor. 5:21; Phil. 3:9, not to speak of other relevant biblical data. Again, faith is displaced from the position which the pervasive witness of Scripture demands, namely, that it is faith, by reason of its specific character in distinction from works as well as from all the other graces of the Spirit, and faith alone

361

that is brought into the instrumental relation to justification. Furthermore, the emphasis of Scripture upon the purely gratuitous character of justification is made of no effect in the Romish construction because the place accorded to human satisfaction and merit violates the concept of grace. And, finally, the definitive character of justification is rejected in favour of justification as an intrinsic process in virtue of which, as the Council of Trent affirmed, the justified increase in the righteousness received in justification and are still further justified (Chapter X). It is apparent how the various aspects of the Romish doctrine cohere with one another and how the basic error of failure to recognize the distinguishing character and grace of justification has made it not only possible but necessary for Rome to controvert what is set forth so patently in the witness of Scripture.

FROM FAITH TO FAITH

More recently Gabriel Hebert in an article "'Faithfulness' and 'Faith'" in *Theology* (Vol. LVIII, No. 424, Oct. 1955, pp. 373–379) maintains that, in accord with the meaning of *'emunah* in the Old Testament, πίστις should be understood in several instances in the New Testament as referring, not to our faith, but to the faithfulness of God and of Christ. Hence in Rom. 1:17 "from faith to faith" is to be interpreted as meaning "from the faithfulness of God to man's faith". Likewise in Rom. 3:22 the expression, "through the faith of Jesus Christ", is to be interpreted as referring to the faithfulness of Jesus Christ. He applies the same interpretation to such passages as Rom. 3:26; Gal. 2:16; 3:22; Eph. 3:12; Phil. 3:9; Col. 2:12.

Thomas F. Torrance, on the basis of a more extensive study of Old Testament terms, propounds the same thesis and applies this same interpretation to such passages as Rom. 1:17; 3:22; Gal. 2:16, 20; 3:22; Phil. 3:9 (*The Expository Times*, Vol. LXVIII, No. 4, Jan. 1957, pp. 111–114, under the title, "One Aspect of the Biblical Conception of Faith"). Torrance maintains, however, that "in most of these passages *pistis Iesou Christou* does not refer only either to the faithfulness of Christ or to the answering faithfulness of man, but is essentially a polarized expression denoting the faithfulness of Christ as its main ingredient but also involving or at least suggesting the answering faithfulness of man" (p. 113).

These are stimulating articles. The criticism offered in the succeeding pages is not to be interpreted as due to any lack of appreciation of the significance of the usage of the Old Testament in respect of those terms which so closely bear upon the meaning of faith in both Testaments. Both Hebert and Torrance bring to the forefront all-important considerations. The conclusions which are herewith presented are simply those which, in the esteem of the writer, examination of the evidence constrains. On the central question as it pertains to such passages as Rom.

1:17; 3:22, 26; Gal. 2:16, 20; Phil. 3:9 the thesis propounded by Hebert and Torrance does not appear to me to derive support from the passages concerned nor from other relevant New Testament data. The study that follows is largely oriented against the presentation of Torrance, and the charge of confusing a polarized situation with a "polarized expression" applies not to Hebert—he does not employ this latter expression nor is it entirely clear that he would have endorsed the use of it, though in one paragraph he may have the same thought in mind (p. 378).

It is quite true that πίστις is used to denote the faithfulness of God. There happens to be only one instance in the New Testament where this is patent (Rom. 3:3). But it is so perspicuous in this instance and πιστός is used so often with reference to God (I Cor. 1:9; 10:13; II Cor. 1:18; I Thess. 5:24; II Tim. 2:13; Heb. 10:23; I Pet. 4:19; I John 1:9) that there is no reason why πίστις should not designate the faithfulness of God in other passages where this denotation is not as patent as in Rom. 3:3 but where contextual considerations would favour this interpretation. Likewise, though πίστις does not expressly denote the faithfulness of Christ in any passage, yet πιστός is frequently enough predicated of him (II Thess. 3:3; Heb. 2:17; 3:2; Rev. 1:5; 3:14; 19:11) and there is no reason why "the faith of Jesus" should not refer to his faithfulness.

Furthermore, there need be no doubt but the faithfulness of God and of Christ are brought to bear upon our justification, and there is a variety of respects in which this could be conceived of as true and relevant. For example, if God is faithful and just to forgive our sins (I John 1:9), surely the same may be said of our being justified. And if the obedience of Christ is our justification (Rom. 5:19), this obedience cannot be divorced from his faithfulness to the commission and commandment of the Father. Hence if, in Rom. 1:17, ἐκ πίστεως is taken to refer to the faithfulness of God, there would be nothing *per se* contrary to Paul's teaching in such an interpretation, or if, in Rom. 3:22, διὰ πίστεως is taken of the faithfulness of Jesus Christ this could readily be seen to be consistent with the general teaching of Paul respecting the place which the obedience or righteousness of Christ occupies in our justification. In addition, this interpretation would resolve the difficulty of the apparently unnecessary duplication if "faith" is regarded in both instances in both passages as referring to our faith in Christ, the difficulty which has given so much trouble to commentators and on which diversity of interpretation has arisen.

Moreover, there need be no question but the correlativity of God's faithfulness and our "answering faithfulness", to use Torrance's expression, obtains in the matter of justification, and, if 'πίστις should sometimes be a "polarized expression" denoting both ingredients, there would be nothing intrinsically objectionable to such a supposition. Our faith is indeed the answer to God's faithfulness and to the faithfulness of Christ.

The question is not then whether in these passages, to which appeal is made, the view that πίστις refers to the faithfulness of God or of Christ would be incompatible with biblical doctrine or with Pauline doctrine in particular but whether this finding is borne out by the pertinent New Testament data. It is to this question that we must now address ourselves. In the nature of the case we shall be largely concerned with Paul's usage.

I. First of all it is necessary to adduce those passages in which πίστις is *obviously* faith on our part and cannot mean the faithfulness of God. In Rom. 1:8 it is quite obvious that it is the faith of the believers in Rome that is in view. And the same must also be true in the following instances: Rom. 14:1, 22, 23; I Cor. 2:5; 12:9; 13:2, 13; 15:14, 17; II Cor. 1:24; 10:15; Gal. 5:6, 22; Eph. 6:23; Phil. 2:17; I Thess. 1:3, 8; 3:2, 5, 6, 7, 10; II Thess. 1:3, 4; 3:2; I Tim. 1:5, 19; 2:15; 4:12; 6:11; II Tim. 1:5; 2:18, 22; Tit. 2:10; Phm. 5, 6; Heb. 4:2; 6:1; 11:1, 3, 4, 5, *passim*; James 1:3, 6; 2:5, *passim*; I Pet. 1:7; II Pet. 1:1, 5; I John 5:4; Rev. 2:19; 13:10. This is not an exhaustive list nor does it include other instances with which we shall deal presently where the same import appears. But these instances are selected to show the frequency with which πίστις appears in the sense of that exercise of heart and mind on our part directed to God or Christ and as instances to which the notion of the faithfulness of God cannot be attached as an ingredient in the term itself.

II. The next classification is that of those instances of πίστις where some contextual consideration, particularly that of contrast with works, makes it apparent that the activity on the part of the human subject is the activity specifically in view. One of the most significant passages in this group is Rom. 4 where Paul appeals to Gen. 15:6 in order to vindicate justification by faith in contrast with justification by works. Verses 3 and 4 indicate the crux of Paul's argument. "Abraham believed God and it was reckoned to him for righteousness" (vs. 4). It is Abraham's *believing* in God that is in the forefront as demonstrating justification by grace in contrast with one of debt on the basis of working (*cf.* vs. 4). The faith *(πίστις)* that is in view throughout (vss. 5, 9, 11, 12, 13, 14, 16, 20) is therefore the faith which Abraham placed in God. This is confirmed, if confirmation were required, by the constant interchange in this passage of the verb "believe" for the substantive "faith". "But to him that worketh not but believeth upon him who justifieth the ungodly, his faith is reckoned for righteousness" (vs. 5; *cf.* also vss. 3, 11, 17, 18, 24). Now that believing has reference exclusively to faith as exercised by Abraham and by those who walk in the footprints of his faith needs no demonstration. Hence πίστις in this passage cannot be understood to include in its connotation the faithfulness of God, although it was preeminently to the faithfulness and power of God that Abraham's faith was directed. It would be not only contrary to the sustained appeal to Abraham's believing but also contrary to the nature of this believing to include within its definition that of which God himself is specifically the agent. The same considerations bear upon the interpretation of πίστις in Gal. 3:2-14.

If in these passages the contrast with working and the emphasis placed upon the activity of believing fix for us the precise import of πίστις, when used in the same contexts, this conclusion bears upon the significance, in these contexts at least, of the expression ἐκ πίστεως. Torrance's contention is concerned to a considerable extent with the significance of ἐκ πίστεως. But in these contexts ἐκ πίστεως cannot reflect on anything more than the faith of Abraham and of those who walk in his footsteps. Concretely, this means that the expression in Rom. 4:16; Gal. 3:7, 8, 9, 11, 12 must have the same precise and restricted reference as πίστις and πιστεύω have in these same contexts. And in Rom. 5:1 ἐκ πίστεως cannot be otherwise interpreted in view of the preceding context.

In Rom. 10:3-12 Paul is again dealing with the contrast between the righteousness that is of works of the law and that which is of faith. His argument takes the form of an indictment against Israel that they "being ignorant of God's righteousness, and seeking to establish their own, did not subject themselves to the righteousness of God" (vs. 3), and then adds that "Christ is the end of the law for righteousness to every one that believeth" (vs. 4). This "to every one that believeth" is significant for our present interest because, along with the repeated use of the same term in verses 9, 10, 11, 14, it points to the sense in which we are to understand the term "faith" (πίστις) in this context. In the expression "the righteousness of faith" (vs. 6) faith must be understood in terms of the exercise of faith on our part and here again we have ἐκ πίστεως. The faithfulness of God cannot, for the same reasons as already indicated, be included in our definition of the term. The same must hold true of the same term in Rom. 9:30, 32 because of the continuity of Paul's argument at these points.

It may not be irrelevant to note that Paul has a distinct preference for the expression ἐκ πίστεως—it occurs more frequently than any other one form of prepositional construction, particularly in connection with justification. We are compelled to take account of the precise scope attaching to its use in these foregoing contexts and strong presumption is created for this signification throughout the Pauline epistles. It is also worthy of note that in Gal. 3:14 we find διὰ τῆς πίστεως and in this context, for the reasons given, "faith" with this construction must likewise have the same import—it is the faith of *our believing* in God.

III. There are some passages in which faith is said to be *in* Christ Jesus. "For ye are all sons of God through the faith in Christ Jesus" (Gal. 3:26). "Having heard of your faith in the Lord Jesus ... I do not cease to give thanks for you" (Eph. 1:15; cf. Col. 1:4). Deacons who have served well purchase to themselves "great boldness in the faith which is in Christ Jesus" (I Tim. 3:13; cf. II Tim. 1:13). The Scriptures are able to "make wise unto salvation through the faith which is in Christ Jesus" (II Tim. 3:15). In each of these instances the preposition ἐν is used. In Col. 2:5 where Paul speaks of beholding "the stedfastness of your faith in Christ" the preposition εἰς is used and there can be no doubt but the faith in view is faith directed to Christ on the part of these believers. Christ is the object of the faith in view and not its subject. In these other passages, however, it is possible that the preposition does not indicate the person *to whom* faith is directed but rather the person *in whom* faith has its sphere of operation; faith is exercised in union with Christ. In either case it is the faith exercised by believers that is in view. With the exception of I Tim. 3:13, where it would not be entirely out of the question to think of the faithfulness of Christ, πίστις in these instances cannot be defined in terms of Christ's faithfulness nor can the faithfulness of Christ be regarded as an ingredient of that denoted by πίστις. When the analogy of Col. 2:5 is taken into account and when the usage in respect of the verb πιστεύω in similar connections is duly weighed (*cf.* Matt. 18:6; John 2:11; 3:15, 16, 18—where ἐν αὐτῷ in vs. 15 must have the same force as εἰς αὐτόν in vss. 16, 18, as far as our present interest is concerned—4:39; 6:29, 35, 40; 7:5, 31, 38, 39; 8:30, 31; 14:1; 16:9; Acts 9:42; 10:43; 11:17; 16:31; 18:8; Rom. 4:24; 9:33; 10:11, 14; Gal. 2:16; Phil. 1:29; I Tim. 1:16; II Tim. 1:12; I Pet. 2:6; I John 5:10, 13), there is very good reason to think that in these passages Christ is viewed as the one to whom faith is directed. Besides, this is the more natural interpretation in these contexts (*cf.* especially Gal. 3:26; Eph. 1:15; Col. 1:4; II Tim. 3:15).

IV. We come now to those passages which offer more plausibility to the contention that πίστις reflects upon the faithfulness of Christ or of God and includes the same in its connotation. They are those passages where πίστις occurs in construction with the genitive of Jesus Christ (Rom. 3:22, 26; Gal. 2:16(2), 20; 3:22; Eph. 3:12; Phil. 3:9). To most of these Torrance appeals as instances illustrating his thesis. And the question is whether the genitive in these cases is a genitive of the subject or a genitive of the object. It is admitted, of course, that it could be a genitive of the subject just as the expression "the faith of God" in Rom. 3:3, as found already, is a case of the genitive of the subject. And, furthermore, there need be no question but the faithfulness of Christ is eminently relevant to the subject of justification. The only question is whether this interpretation is borne out by the evidence directly pertinent to the question. The following considerations are to be taken into account.

1. There are several instances in the New Testament where πίστις occurs in this genitival construction and where the genitive

is obviously that of the object. In Mark 11:22 we have the word of Christ to the disciples, ἔχετε πίστιν θεοῦ—"have faith in God". Obviously it is the faith that has God as its object. It could possibly be the genitive of source, the faith that proceeds from God. But this is rather far-fetched in the context and, besides, even then it would not be the genitive of the subject. Again in Acts 3:16, "by the faith of his name", namely, of Jesus, faith must be "faith in his name". In James 2:1—"have not the faith of our Lord Jesus Christ with respect of persons"—the genitive is just as clearly as in Mark 11:22 not that of the subject. In both passages it is the faith we entertain or exercise that must be in view. In Rev. 2:13—"thou hast not denied my faith"— the genitive could conceivably be that of the subject—"thou hast not denied my faithfulness". But this rendering is artificial and there is nothing to support it. It is most probable that "faith" is used here in the objective sense of the word of faith, the truth of the gospel, as frequently in the New Testament. If faith is used in the sense of faith in exercise, then, of course, the genitive is that of the object and the clause means "thou hast not proved unfaithful to thy faith in me". But in any event there is no warrant for thinking of the genitive as that of the subject. In Rev. 14:12 —"those who keep the commandments of God and the faith of Jesus"—"faith" is no doubt used again in the sense of the gospel believed, the message concerned with Jesus. If "faith" is the subjective exercise, then the genitive is that of the object. But, in any case, the interpretation "the faithfulness of Jesus" does not in the least comport with the sense—we do not keep the faithfulness of Christ. We keep faith with Jesus or we keep the faith (II Tim. 4:7). The latter is the more suitable alternative here. We thus see that in none of these passages is the genitive of the subject apparent. In only one instance is it possible but even in this case it would be artificial and arbitrary. Therefore it is not borne out in any and it is positively ruled out in all but one. These instances are, furthermore, the closest parallels in the New Testament to the other passages which we are now considering, namely, Rom. 3:22, 26; Gal. 2:16, 20; 3:22; Eph. 3:12; Phil. 3:9. If the closest parallels do not offer any support to the view in question, namely, that the genitive is the genitive of the subject, there are two observations necessary. First, analogy creates no presumption in favour of the interpretation in question. Second, analogy provides the strongest support for the view that the genitive is that of the object, namely, that "the faith of Jesus Christ" is faith in him. To say the least, the way is wide open for this interpretation in Rom. 3:22, 26, *etc.*

2. Torrance does not appeal to Eph. 3:12 in the article concerned. Here, however, we have a construction which is identical with that of the other passages—"in whom we have boldness and access in confidence through the faith of him" (Christ Jesus our Lord). If the faithfulness of Christ is reflected on in the other passages, it would be reasonable to assume the same here also. And, ostensibly, to think of the faithfulness of Christ in this case is not out of the question. But there are exegetical reasons for regarding the genitive here as that of the object, namely, faith in Christ. The strongest consideration is that of the near parallel in Rom. 5:2. There Paul says, referring to Jesus Christ, "through whom also we have access by faith into this grace in which we stand". The faith mentioned here is undoubtedly our faith in Christ. In Eph. 3:12 we should expect the faith mentioned to be the same as in Rom. 5:2. Again, the stress which falls upon boldness, access, and confidence in Eph. 3:12 would require allusion, in terms of Paul's thinking, to that faith in Jesus upon which so much emphasis is placed elsewhere. And when we find "faith" expressly mentioned, every consideration points to the conclusion that the faith indispensable to confidence and access is precisely that intended. Hence in Eph. 3:12, to say the least, the balance of considerations favour the genitive of the object and so this passage also offers no support to the interpretation with which we are concerned.

3. When we turn to the passages in question we find no evidence in the contexts to support the supposition that the faithfulness of Christ is contemplated. On the contrary there are considerations which point to the more generally accepted interpretation. In Rom. 3:22, 26, what "faith" is being dealt with in the context? In this whole passage (vss. 21–31), apart from the two occurrences in question in verses 22, 26, faith is mentioned six times. It is sufficient to appeal to verse 28—"therefore we reckon that a man is justified by faith apart from the works of the law"—to show that faith here is our faith in contrast with works. And surely this import and this alone appears in the other five instances—no argument is needed to prove this. For

what reason then may we insist that in verses 22, 26 "faith" means the "faithfulness" of Jesus"? Furthermore, the sustained appeal in the following chapter to the faith of Abraham, in support of justification by *faith* in contrast with *works*, fixes for us the definition of the "faith" with which the whole argument of the apostle from 3:21 to 5:11 is so much concerned. We found also that the passages where the same kind of construction appears (Mark 11:22; Acts 3:16; James 2:1; Rev. 2:13; 14:12), so far from requiring an interpretation in terms of a genitive of the subject, point definitely in the other direction. If then analogy does not support a genitive of the subject but rather that of the object and if the context of Rom. 3:22, 26 has plainly in view faith as directed to God or Christ, the case is such that there is no evidence to substantiate another view of the "faith" mentioned in these two verses nor is there any evidence to suppose that the "faithfulness" of Christ is an ingredient belonging to the definition of the "faith" which the apostle has in view.

When we turn to Gal. 2:16 we find that the same considerations which have been discussed already bear directly upon the interpretation of the two expressions occurring in this verse, namely, "the faith of Jesus Christ" and "the faith of Christ". It will suffice to be reminded that in this immediate context the apostle is again arguing the antithesis between justification by works and that by faith—"knowing that a man is not justified from works of law, but through the faith of Jesus Christ, even we have believed in Christ Jesus in order that we might be justified from the faith of Christ and not from works of law". What is true in the case of Rom. 4 is surely true here also, namely, that it is faith after the pattern of Abraham's faith in the Lord that provides the antithesis to justification by works. In addition, when Paul says, "even we have believed in Christ Jesus", we have no warrant to assume that any other faith than the faith thus defined is in view in the other two references to faith. And it is by no means superfluous for Paul to say, "even we have believed in Christ in order that we might be justified by faith in Christ". It is not superfluous because what Paul is insisting upon here is that we have believed in Christ for no other reason more specifically or relevantly than that we might be justified, and in order to drive home his emphasis it is necessary, because of the complete exclusion of works, to say not only "we have believed in Christ Jesus in order that we

371

might be justified" but also "that we might be justified by faith". That is to say, we have believed in Christ for this reason that it is by such faith we are justified. Thus in Gal. 2:16 as well as in Rom. 3:22, 26 we find the case to be such that not only is there no evidence in favour of the interpretation in question; exegetical considerations militate against it and point to the view that here likewise we have a genitive of the object.

It is not necessary to deal specifically with the other instances (Gal. 2:20; 3:22; Phil. 3:9) other than to observe that similar considerations can be adduced in these instances as have been pleaded in connection with Rom. 3:22, 26; Gal. 2:16. A glance at Phil. 3:9 will show this to be the case. And with reference to Gal. 2:20 the rather unusual construction, "the faith which is of the Son of God", offers no evidence in support of the thesis in question. If, as we found, this genitival construction elsewhere does not favour this view but rather a genitive of the object and if in I Tim. 3:13; II Tim. 3:15 the expression, "faith which is in Christ Jesus", can refer to the faith of which Christ is the object, then there is every good reason to interpret Gal. 2:20 as referring to the faith which is directed to the Son of God

V. With reference to Rom. 1:17 and the expression "from faith to faith", it should be apparent that, if the foregoing conclusions are valid, there is no good reason for maintaining that in this instance ἐκ πίστεως must refer to the faithfulness of God. We have found that ἐκ πίστεως is a favourite Pauline expression to denote the faith of the believer as directed to God or Christ. Hence the expression of itself provides no presumption in favour of the meaning "the faithfulness of God". On the contrary, usage favours reference to the faith exercised by the believer. Our findings with respect to Rom. 3:22 are particularly relevant to Rom. 1:17. As has been shown in the exposition at these points, there is every good reason why in Rom. 3:22 Paul should have used the formula "through faith of Jesus Christ unto all who believe" in order to emphasize both aspects of truth, namely, that it is by faith we are justified and that justification takes place wherever there is faith. In like manner in Rom. 1:17 it is appropriate that this same emphasis should appear. It is but the reiteration of what is implicit in Rom. 1:16 that the gospel is the power of God unto salvation "*to every one that believes*, to the Jew first and to the Greek".

VI. It may be objected that the foregoing detailed argument is irrelevant because the thesis being controverted is not interested in denying that πίστις, in the instances concerned, reflects on the faith of the believer but maintains simply that πίστις is a "polarized expression" comprising both elements, the faithfulness of Christ and the answering faith of the believer. Hence, merely to demonstrate the latter is beside the point, for its presence is not denied. In answer a few observations should suffice.

1. It is fully admitted that wherever there is faith there is always the faithfulness of God and of Christ to which that faith is directed and from which it takes its origin. In other words, faith always involves this *polarized situation*. This is not, therefore, in question.

2. The examination of the evidence has shown, we believe, that what is reflected on in the passages concerned is the faith that is directed to Christ, if we may use the expression, πίστις εἰς Χριστόν or ἐν Χριστῷ. Now, faith that is directed to Christ cannot *consist* in any respect in the faithfulness of Christ himself. *This* faithfulness resides entirely in Christ as the one to whom faith is directed and it is confusion to inject into the faith itself the faithfulness which belongs to the person to whom the faith is directed and in whom it rests. Therefore, once it is demonstrated that the faith of the believer is reflected on in the passages concerned, that means that the faithfulness of Christ is not *included* in the faith that is reflected on. In other words, it is one thing to say that our faith always involves a *polarized situation*; it is another thing altogether to say that *faith* is a polarized *expression*. It is this confusion that the argument has sought to expose.

3. If faith in these instances is a "polarized expression", how can this hold true in instances like Rom. 1:17; 3:22? For, in the premises, surely ἐκ πίστεως in the former case refers to the faithfulness of God and εἰς πίστιν to the faith of men. And in the latter case διὰ πίστεως refers to the faithfulness of Christ and εἰς πάντας τοὺς πιστεύοντας to the faith of men. The polarized situation would indeed be covered by the respective formulae. But in no instance would the term πίστις itself be a polarized *expression*—in one instance it would refer to God's or Christ's faithfulness and in

the other to the faith of man, but in no instance to both at the same time.

We can only conclude, therefore, that the thesis in question is not supported by the evidence and that, so far from contributing to a better understanding of the meaning of πίστις, it confuses a polarized situation (in which our πίστις is one of the factors) with a polarized expression.

ISAIAH 53:11

The clause in which we are particularly interested is the last—"by his knowledge shall the righteous one, my servant, justify many" (בדעתו יצדיק צדיק עבדי לרבים). Assuming for the reasons intimated already in Appendix A that the Hiphil יצדיק is to be interpreted forensically, the question is whether בדעתו is to be interpreted as the knowledge on the part of the servant or the knowledge of the servant on the part of those justified.

I. There can be no question but that the suffix in the expression בדעתו refers to the righteous servant whether it is the knowledge he possesses or the knowledge of him possessed by others.

II. The דעת involved could be a noun or an infinitive construct Qal, that is, knowledge or knowing. Clear instances of the latter are Gen. 38:26; Deut. 9:24; Isa. 7:15 and, more probably than otherwise, Job 9:24; Isa. 48:4. Instances of דעת as a noun are Prov. 3:20; 22:17; Isa. 44:25; 47:10. Job 13:2 is probably in the same category but the infinitive construct is also possible. It would be much more natural to understand דעת in Isa. 53:11 as a noun; there is nothing to suggest the other alternative and "by his knowledge" is the natural and common rendering.

III. The question then is: How are we to understand the suffix? Is the knowledge subjective or objective in respect of the person in view? Is it the knowledge the Servant possesses, his own knowledge (subjective) or is it the knowledge others possess of him, knowledge of him (objective). Some commentators use the terms active and passive to denote these two distinct senses respectively, "active" implying that the knowledge is that which involves activity on the part of the Servant, "passive" implying that the knowledge is that of which he is the object and of which others are the agents.

In dealing with this question it is well to examine Old Testament usage as it applies to suffixes combined with the infinitive construct or the noun.

In Gen. 38:26 the suffix is obviously objective in the sense defined above. It is not the knowing of Judah on the part of the person denoted by the suffix but the knowing on the part of Judah—"he did not know her [Tamar] again". Since Tamar is the person denoted by the suffix it is the knowing of which she is the object. In Deut. 9:24 Moses is the speaker and he is the person denoted by the suffix—"ye have been rebellious against the Lord from the day I knew you". Here it is subjective; it is not their knowing of Moses but Moses' knowing of them. In Job 10:7 the person referred to in the suffix is God. Job is the speaker—"upon thy knowing that I am not wicked". Again the meaning is subjective—it is God's knowledge of Job. Job 13:2 is clearly an instance of the subjective whether רעת is a noun or infinitive construct. In Isa. 7:15 it is the child that is in view in the suffix—"until his knowing to refuse the evil and to choose the good". It is apparent that it is the child's own knowledge that is reflected on and the thought is subjective. In Isa. 48:4—because I know that thou art obstinate"—it is the speaker's own knowledge that is referred to and the subjective force is apparent. Of these instances, where the infinitive construct is present, the subjective prevails.

In cases where we have the substantive use of רעת the subjective sense is again preponderant. God is referred to in the suffix in Prov. 3:20—"by his knowledge the depths were broken up"—and the subjective is obvious. As regards Prov. 22:17—"apply thy heart unto my knowledge"—this instance could be subjective. In that event it would reflect upon the necessity of our giving heed to what God knows rather than to what we know, that is, to God's understanding and judgment rather than to our own. But it would appear to be more natural to understand it objectively as referring to our knowledge of God and the thought would be that we are to apply our hearts to that knowledge which we should have of God. We are to give heed to knowing him. In Isa. 44:25; 47:10 we have clear instances of the subjective.

The conclusion is, therefore, that when we find רעת with a suffix, whether רעת is verbal or substantival, the evidence clearly establishes the prevalence of the subjective sense. That is to say, what is in view is the knowledge possessed or the knowing exercised by the person denoted by the suffix. Hence in Isa. 53:11 usage elsewhere demonstrates that the knowledge or knowing referred to in בדעתו can well be the knowledge possessed by the righteous Servant himself and that it is by that knowledge predicated of him that he is said to justify many. It is, of course, also possible that the objective meaning is in view, namely, the knowledge the justified have of him. The purpose of this appeal to other passages is simply to show that usage does not cast the scales in favour of the objective sense and, as far as usage is concerned, the subjective is altogether feasible. Nothing determinative one way or the other can be elicited from the bare expression itself.

IV. Some of the ablest commentators take the expression in question in the objective sense; as, for example, Hengstenberg, Alexander, and Barnes. Franz Delitzsch adopts the subjective. E. W. Hengstenberg says: "The knowledge does not belong to the Servant of God, in so far as it dwells in Him, but as it concerns Him. . . . 'By His knowledge' is thus equivalent to: by their knowing Him, getting acquainted with Him. This knowledge of the Servant of God according to His principal work, as it was described in what precedes, viz., mediatorial office, or *faith*, is the subjective condition of justification. As the efficient cause of it, the vicarious suffering of the Servant of God was represented in the preceding context. . . . In the whole prophecy, the Servant of God does not appear as a Teacher, but as a Redeemer; and the relation of צדיק to הצדיק shows that here, too, He is considered as such" (*Christology of the Old Testament*, E. T., Edinburgh, 1861, vol. II, p. 304). It is to be granted, of course, that in this context the righteous servant appears as Redeemer. But it is an impoverished view of the equipment necessary to the discharge of his messianic work as Redeemer that does not recognize the place of knowledge and understanding on the part of the righteous Servant himself. To suppose that knowledge on the part of the Servant is not relevant to his redeeming function is baseless. Besides, as we shall see later, the context does reflect on his wisdom, and why not then on his knowledge? Hengstenberg's arguments have little force.

377

Joseph Addison Alexander is dogmatic and summary, "The only satisfactory construction is the passive one which makes the phrase mean *by the knowledge of him* upon the part of others; and this is determined by the whole connexion to mean practical experimental knowledge, involving faith and a self-appropriation of the Messiah's righteousness, the effect of which is then expressed in the following words" (*The Later Prophecies of Isaiah*, New York, 1847, p. 273).

Albert Barnes is equally decisive in his judgment. "*By his knowledge.* That is by the knowledge of him. The idea is, by becoming fully acquainted with him and his plan of salvation. The word *knowledge* here is evidently used in a large sense to denote *all* that constitutes acquaintance with him" (*Notes: Critical, Explanatory, and Practical on the Book of the Prophet Isaiah*, Boston, 1840, vol. III, pp. 455f.).

Edward J. Young says of the view that the knowledge is that which the Servant himself possesses: "Such a conception . . . appears to be quite foreign to the context. The justification of the many is accomplished, according to this verse, not by means of the knowledge which the Servant has, but by means of his bearing their iniquities. . . . It is knowledge, therefore, not which He Himself has, but which is possessed by those whom He would justify . . . It is a personal, intimate knowledge such as one person has of another. It involves faith, trust, intellectual apprehension and belief" (*Isaiah Fifty-Three*, Grand Rapids, 1953, p. 74).

On the other hand Franz Delitzsch, while acknowledging that the preceding view, which regards the suffix as objective, affords "a meaning which is correct in actual fact", nevertheless prefers with Cheyne, Bredenkamp, and Orelli to take the suffix subjectively as in Prov. 22:17 and pleads that this view is favoured by Mal. 2:7; Dan. 12:3; 11:2; Matt. 11:27 (*Biblical Commentary on the Prophecies of Isaiah*, E. T., Edinburgh, vol. II, pp. 309f.).

V. Though it is not a question that radically affects the interpretation of Isa. 53 nor the teaching of the Old Testament on the subject of justification, yet it may not be doing a disservice to exposition and doctrine if we present the reasons for thinking that there is nothing contrary to the context nor to the analogy of Scripture in the view that the knowledge in question is the knowledge possessed by the Servant himself, knowledge brought to bear upon his justifying function.

There are numerous respects in which knowledge may be viewed as an essential part of the equipment of the righteous Servant in the expiatory accomplishment which is the burden of this passage. It could be the knowledge of his commission, the knowledge of its implications as they bore upon the discharge of the precise action denoted by the verb "justify" which immediately follows. It could be the knowledge of the purpose to be served by his undertaking and of the successful issue of his accomplishment. Or the understanding by which he was able to carry out his commission could be reflected on. From whatever angle the task assigned to him and perfected by him as the Servant of the Lord may be viewed, knowledge is an indispensable ingredient of the obedience which his servanthood entailed. For obedience without knowledge would have none of the virtue which attaches itself to his unique and transcendent fulfilment of the Lord's will. To be obedience of that quality it had to be obedience of *intelligent* will. If the justification in view is that which falls within the application of redemption, then knowledge would likewise be requisite to that continued activity on the part of the Servant. His own knowledge can therefore be conceived of as not only relevant to the Servant's justifying action but also as indispensable to its discharge, whether the action is that of his once-for-all expiatory accomplishment or that of his continued work as the exalted Lord.

VI. We may not overlook the fact that in this prophecy elsewhere and more particularly in this same passage distinct emphasis is placed upon the knowledge which the Messiah possesses. In Isa. 11:2 our attention is drawn to the fact that the spirit of knowledge rests upon him as well as the spirit of wisdom and understanding. In 50:4 are we not justified in applying to the Servant the words: "The Lord God hath given me the tongue of the learned that I may know how to speak a word in season to him that is weary"? In 52:13, when we are introduced to the Servant in his specifically expiatory undertaking, there is express mention of the Servant's wisdom and understanding, "Behold my servant shall deal prudently". To quote Edward J. Young, "In its primary signification, it merely means to act with the understanding or intelligence. Since, however, such intelligent action usually results in success, the verb comes also to include the idea of effective action. Thus, we are to understand that the Servant will act so wisely that abundant fruition will crown His efforts" (*op. cit.*, p. 10). Surely it is appropriate that knowledge should likewise be associated with his justifying action in such a way as to condition its exercise and insure its effectiveness. Furthermore, in 53:3 the expression rendered "acquainted with grief" (וידוע חלי) means literally that he is "known of grief" and reflects upon the extent to which he experienced grief; it accentuates the depth of his knowledge of grief. He was thoroughly conversant with it and grief was, as it were, at home with him. That there should be this reflection upon the Servant's experience in this passage indicates one way in which his experiential knowledge bore upon his expiatory work or how his expiatory undertaking made necessary this experiential acquaintance with grief. Is not the fact that he was "known" of temptation and that he learned obedience by the things which he suffered integral to the accomplishment of expiation and to the fellow feeling with our infirmities in virtue of which he continues to be a merciful and faithful high priest? And, finally, in the immediate context there is reflection upon psychological activities of the Servant as a result of the travail of his soul—"he shall see, he will be satisfied".

Hence we may conclude that the emphasis in the passage as a whole upon the experiences of soul involved in the work of the Servant would make it signally appropriate that the state of experiential cognition involved in these experiences and resulting from them should be brought into effective operation in his justifying activity, indeed that it should be causally active in the justification of the many. And this we must reckon with whether the justifying action contemplated is the once-for-all expiation of sin or the continued activity in actual justification. The latter cannot be conceived of apart from the knowledge that belongs to him in the capacity in which he exercises this prerogative. Furthermore, we must make allowance for the pregnant meaning so frequently associated with knowledge in the usage of the Old Testament (see the exposition *ad* Rom. 8:29). This concept in such cases is not barely cognitive; it has its emotive and volitive ingredients. And there is no reason why we should not find that notion in this instance as expressing the cognitive, emotive, and volitive activity which lies back of and is brought to bear upon the Servant's justifying action, the knowledge of loving interest and decision. It may be the counterpart in the Old Testament of Heb. 10:10, "By which will we are sanctified through the offering of the body of Jesus Christ once for all". When viewed in the light of all these considerations there does not appear to be any good reason for the summary dismissal of the subjective interpretation, the Servant's own knowledge in all the reaches of its reference as it applies to the work of the Servant as the sin-bearer, as the trespass-offering, and as the high priest offering himself.

VII. If the justification referred to is that which belongs to the sphere of once-for-all objective accomplishment and is therefore the virtual synonym of expiation, the knowledge could be none other than that possessed by the Servant himself. For, obviously, our knowledge of him could have no instrumentality in his expiatory action. The possibility of this meaning of the term "justify" is not to be ruled out and there are weighty considerations in its favour.

1. It is apparent that this chapter deals particularly with the expiatory work of the Servant. The immediate context has distinctly expiatory references—"when his soul shall make a trespass-offering" (vs. 10), "he shall bear their iniquities" (vs. 11). It is not unreasonable to think of the clause in question as having similar import, more particularly when taken in conjunction with the clause which immediately follows. If these two clauses are taken as expressing coordinate ideas, which is distinctly possible, then both would have expiatory signification because the second is unquestionably expiatory. It is not being argued that the clause in question must refer to the expiatory aspect of the Servant's work. Other clauses in the immediate context have reference to the sequel of his expiatory work. And this one may likewise. All that is being maintained is that the context makes the expiatory interpretation distinctly feasible, if indeed it does not create a presumption in its favour.

2. If the expression "by his knowledge" is taken in the objective sense, then we are faced with an awkward way of expressing the truth concerned. For, in that event, what is alluded to is actual justification and not the expiatory action, and,

in regard to actual justification, this would be a strange and probably unparalleled way of stating the relation of faith to justification. The strangeness will appear if we paraphrase the sense supposed on this interpretation. It would be, "By faith in Christ, Christ will justify the many". There does not appear to be any parallel to this type of formula. But if the knowledge is that on the part of those justified, it is some such pattern that would have to be supposed in order to express the thought intended.

3. In the usage of Scripture it is faith that is brought into relation to justification. Gen. 15:6 points up this fact in the Old Testament and this text is central in the Pauline doctrine. It is true enough that faith implies knowledge and specifically knowledge of Christ, to use Alexander's words, "practical experimental knowledge, involving faith and a self-appropriation of the Messiah's righteousness" (*op. cit.*, *ad loc.*). But to substitute the word "knowledge" for faith in dealing with the instrument of justification is without warrant in the analogy of Scripture. This deviation from the usage of Scripture elsewhere could be entertained as the necessary interpretation only if there is some compelling reason for adopting it. For the reasons given above this compelling consideration does not exist. And when we keep in view the reasons why it is faith that is brought into this instrumental relation to justification, particularly because faith has the specific quality which makes it congruous with a gracious justification, it is exceedingly difficult to entertain the view that there should be deviation from this sustained emphasis of the Scripture in general.

4. For the reason given above it is only in reference to actual justification that the objective interpretation could obtain. Those espousing this view assume that fact. But it is not without relevance to the question, when viewed in the light of the analogy of Scripture, that actual justification is not represented as specifically the action of Christ but as that of the Father in distinction from the Son and, in accord with that analogy, we should expect it to be the action of the Lord (*cf.* vss. 1, 6, 10) in distinction from the Servant. If the subjective interpretation is adopted, then the way is open for applying the justification involved to the expiatory work of the Servant and, in this event, nothing divergent from the analogy of Scripture is intimated; expiation in specifically Messiah's work.

To conclude, the strongest considerations would require to be produced if we are to maintain that the pattern of Scripture usage is not followed in this instance. Such considerations cannot be pleaded; there are numerous respects in which knowledge on the part of the Servant may be regarded as contributive and indispensable to the Servant's justifying action, whether this falls within the category of expiation or of its application. There are some weighty considerations which tell against the objective interpretation and favour the subjective. Hence the preponderance lies with the view that in Isa. 53:11 it is the knowledge possessed by the Servant that is contemplated.

APPENDIX D

KARL BARTH ON ROMANS 5

Under the title *Christus und Adam nach Röm. 5*, published in
1952 as Heft 35 of *Theologische Studien*, Karl Barth has provided us
with a challenging and stimulating study of Romans 5. T. A.
Smail has favoured us with an English translation of this study
and it has recently been published by Harper and Brothers
Publishers (New York, 1957) under the title *Christ and Adam:
Man and Humanity in Romans 5*. In the present evaluation of
Barth's position the quotations and citations are taken from this
edition of Smail's translation. In submitting this appendix I have
reproduced to a large extent what has already been published in
the form of a review in *The Westminster Theological Journal* for
May 1958 (Vol. XX, No. 2, pp. 198 ff.).

The points dealt with in the pages which follow are those which
are, in the esteem of the writer, central in Barth's exegesis of
Romans 5 and they illustrate pivotal elements in Barth's thinking
on anthropology and soteriology. The adverse criticism offered is
exegetically oriented. This is demanded by the nature of Barth's
own study in this treatise as well as by the character of this
present volume.

At the outset Barth properly recognizes that the leading theme
of the first part of Romans is the revelation of the righteousness
of God. This he defines as "the final righteous decision of God,
which for everyone who acknowledges it in faith, is the power of
God unto salvation" (p. 20). This definition in terms of righteous
decision (*Rechtsentscheidung*) is maintained throughout and is
determinative of what Barth conceives the blood of Christ to have
wrought and justification to be. The definition indicates that for
Barth justification is something that occurs in the judgment of
God prior to the event of faith. For faith is simply the acknowledgment or grasp of it; by faith it becomes known to believers.
"In believing, they are only conforming to the decision about
them that has already been made in Him [Christ]" (p. 24). And
that this is applied to justification is made abundantly clear by the

384

following: "In sovereign anticipation of our faith God has justified us through the sacrificial blood of Christ" (p. 22). There are at least two respects in which this construction fails to represent Paul's teaching. According to Paul we are justified by faith, and to apply the terms for justification without discrimination to anything else than to that which is correlative with faith and therefore coincident with it is to deviate radically from the sustained emphasis of the apostle. It is true that there is the once-for-all accomplishment in the blood of Christ which is antecedent to faith. Paul calls it the propitiation, the reconciliation, and redemption. But the all but uniform, if not uniform, use of the term "justification" and its equivalent is to designate that judgment of God of which faith is the instrument. This act of faith is not directed to the fact that we have been justified but is directed to Christ in order that we may be justified (*cf.* Gal. 2:16). It is not to be assumed that in the epistle to the Romans the terms δικαιοσύνη, δικαίωσις, δικαίωμα are used synonymously, as Barth apparently assumes (*cf.* p. 20). In 5:16 δικαίωμα and in 5:18 δικαίωσις refer to God's justifying act. But exegesis neither requires nor allows identification of this act with the δικαιοσύνη θεοῦ of 1:17; 3:21, 22; 10:3. The latter is the justifying righteousness but is to be distinguished from the justifying act. Again, universalism not only in respect of atonement but also of justification is implicit in Barth's construction. Integral to his interpretation of the relation that Christ sustains to Adam is the position that Christ, in respect of his saving office, must sustain to mankind as inclusive a relation as Adam. The implications of this will appear later.

It is with Romans 5:12–21 and the parallel between Adam and Christ that Barth is mainly concerned. It should be understood that for Barth Adam is not to be regarded as a single historical personage who *as such* at the beginning of human history committed a particular sin which is unique in its relationships and effects as the one trespass in which all other members of the race are involved and are therefore related to it as to no other sin. Barth is explicit to the effect that Adam is the typical man and that other men share in his sin because his sin is *repeated* in them and they sin as Adam did. The sins of all other men "are anticipated" in the sin of Adam and "the lives of all other men after Adam have only been the repetition and variation of

his life, of his beginning and his end, of his sin and his death"
(p. 29). "In v. 12, Paul already has made it clear that 'all have
sinned,' that is to say, that all have repeated Adam's sinful act"
(p. 62). Though then for Barth Adam is the representative man
and though in that sense he can speak of him as the "responsible
representative" of mankind, yet it is not because he accepts the
historicity of Genesis 2 and 3 or regards Adam's sin in Eden as a
unique sin by reason of its implications and relations but simply
because Adam's sin is repeated and Adam in his sin and death as
primus inter pares is the representative man (*cf.* pp. 92 f.). "We are
what Adam was and so are all our fellow men. And the one Adam
is what we and all men are. Man is at once an individual and
only an individual, and, at the same time, without in any way
losing his individuality, he is the responsible representative of all
men" (pp. 90 f.). Thus the *unique* individuality of Adam and the
speciality of his sin by reason of the distinctive relations which he
sustained to all other men and the distinguishing involvement of
other men in his sin are eliminated. We are all Adam.

It cannot be too plainly said that if we adopt this construction
of Romans 5:12–19 we must abandon exegesis. If Paul emphasizes
one thing it is that by the one trespass of the one man Adam
the many were accounted sinners and death came to exercise its
lordship over all. Paul's sustained emphasis upon the one trespass
and the one man, the one trespass of the one, is the very opposite
of the idea of *repetition* upon which Barth's construction hinges.
The only exegesis that is compatible with Paul's reiterated
emphasis upon the one trespass is the solidarity of all men in that
one trespass in a way that cannot be equated with the inter-
involvements in sin which appear in our other solidaric relationships. It is this unique character of Adam and this unique
involvement in his trespass that Barth eliminates. For Barth,
as he explains also in his *Church Dogmatics*, it is a case of "the
individual and the many, each with his own responsibility, each
with his own particular form of pride, each in his own fall, each
in his own specific and distinctive way" (IV, 1, E. T., p.
504).

The most distinctive feature of Barth's interpretation appears
in connection with his view of the identity of ordering principle
(*Ordnung*) underlying the analogy instituted between Adam and
Christ. Since Adam is the *type* of him who was to come, Barth

is insistent that the relationship between Adam and all of us had not only been ordered so as to correspond to the relationship between Christ and us but that the latter is the primary anthropological truth and ordering principle. "Man's essential and original nature is to be found, therefore, not in Adam but in Christ. . . . Adam can therefore be interpreted only in the light of Christ and not the other way round" (p. 29). Thus "human existence, as constituted by our relationship with Adam. . . . has no independent reality, status, or importance of its own" and the relationship between Adam and us is "the relationship that exists originally and essentially between Christ and us" (p. 30). In view of the commanding place which this construction of the analogy and of the ordering principle on which the analogy is based occupies in Barth's anthropology and soteriology, it is necessary to focus attention upon it.

(1) As indicated above, this implies that the relation of Christ to men is as inclusive as the relation of Adam to men and therefore the "righteous decision" passes upon all men just as the condemnation passed upon all through Adam. "In the existence of the One, there in Christ, the result for all men is the lordship of grace exercised in the divine righteous decision and the promise of eternal life" (p. 32). Not only does Barth's repeated expressions in such universal terms (*cf.* pp. 26, 31, 32, 46, 48, 49, 51, 53, 72, 84, 88, 89) imply this universality but the priority posited for Christ's relationship to men, without which the Adamic relationship has no validity or meaning, demands this universal relationship of Christ to man in respect of that which he (Christ) most characteristically is as representative and revealer (*cf.* p. 31). And, unless exegesis of Paul is evacuated completely at the most vital point, this means that all men without exception must be ultimately the beneficiaries of that grace which reigns through righteousness unto eternal life (5:21). Barth cannot hold to universalism at one point in the relationship to Christ without carrying out the implications for the ultimate salvation of all men. For if there is distributive universalism in the apodoses of verses 18 and 19, as Barth's interpretation demands, there must also be in the apodosis of verse 21, and the reign of grace through righteousness unto eternal life must embrace all men without exception. This is not Paul's teaching (*cf.* II Thess. 1:9; 2:10–14) and to maintain that the universalistic terms of Rom. 5:18b demand

the ultimate salvation of all is to fail to apply to this text the canons of exegesis which obviously obtain in the interpretation of numberless universalistic expressions.

(2) It cannot be questioned that Adam is the type of Christ (vs. 14). There is undoubtedly a similarity of relationship and there is no objection to speaking of the identity of ordering principle. Our relation to Adam in respect of sin, condemnation, and death follows the pattern of our relation to Christ in respect of righteousness, justification, and life. And that it was designed of God to be thus we must recognize. Soteriology is built upon the same kind of relationship as that which is exemplified in our sin and loss. And the ordering principle by which sin, condemnation, and death came to lord it over mankind required that the ordering principle of saving righteousness be of the same kind or pattern. But Paul's teaching in this passage does not establish the primacy or priority which Barth claims for the relationship to Christ. Adam could be the type of Christ, as Paul says, without drawing all the inferences which Barth elicits from this relationship. All that could feasibly be derived from the typological datum mentioned in verse 14 and applied expressly in the succeeding verses is simply that there is an analogy between our relation to Adam in the realm of sin and death and our relation to Christ in the realm of righteousness and life. In the absence of additional data it is an importation, adopted on our own responsibility, to infer more. And Paul's own teaching in I Cor. 15:45–49 to the effect that Adam was the first man and Christ the second and last Adam, teaching than which nothing is more pertinent to the subject at hand, should at least caution us against a construction in terms of priority and primacy that runs counter to Paul's own express formula in this latter passage. Barth's own treatment of I Cor. 15:45–49 in no way relieves the discrepancy between Paul and Barth. It is true enough that according to Paul's teaching "Christ is above, Adam is beneath. Adam is true man only because he is below and not above" (p. 34). But it does not help Barth in dealing with the order which Paul establishes in regard to Adam as the first and Christ as the second and last to say that Adam's "claim to be the 'first man' and the head of humanity like Christ is only apparent" (*idem*). Besides, the question is not that of "Adam's claim to be our head and to make us members in his body" (*idem*) but .the

relationship in respect of order set forth in Paul's statements. (3) Barth's argument based on the πολλῷ μᾶλλον of verses 15 and 17 illustrates the exegetical method by which he supports his thesis. In Romans 5:9, 10 this same expression occurs in Paul's *a fortiori* argument from reconciliation to the eschatological salvation. And Barth rightly exegetes this to mean that "it is because we are sure that Christ achieved our reconciliation that we can be 'so much more' sure that He has achieved our salvation as well" (p. 45). The same line of thought he applies to the πολλῷ μᾶλλον in verses 15 and 17 and concludes that "the same Jesus Christ is already involved in the truth in Adam", that "Jesus Christ suffered and died for the sin of Adam and the sin of all men" and that by the cross "Adam and all men are reconciled and pardoned" (pp. 47 f.; *cf.* pp. 43–49). Now it is quite plain that the πολλῷ μᾶλλον of verses 9 and 10 implies that *because* we are reconciled we shall all the more be finally saved—the latter is a necessity arising from the former. But does it therefore follow that πολλῷ μᾶλλον in verses 15 and 17 must have the same effect and establish the same kind of causal relationship between the two elements in the comparison? Does verse 15 mean that *because* by the trespass of the one the many died *therefore* the grace of God will abound unto the many? Or does verse 17 mean that *because* death reigned by the trespass of the one *therefore* many will reign in life through Jesus Christ? At the outset it would be preposterous to insist that πολλῷ μᾶλλον must always carry with it the same effect as it has in verses 9 and 10. Language is not so stereotyped as to demand that canon and particularly is it not so in Paul's usage. What Paul is surely emphasizing in these verses (15, 17) is the superabundance of grace. There is indeed the similitude of *modus operandi*. And it is true enough that if, in terms of this *modus operandi*, the many died by the trespass of the one, then, when grace comes into operation and follows the pattern of the same *modus operandi*, how much more will the many reign in life. But we may not infer from this *a fortiori* that "Jesus Christ is already involved in the truth in Adam" and "that Adam and all men are reconciled and pardoned". The identity of *ordering principle* or, we should prefer to say, of *modus operandi* does not involve these inferences and the *a fortiori* in this instance does not by any means establish the connection which we find in verses 9 and 10. If we have been reconciled by the death of Christ it necessarily follows that we shall be saved by his life—the one guarantees the other. But the fact that by the trespass of one the many died does not carry with it the assurance that by grace the many will reign in life. The commanding thought of the apostle in verses 15 and 17 is the superabundant freeness and graciousness of God's grace in contrast with the processes of punitive judgment. And it is just the relentless logic with which judgment unto the reign of death proceeds from one trespass that sets off the magnitude and efficacy of grace as brought to bear upon numberless trespasses unto pardon, justification, and life. The *a fortiori* is basically diverse from that of verses 9 and 10, for in the latter both protasis and apodosis are within the ambit of grace and grace alone. And the force of the *a fortiori* in verses 15 and 17 is not that of necessary consequence to the effect that the penal judgment unto death through the trespass of Adam insures the saving judgment unto life through the righteousness of Christ but simply that, since the same *modus operandi* is brought to bear upon our justification as was exemplified in our condemnation, the one in Christ and the other in Adam, how much more, in view of the nature of grace, must this same ordering principle be effective unto justification and life. It is the unexampled plenitude and efficacy of grace that is in the forefront and not any inference to be drawn from the fact of judgment to the necessity of grace. The kind of connection which Barth finds in the πολλῷ μᾶλλον is both extraneous and alien to the emphasis of the passage.

INDEX OF CHIEF SUBJECTS

391

INDEX OF PERSONS AND PLACES

INDEX OF AUTHORS

INDEX OF SCRIPTURE REFERENCES
OLD TESTAMENT

INDEX OF SCRIPTURE REFERENCES
NEW TESTAMENT

THE NEW INTERNATIONAL COMMENTARY ON
THE NEW TESTAMENT — F. F. BRUCE, *General Editor*

THE EPISTLE TO THE ROMANS

THE EPISTLE TO THE ROMANS

THE ENGLISH TEXT WITH INTRODUCTION,
EXPOSITION AND NOTES

by

JOHN MURRAY

*Professor of Systematic Theology, Westminster Theological Seminary
Philadelphia, Pennsylvania*

VOLUME II
Chapters 9 to 16

WM. B. EERDMANS PUBLISHING CO.
GRAND RAPIDS, MICHIGAN

CONTENTS

v

EDITOR'S PREFACE

Ever since the appearance of Volume I of Professor Murray's Commentary on Romans we have looked forward eagerly to the publication of Volume II. Now it lies before us, and the patience with which we waited for it is amply rewarded. Professor Murray has devoted the same degree of meticulous and unhurried care to the exposition of Chapters 9–16 as he did to the exposition of Chapters 1–8. Whether he is engaged in the interpretation of the theological arguments of Chapters 9–11, or in the practical application to present-day life of the ethical injunctions of the chapters that follow, or in the elucidation of the textual problems that beset the study of the conclusion of the Epistle, he takes all the factors into consideration and expresses his judgment in terms which command the reader's respect. Above all, he is concerned to bring out Paul's meaning, without trying to make him say what the commentator himself, or the twentieth-century climate of opinion, would prefer him to say. Thus the user of this commentary will be greatly helped towards hearing and obeying the Word of God spoken through the Apostle to the Gentiles.

I need say nothing by way of introducing Professor Murray to his readers. Dr. Stonehouse did all that was necessary in this regard in the Editor's Preface to Volume I, and Professor Murray is already well enough known by his other publications among those who appreciate Reformed theology. But I do esteem it an honour to be associated editorially with a work of this high quality—the work, moreover, of a fellow-Scot who worthily maintains the noble tradition of theological exegesis which has for long been one of the glories of our native land.

F. F. BRUCE
General Editor

AUTHOR'S PREFACE

Several years have passed since the publication of Volume I, Chapters 1 to 8, of this commentary. I wish to express to the Wm. B. Eerdmans Publishing Company my deep appreciation of the patience shown to me during this interval and I also extend my warmest thanks for all the courtesies conferred upon me by the Company.

I gratefully acknowledge indebtedness to the following publishers for permission to quote from the copyrighted books cited: Wm. B. Eerdmans Publishing Company, Grand Rapids—F. F. Bruce: *The Epistle of Paul to the Romans* (1963), *Commentary on the Epistle to the Colossians* (1957); John Calvin: *The Epistle of Paul to the Romans* (1961) as translated by Ross Mackenzie; Harper & Brothers, New York—C. K. Barrett: *A Commentary on the Epistle to the Romans* (1957); The Westminster Press, Philadelphia—Oscar Cullmann: *Christ and Time* (1950); Charles Scribner's Sons, New York—Oscar Cullmann: *The State in the New Testament* (1957); Lutterworth Press, London—Franz J. Leenhardt: *The Epistle to the Romans* (1961).

I submit this volume for publication in gratitude to God for the privilege of attempting by his grace to make some contribution to a better understanding of this portion of his precious Word. Exposition of the Word of God is an arduous task. It is also great joy. No undertaking is more sacred. For that reason it is demanding. But by the same token it is rewarding. It is the voice of the eternal God we hear in Scripture and his glory is revealed. When the day will dawn and the day star arise in our hearts, we shall find no discrepancy between the witness of Holy Scripture and the glory then manifested. This faith demands the care and reverence with which Scripture should be handled and it undergirds the confidence with which its testimony is to be received and obeyed.

JOHN MURRAY

Philadelphia, March 25, 1964

ix

INTRODUCTION

Purpose of Chapters 12–16

If chapters 12 to 16 had immediately succeeded chapter 8 in this epistle, the sequence would accord with a pattern easily understood and consonant with the order that we might expect. As observed in the commentary that follows, the section extending from 12:1 to 15:13 deals with concrete and practical duties devolving upon believers. These are particularly concerned with their relations to one another in the community and fellowship of the saints. Also, since believers sustain relations to other men and institutions, Paul deals with the conduct that becomes saints in the exercise of their societal and political responsibilities. In the latter part of chapter 15 the apostle sets forth his missionary policy and plans in pursuance of his Gentile ministry. It is highly appropriate that he should do this in a letter to the church or churches at Rome.

Since Paul was not the agent in founding the church at Rome, it might seem that the more expanded reflection on his policy as apostle of the Gentiles is his apology for addressing an epistle to the saints at Rome and for the boldness with which he had written (*cf.* 15:15). The evidence furnished by the epistle does not support this construction. At the outset of the epistle his apology is concerned with the delay in fulfilling his earnest desire to visit Rome (1:11–13) and he insists that as much as lay in him he was ready to preach the gospel there (1:15). He takes occasion to resume that same subject in chapter 15 and gives additional information explanatory of the delay in fulfilling his desire and intent (15:22–26). Furthermore, as the greetings in chapter 16 indicate, Paul had many friends at Rome and among these were close associates in the work of the gospel. These friends and particularly such co-labourers as Aquila and Prisca would be ardently desirous that Paul should go to Rome and we may reasonably suppose that this desire was expressed to and concurred in by the Christian community in the imperial city. There may have been urgent communications to that effect. Hence the assurance of desire and purpose in chapter 1, reiterated and expanded in chapter 15. There was another reason for delineating his missionary policy and plans. Rome occupied an important place in his projected itineraries for the extension of his Gentile ministry. It was necessary, therefore, that his visit to Rome be set in the context of this broader vision of pursuing his labours to the western bounds of Europe (15:28). And not only so. It was necessary to define more clearly the character of his visit to Rome lest the saints there should entertain wrong notions respecting the purpose or length of his visit. Rome was to be but a resting place on his way to Spain and the church at Rome would send him forth on his new missionary undertaking (15:24, 28).

Chapter 16 is largely devoted to greetings (16:1–16; 21–23). There are also the final warnings against corrupters of the gospel (16:17–20) and a closing doxology eminently consonant as respects length and content with the character and scope of the epistle as a whole (16:25–27).

Purpose of Chapters 9–11

But what of chapters 9 to 11? It might seem that there is discontinuity in this portion of the epistle and its length appears to aggravate the question raised. It is only as we fail to discern or overlook the relation that these chapters sustain to the thesis of this epistle that any thought of irrelevance or discontinuity is entertained. On closer inspection this part of the epistle is seen to bring to climactic vindication the thesis stated in 1:16, 17 and correlative doctrines unfolded later in chapters 1 to 8. If this section of the epistle were absent, there would be a hiatus leaving us with unanswered questions and the corresponding perplexity. It is not that we may demand or expect answers to all questions. But in this instance we may be profoundly grateful that the supreme author of Scripture inspired the apostle to deal with questions so germane to the grand theme of this epistle and urgently pressing upon the minds of intelligent readers.

It is, however, not merely the questions which emerge from this epistle that are answered in chapters 9 to 11. They are the questions which the biblico-theological perspective derived from the whole of Scripture necessarily provokes. It is noteworthy to what an extent Paul appeals to the Old Testament in this part of the epistle. This appeal shows that the subjects with which he deals are those which have their roots in the Old Testament and are, therefore, to be understood in the light of the apostle's interpretation and application. In other words, the apostle, writing in the full light of the fulfilment which the advent of Christ brought and by the inspiration of the Spirit of Pentecost, furnishes us with the orientation in terms of which the prophetical Scriptures are to be understood.

Furthermore, these chapters delineate for us the worldwide design of God in reference to Jew and Gentile. They disclose to us in a manner that is without parallel in the New Testament revelation the ways in which God's diverse providences to Jew and Gentile react upon and interact with one another for the promotion of his saving designs. It is as the apostle leads us on through this delineation and reaches the climax at 11:32: "For God hath shut up all unto disobedience, that he might have mercy upon all" that we with him reach the apex of adoring wonder and exclaim: "O the depth of the riches both of the wisdom and the knowledge of God!" That Paul, at the conclusion of the section of the epistle concerned, should have occasion to burst forth in such unsurpassed exclamatory doxology is of itself demonstration that the themes of these chapters are the fitting sequel to the great theses of the gospel developed in the first eight chapters.

The question encountered at the beginning of chapter 9 is one that arises from the terms in which the theme of the epistle is stated. The gospel "is the power of God unto salvation to every one that believeth; to the Jew first, and also to the Greek" (1:16). "To the Jew first." It is this priority that appears to be contradicted by the large-scale unbelief and apostasy of Israel. The priority of relevance and application seems to have no verification in the sequel of history. Hence the necessity of dealing with the question which Jewish unbelief poses. This, of itself, would be sufficient reason for chapters 9 to 11. But this is not the only angle from which the coherence can be shown. In the earlier chapters Paul had made appeal to Abraham as the "father of all them that believe" (4:11) and in this context refers to the promise given to Abraham (4:13). Although all the implications of this promise are not reflected on in the context in which this reference occurs, nevertheless these implications cannot be forgotten nor the questions pertinent thereto suppressed. So in chapter 9 when we read: "But it is not as though the word of God hath come to nought" (9:6), it is the word of promise to Abraham that is in view.

In chapters 9 to 11 the apostle deals with these questions which emerge from the themes of the earlier part of the epistle as these are related to Israel's unbelief. In summary, his answers are that the promise to Abraham and to his seed was not to all proceeding from Abraham by natural descent. It is to the *true* Israel the promises are made and the purpose of God according to election stands fast (9:6–13); there is always a remnant according to the election of grace (11:5, 7). In this remnant the word of the promise is fulfilled. So it is not as though the word of God has come to nought. This constitutes the first answer to the problem of the mass unbelief of Israel and of their casting away. But it is not the whole answer. The apostle proceeds in chapter 11 to unfold another aspect of God's counsel respecting Israel. In chapter 9 it is sufficient to demonstrate that Israel's unbelief and rejection were not *total*; there was a remnant. In chapter 11:11–32 Paul discloses what at 11:25 he calls "this mystery" that the rejection of Israel is not *final*. There is a further implication of the Abrahamic covenant which the future will verify and vindicate, an implication that goes beyond the reserving of a remnant in all generations. As a result of the covenant with Abraham a favour and love on God's part toward Israel *as a people* are still in exercise. They are beloved for the fathers' sake, and this is so even though they are alienated from God's favour and blessing (11:28). The privileges of Israel enumerated in 9:4, 5 have abiding relevance because "the gifts and the calling of God are not repented of" (11:29). In accordance with these implications of the covenant promise there will be restoration of Israel to the faith and blessing of the gospel. This Paul calls "their fulness" (11:12), a fulness in overt contrast with their trespass and loss and, therefore, characterized by a proportion that will be commensurate in the opposite direction. He also calls this their "receiving" and it is likewise in contrast with their "casting away" (11:15). It is their grafting in again into their own olive tree (11:23, 24). Finally, the restoration is expressed in these terms: "all Israel shall be saved" (11:26).

In this unfolding of the prophecy and promise of Israel's

reclamation Paul not only shows how the Abrahamic covenant as it respects Israel will be fulfilled and finally vindicated but he also shows how the counsel of God respecting the Gentiles is interwoven with the various phases of Israel's history. The trespass of Israel is the riches of the world, their loss the riches of the Gentiles, their casting away the world's reconciliation (11:12, 15). Again, the fulness of Israel and their receiving will bring incomparably greater blessing to the Gentile world. And not only so. The blessing accruing to the Gentiles from Israel's loss, on the one hand, and from Israel's fulness and restoration, on the other, reacts upon Israel to the promotion of their salvation. They are thereby provoked to jealousy (11:11) and the fulness of the Gentiles marks the terminus of Israel's hardening (11:25). Thus is delineated for us God's worldwide design for the realization of his saving purposes. What chapter 11 provides is an insight into the divine philosophy of history as it pertains to the salvation of Jew and Gentile. When we gain this perspective we must exclaim with Paul, "O the depth of the riches both of the wisdom and the knowledge of God!" (11:33).

Summary of Contents[1]

---

[1]   Continued from Summary of Contents of Chapters 1–8, Volume I, p. xxii.

XIV. THE UNBELIEF OF ISRAEL
(9:1-5)

9:1-5

1 I say the truth in Christ, I lie not, my conscience bearing witness with me in the Holy Spirit,
2 that I have great sorrow and unceasing pain in my heart.
3 For I could wish that I myself were anathema from Christ for my brethren's sake, my kinsmen according to the flesh:
4 who are Israelites; whose is the adoption, and the glory, and the covenants, and the giving of the law, and the service *of God*, and the promises;
5 whose are the fathers, and of whom is Christ as concerning the flesh, who is over all, God blessed for ever. Amen.

1, 2 "I say the truth" would have been sufficient certification on the apostle's part to arrest the attention of his readers (*cf.* I Tim. 2:7). But Paul adds what gives ultimate sanction to the veracity of assertion; it is "in Christ" he speaks the truth about to be stated. "In Christ" here refers to union with Christ. It is not a formula of adjuration nor in this instance is he appealing to the agency of Christ. Union with Christ is the orbit within which his emotions move and the spring from which they proceed. Thus the thing spoken of as "the truth" derives its impulse and the guarantee of its propriety from this union. If we ask: why this form of certification? there are two reasons that may reasonably be suggested. (1) Paul's denunciation of Jewry in the earlier part of the epistle must not be regarded as estrangement from his kinsmen. (2) This form of certification is necessary to support the almost unparalleled optative with which he continues, "I could wish that I myself were anathema from Christ" (vs. 3). But, in any case, it is characteristic of the apostle to support his statements by this formula (*cf.* 14:14; II Cor. 2:17; 12:19; Eph. 4:17; I Thess. 4:1).

1

The negative "I lie not" is likewise added, according to Paul's pattern, to emphasize the veracity of his utterance (*cf.* II Cor. 11:31; Gal. 1:20; I Tim. 2:7). The truth stands in absolute antithesis to the lie, and, as Christ is "the truth", what receives its impulse and guarantee from union with him cannot partake of the lie (*cf.* I John 2:21, 27). In Godet's words, "in the eyes of Paul there is something so holy in Christ, that in the pure and luminous atmosphere of His felt presence no lie, and not even any exaggeration, is possible".[1]

It would seem that the apostle had said enough to certify his truthfulness. It is the more striking, therefore, that he should appeal to the witness of his conscience. A glance at Paul's appeal to conscience elsewhere in his epistles will evince that the clause appended, "my conscience bearing witness with me in the Holy Spirit", is not superfluous (*cf.* Acts 23:1; II Cor. 1:12; 4:2; 5:11; I Tim. 1:5, 19; 3:9; II Tim. 1:3; Tit. 1:15). Conscience is the activity by which we judge ourselves and bring our own conduct under moral and religious scrutiny. Conscience may approve or disapprove. When it approves we have a good or pure conscience (*cf.* Acts 23:1; I Tim. 1:5, 19; 3:9; Heb. 13:18; I Pet. 3:16, 21). When conscience disapproves and convicts of sin then we have a bad or guilty conscience (*cf.* John 8:9; Rom. 2:15; Tit. 1:15; Heb. 10:22). It is to the approval of conscience that Paul here appeals. He states this, however, in terms of the confirmatory witness borne by conscience. It is most significant that he regards this witness as borne "in the Holy Spirit". Just as the certification of his earlier assertion is derived from union with Christ, so the veracity of the witness of his conscience is certified by the Holy Spirit. It is only as we are indwelt by the Spirit and live in the Spirit, only as our minds are governed by the Spirit may we be assured that the voice of conscience is in conformity with truth and right. "In Christ" and "in the Holy Spirit" are correlative and mutually dependent in Paul's thinking and they are introduced in these consecutive clauses for the purposes indicated and in appropriate connections.

The truth referred to in verse 1 is now stated: "I have great sorrow and unceasing pain in my heart". That Paul should have

---

[1] F. Godet: *Commentary on St. Paul's Epistle to the Romans* (E. T., Edinburgh, 1881), II, p. 131.

2

adduced the ultimate sanctions of veracity to certify his own subjective state of mind points up the seriousness of that which constrains this state of mind and the relevance of his anguish to the situation in view. In a word, Paul's sorrow is the reflection of the gravity pertaining to Israel's unbelief. The intensity of the apostle's sorrow, as Liddon observes, is marked by its greatness, its continuance, and its depth.[2]

3 "Anathema from Christ"[3] means to be separated from Christ and devoted to destruction (cf. LXX, Lev. 27:28, 29; Deut. 7:26; 13:16, 18; Josh. 6:17; 7:1, 11, 12). In the New Testament "anathema" has similar force and means accursed (cf. Acts 23:14; I Cor. 12:2; 16:22; Gal. 1:8, 9). Any difficulty attaching to this verse cannot be relieved by toning down the force of the expression. It means to be abandoned to perdition. Did Paul then wish to be thus devoted to destruction and separated from Christ?

It would not be proper to refer this clause to the past attitude of the apostle when he was persecuting Christ and the church. His opposition to Christ could not with any warrant be construed as wishing himself anathema from Christ. Neither can we suppose that Paul considered it possible for him to be separated from Christ. This would contradict the assured confidence expressed in the preceding chapter (8:38, 39). Furthermore, the expression does not mean that he *actually* wished or prayed that he would be anathema from Christ. The tense used in the Greek is well expressed by the version in the words "I could wish".[4] It is hypothetical to the effect that if it were possible and of avail for the salvation of his kinsmen he would be willing to be accursed on their behalf. The intensity of the apostle's love for his own people

---

[2] H. P. Liddon: *Explanatory Analysis of St. Paul's Epistle to the Romans* (New York, 1897), p. 148.

[3] The reading ὑπὸ τοῦ Χριστοῦ, supported by D G, is not to be followed. ἀπό is strongly attested.

[4] ηὐχόμην is Imperfect and clearly expresses this idea in other instances in the New Testament. *Cf.* E. DeWitt Burton: *Syntax of the Moods and Tenses in New Testament Greek* (Edinburgh, 1955), § 33; F. Blass and A. Debrunner: *A Greek Grammar of the New Testament and Other Early Christian Literature* (E. T., Chicago, 1961), § 359; G. B. Winer: *A Grammar of the Idiom of the New Testament* (E. T., Andover, 1892), p. 283. Examples given by Burton are Acts 25:22; Gal. 4:20; Phm. 13, 14. *Cf.* also J. B. Lightfoot: *St. Paul's Epistle to the Galatians*, ad 4:20; M. J. Lagrange: *Épître aux Romains* (Paris, 1950), p. 225; F. F. Bruce: *The Epistle of Paul to the Romans* (Grand Rapids, 1963), ad loc.

is hereby disclosed. It is love patterned after the love of the Saviour who was made a curse and sin for the redemption of men (*cf.* Gal. 3:13; II Cor. 5:21). "It was, therefore, a proof of the most fervent love that Paul did not hesitate to call on himself the condemnation which he saw hanging over the Jews, in order that he might deliver them."[5] "It is objected that the wish must thus be irrational... but the standard of selfish reflection is not suited to the emotion of unmeasured devotedness and love out of which the apostle speaks."[6] The use of the term "brethren" bespeaks the bond of affection which united the apostle to his kinsmen. "According to the flesh" is added to show that those for whom he had concern were not contemplated as brethren in the Lord (*cf. contra* 14:10, 13, 15, 21; 16:14) but it also expresses what is implicit in the term "kinsmen" and supplies an additional index to the bond of love created by this natural, genetic relationship.

4, 5 The attachment to Israel is not due merely to natural ties. It is accentuated by the place Israel occupied in the history of revelation. Apart from this identity the great question with which the apostle proceeds to deal would not have arisen. Hence he proceeds to enumerate the distinguishing privileges of the Jewish people.

The first mentioned is that they were "Israelites". This name harks back to Genesis 32:28 and is reminiscent of the dignity bestowed upon Jacob in the reception of the name "Israel", a dignity conferred also upon his seed (*cf.* Gen. 48:16; Isa. 48:1). Although Paul is jealous for the distinctions drawn in verses 6, 7 that they are not all Israel who are of Israel and that natural descent does not constitute the "seed", yet he in no way discounts the advantages belonging to ethnic Israel (*cf.* 3:1, 2; 11:28). The term "Israelite" conveniently expressed this distinguishing character (*cf.* John 1:47; Acts 2:22; 3:12; 5:35; 13:16; 21:28; Rom. 11:1; II Cor. 11:22; and "the stock of Israel" in Phil. 3:5). "Adoption" is the filial relation to God constituted by God's grace (*cf.* Exod. 4:22, 23; Deut. 14:1, 2; Isa. 63:16; 64:8; Hos. 11:1; Mal. 1:6; 2:10). This adoption of Israel is to be distinguished from that spoken of as the apex of New Testament privilege

---

[5] John Calvin: *The Epistle of Paul the Apostle to the Romans* (E. T. by Ross Mackenzie, Grand Rapids, 1961), *ad loc.*

[6] Heinrich A. W. Meyer: *Critical and Exegetical Handbook to the Epistle to the Romans* (E. T., Edinburgh, 1881), II, *ad loc.*

(8:15; Gal. 4:5; Eph. 1:5; *cf.* John 1:12; I John 3:1). This is apparent from Galatians 4:5, for here the adoption is contrasted with the tutelary discipline of the Mosaic economy. Israel under the Old Testament were indeed children of God but they were as children under age (*cf.* Gal. 3:23; 4:1-3). The adoption secured by Christ in the fulness of the time (Gal. 4:4) is the mature, full-fledged sonship in contrast with the pupilage of Israel under the ceremonial institution. This difference comports with the distinction between the Old Testament and the New. The Old was preparatory, the New is consummatory. The adoption of the Old was propaedeutic. The grace of the New appears in this, that by redemption accomplished and by faith in Christ (*cf.* Gal. 3:26) all without distinction (*cf.* Gal. 3:28) are instated in the full blessing of sonship without having to undergo tutelary preparation corresponding to the pedagogical discipline of the Mosaic economy.

"The glory" should be regarded as referring to the glory that abode upon and appeared on mount Sinai (Exod. 24:16, 17), the glory that covered and filled the tabernacle (Exod. 40:34-38), the glory that appeared upon the mercy-seat in the holy of holies (Lev. 16:2), the glory of the Lord that filled the temple (I Kings 8:10, 11; II Chron. 7:1, 2; *cf.* Ezek. 1:28). This glory was the sign of God's presence with Israel and certified to Israel that God dwelt among them and met with them (*cf.* Exod. 29:42-46).

"The covenants"—[7] the plural could refer to the two distinct covenantal administrations to Abraham (Gen. 15:8-21; 17:1-21). Though these two covenant dispensations are closely related yet the distinctions in respect of time, character, and purpose are not to be overlooked. It is more reasonable, however, to regard the plural as denoting the Abrahamic, Mosaic, and Davidic covenants. No feature of Israel's history marked their uniqueness as the recipients of redemptive revelation more than these covenants. The progressive covenantal disclosure advanced apace with the fulfilment of redemptive promise (*cf.* Exod. 2:24; 6:4, 5; Deut. 8:18; Luke 1:72, 73; Acts 3:25; Gal. 3:17-19; Eph. 2:12).

---

[7] The singular ἡ διαθήκη, though supported by P⁴⁶, B, D, G and other authorities, is not probably to be preferred. Internal evidence would favour the plural. In citing the privileges of Israel we should expect mention of more than one covenant and, besides, "the covenant" without any further specification would be so unusual as to be ambiguous, and this we would not expect (*cf.* Eph. 2:12 and the plural "promises" in this same verse).

5. ("The giving of the law") refers to the Sinaitic promulgation
6. and ("the service of God") to the worship of the sanctuary (*cf.*
7. Heb. 9:1, 6). ("The promises") are those which found their focus
in the Messiah (*cf.* Gal. 3:16). ("The fathers") would certainly
8. include Abraham, Isaac, and Jacob (*cf.* 4:1, 11, 12, 16, 17; 9:10;
15:8; Acts 3:13, 25). But it would not be proper to restrict the
denotation to these patriarchs (*cf.* Mark 11:10; Acts 2:29; I Cor.
10:1; Heb. 1:1; 8:9). The next clause would require the inclusion
of David. In 1:3 Paul had spoken of Jesus as "born of the seed
of David according to the flesh". It would not appear reasonable
to exclude the father expressly mentioned in 1:3.[8] Thus we should
have to extend the line beyond Jacob and conclude that the
fathers of distinction in redemptive history from Abraham onwards
are in view. The term could be used to designate those whose
names are in an outstanding way associated with the unfolding of
Israel's covenantal history, a history that reached its climax in
Christ, "born of the seed of David according to the flesh" and
"constituted the Son of God with power, according to the spirit of
holiness, by the resurrection from the dead" (1:3, 4).

9. ("Of whom is Christ as concerning the flesh.") At this point
there is a change in the relationship. After "Israelites" all the
privileges mentioned are stated as *belonging* to the Jewish people.
Even "the fathers" are represented thus. But when Paul reaches
the climax he does not say that Christ belonged to them but that
Christ came from the Jewish stock.[9] The antecedent of "whom" is
not "the fathers" but the Israelites. "Concerning the flesh" has
the same import as the similar expression in 1:3 (*cf.* comments at
that point). The next two clauses are to be taken as referring to
Christ and defining what he is in his divine identity as Lord of all
and God blessed for ever (see Appendix A, pp. 245 ff., for fuller
treatment of this disputed question). It is altogether appropriate
that there should be this reflection upon the supereminent dignity
of Christ at this climactic point in the enumeration of Israel's
privileges. The chief reason for the apostle's anguish was the

---

[8] It may well be that "the fathers" in 11:28 should be restricted to Abraham, Isaac, and Jacob in view of 11:16. But the denotation in 11:28 does not decisively determine the same in 9:5. *Cf. contra* F. A. Philippi: *Commentary on St. Paul's Epistle to the Romans* (E. T., Edinburgh, 1879), II, p. 67; Meyer: *op. cit., ad loc.*; Bruce: *op. cit., ad loc., et al.*

[9] The ἐξ ὧν is to be noted in this case in distinction from the simple ὧν in two instances preceding.

rejection on Israel's part of that which brought to fruition the
covenantal history which constituted their distinctiveness. The
gravity of this rejection was pointed up by the uniqueness of
Jesus' person. In view of the situation with which the apostle
is dealing there could not be any context in this epistle which
would more appropriately, if not necessarily, call for the declaration of Christ's supreme dignity.

XV. VINDICATION OF GOD'S FAITHFULNESS
AND RIGHTEOUSNESS
(9:6-33)

9:6-13

6 But *it is* not as though the word of God hath come to nought. For they are not all Israel, that are of Israel:
7 neither, because they are Abraham's seed, are they all children: but, In Isaac shall thy seed be called.
8 That is, it is not the children of the flesh that are children of God; but the children of the promise are reckoned for a seed.
9 For this is a word of promise, According to this season will I come, and Sarah shall have a son.
10 And not only so; but Rebecca also having conceived by one, *even* by our father Isaac—
11 for *the children* being not yet born, neither having done anything good or bad, that the purpose of God according to election might stand, not of works, but of him that calleth,
12 it was said unto her, The elder shall serve the younger.
13 Even as it is written, Jacob I loved, but Esau I hated.

6, 7 Literally rendered "But it is not such that the word of God has failed" and means that the case is not such that the faithfulness of God is impugned. The question arises: what in the preceding context requires this reservation? Some have found this in verses 4 and 5 and have supposed that "the word of God" alluded to is the word of threatening.[10] It is to be borne in mind, however, that the leading thought of the preceding verses is the grief the apostle entertains. The certifications we found in verse 1 are for the purpose of assuring the veracity of what is stated in verse 2, and verse 3 demonstrates the intensity of the apostle's anguish. Verses 4, 5 are attached to verse 3 for the purpose of explaining this grief and the zeal for Israel. However significant is the catalogue of privileges enumerated in verses 4, 5 it must not

---

[10] *Cf.* James Morison: *An Exposition of the Ninth Chapter of Paul's Epistle to the Romans* (Kilmarnock, 1849), pp. 164ff.

8

be dissociated from its purpose in relation to verses 2, 3. Hence it is to the apostle's grief that the reservation of verse 6 is to be attached. This grief is the reflection in Paul's consciousness of an objective situation; it has compelling grounds and its reality is certified by ultimate sanctions. In the context of the history referred to in verses 4, 5, the anticlimax of Israel's unbelief and of Paul's anguish incident thereto might appear to contradict the covenant promises of God. It is this inference that Paul denies. The word of God has not fallen to the ground.

"The word of God" should be understood in a more specific sense and not in the sense of Scripture as a whole or of the word of the truth of the gospel. It is the word of promise in the covenants alluded to in verse 4. Covenant in Scripture is synonymous with oath-bound promise and the statement here is to the same effect as saying "God's covenant has not come to nought". Then the reason is given: "they are not all Israel who are of Israel". Those "of Israel" are the physical seed, the natural descendants of the patriarchs. It is not necessary to identify "Israel" here as Jacob specifically. It makes no difference to the sense whether we regard "Israel" as those descended from Jacob or go back further to include Abraham and Isaac. The main thought is that of children according to the flesh. In the other expression, "they are not all Israel", obviously the denotation is much more limited and the thought is that there is an "Israel" within ethnic Israel. This kind of distinction appears earlier in this epistle in connection with the term Jew and circumcision (2:28, 29). If the terms of the present passage were applied to the earlier the formulae would be, "they are not all Jews who are of the Jews" and "they are not all circumcised who are of the circumcision". Thus we have been prepared by the patterns of Paul's thought and usage for what we find here in 9:6.

The Israel distinguished from the Israel of natural descent is the *true Israel*. They are indeed "of Israel" but not coextensive with the latter. It is in accord with our Lord's usage to make this kind of distinction within a designated class. He distinguished between those who were disciples and those *truly* disciples (*cf.* John 8:30-32). He spoke of Nathanael as "truly an Israelite" (John 1:47). If we use Paul's own language, this Israel is Israel "according to the Spirit" (Gal. 4:29) and "the Israel of God" (Gal. 6:16), although in the latter passage he is no doubt in-

9

cluding the people of God of all nations. The purpose of this distinction is to show that the covenantal promise of God did not have respect to Israel after the flesh but to this *true* Israel and that, therefore, the unbelief and rejection of ethnic Israel as a whole in no way interfered with the fulfilment of God's covenant purpose and promise. The word of God, therefore, has not been violated. The argument of the apostle here is not *in principle* different from that which we find earlier in this epistle. There is a parallel between his present contention and his polemic that "not through the law was the promise to Abraham or to his seed" (4:13) and that the children of Abraham were those "who walk in the steps" of Abraham's faith (4:12). Now the interest is centred upon a coordinate facet of truth that not through natural descent are the promises inherited and that God's covenant promise was not made so as to include all of ethnic Israel. Thus the exclusion of Israelites from God's covenant favour does not negate the word of the oath.

In verse 7 Paul continues to support this same distinction and expressly carries it back to the seed of Abraham. He is still speaking of those "of Israel" and now draws the distinction in terms of that between "Abraham's seed" and "children". In this instance "Abraham's seed" denotes the natural posterity and "children" is equivalent to the *true* Israel, and in that sense the *true* children as inheritors of the promise. Later on these children are called "children of God" (vs. 8) and this fixes their identity even though in verse 7 they are contemplated simply as the *true* children of Abraham.

The foregoing differentiation is now supported by appeal to Scripture. "In Isaac shall thy seed be called" (Gen. 21:12).[11] Isaac must here be taken of the person and not collectively. Thought is focused on the choice of Isaac in contrast with Ishmael: the proposition to be demonstrated is that natural descent does not make children in the sense of *true* children, children to whom the promise belongs. The choice of Isaac to the exclusion of Ishmael is sufficient to prove this thesis. Furthermore, it may not be taken for granted that "thy seed" in this instance is to be understood

---

[11] The literal rendering is: "In Isaac shall a seed be called to thee". The reference does not appear to be to the descendants of Isaac but to Isaac himself as the son of promise. The *true* seed of Abraham will in every instance be such after the pattern or principle thus exemplified in Isaac as distinct from Ishmael.

collectively.   The English rendering creates the impression that
"seed" is here collective.   But it may well be understood in the
sense "Isaac shall be thy seed" and "seed" understood in this case
in contrast with "Abraham's seed" and in the sense of *true* seed.[12]
If we take "seed" in verse 7b collectively, then the meaning is that
in Isaac will your true descendants be reckoned, as Sanday and
Headlam take it.   If this is the intent the central thought of the
passage, namely, that natural descent does not make children of
God and of promise, cannot be suspended at this point any more
than in the case of Abraham.   The meaning, on this supposition,
would have to be that in reckoning the true seed from Isaac the
same principle of differentiation would have to apply to Isaac's
seed as was operative in the case of Isaac himself.   That is to say,
the collective "seed" are not those descended from Isaac but those
"of Isaac" who like him are children of the promise.   But we may
not be dogmatic to the effect that "thy seed" in this case is
collective; it may be singular and personal.

8, 9   "That is" at the beginning of verse 8 means that what
had been said is now explicated still further.   "The children of
the flesh" has the same import and extent as "Abraham's seed"
in verse 7.   "The children of God" has the same reference as
"children" in verse 7.   But now there is the additional definition
whereby their identity as those brought into the adoptive relation
to God is clearly indicated (*cf.* 8:16, 17, 21; Phil. 2:15).   "The
children of the promise" are the same as the children of God and
this designation is placed in contrast with "the children of the
flesh".   The latter are those born after the flesh but the children
of the promise are those who derive their origin from the promise
of God.   The promise in this instance is the promise given to
Abraham, quoted in verse 9 and drawn from Genesis 18:10, 14.
Isaac was born in pursuance of that promise.   To that promise
the faith of Abraham attached itself (*cf.* 4:19–21).   In the case
of Ishmael there were no such factors.   He was begotten, conceived, and born in accordance with natural procreative powers.
It is this radical difference in the birth of the respective sons that

---

[12]   *Cf.* Philippi: *op. cit., ad loc.*; Liddon: *op. cit.*, p. 157; Charles Hodge:
Commentary on the Epistle to the Romans, ad loc.   Sanday and Headlam are insistent
that "seed" is here collective; *cf.* W. Sanday and A. C. Headlam: *A Critical
and Exegetical Commentary on the Epistle to the Romans* (New York, 1926), *ad loc.*

is summed up here in the word "promise". Isaac was a child of promise. This same criterion is used to define the differentiation that is maintained between those who are "of Israel" and the *true* Israel (vs. 6), between "Abraham's seed" and the *true* children (vs. 7), between the children of the flesh and the children of God (vs. 8), and between the natural seed and the *true* seed (vss. 7, 8). In the sequence of thought, therefore, this word "promise" specifies that which is explanatory of the sustained distinction between the more inclusive and the restricted use of the various terms "Israel", "seed", and "children". In each case the restricted use is defined by what is implicit in God's promise. This brings us back to verse 6: "But it is not as though the word of God hath come to nought". The "word of God" is God's covenant promise.[13] It has not come to nought because it contemplates those whose identity is derived from that same covenant promise. The seed to whom the promise was given or, at least, the seed whom the promise had in view are those in whom the promise takes effect; they are "children of the promise".[14]

10–13 In these verses appeal is made to another instance of the same kind of differentiation in patriarchal history. The thesis being established, it must be remembered, is that not by natural descent did the descendants of Abraham become partakers of God's covenant grace and promises. This was proven in Abraham's own sons in the differentiation between Isaac and Ishmael. But it was not only in Abraham's sons that this discrimination appeared; it enters also into Isaac's own family. The argument of the apostle becomes cumulative as it proceeds. There are new factors exemplified in Isaac's family that do not appear in the case of Abraham's sons and these considerations point up more forcefully and conclusively the differentiation that must be recognized in the fulfilment of God's covenant purposes. These considerations may be listed as follows.

1. If the discrimination which God's covenant promise contemplates were exemplified only in the case of Isaac in the history

---

[13] This is also borne out by verse 9: "This is a word of promise". The genitive ἐπαγγελίας is appositional, the word that consisted in the promise.
[14] "κατὰ τὸν καιρὸν τοῦτον is shown clearly by the passage in Genesis to mean 'at this time in the following year,' i.e. when a year is accomplished" (Sanday and Headlam: *op. cit., ad loc.*).

of the patriarchs, then the proposition, "they are not all Israel who are of Israel", would not have as much ostensible support. It could be pleaded that the promise, "in Isaac shall thy seed be called", guarantees that the promise is to all of Isaac's seed without distinction. The fact that differentiation becomes operative within Isaac's seed shows that the same discrimination exemplified in the case of Isaac himself continues within his progeny.

2. Ishmael was the son of the bondmaid, not of the freewoman. The discrimination, therefore, appeared to reside in a natural factor and this reason would appear to detract from the interest which is paramount in this whole passage, namely, the pure sovereignty of the discrimination which the covenant promise implies. This consideration connected with Ishmael as the son of Hagar is completely eliminated in the case of Esau and Jacob as the sons of Rebecca. The sons are of the same mother and she a freewoman.[15] This is still more accentuated by the fact that they were conceived by her at the same time and their foetal development was concurrent.

3. Though Esau and Jacob were twins, yet Esau was the first-born. The choice of Jacob went counter to the priority which primogeniture would have required. This illustrated still further the sovereignty of the discrimination in actual operation.

4. The apostle draws attention not only to these foregoing facts that Rebecca "conceived by one, even by our father Isaac" but also to the fact that the oracle which bespoke the discrimination was uttered *before the children were born* and before they had done anything good or evil. The word of God to Abraham, quoted in verse 7 with respect to Isaac, reflects a radically different situation (*cf.* Gen. 21:8–12). As was noted earlier, the thesis of the apostle in this passage that physical descent does not determine the objects of God's covenant promise is parallel to his earlier contention that "not through the law was the promise to Abraham or to his seed" (4:13).[16] This is demonstrated in the present passage: the oracle

---

15   It may not be irrelevant to note that Isaac had only one wife.

16   Philippi claims that τέκνα τῆς σαρκός (vs. 8) reflects on this, that "in consonance with the more comprehensive notion of the word σάρξ in Paul" the term refers "to the entire sphere of sensuous, visible profession upon which man might possibly found a claim of right in the presence of God" (*op. cit.*, p. 86).

was spoken to Rebecca[17] before the children did good or evil. This shows that the discrimination did not proceed "of works, but of him that calleth" (vs. 11). "Not of works" and "not of natural descent" are correlative and point to the same principle. Thus the apostle can adduce the one in an argument that is mainly concerned with the other without any sense of incongruity.

There are three features of this passage which require special comment. The first is that the discrimination expressed in the oracle is said to be "that the purpose of God according to election might stand". This is the first time that "election" is expressly mentioned in this passage. Previously the emphasis fell on "promise" as the principle of differentiation and implicit in this term is the sovereign will and grace of God. Promise is in contrast with natural descent and with any right or privilege arising therefrom. Thus promise as a determining factor is coordinate with election. But now the accent falls on election or, more accurately, "the purpose of God according to election". In order to gain the import of this clause several observations are necessary.

1. The oracle spoken to Rebecca[18] is directed to the end of establishing the purpose of God according to election. Verse 11 is not a parenthesis but, syntactically, stands in close relation to verse 12. It is in pursuance of God's electing purpose that the disclosure was made to Rebecca before the children were born. The electing purpose is the plan of God which the oracle serves to bring to expression and fruition.

2. The immutability of the electing purpose is intimated in the words "might stand".[19] The false inference drawn from the unbelief of Israel, namely, that "the word of God hath come to nought" (vs. 6), the apostle is refuting in this passage. In verse 11 he is asserting the security and immovability of the electing purpose in eloquent contrast to the supposition that the word of

---

[17] Why Rebecca received the promise rather than Isaac it may be vain to speculate. It is, however, to be noted that the deception she designed and practised serves also to demonstrate the sovereign grace of God as overcoming and going counter to all human demerit.

[18] The construction in verses 10–12 is not easy to determine. Probably the best proposal is that Ρεβεκκα ἐξ ἑνὸς κοίτην ἔχουσα is to be taken as nominative absolute and thus provides the introduction to what is stated in verses 11, 12a and the antecedent of αὐτῇ in verse 12b.

[19] The present tense μένῃ may more adequately express the "abiding condition" (Philippi, ad loc.). The purpose of God always stands firm.

14

God could be invalidated, the word of God being understood as referring to his covenant promise and purpose.

3. There are various ways of construing the words "the purpose of God according to election". It has been assumed that, since the election and the purpose are eternal and, therefore, before time, there cannot be any order of priority whereby election could be conceived of as prior to purpose or purpose as prior to election.[20] This consideration that the electing purpose is supratemporal does not, however, rule out the thought of priority; there can be priority in the order of thought and conception quite apart from the order of temporal sequence. We find this elsewhere in Paul (*cf.* 8:29; Eph. 1:4–6). The preposition rendered "according to" in the version frequently expresses in Paul's epistles and elsewhere the thought of priority as that in accordance with which something occurs, whether it be the order of time or simply that of logical relationship (*cf.* 8:28; Gal. 1:4; 2:2; 3:29; Eph. 1:5, 11; II Tim. 1:9; Heb. 2:4; I Pet. 1:2). Hence there is no reason why, in the present instance, the purpose of God should not be conceived of as the purpose determined in accordance with election and election would be prior in the order of causation. The purpose would be that which springs from election and fulfils its design. This is the interpretation that has most in its favour on the grounds of usage and Paul's teaching elsewhere. But, since the purpose could be thought of as that which comes to expression in election, dogmatism would not appear to be warranted. In any case, the whole expression cannot mean less than electing purpose. It is a purpose characterized by election and an election with determinative purpose. Both terms, "election" and "purpose", must be given the full force of their biblical and particularly Pauline connotation.

4. The question now is: what is this electing purpose? It is maintained by several commentators older and more recent that the election of which Paul here speaks is not that of individuals but of Israel as a people and that he is thinking not of the destiny of

---

[20] ἡ κατ' ἐκλογὴν πρόθεσις, says Meyer, "can neither be so taken, that the ἐκλογή *precedes* the πρόθεσις in point of time (comp. viii. 28), which is opposed to the nature of the relation, especially seeing that the πρόθεσις pertains to what was antecedent to time... nor so that the ἐκλογή follows the πρόθεσις". The ἐκλογή, he continues, "must be apprehended as an essential *inherent* of the πρόθεσις, expressing the *modal character* of this divine act" (*op. cit.*, *ad loc.*).

individuals but in terms of collectives.[21] This thesis requires expanded examination.

(*a*) It is true that the Scripture speaks of the election of Israel as a people and in numerous passages it is the relationship of God to the people collectively that is in view (*cf.* Deut. 4:37; 7:7, 8; 10:15; 14:2; I Kings 3:8; Psalm 33:12; 105:6, 43; 135:4; Isa. 41:8, 9; 43:20–22; 44:1, 2; 45:4; Amos 3:2). In fact, so much was Paul aware of this and of all its implications that the problem with which he is dealing in this chapter presupposes this election of Israel as a people. The catalogue of privileges mentioned in verses 4, 5 is but a fuller and more pointed way of harking back to the "election" of Israel. We need go no further than the clause "who are Israelites" to be reminded of what the apostle has in view: it is Israel's election.

(*b*) There is no doubt but the oracle to Rebecca contemplated more than the individuals Esau and Jacob. This lies on the face of the Old Testament passage from which Paul quotes in verse 12. "And the Lord said unto her, Two nations are in thy womb, and two peoples shall be separated from thy bowels: and the one people shall be stronger than the other people; and the elder shall

---

[21] "In the context the apostle is not speaking of that specific plan of election in accordance with which he elects certain individuals... He is speaking of a totally different scheme of election,—that scheme, to wit, in accordance with which he selected from among the various races, which sprang out of the loins of Abraham, the peculiarly favoured Messianic seed" (Morison: *op. cit.*, p. 212). With respect to the names Jacob and Esau, Leenhardt says, "the names mentioned certainly do not connote individuals so much as peoples who are thus named after their eponymous ancestors, according to Old Testament practice. It is best to understand the names in this way, since the argument which they are quoted to support concerns the destiny of Israel as a whole, and not the destiny of individuals who compose Israel. Paul thinks in terms of collectives" (Franz J. Leenhardt: *The Epistle to the Romans* [E. T., London, 1961], p. 250). *Cf.* F. F. Bruce: *op. cit., ad* 9:13; Ernst Gaugler: *Der Römerbrief* (Zurich, 1952), II Teil, pp. 38f.; G. C. Berkouwer: *Divine Election* (Grand Rapids, 1960), pp. 210–217; Herman Ridderbos: *Aan de Romeinen* (Kampen, 1959), pp. 227–231. Karl Barth's view of election is so diverse that it could not properly be examined without taking into account his more extensive treatment of the subject in *Church Dogmatics.* The following quotation, however, illustrates the dialectic in terms of which election is construed: "He [God] makes himself known in the parable and riddle of the beloved Jacob and hated Esau, that is to say, in the secret of eternal, twofold predestination. Now, this secret concerns not this or that man, but all men. By it men are not divided, but united. In its presence they all stand on one line—for Jacob is always Esau also, and in the eternal 'Moment' of revelation Esau is also Jacob" (*The Epistle to the Romans*, [E. T., London, 1933], p. 347).

16

serve the younger" (Gen. 25:23). It is also apparent from the
context of what Paul quotes from Malachi 1:2, 3 (vs. 13) that the
peoples of Israel and of Edom are contemplated (*cf.* Mal. 1:1, 4,
5). In terms of biblical teaching it could not be otherwise. Human
relationships and the relations of God to men are governed by the
principle of solidarity and in the history of redemption it could
not be otherwise than that the election of Jacob and the rejection
of Esau should have had radical bearing upon their respective
progenies. In other words, it would be contrary to the principles
that govern history according to the biblical witness to suppose
that the election of such a pivotal personage in the history of
salvation as Jacob would have any other sequel than the election
of Israel as a people. The only question is therefore: is this the
exclusive interest of the apostle in this passage? Is the case such
that the phrase "the purpose of God according to election" is not
applied in this context to the sphere of individual destiny? The
following data bear upon this question and supply the answer.

(i) The two components of the phrase should be given the
meaning which the usage of Paul determines. There is, first of all,
the term "election". Not only the noun but also the verbal forms
have to be taken into account. With respect to the noun it is
possible that in 11:28 it is used with reference to the election of
Israel collectively. This passage as well as 11:5, 7 will be discussed
later. In the other one remaining passage in Paul (I Thess. 1:4)
it refers unquestionably to election to everlasting life (*cf.* II Pet.
1:10). The term "elect" occurs more frequently and, apart from
16:13 where it is used in a specialized sense but with the implication
of elect in the ultimate sense, all the instances[22] refer to particular
election to salvation and life (8:33; Col. 3:12; II Tim. 2:10;
Tit. 1:1; *cf.* Matt. 22:14; 24:22, 24, 31; Mark 13:20, 22, 27;
Luke 18:7; I Pet. 1:1; 2:9; Rev. 17:14). The verb "to elect"
occurs infrequently in Paul and probably Ephesians 1:4 is the
only directly relevant passage where it refers unmistakably to
soteric election (*cf.* Mark 13:20; James 2:5). This application
of the term in its various forms to the election unto salvation makes
it indefensible to understand it in another sense unless there is a
compelling contextual reason. There is, secondly, the term
"purpose". This term when used with reference to God uniformly

---

[22] I Tim. 5:21 is not included because it refers to the elect angels.

17

denotes the determinate will of God (8:28; Eph. 1:11; 3:11; II Tim. 1:9). Thus the whole expression means nothing less than the determinate will of God in election and all that is involved in the expression is confirmed by the verb of which it is the subject, "might stand".

(ii) The thesis that Paul is dealing merely with the election of Israel collectively and applying the clause in question only to this feature of redemptive history would not meet the precise situation. The question posed for the apostle is: how can the covenant promise of God be regarded as inviolate when the mass of those who belong to Israel, who are comprised in the elect nation in terms of the Old Testament passages cited above (Deut. 4:37 et al.), have remained in unbelief and come short of the covenant promises? His answer would fail if it were simply an appeal to the collective, inclusive, theocratic election of Israel. Such a reply would be no more than appeal to the fact that his kinsmen were Israelites and thus no more than a statement of the fact which, in view of their unbelief, created the problem. Paul's answer is not the collective election of Israel but rather "they are not all Israel, who are of Israel". And this means, in terms of the stage of discussion at which we have now arrived, "they are not all elect, who are of elect Israel". As we found above, there is the distinction between Israel and the *true* Israel, between children and *true* children, between the seed and the *true* seed. In such a distinction resides Paul's answer to Israel's unbelief. So now the same kind of distinction must be carried through to the problem as it pertains to the collective, theocratic election of Israel. In terms of the debate we are now considering we should have to distinguish between the elect of Israel and elect Israel. The conclusion, therefore, is that when Paul says "the purpose of God according to election" he is speaking of the electing purpose of God in a discriminating, differentiating sense that cannot apply to all who were embraced in the theocratic election. This is to say the clause in question must have a restrictive sense equivalent to "Israel" as distinguished from "of Israel" in verse 6.

(iii) In 11:5, 7 the same term for election is again used: "a remnant according to the election of grace" (11:5); "the election obtained it, and the rest were hardened" (11:7). The apostle is dealing with the remnant of ethnic Israel who had obtained the righteousness of faith. Hence the "remnant" and "the election"

18

are those conceived of as possessors and heirs of salvation. The election, therefore, is one that has saving associations and implications in the strictest sense and must be distinguished from the election that belonged to Israel as a whole. It is this concept of election that accords with the requirements of Paul's argument in 9:11 and its context. Since it appears without question in 11:5, 7, we have this additional confirmation derived from Paul's own usage in the general context to which 9:11 belongs.

(iv) The clause, "not of works, but of him that calleth", is closely related to the clause in question. Whatever may be the precise connection, the two clauses are intended to express correlative ideas. But "calling" in Paul's usage, when the call of God is in view and when applied to the matter of salvation, is the effectual call to salvation (*cf.* 8:30; 9:24; I Cor. 1:9; 7:15; Gal. 1:6, 15; 5:8, 13; Eph. 4:1, 4; Col. 3:15; I Thess. 2:12; 4:7; 5:24; II Thess. 2:14; I Tim. 6:12; II Tim. 1:9).[23] If the Pauline concept of God's call is to govern our exegesis, it must be given in this instance (9:11) the definition that the total evidence requires. This is all the more necessary when it is conjoined with the negative "not of works"; this stresses the freeness and sovereignty as well as efficacy which are in such prominence elsewhere in connection with God's call. Since, therefore, the clause that is correlative with that bearing on election has this strictly soteric import, "the purpose of God according to election" cannot be given any lower significance and understood of election merely to privilege such as Israel as a people enjoyed.

For all these reasons the interpretation which regards the election as the collective, theocratic election of Israel as a people must be rejected and "the purpose of God according to election" will have to be understood as the electing purpose that is determinative of and unto salvation and equivalent to that which we find elsewhere (Rom. 8:28–33; Eph. 1:4; I Thess. 1:4 *et al.*).

The second feature of this passage (vss. 10–13) that needs to be considered is the clause "not of works, but of him that calleth" (vs. 11). The question is that of its relation to what immediately

---

[23] The same is true of κλῆσις and κλητός (*cf.* 1:6, 7; 8:28; I Cor. 1:2, 24, 26; Eph. 1:18; 4:1, 4; Phil. 3:14; II Thess. 1:11; II Tim. 1:9; Heb. 3:1; II Pet. 1:10). Matt. 22:14 apparently refers to the external call of the gospel. Rom. 11:29 is discussed at that point (p. 101).

precedes.[24] It would appear that it may best be taken as an additional characterization of the electing purpose of God and emphasizes or confirms what is intrinsic to the purpose of God, namely, that it does not proceed from nor is it conditioned by the human will but by the determinate will of God (*cf.* Eph. 1:5, 11). In order to express this negatively no formula is more suited than "not of works" and to express it affirmatively no concept is more appropriate than that denoted by calling. The sovereign initiative and agency of God are nowhere more in evidence than in the call. God alone calls and its definition derives no ingredient from human activity. We see, therefore, how congruous is this amplificatory clause with what precedes whether we take it more particularly with "might stand" or, preferably, with the electing purpose.

The third feature of this passage requiring more detailed comment is the appeal to Malachi 1:2, 3 in verse 13: "Jacob I loved, but Esau I hated". There are two questions that arise in the interpretation.

1. Does this apply to the individuals Jacob and Esau or simply to the nations springing from Jacob and Esau? It must be observed that in Malachi 1:1-5 the peoples of Israel and Edom are distinctly in view. The prophecy is introduced as "the burden of the word of the Lord to Israel" (vs. 1) and verses 3-5 clearly refer to the Edomites, to the desolation of their country, and as the people against whom the Lord hath indignation for ever. This collective or ethnic reference is parallel to what we find in connection with the preceding oracle spoken to Rebecca, as noted earlier. Thus there is no doubt that this word as originally spoken had application to the nations of Israel and Edom. It must not be assumed, however, from this patent fact that the question of its relevance to the individuals Jacob and Esau is thereby determined and determined for the most part negatively. Certain considerations must be kept in mind.

(*a*) Although the respective peoples proceeding from Jacob and Esau are in the forefront in Malachi 1:1-5 (*cf.* also Gen. 25:23), yet we may not discount the relevance to Jacob and Esau themselves. Why was there this differentiation between Israel and Edom? It was because there was differentiation between

---

[24] Philippi rightly criticizes what he quotes from Luther to the effect that the clause is to be attached to ἐρρέθη αὐτῇ.

Jacob and Esau. It would be as indefensible to dissociate the fortunes of the respective peoples from the differentiation in the individuals as it would be to dissociate the differentiation of the individuals from the destinies of the nations proceeding from them. So the question cannot be dismissed: what is the character of the differentiation as it affects the individuals, Jacob and Esau?

(*b*) As observed in connection with verse 11, the differentiation which belongs to Israel as a whole in virtue of the theocratic election does not meet the question the apostle encounters in this whole passage, namely, the unbelief of the mass of ethnic Israel. There must be another factor at work which will obviate the inference that the word of God has come to nought. This factor is found in the particularity of election, that is, in a more specific and determinative election than is exemplified in the generic election of Israel as a people. So now, in terms of *love*, the only criterion that will meet the demands of the situation is a more specific love than that exemplified in the love that distinguished Israel as a people from Edom as a people. The conclusion, therefore, must be that in respect of the persons Jacob and Esau Paul pushes his analysis and application of love and hate to their ultimate in order to discover the kind of differentiation that will satisfy the demands of the problem with which he is dealing. As he had done earlier with God's electing purpose so he now does with the love of God for Jacob.[25]

2. The next question is the meaning of the love and hate of which Jacob and Esau are respectively the objects. It has been maintained that the word "hate" means "*to love less, to regard and treat with less favour*".[26] Appeal can be made to various passages where this meaning holds (*cf.* Gen. 29:32, 33; Deut. 21:15; Matt. 6:24; 10:37, 38; Luke 14:26; John 12:25).[27] It would have to be admitted that this meaning would provide for the differentiation which must be posited. Without embarking on the question of God's love for the reprobate, this view would imply that Esau was not the object of that love which God exercised toward Jacob, namely, the specific distinguishing love which alone would account for the differentiation. The text, it must be said, could not mean

---

[25]   *Cf. contra*, e.g., Sanday and Headlam: *op. cit.*, *ad* 9:11; F. F. Bruce: *op. cit.*, *ad* 9:12, 13; Philippi: *op. cit.*, *ad* 9:13.
[26]   Charles Hodge: *op. cit.*, *ad* 9:13.
[27]   Prov. 13:24 is sometimes cited also. But it is questionably relevant.

anything less than this. Esau could not be the object of the love borne to Jacob for, if so, all distinction would be obliterated, and what the text clearly indicates is the radical distinction.

It is, however, questionable if this privative notion adequately expresses the thought in either Hebrew or Greek as it applies to our text. It can readily be suspected that in the original context, as it pertains to the Edomites (Mal. 1:1–5), the mere absence of love or favour hardly explains the visitations of judgment mentioned: "Esau I hated, and made his mountains a desolation, and gave his heritage to the jackals of the wilderness" (vs. 3); "they shall build, but I will throw down; and men shall call them the border of wickedness, and the people against whom the Lord hath indignation for ever" (vs. 4). These judgments surely imply disfavour. The indignation is a positive judgment, not merely the absence of blessing. In Scripture God's wrath involves the positive outflow of his displeasure. What we find in Malachi 1:1–5 is illustrated by instances in the Old Testament where God's hatred is mentioned and where either persons or things are the objects (cf. Psalms 5:5; 11:5; Prov. 6:16; 8:13; Isa. 1:14; 61:8; Jer. 44:4; Hos. 9:15; Amos 5:21; Zech. 8:17; Mal. 2:16). The divine reaction stated could scarcely be reduced to that of not loving or loving less. Thus the evidence would require, to say the least, the thought of disfavour, disapprobation, displeasure. There is also a vehement quality that may not be discounted. We must not predicate of this divine hate those unworthy features which belong to hate as it is exercised by us sinful men. In God's hate there is no malice, malignancy, vindictiveness, unholy rancour or bitterness. The kind of hate thus characterized is condemned in Scripture and it would be blasphemy to predicate the same of God. But there is a hate in us that is the expression of holy jealousy for God's honour and of love to him (cf. Psalms 26:5; 31:6; 139:21, 22; Jude 23; Rev. 2:6). This hate is the reflection in us of God's jealousy for his own honour. We must, therefore, recognize that there is in God a holy hate that cannot be defined in terms of not loving or loving less. Furthermore, we may not tone down the reality or intensity of this hate by speaking of it as "anthropopathic" or by saying that it "refers not so much to the emotion as to the effect".[28] The case is rather, as in all virtue, that this holy hate in us is patterned after holy hate in God.

---

[28] Philippi: *op. cit., ad* 9:13.

It is difficult for us to find terms adequately to express this holy hate as it is exercised by us. It is still more difficult to express this hate as it belongs to God. And it is not to be supposed that an appeal to the analogy between our holy hate and that of God resolves for us the precise character of the hate specified in the proposition, "Esau I hated". The hate of verse 13 belongs to the transcendent realm of God's sovereignty for which there is no human analogy. The purpose of appeal to holy hate in us is merely for the purpose of showing that even in us men there is a hate that is entirely distinct from malicious and vindictive hatred. It is in this direction that we are to construe God's hate and we may not tone it down to a negative or comparative notion.

On the basis of biblical patterns of thought and usage, therefore, the statement "Esau I hated" is not satisfactorily interpreted as meaning simply "not loved" or "loved less" but in the sense that an attitude of positive disfavour is expressed thereby. Esau was not merely excluded from what Jacob enjoyed but was the object of a displeasure which love would have excluded and of which Jacob was not the object because he was loved. This quotation by Paul from Malachi 1:2, 3 is for the purpose of elucidating or confirming what had just been quoted from Genesis 25:23. It must, therefore, be construed as having relevance to the same situation as that to which the oracle to Rebecca applies. Since the oracle points to a discrimination that existed before the children were born or had done good or evil (vs. 11), so must the differentiation in the present instance. Thus the definitive actions denoted by "loved" and "hated"[29] are represented as actuated not by any character differences in the two children but solely by the sovereign will of God, "the purpose of God according to election" (vs. 11). In accord with what we have found above, however, respecting biblical usage it must be interpreted as hate with the positive character which usage indicates, a hate as determinative as the unfailing purpose in terms of which the discrimination between Jacob and Esau took place. In view of what Paul teaches elsewhere respecting the ultimacy of the counsel of God's will, it would not be proper to say that the ultimate destinies of Jacob and Esau were outside his purview. Besides, in this passage (vss. 6–13) the apostle is making the distinction between the *true* Israel and Israel after

---

[29] The aorists are to be noted.

the flesh, between *true* children and children by descent, between the *true* seed and the natural seed. He is doing this to show that the covenant promise of God has not failed. The promise comes to fruition in the *true* Israel, in the remnant according to the election of grace. It would nullify the whole argument and interest of the passage to suppose that the *true* Israel, the *true* seed, are not conceived of as partakers of the promise in the fullest soteric sense. The appeal to the electing purpose of God, to the oracle spoken to Rebecca in pursuance of that purpose, and to the word "Jacob I loved, but Esau I hated" is for the purpose of confirming this same distinction between those who are partakers of the promise and those who are not. To suppose that the final word of differentiation in this passage is not intended to bear out the distinction between salvation and the coming short of the same is to suppose something that would make this word irrelevant to the apostle's thesis. We are compelled, therefore, to find in this word a declaration of the sovereign counsel of God as it is concerned with the ultimate destinies of men.

9:14–18

14 What shall we say then? Is there unrighteousness with God? God forbid.
15 For he saith to Moses, I will have mercy on whom I have mercy, and I will have compassion on whom I have compassion.
16 So then it is not of him that willeth, nor of him that runneth, but of God that hath mercy.
17 For the scripture saith unto Pharaoh, For this very purpose did I raise thee up, that I might show in thee my power, and that my name might be published abroad in all the earth.
18 So then he hath mercy on whom he will, and whom he will he hardeneth.

14–16 In verses 6–13 Paul's argument is that God's faithfulness to his covenant is not to be judged by the extent to which those physically descended from Abraham are partakers of salvation. God's faithfulness is vindicated by the fact that the covenant promise contemplates those who had been sovereignly chosen by God to be possessors and heirs of his covenant grace. The purpose of God according to election stands firm and this insures that the

24

covenant promise has not come to nought. The word of God has not failed. So these verses are a vindication of God's veracity. At verse 14 the apostle deals with another objection that is anticipated or that might be urged. It is the question of the justice of God. The two questions asked are similar to those of 3:5. The form of the second question is in this case different and points up the ultimate and decisive question of justice. "Is there unrighteousness with God?"[30] A negative answer is implied and Paul answers with the strongest form of denial at his disposal.[31] The thought of injustice with God is so intolerable that it must be dismissed with abrupt and decisive denial. Verse 15 is an appeal to Scripture in support of "God forbid". As illustrating Paul's conception of the place of Scripture it is significant that in answering so basic a question as that of God's justice he should be content to adduce the witness of Scripture. He quotes from Exodus 33:19.[32] This is God's answer to Moses' request, "Show me, I pray thee, thy glory" (Exod. 33:18) but, perhaps of greater relevance, to the anxiety of Moses expressed in verses 13–16 that he should find favour in God's sight and that God's presence would prove that Israel were God's people separated from all other people upon the face of the earth. Although Paul quotes this word without in any way restricting its application to the question at issue, the force is increased when we take into account the particular occasion on which it was spoken. The favour shown to Moses is hereby certified to proceed from God's sovereign mercy. Even Moses and with him God's people can lay no claim to any favour; it is altogether a matter of God's free choice and bestowment.

It is not necessary to press the distinction between the two terms "have mercy" and "have compassion". There are two emphases in the text. The first is the reality, security, and effectiveness of God's mercy. This is accented by the two parallel clauses, the one expressing his favour in terms of mercy, the other in terms of compassion. The second emphasis is primary. It is not so well expressed in English unless we render "on whom" as "on whomsoever", accentuating God's free and sovereign choice.[33]

---

[30] The form παρὰ τῷ θεῷ emphasizes the blasphemy of the suggestion.

[31] On the negative μὴ γένοιτο see comments on 3:4, 6 (Vol. I, pp. 93f., 97).

[32] With a slight difference of spelling in the verb οἰκτίρω the question is verbatim as in the LXX.

[33] The emphasis is upon the ὃν ἄν.

In this context we may not tone down the soteric import. This is Paul's answer to the question of justice that arises from the sovereign discrimination on God's part on which Paul had based his argument in verses 6–13. This differentiation, as shown above, is concerned with the realization of God's covenant promise in those who are the beneficiaries of the election of grace. If lesser import were given to the mercy and compassion of God, the apostle's answer would fall short of the question with which he is dealing.

The all-important aspect of verse 15 is that in support of the "God forbid" of verse 14 the mercy of God is not a matter of justice to those who are partakers of it but altogether of free and sovereign grace. This is true whether the mercy be viewed as the theocratic election of Israel to covenant privileges or, in terms of what is the apostle's particular interest, as the mercy that is unto salvation. Justice presupposes rightful claims, and mercy can be operative only where no claim of justice exists. Since mercy alone is the constraining consideration, the only explanation is God's free and sovereign determination. He has mercy as he pleases. This is the emphasis of Exodus 33:19 and to this Paul makes his definitive appeal. Back of this thesis is the polemic of the apostle in the earlier part of the epistle for the principle of grace.

Verse 16 can be regarded as the inference drawn from the Scripture quoted in verse 15 but it is preferably regarded as a statement of what is involved in the truth just asserted. The relation would then be as follows: if God has mercy on whomsoever he wills, "then it is not of him that willeth, nor of him that runneth, but of God that hath mercy". The emphasis falls here on the exclusion of man's determination as the negative counterpart to God's exercise of mercy. The first negation refers to human volition, the determination belonging to man's will; the second refers to man's active exertion (cf. I Cor. 9:24, 26; Gal. 2:2; 5:7; Heb. 12:1). The mercy of God is not an attainment gained by the most diligent labour to that end but a free bestowal of grace. No statement could be more antithetic to what accrues from claims of justice or as the awards of labour.

17, 18 Here another proof from Scripture is introduced. The most distinctive feature of this passage is that it expressly mentions the opposite of mercy. Verses 15, 16 had referred only to the

26

exercise of mercy. If all men were the recipients of this mercy there would be no interference with the sovereignty of its exercise. It would have been of God's free choice that he determined to make all men its beneficiaries. We could not but think, however, of differentiation in the bestowal of mercy in such a context as this because it is with such the apostle is dealing. So in this second appeal to Scripture the negative of mercy is expressly stated—"whom he will he hardeneth" (vs. 18). The sovereignty of which the apostle is speaking is, therefore, not an abstract sovereignty but that which was concretely exemplified in the history connected with Moses in the twofold exercise of this determinative will of God, "he hath mercy on whom he will, and whom he will he hardeneth". In view of the sustained emphasis on the free, sovereign will of God we must recognize that this sovereignty is just as inviolate in the hardening as it is in showing mercy. Otherwise the relevance to the subject in hand would be impaired. This is but another way of saying that the sovereignty of God is ultimate in both cases and as ultimate in the negative as in the positive.

The way in which the instance of Pharaoh is introduced is again significant for the apostle's use of Scripture. The words quoted are the word of God spoken to Pharaoh through Moses. But here the formula is not "he saith", as in verse 15, but "the scripture saith", indicating that this has the same effect as "God saith".

The word quoted (Exod. 9:16) is that spoken through Moses after the sixth plague, that of boils upon man and beast. In view of the preceding verse (Exod. 9:15), the verse quoted could be understood of the preservation of Pharaoh from being cut off from the earth in that particular instance by the pestilence of boils. But the term that Paul uses here, "raise up",[34] is one that is used in the Greek Old Testament in the sense of raising up on the scene of history for a particular purpose (cf. Numb. 24:19; II Sam. 12:11; Job 5:11; Hab. 1:6; Zech. 11:16). So, with many commentators, the quotation is best taken here as referring to the position Pharaoh occupied by the providence of God on the scene of history and to the role he played in connection with the redemption of Israel from Egypt. The adamant opposition of

---

[34] The verb ἐξεγείρω used by Paul differs from the LXX and is closer to the Hebrew "caused thee to stand".

Pharaoh became the occasion for the display of God's great power in the plagues visited upon Egypt and particularly in the distruction of Pharaoh's hosts in the Red Sea and the passage of Israel as on dry land. That God's name was thus published abroad in all the earth is abundantly verified and this signal manifestation of his power is the theme of Scripture elsewhere (*cf.* Exod. 15:13–16; Josh. 2:9, 10; 9:9; Psalms 78:12, 13; 105:26–38; 106:9–11; 136:10–15).

In verse 18 we have the same kind of explicatory conclusion as we found in verse 16: "So then he hath mercy on whom he will". This is to the same effect as verse 15 in its emphasis upon God's sovereignty in the exercise of his mercy. But there is the new feature in this case, that the sovereign and determinative *will* of God is mentioned and bears the emphasis. Like verse 15 it is a statement that has general application to God's exercise of mercy; whoever is the recipient of mercy owes this favour to God's sovereign will. The main question in this verse is the kind of action implied in the words "whom he will he hardeneth". Like verse 15 and the first part of verse 18 this is a statement with general application to every case that falls into this category. But since this verse is an inference from verse 17 or, preferably, an explication of what is involved in the providence of God referred to in verse 17, we must regard Pharaoh as an example and the example particularly in view. As Moses, in this context, exemplifies mercy, so Pharaoh hardening. Furthermore, since the hardening of Pharaoh's heart is so frequently mentioned in the general context from which verse 17 is taken, there can be no doubt but Pharaoh's hardening is in view. What then is this hardening?

The harshness of the term could be relieved by the view that God is said to do what he permitted. God allowed Pharaoh to harden his own heart but the action of hardening was Pharaoh's own. Analogy could be appealed to in support of such an interpretation (*cf.* II Sam. 12:11; 16:10; Psalm 105:25). As Hodge says, "from these and similar passages, it is evident that it is a familiar scriptural usage, to ascribe to God effects which he allows in his wisdom to come to pass".[35]

There can be no question but Pharaoh hardened his own heart. Although the instances are comparatively few in which the activity

---

[35] *Op. cit., ad loc.*

of Pharaoh is expressly mentioned (cf. 7:13; 8:32(28); 9:34), yet they are sufficient. But, preponderantly, the terms are to the effect that the Lord hardened Pharaoh's heart (cf. Exod. 4:21; 7:3; 9:12; 10:1, 20, 27; 11:10; 14:4, 8). The term used by Paul is the same term as occurs in each of these latter instances in the Greek Old Testament.[36] With this sustained emphasis on the Lord's action it would not be proper to dismiss the interpretation that God did harden Pharaoh's heart unless there were compelling biblical grounds to the contrary. A contextual consideration and the teaching of Paul earlier in this epistle constrain the conclusion that God's action is in view. The text is concerned with the sovereignly determinative will and action of God. This is patent in connection with his mercy: "he hath mercy on whom he will". The determinative will comes to effect in the act of having mercy. These same emphases must be carried over to the hardening: "whom he will he hardeneth". The parallel must be maintained; determinative will comes to effect in the act of hardening. Furthermore, Paul had prepared us for such a conception by his teaching in 1:24, 26, 28 where he deals with judicial abandonment to lust, to the passions of dishonour, and to a reprobate mind (cf. comments on these verses). Thus a positive infliction on God's part is the only interpretation that fits the various considerations.

The hardening, it should be remembered, is of a judicial character. It presupposes ill-desert and, in the case of Pharaoh, particularly the ill-desert of his self-hardening. Hardening may never be abstracted from the guilt of which it is the wages. It might appear that the judicial character of hardening interferes with the sovereign will of God upon which the accent falls in this text. It would be sufficient to say that this cannot be the case in the counsel with which the apostle is dealing. It is impossible to suppress or tone down the sovereign determination of God's will any more than in the first part of the verse, as noted earlier. But it should also be observed that the sin and ill-desert presupposed in hardening is also presupposed in the exercise of mercy. Both parts of this verse rest upon the premise of ill-desert. Indeed, the whole argument of the apostle in this section in refutation of the objection that there is unrighteousness with God (vs. 14) is conducted on the premise that salvation is not constrained by the

---

[36] σκληρύνω.

dictates of justice, that it proceeds entirely from the exercise of sovereign mercy, that God has mercy on whomsoever he wills. The differentiation, therefore, overtly expressed in verse 18, is altogether of God's sovereign will and determination. In reference to the judicial act of hardening the sovereignty consists in the fact that all, because of the sin and ill-desert presupposed in mercy as well as in final judgment, deserve to be hardened and that irretrievably. Sovereignty pure and simple is the only reason for the differentiation by which some are consigned to hardening while others equally ill-deserving are made the vessels of mercy. There is thus no escape from sovereignty in the will to harden or in the action which brings this will to effect. Hence Paul can say without any more reserve than in the case of mercy, "whom he will he hardeneth".

9:19–26

19 Thou wilt say then unto me, Why doth he still find fault? For who withstandeth his will?
20 Nay but, O man, who art thou that repliest against God? Shall the thing formed say to him that formed it, Why didst thou make me thus?
21 Or hath not the potter a right over the clay, from the same lump to make one part a vessel unto honor, and another unto dishonor?
22 What if God, willing to show his wrath, and to make his power known, endured with much longsuffering vessels of wrath fitted unto destruction:
23 and that he might make known the riches of his glory upon vessels of mercy, which he afore prepared unto glory,
24 *even* us, whom he also called, not from the Jews only, but also from the Gentiles?
25 As he saith also in Hosea,
I will call that my people, which was not my people;
And her beloved, that was not beloved.
26 And it shall be, *that* in the place where it was said unto them, Ye are not my people,
There shall they be called sons of the living God.

The objection here is one that arises from the assertion at the end of verse 18 that God hardens whom he will. If God determinatively wills to harden men and puts that will into effect, how can those subjected to this hardening be condemned? Are they not in that state by the will of God? This question is reinforced by the consideration that no one can frustrate this will of God. The will of which Paul is speaking in the preceding context and which the objector has in view is not the will of precept but the will of determinate purpose. The way in which the objection, as it pertains to the irresistibility of this will, is stated should be noted. We might expect the question to be: who *can* resist his will? But the tense used has the force of a present condition and is properly rendered: "who withstandeth his will?" The objector implies that in the premises of the apostle's teaching there is no one who has placed himself in the position of withstanding God's will. It is not necessary to particularize the objector as Philippi does and say that Paul is "thinking of an arrogant Jew, such as alone he has to do with in the whole of the present exposition".[37] The objection is the common one, inevitably encountered when dealing with reprobation. How can God blame us when we are the victims of his irresistible decree?

20 The answer is the appeal to the reverential silence which the majesty of God demands of us. The eloquence of the contrast between "O man" and "God" must be observed. On this contrast the other emphases rest. The conjunction rendered "nay but" (*cf.* 10:18; Luke 11:28; Phil. 3:8) in this instance serves to correct the self-vindication implied in the preceding questions. Based on the contrast between man in his weakness and ignorance and God in his majesty the emphasis falls on *thou:* who art *thou?* And then the presumption of man's attitude appears in the arrogance of replying against God. The method of answering the objection is similar to what we found earlier in 3:6. There Paul's appeal was to the universal judgment as an ultimate datum of revelation. When we are dealing with ultimate facts categorical affirmation must content us. So here, when dealing with the determinate will of God, we have an ultimate on which we may not interrogate him nor speak back when he has uttered his verdict. Who are *we* to dispute his government?

The apostle's answer is significant not only as illustrating his method and the assumptions upon which this method is based but

---

[37] *Op. cit., ad loc.*

also for what he does not say. If, in the matter concerned, the determinative will of God were not ultimate, if the differentiation of verse 18 were not due solely to God's sovereign will, then the apostle would have to deny the assumption on which the objection is based. This he does not do. In Calvin's words: "Why, then, did he not make use of this short answer, but assign the highest place to the will of God, so that it alone should be sufficient for us, rather than any other cause? If the objection that God reprobates or elects according to His will those whom He does not honour with His favour, or towards whom He shows unmerited love—if this objection had been false, Paul would not have omitted to refute it."[38]

The latter part of verse 20 goes more conveniently with verse 21.

21 The thought here is the reproduction of what we find repeatedly in the Old Testament (*cf.* Isa. 29:15, 16; 45:9; 64:8, 9; Jer. 18:1–6). God's sovereign right, pleaded here after the pattern of the potter's right over the clay, belongs to God as Creator in the disposal of his creatures as creatures. It must be borne in mind, however, that Paul is not now dealing with God's sovereign rights over men as men but over men as sinners. He is answering the objection occasioned by the sovereign discrimination stated in verse 18 in reference to mercy and hardening. These, it must be repeated, presuppose sin and ill-desert. It would be exegetically indefensible to abstract verse 21 and its teaching from these presupposed conditions. In other words, Paul is dealing with God's actual government and with the sovereign determinations of his will actualized in this government. The same is true of the Old Testament passages of which verse 21 is reminiscent. Suffice it to refer to Isaiah 64:7, 9 which supplies the context of verse 8.

The similitude is that of the potter making vessels of different character from the same lump of kneaded clay, one to serve a high purpose, another a purpose less noble. No one questions his right to make these distinctions. He has not merely the power; he has the *authority*. There is no warrant for the interpretation or objection that Paul represents God as esteeming mankind as clay and dealing with men accordingly. He is using an analogy and the

---

[38] *Op. cit., ad loc.*

meaning is simply that, in the realm of his government, God has the intrinsic right to deal with men as the potter, in the sphere of his occupation, deals with clay. But the kind of differentiation is as great as is the difference between God and the potter, on the one hand, and between men and clay, on the other.

22-24 These verses are an unfinished sentence (*cf.* Luke 19:42; John 6:62; Acts 23:9). Literally the Greek terms are "but if" and their force is properly rendered by "what if", as in the version, or, as Sanday and Headlam observe, "like our English idiom 'what and if'".[39] Understood thus the three verses are an expansion and application of what underlies the analogy appealed to in verses 20b, 21. If God in the exercise of his sovereign right makes some vessels of wrath and others vessels of mercy what have we to say? It is a rhetorical way of reiterating the question of verse 20.

The interpretation of these verses may more suitably be discussed in the order of the following details.

1. "Vessels of wrath" and "vessels of mercy" are best regarded in terms of verse 21. The potter makes vessels for certain purposes. So here the vessels are *for* wrath and mercy.[40] It is true that they are vessels deserving wrath but this cannot apply in respect of mercy to the vessels of mercy. Hence both should be taken in a sense that can apply to both. This view is to the same effect as that of Calvin who says that vessels are to be taken in a general sense to mean instruments and therefore instruments for the exhibition of God's mercy and the display of his judgment.[41]

2. The participle "willing" has been interpreted in two ways: "because willing" or "although willing". In the former case the thought would be that because God wishes to give more illustrious display of his wrath and power he exercises his longsuffering. In the latter case the meaning would be: although God wills to

---

[39] *Op. cit., ad loc.*

[40] δέ at the beginning of verse 22 is transitional, not adversative. As Godet says it is "the transition from the figure to the application" (*op. cit., ad loc.*). *Cf. contra* Sanday and Headlam: *op. cit., ad loc.*

[41] *Op. cit., ad loc.; cf. contra* Sanday and Headlam who maintain that "'destined for God's anger' would require σκεύη εἰς ὀργήν: and the change of construction from the previous verse must be intentional" (*ibid.*). This is not necessary. "Vessels of mercy" corresponds to εἰς τιμήν and "vessels of wrath" to εἰς ἀτιμίαν.

execute his wrath he nevertheless restrains and postpones the execution from the constraint of longsuffering. In the one case longsuffering serves the purpose of effective display of wrath and power, in the other case longsuffering inhibits the execution of the just desert. In favour of the latter it could be said that according to 2:4 God's longsuffering is a manifestation of the goodness of God directed to repentance and could hardly be represented as the means of promoting the demonstration of God's wrath. Before reaching a decision on this question other considerations bearing on the interpretation of verses 22, 23 have to be taken into account.

3. The governing thought of these verses, as of the preceding, is the twofold way in which the sovereign will of God comes to expression. This is apparent from several considerations but from none more than from the two designations, "vessels of wrath" and "vessels of mercy". This same emphasis upon God's determinative will must be present in the word "willing" at the beginning of verse 22. It harks back to verse 18 and also to the term "will"[42] in verse 19. So "willing" is not simply wishing but determining.

4. It would not be proper to suppress the parallel[43] between "to show his wrath, and to make his power known" (vs. 22) and "that I might show in thee my power" (vs. 17). There is surely reminiscence of the latter in the former. Hence what God did in the case of Pharaoh illustrates what is more broadly applied to vessels of wrath in verse 21. Pharaoh was raised up and hardened, in the sense explained above, for the purpose of demonstrating God's power and publishing his name in all the earth. If we interject the term "forbearance", we must say it was exercised in this case in order that God's great power might be displayed. From this consideration, namely, that of the parallel, there appears to be a compelling reason to subordinate the longsuffering of verse 22 to the purpose of showing his wrath and making his power known. If we bear in mind the determinate purpose of God upon which the accent falls and that those embraced in this purpose are vessels of wrath and therefore viewed as deserving of wrath to the uttermost, the "much longsuffering" exercised towards them is not deprived of its real character as such. It is only because God is forbearing that he delays the infliction of the full measure of ill-

---

[42] βούλημα refers to determinate purpose in verse 19.
[43] *Cf.* Lagrange: *op. cit., ad* 9:22.

desert. Furthermore, the apostle has in view the unbelief of Israel and the longsuffering with which God endures their unbelief. He is reminding his unbelieving kinsmen that God's longsuffering is not the certificate of God's favour but that, awful though it be, it only ministers in the case of those who are the vessels of wrath to the more manifest exhibition of their ill-desert in the infliction of God's wrath and the making known of his power. In the light of these considerations the participle "willing" (vs. 22a) can and should preferably be understood in the sense "because willing" rather than "although willing". The total thrust of the context indicates the subordination which the former alternative implies.

5. The "willing" (vs. 22), as indicated already, has a twofold reference. The first is "to show his wrath, and to make his power known". The second is "that he might make known the riches of his glory upon vessels of mercy" (vs. 23).[44] This is parallel to other expressions earlier in this chapter, especially to verses 16b, 18a. But no expression used hitherto is of comparable richness. The same term is used for making known as is used in verse 22 for making known his power upon vessels of wrath. Yet there is an eloquent contrast in respect of what is made known. Now it is "the riches of his glory". God's glory is the sum of his perfections and "the riches" refer to the splendour and fulness characterizing these perfections. It is to be borne in mind that in the bestowal of mercy there is no prejudice to any of God's attributes. But it is not this negative that bears the emphasis. It is that the perfections are magnified in the work of mercy and in no action is there so effulgent an exhibition of God's glory (*cf.* Psalm 85:9–11; Rom. 11:33; Eph. 1:7, 12, 14; 2:4, 7; 3:8, 16; Col. 1:27; I Tim. 1:11). Glory in this instance is not to be identified with the glory mentioned at the end of verse 23. The latter is the glory bestowed, the former the glory of God manifested. The correlation, however, is noteworthy. The grandeur of believers' bliss will consist in the fact that therein the richness of God's glory will be manifest and it would fall short of "glory" if this were not the case.

---

[44] There is no good reason for opposing this construction. καὶ ἵνα has this force in Greek, especially after such verbs as willing. *Cf.* William F. Arndt and F. Wilbur Gingrich: *A Greek-English Lexicon of the New Testament and Other Early Christian Literature* (Chicago, 1957), *ad* ἵνα, II, 1, a. The change from the infinitive γνωρίσαι (vs. 22) to ἵνα γνωρίσῃ (vs. 23) is, therefore, no obstacle.

6. The vessels of wrath are "fitted unto destruction". The question disputed is whether they are represented as fitted or prepared by God for destruction or whether they are viewed as fitting themselves for destruction. It is true that Paul does not say that God prepared them for destruction as he does in the corresponding words respecting the vessels of mercy that "he afore prepared" them unto glory. It may be that he purposely refrained from making God the subject. However, we may not insist that God is not viewed as fitting them for destruction. In verse 18 there is the agency of God in hardening. In verses 22, 23 the analogy of verse 21 is being applied and the vessels of wrath correspond to the potter's vessel unto dishonour which he prepares for this purpose. They are also vessels of wrath and, therefore, as observed above, vessels for wrath, and wrath corresponds to destruction. For these reasons there is nothing contrary to the teaching of the context if we regard God as the agent in fitting for destruction. At the same time we may not dogmatize that the apostle intended to convey this notion in this case. The main thought is that the destruction meted out to the vessels of wrath is something for which their precedent condition suits them. There is an exact correspondence between what they were in this life and the perdition to which they are consigned. This is another way of saying that there is continuity between this life and the lot of the life to come. In the general context of the apostle's thought there is no release from human responsibility nor from the guilt of which perdition is the wages.

7. The vessels of mercy God "afore prepared unto glory". In this case there is no question as to the agent. The vessels of wrath can be said to fit themselves for destruction; they are the agents of the demerit which reaps destruction. But only God prepares for glory. The figure of the potter is applied without reserve; vessels unto honour correspond to vessels prepared unto glory. The "afore prepared" points to the parallel truth indicated in "fitted unto destruction" that there is continuity between the process of operative grace in this life and the glory ultimately achieved. The glory meted out is something for which the precedent state and condition prepared the vessels of mercy (cf. II Tim. 2:20, 21).

8. Verse 24 must be understood in the light of the differentiation which permeates this whole passage from verse 6 onwards. This differentiation is the answer to the objection that the word of God

might appear to have come to nought. It is the differentiation which the purpose of God according to election causes to be, exemplified in "Jacob I loved, but Esau I hated", vindicated in God's sovereign prerogative to have mercy on whom he will and to discriminate between vessels of wrath and vessels of mercy. Since the apostle is not thinking abstractly nor dealing merely with the past, he brings this to bear upon the concrete situation which he encounters and upon the way in which God's sovereign will unto salvation is realized in the present. So he says "even us, whom he also called, not from the Jews only, but also from the Gentiles". This is the conclusion to what in English has been rendered as a question (vss. 22–24) with the implied answer that we have no reply against God (*cf.* vs. 20). Paul applies what he had said respecting vessels of mercy prepared beforehand unto glory to actual experience in his own case and that of others. He finds in the call of Jews and Gentiles the illustration of God's working grace.

Although in verses 22, 23 there is not direct reference to the decretive foreordination of God in the expressions "fitted unto destruction" and "afore prepared unto glory", it is not possible to dissociate verse 24 from the earlier passage in which calling is given its locus in relation to predestination (8:28–30). Never in Paul is calling anything else than according to purpose and, therefore, the mention of calling in this passage harks back to the sovereign will and purpose of God repeatedly appealed to in the preceding verses. Thus the predestinarian background cannot be denied.

Calling here has the same meaning as elsewhere, the effectual call to salvation (1:7; 8:28, 30; I Cor. 1:9; Gal. 1:15; II Tim. 1:9). It is neither necessary nor proper to think that the preparation mentioned in verse 23 preceded the actual call.[45] The call would rather be the inception of the preparatory process.

The reference to both Jews and Gentiles is all-important. That there should be the called from Jewry belongs to the argument of the passage as a whole. The covenant promise has not failed but comes to effect in the *true* Israel, the *true* children, the *true* seed (*cf.* vss. 6–9, 27, 29; 11:5, 7). This is expressed in the words "not from the Jews only". The form, however, signifies that the covenant

---

[45]   *Cf. contra* E. H. Gifford: *The Epistle of St. Paul to the Romans* (London, 1886), *ad* 9:24 who says: "We here see that the preparation mentioned in v. 23 preceded the actual call".

37

promise and the electing grace of God have broader scope than
Jewry. So "but also from the Gentiles" is added. In 4:12–17 the
interest of the apostle differs from that of the present passage.
There the polemic is focused upon justification by faith in opposition
to works; here the interest is the fulfilment of the covenant promise.
But there is a close relationship between the two passages, as may
be seen particularly from 4:16. Basic in Paul's thought is the
promise given to Abraham that in his seed *all the families of the
earth* would be blessed.

25, 26 These verses are an appeal to Old Testament passages in
confirmation of the call of the Gentiles, drawn from Hosea 2:23;
1:10.[46] There might appear to be a discrepancy between the
purport and reference of these passages in the prophecy and as
applied by Paul. In Hosea they refer to the tribes of Israel and not
to the Gentile nations. There should be no difficulty. Paul
recognizes that the rejection and restoration of Israel of which
Hosea spoke have their parallel in the exclusion of the Gentiles
from God's covenant favour and then their reception into that
favour. Of Israel it had been said "Lo-ruhamah; for I will no more
have mercy upon the house of Israel" (Hos. 1:6). But this is not the
final word. God will again betroth in lovingkindness and "in the
place where it was said unto them, Ye are not my people, it shall
be said unto them, Ye are the sons of the living God" (Hos.
1:10). So it is with the Gentiles, once forsaken of God but later
embraced in covenant love and favour. The same procedure is
exemplified in both cases and Paul finds in the restoration of
Israel to love and favour the type in terms of which the Gentiles
become partakers of the same grace.[47] "In the place where"
(vs. 26) may best be taken as referring in Paul's application to
"every place, where the people had been regarded as aliens, they

---

[46] Verse 26 is a verbatim quotation of the LXX and with the exception of
ἐκεῖ, which nevertheless is implied, is a literal rendering of the Hebrew (Hos.
2:1 in both Hebrew and LXX). But verse 25 does not exactly correspond to
the Hebrew or LXX of Hosea 2:23. The LXX is a rather close rendering
of the Hebrew which in translation reads: "And I will sow her to me in the
earth, and I will have mercy upon her who had not obtained mercy, and I will
say to them who were not my people, Thou art my people, and he will say,
Thou art my God". Paul has retained the thought but has adapted the actual
terms. It may be that the reason is to assimilate the thought of Hosea 2:23
more closely to the terms of Hosea 1:10 which is quoted verbatim in verse 26.
[47] *Cf.* Meyer, Hodge, Sanday and Headlam: *op. cit., ad* 9:25.

should be called the children of God".[48] Thus "the utterance *of God . . . is conceived, in the plastic spirit of poetry, as resounding in all Gentile lands*".[49] "I will call" in this case should be understood not precisely in the sense of "called"in verse 24 but as "named". It is the new denomination that is expressed and the significance resides in the designation "my people" (*cf.* Numb. 6:27). The various designations, "my people", "beloved", "sons of the living God" express differing aspects of the new relationship and, correlative with the effectual call (vs. 24), are all soteric in their import.

9:27–33

27 And Isaiah crieth concerning Israel, If the number of the children of Israel be as the sand of the sea, it is the remnant that shall be saved:
28 for the Lord will execute *his* word upon the earth, finishing it and cutting it short.
29 And, as Isaiah hath said before,
Except the Lord of Sabaoth had left us a seed, We had become as Sodom, and had been made like unto Gomorrah.
30 What shall we say then? That the Gentiles, who followed not after righteousness, attained to righteousness, even the righteousness which is of faith:
31 but Israel, following after a law of righteousness, did not arrive at *that* law.
32 Wherefore? Because *they sought it* not by faith, but as it were by works. They stumbled at the stone of stumbling;
33 even as it is written,
Behold, I lay in Zion a stone of stumbling and a rock of offence:
And he that believeth on him shall not be put to shame.

27-29 In the two preceding verses the call of the Gentiles had been supported by and represented as the fulfilment of Old Testament promises. In these three verses the Isaianic witness is adduced to confirm Paul's thesis that the covenant promise did not contemplate or guarantee the salvation of all ethnic Irsael.

---

48 Hodge: *op. cit.*, *ad* 9:26.
49 Meyer: *op. cit.*, *ad* 9:26.

This is the proposition with which Paul began: "they are not all Israel, that are of Israel" (vs. 6). It is the thesis implicit in the statement of verse 24, "not from the Jews only". If all Jews were *ipso facto* heirs of the promise, this *form* of statement, identical with "also of the Gentiles" and coordinate with it, could not be used. The apostle is showing now from the Old Testament that prophecy itself had spoken of the remnant and of the seed as those to whom salvation belonged and apart from whom the nation would have suffered the destruction of Sodom.

Verses 27, 28 are taken from Isaiah 10:22, 23.[50] This passage occurs in the context of the Lord's indignation executed upon Israel through the instrumentality of Assyria as the rod of God's anger and the staff of his indignation (*cf.* Isa. 10:5). From the desolation only a remnant of Israel would escape. This is spoken of as the return of "the remnant of Jacob, unto the mighty God" (vs. 21). Paul's quotation follows the Greek version with some modification and contraction. In verse 22 he changes "the people of Israel" to "the number of the children of Israel" and verse 23 he condenses. These adaptations do not interfere with the sense. In all cases, as Philippi says, "the fundamental thought is still this, that in the destruction of Israel and the salvation merely of a holy remnant, a divine judicial punishment is carried out".[51] Here again Paul finds in escape from the Assyrian conquest an example of God's government of Israel as it applies to the actual situation with which he is dealing. This scripture demonstrates that God's promises do not pertain to the mass of Israel but are fulfilled in the remnant.

The main thought of verse 28[52] is the efficacy with which God accomplishes his word and the decree of which the word is the utterance. It is the emphasis of Isaiah 14:24: "Surely as I have thought, so shall it come to pass; and as I have purposed, so shall it stand". "Finishing it" refers to accomplishment, "cutting it short" to the expeditious despatch with which the accomplishment takes place. The reference in Isaiah 10:22b, 23 is to the thorough-

---

[50] "His description of Isaiah as *exclaiming*, and not speaking, is deliberately intended to arouse greater attention" (Calvin: *op. cit., ad loc.*).

[51] *Op. cit., ad loc.*

[52] The addition after συντέμνων of the words ἐν δικαιοσύνῃ ὅτι λόγον συντετμημένον found in D G and some versions and in the textus receptus is not supported by P⁴⁶, ℵ, A, B, 1739 and some others. These words are found in these identical terms in the LXX of Isaiah 10:23.

ness and the despatch with which God's punitive judgment will be executed. Also, so widespread will be the destruction that only a remnant will escape. This same emphasis should be understood in the apostle's quotation. The salvation of the remnant and the significance of the remnant are thrown into bold relief by the dark background of judgment with which this salvation is contrasted (*cf.* Amos 3:12).

Verse 29 is quoted from Isaiah 1:9 and adheres to the Greek version without modification. The only difference from the Hebrew is that "a little remnant" is rendered "a seed" in the Greek. In Paul's teaching here "seed" and "remnant" have the same denotation. "Seed", occurring here for the first time after verse 8, points back to that same meaning, namely, the seed who are partakers of the promise. The reference to the remnant is to the same effect as in verse 27 but the accent of the two verses differs. In verse 27 it is that only a remnant will be saved, in verse 29 that the remnant is the preserving seed apart from which the nation would have been given up to utter destruction. Both verses are closely related to the thought of verse 28. That only a remnant is saved points up the severity and extent of the judgment executed. That a remnant is saved is the evidence of the Lord's favour and the guarantee that his covenant promise has not failed. It should be noted that it is by God's gracious action that a seed is maintained: "except the Lord of Sabaoth had left us a seed". In accord with the sustained stress upon the sovereign will and determinate purpose of God in the preceding context the same is still applied to the reservation of a remnant and the preserving of a seed.[53]

30-33 In verses 6–13 the apostle showed that the unbelief and rejection of ethnic Israel as a whole did not invalidate God's covenant promise; the promise had respect to and was realized in the election of grace. In verses 14–18 he had vindicated this procedure by appeal to the sovereignty of God's mercy. In verses 19–29 he had answered the objection that God's sovereign determinations relieved men of responsibility and blame. This

---

[53] The verb ἐγκαταλείπω and the substantive ὑπόλειμμα express similar ideas and the latter is the result of God's action in the former.

section closes with proof that the Old Testament itself and the plan of God disclosed therein had in view only a remnant as the partakers of salvation. This remnant, spoken of also as the seed, brings us back to verse 8. Thus a unity of conception ties all these verses (vss. 6–29) together and the paramount consideration pleaded by the apostle is the differentiation which God in the exercise of his sovereign will determines, a differentiation also which insures that his covenant promise never falls to the ground. The electing purpose stands fast; there is the remnant according to the election of grace.

In verses 30–33, however, a new aspect of the situation with which Paul is dealing comes into view. The emphasis upon the sovereign will of God in the preceding verses does not eliminate human responsibility, nor is the one incompatible with the other. It is not as if God's sovereign will runs athwart all that obtains in the sphere of human will and action. The case is rather that what occurs in the one realm is correlative with what occurs in the other, not because the human will governs and determines God's will but because God's will is concerned with men there is a correspondence between what God wills and what men subjectively are. It is with the latter Paul deals in verses 30–33.

"What shall we say then?" is the same form of question as in verse 14 (*cf.* 3:5; 4:1; 6:1; 7:7; 8:31). It scarcely agrees with the construction of the whole passage to regard what follows as anything else than the direct answer to this question. The question arises in connection with the unbelief of Israel so much in the forefront in verses 1–3. But alongside of this unbelief there is also the faith of Gentiles (vss. 25, 26). This diversity provokes the question: What are we to make of it? The answer is given in a form that accentuates the anomaly; the outcome is so different from what God's dealings in the past with the respective peoples would lead us to expect. This strange outcome is that Gentiles not following after righteousness gained righteousness and that Jews, though following righteousness, did not attain to it.

When Gentiles are said not to follow righteousness, there is allusion to the fact that they were outside the pale of special revelation and had been abandoned to their own ways (*cf.* 1:18–32; Acts 14:16; 17:30). But thought is focused on what is central to the theme of this epistle in the earlier chapters and again in Chapter 10, namely, that they did *not seek after the righteousness of justification.* It is not that they were destitute of all moral interest (*cf.* 2:12–15) but that the matter of justification and of the righteousness securing it was not their pursuit. On the other hand, Israel unto whom the oracles of God had been committed did pursue this righteousness. We may not tone down this statement. As possessors of special revelation, epitomized in the Abrahamic covenant, the matter of righteousness with God unto justification was focal in their interest; it was central in their religion. It is this contrast that points up the tragedy of the sequel. Gentiles attained to this righteousness and Israel failed to arrive there.

The change of form used in verse 31 must not, however, be overlooked. Israel is said to "follow after a law of righteousness". This should not be taken as referring to the righteousness of the law, that of works. "Law" in this case is similar to its use in 3:27b; 7:21, 23; 8:2 and means principle or rule or order. Israel is represented as pursuing that order or institution which was concerned with justification. But Israel came short of gaining the righteousness to which that institution bore witness; "they did not arrive at that law"; they did not attain to what was provided in the institution that was their glory. We sense the importunity of the question: why? This is Paul's question: "wherefore?" Verses 32, 33 are the answer.

This answer is already anticipated in verse 30: the Gentiles are said to have "attained to righteousness, even the righteousness which is of faith". In this instance it was necessary to define the righteousness as that of faith because the apostle does not in this context return to the subject of the righteousness to which the Gentiles attained. In verse 32 the question is why *Israel* did *not* attain to the same. The indictment is a reiteration of the thesis set forth earlier in the epistle, especially in 3:27–4:25. No further exposition is necessary other than to observe the way in which the antithesis is stated: "not of faith but as of works".[54] "As of works" indicates the conception entertained by Israel respecting the way by which justification was to be secured and the kind of righteousness constituting this justification. The misapprehension was total. Hence the failure.

---

[54] νόμου after ἔργων is weakly attested and, besides, robs the antithesis of its pungency. The version, furthermore, weakens this force by inserting unnecessarily "it were".

43

The latter part of verse 32 is an expansion of this fatal error in the terms of an Old Testament figure. The Scripture had forewarned of the stumbling which constituted Israel's fall. There is neither need nor warrant to weaken the meaning of the term "stumbled" as if it referred merely to irritation or annoyance.[55] It clearly refers to a fall and "the stone of stumbling" (Isa. 8:14), as the stone over which one stumbles, confirms this interpretation. If the figure of running a race is present in verses 30, 31 and carried on in verse 32, then the picture is the graphic one of stumbling over the hurdle and failing to gain the prize.

Verse 32 is a fuller confirmation from the Old Testament of the allusion to Isaiah 8:14 in verse 33. The quotation is a combination of two passages of different purport in their original contexts (Isa. 8:14; 28:16). In the former the Lord of hosts is said to be "for a stone of stumbling and for a rock of offense to both the houses of Israel". According to the latter the "stone, a tried stone, a precious corner-stone" is laid in Zion for a foundation and serves the purpose of giving stability and security. Paul takes parts of both passages, weaves these parts together into a unit, and by this abridgement and combination obtains the diverse thought of both passages. This twofold aspect he applies to the subject with which he is dealing, the failure of Israel and the attainment of the Gentiles. He thus shows that the Scripture had foretold in effect the twofold outcome. The main interest, however, is confirmation of the stumbling of Israel. It is this tragedy that looms high in the apostle's concern, as is apparent from the preceding and succeeding contexts.[56]

It cannot be doubted that Paul applies both passages to Christ. This is all the more significant in the case of Isaiah 8:14 for there it is the Lord of hosts who is spoken of as being for a stone of stumbling. The apostle had no hesitation in applying to Christ passages which pertained to the Lord of hosts. Since these passages are applied to Christ (cf. also Matt. 21:42; Mark 12:10; Luke 20:17; Acts 4:11; I Pet. 2:6–8), the faith mentioned in verses 30, 32 is the faith specified in verse 33 as believing upon Christ. It is the faith of resting upon him and in the context (cf. vss. 30, 31) is viewed

---

[55] Cf. John 11:9, 10; Rom. 14:13, 20, 21; I Cor. 8:9; I Pet. 2:8.
[56] The twofold reaction is set forth more fully in I Pet. 2:6–8 where the passages are more fully quoted. This is the best commentary on Paul's more condensed quotation and more summary use of both passages.

particularly as the faith directed to justification. The righteousness attained is that of faith in contrast with works. The effect, "shall not be put to shame", taken from Isaiah 28:16, varies from the Hebrew. The latter says: "he that believeth shall not be in haste". Paul in quoting follows the rendering of the Greek translators. The rendering should not be regarded as importing an idea alien to the thought of the Hebrew. The idea expressed by the Greek is that the believer will not be confounded, he will not have occasion to be ashamed of his confidence. And the Hebrew may express the closely related thought that he will not flee in disappointment.

XVI. THE RIGHTEOUSNESS OF FAITH
(10:1–21)

10:1–8

1 Brethren, my heart's desire and my supplication to God is for them, that they may be saved.

2 For I bear them witness that they have a zeal for God, but not according to knowledge.

3 For being ignorant of God's righteousness, and seeking to establish their own, they did not subject themselves to the righteousness of God.

4 For Christ is the end of the law unto righteousness to every one that believeth.

5 For Moses writeth that the man that doeth the righteousness which is of the law shall live thereby.

6 But the righteousness which is of faith saith thus, Say not in thy heart, Who shall ascend into heaven? (that is, to bring Christ down:)

7 or, Who shall descend into the abyss? (that is, to bring Christ up from the dead.)

8 But what saith it? The word is nigh thee, in thy mouth, and in thy heart: that is, the word of faith, which we preach:

1 In this chapter the apostle is concerned with the same subject as that dealt with in the latter part of the preceding chapter. In 9:32, 33 the stumbling of Israel consisted in seeking righteousness by works and not by faith. This is but another way of saying that they sought to establish their own righteousness and did not subject themselves to the righteousness of God, the way it is stated in 10:3. Thus there is no break in the thought at 10:1. It should be noted, however, that into the midst of this treatment of the guilt of Israel the apostle interjects what reminds us of the way in which the whole subject of the unbelief of Israel had been introduced (9:1–3). The terms he uses now do not have the intensity used earlier. But it is the same heartfelt, deep-seated solicitude for his kinsmen according to the flesh. The address with which he begins, "Brethren", is one charged with emotion and affection and draws our attention to a solicitude, expressed in the words that follow, for those who are outside of the fellowship which the term "brethren" implies.

The word rendered "desire" is more properly translated "good-pleasure" (*cf.*, with reference to God, Matt. 11:26; Luke 2:14; 10:21; 12:32; Eph. 1:5, 9; Phil. 2:13 and, with reference to men, Rom. 15:26; II Cor. 5:8; 12:10; I Thess. 2:8; 3:1; II Thess. 2:12). We are reminded of Ezekiel 18:23, 32; 33:11, in which God proclaims it to be his good-pleasure that the wicked turn from his evil way and live. So here Paul asserts the good-pleasure, the delight of his heart with reference to Israel. This is joined with supplication to God for Israel.[1] "That they might be saved" expresses that to which the good-pleasure of his heart and his supplication were directed. The sorrow and pain of heart (9:1) were not, therefore, emotions of hopeless melancholy; they were joined with goodwill toward Israel and the outgoing of specific entreaty to God on their behalf to the end that they might be saved. Here we have a lesson of profound import. In the preceding chapter the emphasis is upon the sovereign and determinative will of God in the differentiation that exists among men. God has mercy on whom he wills and whom he wills he hardens. Some are vessels for wrath, others for mercy. And ultimate destiny is envisioned in destruction and glory. But this differentiation is God's action and prerogative, not man's. And, because so, our attitude to men is not to be governed by God's secret counsel concerning them. It is this lesson and the distinction involved that are so eloquently inscribed on the apostle's passion for the salvation of his kinsmen. We violate the order of human thought and trespass the boundary between God's prerogative and man's when the truth of God's sovereign counsel constrains despair or abandonment of concern for the eternal interests of men.

2, 3 When Paul says "I bear them witness" he is making

---

[1] The reading αὐτῶν is supported by P⁴⁶, ℵ, A, B, D, G, by several versions and fathers; τοῦ Ἰσραήλ ἐστιν by K, L, P, and the mass of the cursives. It is easy to understand how in the course of transmission the longer reading would have been substituted for the simple αὐτῶν in order to make specific the reference which is unquestionably clear from the context.

allowance for the religious interest which Israel possessed and accords to them the credit due on this account. They have "zeal for God". No one knew better than the apostle what such zeal was; in no one had it risen to greater intensity (cf. Acts 26:5, 8; Gal. 1:14). Hence he knew from personal experience the state of mind and conscience with which he credited his kinsmen and his "witness" to that effect takes on added meaning for that reason. The adversative, "but not according to knowledge", points to the criterion by which "zeal for God" is to be judged. Zeal is a neutral quality and can be the greatest vice. It is that to which it is directed that determines its ethical character. The criterion, therefore, is "knowledge". The term used here is one that often expresses the thorough knowledge that is after godliness to be distinguished from the knowledge that puffs up (cf. I Cor. 8:1; 13:2, 8 with Eph. 1:17; 4:13; Phil. 1:9; Col. 1:9; 3:10; I Tim. 2:4; II Tim. 2:25; 3:7; Tit. 1:1).[2] Verse 3 gives the reason why their zeal was not according to knowledge and explains what this lack of knowledge was: they did not know God's righteousness. It is not merely that they did not acknowledge this righteousness while at the same time knowing that it was that to which the Scriptures bore witness; they did not apprehend that which had been revealed. This concept of "God's righteousness" is that introduced at 1:17 and unfolded still further at 3:21, 22 (cf. the exposition at these points). In opposition to God's righteousness Israel sought to establish their own. Thus again Paul institutes the antithesis between a God-righteousness and a human righteousness, a righteousness with divine properties in contrast with that derived from human character and works. This is the theme developed in the early part of the epistle. Just as in 9:11, 30–32 there is distinct allusion to what had been argued at length in 3:21–5:21, so here also. The basic error of Israel was misconception respecting the righteousness unto justification. The righteousness of God as the provision for man's basic need is here viewed as an ordinance or institution requiring subjection. To this ordinance

---

[2] It is, however, unwarranted to draw a hard and fast line of distinction between γνῶσις and ἐπίγνωσις in the usage of the New Testament as if the former always fell short of the richness and fulness of ἐπίγνωσις and the latter always referred to the knowledge that is unto life (cf. for γνῶσις Luke 1:77; Rom. 15:14; I Cor. 1:5; II Cor. 2:14; 4:6; 6:6; 8:7; Eph. 3:19; Col. 2:3; II Pet. 1:5, 6; cf. for ἐπίγνωσις coming short of fulness Rom. 1:28; 3:20 and for ἐπιγινώσκω Rom. 1:32; II Pet. 2:21).

Israel did not subject themselves.[3] It is the "zeal for God" that places in bolder relief the tragedy of Israel's failure to attain to the law of righteousness. And the sin of ignorance is accentuated when by not knowing we miss the central provision of God's grace. How contrary to the popular notion that ignorance is an excuse and good intent the norm of approbation.[4]

4 This verse gives the reason for the thesis of verse 3 that God's righteousness and not man's is the institution of God: "Christ is the end of the law". This has been taken in the sense that the purpose of the law is fulfilled or realized in Christ. The term rendered "end" does on occasion have this meaning (cf. Luke 22:37; I Tim. 1:5). It is also true that if law is understood in the sense of the Mosaic institution, then this institution is fulfilled in Christ (cf. Gal. 3:24). Furthermore, the righteousness which Christ has provided unto our justification is one that meets all the requirements of God's law in its sanctions and demands. There are, however, objections to this interpretation.

1. Though the word "end" can express aim or purpose, preponderantly, and particularly in Paul, it means termination, denoting a terminal point (cf. Matt. 10:22; 24:6, 14; Mark 3:26; Luke 1:33; John 13:1; Rom. 6:21; I Cor. 1:8; 15:24; II Cor. 1:13; 3:13; 11:15; Phil. 3:19; Heb. 6:11; 7:3; I Pet. 4:7).[5]

2. If "end" means purpose then we should expect the apostle to say that the purpose of the law is Christ,[6] the reason being that, on this assumption, the purpose of the law would be the main thought and the real subject of the sentence. But this would give an awkward if not impossible construction as will appear from the

---

[3] ὑπετάγησαν is the form of the aorist passive (cf. 8:20; I Cor. 15:28; I Pet. 3:22) but since the passive and middle often have the same forms this form should be taken as aorist middle. To regard it as passive would yield a virtually impossible sense. In other instances (cf. James 4:7; I Pet. 2:13; 5:5) the passive is not impossible but these are preferably taken as middle after the pattern of the middle in other instances and forms (cf. Col. 3:18; Tit. 3:1; I Pet. 3:1, 5).

[4] "Away then with those empty equivocations about good intention. If we seek God from the heart, let us follow the way by which alone we have access to Him. It is better, as Augustine says, to limp in the right way than to run with all our might out of the way" (Calvin: op. cit., ad 10:2).

[5] If Paul meant purpose or aim there were other terms at his disposal that would have expressed the thought more adequately and less ambiguously as, e.g., τελείωσις or πλήρωμα.

[6] τέλος is surely predicate not subject. In I Tim. 1:5 it is subject but in that case the thought and construction require it to be.

49

translation that would be required: "The end of the law is Christ for righteousness to every one that believeth".

3. In this epistle and in the context the antithesis is between the righteousness of the law as that of works and God's righteousness as the righteousness of faith. The next verse is the clearest demonstration of this antithesis and of the meaning we are to attach to the apostle's concept of the law as the way of attaining to righteousness (cf. also 3:20, 21, 28; 4:13, 14; 8:3; 9:32). The view most consonant with this context is, therefore, that the apostle is speaking in verse 4 of the law as a way of righteousness before God and affirming the relation that Christ sustains to this conception. The only relation that Christ sustains to it is that he terminates it.

4. It needs to be noted immediately, however, that a qualification is added: "to every one that believeth". This qualification implies that only for the believer is Christ the end of the law for righteousness. Paul does not mean that the erroneous conception ceased to be entertained. That was sadly not the case, as verse 3 proves. It is, Paul says, for every one who believes that Christ is the end of the law, and his whole statement is simply to the effect that every believer is done with the law as a way of attaining to righteousness. In this consideration we have an added reason for the interpretation given. If Paul were speaking of the purpose of the law as fulfilled in Christ, we would expect the absolute statement: "Christ is the end of the law for righteousness", and no addition would be necessary or in place.

The foregoing observation regarding the force of the apostle's statement bears also upon an erroneous interpretation of this verse, enunciated by several commentators to the effect that the Mosaic law had propounded law as the means of procuring righteousness. [7]

It is strange that this notion should be entertained in the face of Paul's frequent appeal to the Old Testament and even to Moses and the Mosaic law in support of the doctrine of justification by grace through faith (cf. 3:21, 22; 4:6–8, 13; 9:15, 16; 10:6–8;

---

[7] Cf., e.g., Meyer who says: "τέλος νόμου, which is placed first with great emphasis, is applied to Christ, in so far as, by virtue of His redemptive death... the divine dispensation of salvation has been introduced, in which the basis of the procuring of salvation is no longer, as in the old theocracy, the Mosaic νόμος, but faith, whereby the law has therefore ceased to be the regulative principle for the attainment of righteousness" (op. cit., ad loc.)

15:8, 9; Gal. 3:10, 11, 17–22; 4:21–31). There is no suggestion to the effect that in the theocracy works of law had been represented as the basis of salvation and that now by virtue of Christ's death this method had been displaced by the righteousness of faith. We need but reflect again on the force of the proposition in question: *for the believer* Christ is the end of the law for righteousness. Paul is speaking of "law" as commandment, not of the Mosaic law in any specific sense but of law as demanding obedience, and therefore in the most general sense of law-righteousness as opposed to faith-righteousness.

5–8 The antithesis which had been developed in verses 3, 4 the apostle finds enunciated in the books of Moses. That is to say, Moses speaks of the righteousness which is of the law and defines what it is and he also speaks of the righteousness of faith. For the former Leviticus 18:5 is quoted and for the latter Deuteronomy 30:12, 14. The general purpose of this appeal to these passages is apparent. In characteristic manner Paul adduces the Old Testament witness to support his thesis. At least he derives from Scripture illustrations of the antithesis instituted in the preceding verses and thus confirms from the Jewish Scriptures themselves the argument he is conducting. But there are difficulties connected with the particular passages quoted, especially in the application which Paul makes.

The difficulty with the first (Lev. 18:5) is that in the original setting it does not appear to have any reference to legal righteousness as opposed to that of grace. Suffice it to say now that the formal statement Paul appropriates as one suited to express the principle of law-righteousness. It cannot be doubted but the proposition, "The man that doeth the righteousness of the law shall live thereby", is, of itself, an adequate and watertight definition of the principle of legalism. (See Appendix B, pp. 249 ff., for fuller discussion.)

Since Paul in verses 6-8 does not introduce the allusions to Deuteronomy 30:12–14 with such a formula as "Moses writeth" (vs. 5) or "Isaiah hath said" (9:29) but with the more unusual expression "The righteousness of faith saith"[8], it could be argued

---

[8] There is no reason why the version should have intruded "which is" in the translation.

that he is not here adducing Scripture proof but making his own independent assertion. Also, since he does not quote with close adherence to the Hebrew or Greek but makes alterations and intersperses his own comments which have no parallels in the passage concerned, it has been maintained that here is not strictly *quotation* in support of his argument but "a free employment of the words of Moses, which the apostle uses as an apt substratum for his own course of thought" so that "the independent dogmatic argument" finds only a formal point of support in the Deuteronomic passage.[9] But since there is patent allusion to and partial quotation from Deuteronomy 30:12-14 and since the formula, "the righteousness of faith saith", is immediately followed by quotation (Deut. 30:12), it is difficult to escape the thought that in this passage the apostle finds the language of faith and appeals to it as confirmation of the righteousness of faith as much as Leviticus 18:5 expresses the principle regulative of law-righteousness. The type of adaptation and application we find in this instance is not wholly diverse from what we find in other instances (*cf.* 9:25, 26 and vs. 5 preceding).

We should not perplex the difficulties of this passage by supposing that the apostle takes a passage concerned with law-righteousness and applies it to the opposite, namely, faith-righteousness. It is true that Moses is dealing with the commandments and the statutes which Israel were charged to obey. Of this commandment he speaks when it is said, "it is not too hard for thee, neither is it far off" (Deut. 30:11), and the protestations of the verses that follow are all in confirmation of the nearness and practicality of the covenant ordinances. It would be a complete misconstruction of Deuteronomy to interpret it legalistically. The whole thrust is the opposite (*cf.* Deut. 7:7ff.; 9:6ff.; 10:15ff.; 14:2ff.; 15:15f.; 29:9f., 29; 32:9; 33:29). The words in question, therefore, do not find their place in a legalistic framework but in that of the grace which the covenant bespoke. Their import is that the things revealed for faith and life are accessible: we do not have to ascend to heaven nor go to the utmost parts of the sea to find them. By revelation "they belong to us and our children for ever" (Deut. 29:29) and therefore nigh in our mouth and in our heart. This truth Paul finds exemplified in the righteousness of faith and

---

[9] Philippi: *op. cit., ad loc.*

he applies it to the basic tenets of belief in Christ. These same tenets were a stumblingblock to unbelieving Israel. Thus, when we think of the truth expressed in Deuteronomy 30:12-14, we can see the appropriateness of the use of this passage to show that the same tenets over which the Jews stumbled are the tenets which verify to the fullest extent the truth of the passage from which the apostle quotes. As we proceed we shall discover this relevance.

When Paul says "the righteousness of faith saith", he is personifying the same (*cf.* Prov. 1:20; 8:1; Heb. 12:5). It is to the effect of saying "Scripture says with reference to the righteousness of faith". The main question in verse 6 is the meaning of Paul's own statement: "that is, to bring Christ down" and in verse 7: "that is, to bring Christ up from the dead".

The former has been interpreted to mean: Christ has ascended up to heaven, and the preceding question is the retort of unbelief: who can ascend up to heaven to establish contact with him? This makes good sense of itself but it does not accord with the unbelief of Israel that hovers in the background in this context nor does it suit that which follows in succeeding verses. It is better, therefore, to take the statement as implying that Jesus never came down from heaven and the preceding question as the taunt of unbelief. What Paul is insisting on is the accessibility, the nearness of revelation. That Christ came down from heaven and tabernacled among men is the most signal proof of this fact. We dare not say: who shall ascend to heaven to find the truth? For this question discounts the incarnation and is a denial of its meaning. In Christ the truth came to earth.

The other statement: "that is, to bring Christ up from the dead" (vs. 7) should be interpreted as a denial of the resurrection. The question: "who shall descend into the abyss?"[10] echoes the same kind of unbelief as that of verse 6. It is to the effect: who shall go down to the abyss to find the truth? The abyss as representing that

---

[10] The abyss in this instance may most suitably be taken as the synonym of *sheol* and the latter is frequently in the Old Testament "the grave". As in Matt. 11:23; Luke 10:15 heaven is contrasted with *hades*, so here heaven is contrasted with the abyss and, since it is in reference to Jesus' resurrection that the question is asked, the abyss can most conveniently denote what *sheol* and *hades* frequently denote in the Old Testament. In the LXX ἄβυσσος is very frequently the rendering of the Hebrew תהום the "deep" and in the singular and plural applied to the depths of the sea. In LXX Psalm 70:20 we have "the depths of the earth".

which is below is contrasted with heaven as that which is above. The question, as the language of unbelief, discounts the significance of Christ's resurrection. For the latter means that Jesus went to the realm of the dead and returned to life again. We do not need to go down to the abyss to find the truth any more than we need to ascend to heaven for the same purpose. For as Christ came from heaven to earth so also did he come again from the lower parts of the earth (*cf*. Eph. 4:9) and manifested himself to men.

Verse 8 is the assertion of what is the burden of Deuteronomy 30: 12–14 and is, with slight alteration, quotation of verse 14. Paul now specifies what this word is: it is "the word of faith, which we preach". So the word of Deuteronomy 30:14 is applied directly to the message of the gospel as preached by the apostles.[11] "The word of faith" is the word to which faith is directed,[12] not the word which faith utters. It is the word *preached* and therefore the message which brings the gospel into our mouth and heart.

10:9–15

9 because if thou shalt confess with thy mouth Jesus *as* Lord, and shalt believe in thy heart that God raised him from the dead, thou shalt be saved:
10 for with the heart man believeth unto righteousness; and with the mouth confession is made unto salvation.
11 For the scripture saith, Whosoever believeth on him shall not be put to shame.
12 For there is no distinction between Jew and Greek: for the same *Lord* is Lord of all, and is rich unto all that call upon him:
13 for, Whosoever shall call upon the name of the Lord shall be saved.
14 How then shall they call on him in whom they have not believed? and how shall they believe in him whom they have not heard? and how shall they hear without a preacher?
15 and how shall they preach, except they be sent? even as it is written, How beautiful are the feet of them that bring glad tidings of good things!

---

[11] As in verses 17, 18 (*cf*. Eph. 5:26; I Pet. 1:25) the term for word is ῥῆμα.
[12] τῆς πίστεως is objective genitive.

9-11 There are various ways of summarizing the gospel message and of stating the cardinal elements of faith. The way adopted in a particular case is determined by the context and suited to the angle from which the gospel is viewed. In this passage attention is focused upon the lordship and the resurrection of Christ, confession that Jesus is Lord and belief that God raised him from the dead. It appears that the conjunction at the beginning of verse 9 means "that" rather than "because"; it specifies what is in the mouth and in the heart, confession of Jesus' lordship and belief of the resurrection, respectively. The order which the apostle follows corresponds to that of verse 8, "in thy mouth, and in thy heart", the order followed in the text quoted (Deut. 30:14).

The confession "Jesus as Lord" or "Jesus is Lord" refers to the lordship which Jesus exercises in virtue of his exaltation (*cf.* 1:4; 14:9; I Cor. 12:3; Eph. 1:20–23; Phil. 2:11; also Matt. 28:18; Acts 2:36; 10:36; Heb. 1:3; I Pet. 3:21, 22). This lordship presupposes the incarnation, death, and resurrection of Christ and consists in his investiture with universal dominion.[13] It can readily be seen how far-reaching are the implications of the confession. On several occasions Paul had reflected earlier in this epistle on the significance of Jesus' resurrection (*cf.* 1:4; 4:24, 25; 5:10; 6:4, 5, 9, 10, and the exposition at these points). In this instance the accent falls upon believing in the heart that God raised him. The heart is the seat and organ of religious consciousness and must not be restricted to the realm of emotions or affections. It is determinative of what a person is morally and religiously and, therefore, embraces the intellective and volitive as well as the emotive. Hence believing with the *heart* that God raised Jesus means that this event with its implications respecting Jesus as the person raised and the exceeding greatness of God's power as the active agency has secured the consent of that which is most decisive in our persons and is correspondingly determinative of religious conviction. The effect of this confession and belief is said to be salvation—"thou shalt be saved". We are not to regard confession and faith as having the same efficacy unto salvation. The contrast between mouth and heart needs to be observed. But we may not tone down the importance of confession with the

---

13 "The whole acknowledgement of the heavenly κυριότης of Jesus as the σύνθρονος of God is conditioned by the acknowledgement of the preceding descent from heaven, the incarnation of the Son of God" (Meyer: *op. cit.*, *ad loc.*).

mouth. Confession without faith would be vain (*cf.* Matt. 7:22, 23; Tit. 1:16). But likewise faith without confession would be shown to be spurious. Our Lord and the New Testament in general bear out Paul's coordination of faith and confession (*cf.* Matt. 10:22; Luke 12:8; John 9:22; 12:42; I Tim. 6:12; I John 2:23; 4:15; II John 7). Confession with the mouth is the evidence of the genuineness of faith and sustains to the same the relation which good works sustain (*cf.* 12:1, 2; 14:17; Eph. 2:8–10; 4:1, 2; James 2:17–22).

In verse 10 the order is inverted; faith is mentioned first and then confession. This shows that verse 9 is not intended to announce the order of priority whether causal or logical. Obviously there would have to be belief with the heart before there could be confession with the mouth. This verse is explanatory of the preceding. A few features deserve comment. (1) Literally the rendering would be: "For with the heart it is believed unto righteousness, and with the mouth it is confessed unto salvation". This can be taken, as in the version, as equivalent to "one believes" and "one confesses". But the subjects can be taken over from the preceding verse and so the resurrection would be the subject of "is believed" and the lordship of Christ of "is confessed". This would particularize the tenets believed and confessed as in verse 9. It may be, however, that Paul intended a more general statement and focused attention upon the heart as the organ of faith and the mouth as the organ of confession. "Heart" and "mouth" have the positions of emphasis. In either case this emphasis must not be overlooked, and thus again the stress falls upon the necessity of confession with the mouth as well as belief of the heart. (2) There is a specification in this verse that does not appear in verse 9. Faith is unto *righteousness*, confession is unto *salvation*, whereas in verse 9 salvation is said to be the common effect of both. In accord with 9:30–33; 10:2–6 the righteousness contemplated must be that which is unto justification and it is consonant with the teaching of the epistle throughout that faith should be represented as the instrument. Thus when Paul becomes more analytic than in verse 9 we find what we would expect—that faith is directed to *righteousness* (for exposition *cf. ad* 1:16, 17; 3:22; 4:1–12 *passim*). Confession is unto salvation as faith is unto righteousness. This cannot mean confession to the exclusion of faith. Such a supposition would be contrary to verse 9 and other passages (*cf.* 1:16; Eph. 2:8).

It does, however, draw attention to the place of confession with the mouth. Confession verifies and confirms the faith of the heart. Verse 11 is another appeal to Isaiah 28:16 (*cf.* 9:33) with the insertion on the apostle's part of "whosoever". This emphasis, implied though not expressed in Isaiah, is supplied in anticipation of verses 12, 13.

12, 13 "For there is no distinction" gives the reason for the "whosoever" of verse 11. Upon the absence of differentiation in respect of sin and condemnation, on the one hand, and opportunity of salvation, on the other, Paul had repeatedly reflected (*cf.* 1:16; 3:9, 19, 22, 23, 29, 30; 4:11, 12; 9:24). The distinctive feature of this text is the reason given in the latter half. In 3:29, 30 the oneness of God is given as the reason why God justifies Jews and Gentiles through faith. Here in verse 12 the same kind of argument is derived from the lordship of Christ: "the same *Lord* is Lord of all".[14] That Christ is in view should be apparent from the immediately preceding context as well as from Paul's usage in general (*cf.* vs. 9). When it is said that he "is rich unto all that call upon him", the thought is not so much that of the riches that reside in Christ (*cf.* Eph. 3:8) as that of the readiness and fulness with which he receives those who call upon him. Verse 13 is again confirmation from the Old Testament (Joel 2:32; Heb. and LXX 3:5). This formula "call upon the name of the Lord" is a characteristic Old Testament way of expressing the worship that is addressed to God and applies specifically to the worship of supplication (*cf.* Gen. 4:26; 12:8; 13:4; 21:33; 26:25; I Kings 18:24; II Kings 5:11; Psalms 79:6; 105:1; 116:4, 13; Isa. 64:7). Joel 2:32 has the same significance as belongs to it elsewhere. When Paul applies the same to Christ this is another example of the practice of taking Old Testament passages which refer to God without qualification and applying them to Christ. It was the distinguishing mark of New Testament believers that they called upon the name of the Lord Jesus (*cf.* Acts 9:14, 21; 22:16; I Cor. 1:2; II Tim. 2:22) and therefore accorded to him the worship that belonged to God alone. In the present text the formula is applied to initial faith in Christ but should not be restricted to the act of commitment to Christ which believing in Christ specifically denotes.

---

14 αὐτός is subject and κύριος is predicate.

57

Calling upon the name of the Lord is a more inclusive act of worship that presupposes faith.

14, 15 These two verses are obviously related to the preceding. They are an analysis of the process involved in calling upon the Lord's name. But in the development of the apostle's thought they sustain a closer relation to what follows and prepare for the statement in verse 16: "But they did not all obey the gospel". The logical sequence set forth in these two verses scarcely needs comment. The main point is that the saving relation to Christ involved in calling upon his name is not something that can occur in a vacuum; it occurs only in a context created by proclamation of the gospel on the part of those commissioned to proclaim it. The sequence is therefore: authorized messengers, proclamation, hearing, faith, calling on the Lord's name. This is summed up in verse 17: "faith is of hearing, and hearing through the word of Christ".

The faith referred to in the first part of verse 14 is the faith of trust, of commitment to Christ,[15] and the proposition implied in the question is that there must be this trust in Christ if we are to call upon his name. The richness of calling upon Christ is thus again indicated and means that there is the relinquishment of every other confidence and abandonment to him as our only help (*cf.* Psalm 116:3, 4; Jonah 2:2). In the next clause, "how shall they believe him[16] whom they have not heard?", it is not likely that any weaker sense is given to the word "believe" than in the preceding clause though the construction differs.[17] A striking feature of this clause is that Christ is represented as being heard in the gospel when proclaimed by the sent messengers. The implication is that Christ speaks in the gospel proclamation. It is in this light that what precedes and what follows must be understood. The personal commitment which faith implies is coordinate with the encounter with Jesus' own words in the gospel message. And the dignity of the messengers, reflected on later, is derived from the fact that they are the Lord's spokesmen. In the last clause of verse 14 the apostle is thinking of the institution which is the ordinary and most effectual means of propagating the gospel,

---

[15] The $\varepsilon i\varsigma$ goes with $\dot{\varepsilon}\pi i\sigma\tau\varepsilon\upsilon\sigma\alpha\nu$. $\dot{\varepsilon}\pi\iota\kappa\alpha\lambda\dot{\varepsilon}\omega$ takes a direct object, as in verses 12, 13.

[16] There is no need to insert the preposition "in" before "him".

[17] That is to say "believe" is not to be given the bare sense of crediting.

namely, the official preaching of the Word by those appointed to this task.[18] Verse 15 reflects on the necessity of God's commission to those who undertake this office. The presumption of arrogating to oneself this function is apparent from what had just been stated. Those who preach are Christ's spokesmen and only the person upon whom he has laid his hand may act in that capacity. But if the emphasis falls on the necessity of Christ's commission, we may not overlook the privilege and joy involved in being sent. It is the sanctity belonging to the commission that enhances its dignity when possessed. This is the force of the quotation which the apostle appends, derived from Isaiah 52:7 but an abridgement of the same and expressing its central feature. In the original setting the passage is one of consolation to Israel in the Babylonish captivity and may well be regarded as the prophecy of restoration (*cf.* vss. 4, 5, 9, 10). It has broader reference and can be applied to the more ultimate salvation accomplished by the Messiah. In its immediate reference the messenger is viewed as swift-footedly[19] coming over the mountains with the good tidings of peace and salvation to Zion. The feet are said to be beautiful because their movements betray the character of the message being brought. The essential thought the apostle expresses by saying, "how beautiful are the feet of them that preach good tidings!" The purpose is to declare the inestimable treasure which the institution of gospel proclamation implies, a treasure that consists in the sending of messengers to preach the Word of Christ. The word from Isaiah is thus applied to that of which the restoration from Babylon was typical. And as the prophecy found its climactic fulfilment in the Messiah himself so it continues to be exemplified in the messengers whom he has appointed to be his ambassadors (*cf.* II Cor. 5:20).

10:16–21

> 16 But they did not all hearken to the glad tidings. For Isaiah saith, Lord, who hath believed our report?

---

[18] "By this very statement, therefore, he has made it clear that the apostolic ministry..., by which the message of eternal life is brought to us, is valued equally with the Word" (Calvin: *op. cit., ad loc.*).

[19] *Cf.* Franz Delitzsch: *Biblical Commentary on the Prophecies of Isaiah* (E. T., Edinburgh, 1881), II, *ad Isa.* 52:7.

17 So belief *cometh* of hearing, and hearing by the word of Christ.
18 But I say, Did they not hear? Yea, verily,
Their sound went out into all the earth,
And their words unto the ends of the world.
19 But I say, Did Israel not know? First Moses saith,
I will provoke you to jealousy with that which is no nation,
With a nation void of understanding will I anger you.
20 And Isaiah is very bold, and saith,
I was found of them that sought me not;
I became manifest unto them that asked not of me.
21 But as to Israel he saith, All the day long did I spread out my hands unto a disobedient and gainsaying people.

16, 17 At verse 16 the apostle returns to that subject which permeates this section of the epistle, the unbelief of Israel. "But they did not all obey the gospel". Although stated in a way that would hold true if only a minority had been disobedient, yet the mass of Israel is viewed as in this category. In the next part of the verse the paucity of the number of the obedient is implied in the question quoted from Isaiah. The unbelief of Israel is corroborated by the word of the prophet: "Lord, who hath believed our report?" (Isa. 53:1). Paul quotes from the Greek version. The term for "report" is the same as appears twice in verse 17 and is there rendered "hearing". It is apparent that in verse 16 this term must mean message or report, namely, that which was heard. It is not impossible to carry over this same meaning to verse 17 and the thought would be that faith arises from the message proclaimed and this message is through or consists in the word of Christ. But it is preferable to take the word in verse 17 in the sense of hearing. It is characteristic of Paul to change from one shade of meaning to another in the use of the same term in the same context (*cf.* 14:4, 5, 13). The verb corresponding to the term in question is used of hearing in verse 14 and again in verse 18. On the assumption that the act of hearing is the sense in verse 17 there are two observations. (1) That faith comes from hearing is a reiteration of what is implied in verse 14: "how shall they believe him whom they have not heard?" and means that there cannot be faith

60

except as the gospel is communicated in proclamation and comes within our apprehension through hearing.[20] (2) It might seem to be redundant to add the second clause of verse 17. For is not the word of Christ that which constitutes the gospel of which Paul had been speaking in verses 14–16? There is, however, an eloquent reiteration of what is implied but is now expressly stated to be "the word of Christ" in order to eliminate all doubt as to what is encountered in the gospel proclamation. It is the word in the sense used in verse 8, but the special interest now is to show that this word is that which Christ speaks (cf. John 3:34; 5:47; 6:63, 68; 12:47, 48; 17:8; Acts 5:20; Eph. 5:26; 6:17; I Pet. 1:25).

18 It might appear from verse 17 that hearing produces faith or at least that hearing is used in the sense of hearkening. The present verse obviates this misapprehension. "But I say, Did they not hear?" The answer is in effect: yes indeed they heard but, nevertheless, they did not hearken. In order to support the universalism of the gospel proclamation Paul quotes from Psalm 19:4 in the exact terms of the Greek version (LXX, Psalm 18:5). It has raised a difficulty that the psalmist here speaks of the works of creation and providence and not of special revelation. Was this due to a lapse of memory or to intentional artifice?[21] It is not necessary to resort to either supposition. We should remember that this psalm deals with general revelation (vss. 1–6) and with special revelation (vss. 7–14). In the esteem of the psalmist and in the teaching of Scripture throughout these two areas of revelation are complementary. This is Paul's own conception (cf. Acts 17:24–31). Since the gospel proclamation is now to all without distinction, it is proper to see the parallel between the universality of general revelation and the universalism of the gospel. The former is the pattern now followed in the sounding forth of the gospel to the uttermost parts of the earth. The application which Paul makes of Psalm 19:4 can thus be seen to be eloquent not only of this parallel but also of that which is implicit in the parallel, namely, the widespread diffusion of the gospel of grace. Its sound

---

[20] We are not to regard the apostle as excluding or disparaging other means of communication. But this is an index to the special place accorded to the *preaching* of the gospel.

[21] *Cf.* Leenhardt: *op. cit., ad loc.*

goes out to all the earth and its words to the end of the world. It cannot then be objected that Israel did not hear.

19–21 At the beginning of verse 19 the same form of expression is used as in verse 18, the only difference being that Israel is now specified and the word "hear" is changed to "know": "But I say, Did Israel not know?". As verse 18 is concerned with the question whether or not Israel *heard*, so verse 19 is concerned with the question whether or not Israel *knew*. The answer to the first was that Israel did hear; so to the second it is that Israel did know.[22] The only question is: *what* did Israel know? The answer is indicated in the quotations which follow (Deut. 32:21; Isa. 65:1, 2). The first is quoted as in the Greek version, which is close to the Hebrew, with the exception that the object of the verbs is changed from the third person plural to the second person. This word from the Song of Moses appears in a context in which Israel is being upbraided for unfaithfulness and perversity. This context corresponds to the situation with which Paul is dealing. The meaning of the quotation, particularly as interpreted and applied by the apostle, is that Israel would be provoked to jealousy and anger because another nation which had not enjoyed God's covenant favour as Israel had would become the recipient of the favour which Israel had despised. This implies the extension of gospel privilege to all peoples, the particular truth emphasized in verse 18. But the distinctive feature of verse 19 is not the universal diffusion of the gospel; it is the provocation of Israel as the by-product of this diffusion. Strangers and aliens will become partakers of covenant favour and blessing. This, therefore, is what Israel *knew*; they had been apprized and forewarned of the outcome, that the kingdom of God would be taken from them and given to a nation bringing forth its fruit. All the more forceful as proof of this knowledge is the appeal to the word of Moses.[23] Nothing could have more cogency for Israel than the testimony of Moses.

---

[22] In μὴ 'Ισραὴλ οὐκ ἔγνω the μή implies a negative answer to the negative οὐκ ἔγνω and a negative of the negative is the positive, "Israel did know". An alternative possibility is that μή is used in the sense "perhaps"; Paul, that is to say, envisages an interlocutor as saying, "Perhaps Israel did not know."
[23] πρῶτος could be understood as stylistic. This is the first instance that Paul adduces. But it should rather be taken as referring to the fact that Moses was the first to bear witness to the provoking of Israel to envy.

The next passage quoted to confirm the thesis that Israel knew is Isaiah 65:1. There is a transposition of the two clauses in the apostle's quotation but otherwise it adheres substantially to the Greek version. The lesson for Israel is that they had been informed by God through the prophet that favour would be shown to the Gentiles. The way in which this quotation is introduced implies that Isaiah had spoken with forthrightness and, since God is directly the speaker in this prophecy, the words "is very bold" point to the plainness with which the reception of the Gentiles had been foretold. There is a close similarity between this verse and 9:30. The Gentiles had not followed after righteousness. This is correlative with the terms now used that they had not sought or asked after the Lord.[24] As faith is said to be the way of attaining to righteousness in 9:30, so now the grace of God is manifest in the bestowal of what was not asked for or sought.

Verse 20 must not be dissociated in interpretation and application from verse 21. It is the contrast that is particularly relevant to the present interest. The contrast is that between the favour shown to the Gentiles and the disobedience of Israel. The aggravated character of the latter is made apparent by the terms that are used to express God's longsuffering and lovingkindness: "All the day long did I stretch out my hands". In Gifford's words, "it is a picture of *the everlasting arms* spread open in unwearied love".[25] The overtures of grace are not merely represented as rejected but as made to "a disobedient and gainsaying people". The perversity of Israel, on the one hand, and the constancy and intensity of God's lovingkindness, on the other, are accentuated by the fact that the one derives its character from the other. It is to a disobedient and contradicting people that the outstretched hands of entreaty are extended. The gravity of the sin springs from the contradiction offered to the overtures of mercy.

In this chapter the apostle is dealing with the failure of Israel. His analysis begins with the indictment that their zeal was not according to knowledge, that they were ignorant of God's righteousness and did not subject themselves to it. He continues this accusation by noting that they did not give obedience to the

---

[24] The paradox of being found when not sought indicates the sovereignty of grace.
[25] *Op. cit., ad loc.*

63

gospel. But the climax is reached in verse 21 when Israel is characterized as a disobedient and gainsaying people. The apostle demonstrates the inexcusableness of Israel and does so by appeal to their own Scriptures. They had heard the gospel. They knew beforehand the design of God respecting the call of the Gentiles. They had been forewarned of the very situation that existed in Paul's day and with which he is concerned in this part of the epistle. Verse 21 brings us to the terminus of the condemnation. We may well ask: what then? Is this the terminus of God's lovingkindness to Israel? Is verse 21 the last word? The answer to these questions chapter 11 provides.

XVII   THE RESTORATION OF ISRAEL
(11:1–36)

A.   THE REMNANT AND THE REMAINDER
(11:1–10)

11:1–10

1 I say then, Did God cast off his people? God forbid.
For I also am an Israelite, of the seed of Abraham, of the
tribe of Benjamin.

2 God did not cast off his people which he foreknew. Or
know ye not what the scripture saith of Elijah? how he
pleadeth with God against Israel:

3 Lord, they have killed thy prophets, they have digged
down thine altars; and I am left alone, and they seek
my life.

4 But what saith the answer of God unto him? I have left
for myself seven thousand men, who have not bowed the
knee to Baal.

5 Even so then at this present time also there is a remnant
according to the election of grace.

6 But if it is by grace, it is no more of works: otherwise
grace is no more grace.

7 What then? That which Israel seeketh for, that he
obtained not; but the election obtained it, and the rest
were hardened:

8 according as it is written, God gave them a spirit of
stupor, eyes that they should not see, and ears that they
should not hear, unto this very day.

9 And David saith,
Let their table be made a snare, and a trap,
And a stumblingblock, and a recompense unto them:

10 Let their eyes be darkened, that they may not see,
And bow thou down their back always.

1   The question posed by the unbelief of Israel as a people

pervades this section of the epistle.[1] It comes to the forefront at various points and in different forms (*cf.* 9:1–3, 27, 29, 31, 32; 10:2, 3, 21). At 11:1 another aspect of the sáme question is introduced. At 9:6ff. the apostle dealt with what might appear to be the effect of Israel's unbelief, namely, that God's word of promise had come to nought, at 9:14ff. with the question as it pertains to God's justice. Now the question is whether the apostasy of Israel means God's rejection of them. It is not, however, in these terms that the question is asked. It is asked in a way that points up the gravity of the issue and anticipates what the answer must be: "did God cast off his people?" The answer, as repeatedly in this epistle (*cf.* 3:4, 6, 31; 6:2, 15; 7:7, 13; 9:14), is the most emphatic negative available. The ground for this negative answer is implicit in the terms used in the question. For Paul's question is in terms that are reminiscent of the Old Testament passages which affirm that God will not cast off his people (I Sam. 12:22; Psalm 94:14 (LXX 93:14); *cf.* Jer. 31:37).

The second part of verse 1 is an additional reason for the negative reply. There are two views of the force of the apostle's appeal to his own identity as an Israelite, of the seed of Abraham and of the tribe of Benjamin. One is that, since he is of Israel, his acceptance by God affords proof that God had not completely abandoned Israel.[2] The appeal to his own salvation would be of marked relevance because of his previous adamant opposition to the gospel (*cf.* Gal. 1:13, 14; I Tim. 1:13–15). The unbelief of Israel (*cf.* 10:21) had been exemplified in no one more than in Saul of Tarsus. The mercy he received is proof that God's mercy had not forsaken Israel. On this view, "of the seed of Abraham, of the tribe of Benjamin" would serve to accentuate his identity as truly one of that race with which he is now concerned. The other view is that the appeal to his own identity is the reason given for the *vehemence* of his negative reply "God forbid" and, therefore, the reason why he recoils from the suggestion that God had cast off his people.[3] His own kinship with Israel, his Israelitish identity,

---

[1] The addition of ὃν προέγνω after τὸν λαὸν αὐτοῦ in P⁴⁶, A, D* is no doubt an insertion following the pattern of verse 2 and should not be accepted as genuine.

[2] Perhaps the most pronounced exponent of this view is Philippi in *op. cit.*, *ad loc.*; *cf.* also Luther, Calvin, Hodge, Godet, Liddon, Gaugler, *et al.*

[3] *Cf.* particularly Meyer: *op. cit.*, *ad loc.* but also Sanday and Headlam, Gifford, and apparently C. H. Dodd.

constrains the reaction, "may it not be". More meaning can be attached to "of the seed of Abraham, of the tribe of Benjamin" on this interpretation. These additions would drive home the depth of his attachment to Israel and emphasize the reason for his revulsion from the proposition that God had cast off his people. Both views are tenable and there does not appear to be enough evidence to decide for one against the other.

2 It might seem that no more than what is stated in the second part of verse 1 would have been necessary to answer the question at the beginning. But the negative reply is now confirmed by direct denial. The denial is in the express terms used in the question with the addition of the clause "which he foreknew". The qualification which this clause provides offers the strongest reason for the denial; the "foreknowing" is the guarantee that God has not cast off his people. The question on which expositors are divided is whether the clause applies to the people of Israel as a whole or whether it is to be understood restrictively as applying only to the elect of Israel in distinction from the nation as a whole.[4] The strongest consideration in support of the latter view is the appeal on the part of the apostle to the differentiation and, therefore, to the restriction involved in particular election in verses 4-7. It may not be doubted but it is the election of a remnant from Israel (vs. 5) that offers proof that God had not cast off Israel as a people. The same type of argument is present in this chapter as is found earlier in 9:6ff. In 9:6ff. the proof that the word of God had not failed resides in the differentiation between the true Israel and those of Israel, between the true seed and those of mere descent. So in the present instance the election of grace is the demonstration that Israel as a people had not been completely cast off by God. But it is not apparent that the qualifying clause in 11:2 must be understood as referring only to the specific and particular election of verses 4-7. As noted above, it is Israel as a whole that is in view in verse 1.[5] The answers in the latter part of verse 1 apply to Israel as a whole. The first part of verse 2 is the direct reply unfolding what is implicit in the latter

---

[4] The arguments in support of this interpretation are most ably presented by Hodge: *op. cit., ad loc.*; *cf.* Calvin, Haldane, *et al.* and *contra* Meyer, Philippi, Liddon, Gifford, Godet, Sanday and Headlam.
[5] Likewise in 10:21 it is the people as a whole who are in view.

part of verse 1. It would be difficult to suppose that the denotation is abruptly changed at the point where this direct denial is introduced. It is more tenable, therefore, to regard "his people" (vs. 1) and "his people which he foreknew" (vs. 2) as identical in their reference and the qualifying clause in verse 2 as expressing what is really implied in the designation "his people". If Israel can be called God's "people", it is only that which is implied in "foreknowledge" that warrants the appellation. There should be no difficulty in recognizing the appropriateness of calling Israel the people whom God foreknew. Israel had been elected and peculiarly loved and thus distinguished from all other nations (*cf.* the evidence adduced and comments thereupon under 9:10–13, pp. 12ff). It is in this sense that "foreknew" would be used in this case.[6] Paul then proceeds to adduce an example from the Old Testament. This instance is relevant because it provides a parallel to the situation with which he is dealing and furnishes a fitting illustration of what is his main interest in succeeding verses, namely, that notwithstanding widespread apostasy in Israel there is "a remnant according to the election of grace".

"Or know ye not" is an arresting way of indicating what the readers are assumed to know or, at least, ought to know and is a favourite expression in Paul (*cf.* 6:16; I Cor. 3:16; 5:6; 6:2, 3, 9, 15, 16, 19, and also to the same effect Rom. 6:3; 7:1). "Of Elijah" refers to that section of Scripture which deals with Elijah and in the Greek, for this reason, reads "in Elijah". Elijah's pleading with God against Israel is not to be understood as making intercession to God for Israel but, as the term "against" indicates, refers to the appeal made against Israel and therefore to the *accusation* quoted in verse 3 from I Kings 19:10, 14.

3, 4 Apart from inversion of order and some abridgement the quotation in verse 3 follows the Hebrew and Greek of the passage concerned. The particular interest of these verses is focused in the reply to Elijah's complaint and the relation of this answer to the apostle's theme. The answer[7] (vs. 4) is taken from I Kings 19:18.

---

[6] See 8:29 for the meaning of προέγνω. It has inherent in itself the differentiating ingredient. But in this instance it has the more generic application as in Amos 3:2 and not the particularizing and strictly soteric import found in 8:29 (*cf.* πρόγνωσις in I Pet. 1:2).

[7] χρηματισμός is used only here in the New Testament but for the corresponding verb *cf.* Matt. 2:12, 22; Acts 10:22; Heb. 8:5; 11:7. The answer is the oracular reply; *cf.* Sanday and Headlam: *op. cit., ad loc.*

The reproduction, though conveying the thought, is modified from both the Hebrew and the Greek in accord with the freedom the apostle applies in other cases. The oracle is not merely that there were seven thousand left who had not bowed to Baal. Emphasis is placed upon God's action; he had reserved these. And Paul introduces the thought that God had kept *for himself* the seven thousand.[8] There is the note of efficacious grace and differentiation. The effectiveness of the discrimination is indicated by the way in which the result of God's preserving grace is stated: they are men of such sort that they did not bow the knee to Baal.

Though the number corrects Elijah's mistaken estimate of the situation and is far in excess of what his complaint would imply, yet it should be noted that the seven thousand were only a remnant. This fact underscores the widespread apostasy in Israel at that time and points to the parallel between Elijah's time and the apostle's. This is a consideration basic to the use Paul makes of the Old Testament passage. Notwithstanding the apostasy of Israel as a whole, yet there was a remnant, though only a remnant, whom God had kept for himself and preserved from the idolatry of Baal's worship. This example is adduced to prove that God had not cast off Israel as his chosen and beloved people. The import, therefore, is that the salvation of a small remnant from the total mass is sufficient proof that the people as a nation had not been cast off.

5, 6   From the parallel situation in the days of Elijah Paul makes the application to his own time and concludes that there is a remnant according to the election of grace. According to the argument there is a necessity for a remnant, however widespread may be Israel's unbelief and apostasy. The necessity resides in the fact that Israel God had loved and elected. For that reason they are "his people which he foreknew". That he should utterly cast them off is incompatible with electing love. The guarantee that this abandonment had not occurred is not denial of the widespread apostasy with its resultant rejection on God's part but the existence

---

[8] "There is nothing in the Hebrew corresponding to the words '*for myself*' (ἐμαυτῷ), which St. Paul adds to bring out more emphatically the thought that the remnant is preserved by God Himself for His own gracious purpose" (Gifford: *op. cit., ad loc.*).

of a remnant. Therefore, since God's "foreknowledge" cannot fail of its purpose, there is always a remnant. The seven thousand in Elijah's day exemplify the operation of this principle because it was a time of patent and aggravated apostasy in Israel. But as it was in Elijah's day so also is it now.

The idea of a remnant is present in verse 4.[9] In 9:27 this notion appears in the quotation from Isaiah 10:22. Now, however, the term is used expressly to designate the distinctive segment of Israel defined by the election of grace. The precise form of expression is that there has come to be a remnant according to the election of grace[10] and this means that the distinguishing identity of those thus characterized proceeds from God's gracious election. This description of the source shows of itself that the differentiation finds its whole explanation in the sovereign will of God and not in any determination proceeding from the will of man. Either term bears this implication and the combination "the election of grace" makes the emphasis cumulative. In verse 6 the apostle adds further definition of what is implicit in the expression "election of grace", and he does so by setting up the antithesis between grace and human performance. If grace is conditioned in any way by human performance or by the will of man impelling to action, then grace ceases to be grace. This verse as specifying the true character of grace in contrast with works serves the same purpose at this point as does "not of works, but of him that calleth" in 9:11 (*cf.* also Eph. 2:8b).[11]

7–10 "What then?" is the way of asking: what is the conclusion to be drawn from what precedes? The situation in view with respect to which the question is asked is that dealt with in the six verses preceding. The apostle is concerned with the apostasy of Israel as a whole. This constrains the question: has God therefore cast off his chosen people? The answer is negative but not negative in such a way as to deny the empirical fact of Israel's apostasy. The answer finds its validation in the fact that there is still a

---

[9] λεῖμμα (vs. 5) is cognate with κατέλιπον (vs. 4).

[10] The perfect γέγονεν has this force.

[11] Verse 6 ends with οὐκέτι γίνεται χάρις in P⁴⁶, ℵ*, A, D, G, and other uncials as well as several versions. The longer ending is supported by ℵᶜ, L, and most of the cursives. B has a shorter form of the longer ending. The longer ending expands the thought of the shorter form of verse 6 and was probably a marginal note that found its way into the text in the course of transmission.

remnant of Israel whom God has elected and reserved for himself. This is just saying that the negative answer is demanded because of the differentiation between the mass and the remnant. The answer to "what then?" is, therefore, a summary assessment of the total situation unfolded in verses 1–6 and viewed from the perspective of Israel's *failure* as the way of interpreting the unbelief with which the whole passage is concerned. The way of stating Israel's failure—"that which Israel seeketh for, that he obtained not"—is similar to, and substantially to the same effect as, what we found already in 9:31, 32; 10:2, 3. It is reasonable to infer that what Israel is represented as seeking for, though not stated in this verse, is the righteousness mentioned in 9:31; 10:3. This righteousness Israel did not obtain and the reason is given in 9:32; 10:3.

When Paul says "the election obtained it" he means the elect. But he uses the abstract noun in order to lay stress on "the idea rather than on the individuals"[12] and thus accentuates the action of God as the reason. "The election", in the evaluation of the situation given in this verse, is parallel to "I have left for myself seven thousand men" in verse 4 and "a remnant according to the election of grace" in verse 5 and fulfils the same purpose in pointing to the act of God's grace by which is obviated the inference that God has cast off his people. What the elect have obtained is the righteousness of God and with it God's favour and acceptance.

"The election of grace" and "the election" of verses 5 and 7 must refer to the particular election of individuals in distinction from the theocratic election referred to in "his people" (vs. 1) and "his people which he foreknew" (vs. 2). This distinction we found earlier in the exposition of 9:10–13. But the reasons for the same conclusion in this context are to be noted. (1) There is sustained differentiation in the whole passage, in verse 4 between the mass of Israel and the seven thousand, in verse 5 between the mass and the remnant, in verse 7 between the hardened and the election. We are compelled to inquire as to the source, implications, and consequences of this distinction. (2) The election is said to be "of grace" (vs. 5) and the apostle in verse 6 is careful to define the true character of grace in contrast with works. When Paul emphasizes grace in this way it is the grace unto salvation that is in view (*cf.* 3:24; 4:16; 5:20, 21; Gal. 2:21; Eph. 2:5, 8; I Tim.

---

[12] Sanday and Headlam: *op. cit., ad loc.*

1:14; II Tim. 1:9). (3) "The election" (vs. 7) is said to have obtained it and, as noted abo̔ve, the thing obtained cannot be anything less than the righteousness unto eternal life (*cf.* 5:18, 21). (4) The seven thousand (vs. 4) are said to have been kept for God himself and as not having bowed a knee to Baal. As characterizations these imply a relation to God similar to the obtaining of righteousness, favour, and life of verse 7. These reasons render it impossible to think of the election as anything other than the election unto salvation of which the apostle speaks elsewhere in his epistles (*cf.* 8:33; Eph. 1:4; Col. 3:12; I Thess. 1:4; II Tim. 2:1; Tit. 1:1). These considerations derived from this context are confirmatory of what we have found above regarding the election referred to in 9:11.

"The rest were hardened." The contextual emphasis upon election as entirely of grace and therefore upon the free and sovereign will of God as the determining cause of the differentiation involved requires us to apply in this case the same doctrine stated earlier in 9:18: "so then he hath mercy on whom he will, and whom he will he hardeneth".[13] Furthermore, ultimate issues are bound up with this hardening. There are several reasons for this conclusion. (1) Election is bound up with the issue of righteousness unto life and therefore with salvation; hardening as the antithesis cannot have a less ultimate issue in the opposite direction. (2) The hardened are those in view in verse 7 when we read: "that which Israel seeketh for, that he obtained not"; "obtained not" means coming short of the righteousness that is unto life and therefore of salvation. (3) The parallel in 9:18 means, because of the antithesis, that the hardened are not the partakers of God's mercy and thus not of the salvation of which mercy is the only explanation.

The subject of the hardening is not mentioned in this verse as in 9:18. But, as we shall discover in the verses which follow, there does not need to be doubt that the same subject, namely, God is in view as in 9:18. We may not abstract this hardening from the sustained indictment brought against Israel in the preceding context. "Israel, following after a law of righteousness, did not arrive at that law. Wherefore? Because they sought it not by

---

[13] In 9:18 the verb is σκληρύνω; in 11:7 it is πωρόω which can be rendered "blinded" (*cf.* II Cor. 3:14). But the meaning is not essentially different. Both terms refer to moral and religious insensitivity.

faith, but as it were by works" (9:31, 32). "Being ignorant of God's righteousness, and seeking to establish their own, they did not subject themselves to the righteousness of God" (10:3). "But they did not all hearken to the glad tidings" (10:16). "But as to Israel he saith, All the day long did I spread out my hands unto a disobedient and gainsaying people" (10:21). It is judicial hardening and finds its judicial ground in the unbelief and disobedience of its objects. This does not, however, interfere with the sovereign will of God as the cause of the differentiation which appears here as at 9:18. The elect have not been the objects of this hardening. But the reason is not that they had made themselves to differ. Election was all of grace and the elect deserved the same hardening. But of mercy (9:18) and of grace (vss. 5, 6) they were not consigned to their ill-desert. Thus grace as the reason for differentiation and unbelief as the ground of the judicial infliction are both accorded their proper place and emphasis.

In verses 8–10 Old Testament passages are adduced to support and confirm the proposition in verse 7 that "the rest were hardened". Verse 8 is for the most part taken from Deuteronomy 29:4 (LXX 29:3). Instead of the negative form of Deuteronomy, "the Lord hath not given you a heart to know", the positive form, "God gave them a spirit of stupor",[14] is adopted and this corresponds more closely to Isaiah 29:10 where God is the agent in pouring out the spirit of deep sleep. This form is taken over because the apostle wishes to represent the hardening as wrought by God himself. The action of God is likewise carried over to the two clauses which follow. He gave eyes so that they would not see and ears so that they would not hear.[15] God's hardening of Israel in Paul's day is parallel to that in the days of Moses and Isaiah. Verses 9 and 10 are taken from Psalm 69:22, 23 (LXX 68:23, 24) and with slight modification in verse 9 follows the terms of the Greek version. The messianic reference of Psalm 69:21 is apparent (cf. Matt. 27:34, 48). In the succeeding verses we have David as

---

14 πνεῦμα κατανύξεως may best be taken as a spirit characterized by stupor. As Gifford says, "'spirit' is used for the pervading tendency and tone of mind, the special character of which is denoted by the Genitive which follows" (op. cit., ad loc.).
15 "Unto this very day" may be compared with Stephen's indictment, "ye do always resist" (Acts 7:51).

God's mouthpiece uttering imprecatory curses.[16] The words "snare", "trap",[17] and "stumblingblock" are closely related and distinction of meaning is not to be pressed. The combination serves to enforce the purpose and effect of turning "their table" into the opposite of its intent. The table stands for the bounties of God's providence placed upon it and the thought may be that those concerned are conceived of as partaking of these gifts in ease and content but instead of peaceful enjoyment they are caught as in a trap or snare (cf. Dan. 5:1, 4, 5), overtaken by the judgments of God. In any case the table as intended for comfort and enjoyment is turned to be the occasion of the opposite. The word "recompense" bespeaks the retribution meted out and therefore confirms the judicial character of the hardening (vs. 7) and of the spirit of stupor (vs. 8). The judicial blinding, already expressed in verse 8, is reiterated in the first part of verse 10 in stronger terms. The last clause in verse 10 differs from the Hebrew though identical with the Greek version. It is difficult to know whether the figure of a back bowed down portrays the bondage of slaves bending under a heavy burden or represents the bowing down under grief, especially that of terror. The Hebrew, "make their loins continually to shake", suggests the latter.

The application of these Old Testament passages to the unbelief of Jewry in Paul's day has relevance surpassing anything that could have been true in Israel's earlier history. The movements of redemptive revelation and history had reached their climax in the coming and accomplishments of Christ, and the contradiction (cf. 10:21) which Israel offered correspondingly climaxed the gravity of the sin which had been exemplified in the successive stages of Israel's history.

---

[16] "In this, as in Ps. cix and Ps. cxxxix. 21 'Do not I hate them, O Lord, that hate Thee?' the Psalmist regards the enemies of the Theocracy as his own, and his own enemies as enemies only so far as they fought against the Divine order of the world. The imprecations, therefore, are only the form which 'Thy Will be done' necessarily assumes in the presence of aggressive evil. They are a prayer that the Divine Justice might be revealed in action for the protection of the cause of Truth and Righteousness against its enemies. So far are they from being 'peculiar to the moral standard of Judaism,' that they are, as here, deliberately adopted by the inspired teachers of Christianity" (Liddon: op. cit., p. 202).

[17] καὶ εἰς θήραν is added by Paul.

74

B. THE FULNESS OF ISRAEL
(11:11-24)

11 I say then, Did they stumble that they might fall? God forbid: but by their fall salvation *is come* unto the Gentiles, to provoke them to jealousy.

12 Now if their fall is the riches of the world, and their loss the riches of the Gentiles; how much more their fulness?

13 But I speak to you that are Gentiles. Inasmuch then as I am an apostle of Gentiles, I glorify my ministry;

14 if by any means I may provoke to jealousy *them that are* my flesh, and may save some of them.

15 For if the casting away of them *is* the reconciling of the world, what *shall* the receiving *of them be*, but life from the dead?

11, 12 In the preceding verses the thesis is that although Israel as a whole had been disobedient yet a remnant was left and therefore God had not cast off his people. Israel's rejection was not *complete*. The thesis in the verses which follow is that the rejection is not *final*. Both considerations–not complete but partial, not final but temporary–support the proposition that God had not cast off his people.

"I say then", as in verse 1, is Paul's way of introducing a question intended to obviate a conclusion which might seem to follow from what precedes. The question: "did they stumble that they might fall?" is answered with the usual emphatic negative, "God forbid". It cannot be doubted but the mass of Israel stumbled (*cf.* 9:32, 33), and it cannot be doubted that this meant a fall with the gravest consequences (*cf.* vss. 7–10). So neither the stumbling nor the corresponding fall[18] is denied. What then is the

---

[18] If πέσωσιν is taken to mean "fall utterly and permanently" (*cf.* Philippi and Liddon), then what would be denied would be the permanent rejection of Israel and in this way, as Philippi says, "the apostle intimates by anticipation the closing thought of the subsequent exposition" (*op. cit., ad loc.*). This does not appear to be the thought at this point. Surely those who stumbled did fall with ultimate consequences. Is not the denotation of those in view the same as those mentioned in verse 7: "the rest were hardened"? And is not Paul thinking here of those contemplated in verse 22: "toward them that fell, severity"? The interpretation, therefore, appears to be required that what Paul is reflecting on here is the more ultimate and gracious design of God in the stumbling and fall of the mass of Israel at the time with which he was dealing.

meaning of the negative reply? The construction supplies the answer. The question is not: "did they stumble and fall?" To that question an affirmative answer would be required. Everything here turns on the clause, "that they might fall". The negative answer means that the purpose of their stumbling was not that they might fall but was directed to and designed for another end, the end immediately appended in the latter part of the verse. This purpose is not viewed as that entertained by Israel when they stumbled as if they stumbled with the intent of thereby promoting the salvation of the Gentiles. It is on God's purpose the apostle is reflecting and the purpose of Israel in stumbling is not within the purview of the passage either negatively or positively. We are here advised, therefore, of the overriding and overruling design of God in the stumbling and fall of Israel. This is that "by their fall salvation is come unto the Gentiles, to provoke them to jealousy". The rendering is unfortunate. It is "by their trespass" rather than "by their fall". What is in view is the stumbling of Israel, their rejection of Christ as Saviour. This was their trespass and it is by this that salvation came to the Gentiles. This development is exemplified in Jesus' prediction and in the history of the apostolic era (cf. Matt. 8:12; 21:43; Acts 13:46; 18:6; 28:28). The same fact is referred to again in verses 15, 25. The salvation of the Gentiles is itself of sufficient magnitude to evince the gracious design fulfilled through the trespass of Israel and therefore sufficient to warrant denial of the proposition that Israel stumbled merely for the purpose that they might fall. In the construction of the sentence, however, the salvation of the Gentiles is subordinate to another design. This subordination is not to depreciate the significance of the Gentiles' salvation. To this Paul returns repeatedly later on. But it is striking that this result should here be represented as subserving the saving interests of Israel. It is "to provoke them to jealousy". Several observations are to be elicited from this latter part of verse 11.

(1) The ethnic distinction between the Gentiles and Israel appearing earlier in these chapters (cf. 9:25, 26, 30, 31; 10:19, 20) is here again brought to the forefront. The saving design contemplated in "to provoke them to jealousy" has in view, therefore, the salvation of Israel viewed in their distinct racial identity. This obviates any contention to the effect that God's saving design does not embrace Israel as a racial entity distinguished by the place

which Israel occupied in the past history of redemption. While it is true that in respect of the privileges accruing from Christ's accomplishments there is now no longer Jew or Gentile and the Gentiles "are fellow-heirs, and fellow-members of the body, and fellow-partakers of the promise in Christ Jesus through the gospel" (Eph. 3:6), yet it does not follow that Israel no longer fulfils any *particular* design in the realization of God's worldwide saving purpose. (2) Paradoxically, the unbelief of Israel is directed to the restoration of Israel's faith and the fall of Israel to their reclamation. We already anticipate Paul's adoring amazement: "O the depth of the riches both of the wisdom and the knowledge of God!" (vs. 33). (3) Provoking to jealousy[19] is not an unworthy incentive to repentance and faith. It is here incorporated in God's design. Later (vs. 14) the apostle says that he conducts his ministry to the Gentiles with the same end in view. The idea is that the Jews observing the favour and blessing of God bestowed upon the Gentiles and the privileges of the kingdom of God accruing therefrom will be moved to emulation and thereby induced to turn to the Lord. It is eminently proper to emulate such gifts as the faith of the gospel secures. (4) The unbelief of Israel is ordained to promote the salvation of the Gentiles. But this implied faith on the part of the Gentiles is not, in turn, to be prejudicial to Israel's salvation; it is to promote the same.

In verse 12 the translation should again be: "now if their trespass is the riches of the world". The trespass is the same as in verse 11b and pointing back to the stumbling of verse 11a. Verse 12 is the beginning of an *a fortiori* argument and uses the fact stated in verse 11b to press home the greater result that will accrue for the Gentile world by the faith of Israel in contrast with their unbelief. "The riches of the world" is the salvation that has come to the Gentiles by the trespass (unbelief) of Israel and in this verse "the world" and "the Gentiles" are synonymous in their denotation.[20] Since this is so the accent must largely fall upon the distinction between "trespass" and "loss". At least it would be difficult to explain the virtual repetition "the riches of the world" and "the riches of the Gentiles" unless distinction resides in that

---

[19] In using this term Paul harks back to Moses' word in Deut. 32:21 quoted at 10:19.

[20] This does not mean that no purpose is served by varying the expression. κόσμος serves to emphasize the ethnic universalism.

with which these are conjoined respectively. The word rendered "loss" has been variously interpreted. The rendering "diminishing" (AV) is not supported by usage and the only apparent reason for adopting the same is that it provides a fitting contrast with fulness. The evidence indicates that the term means defeat, overthrow, discomfiture (cf. Isa. 31:8; 51:7; I Cor. 6:7; II Pet. 2:19, 20).[21] Besides, "diminishing" would not agree with the parallels in the passage. If "diminishing" were in view this would apply only to the small number of the remnant. But that of which Paul is speaking here is that which has befallen the mass of Israel, their stumbling and fall (vs. 11a), their trespass (vss. 11b, 12a); and so the "loss" must be that of the mass of Israel and not anything characterizing the remnant. Furthermore, the meaning "defeat" is sufficiently distinct from trespass to warrant and explain the sequence, "their trespass the riches of the world and their defeat the riches of the Gentiles". What is in view is the great loss, as by overthrow in battle, sustained by Israel when the kingdom of God was taken from them. They are viewed after the figure of a defeated host and deprived of their heritage.[22]

"How much more their fulness." There should be no question but this is the fulness of Israel as a people. The stumbling was theirs, the fall was theirs, theirs was the trespass, and theirs the loss. The fulness, therefore, can have no other reference. What is "their fulness"? This word has a variety of meanings and applications. It often means the plenitude or totality. It can be the full complement. In this instance it is not merely contrasted with "loss" but also with "trespass". Whatever might be the precise term by which to express the import here, it is obvious that the condition or state denoted is one that stands in sharp contrast with the unbelief, the trespass, and the loss characterizing Israel when the apostle wrote. It points, therefore, to a condition marked by antithesis in these respects. This means that Israel is contemplated

---

[21] Cf. Frederick Field: *Notes on the Translation of the New Testament* (Cambridge, 1899), pp. 160f.; Lagrange: op. cit., p. 276; Gaugler, op. cit., p. 183; Philippi: op. cit., pp. 193ff. The only other instance of ἥττημα in the New Testament is I Cor. 6:7 but cf. ἡττάομαι in II Pet. 2:19, 20 and in LXX ἥττημα in Isa. 31:8 and the verb in Isa. 8:9; 13:15; 19:1; 20:5; 30:31; 31:4; 33:1; 51:7; 54:17.
[22] It would not be altogether out of the question to regard loss in verse 12 as parallel to the fall of verse 11 (πέσωσιν) just as trespass (παράπτωμα, vs. 12) corresponds to the stumbling (ἔπταισαν) of verse 11.

as characterized by the faith of Christ, by the attainment of righteousness, and by restoration to the blessing of God's kingdom as conspicuously as Israel then was marked by unbelief, trespass, and loss. No word could serve to convey the thought of the thoroughness and completeness of this contrast better than the term "fulness". For if "fulness" conveys any idea it is that of completeness. Hence nothing less than a restoration of Israel as a people to faith, privilege, and blessing can satisfy the terms of this passage. The *argument* of the apostle is not, however, the restoration of Israel; it is the blessing accruing to the Gentiles from Israel's "fulness". The "fulness" of Israel, with the implications stated above, is presupposed and from it is drawn the conclusion that the fulness of Israel will involve for the Gentiles a much greater enjoyment of gospel blessing than that occasioned by Israel's unbelief. Thus there awaits the Gentiles, in their distinctive identity as such, gospel blessing far surpassing anything experienced during the period of Israel's apostasy, and this unprecedented enrichment will be occasioned by the conversion of Israel on a scale commensurate with that of their earlier disobedience. We are not informed at this point what this unprecedented blessing will be. But in view of the thought governing the context, namely, the conversion of the Gentiles and then that of Israel, we should expect that the enlarged blessing would be the expansion of the success attending the gospel and of the kingdom of God.

13, 14 The two preceding verses have been concerned with the grace bestowed upon the Gentiles by Israel's unbelief and with the promise of greater blessing for the Gentiles when Israel turns to the Lord. The salvation of the Gentiles is thus the theme. In now addressing the Gentiles directly[23] Paul is impressing upon them the significance for their own highest well-being of Israel's conversion. There can be no segregation of interest. As apostle of the Gentiles (*cf.* 1:5; 12:3; 15:15, 16; Gal. 2:7-9; Acts 26:17, 18), his labours to fulfil that ministry in no way conflict with the interests of Israel. The more this ministry to the Gentiles is crowned with success the more is furthered the cause of Israel's salvation. This is why he says "I glorify my ministry" as apostle of the

---

[23] The clause "that are Gentiles" is not restrictive as might appear. Paul is addressing his readers as Gentiles. It is hard to suppress the inference that the Christian community at Rome was preponderantly Gentile.

Gentiles. The reason for this intimate relationship is that which had been stated in verse 11 respecting the purpose and providence of God, that the salvation of the Gentiles is directed to the end of moving Israel to jealousy. This same aim the apostle now states to be his own in the magnifying[24] and promoting of his Gentile ministry. What was said above (vs. 11) respecting the propriety of this impulsion applies in this case to the motivation of the apostle.

In verse 12 a mass restoration of Israel is in view. But here in verse 14 Paul does not say that his activity in provoking Israel to jealousy is in order that the fulness of Israel may be attained. He is much more modest. What he strives for is to stir up this emulation and "save some of them".[25] The same affection for his kinsfolk and zeal for their salvation, voiced on earlier occasions (*cf.* 9:2, 3; 10:1), appear again in this verse. But his zeal does not spill over into any excessive claims for the success of his ministry nor does he presume to state how his ministry of provoking to jealousy is related either causally or temporally to the "fulness" of Israel.

15 Although the apostle does not state in verse 14 how his ministry is causally related to the "fulness" of Israel, there is nevertheless a close relation between verses 13, 14 and verse 15. This is indicated by the terms with which verse 15 begins, "for if". The thesis in this section (vss. 11ff.) is that the apostasy of Israel is not final. This consideration provides the apostle with the incentive to pursue his ministry to the Gentiles and to glory in that office. For the more successful is that ministry the more Israel's salvation is promoted by their being moved to jealousy, and the salvation of Israel reacts for the more abundant blessing of the Gentiles. Thus the thought of verse 12 is reiterated in verse 15 and resumed in this instance in order to support the emphatic assertion of his ministry to the Gentiles in verses 13, 14. Though there is this reiteration in verse 15 the different terms are significant.

---

[24] The expression "glorify my ministry" involves the zealous pursuit of the Gentile ministry. But the term "glorify" does not itself express this; it means that he exalts his office.

[25] Since the provoking to jealousy is a factor in the conversion of Israel (vs. 11) and since Paul pursues his ministry to that end, his saving of some no doubt contributes to the "fulness" of Israel. But this he does not say.

For the first time Paul speaks of the "casting away"[26] of Israel. Hitherto he had spoken of their disobedience, their stumbling, their trespass, their defeat. The thought of rejection by God is no doubt implied, especially in the term "defeat". The accent falls, however, upon the action or failure of action on Israel's part. Now the accent is placed upon the action of God in having cast off Israel. The kingdom of God was taken from them (*cf.* Matt. 21:43). And just as the stumbling and trespass refer to the mass of Israel, so must the rejection. When the rejection is said to be the reconciling (preferably reconciliation) of the world, this is parallel to the result expressed in verses 11, 12, namely, the salvation of the Gentiles, the riches of the world, and the riches of the Gentiles. The term, however, has its own specific meaning and this is germane to the teaching of this verse in distinction from verses 11, 12. "Reconciliation" is contrasted with "casting away". The latter means rejection from the favour and blessing of God and reflects therefore on the attitude of God to Israel and the relation he sustains to them. So the accent falls distinctly upon God's attitude and action thereanent. Reconciliation is in contrast and likewise reflects on the attitude, relation, and action of God. The Gentiles are viewed as previously alienated from God and excluded from his favour. By God's action this alienation was exchanged for reconciliation and the attitude of disfavour exchanged for favour. This is a clear index to that on which the term "reconciliation" focuses attention.

In this verse again we have an *a fortiori* argument as in verse 12. The "receiving" is contrasted with the "casting away" and must, therefore, mean the reception of Israel again into the favour and blessing of God. In terms of the whole passage, as noted repeatedly, this must refer to Israel as a whole and implies that this restoration is commensurate in scale with Israel's rejection, the restoration of the mass of Israel in contrast with the "casting off". Again the accent falls on the action of God, in this case that of grace in contrast with judgment, and on the changed attitude of God to the mass of Israel. This restoration of Israel will have a marked beneficial effect, described as "life from the dead". Whatever this result may be it must denote a blessing far surpassing in its

----

[26] ἀποβολή means more than loss (*cf.* Philippi: *op. cit., ad loc.*). Any harshness belonging to the term is not to be eliminated. The meaning is fixed by the contrast with πρόσλημψις.

proportions anything that previously obtained in the unfolding of God's counsel. In this respect it will correspond to the effect accruing from the fulness of Israel (vs. 12).

The change of construction in verse 15 as compared with verse 12 is noteworthy. Paul does not say "how much more their receiving" as in verse 12 he says "how much more their fulness". In verse 12 we have to infer what the "how much more" has in view; it is not expressly defined. But in verse 15 we read instead: "what shall the receiving of them be, but life from the dead?" and thus the greater blessing is specified for us. What is this "life from the dead"?

It must be accorded its full force as that which brings "the reconciliation of the world" to climactic realization. There is a note of finality belonging to the expression. Many commentators ancient and modern regard it as denoting the resurrection, holding that nothing less than this consummatory event can satisfy the climactic character involved nor accord with the actual terms, "life from the dead".[27] It cannot be doubted that the resurrection from the dead and the accompanying glories would provide the fitting climax to the unfolding of God's saving counsels with respect to Jew and Gentile so much in view in this context. Furthermore, the actual terms, "life from the dead", could denote resurrection. There are, however, weighty considerations which, to say the least, indicate that the foresaid interpretation is not proven. (1) While it is true that the word used for "life" can refer specifically to the resurrection (*cf.* John 5:29; 11:25; II Cor. 5:4) and the corresponding verb likewise to the act of rising from the dead or of having risen (*cf.* Matt. 9:18; Luke 20:38; John 4:50, 51; 11:25; Rom. 14:9; II Cor. 13:4; Heb. 7:25; Rev. 1:18;

---

[27] "The προσληψις of the still unconverted Jews, Paul concludes, will be of such a kind..., will be of so glorious a character (comp. Eph. i. 18), that it will bring with it the last most blessed development, namely, the life beginning with the resurrection of the dead in the αἰὼν ὁ μέλλων, the ζωὴ αἰώνιος, which has the awakening from death as its causal premiss" (Meyer: *op. cit., ad loc.*). "The climacteric nature of the event to be expected as the issue of the unfolding ways of God forbids to tone down this phrase (ζωὴ ἐκ νεκρῶν) to the purely-metaphorical, making it fall within the terms of mere spiritual revival. 'Life from the dead' must refer to the resurrection specifically so named, and so understood it presupposes the beginning of the closing act of the eschatological drama" (Geerhardus Vos: *The Pauline Eschatology* [Princeton, 1930], pp. 87f.). *Cf.* Barrett: *op. cit., ad loc.*; Lagrange: *op. cit., ad loc.*; as the preferred interpretation Sanday and Headlam: *op. cit., ad loc.*

2:8; 20:5), and while the term used for "dead" frequently refers to literal death, yet these same terms are also used in the figurative sense of spiritual life and death. "Life" frequently denotes the new life in Christ (*cf.* Acts 11:18; Rom. 5:18; 6:4; 8:6; II Cor. 2:16; Eph. 4:18; Phil. 2:16; I John 3:14; 5:11-13). The corresponding verb also is used in this religious sense (*cf.* Rom. 6:10, 11, 13; 8:12, 13; 10:5; II Cor. 5:15; I John 4:9). The word "dead" has also this same figurative meaning on many occasions (*cf.* Luke 15:24, 32;[28] Rom. 6:11, 13; Eph. 2:1, 5; Col. 2:13; Heb. 6:1; 9:14; James 2:17; Rev. 3:1). It is significant that so many of these instances occur in Paul's epistles and not a few in the epistle to the Romans. Most noteworthy is Romans 6:13: "but present yourselves unto God, as alive from the dead, and your members as instruments of righteousness unto God". The expression "alive from the dead" is as close to "life from the dead" as could be when the verb "live" is substituted for "life".[29] But "alive from the dead" refers not to the resurrection but to newness of life in Christ. (2) If Paul meant the resurrection, one wonders why he did not use the term occurring so frequently in his epistles and elsewhere in the New Testament to designate this event when referring both to the resurrection of Christ and to that of men (Rom. 1:4; 6:5; I Cor. 15:12, 13, 21, 42; Phil. 3:10; *cf.* Acts 4:2; 17:32; 23:6; 24:15, 21; 26:23; Heb. 6:2; I Pet. 1:3).[30] This expression "resurrection from the dead" is the standard one with Paul and other New Testament speakers and writers to denote the resurrection. It could be that Paul varied his language in order to impart an emphasis appropriate to his purpose. But no such consideration is apparent in this case, and in view of his use of the terms "life" and "dead", particularly in this epistle, we would expect the word "resurrection" in order to avoid all ambiguity if the apostle intended the expression in question to denote such. Besides, nowhere else does "life from the dead" refer to the resurrection and its closest parallel "alive from the dead" (6:13) refers to spiritual life.

For these reasons there is no place for dogmatism respecting the

---

[28]   Luke 15:24, 32 is cited not because it has precisely the same reference as "dead" in the other passages but because it illustrates a non-literal use of the term.

[29]   ἐκ νεκρῶν ζῶντας as compared with ζωὴ ἐκ νεκρῶν.

[30]   ἀνάστασις.

interpretation so widely held that the resurrection is in view. The other interpretation, that of an unprecedented quickening for the world in the expansion and success of the gospel, has much to commend it. The much greater blessing accruing from the fulness of Israel (vs. 12) would more naturally be regarded as the augmenting of that referred to in the preceding part of the verse. Verse 15 resumes the theme of verse 12 but specifies what the much greater blessing is. In line with the figurative use of the terms "life" and "dead" the expression "life from the dead" could appropriately be used to denote the vivification that would come to the whole world from the conversion of the mass of Israel and their reception into the favour and kingdom of God.[31]

11: 16–24

16 And if the firstfruit is holy, so is the lump: and if the root is holy, so are the branches.

17 But if some of the branches were broken off, and thou, being a wild olive, wast grafted in among them, and didst become partaker with them of the root of the fatness of the olive tree;

18 glory not over the branches: but if thou gloriest, it is not thou that bearest the root, but the root thee.

19 Thou wilt say then, Branches were broken off, that I might be grafted in.

20 Well; by their unbelief they were broken off, and thou standest by thy faith. Be not highminded, but fear:

21 for if God spared not the natural branches, neither will he spare thee.

22 Behold then the goodness and severity of God; toward them that fell, severity; but toward thee, God's goodness, if thou continue in his goodness: otherwise thou also shalt be cut off.

23 And they also, if they continue not in their unbelief, shall be grafted in: for God is able to graft them in again.

24 For if thou wast cut out of that which is by nature a wild olive tree, and wast grafted contrary to nature into a good olive tree; how much more shall these, which are the natural *branches*, be grafted into their own olive tree?

---

[31] *Cf.* Calvin, Philippi, Hodge, Gifford, Godet, Leenhardt: *op. cit.*, *ad loc.*; H. C. G. Moule: *The Epistle of St. Paul to the Romans* (New York, n. d.), *ad loc.*; David Brown: *The Epistle to the Romans* (Edinburgh, n. d.), *ad loc.*

16 The idea of this verse is drawn from Numbers 15:17-21. The first of the dough given unto the Lord meant the consecration of the whole lump. In the application of this figure "the firstfruit" is the patriarchs rather than the remnant. The firstfruit and the lump are parallel to the root and the branches. The root is surely the patriarchs. Furthermore, in verse 28 Israel are said to be "beloved for the fathers' sake". In the one case it is the consecration belonging to Israel, in the other it is the love borne to Israel. But both are derived from the patriarchal parentage. Here again we are apprized of the distinguishing character of Israel in the relation of God to them and of his counsel respecting them. This fact of consecration derived from the patriarchs is introduced here by the apostle as support for the ultimate recovery of Israel. There cannot be irremediable rejection of Israel; the holiness of theocratic consecration is not abolished and will one day be vindicated in Israel's fulness and restoration.

17-21 The figure of the tree with its root and branches is continued throughout these five verses and also in verses 22-24. The figure of the olive tree to describe Israel is in accord with the Old Testament usage (*cf.* Jer. 11:16, 17; Hos 14:6).[32] The act of judgment upon Israel spoken of in verse 15 as the "casting away" is now represented as breaking off of branches. This is the appropriate representation in terms of the figure now being used. The expression "some of the branches" does not seem to agree, however, with the fact that the mass of Israel had been cast away. It is a sufficient answer to this difference to bear in mind that the main interest of the apostle now is focused on the grafting in of the Gentiles and the cutting away of Israel and it is not necessary to reflect on the extent to which the latter takes place.

Israel with its rootage in the patriarchs is viewed as the cultivated olive tree (*cf.* vs. 24) and the Gentiles as the wild olive. The latter is grafted into the former. It would press the language and the analogy too far to think of the wild olive as grafted in its entirety into the good olive. As indicated in verse 24 the *branches* of the wild olive are viewed as grafted in. It is not necessary to debate at length the question arising from the kind of olive-culture to which Paul here refers. The common form of tree-culture is to

---

[32] *Cf.* also Psalm 80:8-16; Isa. 5:1-7; John 15:1ff.

take a shoot from a good tree and graft it into the young tree so that the latter might derive from the fatness of the graft the vitality necessary to fruitbearing. That to which Paul refers is the reverse of this practice. It has been shown, however, that grafting from a wild olive to a cultivated olive was a practice also followed for certain purposes[33] and that Paul could have been acquainted with this type of olive-culture and have applied it in this instance. But even if the apostle were not alluding to a practice known to him and even supposing that he was aware of the discrepancy between common practice and the figure he uses, this would not in the least interfere with the propriety of his figure. He could be interpreted as using an analogy diverse from the usual pattern of olive-culture in order to make more striking the super-natural character of the ingrafting in the application of his figure. It should be remembered that Paul is dealing with what he says is "contrary to nature" (vs. 24). Besides and more to the point is the consideration that he conceives of the branches that were broken off as grafted in again into the olive from which they were taken (vss. 23, 24), something out of the question in horticulture.

Two statements in verse 17 bear significantly upon the warning directed to the Gentiles in subsequent verses. The first is: "grafted in among them". The privilege enjoyed by Gentiles is one in this intimate association with Jews; there is always the remnant according to the election of grace. The way in which the breaking off is stated, namely, "some of the branches were broken off" accentuates the fact that not all were. The second is: "partaker of the root and fatness of the olive tree". Gentiles are reminded that they draw all the grace they enjoy from the tree whose root is Israel's patriarchs. Gentiles and Jews partake together of the privilege that stems from the same root.[34] This same lesson is pressed home more forcefully in verse 18: "it is not thou that bearest the root, but the root thee". The warning is then issued: "boast not against the branches". The branches in this case must be the branches broken off, for in verse 19 the Gentile is represented as saying, "branches were broken off that I might be grafted

---

[33] Cf. W. M. Ramsay: "The Olive-Tree and the Wild-Olive" in The Expositor, Sixth Series, Vol. XI (1905), pp. 16–34, 152–160.

[34] τῆς ῥίζης τῆς πιότητος, supported by א*, B, is the more difficult reading and the insertion of καί can be explained as an attempt to relieve the difficulty τῆς πιότητος when taken as a genitive of quality is quite intelligible.

in". The boasting condemned is the arrogance and presumptuous confidence to which believing Gentiles are liable when they consider the place of privilege and honour they occupy in the kingdom of God by the displacement of Israel. The self-adulation can be sensed in the contrasts of verse 19, between "broken off" and "grafted in", between "branches" and "I".[35] A streak of contempt for the Jew may also be detected. It is not difficult to find parallels in the life of the church. The person who is called upon to fill a place vacated by the exercise of discipline upon another is liable to gloat self-righteously over this advancement and look with disdain upon the fallen.

In verse 20 the reference to the unbelief of the branches broken off harks back to the repeated mention of the stumbling and trespass of Israel (9:32; 10:21; 11:11, 12) and reminds us again of the judicial character of the hardening (11:7) and "casting away" (11:15). The observation that "by their unbelief they were broken off" is made in this instance, however, to emphasize that by which Gentiles have come to stand and occupy a place in the olive tree, namely, by faith. The main interest of the context is to rebuke and correct vain boasting.[36] The emphasis falls on "faith" because it is faith that removes all ground for boasting. If those grafted in have come to stand by faith,[37] then all thought of merit is excluded (cf. 9:32; 11:6). "Where then is the glorying? It is excluded. By what manner of law? of works? Nay: but by the law of faith" (3:27). Furthermore, the accent on faith and the contrast with unbelief serve to enforce the necessity of maintaining this faith and of taking heed lest by the presumptuous confidence which is its opposite the Gentiles may fall under the same judgment. In faith there is no discrimination. The gospel is the power of God unto salvation to every one that believes (cf. 1:16; 3:22). In unbelief there is no respect of persons (cf. 2:11). God did not spare the natural branches and neither will he spare the Gentiles (vs. 21). If they continue not in faith, they also will be cut off (vs. 22). It is noteworthy that the attitude compatible with and promotive of faith is not only lowliness of mind but one of fear

---

[35] Note the ἐγώ expressing the egoism and vainglory of this boasting.
[36] That against which Paul is warning is that for which Israel fell and the same judgment will overtake the Gentiles if they fall into the same kind of self-righteous confidence (cf. 9:32, 33; 10:3, 21).
[37] It is not necessary to suppose that "stand" refers to standing in the live tree, though this is not an entirely impossible figure.

(vs. 20). Christian piety is constantly aware of the perils to faith, of the danger of coming short, and is characterized by the fear and trembling which the high demands of God's calling constrain (*cf.* I Cor. 2:3; Phil. 2:12; Heb. 4:1; I Pet. 1:17). "Let him that thinketh he standeth take heed lest he fall" (I Cor. 10:12).[38]

22 This is an appeal to Gentiles to consider the import of the twofold action of God delineated in the preceding verses, the breaking off and the grafting in. It is the lesson of conjunction in God of goodness and severity, a conjunction which cannot be restricted to execution but must apply also to the disposition of which execution is the expression. This can readily be seen in the case of "goodness"; it refers to the lovingkindness characterizing him by which he is actuated in the dispensing of favour. Although the word for severity occurs only here in the New Testament,[39] yet it denotes that which is involved in his wrath and retributive justice (*cf.* 1:18; 2:4–16).[40] The conditional clause in this verse, "if thou continue in his goodness", is a reminder that there is no security in the bond of the gospel apart from perseverance. There is no such thing as continuance in the favour of God in spite of apostasy; God's saving embrace and endurance are correlative. In another connection Paul enunciates the same kind of condition. We are reconciled to God and assured of being presented holy and unreprovable only if we "continue in the faith, grounded and stedfast, and not moved away from the hope of the gospel" (Col. 1:23; *cf.* Heb. 3:6, 14). The "goodness" in which the Gentile must continue is the goodness of God referred to in the preceding clause as bestowed. It is not here the ethical uprightness which the believer must exhibit and which is involved in perseverance. The thought is that he must continue in the enjoyment of God's goodness and is identical with that of Acts 13:43 where the devout are urged to "continue in the grace of God". The implication, however, is that this continuance is conditioned upon the lowliness of mind and the stedfast faith upon which the accent falls in the preceding verses. There is the note of *severity* in the way by which

---

[38] The insertion of μήπως before οὐδέ in verse 21 in accord with P⁴⁶, D, G *et al.* would weaken the categorical statement.
[39] *Cf.* for the adverb II Cor. 13:10; Tit. 1:13.
[40] This complementation of goodness and severity is characteristic of the Old Testament (*cf.* Psalm 125:4, 5; Isa. 42:25–43:1; 50:10, 11; Nah. 1:5, 6).

the alternative is expressed: "otherwise thou also shalt be cut off", a severity with the same character and decisiveness as that mentioned in the earlier part of the verse.

23, 24   The alternatives stressed in the preceding verse and applied with warning to the Gentile believers in the privileged position they occupy are now applied to Israel in their fallen condition but applied in the direction of encouragement and hope. Thou (Gentile) wilt be cut off if thou dost not continue in *faith*; they (Israel) will be grafted in if they do not continue in *unbelief*. No assurance is given in this verse that Israel will desist from unbelief; the stress falls on the certainty of the complementation, faith and grafting in, if and when Israel turn to faith. The last clause in the verse gives the reason why they will be grafted in, more particularly the reason why the grafting in will not fail when unbelief is renounced. The emphasis falls upon the power of God. Different views are held as to the reason for this emphasis. In verse 24 the argument is that it is more natural for Israel to be grafted into their own olive tree than for Gentiles taken from a wild olive to be grafted contrary to nature into a good olive. Thus there would appear to be no need to stress the power of God once the unnatural grafting in of the Gentiles is assumed as it is in the preceding verses. The best view, it would appear, is that the appeal to the power of God in verse 24 is to obviate or answer what is liable to be, if not actually is, the assumption entertained by Gentiles, when actuated by the presumptuous confidence condemned in the preceding verses, that Israel, once disinherited and cast off, cannot again be established in God's covenant favour and blessing. It is the assumption that to restore Israel is contrary to the implications of their "casting away" (vs. 15) and that consequently grafting in again would violate the divine ordinance. This Paul contradicts by saying "God is able". Though the power of God is placed in the forefront, underlying the exercise of power is the recognition that the grafting in again is consonant with his counsel and the order he has established.[41]   The erroneous assumption Paul meets directly by appeal to God's omnipotence and verse 24 is an additional *argu-*

---

[41]   In δυνατός there is no necessary reflection upon the fact that faith is the gift of God (*cf.* Eph. 2:8; Phil. 1:29).

ment to offset the fallacious inferences drawn from the rejection of Israel.

The point of the argument in verse 24 is obvious. If God's action of grace in the reception of the Gentiles is analogous to the unnatural ingrafting of branches from a wild olive into a cultivated olive, how much more compatible to receive Israel again after the pattern of grafting cultivated branches into a cultivated olive. There are, however, two observations. (1) It is to be noted that the figure is not that merely of grafting branches of a cultivated olive into a cultivated olive; it is that of grafting in the branches of the same olive. This is the force of "grafted into their own olive tree". The thought of compatibility in receiving Israel again is thus accentuated. The doctrine involved in this argument is the one pervading this passage, that the provisions of God's redemptive grace for Jew and Gentile have their base in the covenant of the fathers of Israel. To use Paul's figure here, the patriarchal root is never uprooted to give place to another planting and thus it continues to impart its virtue to and impress its character upon the whole organism of redemptive history. The ingrafting of Israel is for this reason the action which of all actions is consonant with the unfolding of God's worldwide purpose of grace. This signally exemplifies the great truth that the realization of God's saving designs is conditioned by history. (2) It is in the light of the foregoing that we should understand the "how much more" of verse 24. The thought is not attached in a restricted sense to the power of God stressed in verse 23 as if it were *easier* for God to graft in Israel than to graft in Gentiles. It is the "how much more" of consonance with the basic Israelitish character of the covenant in terms of which salvation comes to the world.

C. THE FULNESS OF THE GENTILES AND THE SALVATION OF ISRAEL
(11:25–32)

11:25–32

25 For I would not, brethren, have you ignorant of this mystery, lest ye be wise in your own conceits, that a hardening in part hath befallen Israel, until the fulness of the Gentiles be come in;

26 and so all Israel shall be saved: even as it is written,
There shall come out of Zion the Deliverer;
He shall turn away ungodliness from Jacob:

27 And this is my covenant unto them,
When I shall take away their sins.

28 As touching the gospel, they are enemies for your sake: but as touching the election, they are beloved for the fathers' sake.

29 For the gifts and the calling of God are not repented of.

30 For as ye in time past were disobedient to God, but now have obtained mercy by their disobedience,

31 even so have these also now been disobedient, that by the mercy shown to you they also may now obtain mercy.

32 For God hath shut up all unto disobedience, that he might have mercy upon all.

25 The words, "For I would not, brethren, have you ignorant", as in other instances (1:13; I Cor. 10:1; 12:1; II Cor. 1:8; I Thess. 4:13), draw attention to the importance of what is about to be said and the necessity of taking full account of it. The apostle is still speaking to Gentiles and has in view the liability to erroneous assumptions and vain conceits on their part. This is evident from the purpose for which he gives them the disclosure concerned, namely, "lest ye be wise in your own conceits" (*cf.* vss. 18–21). The disclosure he is about to make he calls a "mystery". This term appears frequently in Paul's epistles but this is the first occasion in this epistle and it occurs again in 16:25. The latter instance virtually furnishes a definition.[42] We are liable to

---

[42] *Cf.* exposition at 16:25.

associate with the term the idea of secrecy or of unintelligible mysteriousness. This is not the meaning in Paul's use of the term. As appears in 16:25, there is in the background the thought of something hid in the mind and counsel of God (*cf.* Eph. 3:9; Col. 1:26, 27) and therefore not accessible to men except as God is pleased to make it known. But, as is obvious in this verse, it is not the hiddenness that defines the term but the fact that something has been *revealed* and thus comes to be known and freely communicated. Paul is jealous that his readers be not ignorant of the mystery and therefore that they know it. But, in addition to the emphasis upon revelation and knowledge, "mystery" draws attention to the greatness and preciousness of the truth revealed. In several instances the unsurpassed sublimity of that denoted by mystery is apparent (*cf.* I Cor. 2:7; 4:1; 15:51; Eph. 1:9; 3:3, 4; 5:32; Col. 1:27; 2:2; 4:3; I Tim. 3:16).[43] It is not necessary to suppose that the revelation in this instance (vs. 25) was given only to Paul.[44] The truth denoted as "this mystery" is that "hardening in part hath befallen Israel, until the fulness of the Gentiles be come in". Both elements are clearly expressed: the hardening of Israel is partial not total,[45] temporary not final, "in part" indicating the former, "until the fulness of the Gentiles be come in"

---

[43] *Cf.* Sanday and Headlam: *op. cit.*, p. 334.

[44] In Eph. 3:5 Paul associates other apostles and prophets with himself as organs of revelation. Besides, Paul's appeal to the Old Testament for confirmation (vss. 26, 27) shows that the truth denoted by "mystery" was not entirely undisclosed in the Old Testament. It is upon the fulness and clarity of the revelation that the accent falls in the New Testament disclosure.

[45] "In part" does not refer to the degree of hardening but to the fact that not all were hardened (*cf.* vss. 7, 17). The last clause in this verse should surely be taken as referring to a point of eventuation that brings the hardening of Israel to an end. There is not good warrant for the rendering: "while the fulness of the Gentiles is coming in". It is true that in Heb. 3:13 ἄχρις οὖ has the meaning "while". But there it is used with the present tense καλεῖται and no other rendering is possible. In Acts 27:33 the conjunction would likewise mean "while": "while the day was coming on". In Luke 21:24 it would not yield an impossible sense to render the clause with ἄχρι οὖ: "while the times of the Gentiles are being fulfilled". But this is an unnatural rendering and, to say the least, questionable in view of the aorist passive subjunctive πληρωθῶσιν. In every other instance in the New Testament, whether used with the aorist or future, the meaning "until" is the necessary rendering and indicates a point of eventuation or a point at which something took place (*cf.* Acts 7:18; I Cor. 11:26; 15:25; Gal. 3:19; Rev. 2:25). Hence in Rom. 11:25 it would require a departure from pattern to render the clause other than "until the fulness of the Gentiles will come in". The context makes this the necessary interpretation of the force of the clause in question.

the latter. The restoration of Israel was implied in verse 24 but not categorically stated. Now we have express assurance. The word "mystery" is itself certification of the assurance which divine revelation imparts.

The partial hardening of Israel will have a terminus. This is marked as "the fulness of the Gentiles". What is this "fulness"? The term as applied to Israel (vs. 12) has the complexion of meaning appropriate to that context. It is contrasted with their trespass and loss. Without doubt the present context yields its own complexion to the term as applied to the Gentiles. But it would not be proper to discard the basic meaning found in verse 12. There "fulness", like the "receiving" in verse 15, refers to the mass of Israel in contradistinction from a remnant, the mass restored to repentance, faith, the covenant favour and blessing of God, and the kingdom of God. In other words, the numerical cannot be suppressed. To exclude this notion at verse 25 would not be compatible with the indications given in this chapter as to the import of the term in question. To say the least, we would expect that the "fulness" of the Gentiles points to something of enlarged blessing for the Gentiles comparable to that expansion of blessing for Israel which "their fulness" (vs. 12) and their "receiving" (vs. 15) clearly involve.

There are, in addition, other considerations which have to be taken into account, derived from the immediate context. (1) The verb, of which "the fulness of the Gentiles" is the subject, namely, "be come in", is the standard term in the New Testament for entering into the kingdom of God and life (cf. Matt. 5:20; 7:13; 18:3; Mark 9:43, 45, 47; Luke 13:34; John 3:5; Acts 14:22).[46] The thought is, therefore, that of Gentiles entering into the kingdom of God. The perspective is that of the future, at least from the standpoint of the apostle. The only way whereby those who had already entered could be included is to suppose that "the fulness of the Gentiles" means the total number of elect from among the Gentiles, a supposition that will be dealt with presently. The chief point now is, however, that it is impossible to exclude from the expression "be come in" the thought of numbers entering God's kingdom. (2) In the words "hardening in part" there is an intimation of the numerical. Not all were hardened;

---

[46] Sometimes the verb is used absolutely as here.

there was always a remnant; the hardening was not complete. (3) "All Israel" in verse 26, as will be noted, refers to the mass of Israel in contrast with a remnant. In view of these considerations it would be indefensible to allege that to the expression "the fulness of the Gentiles" no thought of numerical proportion may be attached.

It has been maintained that the designation means the full tale of the elect from among the Gentiles[47] or the added number necessary to make up the full tale of elect Gentiles. On this view the signal for the restoration of Israel would be the completion of the full number to be saved from the Gentiles. Admittedly, "fulness" could *of itself* denote such completion. But contextual considerations militate against this interpretation. (1) Israel's "fulness" (vs. 12) cannot be the total of the elect of Israel. The "fulness" is contrasted with Israel's trespass and loss and must refer to the restoration to faith and repentance of Israel as a whole. The total number of the elect of Israel or the number necessary to make up this total would not provide this contrast nor express the restoration which the passage requires. The total number of the elect or the number remaining to make up that total would require nothing more than the total of a remnant in all generations. Verse 12, however, envisions a situation when it is no longer a saved remnant but a saved mass. Applying this analogy in the use of the term "fulness" in verse 12 to the instance of verse 26 we are, to say the least, pointed in the direction of an incomparably greater number of Gentiles entering into the kingdom of God. But, in any case, the "fulness" of Israel cannot mean simply the full tale of the elect of Israel nor the added complement necessary to complete that tale. And so there is no warrant to impose that concept upon the same term in verse 25. The evidence is decidedly against it. (2) The idea that "fulness" means the added number necessary to complete the elect of the Gentiles would agree with the expression "be come in". But the view that "fulness" means the full tale of elect Gentiles does not comport with the perspective indicated in the clause "until the fulness of the Gentiles be come in", the reason being that this clause refers to an entering in that takes place in the future and provides this perspective. The full tale includes those who had already entered in and it would be

---

[47] *Cf.* Barrett: *op. cit., ad loc.*

unnatural to speak of those who had entered in as contemplated in such an expression as "until they have entered in". Thus the interpretation "full tale" is ruled out. But even if we adopt the view that "fulness" means the added number, a view compatible with "be come in", we have still to reckon with the analogy of verse 12, namely, that "fulness" intimates a proportion such as supplies contrast with what goes before. In other words, we cannot exclude from "fulness" the enhancement and extension of blessing which "fulness" in verse 12 necessarily involves. In this case this increase would have to be interpreted in terms of entering into the kingdom of God and this, in turn, means a greatly increased influx of Gentiles into God's kingdom. (3) In verse 12 the fulness of Israel is said to bring much greater blessing to the Gentiles. As observed above, the interpretation most consonant with the context is the greater expansion of the blessing mentioned in the same verse as the riches of the world and of the Gentiles. But if "the fulness of the Gentiles" means the full tale of the elect of Gentiles, then the fulness of Israel would terminate any further expansion among the Gentiles of the kind of blessing which verse 12 suggests.

The contextual data, therefore, point to the conclusion that "the fulness of the Gentiles" refers to blessing for the Gentiles that is parallel and similar to the expansion of blessing for Israel denoted by "their fulness" (vs. 12) and the "receiving" (vs. 15).

It could be objected that the foregoing interpretation brings incoherence into Paul's teaching. On the one hand, the "fulness" of Israel brings unprecedented blessing to the Gentiles (vss. 12, 15). On the other hand, "the fulness of the Gentiles" marks the terminus of Israel's hardening and their restoration (vs. 25). But the coherence of these two perspectives is not prejudiced if we keep in mind the mutual interaction for the increase of blessing between Jew and Gentile. We need but apply the thought of verse 31 that by the mercy shown to the Gentiles Israel also may obtain mercy. By the fulness of the Gentiles Israel is restored (vs. 25); by the restoration of Israel the Gentiles are incomparably enriched (vss. 12, 15). The only obstacle to this view of the sequence is the unwarranted assumption that "the fulness of the Gentiles" is the consummation of blessing for the Gentiles and leaves room for no further expansion of gospel blessing. "The fulness of the Gentiles" denotes unprecedented blessing for them but does not exclude even greater blessing to follow. It is to this subsequent blessing that the restoration of Israel contributes.[48]

It must not be forgotten that the leading interest of the apostle in verse 25 is the removal of the hardness of Israel and their conversion as a whole.[49] This is the theme of verses 11–32. It is stated expressly in verse 12, is reiterated in different terms in verse 15, and is resumed again in verse 25. In verses 17–22 Paul found it necessary to warn Gentiles against vain boasting. But he returns to the theme of Israel's restoration at verse 23, pleads considerations why Israel could be grafted in again in verses 23, 24, and in verse 25 appeals to divine revelation in final confirmation of the certainty of this sequel. This prepares us for the interpretation of verse 26.

26, 27 "And so" with which verse 26 begins indicates that the proposition about to be stated is either one parallel to or one that flows from the revelation enunciated in the preceding verse. It means "and accordingly", continuing the thought of what precedes or drawing out its implications.[50] "All Israel shall be saved" is the proposition thus involved. It should be apparent from both the proximate and less proximate contexts in this portion of the epistle that it is exegetically impossible to give to "Israel" in this verse any other denotation than that which belongs to the term throughout this chapter. There is the sustained contrast between Israel and the Gentiles, as has been demonstrated in the exposition preceding. What other denotation could be given to Israel in the preceding verse? It is of ethnic Israel Paul is speaking and Israel could not possibly include Gentiles. In that event the preceding verse would be reduced to absurdity and since verse 26 is a parallel or correlative statement the denotation of "Israel" must be the same as in verse 25.[51]

---

[48] "We must remember, that Paul is here speaking as a prophet, ἐν ἀποκαλύψει, 1 Cor. xiv. 6, and therefore his language must be interpreted by the rules of prophetic interpretation. Prophecy is not proleptic history" (Hodge: *op. cit.*, p. 588).

[49] Together with Israel's restoration goes also the great advantage accruing to the Gentiles from this restoration (*cf.* vss. 12, 15).

[50] The force of καὶ οὕτως could also be that it introduces something correlative with what precedes.

[51] "It is impossible to entertain an exegesis which takes 'Israel' here in a different sense from 'Israel' in verse 25" (F. F. Bruce: *op. cit.*, *ad loc.*; *cf. contra* Calvin: *op. cit.*, *ad loc.*). It is of no avail to appeal, as Calvin does, to Gal.

The interpretation by which "all Israel" is taken to mean the elect of Israel, the true Israel in contrast with Israel after the flesh, in accord with the distinction drawn in 9:6, is not tenable for several reasons. (1) While it is true that all the elect of Israel, the true Israel, will be saved, this is so necessary and patent a truth that to assert the same here would have no particular relevance to what is the apostle's governing interest in this section of the epistle. Furthermore, while true that the fact of election with the certainty of its saving issue is a truth of revelation, it is not in the category that would require the special kind of revelation intimated in the words "this mystery "(vs. 25). And since verse 26 is so closely related to verse 25, the assurance that "all Israel shall be saved" is simply another way of stating what is expressly called "this mystery" in verse 25 or, at least, a way of drawing out its implications. That all the elect will be saved does not have the particularity that "mystery" in this instance involves. (2) The salvation of all the elect of Israel affirms or implies no more than the salvation of a remnant of Israel in all generations. But verse 26 brings to a climax a sustained argument that goes far beyond that doctrine. Paul is concerned with the unfolding of God's plan of salvation in history and with the climactic developments for Jew and Gentile that will ensue. It is in terms of this historical perspective that the clause in question is to be understood. (3) Verse 26 is in close sequence with verse 25. The main thesis of verse 25 is that the hardening of Israel is to terminate and that Israel is to be restored. This is but another way of affirming what had been called Israel's "fulness" in verse 12, the "receiving" in verse 15, and the grafting in again in verses 23, 24. To regard the climactic statement, "all Israel shall be saved", as having reference to anything else than this precise datum would be exegetical violence.[52]

6:16. In the present passage there is the sustained contrast between Israel and the Gentiles. There is no such contrast in the context of Gal. 6:16. Although Calvin regards "all Israel" as referring to all the people of God including Jews and Gentiles, yet he does not exclude the restoration of Israel as a people to the obedience of faith. "When the Gentiles have come in, the Jews will at the same time return from their defection to the obedience of faith. The salvation of the Israel of God, which must be drawn from both, will thus be completed, and yet in such a way that the Jews, as the first born in the family of God, may obtain the first place" (*op. cit., ad loc.; cf.* also his comment *ad* 11:15).

[52] Besides, how anticlimactic in this context would be the general truth implicit in all of Paul's teaching that all the elect will be saved!

If we keep in mind the theme of this chapter and the sustained emphasis on the restoration of Israel, there is no other alternative than to conclude that the proposition, "all Israel shall be saved", is to be interpreted in terms of the fulness, the receiving, the ingrafting of Israel as a people, the restoration of Israel to gospel favour and blessing and the correlative turning of Israel from unbelief to faith and repentance. When the preceding verses are related to verse 26, the salvation of Israel must be conceived of on a scale that is commensurate with their trespass, their loss, their casting away, their breaking off, and their hardening, commensurate, of course, in the opposite direction. This is plainly the implication of the contrasts intimated in fulness, receiving, grafting in, and salvation. In a word, it is the salvation of the mass of Israel that the apostle affirms. There are, however, two reservations necessary to guard the proposition against unwarranted extension of its meaning. (1) It may not be interpreted as implying that in the time of fulfilment every Israelite will be converted. Analogy is against any such insistence. The apostasy of Israel, their trespass, loss, casting away, hardening were not universal. There was always a remnant, not all branches were broken off, their hardening was in part. Likewise restoration and salvation need not include every Israelite. "All Israel" can refer to the mass, the people as a whole in accord with the pattern followed in the chapter throughout.[53] (2) Paul is not reflecting on the question of the relative proportion of saved Jews in the final accounting of God's judgment. We need to be reminded again of the historical perspective in this section. The apostle is thinking of a time in the future when the hardening of Israel will terminate. As the fulness, receiving, ingrafting have this time reference, so must the salvation of Israel have. Therefore the proposition reflects merely on what will be true at this point or period in history.

As is characteristic of this epistle and particularly of chapters 9–11, appeal is made to Scripture for support (cf. 9:12, 15, 17, 25, 27, 29, 33; 10:5, 8, 11, 18, 19, 20, 21; 11:8, 9). The first part of the quotation is from Isaiah 59:20, 21 and the last part derived from

---

[53] "πᾶς must be taken in the proper meaning of the word: 'Israel, as a whole, Israel as a nation,' and not as necessarily including every individual Israelite. Cf. I Kings xii. 1... 2 Chron. xii. 1... Dan. ix. 11" (Sanday and Headlam: op. cit., ad loc.).

Jeremiah 31:34.[54] There should be no question but Paul regards these Old Testament passages as applicable to the restoration of Israel. In the earlier portions of this section of the epistle Scripture had been adduced to support various theses and arguments. There may be veiled allusion to the conversion of Israel on some of these occasions (cf. 10:19; 11:1, 2). But this is the first instance of express appeal to Scripture in support of the large-scale reclamation and it is questionable if there is even oblique reference in these earlier passages. This express application is an index to the principle of interpretation which would have to be applied to many other Old Testament passages which are in the same vein as Isaiah 59:20, 21, namely, that they comprise the promise of an expansion of gospel blessing such as Paul enunciates in verses 25, 26.[55] The elements of these quotations specify for us what is involved in the salvation of Israel. These are redemption,[56] the turning away from ungodliness, the sealing of covenant grace, and the taking away of sins, the kernel blessings of the gospel, and they are an index to what the salvation of Israel means. There is no suggestion of any privilege or status but that which is common to Jew and Gentile in the faith of Christ.

The clause, "this is my covenant unto them", warrants further comment. Apart from 9:4, where the patriarchal covenants are mentioned, this is the only reference to covenant in this epistle. In

---

[54] In Isa. 59:20 the Greek differs from the Hebrew in the second clause. Paul quotes the Greek verbatim but the Hebrew reads "and unto them that turn from transgression in Jacob". The first clause in Paul's quotation does not exactly correspond to either the Hebrew or Greek. The former reads "to Zion" or "for Zion" (לְצִיּוֹן) and the Greek renders this quite properly "on behalf of Zion" (ἕνεκεν Σιων). But Paul renders "out of Zion", as in Psalm 14:7 (LXX 13:7). There should not be any great difficulty. The preposition involved in Hebrew is capable of both renderings and Paul was at liberty to use the one he did. Both significations are true, that the Redeemer came out of Zion and for its deliverance. The accent in Paul's teaching in this passage is on what the Redeemer will do *for* Zion. But in the first clause the thought is focused on the relation of the Redeemer to Zion after the pattern of 9:5. This is germane to the total emphasis of this context and underscores the relevance of the Redeemer's saving work to Israel as a people.

[55] Cf. Psalms 14:7; 126:1, 2; Isa. 19:24, 25; 27:13; 30:26; 33:20, 21; 45:17; 46:13; 49:14–16; 54:9, 10; 60:1–3; 62:1–4; Mic. 7:18–20. This is more particularly apparent when Isa. 59:20, 21 is seen to provide the basis for 60:1–3 and in 54:9, 10 the same emphasis upon covenant faithfulness appears as in 59:20, 21 which is the text to which the apostle here appeals.

[56] גָּאַל used in the Hebrew is one of the standard terms with redemptive meaning in the Old Testament.

99

accordance with the biblical conception of covenant as oath-bound confirmation there is here certification of the faithfulness of God to his promise and the certainty of fulfilment. We cannot dissociate this covenantal assurance from the proposition in support of which the text is adduced or from that which follows in verse 28. Thus the effect is that the future restoration of Israel is certified by nothing less than the certainty belonging to covenantal institution. It is to be observed that the other clauses coordinate with the one respecting covenant refer to what God or the Deliverer will do. In a way consistent with the concept of covenant the accent falls upon what God will do, upon divine monergism. In Isaiah 59:21 the covenant is stated in terms of perpetual endowment with the Spirit and words of God, another index to the certitude which covenant grace involves.[57]

28, 29 The first clause of verse 28 has reference to what the apostle had noted earlier in verses 11, 12, 15. The only feature calling for additional comment is the force of the word "enemies". This is not to be understood subjectively of the enmity entertained by Jews toward Gentiles or by Gentiles toward Jews. It refers to the alienation from God's favour and blessing. This is proven by the contrast with "beloved" in the next clause. "Beloved" must be beloved of God. "Enemies" has in view the same relationship as is denoted by "casting away" in verse 15 where it is contrasted with reconciliation and receiving, both of which mean reception into the favour and blessing of God. Hence "enemies" points to that rejection of Israel with which Paul is dealing throughout this chapter. It was the occasion of bringing the gospel to the Gentiles. As in the context, Gentiles are being addressed.

The second clause in verse 28 raises more difficulty. It must be observed that the two clauses refer to relationships of God to Israel that are contemporaneous. Israel are both "enemies" and "beloved" at the same time, enemies as regards the gospel, beloved as regards the election. This contrast means that by their rejection of the gospel they have been cast away and the gospel had been given to the Gentiles but that nevertheless by reason of

---

[57] It is worthy of note that although Paul distinguishes between Israel and Israel, seed and seed, children and children (*cf.* 9:6–13) he does not make this discrimination in terms of "covenant" so as to distinguish between those who are in the covenant in a broader sense and those who are actual partakers of its grace.

election and on account of their relation to the fathers they were beloved. "The election" in this instance is not the same as that in 11:6, 7. In the latter the election belongs only to the remnant in distinction from the mass who had been rejected and hardened and so denotes the particular election which guarantees the righteousness of faith and salvation. But in this instance Israel as a whole are in view, Israel as alienated from the favour of God by unbelief.[58] The election, therefore, is the election of Israel as a people and corresponds to the "people which he foreknew" in verse 2, the theocratic election. This is made apparent also by the expression "for the fathers' sake". It is another way of saying what had been said in terms of the firstfruit and the root in verse 16. "Beloved" thus means that God has not suspended or rescinded his relation to Israel as his chosen people in terms of the covenants made with the fathers. Unfaithful as Israel have been and broken off for that reason, yet God still sustains his peculiar relation of love to them, a relation that will be demonstrated and vindicated in the restoration (vss. 12, 15, 26).

It is in this light that verse 29 is to be understood. "The gifts and the calling of God" have reference to those mentioned in 9:4, 5 as the privileges and prerogatives of Israel. That these "are not repented of" is expressly to the effect that the adoption, the covenants, and the promises in their application to Israel have not been abrogated. The appeal is to the faithfulness of God (cf. 3:3). The veracity of God insures the continuance of that relationship which the covenants with the fathers instituted, another index of the certitude belonging to covenantal confirmation.

30, 31 The apostle is still addressing the Gentiles. Verse 30 is a repetition in different terms of what had been stated already in verses 11, 12, 15, 28 that the Gentiles had become the partakers of God's mercy by the disobedience of Israel. Verse 31, though not without parallel in the preceding verses (cf. vss. 11b, 14, 25b), expressly enunciates the relation which the salvation of the Gentiles sustains to the restoration of Israel. The salvation of the Gentiles was promoted by the disobedience of Israel. But it is the reverse of this that obtains in the promotion of Israel's salvation.

---

[58] "He is not, we must remember, dealing now with the private election of any individual, but the common adoption of a whole nation" (Calvin: *op. cit.*, *ad loc.*)

It is by the mercy shown to the Gentiles,[59] not by their disobedience or defection, that Israel's conversion is realized. The grace of God's plan for the salvation of Jew and Gentile is shown by this progression, and the occurrence on three occasions of the terms for mercy in these two verses (*cf.* 9:15, 16) brings more clearly into focus the emphasis upon God's sovereign beneficence in the whole process here described. We are thus prepared for the statement of God's merciful design in verse 32.

32 In the two preceding verses the triple occurrence of the terms for mercy brings to the forefront the place that God's mercy occupies in the salvation of men. But no less noteworthy is the triple reference to disobedience. The lesson is obvious. It is only in the context of disobedience that *mercy* has relevance and meaning. Mercy is of such a character that disobedience is its complement or presupposition and only as exercised to the disobedient does it exist and operate. It is this truth that comes to expression in verse 32 in terms of the providential *action* of God. It is not simply that men are disobedient, are therefore in a condition that gives scope for the exercise of mercy, and by God's sovereign grace become the objects of mercy. The accent now falls upon the determinate action of God. He "hath shut up all unto disobedience". It is so ordered in the judgment of God that all are effectively inclosed in the fold of the disobedient and so hemmed in to disobedience that there is no possibility of escape from this servitude except as the mercy of God gives release. There is no possibility of toning down the severity of the action here stated.

It is, however, the severity that exhibits the glory of the main thought of this verse. It is "that he might have mercy upon all". The more we reflect upon the implications of the first clause the more enhanced becomes our apprehension of the marvel of the second. And it is not mere correlation of disobedience and mercy that we have now; it is that the shutting up to disobedience, without any amelioration of the severity involved, is directed to the end of showing mercy. The former is for the purpose of promoting the latter. The apostle advances from the thought of complementation to that of subordination. If we are sensitive to

---

[59] τῷ ὑμετέρῳ ἐλέει is to be construed with the ἵνα that follows; *cf.* the same construction in II Cor. 2:4b; Gal. 2:10.

the depths of the design here stated, we must sense the unfathomable, and we are constrained to say: God's way is in the sea and his paths in the great waters: his footsteps are not known (*cf.* Psalm 77:19). This was the reaction of Paul himself. Hence the exclamations: "O the depth of the riches both of the wisdom and knowledge of God! how unsearchable are his judgments, and his ways past finding out!" (vs. 33). It is not the reaction of painful bewilderment but the response of adoring amazement, redolent of joy and praise. When our faith and understanding peer to the horizons of revelation, it is then our hearts and minds are overwhelmed with the incomprehensible mystery of God's works and ways.

In terms of Paul's own teaching (*cf.* 2:4–16; 9:22; II Thess. 1:6–10) it is impossible to regard the final clause in verse 32 as contemplating the salvation of all mankind. The context determines the scope. The apostle is thinking of Jews and Gentiles. In the preceding context he had dealt with the differentiating roles of Jew and Gentile in the unfolding of God's worldwide saving purpose (*cf.* vss. 11, 12, 15, 25–28). Even in the two preceding verses this differentiation is present to some extent. Gentiles obtained mercy by Israel's disobedience and Israel obtains mercy by the mercy shown to the Gentiles. But in verse 32 the emphasis falls upon that which is common to all without distinction, that they are shut up to unbelief and fit objects for that reason of *mercy*. This, however, is no more all without exception than do verses 30 and 31 apply to all Gentiles and Jews nor verse 26 to all of Israel past, present, and future. Thus "mercy upon all" means all without distinction who are the partakers of this mercy. Although the first clause of verse 32 is true of all without exception (*cf.* Gal. 3:22), it is not apparent that in this instance Paul is reflecting upon that fact but, after the pattern of the context and in accord with the last clause, emphasizing that Gentiles and Jews without any difference are shut up to disobedience.

D. THE DOXOLOGY
(11:33–36)

33 O the depth of the riches both of the wisdom and the knowledge of God! how unsearchable are his judgments, and his ways past tracing out!

34 For who hath known the mind of the Lord? or who hath been his counsellor?

35 or who hath first given to him, and it shall be recompensed unto him again?

36 For of him, and through him, and unto him, are all things. To him *be* the glory for ever. Amen.

33–36 The theme of verses 33, 34 may be stated as the incomprehensibility of God's counsel. The terms "unsearchable" and "past tracing out" indicate this. It is a mistake, however, to think that God's incomprehensibility applies only to his secret, unrevealed counsel. What God has not revealed does not come within the compass of our knowledge; it is inapprehensible. What is not apprehended is also incomprehensible. But the most significant aspect of incomprehensibility is that it applies to what God has revealed. It is this truth that is conspicuous in this passage. What constrains the doxology is the revealed counsel, particularly that of verse 32. The apostle is overwhelmed with the unfathomable depth of the scheme of salvation which has been the subject of discourse in the preceding context. Besides, the riches and the wisdom and the knowledge of God which he views as a great deep are not unrevealed. They are the riches of grace and mercy, the deep things of God revealed by the Spirit, and the wisdom not of this world disclosed to the saints (*cf.* I Cor. 1:24; 2:6–8). Furthermore, the judgments that are unsearchable and the ways past tracing out are those of which the apostle had given examples.

It is not certain to how much of the preceding part of the epistle this doxology is intended to be the conclusion. It could be the whole of the epistle up to this point. There is an obvious transition at the end of this chapter to concrete and practical application in the spheres of Christian life and behaviour. The doxology is a fitting conclusion to all that precedes. It could also be the climax to this well-defined section of the epistle (9:1–11:36). There can be no dogmatism on this question. If a preference might be suggested it is for the second of these alternatives. The question of Israel is the one with which this section began. The apostle had dealt with various facets of God's counsel as they bear upon the unbelief and rejection of Israel. In the latter part of chapter 11 (vss. 11ff.) he comes to deal with Israel in relation to God's world-wide redemptive design and shows how both the rejection of Israel and their restoration promote the salvation of the nations of the earth. Casting his eye on the future unfolding of this saving design he sees the fulness of both Gentiles and Israel, and these in their conditioning of one another. It is this sequel of abounding grace that is the final answer to the problem of Israel, a sequel that is brought to fruition by God's mercy and by that alone. In the unfolding of this prophetic survey he places even the unbelief of Israel in the perspective of God's merciful design and not only the unbelief of Israel but that of all nations and makes the astounding statement of verse 32. This is the grand climax. It is this climax in particular that evokes the doxology and the latter is thus directly related to the theme of this section (9:1–11:32).

The word "riches" in verse 33 could be taken, as in the version, to denote the riches of God's wisdom and knowledge. When Paul uses this term, most frequently he speaks of the riches of some attribute of God or of his glory (*cf.* 2:4; 9:23; Eph. 1:7; 2:7; 3:16) or of the riches of something else (*cf.* II Cor. 8:2; Eph. 1:18; 2:4; Col. 1:27; 2:2). But he can also speak of God's riches directly (Phil. 4:19) as also of the riches of Christ (Eph. 3:8; *cf.* II Cor. 8:9). Hence the three terms can be taken as coordinate and so the rendering would be: "O the depth of the riches and the wisdom and the knowledge of God". In this event the "riches" would have in view particularly God's grace and mercy upon which so much stress falls in the preceding context. The challenge of verse 35a would thus find its appropriate antecedent and reason in the word "riches", and this would be the strongest argument in favour of the second rendering. On the other hand, it could be said that the riches of God without any specification would be expected to include wisdom and knowledge and, since these are mentioned separately, the intent of the apostle was to characterize God's wisdom and knowledge by the exclamation "O the depth of the riches". Furthermore, the apostle proceeds to speak of God's judgments and ways and then utters the challenges of verse 34 which are concerned with knowledge and wisdom in that order. There is good reason, therefore, why the accent in these two verses should be placed upon wisdom and knowledge. For in God's providential ordering of events to their designed end (cf. vs. 32) it is the wisdom and knowledge of God that come to the forefront for adoration and admiration. The question, however, may not be settled with certainty. Both renderings are appropriate to the context.

Knowledge refers to God's all-inclusive and exhaustive cognition and understanding, wisdom to the arrangement and adaptation of all things to the fulfilment of his holy designs. In God these are correlative and it would be artificial to press the distinction unduly. His knowledge involves perfect understanding of interrelationships and these, in turn, are determined by his wisdom; the relations of things exist only by reason of the designs they are to promote in his all-comprising plan.

"Judgments" can be used in the sense of decisions or determinations. This meaning appears frequently in the use of the corresponding verb (cf. 14:13b; I Cor. 2:2; 7:37; 11:13; II Cor. 2:1; Tit. 3:12). But preponderantly, if not uniformly, in the New Testament "judgment" refers to judicial decisions or sentences. In the preceding contexts there are several examples of this kind of judgment on God's part (cf. 9:18, 22; 11:7b, 8–10, 20–22, 25, 32). Thus God's judicial acts may be in view. In any case these may not be excluded. The "ways" of God are not to be understood in the restrictive sense of the ways of God revealed for our salvation and direction (cf. Matt. 21:32; Luke 1:76; Acts 13:10; 18:25, 26; Rom. 3:17; I Cor. 4:17; Heb. 3:10). They refer in this instance to God's dealings with men and are to be understood inclusively of the diverse providences in which his decretive will is executed. God's judgments are unsearchable and his ways past tracing out (cf. Eph. 3:8). The praise of the riches of God's wisdom and knowledge preceding is eloquent witness to the contrast between God's knowledge and ours. It is of our understanding Paul speaks when he says unsearchable and past tracing out. But it is the *depth* of God's wisdom and knowledge that makes it so for our understanding.

Verses 34, 35 are confirmation drawn from the Old Testament after the pattern so frequently occurring in this section of the epistle. Verse 34 is practically a verbatim quotation from the Greek version of Isaiah 40:13. This quotation may attach itself to wisdom and knowledge in verse 33, though in reverse order. "Who hath known the mind of the Lord?" witnesses to the unfathomable depth of God's knowledge. "Who hath been his counsellor?" implies that God alone, without dependence on any creature for counsel, devised the plan of which providence is the execution. With change of person from the first to the third, verse 35 appears to be from Job 41:11 (Heb. 41:3).[60] As indicated above, this may refer back to God's riches (vs. 33). This is not necessary, however, and may be artificial. In the preceding context there has been repeated appeal to the grace and mercy of God and no instance is more relevant than the climax which introduced the doxology (vs. 32). God is debtor to none, his favour is never compensation, merit places no constraints upon his mercy. The three rhetorical questions, all implying a negative answer, have their positive counterparts in the self-sufficiency, sovereignty, and independence of God. This truth finds its reason in what brings the doxology to its own climax: "For of him, and through him, and unto him, are all things" (vs. 36).

Verse 36 should be compared with other Pauline texts in which similar sentiments are expressed (I Cor. 8:6; Eph. 4:6; Col. 1:16; *cf.* Heb. 2:10). The view of older interpreters, however, that there is reference in this text to the Father as the one *of* whom are all things, the Son as the one *through* whom are all things, and the Holy Spirit as the one *unto* whom are all things is without warrant. The fallacy can be readily seen in the fact that the Holy Spirit is not represented elsewhere as the person of the Godhead unto whom by way of eminence are all things. Paul is here speaking of God inclusively designated and understood and not by way of the differentiation evident in other passages (*cf.* I Cor. 8:6; Eph. 4:5, 6). Of God as the Godhead these ascriptions are predicated. He is the source of all things in that they have proceeded from him;

---

[60] In both Hebrew and LXX the text is Job 41:3. Paul here does not follow the LXX. He is closer to the Hebrew which reads literally: "who has anticipated me that I should make recompense?" This thought Paul reproduces in his rendering. The LXX has τίς ἀντιστήσεται μοι καὶ ὑπομενεῖ. The ἀντιστήσεται could be derived from the Hebrew verb קדם but otherwise there appears to be no similarity to the Hebrew.

he is the Creator. He is the agent through whom all things subsist and are directed to their proper end. And he is the last end to whose glory all things will redound. The apostle is thinking of all that comes within the created and providential order. God is the Alpha and the Omega, the beginning and the end, the first and the last (*cf.* Prov. 16:4; Rev. 4:11). And to him must not only all glory be ascribed; to him all glory will redound.

XVIII.   THE CHRISTIAN WAY OF LIFE
(12:1–15:13)

A.   MANIFOLD PRACTICAL DUTIES
(12:1–21)

12:1, 2

1 I beseech you therefore, brethren, by the mercies of God, to present your bodies a living sacrifice, holy, acceptable to God, *which is* your spiritual service.

2 And be not fashioned according to this world: but be ye transformed by the renewing of your mind, that ye may prove what is the good and acceptable and perfect will of God.

A change of theme is apparent at the beginning of this chapter. That the apostle is concerned with the subject of sanctification is evident from the outset. "Be ye transformed by the renewing of your mind" (vs. 2) is exhortation to the sanctifying process and the terms used are specially adapted to a definition of that in which this process consists.   Paul did not, however, postpone to this point in the epistle his teaching on the subject of sanctification. Chapters 6–8 had been concerned with that topic, and the basis of sanctification as well as the exhortations particularly relevant thereto had been unfolded in 6:1–7:6. What then is the difference between these earlier chapters and that to which we are introduced at chapter 12?   At this point the apostle comes to deal with concrete practical application. It is important to note the relationship and to appreciate the priority of the aspect developed in 6:1–7:6. It is futile to give practical exhortation apart from the basis on which it rests or the spring from which compliance must flow.

The basis and spring of sanctification are union with Christ, more especially union with him in the virtue of his death and the power of his resurrection (*cf.* 6:2–6; 7:4–6).   It is by this union with Christ that the breach with sin in its power and defilement was effected (*cf.* 6:14) and newness of life in the efficacy of Jesus' resurrection inaugurated (*cf.* 6:4, 10, 11). Believers walk not after the flesh but after the Spirit (*cf.* 8:4). And not only is there this virtue in the death and resurrection of Christ but, since union with Christ is permanent, there is also the virtue that constantly emanates from Christ and is the dynamic in the growth unto holiness. The Holy Spirit is the Spirit of the ascended Lord (*cf.* 8:4, 9). Hence, when Paul at 12:1 enters the sphere of practical application, he does so on the basis of his earlier teaching. The formula with which he begins, "I beseech you therefore" (*cf.* I Cor. 4:16; Eph. 4:1; I Tim. 2:1), points to a conclusion drawn from the preceding context and although the climactic exclamation of the preceding verses in adoration of the riches of God's free and unmerited grace is of itself sufficient to constrain the exhortation with which chapter 12 begins yet it would not be feasible to exclude the whole more doctrinal parts of the epistle, especially the part devoted to sanctification, from that which underlies the "therefore" of 12:1. This illustrates what is characteristic of Paul's teaching, that ethics must rest upon the foundation of redemptive accomplishment. More specifically stated it is that ethics springs from union with Christ and therefore from participation in the virtue belonging to him and exercised by him as the crucified, risen, and ascended Redeemer. Ethics consonant with the high calling of God in Christ is itself part of the application of redemption; it belongs to sanctification. And it is not as if ethics is distinct from doctrine. For ethics is based on ethical teaching and teaching is doctrine. A great deal of the most significant doctrine is enunciated in the teaching concerned with the most practical details of the Christian life.

1, 2 It is important to observe that when the apostle enters upon practical exhortation he deals first with the human body—"present your bodies a living sacrifice". It has been maintained that he uses the term "body" to represent the whole person so that the meaning would be "present your persons". Undoubtedly there is no intent to restrict to the physical body the consecration here enjoined. But there is not good warrant for taking the word "body" as a synonym for the whole person. Paul's usage elsewhere would indicate that he is thinking specifically of the body (*cf.* 6:6, 12;

8:10, 11, 23; I Cor. 5:3; 6:13, 15–20; 7:4, 34; 9:27; 15:44; II Cor. 5:6, 8, 10). A study of these passages will show how important was the body in Paul's esteem and, particularly, how significant in the various aspects of the saving process. It is not without necessity that he should have placed in the forefront of practical exhortation this emphasis upon consecration of the body. In Greek philosophy there had been a depreciation of the body. The ethical ideal was to be freed from the body and its degrading influences. This view of the body runs counter to the whole witness of Scripture. Body was an integral element in man's person from the outset (cf. Gen. 2:7, 21–23). The dissolution of the body is the wages of sin and therefore abnormal (cf. Gen. 2:17; 3:19; Rom. 5:12). The consummation of redemption waits for the resurrection of the body (cf. Rom. 8:23; I Cor. 15:54–56; Phil. 3:21). Hence sanctification must bring the body within its scope. There was not only a necessity for this kind of exhortation arising from depreciation of the body but also because indulgence of vice closely associated with the body was so prevalent and liable to be discounted in the assessment of ethical demands. It is in the light of this practical situation that the injunction of the apostle is to be appreciated. Paul was realistic and he was aware that if sanctification did not embrace the physical in our personality it would be annulled from the outset.

What is Paul's injunction? "Present your bodies a living sacrifice." The language is that of sacrificial ritual. The difference, however, is striking. Any animate offering in the Old Testament ritual had to be slain and its blood shed. The human body is not presented to be slain. It is true that in union with Christ believers were put to death (cf. Rom. 6:2; 7:4, 6) and this also applies to the body of sin (cf. Rom. 6:6). But it is not this body of sin or sinful body that they are to present as a living sacrifice. Romans 6:13 is the index to Paul's meaning here: "Neither present your members as instruments of unrighteousness to sin, but present yourselves to God as those alive from the dead and your members instruments of righteousness to God". It is a body alive from the dead that the believer is to present, alive from the dead because the body of sin has been destroyed. The body to be presented is a member of Christ and the temple of the Holy Spirit (cf. I Cor. 6:15, 19). It is possible that the word "living" also reflects on the permanence of this offering, that it must be a constant dedication.

111

"Holy, acceptable to God." Holiness is contrasted with the defilement which characterizes the body of sin and with all sensual lust. Holiness is the fundamental character and to be well-pleasing to God the governing principle of a believer. These qualities have reference to his body as well as to his spirit and show how ethical character belongs to the body and to its functions. No terms could certify this fact more than "holy" and "well-pleasing to God". When we take account of the sexual vice in all its forms, so prevalent in Paul's day as well as in ours, we see the contradiction that it offers to the criteria which are here mentioned.

"Your spiritual service." The term used here is not the term which is usually rendered by the word "spiritual" in the New Testament. Reasonable or rational is a more literal rendering. No doubt the presenting of the body as a living sacrifice is a spiritual service, that is to say, a service offered by the direction of the Holy Spirit (cf. I Pet. 2:5). But there must have been some reason for the use of this distinct term used nowhere else by Paul and used only once elsewhere in the New Testament (I Pet. 2:2). The service here in view is worshipful service and the apostle characterizes it as "rational" because it is worship that derives its character as acceptable to God from the fact that it enlists our mind, our reason, our intellect. It is rational in contrast with what is mechanical and automatic. A great many of our bodily functions do not enlist volition on our part. But the worshipful service here enjoined must constrain intelligent volition. The lesson to be derived from the term "rational" is that we are not "Spiritual" in the biblical sense except as the use of our bodies is characterized by conscious, intelligent, consecrated devotion to the service of God. Furthermore, this expression is very likely directed against mechanical externalism and so the worship is contrasted, as H. P. Liddon says, "with the external ceremonial of the Jewish and heathen cultus".[1] In any event the term in question shows how related are our bodies and the service they render to that which we characteristically are as rational, responsible beings.

The introductory words of this verse must not be overlooked. They bespeak the tenderness of the appeal. As in I John 2:1 we sense the bowels of earnest solicitude on John's part so here in Paul. "I beseech you therefore, brethren." It is the appeal of

---

[1] *Op. cit.*, p. 229.

loving relationship. But the heart of the exhortation resides in the expression "by the mercies of God". These are the tender mercies of God, the riches of his compassion (*cf.* II Cor. 1:3; Phil. 2:1; Col. 3:12) and are made the plea to present our bodies a living sacrifice. Paul can appeal to the severity of God's judgment in his pleas for sanctification (*cf.* Rom. 8:13; Gal. 6:8). But here we have the constraint of God's manifold mercies. It is the mercy of God that melts the heart and it is as we are moved by these mercies of God that we shall know the constraint of consecration as it pertains to our body (*cf.* I Cor. 6:20). The tenderness of Paul's plea is after the pattern of that which he pleads as the impelling reason.

The leading thought of verse 2 is the pattern of behaviour. In connection with the concrete and practical details of life there is no more searching question than that of the patterns of thought and action which we follow. To what standards do we conform? We know how disconcerting it is to break with the patterns of behaviour that are common in the social environment in which we live. It is to be understood that we should not violate the customs of order, decency, and kindliness. Later in this chapter Paul enjoins: "If it be possible, as much as in you lieth, be at peace with all men" (vs. 18; *cf.* Heb. 12:14). But there are patterns that must not be adhered to. This is the force of "be not fashioned according to this world".

Three things are to be noted about this injunction: (1) It is negative. The Pauline ethic is negative because it is realistic; it takes account of the presence of sin. The pivotal test of Eden was negative because there was liability to sin. Eight of the ten commandments are negative because there is sin. The first evidence of Christian faith is turning from sin. The Thessalonians turned to God from idols to serve the living God (I Thess. 1:9). (2) The term used for this "world" is "age". Its meaning is determined by the contrast with the age to come. "This age" is that which stands on this side of what we often call eternity. It is the temporal and the transient age. Conformity to this age is to be wrapped up in the things that are temporal, to have all our thought oriented to that which is seen and temporal. It is to be a time-server. How far-reaching is this indictment! If all our calculations, plans, ambitions are determined by what falls within life here, then we are children of this age. Besides, this age

113

is an evil age (*cf.* I Cor. 2:6, 8; Gal. 1:4) and if our fashion is that of this age then the iniquity characteristic of this age governs our life. The need for the negative is apparent. (3) The term rendered "fashioned", though it may not of itself reflect upon the fleeting and passing character of this present age, does nevertheless draw our attention to the difference between the pattern of which we are to divest ourselves and the pattern after which we are to be transformed.[2] There is nothing abiding in that by which this age is characterized. "The world is passing away and the lust thereof: but he who does the will of God abides for ever" (I John 2:17). We must have patterns that abide, patterns that are the earnest of and are continuous with the age to come. We do well to examine ourselves by this criterion: are we calculating in those terms which the interests and hopes of the age to come demand?

"But be ye transformed by the renewing of your mind." The term used here implies that we are to be constantly in the process of being metamorphosed by renewal of that which is the seat of thought and understanding. If there is any suggestion of the fleeting fashions of this age in the preceding clause, there is here reflection upon the deep-seated and permanent change wrought by the process of renewal. Sanctification is a process of revolutionary change in that which is the centre of consciousness. This sounds a fundamental note in the biblical ethic. It is the thought of progression and strikes at the stagnation, complacency, pride of achievement so often characterizing Christians. It is not the beggarly notion of second blessing that the apostle propounds but that of constant renewal, of metamorphosis in the seat of consciousness. We must relate the expression here used to Paul's fuller statement of this same process of transformation. "But we all, with unveiled face beholding as in a mirror the glory of the Lord, are transformed into the same image from glory to glory, even as from the Lord the Spirit" (II Cor. 3:18).

The practical and experiential outworking of this renewal of the mind is indicated by that to which the renewal is directed—"that ye may prove what is the good and acceptable and perfect will of God". To "prove" in this instance is not to test so as to find out whether the will of God is good or bad; it is not to examine (*cf.*

[2] *Cf.* J. B. Lightfoot: *Saint Paul's Epistle to the Philippians* (London, 1908), p. 130.

I Cor. 11:28; II Cor. 13:5). It is to approve (cf. Rom. 2:18; Phil. 1:10). But it is this meaning with a distinct shade of thought, namely, to discover, to find out or learn by experience what the will of God is and therefore to learn how approved the will of God is. It is a will that will never fail or be found wanting. If life is aimless, stagnant, fruitless, lacking in content, it is because we are not entering by experience into the richness of God's will. The commandment of God is exceeding broad. There is not a moment of life that the will of God does not command, no circumstance that it does not fill with meaning if we are responsive to the fulness of his revealed counsel for us.

The question arises: is this the will of determinate purpose or the will of commandment? That the term is used in the former sense is beyond question (cf. Matt. 18:14; John 1:13; Rom. 1:10; 15:32; I Cor. 1:1; II Cor. 1:1; Gal. 1:4; Eph. 1:5, 11; I Pet. 3:17; 4:19; II Pet. 1:21). But it is also used frequently in the latter sense (cf. Matt. 7:21; 12:50; 21:31; Luke 12:47; John 4:34; 7:17; 9:31; Acts 13:22; Rom. 2:18; Eph 5:17; 6:6; Col. 4:12; I Thess. 4:3; 5:18; Heb. 10:10; 13:21; I Pet. 4:2; I John 2:17; 5:14). In this instance it must be the latter. It is the will of God as it pertains to our responsible activity in progressive sanctification. The decretive will of God is not the norm according to which our life is to be patterned.

The will of God is regulative of the believer's life. When it is characterized as "good and acceptable and perfect", the construction indicates that these terms are not strictly adjectives describing the will of God. The thought is rather that the will of God is "the good, the acceptable, and the perfect".[3] In respect of that with which the apostle is now dealing the will of God is the good, the acceptable, and the perfect. The will of God is the law of God and the law is holy and just and good (cf. 7:12). We may never fear that the standard God has prescribed for us is only relatively good or acceptable or perfect, that it is an accommodated norm adapted to our present condition and not measuring up to the standard of God's perfection. The will of God is the transcript

---

[3] τὸ ἀγαθὸν καὶ εὐάρεστον καὶ τέλειον may be taken as examples of the substantival use of the adjective or as substantivized adjectives (cf. 1:19; 2:4; 7:18, 21; 8:3). The article τό can be taken as applying to εὐάρεστον and τέλειον though not repeated (cf. G. B. Winer: op. cit., p. 127 and the examples cited by him: Mark 12:33; Luke 1:6; 14:23; Col. 2:22; Rev. 5:12).

of God's perfection and is the perfect reflection of his holiness, justice, and goodness. When we are commanded to be perfect as God is perfect (*cf.* Matt. 5:48), the will of God as revealed to us in his Word is in complete correspondence with the pattern prescribed, namely, "as your heavenly Father is perfect". Hence, when the believer will have attained to this perfection, the criterion will not differ from that now revealed as the will of God. Consummated perfection for the saints is continuous with and the completion of that which is now in process (*cf.* Col. 1:28; 4:12; Psalm 19:7–11).

12:3–8

   3 For I say, through the grace that was given me, to every man that is among you, not to think of himself more highly than he ought to think; but so to think as to think soberly, according as God hath dealt to each man a measure of faith.

   4 For even as we have many members in one body, and all the members have not the same office:

   5 so we, who are many, are one body in Christ, and severally members one of another.

   6 And having gifts differing according to the grace that was given to us, whether prophecy, *let us prophesy* according to the proportion of our faith;

   7 or ministry, *let us give ourselves* to our ministry; or he that teacheth, to his teaching;

   8 or he that exhorteth, to his exhorting: he that giveth, *let him do it* with liberality: he that ruleth, with diligence; he that showeth mercy, with cheerfulness.

3–5 In the two preceding verses the exhortations to sanctification have equal reference to all; there could not be any differentiation. But at verse 3 there is an obvious change. The change is not one that restricts the relevance to all of what Paul is going to say. It concerns every one: "I say . . . to every man that is among you". The change is that the apostle has now in view the differences that exist among believers, differences which God in his sovereign providence and distributions of his grace has caused to exist. These differences are implicit in the various expressions— "according as God hath dealt to each a measure of faith" (vs. 3); "all the members have not the same office" (vs. 4); "having gifts differing according to the grace that was given to us" (vs. 6). So now what is in mind is the diversity in respect of endowment, grace, function, office, faith. We find now the directions pertaining to sanctification in the church of Christ as God's will takes account of this diversity.

At the outset the apostle refers to the grace given to himself— "I say through the grace that was given me". In thinking of the grace given him he could not be unmindful of the grace by which he was saved, the grace common to him and all believers (*cf.* Gal. 1:15; I Tim. 1:13–16). But he is thinking specifically of the grace bestowed upon him in his apostolic commission (*cf.* 1:5; 15:15, 16; I Cor. 3:10; 15:9, 10; Gal. 2:9; Eph. 3:7, 8; I Tim. 1:12). He properly assessed and exercised this grace and it was in pursuance of this office that he was bold to give these directions as they pertain to the recognition of diversity within the unity of the body of Christ and to the maintenance of the order and harmony so liable to be disrupted when the significance of this diversity is not appreciated.

One of the ways in which the design contemplated by the apostle is frustrated is by the sin of pride. Pride consists in coveting or exercising a prerogative that does not belong to us. The negative is here again to be noted and the liability to indulgence is marked by the necessity of directing the exhortation to all— "to every one that is among you". No one is immune to exaggerated self-esteem. In Meyer's words, "He, therefore, who covets a higher or another standpoint and sphere of activity in the community, and is not contented with that which corresponds to the measure of faith bestowed on him, evinces a wilful self-exaltation, which is without measure and not of God".[4]

But that which is commended must be observed no less than that which is forbidden. We are to "think so as to think soberly" Thus humble and sober assessment of what each person is by the grace of God is enjoined. If we consider ourselves to possess gifts we do not have, then we have an inflated notion of our place and function; we sin by esteeming ourselves beyond what we are. But if we underestimate, then we are refusing to acknowledge God's grace and we fail to exercise that which God has dispensed for our own sanctification and that of others. The positive injunction is the reproof of a false humility which equally with over self-

---

4 *Op. cit., ad* 12:3.

esteem fails to assess the grace of God and the vocation which distinguishing distribution of grace assigns to each.

The criterion by which this sobriety of judgment is to be exercised is the "measure of faith" which God has imparted to each one. The meaning is not that the faith of each one determines the degree in which he will exercise sober judgment. It is not the character of the judgment that is reflected on here; the preceding clause takes care of that necessity. The "measure of faith" is that which sober judgment is to take into account in determining the assessment which each is to give of himself and therefore of the function or functions which he may properly perform in the church. The question that does arise is: to what does "faith" refer? Is it faith in the generic sense of faith in Christ by which we have been saved (*cf.* Eph. 2:8)? Or is faith used in a more specific sense of particular gifts which God has imparted to believers and of which there is great diversity?

The term "faith" is not to be understood here in the sense of that which is believed, the truth of the gospel (*cf.* Gal. 1:23; I Tim. 5:8; Jude 3). This could not be spoken of as distributed to each believer by measure, and "faith" must be understood as the faith exercised by the believer. Also, "measure of faith" is not to be understood as if faith were a quantity that could be divided into parts and thus measured out in portions. "Measure of faith" must reflect on the different respects in which faith is to be exercised in view of the diversity of functions existing in the church of Christ. The meaning is to be derived from the various expressions which follow—"but all the members do not have the same function" (vs. 4); "having gifts differing according to the grace that was given to us" (vs. 6), differing functions and gifts which are enumerated in verses 6–8. Each gift requires the grace necessary for its exercise and is itself the certification of this grace, for they are gifts given according to grace (*cf.* vs. 6). There are, therefore, distinct endowments variously distributed among the members of the Christian community and this is spoken of as dealing to each a measure of faith. Each receives what the apostle calls his own "measure". The only question then is: why is this distinguishing endowment, which implies the call to its exercise, spoken of as the "measure of faith"?

It should not be supposed that the strength of the faith that is unto salvation is here in view as if the possession and exercise of certain gifts imply a greater degree of saving faith or a richer exercise of those graces which are the evidence of that faith and which are called the fruit of the Spirit (Gal. 5:22–24). All believers without distinction are called upon to exemplify this faith and the fruit thereof. But that which is here implied in the measure of faith involves, as the succeeding context shows, limitation to the sphere of activity to which each particular gift assigns its possessor. It is called the measure of faith in the restricted sense of the faith that is suited to the exercise of this gift and this nomenclature is used to emphasize the cardinal place which faith occupies not only in our becoming members of this community but also in the specific functions performed as members of it. No gift is exercised apart from faith directed to God and more specifically faith directed to Christ in accordance with the apostle's word elsewhere, "I can do all things in him that strengtheneth me" (Phil. 4:13).

Commentators have properly called attention to the difference in respect of measure between Christ and the members of his body. He is "full of grace and truth" (John 1:14), it pleased the Father that "all the fulness should dwell in him" (Col. 1:19), "in him are hid all the treasures of wisdom and knowledge". There is no *measure* to his endowments. In the church there is distribution of gift and each member possesses his own measure for which there is the corresponding faith by which and within the limits of which the gift is to be exercised.[5]

The diversity of endowment and function referred to at the end of verse 3 is now illustrated and enforced in verse 4 by appeal to the human body. As the body has many members with their own particular function so is it in the church of Christ.[6] The significant feature of this appeal to the human body appears in verse 5: "so we, who are many, are one body in Christ, and severally members one of another". There are two considerations to be noted.

1. Here is expressed the concept of the church as "one body in Christ". This is the only instance of this designation in this epistle. The same thought appears in I Corinthians 10:17: "we, the many,

---

[5] Perhaps the most conspicuous use of the term "faith" in a specific sense is I Cor. 12:9. Here it is comparable to "the word of wisdom", "the word of knowledge", "gifts of healings" *etc.* (*cf.* also 14:22, 23; I Cor. 13:2).

[6] *Cf.* citations in Liddon: *op. cit.*, p. 233 for the use of this comparison in the ancient Roman world with reference to the body social or politic.

are one bread, one body". Although Paul does not in either passage call believers "the body of Christ", yet in I Corinthians 12:27 he says, "ye are the body of Christ, and severally members thereof" and here the thought is so similar that we cannot doubt that the concept of the church as the body of Christ was entertained when he penned the other passages (Rom. 12:5; I Cor. 10:17) although the reason did not arise for that particular form of statement. In the Epistles to the Ephesians and Colossians the doctrine of the church as the body of Christ is more fully unfolded.[7] In these Epistles this doctrine occupies a more prominent place because it is so pertinent to the themes being developed. But we are not to suppose that the doctrine of these later Epistles is not implicit in Romans and I Corinthians. The form of expression, "one body in Christ", is suited to the thought in this instance. The apostle's interest is now centred upon the necessity of carrying into effect in the community of believers that which is exemplified in the human body, namely, that although there are many members they do not all perform the same function. The governing thought of the whole passage, diversity of gift and office exercised according to the measure of faith in the harmony of mutual esteem and recognized interdependence, determines the mode of expression. And in this case there is no need to say more than "one body in Christ".

2. Believers are not only members of the one body but also of one another. This is an unusual way of expressing the corporate relationship (cf. Eph. 4:25). It is not, however, redundant. It points to what is not enunciated in the fact of unity, namely, community of possession, the communion which believers have with one another. They have property in one another and therefore in one another's gifts and graces. This is not the communism which destroys personal property; it is community that recognizes the distinguishing gifts which God has distributed and so individuality is jealously maintained. But the diversity enriches each member because they have communion in all the gifts of the Holy Spirit which God has dispensed according to his own will.

6–8 Verse 6 could be regarded as continuous with verse 5 and thus carrying on its thought: "we, the many, are one body in

---

[7] Cf. Eph. 1:23; 2:16; 4:4, 12, 16; 5:23; Col. 1:18, 24; 2:19; 3:15.

Christ, and severally members one of another, and having gifts differing according to the grace that was given to us". Thus the three clauses are coordinate, going with "the many" as the subject. It is smoother syntax and more in agreement with verses 6b, 7 and 8 to follow the construction underlying the version and regard verse 6 as introducing a new sentence. On this view we would have to supply a verb at the middle of the verse but this is no objection. This is not uncommon in the New Testament. The verb to be supplied would be the one most appropriate to the exercise of the prophetic gift, just as in verses 7 and 8 a verb appropriate to the exercise of ministry, teaching, exhortation, and the other gifts mentioned must likewise be supplied. In verse 6, as the version indicates, the verb "prophesy" is suitable.

In these verses seven distinct gifts are mentioned. In I Corinthians 12:8–10 nine are specified, in I Corinthians 12:28, 29 also nine, in Ephesians 4:11 either four or five according as we regard "pastors and teachers" as one office or as two. Some of the gifts mentioned in these lists are not given here in Romans 12. In I Corinthians 12:28 the order of rank is expressly stated, at least in respect of the order, apostles, prophets, teachers. This same order for apostles and prophets appears in Ephesians 2:20; 3:5; 4:11. In the last cited passage the office of evangelist appears as third and is nowhere else specified in these lists. In all cases where order is intimated apostles are first and prophets second. Hence in this passage (Rom. 12:6–8), since the gift of prophecy is listed and the apostolic office is not, prophecy is mentioned first.

The reasons why Paul does not refer to the apostolic office are apparent. There was no apostle at Rome (*cf.* 15:15–29, esp. vs. 20). He had alluded to his own apostolic commission in verse 3. It would scarcely be in accord with the pattern indicated in the New Testament for one apostle to give directions to another respecting the conduct of his office. The priority of the apostleship makes it thoroughly appropriate, on the other hand, for Paul to enjoin a prophet to exercise his gift "according to the proportion of faith".

As noted, not all the gifts referred to elsewhere are specified in this passage. It would not be proper to infer that only the gifts mentioned were present in the church at Rome. We may infer, however, that those dealt with and the corresponding directions were relevant and that the selection was sufficient to enforce concretely the regulative principles enjoined in verses 3—5.

Prophecy refers to the function of communicating revelations of truth from God. The prophet was an organ of revelation; he was God's spokesman. His office was not restricted to prediction of the future although this was likewise his prerogative when God was pleased to unveil future events to him (*cf.* Acts 21:10, 11). The gift of prophecy of which Paul here speaks is obviously one exercised in the apostolic church as distinct from the Old Testament. In the Old Testament the prophets occupied a position of priority that is not accorded to those of the New Testament (*cf.* Numb. 12:6–8; Deut. 18:15–19; Acts 3:21–24; Heb. 1:1; I Pet. 1:10–12). But the important place occupied by the gift of prophecy in the apostolic church is indicated by the prophecy of Joel fulfilled at Pentecost (Joel 2:28; Acts 2:16, 17), by the fact that prophets are next in rank to apostles, and that the church is built upon "the foundation of the apostles and prophets" (Eph. 2:20). The apostles possessed the prophetic gift; they also were organs of revelation. But the apostles had other qualifications which accorded them preeminence and "prophets" were not apostles.

The regulative principle prescribed for a prophet was that he exercise his gift "according to the proportion of faith".[8] This has been interpreted, as a literal rendering might suggest, "according to the analogy of the faith", faith being taken in the objective sense as the truth revealed and believed. This view would correspond to the expression, the analogy of Scripture, which means that Scripture is to be interpreted in accord with Scripture, that the infallible rule of the interpretation of Scripture is the Scripture itself.[9] Much can be said in support of this interpretation.

1. If the expression means "proportion of faith", it would have the same force as "measure of faith" (vs. 3), and, since every one is to judge himself and exercise his gift in accordance with the measure of faith given, why should this be repeated and directed to the prophet specifically?

2. There is good reason why a prophet should be reminded that the new revelations he has received are never in conflict with existing revelation. This is the mark of a true prophet (*cf.* Deut. 13:1–5; 18:20–22; I Cor. 14:37; I John 4:1–6).

---

[8] There is no possessive pronoun with "faith".

[9] *Cf.* Luther, possibly Calvin, Philippi, Hodge, Shedd and others.

3. The criterion by which men are to judge the claims of a prophet is the canon of revelation which they possess (*cf.* Acts 17:11).

4. There is warrant in classical Greek for the meaning "analogy" in the sense of that which is in agreement or correspondence with something else.[10]

On the other hand, there is not sufficient evidence to confirm this interpretation. The term in question occurs nowhere else in the New Testament. It is used elsewhere of mathematical proportion and progression, also in the sense of ratio and relation. The phrase "out of proportion" also occurs. The idea of proportion appears to be the preponderant one. This meaning, if applied here, is relevant. The prophet when he speaks God's word is not to go beyond that which God has given him to speak. As noted above, every gift must be exercised within the limits of faith and restricted to its own sphere and purpose. There is prime need that a prophet should give heed to this regulative principle because no peril could be greater than that an organ of revelation should presume to speak on his own authority. "The proportion of faith" points also in another direction. The prophet is to exercise his gift to the full extent of his prerogative; he is not to withhold the truth he is commissioned to disclose. Paul asserted his own faithfulness in this regard (Acts 20:20). Furthermore, this is not mere repetition of the "measure of faith" (vs. 3). In that case the accent falls on sober judgment. In verse 6 the emphasis is placed upon the proper discharge of the prophetic function and "proportion of faith" is by way of eminence the appropriate injunction.

The next gift mentioned is "ministry". The term is used of the ministry of the Word and even designates this ministry as performed by an apostle (cf. Acts 6:4; 20:24; 21:19; Rom. 11:13; II Cor. 4:1; 5:18; 6:3; Eph. 4:12; Col. 4:17; I Tim. 1:12; II Tim. 4:5, 11). As far as usage is concerned there is, therefore, abundant support for the view that the ministry of the Word is intended. In addition, this office follows prophecy and precedes that of teaching

---

[10] ἀναλογία occurs only here in the New Testament and rarely, if ever, in the LXX. In classical Greek it is used of mathematical proportion, with ὑπέρ in the sense of out of proportion, and also bears the sense of agreement or correspondence similar to ὁμοιότης.

in the apostle's enumeration. If an order of priority occurs here, then we would be compelled to regard the ministry as that of the Word, because no other phase of the church's ministration could have a higher place than that of teaching except the general ministry of the Word. On this assumption the first four functions would obviously be in the order of rank—prophecy, ministry of the Word, teaching, exhortation. However reasonable is this view we cannot be certain that this was the function in mind.

1. The term is also used in the more restricted sense of the ministry of mercy with reference to physical need (*cf.* Acts 6:1; 11:29; 12:25; II Cor. 8:4; 9:1, 12, 13). Furthermore, in this epistle (15:31) the term is used in this sense of Paul's own mission to Jerusalem, as is apparent from 15:25–27. The flexibility in the use of the term is apparent from I Corinthians 12:5 where Paul speaks of "diversities of ministrations".

2. It is not clear that in this passage the gifts enumerated are in the order of rank (*cf.* I Cor. 12:8–10). If the order of priority is not adhered to, there is no reason why the ministry of mercy should not be mentioned at this point.

3. Although this term is not used to denote the diaconate, yet the corresponding term "servant" is used in the sense of "deacon" and the verb in the sense of exercising the office of a deacon (Phil. 1:1; I Tim. 3:8, 10, 12, 13).

4. If the ministry of the Word is intended, it would be difficult to maintain the distinction of gift and function which in this context must be supposed. If ministry is understood in the broader sense the function would apply to the prophet, on the one hand, and to the teacher, on the other. Hence it would lack the distinguishing specificity which we would expect.

There does not, therefore, appear to be any conclusive reason for rejecting the view that this reference is to the diaconate. If this is the gift contemplated there is good reason why deacons should be exhorted to give themselves to this ministry. It is a ministry of mercy to the poor and infirm. In reference to this office there are two evils which the injunction serves to guard against. Since this office is concerned with material and physical benefits, it is liable to be underestimated and regarded as unspiritual. Hence the office is neglected. The other evil is that for this reason the deacon is liable to arrogate to himself other functions that appear to offer more profitable service. Both neglect and presumption are to be shunned; let the deacon devote himself to the ministration which his office involves. In the proper sense the work of this office is intensely spiritual and the evils arising from underesteem have wrought havoc in the witness of the church. On the contrary, "they that have served well as deacons gain to themselves a good standing, and great boldness in the faith which is in Christ Jesus" (I Tim. 3:13).

"He that teacheth, to his teaching." In dealing with the first two gifts the apostle used the terms "prophecy" and "ministry". Now he becomes more concrete and in the five functions that remain he speaks in terms of the *persons* exercising the gifts. The office of teaching differs from the prophetic. He who expounds the Word of God is not an organ of revelation. The prophet communicates truth and to that extent imparts teaching. But he is not a teacher in the specialized sense of him whose function it is to expound the meaning of that which has been revealed. His work is directed particularly to the understanding. He must devote himself to this task and be content with it.

"He that exhorteth, to his exhortation." As teaching is directed to the understanding, so is exhortation to the heart, conscience, and will. The conjunction of these two aspects of the ministry of the Word is imperative. They are sometimes combined in the ministry of the same person (*cf.* I Tim. 4:13; Tit. 1:9). Prophesying also is said to minister exhortation (I Cor. 14:3) as well as edification and comfort.

The terms used in this case could refer specifically to consolation; they are used in this sense in the New Testament. If thus interpreted the special gift refers to the aptitude to minister consolation, particularly to those in affliction. But even if exhortation is the meaning, the application of this to consolation is necessary. Exhortation needs to be directed to the cultivation of patience and perseverance and these are closely related to consolation.

The next gift mentioned is that of giving and the exhortation is that he do it with simplicity. The term sometimes means liberality (*cf.* II Cor. 8:2; 9:11, 13). But elsewhere it means simplicity, in the sense of singlemindedness of heart, of motive, and of purpose (*cf.* II Cor. 11:3; Eph. 6:5; Col. 3:22). It is not certain which of these meanings is here intended but there is much to be said in favour of simplicity. The giving in this instance is that of private means; it is not the giving from the treasury of the church. This latter is the responsibility of the diaconate and there is no evidence to think that this work of mercy is in view here.[11] Neither liberality nor sincerity of purpose appears to be the most appropriate injunction in reference to the distribution of funds from the treasury of the church. Whereas when one's own possessions are in view either of these virtues is particularly relevant. Besides, if the "ministry" (vs. 7) is that of the diaconate, as the evidence would seem to indicate, there would be duplication or at least additional specification which scarcely agrees with the interest of the apostle in this passage, namely, the exercise of the several gifts which God has distributed in the church. Since the giving is that of personal possession, the inculcation of sincerity of motive and purpose is most pertinent. Giving must not be with the ulterior motives of securing influence and advantage for oneself, a vice too frequently indulged by the affluent in their donations to the treasury of the church and to which those responsible for the direction of the affairs of the church are too liable to succumb.

"He that ruleth, with diligence."[12] There can be no question but those here referred to are those who exercise government and oversight in the church (cf. I Thess. 5:12; I Tim. 5:17). In the latter passage they are called "elders". In I Corinthians 12:28 this office is denoted by another term, namely, "governments". It would be absurd to suppose that there is any allusion here to government as exercised by one man. The other passages imply a plurality of elders (cf. also Acts 15:2, 4, 6, 22, 23; 16:4; 20:17, 28; Tit. 1:5; Heb. 13:7, 17). The apostle uses the singular in this case after the pattern followed in the other four instances without any reference to the number of those who might possess and exercise the several gifts. Hence no support could be derived from this text for the idea of one man as president in the government of the church nor of one man as chief over those who rule. The exhortation to diligence is a reminder of the vigilance that the rulers in the church need to observe. They are to shepherd the church of God and take heed to the flock over which the Holy Spirit has made them overseers (Acts 20:28). They are to watch for the souls of those under their care (Heb. 13:17). No con-

---

[11] The verb used is μεταδίδωμι, "give a share" (cf. Luke 3:11; Rom. 1:11; Eph. 4:28; I Thess. 2:8).

[12] For the verb προΐστημι in the sense of ruling cf. I Thess. 5:12; I Tim. 3:4, 5, 12; 5:17, in the sense of maintaining cf. Tit. 3:8, 14.

sideration adds more force to the apostle's charge than the fact that the church is the pillar and ground of the truth (I Tim. 3:15) and that every infraction upon or neglect of government directly prejudices the witness to the truth of which the church is the pillar.

"He that showeth mercy, with cheerfulness." There is a close relation of this gift to that of giving. But there is in the use of the word "mercy" the thought of more direct, personal ministry to those in need. The giving referred to earlier would not necessarily involve the individual and more intimate service which this ministry of mercy implies. The virtue enjoined in this case indicates this kind of care; it is to be performed with *cheerfulness*. Oftentimes the work of mercy is disagreeable and so it is liable to be done grudgingly and in a perfunctory way. This attitude defeats the main purpose of mercy. In Calvin's words, "For as nothing gives more solace to the sick or to any one otherwise distressed, than to see men cheerful and prompt in assisting them; so to observe sadness in the countenance of those by whom assistance is given makes them to feel themselves despised".[13]

In the case of the first four gifts the exhortation is concerned with the sphere in which the gift is to be exercised but in the case of the last three it is directed to the disposition of heart and will with which the service is to be rendered.[14]

12:9–21

9 Let love be without hypocrisy. Abhor that which is evil; cleave to that which is good.

10 In love of the brethren be tenderly affectioned one to another; in honor preferring one another;

11 in diligence not slothful; fervent in spirit; serving the Lord;

12 rejoicing in hope; patient in tribulation; continuing stedfastly in prayer;

13 communicating to the necessities of the saints; given to hospitality.

14 Bless them that persecute you; bless, and curse not.

15 Rejoice with them that rejoice; weep with them that weep.

---

[13] *Op. cit., ad loc.*
[14] *Cf.* Meyer: *op. cit., ad* 12:8.

16 Be of the same mind one toward another. Set not your mind on high things, but condescend to things that are lowly. Be not wise in your own conceits.

17 Render to no man evil for evil. Take thought for things honorable in the sight of all men.

18 If it be possible, as much as in you lieth, be at peace with all men.

19 Avenge not yourselves, beloved, but give place unto the wrath *of God*: for it is written, Vengeance belongeth unto me; I will recompense, saith the Lord.

20 But if thine enemy hunger, feed him; if he thirst, give him to drink: for in so doing thou shalt heap coals of fire upon his head.

21 Be not overcome of evil, but overcome evil with good.

In the six preceding verses the apostle had dealt with different offices and functions and gives in each case the appropriate exhortation. In verses 9-21 he enjoins those duties which all believers are to observe. The whole chapter is concerned with the concrete and practical aspects of sanctification and so the exhortations must cover the diverse situations of life. But verses 3–8 have in view duties which are not common to all; verses 9–21 deal with duties which no one can afford to neglect. It is easy to see the relevance to all of such virtues as love, brotherly kindness, zeal, hope, patience, prayer, hospitality, forbearance, fellow-sympathy, humility; it is with this gamut of graces the apostle proceeds to deal.

9, 10 "Let love be without hypocrisy." We might expect that the catalogue would begin with love (*cf.* Rom. 13:8–10; I Cor. 13:13; Gal. 5:22). In view of the primacy of love it is of particular interest to note how it is characterized. It is to be unfeigned. We find this emphasis elsewhere (II Cor. 6:6; I Pet. 1:22). No vice is more reprehensible than hypocrisy. No vice is more destructive of integrity because it is the contradiction of truth. Our Lord exposed its diabolical character when he said to Judas, "Betrayest thou the Son of man with a kiss?" (Luke 22:48). If love is the sum of virtue and hypocrisy the epitome of vice, what a contradiction to bring these together! Dissembling affection!

No criterion of our alignments is more searching than the antithesis instituted between the evil and the good. Our reaction to the former in all its forms is to be that of instant abhorrence; we must hate "even the garment spotted by the flesh" (Jude 23). Our attachment to the good is to be that of the devotion illustrated by the bond of marriage.[15] No terms could express the total difference in our attitude more than the recoil of abhorrence from that which belongs to the kingdom of darkness and our bonded allegiance to all that is good and well-pleasing to God (cf. I Thess. 5:22; Phil. 4:8, 9). When the good is the atmosphere of our life we suffocate in the paths of iniquity and the counsels of the ungodly (cf. Psalm 1:1, 2).

In the next series of injunctions there is a similarity of construction and this may be conveyed by the following rendering: "In brotherly love being kindly affectioned to one another, in honour preferring one another, in zeal not flagging, in spirit fervent, serving the Lord, in hope rejoicing, in affliction being patient, in prayer continuing instant, in the needs of the saints partaking, hospitality pursuing".

"In love of the brethren be tenderly affectioned one to another." The love of verse 9 is love to our fellowmen and in the context must refer particularly to the love exercised within the fellowship of the church. But here and in the verses that follow various expressions of that love are mentioned. It is plain that in the present instance the fellowship of the saints is viewed as a family relationship and as demanding therefore that which corresponds in the life of the church to the affection which the members of a family entertain for one another.[16] The particularity of the love believers bear to one another is hereby indicated and sanctioned. Even love on the highest level of exercise is discriminating in quality. This discrimination is exemplified in Paul's word elsewhere, "do good to all men, and especially to them who are of the household of faith" (Gal. 6:10).

"In honor preferring one another." The practical import of this is obvious. But there is a question whether the intent is the same as elsewhere when Paul says, "each counting other better than himself" (Phil. 2:3) or whether the idea is that we are to lead in bestowing honour. That is, the thought can well be that instead of looking and waiting for praise from others we should be foremost

---

[15] On κολλάω see this use in Matt. 19:5; I Cor. 6:16, 17.

[16] Φιλόστοργοι, though not occurring elsewhere in the New Testament, de suis to denote family affection in classical Greek.

in according them honour. We cannot be certain which thought is here present. In either case the exhortation is directed against the conceit by which we assert ourselves above others. The humility commended is not incompatible with the sober judgment commended in verse 3. We are to recognize the gifts God has bestowed upon us and exercise these in the awareness that others do not possess these same gifts and therefore are not qualified to assume the functions or prerogatives which the gifts involve. Humility does not overlook the differentiation that exists in the fellowship of faith nor can it be pleaded as an excuse for indolence. Paul considered himself "less than the least of all saints" (Eph. 3:8) but he did not allow this estimate of himself to keep him from asserting his high prerogatives as an apostle and minister of Christ. Among believers he is the noblest example of what he here commends and of the sobriety of judgment to be exercised "according as God hath dealt to each a measure of faith" (vs. 3).

11 The next three exhortations are closely related:[17] "in diligence not slothful; fervent in spirit; serving the Lord". The first is negative and is directed against weariness in well-doing (cf. Gal. 6:9).[18] The second is the positive counterpart and exhorts to the fervour with which our spirits are to be aglow. The "spirit" has been taken to refer to the Holy Spirit and so the thought would be "fervent in the Holy Spirit".[19] This meaning is appropriate, particularly in view of service to the Lord in the clause that follows. It is also true that only as our spirits are quickened by the Holy Spirit can we be fervent in our spirits. Although the term "spirit" is the personal name of the Holy Spirit and occurs frequently with this denotation, it also designates the human spirit and occurs often in Paul's epistles in this sense (cf. Rom. 1:9; I Cor. 2:11; 5:4; 7:34; II Cor. 7:1; Eph. 4:23; I Thess. 5:23). Since this reference to the human spirit is appropriate here, it is

---

[17] NEB puts the three in close relation by the rendering: "With unflagging energy, in ardour of spirit, serve the Lord".

[18] In Matt. 25:26 ὀκνηροί means "slothful", in Phil. 3:1 "irksome" or "troublesome". Here similar ideas are expressed: "be not indolent", "be not irked by the demands of". σπουδή sometimes means haste (Mark 6:25; Luke 1:39) and σπουδάζω possibly has this sense in II Tim. 4:9, 21; Tit. 3:12. But σπουδή more frequently means diligence or carefulness (cf. II Cor. 7:11, 12; 8:7, 8, 16; Heb. 6:11; II Pet. 1:5; Jude 3) and σπουδάζω has the same import in most cases if not in all.

[19] Cf. Barrett: op. cit., ad loc.

not necessary to refer it to the Holy Spirit. The third defines the service in which sloth is to be shunned and fervour practised.[20] This reminder is the most effective antidote to weariness and incentive to ardour. When discouragement overtakes the Christian and fainting of spirit as its sequel, it is because the claims of the Lord's service have ceased to be uppermost in our thought. Although this exhortation is a general one and applies to every situation of life, it is not out of place in this series of particular exhortations;[21] it expresses that which is calculated to avert sloth, incite to constancy of devotion, and also guard against intrepid zeal which passes beyond the orbit of service to the Lord. "Serving the Lord" has this dual purpose of stirring up from sloth and regulating zeal.

12 The next three are also closely related: "rejoicing in hope; patient in tribulation; continuing stedfastly in prayer". Hope has reference to the future (*cf.* 8:24, 25). The believer must never have his horizon bounded by what is seen and temporal (*cf.* vs. 2). The salvation now in possession is so conditioned by hope that without hope its character is denied; "for in hope were we saved" (8:24). The hope is hope of the glory of God (5:2) and it is one of unalloyed, consummated bliss for the believer. Hope realized will be a morning without clouds; there will be no mixture of good and evil, joy and sorrow. Hence "rejoicing in hope" even now. Hope is not here, however, the object to which rejoicing is directed. In Philippi's words, "the summons meant is not to joy *at* hope . . . but

---

[20] The reading καιρῷ in place of Κυρίῳ is weakly attested as far as external evidence is concerned. Against it are P⁴⁶, א, A, B, L, the mass of the cursives, and other authorities. καιρῷ has been favoured by notable exegetes (*cf.* Meyer, Godet). The idea of serving the time in the sense of accommodating oneself to the circumstances of the time appears in Greek and Latin, and the thought of taking advantage of the opportunity appears in Paul (ἐξαγοραζόμενοι τὸν καιρόν, Eph. 5:16; Col. 4:5; *cf.* also Gal. 6:10). Hence the thought of serving the time is not alien to Paul's teaching nor inappropriate in this context. Furthermore, it is difficult to understand how καιρῷ could have been substituted for Κυρίῳ, whereas the reverse is easily understood. However, the confusion may have arisen from the similarity in writing and the external evidence is such that we may not adopt καιρῷ as the proper text. One cannot but detect the dialectic proclivity in Karl Barth's comment: "*serve the time*: plunge into the KRISIS of the present moment, for the decision is there" (*op. cit., ad loc.*).
[21] *Cf. contra* Godet who says: "The precept: *serve the Lord*, is too general to find a place in a series of recommendations so particular" (*op. cit., ad loc.*).

to joy *by means* or *in virtue of* hope".[22] The hope is the cause or ground of the joy. However tried by affliction the reaction appropriate in view of hope is rejoicing. There is no comfort in sorrow except as it is illumined by hope. How eloquent to this effect is Paul's word elsewhere to believers as they weep over the deceased, "ye sorrow not, even as others, who do not have hope" (I Thess. 4:13).

"Patient in tribulation." As Philippi again points out, this is not *enduring tribulation* but *stedfast in tribulation*.[23] Our attention had been already drawn to the tribulations characterizing the believer's pilgrimage and to his attitude toward them (5:3). Paul refers frequently to the affliction which he himself endured (*cf.* II Cor. 1:4, 8; 2:4; 6:4; 7:4; Eph. 3:13; I Thess. 3:7). It is also noteworthy how often with different aspects of life in view the apostle's teaching takes account of the believers' afflictions (*cf.* 8:35; II Cor. 1:4; 4:17; 8:2; I Thess. 1:6; 3:3; II Thess. 1:4). These often take the form of persecution and we are reminded that "all that would live godly in Christ Jesus shall suffer persecution" (II Tim. 3:12; *cf.* Rom. 8:35; II Cor. 12:10; II Thess. 1:4; II Tim. 3:11) and that "through many tribulations we must enter into the kingdom of God" (Acts 14:22; *cf.* Rev. 7:14). The exhortation of the present text evinces the need for constancy and perseverance in what is so pervasive in the life of faith.

The exacting demands involved in the preceding point up the relevance of the next injunction: "continuing stedfastly in prayer" (*cf.* Acts 1:14; 6:4; Col. 4:2). The measure of perseverance in the midst of tribulation is the measure of our diligence in prayer. Prayer is the means ordained of God for the supply of grace sufficient for every exigency and particularly against the faintheartedness to which affliction tempts us.

It is well to observe the interdependence of the virtues enjoined in this trilogy. How dismal would tribulation be without hope (*cf.* I Cor. 15:19) and how defeatist would we be in persecution without the resources of hope and patience conveyed to us through prayer. The sequence of David's thought reflects the apostle's exhortations: "Hear the voice of my supplications when I cry unto thee, when I lift up my hands towards thy holy oracle ...

---

[22] *Op. cit., ad loc.*
[23] *Ibid.*

Blessed be the Lord, because he hath heard the voice of my supplications. The Lord is my strength and shield; my heart trusted in him, and I am helped. Therefore my heart greatly rejoiceth and with my song will I praise him" (Psalm 28:2, 6, 7).

13 "Communicating to the necessities of the saints."[24] It is true that if we comply with this exhortation we shall distribute and impart our possessions to meet the needs of the saints. But though this is implied as a consequence the precise thought does not appear to be that of communicating but that of participating in or sharing the needs of the saints. The same term rendered here by "communicating" has clearly in other cases the sense of partaking (15:27; I Tim. 5:22; Heb. 2:14; I Pet. 4:13; II John 11) and probably also in Philippians 4:14. The corresponding noun means partaker (Matt. 23:30; I Cor. 10:18, 20; II Cor. 1:17; Phm. 17; Heb. 10:33; I Pet. 5:1; II Pet. 1:4; *cf.* also Luke 5:10; II Cor. 8:23 in the sense of partner and a compound form of the verb in Eph. 5:11; Phil. 4:14; Rev. 18:4).[25] The meaning, therefore, would be that we are to identify ourselves with the needs of the saints and make them our own. We are partakers of the gifts of others in the sense of verse 5 but we are also of their wants and needs.[26] The same identifying of ourselves with the lot of others, enjoined in verse 15, is here applied to the wants of the saints.

The next exhortation is closely related: "given to hospitality". The term translated "given" is one that means to follow after or pursue and implies that we are to be active in the pursuit of hospitality and not merely bestowing it, perhaps grudgingly (*cf.* I Pet. 4:9), when necessity makes it unavoidable. The same kind of activity is here enjoined as elsewhere in reference to love, peace, righteousness, the good, and the attainment of the prize of the high calling of God in Christ Jesus (*cf.* 14:19; I Cor. 14:1; Phil. 3:12, 14; I Thess. 5:15; I Tim. 6:11; Heb. 12:14; I Pet. 3:11). In apostolic times there was urgent need for the practice of this virtue. There were the persecutions by which Christians were

---

[24] The variant μνείαις (for the accepted reading χρείαις, "necessities") is not to be followed on any account, external or internal.

[25] Gal. 6:6 may be an instance of "communicate".

[26] Philippi's remark is to the effect that we do not communicate to the *needs* of the saints but to the saints themselves (*op. cit., ad loc.*).

compelled to migrate. There were other reasons also for which they were moving from place to place. The messengers of the gospel were itinerating in the fulfilment of their commission. The world was inhospitable. Therefore hospitality was a prime example of the way in which believers were to be partakers in the needs of the saints. The conditions prevailing in apostolic times still obtain in various parts of the world and the need for this grace is as urgent as then. But even where economic and social conditions are more favourable, the practice of hospitality is not irrelevant. It is in these circumstances that the force of the verb "pursue" should be heeded. The occasions will present themselves if we are alert to the duty, privilege, and blessing (*cf.* Heb. 13:2; II Tim. 1:16–18).

14 No practical exhortation places greater demands upon our spirits than to "bless them that persecute" us. Implied in persecution is unjust and malicious maltreatment. It is provoked not by ill-doing on our part but by well-doing (*cf.* I Pet. 3:13–17). The reason for persecution is that "the mind of the flesh is enmity against God" (8:7) and is provoked to animosity against those who are God's witnesses to truth and godliness. It is the unreasonableness of this persecution that is liable to provoke resentment in the minds of believers and with resentment thoughts of vindictive retaliation. Herein lies the difficulty of compliance with the injunction. For if we refrain from retaliatory actions, how ready we are to indulge vindictive thoughts. It is not, however, mere abstinence that is here required nor is it simply endurance of the persecution (*cf.* I Pet. 2:20) but the entertainment of the kindly disposition expressed in blessing. To bless has different meanings. When we bless God we ascribe to him the praise that is his due (*cf.* Luke 1:64, 68; 2:28; 24:53; James 3:9). When God blesses us he bestows blessing upon us (*cf.* Matt. 25:34; Acts 3:26; Gal. 3:9; Eph. 1:3). When we bless persons or things we invoke God's blessing upon them (*cf.* Luke 2:34; I Cor. 10:16; Heb. 11:20). It is this last meaning that applies to the exhortation of the text and in numerous other cases where the same duty is commended. The apostle's word is to the same effect as the teaching of our Lord (Matt. 5:44; Luke 6:27, 28). When Paul adds, "bless and curse not", he underlines the fact that our attitude is not to be a mixture of blessing and cursing but one of unadulterated blessing. The demand points up two considerations:

(1) that nothing less than the pattern of God's own lovingkindness and beneficence is the norm for us (*cf.* Matt. 5:45–48) and (2) that only the resources of omnipotent grace in Christ Jesus are equal to the demands of the believer's vocation.[27]

15, 16 We found above that the believer must identify himself with the needs of others (vs. 13).[28] In verse 15 we have another example of this sympathy. We might be ready to think that it is easy and natural to rejoice with those who rejoice. In mutual jollification it is natural to be joyful. But this is not the joy spoken of here. The rejoicing is that which arises from gratification before the Lord and in the Lord (*cf.* Phil. 4:4). In contrast with the weeping of the next clause there must be in view some particular occasion for special joy because of God's favour and blessing, some distinguishing manifestation of grace bestowed upon those who are designated as "them that rejoice". The point of the exhortation is that we are to enter into this rejoicing as if the occasion for it were our own. If we love our neighbour as ourselves, if we appreciate the community within the body of Christ, the joys of others will be ours (*cf.* I Cor. 12:26b). This mutuality is not native to us. Jealousy and envy, hatred and malice are our native bents (*cf.* Gal. 3:20, 21; Tit. 3:3) and this exhortation, as much as any in this catalogue of virtues, demonstrates the transformation (*cf.* vs. 2) that must be wrought in those who are "one body in Christ" (vs. 5).

"Weep with them that weep." This is also directed against a vice that is unspeakable in its meanness, to be glad at the calamities of others (*cf.* Prov. 17:5). Identification of ourselves with the lot of others is here again commended. Weeping means sorrow, pain, and grief of heart. It is not pleasant to weep; no one invites grief. But our love for others will constrain in us the sorrow of heart which the providence of God metes out to our brethren in Christ.

In these cases we are concerned with the emotions of joy and grief and are reminded again of the vicissitudes which belong to a believer's life. To each vicissitude there is the appropriate reaction and to these reactions, emotional or otherwise, fellow-believers must be sensitive and not ride ruthlessly athwart the psychology

---

[27] *Cf.* also I Cor. 4:12; I Pet. 3:9.

[28] χαίρειν and κλαίειν are imperatival infinitives (*cf.* στοιχεῖν in Phil. 3:16).

which the situations of others create. We remember another word in the New Testament. "Is any among you afflicted? let him pray. Is any cheerful? let him sing psalms" (James 5:13), and we appreciate the wisdom of Solomon: "As he that taketh away a garment in cold weather, and as vinegar upon nitre, so is he that singeth songs to an heavy heart" (Prov. 25:20).

"Be of the same mind one toward another."[29] Exhortation to unity of mind and spirit in the Lord is frequent (cf. 15:5; II Cor. 13:11; Phil. 2:2; 4:2). It is possible that the apostle intended to relate this exhortation to the preceding verse and would mean that we are to have so much fellow-feeling towards one another that we shall rejoice with those who rejoice and weep with those who weep (cf. Phil. 2:4). But there is no need to posit this kind of dependence. As in these instances cited above there is sufficient reason for inculcating harmony that will have broader reference than the sympathy contemplated in the preceding verse. There is a difference between being of "the same mind one with another" (15:5) and being of "the same mind one toward another". The latter indicates the thought which each person is to entertain with respect to the other and requires that there be concord in this mutual interplay of thought regarding one another. Let no discordant sentiments be entertained in these reciprocal relations.

The next two clauses are directed against the high-mindedness of vain ambition, the grasping for position and honour. High things are contrasted with the lowly and humble. There is a question whether "the lowly" refer to things or persons; expositors are divided. It is more likely that the former is correct because of the contrast with "high things". If this is the intent then the thought is that we are to be content with a lowly estate and with humble tasks (cf. Phil. 4:11; I Tim. 6:8, 9; Heb. 13:5). The term rendered "condescend" means to be carried away with (cf. Gal. 2:13; II Pet. 3:17) and indicates that our feelings and attitudes are to be so much in line with lowly things that we shall be perfectly at home with these circumstances. If "the lowly" refer

---

[29] There is no need to take the participle φρονοῦντες as dependent upon the preceding infinitives. In the preceding context there are numerous participles with imperative force and later in vss. 17, 18. If we were to insist on dependence of this sort, the same would apply to the next two participles and they will not fit such a construction. Neither are we to construe them with μὴ γίνεσθε (vs. 16b).

to persons,[30] then the thought is that we are to be at home with humble folk. Whatever the denotation of "lowly" may be, the practical import would include both lines of thought, for the one would imply the other. The vice against which the exhortations are directed is a common one and gnaws at the root of that community in the church of Christ on which the apostle lays so much emphasis. There is to be no aristocracy in the church, no cliques of the wealthy as over against the poor, no pedestals of unapproachable dignity for those on the higher social and economic strata or for those who are in office in the church (cf. I Pet. 5:3). How contradictory to all such pretension is the character of the church's head: "I am meek and lowly in heart" (Matt. 11:29).

"Be not wise in your own conceits."[31] Literally rendered it is: "be not wise in your own eyes" (cf. 11:25; Prov. 3:7). Apparently the conceit in view is that self-sufficiency by which our own judgment is so highly esteemed that we will not have regard to wisdom that comes from any other source. It strikes at the opinionated person who has no regard for any one else's judgment. "The wisdom that is from above is first pure, then peaceable, gentle, easy to be entreated" (James 3:17). The opinionated person is intractable and impervious to any advice but his own. Just as there is to be no social aristocracy in the church, so there is to be no intellectual autocrat.

17–21 Misunderstanding of these admonitions arises from failure to see that they are concerned with our private, individual, personal relations to one another and not with magisterial and judicial administration. It is noteworthy that the apostle proceeds immediately after these admonitions to deal with the prerogatives and functions of the magistrate and therefore with the civil, judicial, and penal institution. To the magistrate is given the power of the sword to avenge the evil-doer (cf. 13:4). If he avenges wrongdoing he inflicts the evil of penalty. So for the governing authorities not to render evil for evil and not execute wrath (cf. 13:2, 5, 6) would mean abdication of the prerogative and obligation devolving upon them by God's appointment. It is necessary,

---

[30] In all other instances ταπεινός refers to persons (Matt. 11:29; Luke 1:52; II Cor. 7:6; 10:1; James 1:9; 4:6; I Pet. 5:5).

[31] παρ᾽ ἑαυτοῖς has the force of "in the sight of yourselves", "in the judgment of yourselves" (cf. Arndt and Gingrich: op. cit., ad παρά, II, 2, b).

therefore, to appreciate the difference between what belongs to political jurisprudence and that which is proper in private relationships with our fellow-men. To transfer the prohibitions and injunctions of the respective spheres would be not only distortion but perversion and would lead to the gravest travesties. Here is an appropriate example of the need of observing the universe of discourse in the interpretation and application of each part of Scripture.

"Render to no man evil for evil." This is the negative complement of what we found positively in verse 14. It serves to point up the relevance of this admonition to observe that it applies in our individual relations even to the crimes which are subject to penalty by the civil magistrate; we may not as private citizens take upon ourselves the execution of the demands of justice in the sphere of government. "Avenge not yourselves, beloved" (vs. 19). The essence of the exhortation is, however, that we may never indulge in vindictive retaliation (*cf.* I Thess. 5:15; I Pet. 3:9).

The next appeal does not, as the A.V. might suggest, refer to honesty in our relations with men, though this is an important ingredient in what is commended.[32] The appeal is to "take thought for things honorable in the sight of all men". For the first time in this chapter[33] this type of consideration appears, namely, the need for maintaining a deportment that approves itself to men. The close parallel, "We take thought for things honorable not only in the sight of the Lord but also in the sight of men" (II Cor. 8:21), points up this consideration because emphasis falls upon the necessity of taking care for what is honourable in the sight of men in addition to the Lord's approbation. Elsewhere Paul speaks of commending himself to "every conscience of men in the sight of God" (II Cor. 4:2). He also requires that a bishop "must have a good report from those who are without" (I Tim. 3:7). "All men" in our text must include, therefore, those outside the church. This reminds us that the norms of behaviour governing Christian conduct are norms that even unbelievers recognize as worthy of approval and that when Christians violate these canons they bring reproach upon the name of Christ and upon their own profession. This does not mean that the unbelieving world

---

[32] For similar use of προνοέω *cf.* I Tim. 5:8.
[33] *Cf.* 2:24.

prescribes norms of conduct for the Christian but only that the Christian in proving what is the good, and acceptable, and perfect will of God must have regard to what can be vindicated as honourable in the forum of men's judgment. We may never overlook the effect of the work of the law written on the hearts of all men (cf. 2:15) as also how alert the unbelieving are to inconsistency in the witness of believers.

"If it be possible, as much as in you lieth, be at peace with all men."[34] This must be as inclusive in its scope as the preceding clause; there is no restrictive use of the expression "all men". It is obvious, however, that a reservation is made in this instance respecting the obligation to be at peace. "If it be possible" indicates that it may not always be possible. We may not suppose that the implied impossibility has in view any inability arising from our weakness as, for example, inability to restrain our own impulses of anger or resentment. The impossibility is that of another character; it is "a case of the *objective* impossibility . . . chiefly where truth, right, and duty command resistance".[35] It would violate the witness of Jesus to demand peace at the expense of these priorities (cf. Matt. 10:34–36; Luke 12:51–53). "The wisdom that is from above is first pure, then peaceable" (James 3:17) and we are to follow peace and holiness (cf. Heb. 12:14). As Philippi again observes, "by the side of speaking the truth in love must ever stand loving in truth".[36]

"As much as in you lieth." If the preceding clause alludes to the impossibility proceeding from considerations objective to ourselves, this bears upon the exercise of every means within our power to maintain peace with our fellow-men. The responsibility for discord must to no extent be traceable to failure on our part to do all that is compatible with holiness, truth, and right.

This exhortation as a whole underlines the evil of indulging discord for its own sake or when necessity does not demand it. Peaceableness of disposition and behaviour is a virtue to be cultivated in our relations with all men; there is no circumstance in which our efforts to preserve and promote peace may be suspended.

---

34 To take εἰ δυνατόν with what precedes would be not only indefensible, it would be perverse. There is no qualification applicable to what precedes. It is necessary in what follows.

35 Philippi: *op. cit., ad loc.*

36 *Ibid.*

This is the force of "as much as in you lieth". On the other hand, we may never be at peace with sin and error. If peace means complicity with sin or error or if it encourages these, then peace must be sacrificed. We are to love our neighbour as ourselves and we may not refrain from the rebuke and dissent which may evoke his displeasure but which his highest interest requires.

In verse 19 the tenderness of the appeal with which the chapter begins is here introduced in another form. In verse 1 the entreaty was enforced by appeal to the mercies of God. Now the apostle addresses his readers in terms of the bond of affection that unites him to them; he calls them "beloved". No form of address could bespeak greater love and esteem (cf. 16:5, 9, 12; Eph. 6:21; Col. 1:7; 4:7, 9, 14; II Tim. 1:2; Phm. 1). It underlines the solicitude Paul entertained that believers should not give way to avenging retaliation. There is a close relation between this prohibition and that of verse 17, not to render evil for evil. But there must be some difference. This probably resides, as Calvin suggests, in the more serious kind of injury inflicted and of recompense contemplated in this instance. The fact that in conjunction with the restraint here enjoined there is the imperative added, "give place to the wrath", indicates that it is proper to reckon with the retribution due though we ourselves are not to execute the same. In verse 17 no such retribution necessarily comes into the purview.

What is the wrath to which we are to give place? Various interpretations have been proposed. One is that it is the wrath of our adversary. Give way to his wrath. If wrath is to have a place, if it is to be allowed scope, let it be that of your adversary, not yours. Hence let there be no place for your wrath. This view could derive some support from Luke 14:9: "give this one place". Another view is that we are to give place to our own wrath. Give it time to spend itself, give it a wide berth so that it may be dissipated. Pent-up resentment is always liable to explode. A third view that might be entertained is that the wrath is that referred to in 13:4, 5, namely, the judicial penalty exacted by the civil magistrate in the execution of justice for wrongdoing (cf. 13:2). The fourth view is that the wrath is the wrath of God.

The most conclusive argument against the first view is that the wrath of an adversary is not necessarily contemplated. This is an importation. There could be numerous situations prompting us to vengeful retaliation in which the wrath of the person inflicting injury would not be a factor. Hence to adopt an interpretation that is premised on an arbitrary supposition is without warrant. The second view has little to commend it on the basis of usage.[37] It is apparent that our vindictive anger is not to be vented; this is the force of the prohibition. But if our anger is to be curbed, if it is not to be given entertainment, then, according to the analogy of Ephesians 4:27, we are not to give it place. It would be contrary to the pattern of this latter passage to suppose that the same thought could be expressed by saying "give it place". These foregoing objections do not apply to the third view. And since Paul proceeds to deal immediately with the office of the magistrate as "the servant of God, an avenger unto wrath to him that doeth evil", there is much to commend this interpretation. Vindicatory retribution is the prerogative of the magistrate and the effect of the exhortation would be "Let the place of vengeance be occupied by the magistrate and do not you presume to occupy it". The fourth view, however, has the most to commend it.

1. In Paul's usage "the wrath" and also "wrath" without the article is pervasively the wrath of God (*cf.* 2:5, 8; 3:5; 5:9; 9:22; Eph. 2:3; I Thess. 1:10; 2:16; 5:9). In every instance, with the possible exception of 13:5, where "the wrath" is spoken of without any further specification (3:5; 5:9; 9:22; I Thess. 2:16) it is the wrath of God. No argument so far adduced bears the weight of this consideration.

2. The admonition to "give place to the wrath" is supported by appeal to Scripture. But the Scripture quoted (Deut. 32:35) is the assertion of the divine prerogative: "Vengeance belongeth to me; I will recompense, saith the Lord". This defines the wrath, and only the most conclusive counter-argument could remove the specification which this quotation provides. Suffice it to ask: what wrath other than the wrath of God could be supported by appeal to God's unique prerogative of executing retribution?

Here we have what belongs to the essence of piety. The essence of ungodliness is that we presume to take the place of God, to take everything into our own hands. It is faith to commit ourselves to God, to cast all our care upon him and to vest all our interests in him. In reference to the matter in hand, the wrongdoing of which

---

[37] The Latin *dare irae spatium* has temporal meaning. But τόπος does not lend itself to the temporal idea.

we are the victims, the way •of faith is to recognize that God is judge and to leave the execution of vengeance and retribution to him. Never may we in our private personal relations execute the vengeance which wrongdoing merits. We see how the practical details of the Christian ethic reveal the soul of piety itself. How appropriate likewise is the word of Peter in pleading the example of Christ: "who, when he was reviled, reviled not again; when he suffered, threatened not; but committed himself to him that judgeth righteously" (I Pet. 2:23; cf. Psalm 37:5–13).

The foregoing commitment of judgment to God might appear to leave room for the harbouring of desires for the execution of judgment on God's part upon those who make us the victims of their wrongdoing. This would be inconsistent with verse 14. But it is also countered by verse 20.

It is noteworthy how often the apostle quotes from the book of Proverbs in this chapter (at vs. 16 from Prov. 3:7, at vs. 17 from Prov. 3:4, and here in vs. 20 from Prov. 25:21, 22). The kindness enjoined is a practical and concrete way of exemplifying the disposition to which we are exhorted in verse 14. In the latter text, however, much more is in view than that of supplying physical needs. But if practical generosity is absent the presence of the disposition is suspect (cf. James 2:15, 16). The only question in this verse is the meaning of the last clause, "thou shalt heap coals of fire upon his head".

One interpretation relates the coals of fire to the execution of God's vengeance and recompense (vs. 19b).[38] This would require the thought that our deeds of kindness minister to this end and that, instead of being the executioners of vengeance, we are to be consoled by the fact that kindness only promotes that result. There are two objections to this view. (1) No warrant can be elicited from Scripture by which the execution of God's vengeance could be pleaded as the reason for bestowing kindness upon our enemies. That vengeance belongs to God is the reason why we are not to mete out vengeance but not the reason for acts of benefi-

---

[38] Cf. Psalm 11:6; 140:10; Ezek. 10:2. II Esdras 16:53 is sometimes adduced to support this interpretation. But the section in which this verse occurs is believed to be late. With respect to chapters 15 and 16 W. O. E. Oesterley says: "These chapters may, with some confidence, be assigned to a time between 240 A.D. and 270 A.D." (An Introduction to the Books of the Apocrypha, pp. 155f.); cf. also C. C. Torrey: The Apocryphal Literature (New Haven, 1945), pp. 116f.; Bruce M. Metzger: An Introduction to the Apocrypha (New York, 1957), p. 22.

cence. (2) Verse 21 is closely related to verse 20 and points to the result of our acts of mercy: it is that evil may be overcome. As will be observed, this envisions a saving effect on the perpetrators of the evil which verse 20 has in mind.

A second view, with slight variations respecting the state of mind induced in the enemy,[39] is the one most widely held. It is, that heaping coals of fire on the head refers to the burning sense of shame and remorse constrained in our enemy by the kindness we shower upon him. If the first view mentioned is not acceptable, then this must be the direction in which the interpretation must be sought. Whatever may be the state of mind induced in our enemy, whether that of burning shame or the softening of penitence, it is one that ameliorates his enmity, and the action of heaping coals of fire on his head is for the purpose of constraining that effect.

As indicated above, verse 21 is closely related to verse 20. There is a question whether "the evil" is the wrong perpetrated by our enemy or the wrong to which we may be tempted, namely, that of vindictive retaliation (vs. 19a). If the latter is in view then the thought is that we are not to be overcome by this evil of retaliation but that by resisting the impulse and bestowing kindness upon our enemy rather than vengeance we thereby overcome temptation and promote our sanctification. We achieve victory in the conflict that goes in on our own souls by doing the good of beneficence toward our enemy. This interpretation does not dissolve the connection with the preceding context. "The evil" would hark back to "avenge not yourselves" (vs. 19) and "the good" to the kindness extended to our enemy (vs. 20).

The first view mentioned is more generally accepted and is to be preferred for the following reasons. (1) The evil of the impulse to

---

[39] "Either our enemy will be softened by kindness, or, if he is so ferocious that nothing may assuage him, he will be stung and tormented by the testimony of his conscience, which will feel itself overwhelmed by our kindness" (Calvin: *op. cit., ad loc.*). "The true and Christian method, therefore, to subdue an enemy is, to 'overcome evil with good.' This interpretation, which suits so well the whole context, seems to be rendered necessary by the following verse" (Hodge: *op. cit., ad loc.*). For a more recent illuminating and discriminating study *cf.* William Klassen: "Coals of Fire: Sign of Repentance or Revenge?" in *New Testament Studies*, 9, pp. 337–350. The various views are set forth and examined. Klassen's conclusion is that "the interpretation so widely accepted by interpreters that the coals of fire refer to shame, remorse or punishment lacks all support in the text. In the Egyptian literature and in Proverbs the 'coals of fire' is a dynamic symbol of change of mind which takes place as a result of a deed of love" (p. 349).

retaliation is not in the forefront at this point. It is at verses 17 and 19. But at this stage the thought is concentrated on the well-doing of the believer in contrast with ill-doing on the part of his enemy. The hostility of the latter is in the forefront. (2) This view is a more fitting conclusion to verse 20. If heaping coals of fire refers to a beneficent result, then verse 21b alludes to this beneficent result and the good which overcomes is that of verse 20a. It is a fitting commendation of that enjoined in verse 20. (3) The idea of overcoming is more in accord with an assault that comes from without than with an inward impulse. (4) This section begins with verse 17a. The implication is that we are to render good for evil. If we apply this assumed antithesis, then the evil in mind in verse 21, as in 17a, is the evil perpetrated by another and therefore the evil to be overcome.

The meaning then would be that we are not to be vanquished ethically by the evil heaped upon us. On the contrary, by well-doing we are to be the instruments of quenching the animosity and the ill-doing of those who persecute and maltreat us. How relevant to the believer's high and holy calling! Vengeance, retaliation foments strife and fans the flames of resentment. How noble the aim that our enemy should be brought to repentance, at any rate to the shame that will restrain and perhaps remove the ill-doing which hostility prompts.

B. THE CIVIL MAGISTRATE
(13:1–7)

1 Let every soul be in subjection to the higher powers: for there is no power but of God; and the *powers* that be are ordained of God,

2 Therefore he that resisteth the power, withstandeth the ordinance of God: and they that withstand shall receive to themselves judgment.

3 For rulers are not a terror to the good work, but to the evil. And wouldest thou have no fear of the power? do that which is good, and thou shalt have praise from the same:

4 for he is a minister of God to thee for good. But if thou do that which is evil, be afraid; for he beareth not the sword in vain: for he is a minister of God, an avenger for wrath to him that doeth evil.

5 Wherefore *ye* must needs be in subjection, not only because of the wrath, but also for conscience' sake.

6 For for this cause ye pay tribute also; for they are ministers of God's service, attending continually upon this very thing.

7 Render to all their dues: tribute to whom tribute *is due*; custom to whom custom; fear to whom fear; honor to whom honor.

This section is not a parenthesis in this part of the epistle extending from 12:1 through 15:13. The obligations incident to our subjection to civil authorities belong to "the good and acceptable and perfect will of God" (12:2). The reason for dealing with this topic at this point should not be artificially sought in some kind of connection with what immediately precedes as, for example, that in 12:19–21 Paul is dealing with the injustices Christians may suffer at the hands of their personal enemies and in 13:1–7 with the injustices which they may suffer at the hands of magistrates or which are properly avenged by the magistrate. It is true that the juxtaposition of 12:17–21 and 13:1–7 is most significant for the avoidance and correction of erroneous applications of the teaching in 12:17–21, as was noted earlier.[1] But we may not say that this was the reason for the sequence which Paul follows. It is apparent how diverse are the concrete aspects of the believer's life dealt with in 12:3–21 and particularly how many of the circumstances in his social life come within the apostle's purview. In 13:1–7 we have an all-important relationship affecting the life and witness of a believer and there is good reason why Paul should treat of it, as he does, in this portion of the epistle. There is also sufficient ground for thinking that there was some urgent need for pressing home upon the believers at Rome the teaching which is given here respecting the prerogatives of magistrates and the obligations of subjects in relation thereto.

We know from the New Testament itself that the Jews had questions regarding the rights of the Roman government (*cf.* Matt. 22:16, 17; Mark 12:14; Luke 20:21, 22). We also know that the Jews were disposed to pride themselves on their independence (*cf.* John 8:33). We read also of seditious movements (Acts 5:36, 37). There is also the evidence from other sources respecting the restlessness of the Jews under the Roman yoke.[2] We are told that Claudius "had commanded all the Jews to depart from Rome" (Acts 18:2). This expulsion must have been occasioned by the belief that Jews were inimical to the imperial interests if not the aftermath of Jewish insurrection. In the mind of the authorities Christianity was associated with Judaism and any seditious temper attributed to Judaism would likewise be charged to Christians. This created a situation in which it was necessary for Christians to avoid all revolutionary aspirations or actions as well as insubordination to magistrates in the rightful exercise of their authority.

Not only was there this danger arising from association with Judaism, there was also within the Christian community the danger of perverted notions of freedom, especially in view of the kingship and lordship of Christ. The fact that Paul on three occasions[3] in his epistles found it necessary to reflect on our duties in reference to magistrates and Peter likewise to the same effect in

---

[1] *Cf.* comments *ad* 12:19.
[2] *Cf.* citations in Liddon: *op. cit.*, p. 246.
[3] In addition to Rom. 13:1–7 *cf.* I Tim. 2:1–3; Tit. 3:1.

his first epistle[4] shows that there was a reason for reminding believers of the necessity to be subject to the magisterial authorities.

Furthermore, Christians often suffered at the hands of these authorities and there was greater reason to draw the line between the disobedience which loyalty to Christ demanded (*cf.* Acts 4:19, 20; 5:29) and the obedience which the same loyalty required.

1, 2 "The higher powers" refer without question to the governing authorities in the commonwealth. The term "authorities" is the more literal rendering and points to the right to rule belonging to the persons involved and to the subjection required on the part of the subjects. At the time when Paul wrote civil magistracy was exercised by the Roman government and the direct reference is to the executors of this government. The only question that arises is whether "authorities" denote also invisible angelic powers standing behind the human governors. This question would not arise were it not that in the New Testament and especially in Paul's epistles this same term "authorities" is used to denote suprahuman beings, and Oscar Cullmann has vigorously contended that in this instance the term has a dual reference, to the angelic powers and to the human executive agents.[5] The governing authorities are those in whom are vested the right and the power of ruling in the commonwealth and the evidence does not indicate that any other than human agents are in view.

"Every soul" is to be in subjection. Every soul means every person and does not reflect on the soul in man as distinguished from the body. Frequently in Scripture the word "soul" is used in this sense as synonymous with the whole person and sometimes as equivalent to the personal pronoun (*cf.* Matt. 12:18; Luke 12:19; Acts 2:27, 41, 43; 3:23; 7:14; Rom. 2:9; Heb. 10:38, 39; James 1:21; 5:20; I Pet. 1:9; 3:20; Rev. 16:3). The implication is that no person is exempt from this subjection; no person enjoys special privileges by which he may ignore or feel himself free to violate the ordinances of magisterial authority. Neither infidelity nor faith offers immunity. It is of particular significance that it is to the church Paul is writing. The Westminster Confession of Faith states the case well when it says: "Infidelity, or difference

---

[4]   I Pet. 2:13–17.
[5]   See Appendix C (pp. 252 ff.) for presentation and criticism of this thesis.

in religion, doth not make void the magistrates' just and legal authority, nor free the people from their due obedience to them: from which ecclesiastical persons are not exempted, much less hath the Pope any power and jurisdiction over them in their dominions, or lives, if he shall judge them to be heretics, or upon any other pretence whatsoever".[6]

The term for "subjection" is one more inclusive than that for obedience. It implies obedience when ordinances to be obeyed are in view, but there is more involved. Subjection indicates the recognition of our subordination in the whole realm of the magistrates' jurisdiction and willing subservience to their authority. This is enforced still more if the rendering of the whole clause is given the reflexive form: "Let every soul subject himself to the governing authorities". This rendering, for which much can be said, stresses active participation in the duty of subjection.

The next two clauses give the reason for this subjection.[7] They are explanatory the one of the other. They point to the source whence civil government proceeds and to the sanction by which subjection is demanded. Certain observations will bring out the meaning. (1) Paul is dealing with existing governmental agents. This is the force of "the *powers* that be". He is not now treating of government in the abstract nor entering into the question of the different forms of government. He is making categorical statements regarding the authorities in actual existence. (2) When he says they are "of God", he means that they derive their origin, right, and power from God. This is borne out by several considerations urged later in this passage but here it is expressly stated and excludes from the outset every notion to the effect that authority in the state rests upon agreement on the part of the governed or upon the consent of the governed. Authority to govern and the subjection demanded of the governed reside wholly in the fact of divine institution. (3) The propositions that the authorities are of God and ordained of God are not to be understood as referring merely to God's decretive will. The terms could be used to express God's decretive ordination but this is not their

---

[6] Chapter XXIII, Section IV.

[7] In the first clause ὑπό is more strongly attested. ἀπό is the preposition we might expect and probably explains its occurrence in D, G, and other authorities. In the second clause the addition of ἐξουσίαι after οὖσαι has much authority against it and should not be adopted.

precise import here. The context shows that the ordination of which the apostle now speaks is that of institution which is obliged to perform the appointed functions. The civil magistrate is not only the means decreed in God's providence for the punishment of evildoers but God's instituted, authorized, and prescribed instrument for the maintenance of order and the punishing of criminals who violate that order. When the civil magistrate through his agents executes just judgment upon crime, he is executing not simply God's decretive will but he is also fulfilling God's preceptive will, and it would be sinful for him to refrain from so doing.[8]

For these reasons subjection is required and resistance is a violation of God's law and meets with judgment. Since verse 3 speaks of the "terror" which rulers are to the evil work there must be some reference to the penal judgment which magistrates inflict upon evil-doers. But since all that precedes stresses the ordinance of God there must also be reflection upon the divine sanction by which this penal judgment is executed and therefore upon the judgment of God of which the magistrate's retribution is an expression. We have here in this term "judgment" the twofold aspect from which it is to be viewed. It is punishment dispensed by the governing authorities. But it is also an expression of God's own wrath and it is for this reason that it carries the sanction of God and its propriety is certified.[9]

There are many questions which arise in actual practice with which Paul does not deal. In these verses there are no expressed qualifications or reservations to the duty of subjection. It is, however, characteristic of the apostle to be absolute in his terms when dealing with a particular obligation. At the same time, on the analogy of his own teaching elsewhere or on the analogy of Scripture, we are compelled to take account of exceptions to the absolute terms in which an obligation is affirmed. It must be so in this instance. We cannot but believe that he would have endorsed and practised the word of Peter and other apostles: "We must obey God rather than men" (Acts 5:29; cf. 4:19, 20). The

---

[8] Cf. review by the present writer in *The Westminster Theological Journal*, VII, 2, May 1945, pp. 188ff.

[9] ἑαυτοῖς λήμψονται may express the thought of bringing upon themselves and in that event the responsibility for the penal judgment inflicted would be expressed.

magistrate is not infallible nor is he the agent of perfect rectitude. When there is conflict between the requirements of men and the commands of God, then the word of Peter must take effect.

Again Paul does not deal with the questions that arise in connection with revolution. Without question in these two verses we are not without an index to what we ought to do when revolution has taken place. "The *powers* that be" refer to the *de facto* magistrates. And in this passage as a whole there are principles which bear upon the right or wrong of revolution. But these matters which become acute difficulties for conscientious Christians are not introduced in this passage. The reason lies on the surface. The apostle is not writing an essay on casuistical theology but setting forth the cardinal principles pertaining to the institution of government and regulating the behaviour of Christians.[10]

3, 4 While the first clause of verse 3 attaches itself to the last clause of verse 2, it is scarcely proper to say that it assigns the ground why rebels will bring upon themselves penal judgment.[11] It is preferably taken as enunciating the prerogative of the rulers, arising from the appointment or ordinance of God, and therefore as validating the penal judgment which these rulers administer. It should be observed that in this clause we have an express intimation of the magistrate's function and it is because he exercises this office that he has the authority to inflict punishment.

The "terror" which rulers are to the evil work is the fear of punishment evoked in the hearts of men by reason of the authority vested in rulers to execute this punishment. This fear can be of two kinds, the fear that inhibits wrongdoing and the fear that results when wrong has been committed. It would appear that the latter is particularly in view. In the next clause the question, "wouldest thou have no fear of the power?" enjoins the absence of the fear that is the result of wrongdoing. This is confirmed by verse 4 when it says, "But if thou do that which is evil, be afraid"; it is the fear of the penalty which the magistrate executes as the bearer of

---

[10] "With the origin of a government, or its political form the Apostle does not concern himself: nor does he enter upon the question at what point during a period of revolutionary change a given government is to be considered as οὖσα, or as non-existent; and when a government, originally illegitimate, acquires a prescriptive right. The imperial authority was too old, and too firm to make these questions practical" (Liddon: *op. cit.*, pp. 247f.).

[11] *Cf.* Liddon and Meyer.

the sword. However, there could also be reference to the fear that inhibits wrongdoing. If we are minded only to do that which is good, then we have no reason to be actuated by the fear that restrains wrongdoing.

When it is said that "rulers are not a terror to the good work but to the evil" the good work and the evil are personified. For what is meant is terror to the person performing evil. There are two observations respecting this clause. (1) The thought is focused upon the punishment of evil-doing. It is significant that the apostle mentions this first of all in dealing with the specific functions assigned to the civil magistrate. There is the tendency in present-day thinking to underestimate the punitive in the execution of government and to suppress this all-important aspect of the magistrate's authority. It is not so in apostolic teaching. (2) It is with the *deed* that the magistrate is concerned. Paul speaks of the good and evil *work*. It is not the prerogative of the ruler to deal with all sin but only with sin registered in the action which violates the order that the magistrate is appointed to maintain and promote.

The next clause can be interpreted either as a question or as a statement. In the latter case the rendering would be: "Thou wouldest then have no fear of the power" and means "if thou wouldest have no fear of the power, do that which is good". But it is preferable, with the version quoted, to regard it as a question. The sense is to the same effect. But the question expresses the thought more forcefully. If we do that which is good, then we shall have no reason to fear the ruling authority.

"Thou shalt have praise from the same." The praise given by the magistrate is not reward in the proper sense of the term. Evil-doers receive their punitive reward but those who do well do not receive any meritorious award. The term used for "praise" does not bear this signification but rather that of approval (*cf.* I Cor. 4:5; II Cor. 8:18; Phil. 4:8; I Pet. 2:14) and is used of the praise that redounds to God for the riches of his grace (*cf.* Eph. 1:6, 12, 14; Phil. 1:11). This praise may be followed by reward in certain instances but the idea of reward is not implicit in the term. The praise could be expressed by saying that good behaviour secures good standing in the state, a status to be cherished and cultivated.

The first clause in verse 4 states what is, positively, the chief purpose of magisterial authority. The ruler is the minister of God for good. The term "minister of God" harks back to verses 1 and 2 where the "authority" is said to be of God, ordained of God, and the ordinance of God. But now there is intimated the specific capacity in which this ordination consists. This designation removes every supposition to the effect that magistracy is *per se* evil and serves good only in the sense that as a lesser evil it restrains and counteracts greater evils. The title here accorded the civil ruler shows that he is invested with all the dignity and sanction belonging to God's servant within the sphere of government. This is borne out still further by the purpose for which he is God's servant; he is the minister of God for that which is *good*. And we may not tone down the import of the term "good" in this instance. Paul provides us with a virtual definition of the good we derive from the service of the civil authority when he requires that we pray for kings and all who are in authority "that we may lead a tranquil and quiet life in all godliness and gravity" (I Tim. 2:2). The good the magistrate promotes is that which subserves the interests of piety.

There is a direct, personal address in this clause, expressed in the words "to thee", showing the relevance for the well-being of the individual believer of that service which the magistrate renders.

The second clause, as has been observed above, points to the kind of fear particularly in view in verse 3 and the third clause gives the reason why this fear is to be entertained. This reason is that the magistrate "bears not the sword in vain". The sword which the magistrate carries[12] as the most significant part of his equipment is not merely the sign of his authority but of his right to wield it in the infliction of that which a sword does. It would not be necessary to suppose that the wielding of the sword contemplates the infliction of the death penalty exclusively. It can be wielded to instil the terror of that punishment which it can inflict. It can be wielded to execute punishment that falls short of death. But to exclude the right of the death penalty when the nature of the crime calls for such is totally contrary to that which the sword signifies and executes. We need appeal to no more than New Testament usage to establish this reference. The sword is so frequently associated with death as the instrument of execution

---

[12] The verb is φορέω and is more expressive in this connection than φέρω.

(*cf.* Matt. 26:52; Luke 21:24; Acts 12:2; 16:27; Heb. 11:34, 37; Rev. 13:10) that to exclude its use for this purpose in this instance would be so arbitrary as to bear upon its face prejudice contrary to the evidence.[13] "In vain" means to no purpose.

"For he is a minister of God, an avenger for wrath to him that doeth evil." In the first clause the ruler is said to be the minister of God for good. Now the same office is accorded to him for avenging evil. The parallelism is noteworthy—the same dignity and investiture belong to the ruler's penal prerogative as to his function in promoting good. This penal function is said to consist in being "an avenger unto wrath" to the evil-doer. This is the first time that the term "wrath" is used in reference to the civil magistrate. In verse 2 we found that the "judgment" alludes to the judgment of God of which the retribution executed by the civil magistrate is the expression and from which this retribution derives its sanction. The question would arise here: whose "wrath" is in view, that of God, or that of the magistrate, or that of both? In 12:19, as demonstrated above, "the wrath" is the wrath of God and the usage would point to the same conclusion in this instance. Furthermore, there is not warrant for thinking that the magistrate's reaction to crime is to be construed in terms of wrath. Hence "wrath" should be regarded as the wrath of God. Thus the magistrate is the avenger in executing the judgment that accrues to the evil-doer from the wrath of God. Again we discover the sanction belonging to the ruler's function; he is the agent in executing God's wrath. And we also see how divergent from biblical teaching is the sentimentality that substitutes the interests of the offender for the satisfaction of justice as the basis of criminal retribution.

5 Commentators are divided on the question whether the necessity enunciated here arises from what is stated in verse 4 or harks back to the whole of the preceding context. It makes little difference to the force of the conclusion drawn in this verse and indicated by "wherefore". In the latter part of verse 4 enough is stated to ground the conclusion of verse 5; the designation "minister of God" as well as the allusion to the ruler as agent in executing God's wrath point to an investiture that *demands* subjection. But

---

[13] The sword is the *insignium juris vitae et necis*.

even if we find the immediate grounding of verse 5 in the last clause of verse 4, we cannot dissociate verse 4b from all that had been stated previously respecting the prerogatives of magistrates as proceeding from the ordinance of God. In any case, no proposition in this passage expresses the divine sanction of civil government more than this one, namely, that we must be subject "for conscience' sake". Paul uses this word "conscience" frequently and it is apparent that the meaning is conscience toward God (*cf.* Acts 23:1; 24:16; II Cor. 1:12; 4:2; 5:11; I Tim. 1:5; 3:9; II Tim. 1:3). The meaning here must be that we are to subject ourselves out of a sense of obligation to God. The thought then is that we are not only to be subject because insubjection brings upon us penal judgment but also because there is the obligation intrinsic to God's will irrespective of the liability which evil-doing may entail. God alone is Lord of the conscience and therefore to do anything out of conscience or for conscience' sake is to do it from a sense of obligation to God. This is stated expressly in I Peter 2:13: "be subject to every ordinance of man for the Lord's sake". The necessity, therefore, is not that of inevitable outcome (*cf.* Matt. 18:7; Luke 21:23; I Cor. 7:26) but that of ethical demand (*cf.* I Cor. 9:16).

6 In view of all that is involved in verse 5 regarding the divine sanction by which the magistrate discharges his functions there is no need to seek any remoter basis for the terms with which verse 6 begins, "for for this cause". If the magistrate is to perform the ministry which is given him of God, he must have the material means for the discharge of his labours. Hence the payment[14] of tribute is not a tyrannical imposition but the necessary and proper participation on the part of subjects in the support of government. This reason for the payment of taxes is stated in the latter part of the verse: "for they are ministers of God's service, attending continually upon this very thing".

The term for "ministers" in this instance is different from that used on two occasions in verse 4. But it does not denote a less dignified kind of ministry as if the collection of taxes, since it is a monetary affair, called for the use of a term of inferior signification. This term and its cognates are used in the New Testament, with

---

[14] There is no reason for taking τελεῖτε as imperative.

one possible exception,[15] with reference to the service of God and sometimes of the highest forms of ministry in the worship of God (*cf.* Luke 1:23; Acts 13:2; Rom. 15:16, 27; II Cor. 9:12; Phil. 2:17; Heb. 1:7, 14; 8:2; 10:11). Hence, if anything, this designation enhances the dignity attaching to the ministry of rulers. In the administration associated with taxes and customs there is to be no depreciation of their office. In the version this thought is properly expressed by saying that they are "ministers of God's service", although in the Greek they are simply called "ministers of God".

The "very thing" upon which the rulers are said to attend continually must in the context refer to the taxes. It would not be reasonable to regard the antecedent as the more general functions specified in the earlier verses. The thought is now focused on the payment of taxes and this is the "very thing" in view. The verb used in this clause adds likewise to the emphasis that falls in this verse upon the propriety and dignity of this phase of the magistrate's administration (*cf.* Acts 1:14; 2:42; 6:4; Rom. 12:12; Col. 4:2).[16]

By implication this verse also reflects on the purposes for which taxes are collected and on the uses which they serve. They subserve the ends for which rulers are appointed and not the abuses which are so frequently attendant upon the expenditure of them. In the words of Calvin, rulers "should remember that all that they receive from the people is public property, and not a means of satisfying private lust and luxury".[17]

7 "Render to all their dues." This should not be taken as a general exhortation that we are to discharge our obligations to all men. It is to be understood of the obligations we owe to those in authority in the state. This limitation is required by the context. With our all-inclusive obligations verses 8-10 deal. But within this sphere of obligation to magistrates the exhortation embraces every kind of debt owing. The "dues" are not merely those pertaining to taxes but, as the remaining part of the verse indicates,

---

[15] Phil. 2:25; *cf.* also Phil. 2:30. The Greek word is λειτουργός (as distinct from διάκονος in vs. 4).

[16] προσκαρτερέω. *Cf.* Jesus' own endorsement of custom and tribute in Luke 20:22-25 and the false charge in Luke 23:2.

[17] *Op. cit., ad loc.*

include the debts of veneration and honour. Hence this summary imperative is inclusive of all the obligations to be fulfilled within the sphere of civil government. The form of the imperative underlines the strength accorded to it.

The "tribute" corresponds to our term "tax", levied on persons and property (*cf.* Luke 20:22; 23:2), "custom" refers to the tax levied on goods and corresponds to customs payments.

"Fear to whom fear." The word used here for fear is the same as that rendered "terror" in verse 3. But in the latter verse the behaviour enjoined is that which will obviate the necessity of fear and therefore the absence of fear is commended, at least the absence of that which will be the occasion for fear. Fear is the accompaniment of wrongdoing. For this reason it might be thought that the magistrate is not in view in this present exhortation: two opposing attitudes would not be commended. Hence, it is thought, God is the person to whom fear is to be accorded as in I Peter 2:17: "Fear God. Honor the king". This interpretation is neither necessary nor feasible. (1) The kind of fear contemplated in verse 3, namely, the fear of the punishment executed for wrongdoing, should be absent in reference to God as well as to the magistrate: we are under an even greater obligation to avoid the conduct that will make us liable to divine retribution. Thus to make God the object does not relieve the apparent discrepancy between the two verses. (2) The apostle is dealing with our obligations to the civil authorities and it would be alien to the coordination and sequence to introduce a reference to the fear we owe to God. The identical form of statement in all four imperatives requires us to believe that they all belong to the same sphere. If the fear of God were meant the name of God would have to be mentioned in order to indicate the break in the sequence.

The solution lies in the different connotations. In verse 3 the fear is that of the punishment to be inflicted; in verse 7 it is the fear of veneration and respect. In reference to God this is the fear of reverential awe (*cf.* Acts 9:31; Rom. 3:18; II Cor. 7:1; Eph. 5:21), in reference to men the veneration due on account of their station (*cf.* Eph. 6:5; I Pet. 2:18). It is possible that difference of rank among officers of state is indicated by the terms "fear" and "honor", that the former has in view the respect paid to those on the highest level of authority and the latter that paid to those of lower rank. But there is not sufficient evidence to insist on this distinction. Both

156

terms could be used for the purpose of emphasizing the obligation to exercise not only the subjection due to rulers but also the veneration that belongs to them as ministers of God.

C. THE PRIMACY OF LOVE
(13:8–10)

13:8–10

8 Owe no man anything, save to love one another: for he that loveth his neighbor hath fulfilled the law.

9 For this, Thou shalt not commit adultery, Thou shalt not kill, Thou shalt not steal, Thou shalt not covet, and if there be any other commandment, it is summed up in this word, namely, Thou shalt love thy neighbor as thyself.

10 Love worketh no ill to his neighbor: love therefore is the fulfilment of the law.

8–10

There is transition at this point. Verses 1–7 are strictly concerned with the state and our relations to it. Verses 8–10 are not restricted to this sphere. Just as the imperative with which verse 7 begins is to be understood of the dues rendered to magistrates and their agents, so the imperative of verse 8 applies to every relationship. However, the transition is not an abrupt one. The apostle easily and appropriately passes from the subject of debts paid to rulers in the state to the subject of our obligations to all men. So he proceeds: "owe no man anything". It is necessary to take this as imperative. It could be regarded as indicative. But then the sentence would have to read: "ye owe no man anything but to love one another". The purpose would be to stress the primacy of love. But exegetically this construction is out of the question. It would be strange indeed for Paul to say this after having insisted that we are to pay our debts to the civil authorities. Besides, he does not proceed to say that the only debt we owe to men is love. He goes on to say that love enables us to fulfil our obligations to men but not to teach that love displaces all other commandments.

The force of the imperative is that we are to have no unpaid debts; that we are not to be in debt to any. In accord with the analogy of Scripture this cannot be taken to mean that we may never incur financial obligations, that we may not borrow from others in case of need (*cf.* Exod. 22:25; Psalm 37:26; Matt. 5:42;

Luke 6:35). But it does condemn the looseness with which we contract debts and particularly the indifference so often displayed in the discharging of them. "The wicked borroweth, and payeth not again" (Psalm 37:21). Few things bring greater reproach upon the Christian profession than the accumulation of debts and refusal to pay them.

"Save to love one another." This has frequently, if not generally, been regarded as the one exception to what precedes and would mean that the only unpaid debt is that of love, that love to our neighbour is a debt that can never be discharged. It is true that love is inexhaustible; it is a duty from which we are never relieved. In Philippi's words, "By its very nature, love is a duty which, when discharged, is never discharged, since he loves not truly who loves for the purpose of ceasing from loving ... by loving love is intensified, the more it is exercised the less can it be satisfied".[18] But it appears rather incongruous for the apostle, in a passage which enjoins love and asserts its primacy, to say or imply that love is an unpaid debt. There is, therefore, another way of taking the Greek terms rendered by the word "save". These terms frequently mean "except" and state an exception to that which has been asserted. But they also are used in the sense of "but" or "only" (*cf*. Matt. 12:4; John 17:12; Rom. 14:14; Gal. 1:19) and do not state an express exception to what precedes but only another consideration or reservation relevant to what has been stated. It would seem preferable to follow this usage here. So the thought would be: "Owe no man anything; only do love one another". This is to say, love is not regarded as a debt unpaid, nor is there any reflection upon the inexhaustible debt which love involves, but the apostle is simply reminding us of what we owe in the matter of love. We are to remember that love is a perpetual obligation.[19]

The question arises: what is the love here spoken of? Is it the love believers exercise towards one another within the fellowship of faith or is it the more embracive love to all men? It cannot be doubted that a distinct quality belongs to the mutual love operative among believers. It is of this love Paul speaks in 12:9, 10. And the expression "one another" in the present case would suggest the same. The solution to the question would appear to be as follows.

---

[18] *Op. cit., ad loc.*
[19] *Cf.* Barrett: *op. cit., ad loc.*

In enunciating the primacy of love and writing to the church as Paul now is it would not be possible to think of love on any lower plane than that of love in its highest exercise, love as exercised within the fellowship of the saints. And so Paul says "one another", thus focusing attention upon that circle to which the epistle is addressed. But it is likewise not feasible to restrict the love enjoined to the circle of believers. For the apostle proceeds immediately to show the relation of love to the law of God and the law of God of which he speaks is the law regulative of behaviour in our social relationships with all men. If the love of which he speaks is the fulfilment of the law, then the love must be as broad as the law itself and the law has respect to our relations to all men. This is indicated in the next clause: "for he that loveth the other hath fulfilled the law".[20] "The other" is the person other than oneself and cannot be restricted in this case to believers.[21]

It is apparent that in this passage the apostle is not dealing with love to God. He is dealing exclusively with love to our fellowmen, as the commandments quoted later show. It is just as true that love to God is the fulfilment of the law that pertains to our relation to God (cf. Matt. 22:37, 38; Mark 12:29, 30; Luke 10:27). But here it is love in inter-human relations that is in view (cf. Matt. 22:39; Mark 12:31; Luke 10:29-37). So in this instance the law that love is said to fulfil is the law pertaining to mutual relations among men.

"Hath fulfilled the law" is the perfect of completed action. "Fulfil" is a richer term than "obey". It means that the law has received the full measure of that which it requires. The completeness of conformity is thereby expressed (cf. Gal. 5:14).[22]

We are not to regard love as dispensing with law or as displacing law as if what has misleadingly been called "the law of love" has been substituted under the gospel for the law of commandments or precepts. Paul does not say that the law is love but that love fulfils the law and law has not in the least degree been depreciated or deprived of its sanction. It is because love is accorded this

---

[20] This is the literal rendering. "Neighbor" occurs in verse 9 but not in verse 8.

[21] There is no reason to suppose that "the other" is the other law, that is the rest of the law. The other commandments are not "other"; they are the commandments that love fulfils.

[22] *Cf.* Arndt and Gingrich: *op. cit., ad πληρόω*, 3.

quality and function that the law as correlative is confirmed in its relevance and dignity. It is the law that love fulfils.

Love is emotive, motive, and expulsive. It is emotive and therefore creates affinity with and affection for the object. It is motive in that it impels to action. It is expulsive because it expels what is alien to the interests which love seeks to promote.

If love is the fulfilment of the law this means that no law is fulfilled apart from love. This must apply, therefore, to the law that governs our conduct in the state (vss. 1–7). It is a great fallacy to suppose that in the state we have simply the order of justice but that in other spheres, particularly in the church, we have the order of love. There is no such distinction; far less is there antithesis. It is only through love that we can fulfil the demands of justice. The magistrate cannot properly exercise his authority except as he is animated by love to God and to the subjects of his realm. The subjects cannot render to him the veneration that is his due and be law-abiding for conscience' sake save as they recognize God's institution and with godly fear subject themselves to it. "Fear God. Honor the king" (I Pet. 2:17).[23]

Verse 9 corroborates and expands what is affirmed in verse 8. In the latter verse Paul had referred to the law. Now he gives examples of what the law is. He enumerates four[24] of the ten commandments. The order followed represents the order in which they appear in the Greek version of the Old Testament (*cf.* Deut. 5:17–21). The command respecting adultery precedes that respecting murder elsewhere in the New Testament (Luke 18:20; James 2:11). This enumeration from the decalogue indicates that, in Paul's esteem, the law which love fulfils finds its epitome in the ten commandments. That the precepts mentioned do not comprise the whole law is expressed by the words, "if there be any other commandment". This appeal to the decalogue demonstrates the following propositions. (1) The decalogue is of permanent and

---

[23] "It is as though he had said, 'When I request you to obey rulers, I require only what all believers ought to perform by the law of love. If you wish the good to prosper... you ought to strive to make the laws and judgments prevail, in order that the people may be obedient to the defenders of the laws, for these men enable us to enjoy peace.' To introduce anarchy, therefore, is to violate charity" (Calvin: *op. cit.*, *ad loc.*)

[24] οὐ ψευδομαρτυρήσεις appears after οὐ κλέψεις in א, the mass of the cursives, and some versions but is omitted in P⁴⁶, A, B, D, G, L, and some versions.

abiding relevance. (2) It exemplifies the *law* that love fulfils and is therefore correlative with love. (3) The commandments and their binding obligation do not interfere with the exercise of love; there is no incompatibility. (4) The commandments are the norms in accordance with which love operates.

It should be noted that the commandments mentioned are all negative in form. It is often pleaded that ethics should not be negative but positive. The fallacy here is that the plea is unrealistic; it overlooks the fact of sin. If there were no liability to sin and no fact of sin there would be no need of prohibition. It is because God's law is realistic that eight of the ten commandments are negative and one other has a negative element. God's law must be negative of sin. The one absolute prohibition in Paul's teaching to which there is no reservation is, "abstain from every form of evil" (I Thess. 5:22). Truth is negative of error, right of wrong, righteousness of iniquity. The gospel is good news because it is first of all salvation from sin (*cf.* Matt. 1:21). Even love itself is negative: it "worketh no ill to his neighbor" (vs. 10). And here in verse 9 we have examples of the ills it does not perpetrate: adultery, murder, theft, coveting. The commandment to love is positive and Paul elsewhere gives us a catalogue of its positive qualities. "Love suffereth long and is kind . . . rejoiceth with the truth; beareth all things, believeth all things, hopeth all things, endureth all things" (I Cor. 13:4, 6, 7). But even in this passage we also have negations: "love envieth not; love vaunteth not itself, is not puffed up, doth not behave itself unseemly, seeketh not its own, is not provoked, taketh not account of evil; rejoiceth not in unrighteousness" (I Cor. 13:4, 5, 6). When we translate these into imperatives directed to love they become negatives. Who is to say that the demands of love, both positive and negative, are not to be directed to love and its proper exercise commanded?

"Thou shalt love thy neighbor as thyself." This is an exact quotation from Leviticus 19:18. In the Old Testament passage it comes at the end of a lengthy series of commandments most of which are in prohibitory form (vss. 9–18). When Paul says that all the commandments are "summed up in this word", it is not certain whether he means that they are summarily *repeated*, that is recapitulated, or whether he means simply summed up in the sense of condensed. In any case the main thought is that when love is in exercise, then all the commandments receive their fulfilment and so they can all be reduced to this demand. The person who loves his neighbour as himself will not work towards him the ills prohibited and will, on the contrary, discharge the positive counterpart.

Something frequently overlooked deserves comment. It is the expression "as thyself". This implies that we do love our own selves. Love of oneself is not to be equated with selfishness or egotism. We are selfish when we do not love our neighbours as ourselves, when we are so absorbed with our own selves that we have no regard for others. Unselfish concern for others fulfils the injunction: "not looking each of you to his own things, but each of you also to the things of others" (Phil. 2:4). But this does not say or imply that we may be oblivious of our own things and, particularly, not oblivious of our own persons. It is unnatural and impossible for us not to love ourselves. "No man ever hated his own flesh" (Eph. 5:29) and in accord with this Paul says: "He that loveth his wife loveth himself" (Eph. 5:28). The various injunctions which might appear to contradict this love for oneself are not incompatible (cf. 12:10; Phil. 2:3). When we esteem others better than ourselves or when we sacrifice ourselves for the good of others (cf. John 15:13; Rom. 5:7), we do not thereby cease to love ourselves. The love of God is supreme and incomparable. We are never asked to love God as we love ourselves or our neighbour as we love God. To God our whole being in all relationships must be captive in love, devotion, and service. To conceive of such captivity to our own selves or to any creature would be the essence of ungodliness. Of this distinction our Lord's words are eloquent: "Thou shalt love the Lord thy God with all thy heart, and with all thy soul, and with all thy mind, and with all thy strength . . . Thou shalt love thy neighbor as thyself" (Mark 12:30, 31).

"Love therefore is the fulfilment of the law." The version has advisedly chosen the term "fulfilment" rather than "fulfilling". The latter term suggests process but this is not the force here. In verse 8 the tense of the verb points to the perfect of completed action. So here the noun denotes the full measure. It is common for commentators to regard the use of the noun in this instance as serving the same purpose and expressing the same meaning as the perfect tense of the verb in verse 8. This is questionable. The verb has frequently the sense of "fulfil"[25] and so it is proper to render the

---

[25] Cf. Matt. 1:22; 3:5; Luke 1:20; 4:21; John 12:38; Acts 1:16; Rom. 8:4.

clause in question, "he that loveth the other hath fulfilled the law". But it is doubtful if the noun ever bears the signification expressed by "fulfil".[26] Pervasively, if not uniformly, it has the meaning of that which "fills" or that which is "filled" and frequently the proper rendering is "fulness" (cf. John 1:16; Rom. 15:29; I Cor. 10:26; Gal. 4:4; Eph. 1:10; 3:19; 4:13; Col. 1:19; 2:9). Sometimes it means that which is filled in to make something complete (cf. Matt. 9:16; Mark 2:21).[27] It could mean complement in Ephesians 1:23.[28] Hence usage would suggest that the precise meaning is that of "fulness" and that the apostle has enriched and added to the notion of fulfilment expressed in verse 8 by indicating through the use of the noun in verse 10 that love gives to the law the full measure of its demand. The law looked upon as something to be filled is filled to the brim by love. It is not as if something other than love does part of the filling up and then love enters to complete the process but that love does all of the filling. From beginning to end it is love that fills and so in this sense it is with or by love that the law is filled.

---

[26] Rom. 11:12 has been taken in this sense by some. The noun is $\pi\lambda\acute{\eta}\varrho\omega\mu\alpha$.

[27] In these instances it is that which is filled in to make the garment complete and the thought is that the patch of new cloth on the old garment, intended to complete the garment, only takes away from the completeness which the garment should have.

[28] But, exegetically speaking, this is not to be preferred in the light of Eph. 3:19; 4:13.

D. THE APPROACHING CONSUMMATION
(13:11–14)

13:11–14

11 And this, knowing the season, that already it is time
for you to awake out of sleep: for now is salvation
nearer to us than when we *first* believed.
12 The night is far spent, and the day is at hand: let
us therefore cast off the works of darkness, and let us
put on the armor of light.
13 Let us walk becomingly, as in the day; not in revelling
and drunkenness, not in chambering and wantonness,
not in strife and jealousy.
14 But put ye on the Lord Jesus Christ, and make not
provision for the flesh, to *fulfil* the lusts *thereof*.

11, 12 "And this" means "and indeed" or "and the more"
(*cf.* Eph. 2:8; Phil. 1:28). This introduction therefore indicates
another reason why the readers are to fulfil the royal law, "Thou
shalt love thy neighbor as thyself". The reason is immediately
appended: "knowing the time". "Time" (season) here is not
time in general but a time with distinct significance, a time
charged with issues of practical moment so that it is now high time
to awake out of sleep. How we may further characterize this
"time" depends upon the interpretation of the "salvation" which
is said to be nearer than when we first believed.

The term "salvation" could be used in the sense of deliverance
from some temporal oppression or affliction (*cf.* Phil. 1:19). It
might be supposed, therefore, that the apostle is thinking of some
present distress afflicting the church from which he hopes there
will soon be deliverance. The usage of the New Testament,
however, would point to the conclusion that when this term is
used with reference to the future it denotes the consummation
of salvation to be realized at the advent of Christ (*cf.* Phil. 2:12;
I Thess. 5:8, 9; Heb. 1:14; 9:28; I Pet. 1:5; 2:2). Hence it is the
completion of the salvation process that is said to be nearer than
when we believed. Since this completion is consummatory and is

165

bound up with what is central in the eschatological hope, we would have to regard this passage as having a distinctly eschatological emphasis. The term "season" or "time" should thus be taken in a sense that is relevant to this emphasis. The term does not of itself have eschatological reference.[29] It may denote any particular season or period (*cf*. Matt. 11:25; 12:1; Luke 4:13; 8:13; 21:36; Acts 7:20; 12:1; 14:17; I Cor. 7:5; Gal. 4:10; Eph. 2:12; II Tim. 4:6). Frequently the word is used with reference to an appointed time and therefore to the time fixed for and appropriate to certain events or even duties (*cf*. Matt. 26:18; Luke 19:44; John 7:6, 8; Acts 17:26; Rom. 5:6; 9:9; II Cor. 6:2; Gal. 6:9, 10; II Thess. 2:6; I Tim. 2:6; 6:15; Tit. 1:3; I Pet. 5:6). It is sometimes used to denote a definite period of climactic significance in the unfolding of God's redemptive plan (*cf*. Matt. 26:18; Mark 1:15; Rom. 3:26; Rev. 1:3). The plural is also used with similar signification (*cf*. I Tim. 2:6; Tit. 1:3). But the term has also expressly eschatological application (*cf*. Mark 13:33; Luke 21:8; I Pet. 1:5; Rev. 11:18). A distinctly eschatological aspect appears also in the use of the plural in such passages as Luke 21:24; Acts 3:20; I Timothy 4:1; 6:15. With these diverse uses of the term in view the application in the passage before us would appear to be that the apostle is thinking of the present time in which he is writing as the period that has its terminus in the consummation. It is the last epoch in this world's history, the time in which the complex of consummating events is impending. These are the last days (*cf*. Acts 2:17; II Tim. 3:1; Heb. 1:2; James 5:3; I Pet. 1:20; II Pet. 3:3; I John 2:18). With this perspective in reference to the readers' place in history Paul assumes they are familiar and he is reminding them of its meaning for practical godliness. They have their place in "the fulness of the time" (Gal. 4:4), in the "dispensation of the fulness of the times" (Eph. 1:10), in "the ends of the ages" (I Cor. 10:11), in "the consummation of the ages" (Heb. 9:26). The exhortation is, therefore, to much the same effect as that of Paul elsewhere (Tit. 2:12, 13) and of Peter (II Pet. 3:14). The "season" is that

---

[29] For a recent study of καιρός and for a discriminating and searching criticism of the viewpoint whereby χρόνος and καιρός are sharply distinguished and the latter regarded as time considered in relation to personal action *cf*. James Barr: *Biblical Words for Time, Studies in Biblical Theology No. 33* (Naperville, 1962); *cf*. also by the same author *The Semantics of Biblical Language* (London, 1961).

which derives its character from the consummating events towards which the present age is hastening, events which have their focus in "the appearing of the glory of the great God and our Saviour Jesus Christ" (Tit. 2:13). The foregoing interpretation of the "salvation" and "season" would give the direction for the understanding of other details in verses 11, 12.

"The night is far spent, the day is at hand." "The day", without further characterization or specification, is used by Paul and other New Testament writers as an eschatological designation (*cf.* I Cor. 3:13; I Thess. 5:4; Heb. 10:25; II Pet. 1:19). This use of the simple expression "the day" is defined by closely related expressions such as "that day" and "the great day" (*cf.* Matt. 7:22; 24:36; II Thess. 1:10; II Tim. 1:12, 18; 4:8; Jude 6). That "the day" and "that day" could be used to denote the eschatological day without further specification arises, no doubt, from the frequency with which the word "day" is used in various combinations to designate what is strictly eschatological—"the day of judgment", "the last day", "the day of wrath", "the day of the Lord", "the day of God", "the day when the Son of man is revealed", "the day of Christ" (*cf.* Matt. 10:15; 12:36; Luke 17:24, 30; John 6:39; 14:48; Acts 17:31; Rom. 2:15, 16; I Cor. 1:8; 5:5; Eph. 4:30; Phil. 1:6, 10; I Thess. 5:2; II Thess. 2:2; II Pet. 3:7, 10; I John 4:17). With this copious use of the term "day" in mind, no other interpretation could begin to gather to itself as much support as that which interprets "the day" in the present text as referring to the day when Christ will come with salvation for his people (*cf.* Heb. 9:28). How then could the apostle have said that the day of Christ was at hand?

It is often claimed that the apostle, like other New Testament writers, expected the advent of Christ within a short time and that this expectation was reproduced in his teaching in the form of affirmation to that effect (*cf.* I Cor. 7:29-31).[30] Would not the

---

[30] "Paul's earliest extant epistles, those to the Thessalonians, suggest that at that time he thought that the Advent of the Lord might come within a few months: it would certainly come within the lifetime of most present members of the Church. The same thought is present in I Corinthians, and it affects his judgment on ethical problems (see chap. vii). It is all the more striking that in this epistle there is no mention of the imminence of the Advent, apart from these few verses. The whole argument stands independently of any such expectation... Only in the present passage the old idea of the nearness of the Day of the Lord survives to give point to his moral exhortations" (Dodd: *op. cit.*, p. 209). *Cf.* also Leenhardt: *op. cit.*, p. 339.

events then prove that the apostle was mistaken not simply in his expectation but also in his teaching?

The answer to this question would appear to reside in two considerations. (1) The New Testament does teach that the day of the Lord is at hand (*cf.* Phil. 4:5; James 5:8; I Pet. 4:7; Rev. 22:10–12, 20). This is not to be interpreted, however, in the sense of imminence in our sense of that word. Paul himself who gives expression to this thought of nearness found occasion to warn against the supposition of imminence (II Thess. 2:1–12). And in this epistle he teaches the restoration of Israel, even though at the time of writing there were no apparent signs of Israel's conversion satisfying the terms of his prediction (*cf.* 11:12, 15, 26). And Peter, though he had written that "the end of all things is at hand" (I Pet. 4:7), had occasion to deal with the objections proceeding from the lapse of time. He reminded his readers that "one day is with the Lord as a thousand years and a thousand years as one day" (II Pet. 3:8) and, therefore, that the lapse of a thousand years no more interfered with the fulfilment of the promise nor with the certainty of the Lord's coming than the passage of a single day. It is necessary, therefore, to gain this perspective with reference to the New Testament concept of the nearness of the advent. It is the nearness of prophetic perspective and not that of our chronological calculations. In the unfolding of God's redemptive purpose the next great epochal event, correlative with the death of Christ, his resurrection and ascension, and the outpouring of the Holy Spirit at Pentecost, is Jesus' advent in glory. This is the event that looms on the horizon of faith. There is nothing of similar character between the present and this epochal redemptive event. In this sense it is nigh. And this was as true when the apostle wrote as it is today. (2) Correlative with the nearness of "the day" is the other statement, "the night is far spent". Obviously "the day" and "the night" are contrasted and as "the day" is characterized by light so is the night by darkness. "The day" makes manifest (*cf.* I Cor. 3:13), the night conceals. The Lord's coming is represented as bringing to "light the hidden things of darkness" (I Cor. 4:5) and is associated with light because then the whole panorama of history will be placed in the pure light of God's judgment (*cf.* Rom. 14:10; II Cor. 5:10). In respect of the splendour of this light all that precedes Christ's advent in glory is *relatively* darkness and is thus called "the night". Furthermore, that which precedes Christ's coming is "this age" in contrast with "the age to come" and "this age" is evil (*cf.* Luke 16:8; Rom. 12:2; I Cor. 1:20; 2:6–8; II Cor. 4:4; Gal. 1:4; II Tim. 4:10). This indicates another reason why that which antedates Christ's advent should be called "the night" and associated with darkness. We are also provided with a perspective that throws light upon the statement that "the night is far spent". For "the night" would have to be identified with "this age" and therefore with the whole period of this world's history prior to the advent. And we have good reason to infer that the apostle is reflecting upon the relative brevity of what is yet to run its course of the history of this world, that history is hastening to its terminus. Paul elsewhere speaks of what is past as "the ages and the generations" (Col. 1:26). He identifies the present as "the ends of the ages" (I Cor. 10:11) and in Hebrews 9:26 it is called "the consummation of the ages". In this light not only is it appropriate to say "the night is far spent"; it is also necessary, and it is the bearing of this truth upon practical godliness that the apostle is now stressing. "Let us therefore cast off the works of darkness, and let us put on the armor of light."

Sleep, night, darkness are all co-related in our ordinary experience. The same is true in the moral and religious realm. And what the apostle is pressing home is the incompatibility of moral and religious slumbers with the position which believers now occupy in the great drama of redemption. The basic sanction of love to our neighbour as ourselves applied to the Old Testament as well as to the New (vss. 8–10). But the consideration Paul is now pleading is one that could apply only to the particular "season" contemplated in the present passage and urged as the reason for godly living. The day of Christ, though not yet come, is nevertheless throwing its light backward upon the present. In that light believers must now live; it is the dawning of the day of unprecedented splendour. It is high time to awake to the realization of this fact, to be aroused from spiritual torpor, to throw off the garments of slumber, and to put on the weapons that befit the tasks of such a "season" in redemptive history. Each calendar day brings nearer to us the day of final salvation, and, since it is life in the body that is decisive for eternal issues, the event of death points up for each person how short is "the season" prior to Christ's advent. As "we must all be made manifest before the judgment-seat of Christ" (II Cor. 5:10; *cf.* Rom. 14:10) and Christ is ready to "judge living and dead" (II Tim. 4:1; *cf.* I Pet. 4:5; James 5:9), indulgence of the works of the flesh is contradiction of the believer's faith and hope.

"The works of darkness" are the works belonging to and characteristic of darkness and darkness is to be understood in the ethical sense (*cf.* I Cor. 4:5; 6:14; Eph. 5:8, 11; Col. 1:13). "The armor of light" is likewise to be understood ethically and religiously and suggests by the terms used that the life of the believer is the good fight of faith (*cf.* II Cor. 6:7; Eph. 6:10–18).

13, 14 The excesses which the apostle enumerates in verse 13 were common in the empire at this time and particularly at Corinth from which the epistle was written. The terms indicate abandonment to debauchery and the quarrels which are the sequel. The positive exhortation in verse 14 points up the contrast which the lordship of Christ creates and demands. The figure is that of putting on Christ. Elsewhere Paul speaks of putting on the new man (Eph. 4:24; Col. 3:10), of putting on the armour of God (Eph. 6:11) and the weapons of light (vs. 12), of putting on the breastplate of righteousness, of faith, and bowels of compassion (Eph. 6:14; Col. 3:12; I Thess. 5:8). But none of these measure up to the significance of the present formula. It is used once elsewhere (Gal. 3:27). This latter text is to be interpreted in the light of Romans 6:1–10. To put on Christ is to be identified with him not only in his death but also in his resurrection. It is to be united to him in the likeness of his resurrection life. The full title "the Lord Jesus Christ" underlines the inclusiveness involved in the exhortation. Nothing less than the complete negation of vice and the perfection of purity and virtue exemplified in Christ make up the habitude required of a believer. When we think of Christ as holy, harmless, undefiled, and separate from sinners, we see the total contrast between the vices described in verse 13 and the pattern of verse 14. The negative is as exclusive as the positive is inclusive. We are not to make any provision for the fulfilment of the lusts of the flesh. The flesh is not to be equated with the body but includes all sinful propensions (*cf.* 7:5; 8:5–8; Gal. 5:19–21; 6:8; Eph. 2:3).

170

E. THE WEAK AND THE STRONG
(14:1–23)

14:1-12

1 But him that is weak in faith receive ye, *yet* not for decision of scruples.

2 One man hath faith to eat all things: but he that is weak eateth herbs.

3 Let not him that eateth set at nought him that eateth not; and let not him that eateth not judge him that eateth: for God hath received him.

4 Who art thou that judgest the servant of another? to his own lord he standeth or falleth. Yea, he shall be made to stand; for the Lord hath power to make him stand.

5 One man esteemeth one day above another: another esteemeth every day *alike*. Let each man be fully assured in his own mind.

6 He that regardeth the day, regardeth it unto the Lord: and he that eateth, eateth unto the Lord, for he giveth God thanks; and he that eateth not, unto the Lord he eateth not, and giveth God thanks.

7 For none of us liveth to himself, and none dieth to himself.

8 For whether we live, we live unto the Lord; or whether we die, we die unto the Lord: whether we live therefore, or die, we are the Lord's.

9 For to this end Christ died and lived *again*, that he might be Lord of both the dead and the living.

10 But thou, why dost thou judge thy brother? or thou again, why dost thou set at nought thy brother? for we shall all stand before the judgment-seat of God.

11 For it is written,
As I live, saith the Lord, to me every knee shall bow,
And every tongue shall confess to God.

12 So then each one of us shall give account of himself to God.

171

What extends from 14:1 to 15:13 is another well-defined section of the epistle. This section is coordinate with what precedes in chapters 12 and 13 in that it deals with what is concrete and practical in the life of the believer and, more particularly, with his life in the fellowship of the church. But this section is concerned specifically with the weak and the strong and with the attitudes they are to entertain in reference to one another.

There is a similarity between the subject dealt with and what we find in other epistles of Paul. Most patent is the similarity to situations of which Paul treats in I Corinthians 8:1–13; 10:23–33. But also in the epistles to the Galatians and Colossians there appear to be points of contact. In Romans 14:5 reference is made to distinctions of days and in Galatians 4:10 we read: "Ye observe days, and months, and seasons, and years". In Colossians 2:16, 17 we have reference to feast days, new moons, and sabbath days as a shadow of things to come. Furthermore, in Colossians 2:16, 20–23 we have allusions to a religious scrupulosity concerned with food and drink, and the slogan of the proponents was "handle not, nor taste, nor touch" (Col. 2:21). In the case of these two latter epistles it is not, however, the similarity that is most striking; it is the totally different attitude on the part of the apostle. In these two epistles there is a severely polemic and denunciatory note in reference to these same matters. In Galatians the observance of days and seasons is viewed with grave apprehensions. "I am afraid of you, lest by any means I have bestowed labor upon you in vain" (Gal. 4:11). In Colossians likewise the reproof directed at the ascetics is of the severest character: "If ye died with Christ from the rudiments of the world, why, as though living in the world, do ye subject yourselves to ordinances...? Which things have indeed a show of wisdom ... but are not of any value against the indulgence of the flesh" (Col. 2:20, 23). This polemic severity we do not find in the section with which we are now concerned in Romans. Here there is a tenderness and tolerance that reflect a radically different attitude. "But him that is weak in faith receive ye" (14:1). "One man esteemeth one day above another: another esteemeth every day *alike*. Let each man be fully assured in his own mind" (14:5). Why this difference? The reason is clear. In Galatians Paul is dealing with the Judaizers who were perverting the gospel at its centre. They were the propagandists of a legalism which maintained that the observance of

172

days and seasons was necessary to justification and acceptance with God. This meant a turning back again "to the weak and beggarly rudiments" (Gal. 4:9); it was "a different gospel which is not another", and worthy of the apostle's anathemas (*cf.* Gal. 1:8, 9). In Romans 14 there is no evidence that those esteeming one day above another were involved in any respect in this fatal error. They were not propagandists for a ceremonialism that was aimed at the heart of the gospel. Hence Paul's tolerance and restraint. The Colossian heresy was more complicated than the Galatian. At Colossae the error which Paul controverts was basically gnostic and posited, as F. F. Bruce observes, "a clear-cut dualism between the spiritual and material realms" and regarded salvation as consisting in the liberation of the spiritual from the material. Thus "asceticism was commonly regarded as an important element in the process of this liberation".[1] There was also the worship of angelic beings (*cf.* Col. 2:18) who were conceived of as the media of revelation from God and the mediators through whom "all prayer and worship from man to God could reach its goal".[2] Asceticism was also part of the ritual by which the favour of these angelic powers was to be gained. This heresy struck at the heart of the gospel and its peculiar gravity rested in the denial of Christ's preeminence as the one in whom dwelt the fulness of Godhood (*cf.* Col. 2:9) and as the only mediator between God and man. Hence the vigour of Paul's denunciations. There is not the slightest evidence that the asceticism of the weak in Romans 14 was bound up with the heretical speculations of the Colossian heresy. The climate is, therefore, radically different.

It could be argued with a good deal of plausibility that the weakness contemplated in Romans 14 is identical with that of I Corinthians 8. The latter consists clearly in the conviction entertained by some that food offered to idols had been so contaminated by this idolatrous worship that it was not proper for a Christian to partake of it. The whole question in the Corinthian epistle is focused in food or drink offered to idols. It might seem that the similarity of attitude and injunction in Romans 14 would indicate the same issue. This inference is not established and the evidence would point to the conclusion that the weakness in view

---

[1] F. F. Bruce: *Commentary on the Epistle to the Colossians* (Grand Rapids, 1957), p. 166, n. 10.

[2] *Ibid.*, p. 167.

in Romans 14 is more diversified. This is not to say that weakness of faith respecting meat offered to idols did not come into view in the Roman epistle. The case is simply that more has to be taken into account. The reasons for this conclusion are as follows. (1) In Romans 14 there is no mention of food or wine offered to idols. If this were exclusively the question we would expect an explicit reference as in I Corinthians 8 and 10. (2) Distinction of days comes into view in Romans 14. This is not reflected on in the Corinthian passages. It is very difficult to trace a relationship between scrupulosity respecting days and that concerned with food offered to idols. (3) The weakness of Romans 14 involved a vegetarian diet (*cf.* vs. 2). There is no evidence that the weak in reference to food offered to idols scrupled in the matter of flesh-meat if it had not been offered to idols. For these reasons we shall have to conclude that the weakness in Romans 14 was more generic in character.

There has been much difference of opinion as to the source whence this weakness came and the background that gave to it its precise complexion. To be less positive than some exegetes have been would appear to be necessary. Rome was cosmopolitan and so was the church there. It may have been, and the evidence offers much to favour the thesis, that various types of weakness proceeding from different backgrounds and influences were represented in that situation which the apostle envisaged. It is not necessary to suppose that all within the category of the weak were characterized by the same kind of weakness. Some who were weak in one respect may have been strong in a particular in respect of which others were weak. The diversity may be the explanation of Paul's treatment. This passage deals with the question of the weak and the strong in a way that applies to every instance in which religious scrupulosity arises in connection with such things as those exemplified in this chapter.

1–3 "Receive ye." This exhortation is directed to those who are not themselves in the category of the weak and therefore to those who were strong in faith and did not entertain these scruples. Since it is not in the form, "ye who are strong receive the weak" (*cf.* 15:1), the implication appears to be that the church at Rome was not as a whole characterized by this weakness but that the weak were a minority. This would gather support from the consideration that in this section of the epistle the exhortations are preponderantly directed to the strong. "Receive ye" means that there is to be no discrimination in respect of confidence, esteem, and affection. The strength of the plea is indicated by the use of the same term in verse 3 for God's reception of us and in 15:7 for Christ's reception. The latter text enforces the unrestrained character of this mutual acceptance by enjoining that it is to be patterned after the grace of Christ in receiving us to the glory of God. Nothing exposes the meanness of the discrimination against which the entreaty is directed more than the contradiction it offers to the attitude of the Saviour himself.

"Not for decision of scruples." The general thought expressed is rather clear. It is that the acceptance of the weak is not to be for the purpose of fanning the flames of dissension respecting differences of conviction on the matters in question, namely, eating and drinking, observance or non-observance of days. But what the precise thought is it is difficult to determine. The word rendered "scruples" means "thoughts" and is sometimes used with depreciatory reflection so that it virtually means "evil thoughts" (*cf.* Luke 5:22; 6:8; 9:46, 47; 24:38; Rom. 1:21; I Cor. 3:20; Phil. 2:14; I Tim. 2:8). The other word rendered "decision" is a plural form and refers most probably to the act of distinguishing (*cf.* I Cor. 12:10; Heb. 5:14). Hence the thought would appear to be "not to distinguishing of thoughts". This is to say "nor for the purpose of subjecting the convictions and thoughts of one another to censorious scrutiny". Since this is contrasted with "receive ye" and the latter is directed to the strong, the accent falls upon the necessity of avoiding the provocations which would befall the weak if their scruples were made the subject of analysis and dispute.

In verse 2 one form of the distinction between the strong and the weak is instanced. The weak are vegetarians; the strong are able to eat all kinds of food. In verse 3 the apostle places his finger on the vice so liable to be indulged by the respective groups. That of the strong is the disposition to despise or treat with contempt the weak and that of the weak to judge the strong. Both are condemned with equal vigour. In actual practice these vices appear respectively in the smile of disdainful contempt and in the frown of condemnatory judgment. These exemplify the attitudes which the apostle condemns and they point up their disruptive tendency within the fellowship which "receive ye" contemplates.

175

The concluding clause of verse 3, "for God hath received him" has been taken as referring both to him who does not eat and to him who eats. No doubt it is true that God has received the weak as well as the strong and his reception of the weak provides the reason for the exhortation to the strong stated in verse 1. But in this instance proximity to the exhortation directed to the weak and the more direct relevance of this consideration to the condemnatory judgment in which the weak are disposed to indulge favour the view that the reference is to God's reception of the strong. The wrong of censorious judgment is rebuked by the reminder that if God has received a person into the bond of his love and fellowship and if the conduct in question is no bar to God's acceptance, it is iniquity for us to condemn that which God approves. By so doing we presume to be holier than God. Furthermore, the next verse is directed against the vice of the weak and asserts with reference to the strong something coordinate with God's reception of him, namely, that "he shall be made to stand; for the Lord hath power to make him stand".

4 In this verse the wrong of censorious judgment on the part of the weak is exposed by showing the intrusive presumption that it involves. It is the impropriety of intermeddling in the domestic affairs of other people that is expressed in the question. This is then applied to the relation of a believer to Christ's lordship. It is doubtful whether the next clause, "to his own lord he standeth or falleth" carries on the thought of the question and refers simply to the master of a house or whether the Lord Christ is contemplated.[3] But even if it is the master of the house that is in view, the figure is immediately applied in the succeeding clause to the lordship of Christ over the believer. "Yea, he shall be made to stand; for the Lord[4] hath power to make him stand". The Lord in this case is the Lord Christ and what is affirmed is the certitude of the believer's standing firm in the service of Christ. It has been maintained that the standing firm in this case refers to the final judgment. It is true that the thought of judgment is present in this verse. In the sphere of ordinary domestic relations the servant of

---

[3] It is more likely that κυρίῳ refers to the master in the human household. In Christ's household, as the clauses which follow show, the alternatives of standing or falling are not in view.

[4] Κύριος is supported by P⁴⁶, ℵ, A, B, C, and P.

another is not to be judged by our norms but by those of his own master. He stands well or ill according to the judgment of his master. Likewise in the believer's relation to Christ it is Christ's judgment that is paramount, not ours. But there is no warrant for supposing that the judgment in view is specifically that of the last judgment. The "standing" is that which is directly pertinent by way of rebuke to the censorious judgment on the part of the weak here and now. The weak tended to regard the exercise of liberty on the part of the strong as a falling down in their devotion to Christ and as therefore subjecting them to the Lord's disapproval. The apostle's assurance is to the contrary effect and should, therefore, be regarded as having reference to the standing of the strong believer and of his conduct in the approbation of the Lord Christ. He will stand firm and the reason is given: the power of the Saviour is the guarantee of his stedfastness. This appeal to the power of Christ offers poignant reproof to the sin of censorious judgment. The suspicion which the latter involves is a reflection upon the sustaining power of Christ and overlooks the fact that the conduct which meets with the Lord's approval cannot imperil the stedfastness of the person concerned.

5, 6 In these verses another form of scrupulosity is introduced and is concerned with the sanctity which some believers attached to certain days. The difference resided in the fact that other believers attached no distinguishing religious significance to these particular days. "One man esteemeth[5] one day above another: another esteemeth every day *alike*". That this divergence of opinion is in the same category as that concerned with certain kinds of food appears from the fact that in verse 6 the apostle returns to the subject of eating and not eating and gives the esteeming of a day as an example of the conscientious devotion to the Lord which eating and not eating exemplify.

As will be argued later, the most reasonable, if not the only feasible, view of this scrupulosity on the part of some is that they regarded the holy days of the ceremonial economy as having

---

[5] Here we have a good example of the way in which the apostle can change from one shade of meaning to another in the use of the same term. In verses 3 and 4 κρίνω is used in the depreciatory sense of censorious judgment. In verse 5 it is used in the sense of "esteem" to which no criticism belongs.

abiding sanctity.[6] Others recognized that these ritual observances were abrogated with the passing away of the ceremonial institution.

Since this difference of conviction among believers is in the same category as the difference respecting the use of certain kinds of food, we must conclude that the observance of the days in question did not proceed from any continuing divine obligation. The person who esteems every day alike, that is, does not regard particular days as having peculiar religious significance, is recognized by the apostle as rightfully entertaining this position. This could not be the case if the distinction of days were a matter of divine obligation. Hence it is the person esteeming one day above another who is weak in faith: he has not yet understood the implications of the transition from the old economy to the new. Again, however, we must note the apostle's forbearance and the demand that those who are characterized by this weakness be received into the confidence and fellowship of the church. The diversity of approved conviction is illustrated by the injunction, "Let each man be fully assured in his own mind". This points to the personal persuasion indispensable, in these matters of conduct, to the sense of devotion to the Lord, expressly referred to in the succeeding verses as that by which the believer's life is to be regulated. Whether he eats or does not eat, esteems the day or does not, it is to the Lord (vss. 6-8). The injunction to be fully assured in one's own mind refers not simply to the *right* of private judgment but to the *demand*. This insistence is germane to the whole subject of this chapter. The plea is for acceptance of one another despite diversity of attitude regarding certain things. Compelled conformity or pressure exerted to the end of securing conformity defeats the aims to which all the exhortations and reproofs are directed.

The coordination in verse 6 might lend itself to the view that it is the strong believer who esteems one day above another because the reference to such observance is immediately followed by reference to the strong believer's eating practices. For the reasons already adduced this cannot be the case. Besides, in the other epistles (Gal. 4:10, 11; Col. 2:16, 17) the observance of days, because of its association with the heresies prevalent in the Galatian and Colossian churches, is unsparingly condemned. The observance in the church at Rome is tolerated because it was not

---

[6] See Appendix D (pp. 257ff.) for fuller discussion.

bound up with heresy. But for this reason those observing the days must have been the weak in faith.

The threefold repetition of the words "unto the Lord" in verse 6 expresses the religious conviction, namely, conscience toward the Lord, out of regard for which the diverse practices are followed. This is the vindication in the respective cases. In the realm of liberty a believer's conduct is not unreligious. Whatever he does or refrains from doing is "unto the Lord" and so he may never be destitute of the consciousness that he is serving the Lord Christ (*cf.* I Cor. 10:31). This expression "unto the Lord" anticipates what is unfolded in verses 7, 8.

Proof that the strong believer eats to the Lord is derived from the fact that he gives God thanks. The thought is that thanksgiving implies gratitude to God and the awareness that what he eats is the gift of God to be enjoyed. This state of mind carries with it the conviction that he eats to the Lord. Elsewhere thanksgiving is represented as that which sanctifies food. "For every creature of God is good, and nothing is to be rejected, if it be received with thanksgiving: for it is sanctified through the word of God and prayer" (I Tim. 4:4, 5). This thanksgiving is exemplified in the blessing pronounced before meals (*cf.* Matt. 15:36; Acts 27:35; I Cor. 10:30), though not to be restricted to it.

The consciousness of devotion to the Lord is also true of the weak believer in his abstinence from certain foods: "he that eateth not, unto the Lord he eateth not". There is, therefore, no under-valuation of the weak believer. He is credited with an equal sense of devotion to Christ, and he likewise gives thanks. This is not to be understood as meaning that he gives thanks for what he does not eat nor that he gives thanks to God because he abstains from that of which the strong believer partakes. The words "and giveth God thanks" should be taken as referring to the thanks he offers for that of which he does partake.[7] And this thanksgiving is likewise in his case a manifestation of his sense of indebtedness to God and devotion to Christ. The change from "for he giveth God thanks" to "and giveth God thanks" is striking. The former states a reason, the latter is a statement of fact. The distinction is not, however, to be loaded with the meaning that although the weak does not eat

---

[7] "But the thanks are given neither for *what* he eats not, which were absurd, nor *that* he eats not, which were Pharisaic (Luke xviii. 11), but for what he eats, namely vegetable food" (Philippi: *op. cit., ad loc.*).

nevertheless he gives thanks. If stress is to be laid on the distinction it should not be given more significance than that in the one case giving thanks is adduced as the reason, in the other case it is stated as an all-important and necessary condition.

7, 8 Verse 7 does not mean, as sometimes popularly understood and quoted, that a man is not sufficient to himself in the social and economic spheres. It is not directed against selfish and self-assertive independence in the order of society. In this passage as a whole this attitude is condemned and the demand of considerateness for others is inculcated. But in this verse, as verse 8 clearly shows, what is being asserted is that the believer lives *to theLord*, not to himself. It is a negative way of expressing what is involved in the thrice repeated "unto the Lord" of verse 6 and the living and dying "unto the Lord" of verse 8. In these two verses it is the principle regulating and controlling the believer's subjective attitude that is in view, the disposition of subservience, obedience, devotion to the Lord, and it indicates, as noted earlier (*cf.* 12:2), that the guiding aim of the believer is to be well-pleasing to the Lord. In 12:2 this is stated in terms of pleasing God, now it is the Lord Christ who is contemplated. There is no conflict. If we discover by experience what the will of God is as the good and well-pleasing and perfect, it is because we have come to the recognition of the lordship of Christ in all of our life. The lordship of Christ in his mediatorial capacity is as inclusive and pervasive as is the sovereignty of God (*cf.* Matt. 11:27; 28:18; John 3:35; 5:23; Acts 2:36; Eph. 1:20–22; Phil. 2:9–11; I Pet. 3:22). It is only in the faith of Jesus and obedience to him that we can discover what the will of God is.

It might appear that in verses 7, 8 the thought is no longer that of conscious devotion to the Lord but that of the objective relation which Christ sustains to the believer. For how could our dying be regarded as taking place in the exercise of consecration to the Lord? There are two reasons for rejecting this supposition. (1) The import of the expression "unto the Lord", repeated three times in verse 6, must be carried over to the same expression in verse 8. This appears particularly in the words "whether we live, we live unto the Lord". Verse 7 gives the reason why it is to the Lord we eat or eat not, and verse 8 is the positive counterpart to what is denied in verse 7. So the sequence and close connection of the three verses would require that the conscious service of the Lord, so clearly in view in verses 6, 7, must govern the sense of "unto the Lord" in verse 8. (2) It is true that the event of death is not something *wrought* by our volition. But the same is true of what is here contrasted with it, namely, life. It is not by our will that the tenure of life is determined. There is, therefore, to this extent a parallel between life and death. The thought would thus appear to be that as the believer contemplates death, as well as in all the details of behaviour in this life, he is conscious of the Lord's will and in the act of dying his sense of devotion to the Lord is not suspended. No doubt, as far as the latter is concerned, it is the consciousness of being the Lord's that is uppermost but the accent still falls on what is true in the consciousness of the believer (*cf.* II Cor. 5:8, 9; Phil. 1:20-25). And this conscious resignation to and acceptance of death find their support in the assurance mentioned in the latter part of verse 8 that "whether we live therefore, or die, we are the Lord's".

This assurance, though it is entertained by the believer and is indispensable to his consecration to the Lord in living and dying, refers not to the faith which is consciously exercised by the believer but to the relation which Christ sustains to him, namely, that of possession.[8] It prepares for the assertion of Christ's all-embracive lordship in verse 9.

In these two verses we have witness borne to the transformation wrought in the life of a believer in the attitude to death. It is not because death itself has lost its character as the wages of sin or that it has ceased to be the last enemy. Death does not become good; it is an evil, the abnormality which sin brought into the world. We have in Paul the recognition of this in his own case when he says, "not for that we would be unclothed, but that we would be clothed upon "(II Cor. 5:4). We are also reminded that only in the resurrection will death be swallowed up in victory (I Cor. 15:54). The transformed attitude to death (*cf.* Heb. 2:14, 15) springs not from any change in the character of death but from the faith of what Christ has done to death and from the living hope of what he will do in the consummation of his conquest. It is the

---

[8] "Hence it follows... that he remains in every state of the case the Lord's *property*. As the dative τῷ κυρίῳ, *to the Lord*, in the first part of the verse, expressed consecration; so the genitive τοῦ κυρίου, *of the Lord*, in the last proposition, expresses possession" (Godet: *op. cit., ad loc.*).

resurrection of Christ, the hope of resurrection after the pattern of his, and the removal of sin which is the sting of death that transform the *relation* of the believer to death. So radical is this change that in the faith of it the apostle could "desire to depart and to be with Christ; for it is very far better" (Phil. 1:23).

9 This verse harks back to the latter part of verse 8 and states the ground upon which rests the lordship of possession just enunciated. This ground is stated, however, in terms of the way in which Christ secured this lordship and, more particularly, in terms of the purpose Christ had in view in dying and rising again, namely, that he might secure this lordship. There are several observations respecting this text.

(1) The lordship of Christ here dealt with did not belong to Christ by native right as the Son of God; it had to be secured. It is the lordship of redemptive relationship and such did not inhere in the sovereignty that belongs to him in virtue of his creatorhood. It is achieved by mediatorial accomplishment and is the reward of his humiliation (*cf.* Acts 2:36; Rom. 8:34; Phil. 2:9–11).

(2) It is to the end of securing and exercising this lordship that he "died and lived".[9] The latter does not refer to his life on earth prior to his death but to his resurrection.[10] The sequence indicates this. If the life on earth were in view the order would have been "lived and died". Besides, Paul uses the corresponding noun "life" with reference to the resurrection (5:10; II Cor. 4:10),[11] and mention of the resurrection is demanded here as an integral event of the process by which the lordship was achieved. It is appropriate that this term should have been used rather than other terms denoting resurrection because this same word is used in verses 7, 8 and, more particularly, because "died and

---

[9] ἀπέθανεν καὶ ἔζησεν supported by ℵ*, A, B, C and several versions is to be preferred to ἀπέθανεν καὶ ἀνέστη supported by G and the Vulgate and to various forms of a longer reading the most important of which is ἀπέθανεν καὶ ἀνέστη καὶ ἔζησεν supported by L, P, and the mass of the cursives.

[10] The aorist is adapted to express his becoming alive from the dead. It is inceptive aorist. Most frequently the resurrection of Christ is represented as the action of God the Father. This instance could be taken as referring to the action of Jesus himself after the analogy of John 2:19; 10:17, 18. But it is more likely that there is no reflection on agency. The thought is focused on the fact of his having lived again.

[11] Rev. 1:18; 2:9 are important parallels in which ζάω is used with reference to the resurrection.

lived" is parallel to "the dead and the living" in the latter part of
the text. It is by the life which Jesus lives in his resurrection power
that believers live unto the Lord. Thus there is a correspondence
between Jesus' resurrection viewed as "living" and the life of
devotion to Christ, so much in the forefront in this passage (*cf.*
6:4, 5; II Cor. 4:10–12; Col. 3:1–3).

(3) Christ is represented as achieving dominion over "both the
dead and the living". The order here is determined by correspondence with what is said of Christ that he "died and lived".
The form "both the dead and the living" emphasizes the sovereignty which Christ exercises equally over both spheres. He has a-
chieved this dominion because he himself entered the realm of
death, conquered death, and rose triumphant as the Lord of life.
He established his supremacy in both domains and therefore in
whatever realm believers have their abode they are embraced in
his lordly possession as those for whom he died and rose again. The
idea of this lordship is amplified in Ephesians 4:9, 10 where Christ
is said to fill all things and the process by which the same is secured
is descent into the lower parts of the earth and ascent above all
the heavens.[12]

(4) Although it is proper to think of Christ's dominion as
embracing unbelieving dead and living (*cf.* John 5:26–29), yet
because of the context it would not be feasible to understand this
text as having all-inclusive reference. We cannot interpret the
last clause in verse 8 inclusively and verse 9, it must be remembered, sets forth the basis of the assurance "we are the Lord's",
an assurance belonging only to believers.

10–12 Here the apostle returns to the thought of verse 3 that
the weak are not to *judge* the strong nor the strong to *set at nought*
the weak. But the difference of form adds strength to the indictment of the respective vices. In verse 3 there is exhortation to
abstain from these attitudes. Now we have the interrogative
address (*cf.* vs. 4a) which points up the presumption of judging or
despising a brother. The emphasis may be expressed by saying:
"Who are *you* to judge your brother? or who are *you* to despise
your brother?" The arraignment derives its warrant both from

---

[12] *Cf.* E. K. Simpson: *Commentary on the Epistle to the Ephesians* (Grand
Rapids, 1957), p. 91, n. 17.

what precedes, namely, that Christ is Lord, and from what follows, namely, that it is before God's judgment-seat we all must appear. The sin in each case, therefore, resides in the assumption to ourselves of prerogatives that belong only to Christ and to God.

The reproofs of verse 10 draw their force particularly from the appeal to God's judgment-seat at the end of the verse.[13] We are not to suppose that the appeal to God's judgment has relevance as reproof only to the "judging" on the part of the weak or even that it has more relevance to them. The vice of the strong is equally incompatible with the restraint which the future judgment requires. That all will stand before God's judgment-seat offers the severest kind of rebuke to the impiety of our sitting in judgment upon others whether it be in the form of censorious condemnation or haughty contempt.

The universality of the final judgment for just and unjust the apostle had unfolded earlier in this epistle (2:5–16). In the present text he is addressing believers and therefore of believers it is said "we shall all stand before the judgment-seat of God". In II Corinthians 5:10 it is to believers likewise he speaks when he says, "We must all be made manifest before the judgment-seat of Christ". These two texts therefore place beyond all dispute the certainty of future judgment for believers. It is only by deflection from biblical patterns of thought that doubt could be entertained or the consciousness of the believer fail to be conditioned by it. Furthermore, this judgment is not merely of persons. It is of the behaviour of believers Paul is here speaking and it is for the correction of wrong behaviour that the fact of God's future judgment is adduced. Conduct is to be judged. The other passage puts this beyond question: each one will "receive the things *done* in the body, according to what he hath done, whether it be good or bad" (II Cor. 5:10; *cf.* I Cor. 3:8–15; 4:5; Eccl. 12:14). The judgment embraces not only all persons but also all deeds.

The support from Scripture is derived from Isaiah 45:23. In the part of the verse quoted the only significant change from the Hebrew and Greek is that instead of using the formula, "By myself I have sworn" the apostle uses another Old Testament formula

---

[13] The reading θεοῦ is supported by such uncials that the other reading Χριστοῦ could scarcely be adopted. It may well be that Χριστοῦ in II Cor. 5:10 influenced the text in Rom. 14:10 and this would be another reason for regarding θεοῦ as the proper variant in the latter case.

which has the same effect: "As I live, saith the Lord" (*cf.* Numb. 14:28; Deut. 32:40; Isa. 49:18; Ezek. 33:11). The remainder as quoted corresponds with the Greek version except for a slight alteration in the order of words. The refrain of this chapter in Isaiah is that the Lord is God and there is none else (*cf.* vss. 5–7, 14, 18, 21, 22). This is directly germane to the fact of judgment. It is because God is God and there is none else that he must bring the whole panorama of history before him for final adjudication. Everything must be adjudged with equity. "He will judge the world with righteousness, and the peoples with his truth" (Psalm 96:13; *cf.* 98:9). Reluctance to entertain the reality of this universal and all-inclusive judgment springs from preoccupation with what is conceived to be the comfort and joy of believers at the coming of Christ rather than with the interests and demands of God's glory. The latter should always be paramount in the outlook of the believer. And it should not be forgotten that, although God will bring evil as well as good into judgment, there will be no abatement of the believer's joy, because it is in the perspective of this full disclosure that the vindication of God's glory in his salvation will be fully manifest. It is only in the light of this manifestation that the believer's joy could be complete. Judgment involves severity and by this consideration the believer should always be actuated in the life of faith. But it also is filled with grandeur and a grandeur indispensable to the consummation of redemption as well as to the consummation of all things.[14]

Verse 12 completes the appeal to the fact of judgment by the reminder that implied in the same is the account which each person for himself will render to God. It is to God each will render account, not to men. It is concerning himself he will give account, not on behalf of another. So the thought is focused upon the necessity of judging *ourselves now* in the light of the account which will be given ultimately to God.[15] We are to judge ourselves rather than sit in judgment upon others.

14:13–23

13 Let us not therefore judge one another any more: but judge ye this rather, that no man put a stumbling-block in his brother's way, or an occasion of falling.

---

[14] *Cf.* Phil. 2:10, 11 for another instance of quotation from Isa. 45:23.
[15] There is not good warrant for the omission of τῷ θεῷ at the end o verse 12.

14 I know, and am persuaded in the Lord Jesus, that nothing is unclean of itself: save that to him who accounteth anything to be unclean, to him it is unclean.

15 For if because of meat thy brother is grieved, thou walkest no longer in love. Destroy not with thy meat him for whom Christ died.

16 Let not then your good be evil spoken of:

17 for the kingdom of God is not eating and drinking, but righteousness and peace and joy in the Holy Spirit.

18 For he that herein serveth Christ is well-pleasing to God, and approved of men.

19 So then let us follow after things which make for peace, and things whereby we may edify one another.

20 Overthrow not for meat's sake the work of God. All things indeed are clean; howbeit it is evil for that man who eateth with offence.

21 It is good not to eat flesh, nor to drink wine, nor *to do anything* whereby thy brother stumbleth.

22 The faith which thou hast, have thou to thyself before God. Happy is he that judgeth not himself in that which he approveth.

23 But he that doubteth is condemned if he eat, because *he eateth* not of faith; and whatsoever is not of faith is sin.

This section is directed largely to the strong and enjoins upon them the action which love for the weak requires. In this part of the epistle it has been already noted how much emphasis falls upon love (*cf.* 12:9; 13:8–10). The necessity of walking according to love (vs. 15) is in this section applied to the behaviour which consideration for the well-being of weaker brethren must constrain on the part of the strong.

13, 14 It is not possible in simple translation to bring out the force of the two distinct senses in which the word "judge" is used in verse 13 nor the effect of the different tenses. In the first instance "judge" is used in the sense of censorious judgment, in the second it is used in the good sense to "determine" (*cf.* II Cor. 2:1). We found a similar distinction in verses 4 and 5. Thus we have another example of the way in which the apostle can use the same term with different meaning in successive clauses. The effect of the different tenses may be thus expressed: "do not continue to judge one another any more but come to determine this rather". The coming to be of the right kind of judgment is contrasted with the existing wrong kind of judgment.[16]

Since censorious judgment was the vice of the weak (*cf.* vss. 3, 4, 10), it might be thought that this exhortation is addressed to them. In that event the latter part of verse 13 would have to be applied to the weak and construed as meaning that they could place a stumblingblock in the way of the strong. It is not impossible to think of such an eventuality. A weak person in pressing his pleas for abstinence may cause doubts to arise in the mind of the strong and the strong is thus weakened in his faith and caused to stumble. Questionings are aroused where they ought not to exist and the perplexity resulting is an impediment rather than a help.

It is, however, impossible to carry over this interpretation to verses 14, 15. In these verses it is the weak person who is represented as stumbling and thereby grieved. Verses 14, 15 are so closely related to verse 13 that the latter part of verse 13 must be regarded as referring to the stumbling of the weak and the exhortation, therefore, as directed to the strong. It should be remembered that verses 10–12 contemplate both classes and the vice of both is that of presuming to take upon themselves the prerogative that belongs only to God, namely, that of judgment. In this way even the vice of the strong is regarded as a "judging". In view of this broader implication found in verses 10–12 it is proper to apply the exhortations of verse 13 to the strong and even regard them exclusively as those addressed. It is not out of the question to regard the prohibitive part of verse 13 as directed to both classes. But the positive clause must apply to the strong and, since the negative and positive are interdependent, it is better to take the whole as exhortations addressed to the strong.[17] They are not to place a "stumblingblock" or "occasion of falling" in the way of a weak brother.

A stumblingblock is an impediment in the way over which a person may stumble. An occasion of falling refers literally to a trap. Here these terms are used metaphorically and convey the

---

[16] On the distinction between the present subjunctive with imperative force in κρίνωμεν and the aorist imperative κρίνατε *cf.* Blass and Debrunner: *op. cit.*, pp. 172f.

[17] It is possible that the first exhortation of verse 13 is directed to both parties and then restriction to the strong in the second clause. But for the reasons stated it appears more reasonable to regard both clauses as having the same reference.

same thought, namely, that which becomes the occasion of falling into sin. In the most aggravated sense an occasion of falling is placed before a person when the intention is that of seduction; there is deliberate intent that the person may fall. We are not to suppose that the strong in this case are conceived of as actuated by that express intent. But this only accentuates the care that must be taken by the strong in the circumstance of weakness on the side of their brethren. The strong are regarded as placing a stumblingblock when they do not desist from what becomes an occasion of stumbling for the weak brother. What is condemned is the inconsiderateness that discards the religious interests of the weak.

The conviction underlying abstinence from certain foods and drinks was that these things were intrinsically evil and that the use of them for these purposes was defiling and contrary to the morals which should govern the Christian. The apostle sets forth the biblical principle that nothing is unclean of itself, that, as he says elsewhere, "every creature of God is good and nothing is to be rejected, if it be received with thanksgiving" (I Tim. 4:4). It is the truth affirmed by our Lord (*cf.* Mark 7:15). What is significant about Paul's enunciation of this principle is the way in which he expresses it: "I know, and am persuaded in the Lord Jesus". No form of words could express more fully the certitude of his conviction than "I know, and am persuaded" and no sanction could certify the rightness of this conviction more than to add, "in the Lord Jesus". The latter formula should not be taken as a mere appeal to the teaching of Christ in the days of his flesh (*cf.* Mark 7:19), although this teaching is relevant. Paul refers here to union and fellowship with Christ, and "in Christ Jesus" means that the conviction springs from, is consistent with, and is certified by the union and communion with Christ which, for the apostle, is the most characteristic way of defining his relation to the Saviour.

The word "unclean" is a term that originally means common and then came to mean defiled or impure (*cf.* Mark 7:2, 5; Acts 10:14; Heb. 10:29; Rev. 21:27). That "nothing is unclean of itself" is the justification of the belief entertained by the strong that he may eat all things (vs. 2) and is the reason why abstinence on the part of some is due to weakness of faith. This principle is the refutation of all prohibitionism which lays the responsibility for wrong at the door of things rather than at man's heart. The basic evil of this ethic is that it makes God the Creator responsible and involves both blasphemy and the attempt to alleviate human responsibility for wrong. It was necessary for the apostle to preface his plea to the strong with the insistence that nothing is unclean of itself. Otherwise the plea would lose its character as one based entirely upon consideration for the religious interests of the weak. If certain things were intrinsically evil, then the strong would be required to abstain from their use out of regard to their own religious interests.

Though nothing is unclean of itself, it does not follow that every thing is clean for every one. This is the force of the latter part of verse 14. The conviction of each person must be taken into account. The situation dealt with here is similar to that with which the apostle deals in I Corinthians 8:4, 7. "We know", Paul says, "that no idol is *anything* in the world, and that there is no God but one." However, account must be taken of the fact that "there is not in all men that knowledge". So, in our present text, "nothing is unclean of itself" but not all men have that knowledge or conviction. It is apparent that the distinction is between what is true objectively and what is recognized as true subjectively.

The conjunction rendered "save" does not state an exception to what had been asserted in the first part of the verse. It simply introduces a consideration that belongs to the situation. "There is nothing unclean of itself"; this is a proposition that is absolutely and universally true and there is no exception. But it is also true that not all have sufficient faith to know this.[18]

15 As noted above, the appeal to the strong is not based upon consideration for their own religious interests but upon regard for the religious interests of the weak. They are not to place a stumblingblock in the way of a weak brother, and the latter is weak because he esteems something to be unclean. These considerations explain the words "for if" with which verse 15 begins. They point back to verses 13 and 14 and introduce the reason why the strong believer is to abstain from the use of certain foods. If he discards the scruples of the weak and does not have concern for his religious interests, then he violates the dictates of love.

---

[18] *Cf.* comments at 13:8 for this use of εἰ μή.

The main question in the early part of this verse is the meaning of "thy brother is grieved". It might appear that the grief is the pain of annoyance and displeasure experienced when he sees the strong believer partake of food which he, the weak brother, esteems to be forbidden. He takes offense at the liberty which the strong believer exercises. This interpretation might seem to be supported by 15:1, 2: "Now we that are strong ought to bear the infirmities of the weak, and not to please ourselves. Let each one of us please his neighbor for that which is good, unto edifying". So it could be said: "avoid what is displeasing to others; defer to their wishes and pleasures". It must be admitted that weak believers do often experience acute pain of heart when they observe others exercise liberties that in their esteem are improper, and a strong believer actuated by love will seek to spare his fellow-believer this pain. There are, however, good reasons for rejecting this view of the grief in question.

1. This interpretation will not satisfy what is involved in the terms "stumblingblock" and "occasion of falling" in verse 13. They imply that the weak believer falls into sin. If the grief were merely the painful displeasure in the mind of the weak, this could not be construed as a fall. It is true that his displeasure arises from the censorious judgment in which he indulges, a judgment which is wrong and which Paul condemns (vss. 3, 4, 10). But at verse 13, in the use of the terms "stumblingblock" and "occasion of falling", the apostle introduces something new in the conduct liable to befall the weak and something not reflected on in the preceding verses. It is this new ingredient that is not accounted for by the mere notion of displeasure. The sin on the part of the weak implied in the fall which the stumblingblock occasions is the violation of conscience entailed for the weak when he is induced by the example of the strong to do that which he esteems wrong. He violates his religious scruples; this is the stumbling and falling envisioned in verse 13.

2. Verse 15 indicates the gravity of what is involved in the grief, a gravity that could not apply to mere displeasure at the conduct of the strong. The exhortation "Destroy not by thy food that one on whose behalf Christ died" implies that the grief befalling the weak is morally and religiously destructive. The sin committed, therefore, is of a grievous character and the grief can be nothing less than the vexation of conscience that afflicts a

believer when he violates conscience and does what he esteems to be disloyalty to Christ.

3. Verses 20–23 confirm this same conclusion. Here again the thought of stumbling is introduced and this is clearly indicated to be eating or drinking when, in the place of faith, there is doubt. "Whatsoever is not of faith is sin" (vs. 23).[19]

Hence a weak believer "is grieved" when he has violated his religious convictions and is afflicted with the vexation of conscience which the consequent sense of guilt involves. It is this tragic result for the weak believer that the strong believer must take into account. When the exercise of his liberty emboldens the weak to violate his conscience, then, out of deference to the religious interests of the weak, he is to refrain from the exercise of what are intrinsically his rights. No charge could be weighted with greater appeal than "Destroy not by thy food that one on whose behalf Christ died" (cf. I Cor. 8:11).

When the apostle bases his plea upon the vicarious death of Christ, he is reminding the strong believer of two things: (1) the extent of Christ's love for the weak believer; (2) the death of Christ as the bond of fellowship among believers. If Christ loved the weak believer to the extent of laying down his life for his salvation, how alien to the demands of this love is the refusal on the part of the strong to forego the use of a certain article of food when the religious interests of the one for whom Christ died are thereby imperilled! It is the contrast between what the extreme sacrifice of Christ exemplified and the paltry demand devolving upon us that accentuates the meanness of our attitude when we discard the interests of a weak brother. And since the death of Christ as the price of redemption for all believers is the bond uniting them in fellowship, how contradictory is any behaviour that is not patterned after the love which Christ's death exhibited! "If because of food thy brother is grieved, thou walkest no longer in love."

The imperative "destroy not" is one that implies grave consequences for the weak when he is emboldened to violate his conscience. The accent falls, however, upon the responsibility of

---

[19] The more accentuated would be the adverse judgment of the strong on the part of the weak the more would be excluded the liability to stumble; the greater the grief at the conduct of the strong the less liable would the weak be to follow his example. *Cf.* the pertinent remarks of Philippi: *op. cit., ad loc.*

the strong for the detriment that befalls the weak. In the event that the strong does not refrain from placing a stumblingblock he is charged with this offense. "Destroy" is a strong word (*cf.* Matt. 10:28; 18:14; Luke 9:25; 13:3; John 3:16; 10:28; Rom. 2:12; I Cor. 8:11; 15:18; II Cor. 4:3; II Pet. 3:9) and enforces the responsibility of the strong and the seriousness of the offense in which his failure to respect the infirmity of the weak involves both himself and the weak brother. The strong is not said to be destroyed. In accord with the emphasis of the passage his sin resides entirely in the violation of the demands of love to his brother and in his failure to entertain and exercise concern for the religious well-being of the brother. He has not loved his neighbour as himself (*cf.* 13:8). So both the indictment of the strong (vs. 15a) and the imperative (vs. 15b) show how jealously the requirements of love must be observed even in the realm of what has been called the *adiaphora* or, more properly, in the use of those things that are intrinsically right and good.

The strength of the word "destroy" underlines the serious nature of the stumbling that overtakes the weak brother. Are we to suppose that he is viewed as finally perishing? However grave the sin he commits it would be beyond all warrant to regard it as amounting to apostasy. The exhortation "destroy not" is directed to the strong. In a similar situation the weak person is represented as perishing (I Cor. 8:11). But here likewise it would be beyond warrant to think of apostasy.[20] Furthermore, the destruction contemplated as befalling the weak should not be construed as eternal perdition. All sin is destructive and the sin of the weak in this instance is a serious breach of fidelity which, if not repaired, would lead to perdition. It is upon the character of the sin and its consequence that the emphasis is placed in order to impress upon the strong the gravity of his offense in becoming the occasion of stumbling. It would load the exhortation with implications beyond this intent to suppose that the weak believer by his sin is an heir of eternal destruction. It is a warning, however, to the strong believer that what he must consider is the nature and tendency of sin and not take refuge behind the security of the believer and the final perseverance of the saints.

---

[20] *Cf. contra* Philippi (*ibid.*), who says that this is "a *dictum probans* for the possibility of apostasy".

16, 17 The question in verse 17 is the reference in "your good". Various views have been held—the gospel, the Christian profession, the kingdom of God. But no view suits the context better than the liberty which the strong believer enjoys in regard to eating and drinking. It has been objected that this is too restrictive because it would then be the exclusive property of the strong. This objection, however, has no validity. The strong is being addressed in this context (*cf*. vss. 13, 15, 19–21) and there is no need to broaden the application. Why should not the strong be exhorted here to avoid the consequences of undue exercise of his liberty? In another context Paul protests: "why am I evil spoken of for that for which I give thanks?" (I Cor. 10:30). That for which a strong believer gives thanks (*cf*. vs. 6) may properly be regarded as his "good"; it is his liberty in Christ to enjoy what God has created to be received with thanksgiving. However, when the damage to the weak, mentioned in verse 15, results, then this liberty comes into disrepute and it is this evil the exhortation of verse 16 seeks to prevent.

In verse 17 a reason is given for the exercise of restraint on the part of the strong. No consideration could have greater relevance or force than to be reminded negatively and positively of that in which the kingdom of God consists. The kingdom of God is that realm to which believers belong. Nothing defines their identity more characteristically than that they are members of it (*cf*. John 3:3–8; I Thess. 2:12). It should not be forgotten that the emphasis falls upon the rule of God. It is the sphere in which God's sovereignty is recognized and his will is supreme. Thus the mention of God's kingdom should always have the effect of summoning believers to that frame of mind that will make them amenable to the paramount demand of their calling, the will of God. It is in this perspective that the negation appears in its true light—it "is not eating and drinking".[21] When questions of food and drink become our chief concern, then it is apparent how far removed from the interests of God's kingdom our thinking and conduct have strayed (*cf*. Matt. 6:31–33).[22]

Difference exists among expositors as to the import of "righteousness and peace". Some maintain that these terms are forensic,

---

[21] Note βρῶσις and πόσις, not βρῶμα and πόμα.
[22] *Cf*. I Cor. 8:8 which is Paul's own comment on the negative of the present text.

righteousness referring to the righteousness of justification (*cf.* 1:17; 3:21, 22; 10:3, 6) and peace to peace with God (*cf.* 5:1).[23] Others maintain that these terms are to be understood ethically and therefore refer to righteousness as fulfilled and peace promoted and preserved by believers.[24] While it is true that all uprightness and concord as observed by the believer rest upon justification and peace with God, there is much more to be said in favour of the second view. (1) "Joy in the Holy Spirit" is subjective; it is joy in the believer's heart. Since this joy is coordinated with righteousness and peace we would expect the two latter to be in the same category. (2) Verse 18 points back to verse 17. "Herein" refers to the elements specified in verse 17. In these elements the believer is said to serve Christ, be well-pleasing to God, and approved of men. The service of Christ is, without question, an obligation devolving upon us and the discharge is said to make us well-pleasing to God. These ideas do not accord with forensic righteousness and peace. (3) Likewise in verse 19 we have hortatory terms directed to our responsibility. Of particular relevance are the words, "follow after things which make for peace". This enjoins upon us the promotion of concord in the church and is an index to what is meant by "peace" in verse 17. Furthermore, the demand to follow things that are unto edification points in the same direction. For these reasons "righteousness" and "peace" should be taken as the rectitude and harmony that must govern the attitude and behaviour of the believer within the fellowship of the church. There is, however, a parallel between what obtains in the subjective realm of attitude and conduct and what is true in the sphere of the forensic. This can be seen by comparing 5:1, 2 with 14:17. Justification, peace with God, and rejoicing in hope of the glory of God correspond to righteousness, peace, and joy in the Holy Spirit. The Godward reference of all grace in us is likewise patent. It is joy in *the Holy Spirit*, and the norm by which righteousness is directed and peace cultivated is the will of God.

18 Here again the principle set forth in verses 6–8 is reaffirmed and the same guiding principle of the believer's life as in 12:2. "Approved of men" is the opposite of the disrepute referred to in

---

23   *Cf.* Calvin, Philippi, Hodge: *op. cit.*, *ad loc.*
24   *Cf.* Meyer, Godet, Sanday and Headlam, Barrett: *op. cit.*, *ad loc.*

verse 16. We may not rigidly restrict the approval in view to those who are of the household of faith. The damage which befalls the church by inconsiderate conduct on the part of strong believers has its repercussions in the judgments of those outside and the good name of the church as the community of love and concord should be maintained so that adversaries may not have occasion to speak reproachfully (*cf.* 2:24; I Tim. 3:7; 6:1).

19 The preceding verses make clear the import of this exhortation. It is the strong who are being exhorted, as in the preceding verses and in verses 20–22.

20 Verse 20a is to the same effect as verse 15b. "Overthrow" is the opposite of the building up involved in the word "edify" of verse 19. "The work of God" may most properly be understood as referring to the weak believer who, though weak, is still God's workmanship (*cf.* Eph. 2:10). God is building up. Loveless brandishing of liberty breaks down. How antithetical! Verse 20b is a reiteration in more summary form of verse 14. It is more likely that the "man who eateth with offence" is the weak believer. He stumbles when he eats because it is not of faith and with a clear conscience. This corresponds with verse 14b, and the express mention of the brother who stumbles in verse 21 would support this view.[25] He eats with offence because he violates conscience in so doing.

21 This is also directed to the strong. For the first time we are informed that the drinking of wine was involved in the scruples of the weak.[26]

22 Verse 22a is another exhortation to the strong and means that they are not to parade and protest their rights and liberties to the detriment of the weak and with the evil consequences delineated in the preceding verses. The words "have to thyself before God" is another way of vindicating the strong in the possession and

---

[25] διὰ προσκόμματος is the genitive of attendant circumstance as διὰ γράμματος καὶ περιτομῆς in 2:27.

[26] κρέα is flesh-meat and is more specific than βρῶμα in verse 20. Of course a vegetarian diet is expressly referred to in verse 2. There are variants in verse 21. At the end ἢ σκανδαλίζεται ἢ ἀσθενεῖ is added by B, D, G, the mass of the cursives, and some versions. See also Appendix E (pp. 26off.) on the application of the principle here enunciated.

conviction of their liberty (*cf.* vss. 14a, 20b). They have this conviction in the presence of God and may not surrender it. But they are not to brandish it to the destruction of others. Verse 22b is a further corroboration of what is implicit in the preceding clause, as just noted. It is a particularly forceful way of commending the intelligent and mature faith whereby a Christian entertains no scruples in eating and drinking. It is not a future blessedness that is reflected on but, as Gifford says, "the present blessedness of a clear and undoubting conscience".[27] In pronouncing the strong believer "blessed" there is, however, no retraction of the leading plea of the passage. It is, rather, the blessedness of this state of mind and conscience that underscores the necessity of exercising the restraint which the weakness of others constrains.

23 This verse is concerned with the weak and "the danger of the weak brother is now brought into striking contrast with the happy condition of him who is strong in faith, and so supplies a further motive to the charitable restraint of freedom".[28] We may not tone down the condemnation to which the weak believer is subjected when he eats without clear conscience. It is not merely the condemnation of his own conscience; it is condemnation before God. This is proven by the last clause that "whatsoever is not of faith is sin". Just as the strong believer entertains his conviction of liberty before God (vs. 22a) and is blessed before God (vs. 22b), so the weak is condemned before God when he violates conviction (*cf.* vss. 14b, 15). The concluding clause is to be understood as applying to the subject in hand. It is true that without faith it is impossible to please God (*cf.* 8:7, 8; Heb. 11:6) and thus unbelievers can do nothing that is well-pleasing to God in terms of the criteria of holiness and rectitude. But we may not regard the apostle as stating this general principle in this instance but as reaffirming that a *believer* sins when he does what is not approved in his conviction and faith.[29]

---

[27] *Op. cit., ad loc.* μακάριος is a particularly commendatory term and finds its basis in the principle stated in verse 14a.

[28] Gifford: *op. cit., ad loc.*

[29] On the occurrence of the doxology found in some manuscripts at the end of this chapter see the discussion in Appendix F (pp. 262 ff.).

F. CHRIST'S EXAMPLE
(15:1–6)

15:1–6

1 Now we that are strong ought to bear the infirmities of the weak, and not to please ourselves.

2 Let each one of us please his neighbor for that which is good, unto edifying.

3 For Christ also pleased not himself; but, as it is written, The reproaches of them that reproached thee fell upon me.

4 For whatsoever things were written aforetime were written for our learning, that through patience and through comfort of the scriptures we might have hope.

5 Now the God of patience and of comfort grant you to be of the same mind one with another according to Christ Jesus:

6 that with one accord ye may with one mouth glorify the God and Father of our Lord Jesus Christ.

1, 2 Continuing the same theme as in chapter 14 the obligation of the strong in relation to the weak is developed still further. This is the only instance in which the term used for "strong" appears in the restricted sense applicable in this passage, though the general sense is the same as elsewhere (*cf.* II Cor. 12:10; 13:9). "Bear" is not to be understood in the sense of "bear with" frequent in our common speech but in the sense of "bear up" or "carry" (*cf.* 11:18; Gal. 5:10; 6:2, 5)[1]. The strong are to help the weak and promote their good to edification (vs. 2). Besides, the weak are represented as having "infirmities" and the exhortation of Galatians 6:2 must surely apply. "Let each one please his neighbour", as also the negative "not to please ourselves", must not be interpreted to mean that we are always to defer to the whims and

---

[1] In Rev. 2:2 βαστάζω has the sense of "put up with". It is questionable if it has this meaning anywhere else in the New Testament.

wishes of others, not even those of fellow-believers and thus always follow the course of action that pleases them. To please men is not a principle of the believer's life (*cf.* Gal. 1:10). Paul provides us with an example of the pleasing that he has in mind (I Cor. 10:33) and in the present passage is to be restricted to that situation dealt with. The strong are not to indulge their own liberties so as to be an occasion of stumbling to the weak and thus induce in them the grief and in that sense the displeasure reflected on in 14:15. It is the pleasing that will maintain in the weak the peace of conscience which emulation of the conduct of the strong will disturb and destroy (*cf.* also I Cor. 8:12). The aim specified in this pleasing of the weak, "for that which is good, unto edifying", indicates the considerations by which the strong are to be governed.[2] Disregard for the scruples of the weak breaks down the work of God (*cf.* 14:15, 20) and is fraught with *evil* consequences. Considerateness promotes what, in contrast, is *good* and builds up not only the weak themselves but the whole fellowship (*cf* 14:19).

3 Here is appeal to the supreme example in order to enforce the obligation enjoined in the two preceding verses. It is noteworthy how the apostle adduces the example of Christ in his most transcendent accomplishments in order to commend the most practical duties (*cf.* II Cor. 8:9; Phil. 2:5–8). The thought is focused in this case upon the disinterestedness of Christ. He did not look upon his own things but upon those of others. He identified himself with the supreme interests of those whom he came to save and thus bore the utmost of reproach and shame by commitment to that end in fulfilment of the Father's will. The quotation from Psalm 69:9 specifies the particular aspect of Christ's not pleasing himself which the apostle deems most relevant to the duty being enjoined. This scripture he regards as a forecast of Christ's self-humiliation. The frequency with which this Psalm is alluded to in the New Testament and its details represented as fulfilled in Christ marks it as distinctly messianic.[3] The part quoted must be understood in the light of what immediately precedes in the Psalm: "the zeal of thy house hath eaten me up". It is not our reproaches that are in view but the reproaches of dishonour

---

[2] The distinction drawn by Gifford: *op. cit., ad loc.* between εἰς as marking the aim and πρός the standard of judgment can hardly be maintained.

[3] *Cf.*, for the listing and comparison of passages, Liddon: *op. cit.*, p. 274.

levelled against God.[4] These reproaches vented against God by the ungodly fell upon Christ. This is to say that all the enmity of men against God was directed to Christ; he was the victim of this assault. It is to this Paul appeals as exemplifying the assertion that Christ "pleased not himself". We may well ask then: how does this feature of our Lord's humiliation bear upon the duty of pleasing our neighbour in the situation which Paul has in view? It is the apparent dissimilarity that points up the force of Jesus' example. There is a profound discrepancy between what Christ did and what the strong are urged to do. He "pleased not himself" to the incomparable extent of bearing the enmity of men against God and he bore this reproach because he was jealous for God's honour. He did not by flinching evade any of the stroke. Shall we, the strong, insist on pleasing ourselves in the matter of food and drink to the detriment of God's saints and the edification of Christ's body? It is the complete contrast between Christ's situation and ours that enhances the force of the appeal.[5] The same applies to all the passages in which Christ's example is urged and with the particularity relevant in each case.

4 The "for" at the beginning of this verse intimates the reason for the propriety of appeal to Scripture for support. Paul vindicates the use of Psalm 69:9 in verse 3 by the purpose which Scripture is intended by God to subserve: "whatsoever things were written aforetime were written for our learning" (*cf.* I Cor. 10:6, 10; II Tim. 3:16, 17). The extent to which Paul's thought was governed by this truth is evident from the frequency of appeal to Scripture in this epistle. The form of statement here and in the parallels cited above shows that in Paul's esteem Scripture in all its parts is for our instruction, that the Old Testament was designed to furnish us in these last days with the instruction necessary for the fulfilment of our vocation to the end, and that it is as *written* it promotes this purpose. The instruction which the Scriptures impart is directed to patience and comfort. Patience is endurance and stedfastness.

---

[4] *Cf. contra* Sanday and Headlam: *op. cit., ad loc.*
[5] It may be that the reproaches cast at the strong by weak brethren are in view and thus some parallel between Christ and the strong would be intimated. This, however, seems remote from the thought at this point. But, even if granted, the contrast between Christ and the strong believer would not be eliminated. How incomparably more shameful were the reproaches cast upon Christ!

Both the stedfastness and the comfort[6] are derived from the Scriptures and are, therefore, dependent upon these Scriptures and draw their character and value from them. These are generated by Scripture and their quality is determined by Scripture. However, the stedfastness and consolation are said to be the means of something more ultimate, namely, hope. Hope in this case is to be understood of that which the believer entertains, the state of mind. There cannot be the exercise of hope except as it is directed to an object, that hoped for. But to "have hope" is to exercise hope (cf. Acts 24:15; I Cor. 3:12; 10:15; Eph. 2:12, I Thess. 4:13; I John 3:3). In this text the instruction, stedfastness, and consolation derived from Scripture are all represented as contributing to this exercise of hope and thereby is demonstrated the significance for the believer and for the fellowship of the saints of the prospective outreach which hope implies (cf. 8:23–25 and vs. 13).

5, 6 These verses are not directly in the form of prayer addressed to God. They are in the form of a wish addressed to men that God would accomplish in them the implied exhortation, an eloquent way of doing two things at the same time, exhortation to men and prayer to God. Without the enabling grace of God exhortation will not bear fruit. Hence the combination. No form of exhortation is more effective in address to men than this. The following considerations respecting these verses should be noted. (1) The titles—"God of patience and of comfort" point back to the terms "patience" and "comfort" in verse 4 and mean that God is the source and author of these (cf. II Cor. 1:3).[7] God is characterized and recognized by the grace he imparts to us in the life and fellowship of faith. (2) The close relation of God to the Scriptures is clearly indicated. Patience and comfort are derived from the Scriptures (vs. 4) and they are also derived from God. There is no disjunction. The Scriptures are the abiding Word of God and therefore the living Word. It is through their means that God imparts to us the patience and comfort that are his. Paul's thought cannot be adjusted to any other view than that the

---

[6] παράκλησις is consolation and it is not necessary to adopt the meaning "exhortation".
[7] Cf. "God of peace" (15:33; 16:20; II Cor. 13:11; Phil. 4:9; I Thess. 5:23; Heb. 13:20) and "God of hope" (15:13).

Scriptures sustain to God that abiding relation that they themselves are his Word (*cf*. 3:1, 2). (3) "To be of the same mind one with another" (*cf*. Phil. 2:2, 5)[8] is a plea for the mutual esteem and forbearance which have been the plea from the beginning of this section (14:1) and is addressed to both weak and strong. "According to Christ Jesus" could mean in accordance with the will of Christ. In that event the harmony enjoined is qualified as consonant with Christ's revealed will and is not harmony irrespective of such conformity. In view of the appeal to Christ's example in verse 3 it is more likely that the meaning is "according to Christ's example" though not by any means limiting the thought to the specific particular mentioned in verse 3 (*cf*. Phil. 2:5). But even in this case the implications of the other meaning would be present. What is after Christ's example must always accord with his will. (4) The end to which this harmony is directed is the distinctive feature of these two verses. It is that in unison and unity they might glorify God the Father. The terms "with one accord ... with one mouth" (*cf*. Acts 1:14; 2:46) express the unity with which inwardly and outwardly the glorifying of God is to take place. To glorify God is to exhibit his praise and honour. In the background lurks the thought of the prejudice incurred for the final end to be promoted by the church when the fellowship of the saints is marred by suspicions and dissensions and in this case particularly by the arrogance of the strong and the stumblings of the weak. No consideration could enforce the exhortation more strongly than to be reminded of the glory of God as the controlling purpose of all our attitudes and actions. The form of the title by which the Father is designated could be rendered "God even the Father of our Lord Jesus Christ" or "God and the Father of our Lord Jesus Christ". There is not sufficient reason to insist upon this rendering. The Father is not represented merely as the *Father* of Christ but also as the *God* of our Lord Jesus Christ (*cf*. Matt. 27:46; John 20:17; Eph. 1:17; Heb. 1:9).[9] Hence the rendering of the version is in accord with the New Testament pattern of thought and its propriety should not be contested. In either case, however, our attention is

---

[8] The Greek is ἐν ἀλλήλοις.
[9] *Cf*. for defence of this rendering Sanday and Headlam: *op. cit*., *ad loc*.

here drawn to what is ultimate in our glorifying of God, the glory of God the Father.[10]

---

[10] This ultimacy is exemplified in other cases as, for example, in the love of God. The love of the Father is ultimate and fontal (*cf.* John 3:16; Rom. 5:8; 8:29; Eph. 1:4, 5; I John 4:9, 10).

G. JEWS AND GENTILES ONE
(15:7–13)

7 Wherefore receive ye one another, even as Christ also received you, to the glory of God.

8 For I say that Christ hath been made a minister of the circumcision for the truth of God, that he might confirm the promises *given* unto the fathers,

9 and that the Gentiles might glorify God for his mercy; as it is written,

Therefore will I give praise unto thee among the Gentiles,

And sing unto thy name.

10 And again he saith,

Rejoice, ye Gentiles, with his people.

11 And again,

Praise the Lord, all ye Gentiles;

And let all the peoples praise him.

12 And again, Isaiah saith,

There shall be the root of Jesse,

And he that ariseth to rule over the Gentiles;

On him shall the Gentiles hope.

13 Now the God of hope fill you with all joy and peace in believing, that ye may abound in hope, in the power of the Holy Spirit.

7 As in verses 5, 6 both weak and strong are in view, so here. In 14:1 the same exhortation is addressed to the strong in reference to the weak but now both classes are exhorted to mutual embrace in confidence and love. The necessity is underlined by what Christ has done. If Christ has received us,[11] are we to refuse fellowship to those whom Christ has received? If we place restraints upon our acceptance of believers, we are violating the example of

---

11 ὑμᾶς rather than ἡμᾶς is the more strongly attested variant. The former is supported bij ℵ, A, C, G, the mass of the cursives, and several versions. In view of the textual patterns which appear in this epistle it is difficult to defend ἡμᾶς. Internal evidence would not be a factor in this case.

that redemptive action upon which all fellowship in the church rests. In 14:3 the fact that God has received the strong believer is urged as the reason why the weak should receive him. Christ's reception of all without distinction is the ground upon which fellowship is to be unrestrained. "To the glory of God" should be taken in conjunction with Christ's action in receiving us.[12] In verses 8 and 9 two respects are mentioned in which the glory of God is exhibited in Christ's being made a minister of the circumcision. But we may not limit the glory of God in verse 7. There is a close connection between "to the glory of God" (vs. 7) and the glorifying of the Father (vs. 6). The harmony enjoined is for the glory of God the Father. This, as well as the harmony, is patterned after Christ's example; his receiving of us is to the glory of God and no consideration could enforce the necessity of mutual confidence and love more than that Christ's receiving of all, weak and strong, was not only in perfect accord with God's glory but was directed specifically to that end. The ultimate goal of Christ's action was likewise the glory of the Father (*cf.* John 17:4). We are reminded of the coalescence of supreme grace to us and the promotion of God's glory (*cf.* Eph. 1:14; Phil. 2:11).

8, 9a   These two verses appear to be not so much proof that Christ received all without distinction as additional argument to support the obligation to harmony and fellowship enjoined in the preceding verses. We are here introduced to a distinction not overtly mentioned in this section of the epistle, that between Jews and Gentiles. We may not infer from this that the weak were Jews and the strong Gentiles.[13] The respective parties may well have been drawn from both racial groups. But this reference to Jews and Gentiles does suggest, if it does not show, that the exhortation to mutual acceptance had in view the need to overcome all racial prejudice and discrimination in the communion of the saints at Rome. The stress upon the Gentiles in the succeeding verses makes evident the emphasis which the apostle felt called upon to place upon the world-wide redemptive purpose which Christ fulfilled in his very capacity as "minister of the circumcision". Any

---

[12]   The punctuation in the version quoted is based on the assumption that to "the glory of God" goes with "receive ye one another". This construction is not to be followed. *Cf.* A.V.

[13]   *Cf. contra* Gifford: *op. cit., ad loc.*

tendency to limit to Israel the relevance of this ministry is plainly excluded. The following considerations should be noted. (1) "The circumcision" stands for those of the circumcision, namely, Israel after the flesh (*cf.* 3:1, 30; 4:12; Gal. 2:7–9). The reference to "the fathers" (vs. 8) and to "the Gentiles" (vs. 9) by way of distinction demonstrates this. That Christ has become[14] a minister of the circumcision accentuates again the way in which Israel comes within the purview of Christ's mission (*cf.* Matt. 15:24; John 4:22). (2) It is necessary, however, to find a more significant allusion in the term "circumcision". This was the sign and seal of the covenant with Abraham (Gen. 17:1–21; *cf.* 4:11). Christ is therefore the minister of the covenant of which circumcision was the seal and it is in pursuance of that covenant that he came and fulfilled the office here mentioned (*cf.* Gal. 3:16). (3) The design of his being made a minister of the circumcision was to confirm the promises made unto the fathers.[15] The force of "confirm" is to establish and bring to realization. This is equivalent to bringing the covenant sealed by circumcision to fruition. For the covenant is the certification of promise and to fulfil the covenant is to fulfil its promises. It is in this light that the expression "for the truth of God" is to be understood. The oath-certified promises are God's promises and to their fulfilment his truth is pledged. God's faithfulness cannot fail and so Christ came to vindicate and bring to effect God's faithfulness (*cf.* Matt. 26:54). (4) The relation of verse 9 to verse 8 concerns the question: what is the design for the Gentiles of Christ's office as minister of the circumcision? It might be supposed that his ministry to the Gentiles would be independent and follow a different though parallel line. Such a construction would run counter to all that the apostle had argued in the earlier portions of the epistle (*cf.* 4:11, 12, 16, 17, 23–25; 11:11–32). But not only so. The syntax of these verses is eloquent of the fact that mercy to the Gentiles is likewise the design of Christ's being made a minister of the circumcision. The latter is not only that he might confirm the promises but also that "the Gentiles might glorify God for his mercy". This implies that the Gentiles are partakers of God's mercy. However, in accord with the emphasis upon glorifying God in verses 6 and 7 and in order to provide a more

---

14 The perfect tense should be noted—γεγενῆσθαι.
15 The τῶν πατέρων has the force of the promises belonging to the fathers and is properly understood as the promises given to them.

suitable parallel to "confirm" in the preceding clause as well as to enhance the beneficent result, the apostle expresses the thought by saying "glorify God for his mercy". This Paul then proceeds to demonstrate by a series of quotations from the Old Testament.

9b–12 The first quotation is derived from II Samuel 22:50; Psalm 18:49 and, apart from the omission of the vocative "Lord", is a verbatim quotation of the Greek version of Psalm 18:49 (Heb. 18:50; LXX 17:50) which, in turn, adheres closely to the Hebrew. Verse 10 is taken from Deuteronomy 32:43 and follows the Hebrew rather than the Greek version, verse 11 from Psalm 117:1 and the variation from the Hebrew and the Greek version consists only in the change of person in the second clause, verse 12 from Isaiah 11:10 and with slight abridgement follows the Greek version. Common to all of these quotations in the form quoted by the apostle is the reference to the Gentiles. As is apparent from verse 9 this is the interest that guided the selection of these passages. They all are adduced to support the proposition that one of the designs in Christ's being made a minister of the circumcision was the salvation of the Gentiles and they show the extent to which in the apostle's esteem the Old Testament had envisioned the outreach to all nations of that blessing which lay at the centre of the Abrahamic covenant. These texts quoted by Paul here and numerous others all bear witness to the way in which the outlook of the Old Testament had been regulated and inspired by the promises to Abraham (Gen. 12:3; 22:18). Although the first three quotations do not expressly state that the Gentiles will respond to the witness borne (vs. 9) or to the imperatives addressed (vss. 10, 11) to them, yet they must be understood as implying the subjection to the root of Jesse indicated in the last quotation (vs. 12).[16] Even if this inference were not made, they would still involve on the part of the inspired writers and in Paul's esteem the relevance to the Gentiles of that obligation to praise the Lord and rejoice in him which only covenant relationship could secure.

13 This verse may well be regarded as bringing this section of the epistle to a close. In accordance with the last quoted word

---

[16] This is particularly true in verse 10 in view of the way in which the Hebrew of Deut. 32:43 is rendered.

(vs. 12) the emphasis falls clearly on hope. The clause to which all else is subordinate is the final one, "that ye may abound in hope, in the power of the Holy Spirit". The form of this verse is the same as that of verse 5; it is indirectly prayer to God and combines invocation and exhortation. The title "God of hope" is to be construed after the same pattern as the titles in verse 5 and "the God of peace" (vs.33; *cf.* I Thess. 5:23; Heb. 13:20). God is the God of hope because he generates hope in us. It is, however, difficult to suppress the thought in this instance that the title points also to God as the object of hope. God himself is the ultimate hope of the people of God because he is their portion, their inheritance, and their dwelling-place (*cf.* Psalms 73:24–26; 90:1; Eph. 3:19; Rev. 21:3).

The fulness of joy and peace which the apostle invokes for his readers is based upon what is implied in the title "God of hope". Only the hope created by God gives warrant for joy and peace and when this hope is present joy and peace should be full. The joy is joy in the Lord (*cf.* Gal. 5:22; Phil. 4:4; I John 1:4) and the peace is the peace of God (*cf.* Phil. 4:7).[17] As joy and peace are conditioned by hope, so they are produced by faith and they promote hope. The fulness of joy and peace invoked is to the end that hope may abound more and more in the hearts of those who entertain it. The graces in exercise in believers never reach the point of fulness to which no more can be added. Joy and peace emanate from hope and they contribute to the abounding of the same. The object contemplated in hope far transcends human conception and the discrepancy between what believers are now and what they will be (*cf.* I John 3:2) makes the entertainment of hope presumption except as it is generated and sealed by the Holy Spirit. This is the significance of the concluding words of the invocation, "in the power of the Holy Spirit". The prayer begins and ends with the accent upon divine agency and resource. Within this sphere alone can the grandeur of hope be contemplated and within it hope has the certification which the earnest of the Spirit accords to it (*cf.* Eph. 1:13, 14).

---

[17] It is not peace with God (5:1). We could not suitably be regarded as filled with peace with God and, besides, peace is coordinate with joy.

XIX. PAUL'S GENTILE MINISTRY, POLICY, AND PLANS
(15:14-33)

14 And I myself also am persuaded of you, my brethren, that ye yourselves are full of goodness, filled with all knowledge, able also to admonish one another.

15 But I write the more boldly unto you in some measure, as putting you again in remembrance, because of the grace that was given me of God,

16 that I should be a minister of Christ Jesus unto the Gentiles, ministering the gospel of God, that the offering up of the Gentiles might be made acceptable, being sanctified by the Holy Spirit.

17 I have therefore my glorying in Christ Jesus in things pertaining to God.

18 For I will not dare to speak of any things save those which Christ wrought through me, for the obedience of the Gentiles, by word and deed,

19 in the power of signs and wonders, in the power of the Holy Spirit; so that from Jerusalem, and round about even unto Illyricum, I have fully preached the gospel of Christ;

20 yea, making it my aim so to preach the gospel, not where Christ was *already* named, that I might not build upon another man's foundation;

21 but, as it is written,
> They shall see, to whom no tidings of him came,
> And they who have not heard shall understand.

14 At this point begins the concluding part of this epistle, devoted to encouragement, explanation, greeting, and final doxology. In earlier portions there is oftentimes the severity of rebuke, correction, and warning. But the apostle would not have this feature to be interpreted as implying a low estimate of the attainments of the church at Rome. At the outset he had paid his compliment to the believers there for their faith and for the encouragement which they would impart to him when he would

achieve his desire to visit them (1:8, 12). But now again in stronger
terms he gives his assessment of their virtues. The bond of fellowship
is expressed in the address "my brethren" and he could scarcely
have devised a combination of words that would more effectively
convey to them his own personal conviction of the fruit of the
gospel in their midst: "I myself also am persuaded of you".[18]
They were, he believed, "full of goodness" and "filled with all
knowledge". This complementation and the fulness in each case
show the maturity which characterized the Roman community
of believers. "Goodness" (*cf.* Gal. 5:22; Eph. 5:9; II Thess.
1:11) is that virtue opposed to all that is mean and evil and includes
uprightness, kindness, and beneficence of heart and life. The
"knowledge" is the understanding of the Christian faith and is
particularly related to the capacity for instruction reflected on in the
next clause. It may not be extraneous to suggest that the reference
to these two qualities in particular may have been dictated by their
relevance to the subject dealt with in the preceding section (14:1–
15:13). Goodness is the quality which will constrain the strong to
refrain from what will injure the weak and knowledge is the attainment that will correct weakness of faith. The treatment of differences in 14:1–15:13 was not hypothetical; there must have been a
situation requiring it. But we must not exaggerate the situation;
the church was "full of goodness, filled with all knowledge". Thus
the believers there were themselves able to instruct and admonish
one another.

15 Having given the commendation of verse 14 the apostle
now proceeds to explain the boldness with which he had written.
He is careful, however, to state the true measure of this boldness.
He does not say "boldly" but "more boldly" which in this case
does not mean "more than boldly" but somewhat or rather boldly
and he modifies this still further by saying "in some measure".[19]
All of this indicates his concern that the believers would properly
evaluate the degree of boldness he exercised. The reason for it
was to put them in remembrance and here again there is the

---

[18] There is the assumption that others entertained this esteem. Paul was
not behind others in this respect.

[19] ἀπὸ μέρους surely means "partly" and is properly rendered "in some
measure". To take it as referring to "parts" of the epistle is scarcely warranted,
even though it is true that the apostle's boldness is apparent at points where he
writes in tones of severity.

softening appropriate to the goodness and knowledge already credited to them. It is all-important to note that the main apology resides in the next clause and in what follows in verse 16. It is only because of the grace given him of God that he could dare to write as he did. This is characteristic of Paul. It is in pursuance of divine commission and the enduement with grace which belongs to it that he exercises his ministry (cf. I Cor. 9:16; Eph. 3:7-9).

16 We are now informed of the office alluded to in the last clause of verse 15. Grace was given to the end that he might be the minister of Christ to the Gentiles. Paul had repeatedly referred to this office (1:5; 11:13; 12:3). But in this verse there are distinctive features which ought to be marked. (1) When he calls himself a "minister" of Christ he uses a term which in its various forms is often charged with the sacredness belonging to worship (cf. Luke 1:23; Acts 13:2; Rom. 15:27; II Cor. 9:12; Phil. 2:17; Heb. 1:7, 14; 8:2, 6; 9:21; 10:11). It should be understood with these associations, for this is in accord with and anticipates the ideas expressed later respecting the character of his ministry. (2) When he defines his ministry as "ministering the gospel of God" the apostle uses a word occurring nowhere else in the New Testament which may properly be rendered "acting as a priest". So the ministry of the gospel is conceived of after the pattern of priestly offering. It is not to be supposed that the gospel itself is regarded as the offering. The offering is specified in the next clause. The dignity belonging to this office of preaching the gospel is, however, hereby underlined and the kind of priestly action performed in the exercise of the apostolic office is thus shown to be of an entirely different character from that of the Levitical priesthood and also from that of Christ himself. (3) The expression "the offering up of the Gentiles" is without precise parallel in the New Testament. But it has its parallel in Isaiah 66:20: "And they shall bring all your brethren out of all the nations for an offering unto the Lord".[20] It may be that Paul derived this concept from the Isaianic passage which appears in a context of blessing to all nations and tongues (cf. Isa. 66:18). This then is the offering which Paul as apostle of the Gentiles offers to God in the exercise

---

[20] The Hebrew is מנחה and the LXX δῶρον. But the word used by Paul, προσφορά, would be the more appropriate.

of priestly activity. The Gentiles as converted to the faith of the gospel are regarded as presented holy unto God. Again we see how extraneous to the Levitical pattern is the priestly function exercised by the ministers of the new covenant. (4) Carrying on the ideas associated with priestly activity Paul adds "acceptable" (cf. I Pet. 2:5). An offering to be acceptable to God must conform to conditions of purity. So in this case. The conditions of holiness are created by the Holy Spirit. Hence the clause, "sanctified by the Holy Spirit", stands in apposition to "acceptable". The apostle thinks of his function in the priestly action as ministering that gospel which is efficacious through the grace of the Holy Spirit. Thus the Gentiles become an offering acceptable to God. This is his apology for the boldness he exercised in putting his readers in remembrance. He has said enough to vindicate the epistle and to remove any accusation which his severity might provoke.

17–19a The result specified in the preceding verse, the acceptable offering up of the Gentiles, and the ministration of the gospel contributing by God's grace to that end gave the apostle abundant ground for glorying and he says "I have therefore my glorying".[21] He is referring to the *act* of glorying. The ground is implicit in the "therefore" which points back to verses 15b, 16. He is careful to add, however, "in Christ Jesus". Boasting is excluded except as it is in the Lord (cf. I Cor. 1:29–31; II Cor. 10:17). And he makes a further qualification; his glorying is "in things pertaining to God". This should not be understood in the sense of his personal relation to God but, as the preceding verse and especially the succeeding indicate, of the things pertaining to the gospel and kingdom of God. There is nothing of egoism in his glorying; it is glorying in God's grace and when thus conditioned it cannot be too exuberant.

That Paul is thinking of the gospel triumphs (cf. II Cor. 2:14) wrought through his instrumentality in verse 17 is demonstrated by verse 18. For here he protests that only of the things which Christ wrought through him would he dare to speak. But he does dare to speak of these. He does not say "the things I have wrought through

---

[21] In the Greek there is no possessive pronoun answering to "my". It is τὴν καύχησιν and the article is omitted in P⁴⁶, ℵ, A, and the mass of the cursives. The sense is not materially affected by the omission or insertion of the article in view of the distinct specification given in the words that follow.

Christ". It is Christ's action through the apostle and this action was in both "word and deed". The things of which he dares to speak in the glorying concerned are, however, only those things which had been wrought through the apostle himself rather than through others. C. K. Barrett has expressed both thoughts succinctly: "(i) I would not dare to speak of this if it were not Christ's work (rather than mine); (ii) I would not dare to speak of this if it were not Christ's work through me (rather than any one else)".[22] "Word and deed" are to be construed with "Christ wrought through me" rather than "obedience". This conjunction is eloquent witness to the coordination of word and deed in that which Christ does from his exalted glory. The same applies to what he had done during the days of his flesh upon earth. It also certifies to us that behind Paul's words as well as deeds were the activity and authority of Christ.

Verse 19a is a further specification of things Christ wrought through Paul and is obviously continuous with "by word and deed" of verse 18. This could be taken as specifying the way in which Christ wrought through the apostle in the accomplishment of the things mentioned in verse 18; Christ wrought by the power of signs and wonders. But it is preferable to regard the statement as an additional particularizing of the things Christ wrought through the apostle and we may not even equate the signs and wonders with "deed" in verse 18. The signs and wonders were deeds but not all deeds are in this category. The word "power" in this instance is regarded by commentators as the power derived from signs and wonders. "The power of the Holy Spirit" later is certainly the power derived from the Holy Spirit, more accurately expressed as the power *exercised* by the Spirit. But it may not be out of place to suggest that "power" in the first instance is rather the power *exemplified* in signs and wonders.

The three standard terms for miracles in the New Testament are powers, signs, and wonders. Only two of these are used here; the word "power" is used in construction with signs and wonders for the reason indicated. Signs and wonders do not refer to two different sets of events. They refer to the same events viewed from different aspects. A miracle is both a sign and a wonder. As a sign it points to the agency by which it occurs and has thus certificatory

---

[22] *Op. cit., ad loc.*

character; as a wonder the marvel of the event is emphasized. It might appear from the history recorded that Paul's ministry was not conspicuously marked by miracles. This text corrects any such misapprehension (*cf.* II Cor. 12:12 where all three terms occur; also Gal. 3:5, and see also the general application in Heb. 2:4). "In the power of the Holy Spirit" could be regarded as a further definition of the power mentioned in the earlier part of the verse, for the power of signs and wonders may not be abstracted from the power of the Spirit. But the teaching of Paul in general would militate against this restrictive interpretation. The power of the Spirit is, according to the apostle, the efficiency by which the gospel is effectual in all its aspects. Hence the analogy of this teaching elsewhere would indicate that he is referring to the inclusive agency of the Holy Spirit in virtue of which all phases of his ministry had been crowned with the success of which he dared to speak (*cf.* I Cor. 2:4; I Thess. 1:5, 6; 2:13). It is characteristic to intimate his dependence upon the Holy Spirit whenever he refers to the saving effects of the gospel. And it is also characteristic of him to make no disjunction in this regard between the working of the Spirit and that of Christ (*cf.* 8:9–11; II Cor. 3:6, 17, 18).

It is noteworthy how in verses 16–19a Paul weaves his teaching around the distinctive relations to and functions of the three persons of the Godhead. This shows how Paul's thought was conditioned by the doctrine of the trinity and particularly by the distinguishing properties and prerogatives of the three persons in the economy of salvation. It is not a case of artificially weaving these persons into his presentation; it is rather that his consciousness is so formed by and to faith in the triune God that he cannot but express himself in these terms (*cf.* vs. 30; Eph. 4:3–6).

19b–21 At this point Paul intimates the result of the commitment and enduement dealt with in the preceding context and he speaks of this in terms of the extent of his labours as minister of Christ to the Gentiles. We might have expected that the starting-point of his itineraries would have been stated to be Antioch in Syria (*cf.* Acts 13:1–4). But it is not likely that he has in mind precisely the *startingpoint* when he mentions Jerusalem but the south-eastern limit of his missionary activity. Furthermore, it would have been strange indeed, when mentioning the bounds of his ministrations, that he would have omitted the mention of

Jerusalem. He did preach the gospel there (*cf.* Acts 9:26–30) and since it was from Jerusalem the gospel went forth it was not only appropriate but necessary that he should say "from Jerusalem". The other limit is Illyricum. This is the northwest bound. Illyria was on the eastern shore of the Adriatic, comprising roughly what is now Yugoslavia and Albania and therefore north-west of Macedonia and Achaia, the scene of such intensive labours on Paul's part. It is uncertain whether "unto Illyricum" means that he penetrated into this country or simply reached its borders. He could have preached in Illyria on the journey mentioned in Acts 20:1, 2 or he may have made a preaching excursion into this territory during his stays in Corinth (*cf.* Acts 18:1, 18; 20:3). But of this we cannot be certain. The borders of Illyria satisfy the terms "unto Illyricum". "Round about" should not be understood as referring to the environs of Jerusalem. There is no evidence that Paul had conducted missionary labours round about Jerusalem to an extent that would warrant this kind of reference and, besides, since he is dealing with his ministry to the Gentiles in the territories extending from Jerusalem to Illyria, this restriction of "round about" to the environs of Jerusalem would not comport with the way in which his labours were "round about" in this whole area.[23] He says he "fully preached" the gospel. This means that he had "fulfilled" the gospel (*cf.* Col. 1:25) and does not reflect on the fulness with which he set forth the gospel (*cf.* Acts 20:20, 27). Paul had discharged his commission and fulfilled the design of his ministry within the wide area specified. Neither does "fully preached" imply that he had preached the gospel in every locality and to every person in these territories. "His conception of the duties of an Apostle was that he should found churches and leave to others to build on the foundation thus laid (I Cor. iii. 7, 10)".[24] And, in respect of what he considered to be his function, he

---

[23]   Only here in the New Testament does κύκλῳ occur with μέχρι and this must be taken into account. It is *round about unto Illyricum*, not round about Jerusalem. It is true that Paul preached, according to his own testimony, "throughout all the country of Judaea" (Acts 26:20) and this might be construed as round about Jerusalem. But, for the reason just stated and also for the reason that Paul's ministry in Judaea could scarcely have been an extended one, it is much more in accord with the expression and with the known facts to take "round about" as referring to his missionary activities in the whole area specified.

[24]   Sanday and Headlam: *op. cit.*, p. 409. The whole paragraph should be noted.

proceeds to say (vs. 23) that he had "no more any place in these regions".

In verses 20, 21 we are informed of the policy that guided the apostle in the conduct of his ministry and he elucidates for us the scope, on the one hand, and the limitation, on the other, of his claim in the preceding verse. It was his well-defined and studied procedure not to build upon the foundation laid by another (*cf.* I Cor. 3:10). This indicates the sense in which we are to understand "not where Christ was already named". He does not mean "named" in the loose sense of merely known or reported but in the sense of acknowledged and confessed (*cf.* I Cor. 5:11; Eph. 3:15; II Tim. 2:19). When a foundation is laid the church is conceived of as existing and in such centres it was his policy not to conduct his missionary labours. It would be an unreasonable application of this declared course of action to suppose that Paul would refrain from visiting a church that had been established by the labours of another or that he would refrain from all apostolic witness and activity in such places. He had visited Jerusalem on several occasions and had borne witness to the gospel there. He was at this time about to depart for Jerusalem in order to bring the contribution from the churches of Macedonia and Achaia and to cement the bonds of fellowship between the Gentile churches and those of Jewish composition in Jerusalem. He was determined to visit Rome. There is no contradiction. What he has in mind in verse 20 is that his apostolic activity was directed to the founding of churches and the edifying of churches he had been instrumental in establishing and not to the building up of churches that were the fruit of another man's labours. In verse 21 he draws support from Isaiah 52:15. The quotation varies slightly from the Hebrew text but with the transposition of one word is the same as the Greek version. This text is derived from a context in which the world-wide effects of Messiah's sacrifice are in view and the appropriateness of the application to the apostle's Gentile ministry is apparent. He conceives of his own work as the minister of Christ to be conducted in pursuance of this prophecy and, therefore, as not only in accord with God's design but as specifically demanded by this Scripture.[25]

---

[25] On the objections to verses 19–21 *cf.* the excellent treatment by Sanday and Headlam: *op. cit.*, pp. 408–410.

22 Wherefore also I was hindered these many times from coming to you:
23 but now, having no more any place in these regions, and having these many years a longing to come unto you,
24 whensoever I go unto Spain[26] (for I hope to see you in my journey, and to be brought on my way thitherward by you, if first in some measure I shall have been satisfied with your company)—
25 but now, *I say*, I go unto Jerusalem, ministering unto the saints.
26 For it hath been the good pleasure of Macedonia and Achaia to make a certain contribution for the poor among the saints that are at Jerusalem.
27 Yea, it hath been their good pleasure; and their debtors they are. For if the Gentiles have been made partakers of their spiritual things, they owe it *to them* also to minister unto them in carnal things.
28 When therefore I have accomplished this, and have sealed to them this fruit, I will go on by you unto Spain.
29 And I know that, when I come unto you, I shall come in the fulness of the blessing of Christ.

22-24 In verse 22 we have a virtual repetition of what Paul had said at 1:13. The significant difference is that now he tells the reason why he had been so many times hindered from fulfilling his purpose to go to Rome. This is the force of "wherefore also". He was hindered by the necessities of fulfilling his ministry in the regions more adjacent. He could not leave until he had fully preached the gospel in the territories in which up to date he had laboured. "But now" (vs. 23) the case is different. Having fulfilled the gospel he has no more place for this kind of activity in the regions extending from Jerusalem to Illyricum. Hence he is now free to cast his missionary eyes on more distant horizons. It is not Rome, however, of which he is thinking as the scene of labours complying with the policy set forth in verses 20, 21. Not at all. It is all-important, in view of Paul's declared plan in verses 20, 21, to observe how Rome relates itself to this projected outreach of apostolic labour. It is the region far beyond Rome that comes

---

[26] The addition after Σπανίαν in verse 24 of ἐλεύσομαι πρὸς ὑμᾶς is not supported by sufficient authority.

within his ambition and, as subsequent considerations will show, Rome is envisaged as a resting point on the way. "Whensoever I go unto Spain"—this is Paul's objective and its relation to the principles enunciated in verses 20, 21 is patent. Whether or not Paul ever reached Spain is problematical.[27] But that he properly entertained the desire and hope is beyond question and there are indications in what follows that it was his intent, as soon as he had fulfilled his mission to Jerusalem, to be off on his journey to the western limits of Europe.

In verse 24b he intimates the kind of visit he planned for Rome. It was not to conduct the type of apostolic ministry he had fulfilled at Corinth or Ephesus. "I hope to see you in my journey", that is, on his way to Spain. It was to be, in his design, a passing visit,[28] though not by any means so brief or casual that he would not impart to believers there and derive from them that of which he spoke in 1:11–13. In this verse he expresses the benefit he hopes to derive from his visit as being "satisfied" with their company. The term rendered "satisfied" means to have full enjoyment of. The modification "in some measure" is not probably for the purpose of toning down the enjoyment he anticipates as if he were reflecting on the limitation placed upon the satisfaction derived from a human source but that he is again courteously reminding his readers that he will not be able to enjoy the full measure of satisfaction because his visit will only be a passing one.[29] Perhaps the most significant element in this verse is the clause, preferably rendered, "to be sent forth thither by you". "Thither" refers to Spain. He expects from the church at Rome a sending forth with

---

[27] Probably the strongest support for the supposition that Paul achieved his desire to go to Spain is that derived from The Epistle to the Corinthians by Clement of Rome who says of Paul δικαιοσύνην διδάξας ὅλον τὸν κόσμον καὶ ἐπὶ τὸ τέρμα τῆς δύσεως ἐλθών (V). On the basis of the expression τὸ τέρμα τῆς δύσεως J. B. Lightfoot concludes: "From the language of Clement here it appears that this intention (Rom. 15:24) was fulfilled". He maintains that the expression points to the western extremity of Spain. "It is not improbable also that this western journey of S. Paul included a visit to Gaul (2 Tim. iv. 10; see Galatians, p. 31)" (J. B. Lightfoot: The Apostolic Fathers, London, 1890, Part I, Vol. II, p. 30). The other early reference to Paul's visit to Spain is rom the Muratorian Fragment. The atrocious Latin of the manuscript is amended by Lightfoot to read: "Sed et profectionem Pauli ab urbe ad Spaniam proficiscentis" (ibid.). For a more cautious interpretation of these references cf. Sanday and Headlam: op. cit., ad loc.

[28] διαπορευόμενος has this meaning.

[29] Cf. Meyer, Gifford: op. cit., ad loc.

commendation and blessing comparable to that experienced earlier at the hands of other churches (*cf.* Acts 13:1–4; 14:26; 15:40). How close was the bond of fellowship between the churches and the apostle in the discharge of his specifically apostolic commission!

25, 26 Now is explained the reason why the journey to Rome is postponed and for what purpose he sets out for Jerusalem. He is going there on the ministry of mercy. It may surprise us that Paul would have interrupted his primary apostolic function (*cf.* vs. 16) for what is apparently secondary and concerned with material things. We think so only when we overlook the dignity of the work of mercy. We are reminded of this in that incident which perhaps more than any other reveals apostolic statesmanship in the worldwide missionary enterprise (Gal. 2:7–9). And we must read the appendix: "only they would that we should remember the poor: which very thing I was also zealous to do" (Gal. 2:10). Of this Paul was not neglectful. Hence, "I go unto Jerusalem, ministering to the saints". There is a further implication on which Paul will reflect later (vs. 31).

The contribution he brings to Jerusalem was from the saints in Macedonia and Achaia. The voluntary nature of the collection is implied in the words "it hath been the good pleasure of" (*cf.* II Cor. 8:1–5; 9:1–5). The word "contribution" is the same as that rendered in other cases by the term "fellowship".[30] It has been suggested that "make a certain contribution" should be translated "establish a certain fellowship", in accord with the more usual meaning of the word in question. There does appear, however, to be warrant for the meaning "contribution". So the translation in the version may be retained. But it is difficult to suppress the notion of fellowship as flowing over into the thought of contribution in this instance. It was the bond of fellowship existing between the saints that constrained the offering and it was calculated to promote and cement that fellowship.

27 This verse begins with the same terms as verse 26 and reiterates the voluntary character of the contribution. This is not

---

[30] κοινωνία means "participation" and "fellowship" and so the clause in question has been rendered: "*they have undertaken to establish a rather close relation w. the poor*" (Arndt and Gingrich: *op. cit., ad* κοινωνία, 1; but *cf.* also *idem*, 3). *Cf.* TWNT, III, p. 809.

incompatible with the debt of which Paul then proceeds to speak. Charity is an obligation but it is not a tax. The obligation mentioned in this case is specific. It is not in the same category as a commercial debt incurred which we are under contractual obligation to pay. It is the indebtedness arising from benefits received as when we acknowledge our indebtedness to a great benefactor. The Gentiles were partakers of the spiritual things which emanated from Jewry and from Jerusalem and these spiritual things were of the highest conceivable character. The apostle is here enunciating what belongs to the philosophy of God's redemptive grace. "Out of Zion shall go forth the law, and the word of the Lord from Jerusalem" (Isa. 2:3b; cf. vss. 2, 3a). "In this mountain will the Lord of hosts make unto all peoples a feast of fat things" (Isa. 25:6). It is the Lord's servant, "a shoot out of the stock of Jesse", who "will bring forth justice to the Gentiles" (Isa. 11:1; 42:1). Upon Zion the glory of the Lord is risen "and nations shall come to thy light, and kings to the brightness of thy rising" (Isa. 60:3). "Salvation is of the Jews" (John 4:22). Paul had frequently in this epistle reflected on this relationship (cf. 3:2; 4:16, 17; 9:5; 11:17–24). So now he brings this truth to application in the concrete and practical. Gentiles should minister to the Jews in material things. The term "carnal" is not in this instance to be given any evil associations; it is used with reference to tangible, material possessions. And this ministry is accorded the sanctity of worship by the term the apostle uses.[31]

28, 29 Paul now returns to the design of visiting Rome on his way to Spain. There is a note of despatch in verse 28. "Having, therefore, accomplished this, and having sealed to them this fruit, I shall be off by you into Spain".[32] The contribution is called "this fruit". It was the fruit of the faith and love of the believers in Macedonia and Achaia and a token of the bond of fellowship existing between these believers and the saints at Jerusalem. In view of verse 27, however, it is likely that it is regarded as the fruit accruing from the "spiritual things" which emanated from Jerusalem. The gospel came from the Jews and went into all the world. An example of the fruit borne in distant climes is now being brought

---

[31] λειτουργῆσαι; cf. vs. 16.
[32] "I shall be off to Spain" is Barrett's expressive rendering.

back to Jerusalem in the supply of the wants of the poor saints there, an indication of the close relation between "spiritual" and material things. It is more difficult to understand what is meant by *sealing* to them this fruit. Since Paul represents himself as sealing the fruit, the preferable view surely is that the collections delivered to them at Jerusalem would seal to the churches there the fruit accruing from the gospel and would be to them the certification of the love which constrained these contributions.

In verse 29 there is the note of certitude. We may not say that the certitude applies to his arrival at Rome. There are the indications noted earlier (*cf.* 1:10) and to be noted later (vs. 33) that Paul fully recognized the sovereignty of God in this matter and that he did not know what God had in store for him (*cf.* Acts 20:22–24). He had well-defined designs, and he had solid hope that he would finally reach Rome. But the *certitude* pertains to the blessing with which he would come if God so willed, "the fulness of the blessing of Christ".[33] This is the blessing which Christ imparts and Paul is convinced that his presence in Rome would be accompanied by the *fulness* of this blessing. No term could more appropriately express the full measure of the blessing anticipated. We are liable to think of the rich blessing that would *accompany* his ministry. This is without doubt in view. But we may not restrict the thought thus. The terms indicate that he will come thither in the possession of the fulness of Christ's blessing. This evinces the confidence of Christ's abiding presence in the plenitude of his grace and power. And it is also the key to the boldness with which Paul had planned his journey to the seat of empire and to the limits of the west. Although we may not press the terms of the sentence to convey this meaning, nevertheless, we cannot exclude from Paul's total thought (*cf.* 1:12; 15:24) the assurance that the fulness of Christ's blessing would also be imparted to the believers at Rome.

15:30–33

> 30 Now I beseech you, brethren, by our Lord Jesus Christ, and by the love of the Spirit, that ye strive together with me in your prayers to God for me;

---

[33] The addition after εὐλογίας of τοῦ εὐαγγελίου τοῦ in ℵc, L, the mass of the cursives, and some versions may not be adopted.

31 that I may be delivered from them that are disobedient
in Judaea, and *that* my ministration which *I have* for
Jerusalem may be acceptable to the saints;
32 that I may come unto you in joy through the will of
God, and together with you find rest.
33 Now the God of peace be with you all. Amen.

30–32 The estimate given of the maturity of the Roman
believers (vs. 14) and the refreshment he expects from them on his
visit (*cf.* 1:12; 15:32) would be added ground for entreating their
prayers on his behalf. But it is characteristic of Paul to solicit the
prayers of the saints (*cf.* II Cor. 1:11; Phil. 1:19; Col. 4:3; I
Thess. 5:25; II Thess. 3:1). So he beseeches the Roman believers.
"By our Lord Jesus Christ" could refer to the mediacy through
which he directs his entreaty to them; he could not even beseech
his brethren apart from Christ's mediation. But this does not
appear to be the sense. It is rather that he makes Christ Jesus his
plea for compliance with his request (*cf.* 12:1; II Cor. 10:1). The
fuller title "our Lord Jesus Christ" adds force to the plea. "The
love of the Spirit" is coordinated and would have to be interpreted
as serving the same purpose. Expositors commonly regard this
love as the love which the Spirit instills in us, the fruit of the Spirit
(*cf.* Gal. 5:22).[34] But there is no good reason why it should not be
taken as the love which the Spirit bears to believers.[35] Besides,
since "the love of the Spirit" is coordinated with "our Lord Jesus
Christ" there is good, if not decisive, reason for the view that the
love of the Spirit to us is intended. As the plea is urged on the
basis of what Christ is and, by implication, does, so attention
is also focused on what is true of the Holy Spirit himself. This
imparts a distinctive emphasis. In respect of the Holy Spirit, what
could enforce Paul's request more than to be reminded of the
Spirit's love? As God's love inspires and validates hope (5:5), so
the Spirit's love should incite to prayer.

Paul's request is that "ye strive together with me in your prayers
to God for me; that I may be delivered from them that are disobedient in Judaea" *etc.* The term "strive together" is suggestive of

---

[34] *Cf.* most recently Bruce: *op. cit.*, *ad loc.*: "the love which the Holy Spirit
imparts and maintains".
[35] *Cf.* Barrett: *op. cit.*, *ad loc.*: "the genitive cannot be objective, and the
clue is given by v. 5". It should be borne in mind that the love of God shed
abroad in our hearts (5:5) is the love of God to us and the genitive is subjective.

the wrestling which prayer involves; it is to be persistent and earnest. Truly, as commentators observe, this is necessary because of the resistance offered to persevering prayer by the world, the flesh, and the devil. But there is something more germane to the nature of prayer indicated by the term "strive". It is that earnest and consecrated prayer will be persistent and will wrestle. It is a means ordained of God for the accomplishment of his gracious designs and is the fruit of faith and expectation. That to be prayed for is twofold and pointedly particularized. First, it is to be delivered from the disobedient in Judaea. These are the unbelievers. The sequel shows that there was good ground for the apostle's foreboding (cf. Acts 20:22, 23; 21:27–36). Although he could protest that he did not hold his life as dear to himself (Acts 20:24) and that he was "ready not to be bound only, but also to die at Jerusalem for the name of the Lord Jesus" (Acts 21:13) and, therefore, would not compromise the gospel to save his life (cf. Matt. 16:25; John 12:25), yet he did not crave martyrdom. Furthermore, it was in the interests of promoting the gospel that he sought to be delivered from the murderous plots of unbelievers and, besides, it would be contrary to all Christian principles to resign himself fatalistically to the ungodly designs of men. Hence his earnest petition to the believers at Rome. Though Paul could not have anticipated the exact course of events, we cannot but discover the answer to his own prayers and of those at Rome in the events as they developed (cf. Acts 21:31–33; 23:12–35). The second particular for prayer was that his ministration might be acceptable to the saints. This is surprising. Would a gift to meet the poverty of saints be unacceptable? The apostle had ample evidence of the suspicions with which his Gentile ministry had been regarded and would most probably have heard of the false reports circulating in Jerusalem (cf. Acts 21:20, 21). There was, therefore, ground for fear that the fruit of his ministry in Macedonia and Achaia would not be welcomed. In the esteem of believing Jews still "zealous for the law" and especially for circumcision the contribution would be marked by a ministry prejudicial to what they deemed precious. This is the situation Paul envisioned. We can readily sense his concern and therefore the need for earnest prayer to God that the contribution would be acceptable. What a violation of *fellowship* rejection would be! That the fruit of the gospel that went out from Jerusalem, the fruit of faith and love, the token of the bond of fellowship between believers, a contribution to cement bonds of love and meet the needs of the saints should be rejected, what a tragedy! The repercussions for the cause of the gospel and for the fellowship of which the common redemption was the bond are what the apostle dreads. There is good reason to believe this prayer also was answered (*cf.* Acts 21:17–20).

The prayers to be offered had an additional design (vs. 32). It is that he might come to Rome in joy and together with the believers there find rest. Various factors would contribute to the joy of his contemplated arrival in Rome: the realization of his plans and hopes for many years, deliverance from his enemies at Jerusalem, the success of his visit thither in the grateful acceptance of the contribution, the fellowship with believers at Rome, and the prospect of continuing his apostolic labours in the regions beyond. The rest he hopes for is not that of leisure but the refreshment and encouragement this new fellowship would impart. Most significant is the qualifying expression "through the will of God". The term used for "will" frequently refers in the New Testament to the preceptive will of God, the will revealed to us for the regulation of life and behaviour (*cf.* Matt. 6:10; 12:50; John 7:17; Rom. 2:18; 12:2; Eph. 5:17; 6:6; I Thess. 4:3). But it also refers to the will of God's determinate purpose, his decretive will realized through providence (*cf.* Matt. 18:14; John 1:13; Rom. 1:10; Gal. 1:4; Eph. 1:5, 11; I Pet. 3:17; II Pet. 1:21; Rev. 4:11). It is in this latter sense the term is used in this case. There are two things to be noted. (1) In praying for the particulars mentioned, especially that of reaching Rome, there is the expressed desire that these may prove to be the determinate will of God. There is the prayer that God may bring these requests to pass and therefore that they may be his determinate will unfolded in his providence. (2) There is also the recognition that God is sovereign and that the coming to pass of these events is dependent upon his sovereign will. The apostle in this reflects his resignation to the will and wisdom of God. It was not part of God's revealed will to Paul that he would go to Rome. Hence the reserve of submissiveness to what God determined his providence for Paul would prove to be.

Paul did go to Rome but under circumstances and after delays which he could not have forecast. God answered the prayers but not in the ways that Paul had hoped for or anticipated. The lessons for us to be derived from these verses (30–32) are number-less.

33 God is called the God of peace because he is the author of peace (*cf.* vss. 5, 13). In view of the emphasis upon peace with God (5:1; *cf.* 16:20; Eph. 2:14, 15, 17; I Thess. 5:23; Heb. 13:20) we should infer that peace with God is primary. But we may not exclude what is the consequence, namely, the peace of God (*cf.* Phil. 4:7; Col. 3:15), the peace of heart and mind in stedfast confidence and tranquillity. It is noteworthy how often the apostle in his benedictions calls God the God of peace or invokes upon his readers the peace that is from God (*cf.* 1:7; 15:13; I Cor. 1:3; 13:11; II Cor. 1:2; Gal. 1:3; Eph. 1:2; Phil. 1:2; 4:9; Col. 1:2; I Thess. 1:2; II Thess. 1:2; 3:16; I Tim. 1:2; II Tim. 1:2; Tit. 1:4; Phm. 3). Hence in the benediction which closes this part of the epistle no formula in Paul's repertory could be richer. In the prayer that the God of peace would be with them there is included all of the blessing insured by the presence of the God of peace.[36]

---

[36] On the critical question pertaining to the benediction in this verse see Appendix F (pp. 262 ff.).

XX GREETINGS AND CLOSING DOXOLOGY
(16:1-27)

A. PAUL'S OWN GREETINGS
(16:1-16)

16: 1-16

1 I commend unto you Phoebe our sister, who is a servant of the church that is at Cenchreae:

2 that ye receive her in the Lord, worthily of the saints, and that ye assist her in whatsoever matter she may have need of you: for she herself also hath been a helper of many, and of mine own self.

3 Salute Prisca and Aquila my fellow-workers in Christ Jesus,

4 who for my life laid down their own necks; unto whom not only I give thanks, but also all the churches of the Gentiles:

5 and *salute* the church that is in their house. Salute Epaenetus my beloved, who is the firstfruits of Asia unto Christ.

6 Salute Mary, who bestowed much labor on you.

7 Salute Andronicus and Junias, my kinsmen, and my fellowprisoners, who are of note among the apostles, who also have been in Christ before me.

8 Salute Ampliatus my beloved in the Lord.

9 Salute Urbanus our fellow-worker in Christ, and Stachys my beloved.

10 Salute Apelles the approved in Christ. Salute them that are of the *household* of Aristobulus.

11 Salute Herodion my kinsman. Salute them of the *household* of Narcissus, that are in the Lord.

12 Salute Tryphaena and Tryphosa, who labor in the Lord. Salute Persis the beloved, who labored much in the Lord.

13 Salute Rufus the chosen in the Lord, and his mother and mine.

14 Salute Asyncritus, Phlegon, Hermes, Patrobas, Hermas, and the brethren thàt are witḥ them.
15 Salute Philologus and Julia, Nereus and his sister, and Olympas, and all the saints that are with them.
16 Salute one another with a holy kiss. All the churches of Christ salute you.

1–2 It is highly probable that Phoebe was the bearer of this epistle to the church at Rome. Letters of commendation were a necessity when a believer travelled from one community to another in which he was unknown to the saints. But if Phoebe conveyed the epistle there would be an additional reason. Besides, as will become apparent, Phoebe was a woman who had performed distinguished service to the church and the commendation had to be commensurate with her character and devotion. Cenchreae was one of the ports for Corinth. There was a church there and Phoebe was a servant of this church. It is common to give to Phoebe the title of "deaconess" and regard her as having performed an office in the church corresponding to that which belonged to men who exercised the office of deacon (*cf.* Phil. 1:1; I Tim. 3:8–13). Though the word for "servant" is the same as is used for deacon in the instances cited, yet the word is also used to denote the person performing any type of ministry. If Phoebe ministered to the saints, as is evident from verse 2, then she would be a servant of the church and there is neither need nor warrant to suppose that she occupied or exercised what amounted to an ecclesiastical office comparable to that of the diaconate. The services performed were similar to those devolving upon deacons. Their ministry is one of mercy to the poor, the sick, and the desolate. This is an area in which women likewise exercise their functions and graces. But there is no more warrant to posit an *office* than in the case of the widows who, prior to their becoming the charge of the church, must have borne the features mentioned in I Timothy 5:9, 10. The Roman believers are enjoined to "receive her in the Lord, worthily of the saints". To receive in the Lord is to accept her as one bound to them in the bond and fellowship of union with Christ. "Worthily of the saints" could mean "as a fellow believer should be received". But it is more likely that it means "as it becomes saints to receive a believer", the "worthily" reflecting on what becomes them rather than on what is owing to her. The particular commendation of Phoebe is that she had been a helper of many

226

and of Paul himself.[1] This specification of virtue is, no doubt, mentioned as the outstanding feature of Phoebe's service to the church and indicates that on account of which she was called a servant of the church. But this virtue is also mentioned to enforce the exhortation that she is to be given assistance in every matter in which she may have need. The kind of help rendered by Phoebe is not intimated. She may have been a woman of some wealth and social influence and so have acted as patroness. Her services may have been of another kind such as caring for the afflicted and needy. Under what circumstances she was a helper of Paul we do not know. But her help may well have been of the kind afforded by Lydia at Philippi (Acts 16:15). In any case Phoebe is one of the women memorialized in the New Testament by their devoted service to the gospel whose honour is not to be tarnished by elevation to positions and functions inconsistent with the station they occupy in the economy of human relationships.

3, 4 Prisca, on other occasions also named Priscilla, and Aquila Paul first met at Corinth (Acts 18:2). They had just come from Italy for the reason mentioned. They had given him domicile at Corinth (Acts 18:3). Later they accompanied Paul as far as Ephesus and they remained there (Acts 18:18, 19). There they instructed Apollos in a more accurate understanding of the gospel (Acts 18:26). They are mentioned also in salutations in two other epistles of Paul (I Cor. 16:19; II Tim. 4:19). By the time Paul wrote the epistle to Rome they had returned thither. This

---

[1] The contention of Russell C. Prohl that προστάτις means "one who presides" and is to be understood in the sense of the verb προίστημι (*cf.* 12:8) from which, he says, προστάτις is derived rests upon insufficient evidence. It is true that the masculine προστάτης can mean "ruler", "leader", "president" and the corresponding verbs προστατεύω and προστατέω have similar meaning. But προστάτης can also mean "patron" or "helper". The feminine προστάτις can have the same meaning. Besides, the meaning "president" does not suit in the clause in question. Paul says that Phoebe "became a προστάτις of many and of me myself". Are we to suppose that she exercised rule over the apostle? What she was to others she was to the apostle. The rendering that Prohl adopts "She was made a superintendent of many by me myself" is wholly unwarranted. Furthermore, the believers at Rome are enjoined to "stand by" or "help" Phoebe (παραστῆτε αὐτῇ) and the last clause in verse 2 is given as a reason to enforce this exhortation. "She herself was a helper of many and of me myself". There is exact correspondence between the service to Phoebe enjoined upon the church and the service she herself bestowed upon others. The thought of presidency is alien to this parallel. See Russell C. Prohl: *Woman in the Church* (Grand Rapids, 1957), pp. 70f.

should not be surprising. The Emperor Claudius had died and his decree (Acts 18:2) for this reason or for some other was no longer in effect. Aquila and Prisca were itinerant as the preceding references show and there is no reason why they should not have returned to Rome when the abovementioned restriction had been removed or relaxed. As the incident recorded in Acts 18:26 shows, they were well versed in the faith and Paul calls them his "fellow-workers in Christ Jesus". Since even the secular occupation of believers is in Christ Jesus it would not have been improper for Paul to accord this dignity to the partnership in tentmaking (Acts 18:3). But in view of verses 9 and 21 we must regard the coopera-tion as referring to joint labour in the gospel in the bond of union and fellowship with Christ. Here we have another example of the contribution made by a woman (Prisca) in the work of the gospel and of the church (*cf.* vss. 6, 12) within the limits prescribed by Paul elsewhere (*cf.* I Cor. 11:3–16; 14:33b–36; I Tim. 2:8–15). When Prisca and Aquila placed their lives in jeopardy on Paul's account we do not know. It may have been at Corinth or at Ephesus or elsewhere. Neither are the circumstances known. Laying down their own necks could be even literally interpreted. But this may also be figurative to express the extreme peril at the hands of persecutors to which they subjected themselves to save Paul's life. It may well be that so notable was this incident that it had been reported to all the churches of the Gentiles and that the gratitude of the churches for this act of self-sacrifice is alluded to in the latter part of verse 4. But, in any event, the fame of Prisca and Aquila was so widespread that to them not only Paul gave thanks but "also all the churches of the Gentiles". The data already adduced from Acts 18 are an index to the mobility of this couple as also to their devotion. That they should have returned to Rome is consonant with all that we know of their character and practice.

5 This reference to the church in the house as well as other references (I Cor. 16:19; Col. 4:15; Phm. 2) may not be restricted to the household (*cf.* Acts 10:2; 11:14; 16:15, 31; 18:8; I Cor. 1:16; I Tim. 3:4; 5:13; II Tim. 1:16). It was necessary and appropriate in apostolic times, as on some occasions today, for Christians to make their homes available for the congregations of the saints. It is not without significance that in our totally different present-day situation the practice of the house church is being restored and recognized as indispensable to the propagation of the gospel. In a city like Rome or Ephesus (*cf.* I Cor. 16:19) there would be more than one such congregation. The fact that the church in the house of Aquila and Prisca is particularly mentioned in this list of greetings shows that it did not comprise the whole church at Rome. Hence there would be other *churches* and it would be proper to speak of the churches in Rome.

Epaenetus is called "beloved" as is also Ampliatus (vs. 8), Stachys (vs. 9), and Persis (vs. 12). There could not be any offensive discrimination in calling these "beloved" when others were not. There must have been a particular constraint of affection in these instances which the apostle would assume to be known or readily recognized by others. This can be detected in the case of Epaenetus; he was the firstfruits, that is the first convert, of Asia[2] unto Christ. The bond of peculiar affection is apparent.

6 Mary is another instance of a woman labouring on behalf of the church. There is no validity to the objection that Paul could not have had such intimate knowledge of affairs at Rome[3] so as to be able to particularize thus. He must have received much information from Aquila and Prisca who had just come from Rome when Paul first arrived in Corinth. The "much labor" suggests that Mary was one of the earliest members of the church at Rome and its organization could have been largely due to her influence.

7 Andronicus and Junias were kinsmen of the apostle. This cannot be proven to mean more than that they were Jewish (*cf.* 9:3). But they may have been more closely related as also Herodion (vs. 11), Lucius, Jason, and Sosipater (vs. 21). Since there are other Jews mentioned who are not called kinsmen (*cf.* vs. 3), those who are called kinsmen likely stood in a closer relation of kinship. It would not be necessary to suppose that they were all members of the apostle's *family*. When Andronicus and Junias shared captivity with Paul we do not know. His imprisonments were frequent (*cf.* II Cor. 6:5; 11:23) and on at least one occasion they shared this honour. "Of note among the apostles" may mean that they were apostles themselves. If so then the word "apostles"

---

[2] Ἀχαίας is not the proper reading. Ἀσίας is supported by P⁴⁶, ℵ, A, B, D*, G, and several versions. *Cf.* I Cor. 16:15 for Ἀχαίας.
[3] εἰς ὑμᾶς is to be preferred on both external and internal grounds.

would be used in a more general sense of messenger (*cf.* II Cor. 8:23; Phil. 2:25). Since, however, the term has usually in Paul the more restricted sense, it is more probable that the sense is that these persons were well known to the apostles and were distinguished for their faith and service. The explanation is ready at hand; they were Christians before Paul and, no doubt, were associated with the circle of apostles in Judea if not in Jerusalem. There are thus four reasons why they are selected for greetings.

8 Ampliatus was beloved "in the Lord". All the others mentioned as beloved were likewise. But it was not necessary to amplify in every case. "In the Lord" underscores the relation to Christ that alone establishes the bond of love which beloved in the Christian sense involves.

9 The derivation of the name Urbanus would suggest that he was natively a Roman. He is said to be *our* fellow-worker and was not therefore a companion of the apostle as Prisca and Aquila (vs. 3) and Timothy (vs. 21) who are called his own fellow-workers. Stachys is identified simply as beloved and, like Ampliatus, has no further commendation.

10 Apelles is distinguished as "approved in Christ" and is accorded this distinction because of peculiar trials and temptations perseveringly endured and proven thereby. Aristobulus is mentioned only because there were believers in his household. Like Narcissus (vs. 11) he must have been a man of station in Rome. J. B. Lightfoot maintains that he was a grandson of Herod the Great and a brother of the elder Agrippa and of Herod (king of Chalcis) and on intimate relations with the Emperor Claudius.[4] Those of his household need not have been more than servants or slaves. Although those of the household of Narcissus who are greeted are those "in the Lord", we need not infer that the absence of this restriction in the present instance means that all of Aristobulus' household were Christians. No doubt the same qualification applies in both cases, though mentioned only in one.

---

[4] *Saint Paul's Epistle to the Philippians* (London, 1908), pp. 174f. But *cf.* also F. F. Bruce: "Herod" in *The New Bible Dictionary* (London, 1962), pp. 521–523.

11 The name Herodion and the context in which the reference occurs suggest that he was of the Herod family or household. He was one of the kinsmen, therefore Jewish and, as suggested above, probably related in some way to the apostle. Lightfoot maintains that Narcissus is the powerful freedman by that name put to death shortly after the accession of Nero and therefore some years before Paul wrote this epistle.[5] Though deceased, his household would still go under his name as likewise in the case of Aristobulus.

12 Tryphaena and Tryphosa are supposed to have been sisters. Persis is also a woman. All three are said to have laboured in the Lord. The present tense used in the case of Tryphaena and Tryphosa and the past in the case of Persis should not be unduly pressed. The difference should not be construed as a reflection upon Persis' fidelity. She is called "beloved" and is said to have laboured *much*. In these two respects she is accorded an eminence not given to Tryphaena and Tryphosa. The distinction in tense may be an index to the reserve observed by Paul. He knew that Persis laboured *much* but is not able to say the same as of the time of writing. Or it may be that age or infirmity had overtaken Persis and that she was no longer active as she had been. Epaenetus, Ampliatus, and Stachys he calls "my beloved", Persis he calls "the beloved". It might have been indelicate to call her *my* beloved.

13 It may be that Rufus is the same person mentioned in Mark 15:21, the son of Simon of Cyrene. If so there was good reason for Mark's mention of his name. "Chosen in the Lord" does not refer to election in Christ (*cf.* Eph. 1:4) unto salvation. This would apply to all the saints mentioned in this chapter. It means "choice" and points to some eminence belonging to Rufus. The mother of Rufus was not *literally* Paul's mother. He means that she had performed the part of a mother to him. When or where we do not know.

14 The names listed in this verse and the brethren with them indicate a certain community of believers in a particular location or even vocation, all of the male sex.

---

[5] *Philippians*, as cited, p. 175.

THE EPISTLE TO THE ROMANS

15 Julia is most probably a woman[6] and may have been the wife of Philologus. It is not probable that she was a sister in view of this identification in the next greeting. The five persons mentioned in this verse and the saints with them formed a community and it may well be that here we have another example of a congregational group as in verse 5. This is more likely in this instance than in verse 14 because of the expression "all the saints that are with them" and the fact that both sexes are involved. The absence of reference to a church or to the church in a house does not militate against this supposition. There may not have been any one home extending this hospitality and the distinguishing eminence of Prisca and Aquila in this regard may have been the reason for the mention of their house in verse 5.

16 The holy kiss is enjoined not only in this epistle but in several others (I Cor. 16:20; II Cor. 13:12; I Thess. 5:26). Peter gives the same charge and calls it the kiss of love (I Pet. 5:14). We are advised of the custom of extending friendly greeting by a kiss in the reprimand of Jesus to Simon the Pharisee, "Thou gavest me no kiss" (Luke 7:45). There can be no question but the kiss was practised as the token of Christian love. Peter's designation makes this clear. But a kiss on its own account is the token of love and the hypocrisy of Judas is exposed by the question, "betrayest thou the Son of man with a kiss?" (Luke 22:48). Paul characterizes the kiss as "holy" and thus distinguishes it from all that is erotic or sensual. It betrays an unnecessary reserve, if not loss of the ardour of the church's first love, when the holy kiss is conspicuous by its absence in the Western Church. The final salutation at this point, "All the churches of Christ salute you", might seem more appropriate in verses 21–23 because these verses deal with the greetings of others rather than of Paul himself. But on closer examination we can see the significance of inclusion at this point. Paul is so identified with all the churches, particularly those of the Gentiles as the apostle of the Gentiles, that his greetings may not be dissociated from those of the whole church. His solidarity with the church universal governs his consciousness and as apostle of the Gentiles he represents all the Gentile churches in the conveyance

---

[6] "A common name, found even among slave women in the imperial household" (Arndt and Gingrich: *op. cit., ad loc.*). *Cf.* Lightfoot: *ibid.*, p. 177.

of his greetings. Another observation worthy of note is the plural "churches". We may not tone down the unity of the church. This comes to expression repeatedly in Paul (*cf.* 11:16–24; Eph. 2:16, 18–22; 4:2–16). But Paul is also jealous to maintain that in every instance where the saints are gathered together in Christ's name in accordance with his institution, there the church of Christ is (*cf.* vs. 5). Finally, this salutation, as F. F. Bruce observes, "is a strong argument for the Roman destination of these greetings. Why should Paul send greetings from *all* the churches to another church to which he was writing an ordinary letter? But at a time when one very important phase of his ministry was being concluded he might well send greetings from all the churches associated with that phase of his ministry to a church which not only occupied a unique position in the world . . . but also, in Paul's intention, was to play an important part at the outset of a new phase of his ministry".[7]

---

[7] *Romans*, as cited, p. 276.

B. WARNINGS AGAINST DECEIVERS
(16:17–20)

17 Now I beseech you, brethren, mark them that are
causing the divisions and occasions of stumbling, contrary to the doctrine which ye learned: and turn away
from them.

18 For they that are such serve not our Lord Christ, but
their own belly; and by their smooth and fair speech
they beguile the hearts of the innocent.

19 For your obedience is come abroad unto all men. I
rejoice therefore over you: but I would have you wise
unto that which is good, and simple unto that which is
evil.

20 And the God of peace shall bruise Satan under your
feet shortly.

The grace of our Lord Jesus Christ be with you.

Though this passage differs in content and tone from the rest of
the epistle we should not exaggerate the difference. Severity of
mood and expression appears at various points in the epistle (*cf.*
2:1–5; 3:8; 6:1–3; 9:19, 20; 11:20; 14:15, 16). The warning
note appears throughout. As Sanday and Headlam properly
observe, this "vehement outburst . . . is not unnatural. Against
errors such as these St. Paul has throughout been warning his
readers indirectly, he has been building up his hearers against
them by laying down broad principles of life and conduct, and
now just at the end, just before he finishes, he gives one definite and
direct warning against false teachers."[8] We need not suppose that
these agitators and false teachers had actually invaded the Roman
scene. Probably they had not. If they had we would expect
direct encounter with them in the body of the epistle, as, for
example, in the epistles to the Galatians and Colossians.[9] But

---

[8] *Op. cit.*, p. 429; *cf.* also F. J. A. Hort: *Prolegomena to St. Paul's Epistles to the Romans and Ephesians* (London, 1895), pp. 53–55.

[9] *Cf.* Hort: *ibid.*, pp. 53f. who says: "It is conceivable that just as St. Paul was on the point of finishing or sending his letter, fresh tidings reached him of impending doctrinal troubles at Rome".

234

Paul was well aware of the existence of these heretics and, if their propaganda had not reached Rome, there was good ground for fear that the danger was impending.[10]   The similarity of these warnings to those of Philippians 3:2, 18, 19 is apparent and Colossians 2:16-23 deals with the same or at least closely allied evil.

17, 18   The trouble-makers are by some regarded as antinomian libertines, by others an Judaizing zealots. These two viewpoints, though apparently antagonistic, are in reality and ultimate effect closely related. The person jealous for what God has not commanded soon sets more store by his own ordinances than by those of God. It might be pleaded that verse 18 favours the view that they were of the Epicurean variety. They are said to serve "their own belly". This characterization need not refer, however, to preoccupation with sensuous appetite. It may express the notion of self-service in contrast with the service of the Lord Christ (*cf.* James 3:15; Jude 19) and be virtually equivalent to earthly and sensual. Those condemned in Colossians 2:20-23 whose slogans were "handle not, nor taste, nor touch" (Col. 2:21) could thus come under the same indictment (*cf.* Phil. 3:19). On this interpretation of verse 18 the false teachers could well be Judaizing zealots. These were the apostle's opponents in many instances and they fit the description, "causing the divisions and occasions of stumbling, contrary to the doctrine which ye learned".[11]   The word for "occasions of stumbling" is the same as, in the singular, occurs in 14:13. It does not appear that Paul has the same situation in mind.[12]   In 14:13 a strong believer is for a weak believer the occasion of falling and this is a grave breach of love. But there is no suggestion of the gravity contemplated in the present passage.

---

[10]   *Contra* to the supposition that the heretics had not yet reached Rome *cf.* Dodd: *op. cit.*, p. 242 who says: "He (Paul) knows, or has reason to fear, that the sort of people who have disturbed the peace of his own churches are at work in Rome. He has carefully avoided controversial references to them in the body of the epistle; but when it comes to the final admonition, he cannot refrain from an appeal to the Romans to beware of them."

[11]   It may be that the heretics were of the gnostic variety and similar to those dealt with in the epistle to the Colossians (*cf.* especially Col. 2:4, 8 and Rom. 16:18). "They may have been associated with quasi-gnostic speculations... such as cropped up a little later at Colossae" (Dodd: *op. cit.*, p. 243).

[12]   *Cf. contra* Barrett who says that "possibly the division between weak and strong is still in·mind" (*op. cit., ad. loc.*).

We have here false teachers and propagandists. These are not envisaged in chapter 14. Hence the stumbling is that caused by false doctrine and falls into the category of the error anathematized in Galatians. The injunctions comport with an error of such character: they are to "mark" the proponents so as to avoid them and they are to "turn away from them". No such exhortations are appropriate in chapter 14. These teachers were skilled in the artful device of "smooth and fair speech", a common feature of those who corrupt the purity and simplicity of the gospel. Deceptiveness is the chief peril: "they beguile the hearts of the innocent". The term "innocent" means guileless and refers to the person not given to the wiles of deceit and craft and therefore not suspecting the same in others. The "innocent" person is the unsuspecting and thus readily ensnared by appearance. To the strategems of deception Paul refers in other passages (*cf.* II Cor. 4:2; Eph. 4:14). In view of verse 20 it is difficult to suppress allusion to the beguiling of the serpent (Gen. 3:1-6; *cf.* II Cor. 11:3; I Tim. 2:14).

19, 20 Verse 18 begins with "for" and gives a reason for the preceding exhortations. Verse 19 also begins with "for" but the connection is not the same as in verse 18. The apostle is concerned lest believers at Rome should have their minds corrupted from the simplicity that is unto Christ. The high esteem entertained of the maturity and devotion of the church there (*cf.* 15:14) only intensifies his zeal for the continuance of this fidelity. The fame of the Christian community at Rome had come to all the churches. He speaks of this fame as the report of their "obedience", a term characteristic of this epistle and adapted to the subject of which he now speaks (*cf.* 1:5; 6:16; 15:18; 16:26). The reputation of the Roman church and the crucial place it occupied would correspondingly aggravate the tragedy of corruption. Hence all the more reason for the urgent warnings and injunctions of verse 17. There is also another connection between verse 19 and what precedes. Paul is concerned not to insinuate that the false teaching had entered the church at Rome. He reiterates his assurance of their fidelity and he rejoices over them. Precisely for these reasons they must take heed and he beseeches them to do so. "I would have you wise unto that which is good, and simple unto that which is evil." Though this plea has analogies elsewhere (*cf.* Jer. 4:22;

Matt. 10:16; I Cor. 14:20; Phil. 2:15) and the thought in general is plain enough, it is difficult to ascertain the precise meaning in relation to what precedes. It is obvious that good and evil, wise and simple are contrasted. If a preference may be proposed, the plea is that they would be wise in following what was good and immune to solicitations to evil, that the implied imperative is to the same effect as "hold fast that which is good; abstain from every form of evil" (I Thess. 5:21, 22). The terms "wise" and "simple" are used in order to emphasize the need for alertness and discernment in reference to the craftiness of the false teachers (*cf.* vs. 18a).

In verse 20a there is allusion to Genesis 3:15.[13] The designation "God of peace" (*cf.* 15:33; II Cor. 13:11; Phil. 4:9; I Thess. 5:23; II Thess. 3:16; Heb. 13:20) may well have been used here not merely for the reasons why Paul uses it elsewhere but also because of its particular relevance to the bruising of Satan. The latter envisions the conflict that is to issue in Satan's defeat. The preceding verses have in view the divisions caused by Satan's instruments (*cf.* II Cor. 11:12–15). It is God who bruises Satan and establishes peace in contrast with conflict, discord, and division. He is, therefore, the God of peace. The assurance given in this verse is the encouragement to give heed to the admonitions. Each element is significant. God will *crush* Satan, he will crush him *under the feet* of the faithful, and he will do it *speedily*. The promise of a victorious issue undergirds the fight of faith. The final subjugation of all enemies comes within the horizon of this promise (*cf.* I Cor. 15:25–28). But we may not exclude the conquests which are the anticipations in the present of the final victory (*cf.* I John 2:14; 4:4).

Verse 20b is another example of benediction inserted at the close of a subdivision of the epistle (*cf.* 15:33). It is similar to the closing benediction of several epistles (*cf.* I Cor. 16:23; Gal. 6:18; Phil. 4:23; I Thess. 5:28; II Thess. 3:18; II Tim. 4:22; Phm. 25). But, as noted elsewhere,[14] there are numerous instances of benedictions in the body of an epistle and the occurrence of this one here is not abnormal.

---

13 Following the Hebrew but not the LXX rendering.
14 See Appendix F (pp. 262 ff.).

C. GREETINGS OF FRIENDS
(16:21–23)

16:21–23

21 Timothy my fellow-worker saluteth you; and Lucius
and Jason and Sosipater, my kinsmen.
22 I Tertius, who write the epistle, salute you in the Lord.
23 Gaius my host, and of the whole church, saluteth you.
Erastus the treasurer of the city saluteth you, and
Quartus the brother.

21–23 These verses are the greetings of others associated with the
apostle. The name Timothy needs no comment. Lucius, Jason,
and Sosipater are said to be kinsmen (*cf.* vss. 7, 11). In all there are
six who are called kinsmen, not too large a number for the hypothesis that they were related to Paul by kinship and not merely of
the Jewish race. In the case of Tertius there is direct salutation.[15]
He was Paul's secretary. It is striking that this greeting should be
inserted at this point; Paul is addressing his readers in both what
precedes and what follows. Why Tertius' personal greeting
appears at this point rather than at the end of this section we do not
know. Paul's practice of using an amanuensis is attested in other
epistles (I Cor. 16:21; Gal. 6:11; Col. 4:18; II Thess. 3:17).
Gaius is undoubtedly the Gaius whom Paul baptized at Corinth
(I Cor. 1:14) and there is good ground for thinking that he is the
Titius Justus of Acts 18:7 into whose house Paul entered. Gaius was
not only Paul's host but of the church. If Gaius is to be identified
with Titius Justus, then his being host of the whole church would
probably mean that his home was the meeting place for the as-
semblies of the believers at Corinth (*cf.* vs. 5).[16] But this could also
mean that Gaius' home was open to all Christians visiting Corinth.

---

[15] "We have therefore in this little detail an instance of Paul's characteristic
courtesy, and at the same time a strong proof of the genuineness of the passage:
for what forger would have thought of introducing such an incident?" (Gifford:
op. cit., ad loc.).
[16] If Gaius is to be identified with the Justus of Acts 18:7, then the reading
Titius is to be preferred to Titus in the latter passage: Gaius Titius Justus
being respectively the *praenomen, nomen gentile* and *cognomen* of a Roman citizen.

In this case he would be an outstanding example of the grace of hospitality (*cf.* 12:13). There are not sufficient reasons for identifying this Gaius with the person bearing the same name in any of the other instances (Acts 19:29; 20:4; III John 1). Erastus occupied a position of influence in the city. As in the case of Crispus, the ruler of the synagogue (Acts 18:8), this shows that the church at Corinth comprised men of social station. There is not sufficient evidence to identify this Erastus with the Erastus mentioned elsewhere (Acts 19:22; II Tim. 4:20). Quartus is called the brother. It is more likely that this means brother in Christ rather than brother of Erastus or even of Tertius. The fact that he is distinguished as "the brother", when all the others are brethren in Christ, does not require the ordinary use of the term "brother" any more than does the addition of "in the Lord" in verse 8 in the case of Ampliatus mean that others mentioned as beloved were not beloved in the Lord as well. All the others mentioned in these greetings (vss. 21–23) are not only mentioned by name but identified by some other addition. To end with no more than the name Quartus would be, stylistically if no more, abrupt.[17]

---

[17] The virtual repetition of the benediction found in verse 20 at this point found in D, G, the mass of the cursives, and some versions should not be regarded as impossible from the standpoint of internal evidence. The benediction in verse 20 would close the section devoted to Paul's own greetings and warnings (16:1–20). The benediction at this point would end the section devoted to the greetings of others, conveyed by the apostle (vss. 21–23), and then there would be the closing doxology (vss. 25–27). If such close proximity should seem strange we need but compare with II Thess. 3:16, 18. The question of text depends on the external evidence. The benediction is absent in P⁴⁶, א, A, B, C, the Latin Vulgate and some other versions. In this instance, however, the suspicion can hardly be suppressed that a mistaken notion of incompatibility with the proximate benediction in vs. 20 may have exercised some influence in the omission.

D. DOXOLOGY
(16:25–27)

25 Now to him that is able to establish you according to my gospel, and the preaching of Jesus Christ, according to the revelation of the mystery which hath been kept in silence through times eternal,

26 but now is manifested, and by the scriptures of the prophets, according to the commandment of the eternal God, is made known unto all the nations unto obedience of faith:

27 to the only wise God, through Jesus Christ, to whom be the glory for ever. Amen.

25–27 This concluding doxology is longer than we find in other epistles of Paul. But we find rather close parallels in Hebrews 13:20, 21; Jude 24, 25. At the beginning of the epistle Paul had stated his desire to visit Rome and impart some spiritual gift to the end that believers there might be established. There is an appropriate connection with that aim and the opening words of this doxology. It is God who is able to establish and confirm the saints and of this Paul reminds himself and his readers. But there is a more proximate connection showing the relevance of the introductory words. In verses 17–20 he had warned against the seduction of deceivers and the paramount need is that believers be so established that they would not be the victims of Satan's craft. On God alone must reliance be placed. The confirmation which God gives will be, he says, "according to my gospel and the preaching of Jesus Christ". When he says "my gospel" (*cf.* 2:16; I Thess. 1:5; II Tim. 2:8) he means the gospel that was entrusted to him and which he preached (*cf.* I Cor. 15:1; Gal. 1:11; 2:2, 7; Eph. 3:6; I Thess. 2:4; I Tim. 1:11). "The preaching of Jesus Christ" could mean the preaching on the part of Christ through the instrumentality of Paul (*cf.* 15:18). But it is more likely the preaching concerned with Jesus Christ is in view. The gospel is essentially the preaching which has Christ as its subject; Paul preached Christ (*cf.* I Cor. 1:23; II Cor. 4:5). Thus the establishing is to be in accordance with the gospel of Jesus Christ whom Paul preached and there is no dissonance between Paul's gospel and the preaching of Christ. The term "preaching" is not to be understood as referring merely to the act of preaching. It refers to the *message* preached and so "the preaching of Jesus Christ" is virtually the gospel of which Jesus Christ is the subject.

It is difficult to be certain whether the words "according to the revelation of the mystery" are intended to specify another norm in accordance with which believers are to be established and thus coordinated with "my gospel" and "the preaching of Jesus Christ" or intended to assert that the "gospel" and "preaching" are in accordance with the revelation of the mystery. The latter alternative seems preferable. The gospel Paul preached is in accordance with the mystery revealed. Here "the mystery" is used to include much more than is denoted by the same term in 11:25. There it referred to a restricted aspect of God's revealed counsel (*cf.* I Cor. 15:51). Now it refers to the gospel message inclusively considered. But the term "mystery" has the same connotation as in 11:25.[18] The stress laid upon revelation appears expressly in the present instance as also upon the correlate of revelation, namely, that it had been hid from times eternal. If "times eternal" are to be understood as referring to the earlier ages of this world's history,[19] we have in verse 26 two considerations which do justice to Old Testament revelation, on the one hand, and to New Testament revelation, on the other. (1) The clause "now is

---

[18] *Cf.* comments *ad* 11:25.

[19] It is admittedly very difficult to ascertain the precise reference in χρόνοις αἰωνίοις. In II Tim. 1:9; Tit. 1:2 πρὸ χρόνων αἰωνίων could well mean "before the world began" and "times eternal" would thus be taken as referring to the ages of this world's history. In the present instance "times eternal" could designate the ages extending from creation to the coming of Christ. But this is not so certain. The expression could mean, to use Lagrange's expression, "The eternity of God". He appeals to πρὸ τῶν αἰώνων in I Cor. 2:7 and ἀπὸ τῶν αἰώνων in Eph. 3:9, a sense which, he says, is "indicated by the employment of αἰώνιος in speaking of God in v. 26" (*op. cit., ad loc.*). If this is Paul's meaning, then the thought is that the design was hid in the eternal counsel of God and implies the truth that this grace had been designed by God from eternity. Just as the mystery of election is enhanced by the fact that it took place in Christ before the foundation of the world (Eph. 1:4), so the glory of this mystery is shown by the fact that, though hid, it was not hid to God but was eternally embraced in his design. If χρόνοις αἰωνίοις has this import, then there is no overt reflection in this text on the relative concealment during the Old Testament periods. The relative fulness and expansion of the New Testament revelation would, however, be implicit in verse 26.

manifested", when taken in conjunction with the emphases on "silence" and "revelation" in verse 25, might create the impression that there had been no revelation whatsoever of this mystery in the Old Testament Scriptures. This impression, however, is decisively excluded or corrected by the words "by the scriptures of the prophets". These are the Scriptures to which Paul appeals repeatedly in this epistle for confirmation of the gospel he preached (*cf*. especially in this connection 1:2; 3:21; 11:25, 26). Hence the Old Testament was not silent on this mystery; it was the medium of revelation concerned with this subject. (2) Allowance must also be made for the significance of "now is manifested". There is no suppression of the emphasis upon the New Testament revelation in relation to the "silence through times eternal" (*cf*. Tit. 1:2, 3). The contrast is not absolute but it is *relative*, and this relative contrast must not be discounted. Again we must appreciate the pregnant force of the term "reveal" (*cf*. 1:17). In the Old Testament the ingathering of all nations had been foretold. This promise was given to Abraham (*cf*. Gen. 12:3, 22:18) and had been unfolded progressively. In the Psalms and Isaiah it is a refrain. But only with the coming of Christ and the breaking down of the wall of partition did this promise come to fruition and the implications become apparent. Thus the promise is revealed in fulfilment and operation. All the features of the history of revelation respecting the "mystery" are provided for in the terms here used by the apostle.[20] The "made known unto all the nations" makes clear what has just been said respecting the fulfilment which the New Testament brings. The prophetical scriptures were not the property of all the nations until the gospel went into all the world in accordance with Christ's command and in the power of Pentecost (*cf*. Matt. 28:18-20; Acts 1:4-8). With this worldwide proclamation these scriptures became the property of all without distinction and so *through their medium* the mystery is made known to all nations.

The great change in the ministry of the gospel and of the revelation concerned (*cf*. Acts 17:30) is "according to the commandment of the eternal God" (*cf*. I Tim. 1:1; Tit. 1:3). This points not only to the authority which God's appointment imparts to the

---

[20] *Cf*. the comments of Calvin: *op. cit*., p. 328; Philippi: *op. cit*., *ad* 16:25; Bruce: *op. cit*., *ad* 16:26.

universal proclamation of the gospel but also to the commission with which Paul himself was invested. It also has overtones of grace; it is by God's *commandment* that these overtures come to all men and they come, therefore, with the authority which God's command implies. The aim to which the mystery is directed is "the obedience of faith" (*cf.* 1:5). Though this is not most suitably taken as "obedience of faith unto all the nations", thus meaning *directly* that all nations are summoned to the obedience of faith, yet this thought is implied in the fact that the mystery is made known to all the nations. Wherever the gospel is proclaimed men are called to faith in it.[21]

"To the only wise God" resumes that with which the doxology began, "Now to him that is able "(vs. 25). In the latter, thought is focused on the *power* of God because this is specially relevant to the establishing of believers against all deception and compromise. Now at the close the *wisdom* of God is in the forefront (*cf.* 11:33; Eph. 3:10). The reason for this appears to be that the "mystery" with which verses 25b, 26 are concerned draws attention to and elicits the adoration of God's wisdom (*cf.* I Cor. 2:6–13). The appropriate designation is, therefore, "the only wise God". He is the only God and to him alone can be ascribed the wisdom exhibited in the unfolding of the mystery of his will. According to the reading followed by the version, this doxology presents an unfinished sentence. This should not be regarded as an objection. It is obvious that glory is being ascribed to God and we must not think so pedantically as to require neatly finished syntax. Paul's heart is filled with adoration and what we might regard as broken style does not interfere with the worship expressed. The question does remain, however: to whom is the glory ascribed, to "the only wise God" or to "Jesus Christ"? Other passages have been adduced to support the interpretation that this is a doxology to Christ. In II Timothy 4:18 the same form is used and is ascribed to Christ. It is not so apparent that the doxology is ascribed to Christ in other passages cited in this connection (Heb. 13:21; I

---

[21] No passage in Paul's epistles more than this one places in focus the distinction between mystery as something esoteric and belonging only to the initiated élite, on the one hand, and the Pauline conception, on the other. The features of this mystery as revealed set this distinction in the sharpest relief: (1) it is made known to all nations; (2) it is made known through Scriptures which are the property of all; (3) it is made known to all by God's command; (4) it is revealed to the end of bringing all to the obedience of faith.

Pet. 4:11). There is no reason why doxology in these terms should not have Christ as the object (*cf.* II Pet. 3:18; Rev. 1:6; 5:12, 13). But in this instance there is more to be said in favour of regarding "the only wise God" as the one to whom the glory is ascribed. This is the more frequent pattern (*cf.* 11:36; Gal. 1:5; Eph. 3:21; Phil. 4:20; I Tim. 1:17; I Pet. 5:11; Jude 24, 25).[22] Furthermore, "the only wise God", in apposition to the ascription with which the doxology begins (vs. 25), occupies, as in other similar doxologies, the place of prominence and we should expect that the closing words would apply to him.[23] We may justifiably sense an inappropriateness in the other supposition for it would mean that the titles which are particularly in focus in the earlier stages of the doxology are left without the ascription which expressly enunciates doxology. "Through Jesus Christ" could most suitably be understood as indicating the person through whom glory is ascribed to God and through whom God's glory is made known and extolled. The meaning would be, "to the only wise God be glory through Jesus Christ for ever".

---

[22] I Tim. 1:17 is particularly relevant.
[23] For φ *cf.* Gal. 1:5; Heb. 13:21.

ROMANS 9:5

The interpretation of the two concluding clauses of this verse may be discussed, first of all, in terms of punctuation. There are three alternatives that have been proposed. 1. Place a period or colon after σάρκα and regard what follows to the end of the verse as having reference not to Christ but to God in the form of a doxology. 2. Regard the ὁ ὤν as having its antecedent in ὁ Χριστός and construe all that follows as applied to Christ and rendered, as in the version, "who is over all, God blessed for ever. Amen". 3. A third view had been proposed by Erasmus, namely, to take ὁ ὤν ἐπὶ πάντων with ὁ Χριστός and the remainder Θεὸς εὐλογητὸς εἰς τοὺς αἰῶνας as doxology to God.

It can be said in favour of both alternatives 1 and 3 that doxologies are usually by Paul applied to God in distinction from Christ (II Cor. 1:3; Eph. 1:3; cf. I Pet. 1:3). It is possible to take the latter part of the verse as doxology to God so that in this text the title Θεός would not be predicated of Christ. The following observations should, however, be made.

1. The form of doxology in the LXX and in the New Testament does not follow the pattern we find here in Rom. 9:5.[1] The form for doxology is rather εὐλογητὸς ὁ Θεός. In the LXX this latter form is very frequent and often in the form εὐλογητὸς κύριος ὁ Θεός. In Psalm 67:19 (68:19) we find κύριος ὁ Θεὸς εὐλογητός. But we have not sufficient reason to regard this as intended to be doxology. There is no corresponding clause in the Hebrew. In the following clause (67:20) we have doxology in the usual form εὐλογητὸς κύριος ἡμέραν καθ᾽ ἡμέραν, corresponding to the Hebrew (68:20) ברוך אדני יום יום. So the presumption is that LXX 67:19b is not doxology but affirmation. In LXX Psalm 112:2 (113:2) we find εἴη τὸ ὄνομα κυρίου εὐλογημένον, in III Kings 10:9 γένοιτο κύριος ὁ Θεός σου εὐλογημένος, in II Chron.

---

[1] C. K. Barrett properly recognizes this when he says that "if Paul wished to say 'Blessed be God', he should have placed the word 'blessed' (εὐλογητός) first in the sentence, as he does not" (op. cit., p. 179).

245

9:8 ἔστω κύριος ὁ Θεός σου εὐλογημένος, and in Job 1:21 εἴη τὸ ὄνομα κυρίου εὐλογημένον. But these are not exceptions to the pattern given above; the optative or imperative of these other verbs occurs first and is conjoined with εὐλογημένος. In the New Testament the instances are not as frequent as in the LXX but the same order is followed, whether it be with εὐλογητός or εὐλογημένος (Matt. 21:9; 23:39; Mark 11:9, 10; Luke 1:42, 68; 13:35; 19:38; John 12:13; II Cor. 1:3; Eph. 1:3; I Pet. 1:3). Rom. 1:25 and II Cor. 11:31 are not doxologies but affirmations that God is blessed for ever.

This preponderant usage of both Testaments constitutes a potent argument against the supposition that Rom. 9:5b should be regarded as doxology to God whether it be on the punctuation of alternative 1 or that of 3. The reasons necessary to support the thesis that Paul had here departed from the usual, if not uniform, formula for doxology would have to be conclusive. As we shall see later such reasons are lacking.

2. If the clauses in question were taken as ascription of blessedness to God after the analogy of Rom. 1:25; II Cor. 11:31, then we would expect the name Θεός or an equivalent title to precede, as in the cases just cited. That is, according to this pattern, ὁ ὤν would find its antecedent as ὅς ἐστιν in Rom. 1:25 and ὁ ὤν in II Cor. 11:31 in the person specified in the preceding context. But the only person specified in Rom. 9:5 is ὁ Χριστός. The argument in this case is not that ὁ ὤν could not introduce a new subject (cf. John 3:31; Rom. 8:5, 8)[2] but only that in this instance such a construction would be unnatural, abrupt, and contrary to the analogy of these other Pauline passages. Grammatically or syntactically there is no reason for taking the clauses in question as other than referring to Christ.

3. The interpretation which applies the clauses to Christ suits the context. In the words of Sanday and Headlam "Paul is enumerating the privileges of Israel, and as the highest and last privilege he reminds his readers that it was from this Jewish stock after all that Christ in His human nature had come, and then in order to emphasize this he dwells on the exalted character of Him who came according to the flesh as the Jewish Messiah".[3]

---

[2] See Sanday and Headlam: *op. cit.*, p. 235 to whom I am indebted for these references.

[3] *Op. cit.*, p. 236.

Without some predication expressive of Jesus' transcendent dignity there would be a falling short of what we should expect in this climactic conclusion.

4. With reference to the chief argument in support of the view that these clauses are doxology or ascription of blessedness to the Father, namely, that Paul never predicates Θεός of Christ,[4] the following considerations should be noted. (a) It may not be assumed that Paul never ascribes the title Θεός to Christ. In II Thess. 1:12 it is, to say the least, distinctly possible that τοῦ Θεοῦ ἡμῶν refers to Christ and that Θεοῦ stands in the same relationship to 'Ιησοῦ Χριστοῦ as κυρίου. Likewise in Tit. 2:13, the same holds true of τοῦ μεγάλου Θεοῦ. In this case there is more to be said in favour of this construction than in II Thess. 1:12 (cf. also II Pet. 1:1). It may not be dogmatically affirmed that Paul never uses the predicate Θεός of Christ. (b) Paul uses several expressions which predicate of Jesus the fulness of deity. Perhaps most notable is Phil. 2:6 — ἐν μορφῇ Θεοῦ ὑπάρχων. μορφή means the specific character and in this instance is more eloquent than the simple Θεός because it emphasizes the fulness and reality of deity. To refrain from applying the predicate Θεός to Christ when he is said to have been originally and continued to be "in the form of God" could not possibly have arisen from any hesitation in respect of propriety and, if Paul should, on occasion, speak of Christ as Θεός, this is what we should expect. Of no less significance is Col. 2:9 where πᾶν τὸ πλήρωμα τῆς Θεότητος is said to dwell in Christ. This means "the fulness of Godhood" and no expression could express the fulness of Christ's deity more effectively. Again in Phil. 2:6 the terms τὸ εἶναι ἴσα Θεῷ refer to the dignity of Christ's station as the terms preceding deal with the dignity of his essential being and attribute to Jesus that equality which could belong to no other than to one who is himself also God. Other expressions in Paul could be adduced. These, however, place beyond any doubt the propriety, in terms of Paul's own teaching, of the predicate Θεός after the pattern of John 1:1 and 20:28. (c) Even if we were to discount the possibility of II Thess. 1:12 and the probability of Tit. 2:13 and regard Rom. 9:5 as the only instance where Θεός is expressly applied to Christ by Paul, this should not

---

[4] Cf. Dodd: op. cit., p. 152 who, however, recognizes that Paul "ascribes to Christ functions and dignities which are consistent with nothing less than deity".

be regarded as an obstacle to what is on all accounts the natural interpretation of the clauses in question. We have just found that in Paul's teaching all that is involved in the predicate Θεός belongs to Christ. That he should have usually refrained from the use of the term Θεός as referring to Christ could be adequately explained by Paul's characteristic use of titles, that ὁ Θεός is so frequently the personal name of the Father and ὁ Κύριος that of Christ. But that he should on one occasion (as supposed at this point) have expressly used Θεός of Christ should not be surprising in view of what Paul's conception of Christ not merely allowed but demanded. In II Cor. 3:17 Paul says ὁ δὲ Κύριος τὸ Πνεῦμά ἐστιν. This is unusual and without knowing Paul's theology we would be staggered and ready to question the propriety of the predication. It is his conception of the relation of Christ to the Holy Spirit that explains it, not his characteristic use of titles. So in Rom. 9:5. (d) The clause ὁ ὢν ἐπὶ πάντων as an assertion of Christ's lordship is in accord with Paul's teaching elsewhere (cf. 1:4; 14:9; Eph. 1:20–23; Phil. 2:9–11; Col. 1:18, 19; for parallels cf. Matt. 28:18; John 3:35; Acts 2:36; Heb. 1:2–4; 8:1; I Pet. 3:22). Every consideration would show the relevance of appeal to Christ's sovereignty at this point. The arguments already adduced against the supposition that both concluding clauses refer to the Father would likewise militate against the proposal to apply this clause to Christ and Θεός εὐλογητός to the Father. The most natural rendering would, therefore, be "who is over all, God blessed for ever", so that "God blessed for ever" stands in apposition to what precedes.

We may thus conclude that there is no good reason to depart from the traditional construction and interpretation of this verse and, on the other hand, there are preponderant reasons for adopting the same.

LEVITICUS 18:5

There does not need to be any question but Paul in Rom. 10:5 makes allusion to Lev. 18:5 more directly than to any other Old Testament passage. He places the principle stated in Lev. 18:5 in opposition to the righteousness which is of faith and calls it "the righteousness which is of the law". The problem that arises from this use of Lev. 18:5 is that the latter text does not appear in a context that deals with legal righteousness as opposed to that of faith. Lev. 18:5 is in a context in which the claims of God upon his redeemed and covenant people are being asserted and urged upon Israel. In this respect Lev. 18:1-5 is parallel to Exod. 20:1-17; Deut. 5:6-21. The preface is "I am the Lord your God" (Lev. 18:2) and corresponds to the preface to the ten commandments (Exod. 20:2; Deut. 5:6). The whole passage is no more "legalistic" than are the ten commandments. Hence the words "which if a man do, he shall live in them" (vs. 5) refers not to the life accruing from doing in a legalistic framework but to the blessing attendant upon obedience in a redemptive and covenant relationship to God. In this respect Lev. 18:1-5 has numerous parallels in the Pentateuch and elsewhere (*cf.* Deut. 4:6; 5:32, 33; 11:13-15, 26-28; 28:1-14; Ezek. 20:11, 13). It is the principle expressly enunciated in the fifth commandment (*cf.* Exod. 20:12; Eph. 6:2, 3). Thus the question is: could Paul properly have appealed to Lev. 18:5 as an illustration of works-righteousness in opposition to that of faith? In order to answer the question it is necessary to deal with the three distinct relationships in which the principle "the man that does shall live" has relevance.

1. This principle has the strictest relevance and application in a state of perfect integrity. It is the principle of equity in God's government. Wherever there is righteousness to the full extent of God's demand there must also be the corresponding justification and life. This is the principle on which the argument of the apostle turns in the earlier part of the epistle. Just as sin—condemnation—death is an invariable combination in God's

judgment, so is righteousness—justification—life. It could not be otherwise. God's judgment is always according to truth. Perfect righteousness must elicit God's favour or complacency and with this favour goes the life that is commensurate with it. This would have obtained for Adam in sinless integrity apart from any special constitution that special grace would have contemplated.

This relationship could have no application to mankind after the fall. It can never again be in operation for man's acceptance with God and for the life that accompanies this acceptance. The only combination operative now in terms of simple equity is sin—condemnation—death.

2. The principle "the man who does shall live" must be regarded as totally inoperative within the realm of sin. It is this truth that underlies Paul's whole polemic regarding the justification of the ungodly and the righteousness that is constitutive thereof. Justification by *doing* is the contradiction of justification by faith. *Doing* has human righteousness in view, and the only righteousness that can be operative in our sinful situation is the God-righteousness which the gospel reveals (*cf.* 1:17; 3:21, 22; 10:3). It is this contrast that Paul institutes in Rom. 10:5, 6. In alluding to Lev. 18:5 at this point he uses the formula "the man that doeth . . . shall live thereby" as a proper expression *in itself* of the principle of works-righteousness in contrast with the righteousness of faith. We have no right to contest the apostle's right to use the terms of Lev. 18:5 for this purpose since they do describe that which holds true when law-righteousness is operative unto justification and life and also express the conception entertained by the person who espouses the same as the way of acceptance with God (*cf.* also Gal. 3:12).

3. It must be understood, therefore, that the principle "this do and thou shalt live" can have no validity in our sinful state as the way of justification and acceptance with God. To aver that it has is to deny the reality of our sin and the necessary provision of the gospel. But we must not suppose that doing the commandments as the way of life has ceased to have any validity or application. To suppose this would be as capital a mistake in its own locus as to propound works-righteousness as the way of justification. We must bear in mind that righteousness and life are never separable. Within the realm of justification by grace through faith there is not only acceptance with God as righteous in the righteousness of

Christ but there is also the new life which the believer lives. Pauls had unfolded the necessity and character of this new life in chapters 6 to 8. The new life is one of righteousness in obedience to the commandments of God (*cf.* 6:13, 14, 16, 17, 22; 8:4). In a word, it is one of obedience (*cf.* 13:8–10). So Paul can say in the most absolute terms, "If ye live after the flesh, ye must die; but if by the Spirit ye put to death the deeds of the body, ye shall live" (8:13). In the realm of grace, therefore, obedience is the way of life. He that does the commandments of God lives in them. It could not be otherwise. The fruit of the Spirit is well-pleasing to God and the fruit of the Spirit is obedience. In the renovated realm of saving and sanctifying grace we come back to the combination righteousness—approbation—life. The witness of Scripture to the necessity and actuality of this in the redeemed, covenant life of believers is pervasive. It is this principle that appears in Lev. 18:5 and in the other passages from the Old Testament cited above. "Fear the Lord, and depart from evil: it will be health to thy navel, and marrow to thy bones" (Prov. 3:7, 8).

THE AUTHORITIES OF ROMANS 13:1

Oscar Cullmann contends that "the late Jewish teaching concerning the angels ... of the peoples" belongs "to the solid content of faith in the New Testament"[1] and that on the basis of this faith "the existing earthly political power belongs in the realm of such angelic powers".[2] In Romans 13:1 the ἐξουσίαι, he maintains, must be conceived of, in accordance with Pauline usage, as *"the invisible angelic powers that stand behind the State government"*. "Thus as a result the term has for Paul a double meaning, which in this case corresponds exactly to the content, since the State is indeed the executive agent of invisible powers."[3]

As far as Pauline teaching is concerned Cullmann appeals particularly to I Cor. 2:8; 6:3. In the former passage the analogy, he says, is complete because "it is quite plain", he avers, "that by ἄρχοντες τοῦ αἰῶνος τούτου are meant both the invisible 'rulers of the age' *and* the visible ones, Pilate and Herod".[4] The latter passage, he says, "proves that according to the Primitive Christian view these invisible angelic powers stand behind the earthly states".[5]

It should be understood that Cullmann's argument is based entirely upon the plural form and upon the pluralistic usage of the singular, not upon the usage of the singular.[6] Furthermore, it is not the good angels that Cullmann regards as the invisible angelic beings lying back of the human agents but the evil angels who by "their subjection under Christ ... have rather lost their evil character, and ... now stand under and within the Lordship of Christ".[7] "Of them it can be said in the most positive manner

---

[1] *Christ and Time* (E. T., Philadelphia, 1950), p. 192. *Cf.* also revised edition (London, 1962). In the latter the quotations given and pagination are the same.
[2] *Ibid.*, p. 193.
[3] *Ibid.*, p. 195.
[4] *Ibid.*
[5] *Ibid.*, p. 193.
[6] *Ibid.*, pp. 194f.; *cf.* also pp. 209f.
[7] *Ibid.*, p. 196.

that although they had formerly been enemies they have now become 'ministering spirits sent forth for ministry' (Heb. 1:14)".[8]

In dealing with this thesis it is proper, first of all, to take account of those features of Paul's usage which might lend support to this interpretation of the ἐξουσίαι in Rom. 13:1. It is true that on several occasions this term is used of angelic beings, sometimes viewed as good and sometimes as evil (Eph. 3:10; 6:12; Col. 1:16; 2:15; cf. I Pet. 3:22). In the use of the singular there is reference to satanic authority in Eph. 2:2; Col. 1:13 (cf. Acts 26:18). In those passages which refer to the exalted lordship of Christ there is surely allusion to suprahuman agents (Eph. 1:21; Col. 2:10; cf. Phil. 2:9–11). In I Cor. 15:24, where the final subjugation of all enemies is in view, suprahuman authorities are likewise contemplated. It should also be observed that in such connections the term "authority" is coordinated with the term "principality" (ἀρχή) (Eph. 1:21; 6:12; Col. 1:16; 2:10, 15). In Tit. 3:1, which is closely parallel to Rom. 13:1, Paul uses "principalities" as well as "authorities" in designating magisterial agents.

But, secondly, while it is to be admitted that the term in question (ἐξουσίαι or the pluralistic use of the singular) has suprahuman reference in several instances, yet Cullmann's thesis is not borne out by the evidence. In criticism the following considerations may be pleaded.

1. Cullmann bases his argument upon the use of the plural.[9] But the use of the singular is not totally irrelevant to the question at issue. The argument must take account of the diversity that applies to the use of the singular. The latter is used frequently without reference to suprahuman agency.[10] To say the least, why should not the plural likewise be used without any allusion to invisible angelic beings? It is necessary to preface our examination of the evidence with this caution.

2. Cullmann is confident that in I Cor. 6:3 there is reference to invisible angelic powers. "For it is only on this assumption that it has any meaning when Paul justifies his admonition to the

---

[8] *Ibid.*, p. 198; *cf.* also by Cullmann: *The State in the New Testament* (New York, 1956), p. 66 and the "Excursus" in the same volume, pp. 95–114.

[9] See citations in n. 6.

[10] *Cf.* Matt. 8:9; 10:1; Mark 13:34; Luke 19:7; 23:7; John 1:12; I Cor. 7:37; 8:9; 9:4; 11:10; II Thess. 3:9.

Church, to avoid the State courts in trials among Christians, by reference to the fact that the members of the Church will judge the 'angels' at the end of the days".[11] This assumption is based on far too precarious exegesis. The appeal to the fact that the saints will judge angels is adequately, if not fully, explained by what lies on the face of the text. It is in effect an *a fortiori* argument. If the saints are to judge angels, how much more should they be competent to settle disputes pertaining to things of this life. This only exemplifies the arbitrariness of what Cullmann propounds as proof.

3. I Cor. 2:6, 8, to which Cullmann also appeals with such confidence, does not offer the support required. The rulers of this age who are coming to nought (vs. 6) and who crucified the Lord of glory (vs. 8) cannot be shown, on the basis of the New Testament, to be angelic powers. Nowhere else does the New Testament attribute the *crucifixion* to angelic beings. It does charge men and particularly the rulers with this crime (Acts 2:23; 3:17; 4:26–28; 13:27). It is significant that the same term for rulers is used (Acts 3:17; 4:26; 13:27) as is used in I Cor. 2:6, 8. The relevant evidence, therefore, would identify the rulers of this age as the human potentates who were the agents of the crucifixion. Although in Eph. 2:2 Paul uses this term ruler (ἄρχων) with reference to Satan (*cf.* John 12:31; 14:30; 16:11), apart from the text in question (I Cor. 2:6, 8) and Rom. 13:3, he uses it in no other instance. In the Gospels it is frequently used of human rulers (*cf.* Matt. 9:18; 20:25; Luke 12:58; 23:13; 24:20; John 3:1; 7:26, 48; 12:42). Thus the usage of the New Testament does not indicate that the rulers of this age in I Cor. 2:6, 8 are conceived of as invisible principalities. The usage points in another direction. Again, one of the main props of Cullmann's contention is shown to fall short of the proof claimed for it.

4. Though Christ triumphed over the principalities and powers (Col. 2:15) and wrought judgment upon the prince of this world (John 12:31; Heb. 2:14), yet in Paul's teaching Satan and the demonic powers are exceedingly active in opposition to the kingdom of God (*cf.* II Cor. 4:4; Eph. 6:12). According to Paul's teaching here in Rom. 13:1–7 the governing authorities are represented as God's ministers to promote good and restrain evil

---

[11] *Christ and Time*, p. 193.

and are, therefore, directed against Satanic and demonic influences.[12] Evil powers are represented as subjugated but nowhere are they credited with well-doing. Besides, if the "authorities" are angelic beings that once were evil and now subjugated to Christ and ministers of God, what possible principle of differentiation can be applied to this order of beings whereby this dual and antithetical role can be predicated of the same order of principalities? There is no place for this differentiation in Paul's writings. In the words of Franz J. Leenhardt: "These demonic powers are always presented by the apostle as evil and maleficent. Christ has fought against them and conquered them: He has not placed them in His service, but has rendered them powerless to harm the elect who in spite of everything have still to struggle against them with the strength which Christ the Victor supplies. How can we conceive of these powers as being converted and becoming servants of the good? How could believers be exhorted to obey powers which they have still to fight against? How could Paul himself, who has just mentioned (ch. 8) the powers which seek to separate the believer from his Lord, regard these same powers as the basis of a useful authority worthy of conscientious obedience on the part of the believer?"[13] If the "authorities" were regarded as unfallen angels there would be much more plausibility to the thesis in question. But this is not Cullmann's position. These are "demonic beings" who in the time before Christ "*were destined to be subjected through Jesus Christ*"[14] and now are in subjection to him, "elevated to the highest dignity by the function that is here assigned to them".[15]

5. I Pet. 2:13–17 is closely parallel to Rom. 13:1–7.[16] But Peter calls civil magistracy a "human ordinance" ($\dot{\alpha}\nu\theta\rho\omega\pi\dot{\iota}\nu\eta$ $\varkappa\tau\dot{\iota}\sigma\iota\varsigma$). This characterization militates against Cullmann's thesis. For even though he recognizes that there is the State behind which stand the angelic powers this designation of Peter stands in opposition to any supposition of angelic composition.

6. In Luke 12:11 the terms "principalities" ($\dot{\alpha}\rho\chi\alpha\dot{\iota}$) and "authorities" ($\dot{\varepsilon}\xi o v \sigma\dot{\iota}\alpha\iota$) are used with reference to human rulers.

---

12   *Cf.* Barrett: *op. cit.*, p. 249.
13   *Op. cit.*, p. 329, n.
14   *Christ and Time*, p. 209.
15   *Ibid.*, p. 202.
16   Cullmann calls it the "first exegesis of this Pauline passage" (*ibid.*, p. 197).

This clear instance indicates that the plural of both terms can be used for human authorities. It would require the most conclusive evidence to establish the thesis that when these same terms are used with reference to the political power, as in Rom. 13:1; Tit. 3:1, there are not only the human agents but also invisible angelic powers. The arguments advanced by Cullmann are not sufficient to establish his thesis. It is significant that notwithstanding the vigour of his contention the concluding word of his "Excursus" is that the thesis "is an hypothesis, and naturally we can never say with final certainty that Paul had in mind not only the secular sense of the word ἐξουσίαι, but also the meaning which he himself attributes to it in all other passages. I can only wish, however, that all other hypotheses which we necessarily must use in the field of New Testament science were as well grounded as this one".[17]

---

[17] *The State in the New Testament,* p. 114.

ROMANS 14:5 AND THE WEEKLY SABBATH

The question is whether the weekly Sabbath comes within the scope of the distinction respecting days on which the apostle reflects in Romans 14:5. If so then we have to reckon with the following implications.

1. This would mean that the Sabbath commandment in the decalogue does not continue to have any binding obligation upon believers in the New Testament economy. The observance of one day in seven as holy and invested with the sanctity enunciated in the fourth commandment would be abrogated and would be in the same category in respect of *observance* as the ceremonial rites of the Mosaic institution. On the assumption posited, insistence upon the continued sanctity of each recurring seventh day would be as Judaizing as to demand the perpetuation of the Levitical feasts.

2. The first day of the week would have no prescribed religious significance. It would not be distinguished from any other day as the memorial of Christ's resurrection and could not properly be regarded as the Lord's day in distinction from the way in which every day is to be lived in devotion to and the service of the Lord Christ. Neither might any other day, weekly or otherwise, be regarded as set apart with this religious significance.

3. Observance of a weekly Sabbath or of a day commemorating our Lord's resurrection would be a feature of the person weak in faith and in this case he would be weak in faith because he had not yet attained to the understanding that in the Christian institution all days are in the same category. Just as one weak Christian fails to recognize that all kinds of food are clean, so another, or perchance the same person, would fail to esteem every day alike.

These implications of the thesis in question cannot be avoided. We may now proceed to examine them in the light of the considerations which Scripture as a whole provides.

1. The Sabbath institution is a creation ordinance. It did not begin to have relevance at Sinai when the ten commandments

were given to Moses on two tables (*cf.* Gen. 2:2, 3; Exod. 16:21–23). It was, however, incorporated in the law promulgated at Sinai and this we would expect in view of its significance and purpose as enunciated in Genesis 2:2, 3. It is so embedded in this covenant law that to regard it as of different character from its context in respect of abiding relevance goes counter to the unity and basic significance of what was inscribed on the two tables. Our Lord himself tells us of its purpose and claims it for his messianic Lordship (Mark 2:28). The thesis we are now considering would have to assume that the pattern provided by God himself (Gen. 2:2, 3) in the work of creation (*cf.* also Exod. 20:11; 31:17) has no longer any relevance for the regulation of man's life on earth, that only nine of the ten words of the decalogue have authority for Christians, that the beneficent design contemplated in the original institution (Mark 2:28) has no application under the gospel, and that the lordship Christ exercised over the Sabbath was for the purpose of abolishing it as an institution to be observed. These are the necessary conclusions to be drawn from the assumption in question. There is no evidence to support any of these conclusions, and, when they are combined and their cumulative force frankly weighed, it is then that the whole analogy of Scripture is shown to be contradicted by the assumption concerned.

2. The first day of the week as the day on which Jesus rose from the dead (Matt. 28:1; Mark 16:2, 9; Luke 24:1; John 20:1, 19) is recognized in the New Testament as having a significance derived from this fact of Jesus' resurrection (Acts 20:7; I Cor. 16:2) and this is the reason why John speaks of it as the Lord's day (Rev. 1:10). It is the one day of the week to which belongs this distinctive religious significance. Since it occurs every seventh day, it is a perpetually recurring memorial with religious intent and character proportionate to the place which Jesus' resurrection occupies in the accomplishment of redemption. The two pivotal events in this accomplishment are the death and resurrection of Christ and the two memorial ordinances of the New Testament institution are the Lord's supper and the Lord's day, the one memorializing Jesus' death and the other his resurrection. If Paul in Romans 14:5 implies that all distinctions of days have been obliterated, then there is no room for the distinctive significance of the first day of the week as the Lord's day. The evidence

supporting the memorial character of the first day is not to be controverted and, consequently, in this respect also the assumption in question cannot be entertained, namely, that all religious distinction of days is completely abrogated in the Christian economy.

3.   In accord with the analogy of Scripture and particularly the teaching of Paul, Romans 14:5 can properly be regarded as referring to the ceremonial holy days of the Levitical institution. The obligation to observe these is clearly abrogated in the New Testament. They have no longer relevance or sanction and the situation described in Romans 14:5 perfectly accords with what Paul would say with reference to religious scrupulosity or the absence of such anent these days. Paul was not insistent upon the discontinuance of ritual observances of the Levitical ordinances as long as the observance was merely one of religious custom and not compromising the gospel (cf. Acts 18:18, 21; 21:20–27). He himself circumcised Timothy from considerations of expediency. But in a different situation he could write: "Behold, I Paul say unto you, that if ye be circumcised, Christ will profit you nothing" (Gal. 5:2). Ceremonial feast days fall into the category of which the apostle could say: "One man esteemeth one day above another: another esteemeth every day alike". Many Jews would not yet have understood all the implications of the gospel and had still a scrupulous regard for these Mosaic ordinances. Of such scruples we know Paul to have been thoroughly tolerant and they fit the precise terms of the text in question. There is no need to posit anything that goes beyond such observances. To place the Lord's day and the weekly Sabbath in the same category is not only beyond the warrant of exegetical requirements but brings us into conflict with principles that are embedded in the total witness of Scripture. An interpretation that involves such contradiction cannot be adopted. Thus the abiding sanctity of each recurring seventh day as the memorial of God's rest in creation and of Christ's exaltation in his resurrection is not to be regarded as in any way impaired by Romans 14:5.

THE WEAK BROTHER

It has been common in our modern context to apply the teaching of Paul in Romans 14 to the situation that arises from excess in the use of certain things, especially the excess of drunkenness. The person addicted to excess is called the "weak brother" and those not thus addicted are urged to abstain from the use of that thing out of deference to the weakness of the intemperate. The temperate are alleged to be guilty of placing a stumblingblock in the way of the intemperate because by their use of the thing in question they are said to place before the weak an inducement or perchance temptation to indulgence of his vice.

It will soon become apparent that this application is a complete distortion of Paul's teaching and it is an example of the looseness with which Scripture is interpreted and applied.

1. Paul is not dealing with the question of excess in the use of certain kinds of food or drink. This kind of abuse does not come within his purview in this passage or in the other passages in I Corinthians. The weak of Romans 14 are not those given to excess. They are the opposite; they are total abstainers from certain articles of food. The "weak" addicted to excess do not abstain; they take too much.

2. The "weakness" of those who go to excess is in an entirely different category from that of which Paul treats in this instance. The "weakness" of excess is iniquity and with those who are guilty of this sin Paul deals in entirely different terms. Drunkards, for example, will not inherit the kingdom of God (I Cor. 6:10) and Paul enjoins that if any one called a brother is a drunkard with such an one believers are not to keep company or even eat (I Cor. 5:11). How different is Romans 14:1: "Him that is weak in faith receive ye". Is it not apparent what havoc is done to interpretation of Scripture and to the criteria by which the purity and unity of the church are to be maintained when the weak of Romans 14 are confused with the intemperate and drunkards?

3. Even when we consider the case of one converted from a life of excess and still afflicted with temptation to his old vice, we do not have a situation that is parallel to Romans 14. It is true that sometimes for such a person the cost of sobriety is total abstinence. Every proper consideration should be given and measure used by stronger believers to support and fortify him against the temptation to which he is liable to succumb. But his "weakness" is not that of the weak in the circumstance with which Paul deals. The latter is the weakness of conscientious scruple, the former is that of tendency to excess and conscientious religious scruple does not describe or define his situation.

4. There is the case of a person who has been converted from excess in some particular. It sometimes happens that such a person comes to entertain a religious scruple against the use of that particular which had previously been the occasion of vice and perhaps debauchery. Thus on religious grounds he becomes a total abstainer. He has made an erroneous judgment and has failed to make a proper analysis of responsibility for his former excesses. But the fact remains that on religious grounds he abstains from the use of the particular thing concerned. He is weak in faith and is thus in the category of the weak in Romans 14. The injunctions to the strong would thus apply in this instance. The past excess enters into this situation, however, only as explaining the reason for his religious scruple, and there is no ground for thinking that the origin of the scruples entertained by the weak at Rome was of this character. But the weakness, in the illustration given, is still that of wrongly entertained scruple. It is that religious scruple that the strong must take into account in their relations to this person and not at all his tendency to excess. There is no tendency to excess in the case posited.

It is obvious, therefore, that Paul's teaching in this chapter turns on scruple arising from religious conviction. This is the principle on which the interpretation rests and in terms of which application is relevant. To apply Paul's teaching to situations in which this religious involvement is absent is to extend the exhortations beyond their reference and intent and is, therefore, a distortion of the teaching concerned.

THE INTEGRITY OF THE EPISTLE

The question respecting integrity pertains almost entirely to chapters 15 and 16 of the epistle. Hypotheses divergent from the traditional view that these chapters belonged to the epistle Paul addressed to the Roman church have not always been based on the textual data. But, as the discussion proceeds in the last few decades, hypotheses and opinions advanced are to a large extent related to the textual variants. The most important data can be briefly summarized in order that various questions may be placed in focus in relation to the relevant evidence.

1. At 1:7 ἐν Ῥώμῃ is omitted by G, a Graeco-Latin manuscript of the tenth century. The margins of the minuscules 1739 and 1908 indicate that "in Rome" did not appear in Origen's text and commentary. There is also evidence in other Latin texts that "in Rome" had been restored to the corrupted text represented by G with the result that a combination of both is effected.

2. At 1:15 G again omits τοῖς ἐν Ῥώμῃ and what T. W. Manson calls the "patchwork" in D,[1] a sixth century bilingual, may well attest, as he and others suggest, that the ancestor of both D and G omitted reference to Rome at 1:7, 15.[2]

3. Preponderant evidence supports the ending of chapter 14 with verse 23. But in L, an eighth century uncial, in the minuscules 104, 1175, and in manuscripts known to Origen the doxology of 16:25–27 appears at this point after verse 23.

4. In the uncials A and P and in minuscules 5 and 33 the doxology appears after 14:23 and at the end of the epistle (16:25–27).

5. In G the doxology does not appear at all; but after 14:23 there is a space which probably indicated that the scribe was aware of the doxology and left enough space for its insertion. Marcion's text also omitted the doxology and ended with 14:23.

---

[1] T. W. Manson: *Studies in the Gospels and Epistles*, Manchester, 1962, p. 229.
[2] *Cf.* F. F. Bruce: *Romans*, as cited, p. 26.

6. In P[46], the third century papyrus, the doxology of 16: 25–27 occurs after 15:33 and not at the end of the epistle. This is the only witness for insertion at this point. But the early date of P[46] has led some to attach considerable weight to this reading.

7. There is some evidence that recensions of the epistle came to an end with the doxology after 14:23. Particularly significant is codex Amiatinus of the Vulgate which from its chapter divisions and summaries would indicate that the final chapter, number 51, comprised the doxology which immediately followed what is dealt with in 14:13–23 as chapter 50.

It is not necessary to review a great many of the theories that have been propounded. For example, E. Renan's theory of a quadripartite epistle on the basis of what he alleges to be four distinct endings (15:33; 16:20; 16:24; 16:25–27) has been so thoroughly dealt with and in its main contentions so effectively refuted by J. B. Lightfoot (cf. Biblical Essays [London, 1893], pp. 293–311) that it would be wasteful expenditure of space to repeat the arguments. Suffice it to say that Lightfoot's masterful treatment of relevant data must always be taken into account in dealing with the questions at stake.

It needs to be stated at the outset that as far as the textual evidence is concerned there is no ground for disputing the genuineness of the text "in Rome" (1:7), "who are in Rome" (1:15), the doxology (16:25–27). The only questions requiring discussion are those that arise from the omission of reference to Rome in some authorities at 1:7, 15 and the different positions which the doxology occupies in the traditions referred to above. Though the doxology does not appear in G and though Marcion's text did not contain it, this does not give any ground for assailing its genuineness as Pauline.

It is not difficult to discover reasons for Marcion's recension, namely, the exclusion of all that follows 14:23. It is apparent that 15:1–13 is continuous with 14:1–23. But no texts in Paul are more antithetical to Marcion's depreciation of the Old Testament than 15:4, 8, 9. The same applies to 16:26.[3]

The evidence does indicate that a shorter recension of the epistle was in circulation. Codex Amiatinus, as referred to above, is an example of this type of text. Furthermore, Cyprian in his

---

[3] Cf. Manson: op. cit., p. 230.

Testimonia, in which he gives "an arsenal of proof texts for various dogmas",[4] does not clearly adduce texts from Romans 15 and 16 even though some of these are directly germane to some of his headings.[5] Likewise Tertullian in his books *Against Marcion* does not quote from these two chapters even though, as F. F. Bruce observes, they are "full of potential anti-Marcionite ammunition"[6] and, after quoting 14:10, Tertullian also says that this comes in the closing section of the epistle.[7] This kind of evidence would favour the view that the shorter recension ended with 14:23 with or without the doxology of 16:25–27. The question arises: how is this shorter recension to be explained?

Scholars of the highest repute, without disputing the genuineness of chapters 15 and 16 as Pauline, have taken the position that Paul himself was responsible for the discrepancy between the longer and shorter forms in which the epistle was in circulation. J. B. Lightfoot took the position that Paul first wrote the epistle in the longer form, including chapters 15 and 16, and addressed it to the church at Rome. But since "the epistle, though not a circular epistle itself, yet manifested the general and comprehensive character which might be expected in such" and therefore "is more of a treatise than a letter",[8] Paul himself made it also available as a circular or general letter and thus omitted the two last chapters in order to divest it of personal matter and make it suitable for the churches in general. This circular letter, Lightfoot supposes, omitted the reference to Rome in 1:7, 15 and added the doxology which is now found in most manuscripts and versions at the end of the epistle but which, he thinks, did not belong to the original letter addressed to Rome.

It would not be prejudicial to the Pauline authorship of the received text of the epistle to accept this hypothesis. But on the premises assumed by Lightfoot there is one formidable, if not insurmountable, objection to the supposition. This objection has been advanced by several competent critics and is to the effect that 14:1–23 and 15:1–13 are so much of a unit that for Paul to divide his own work at 14:23 would be most unnatural. In the

---

[4] Kirsopp Lake: *The Earlier Epistles of St. Paul*, London, 1927, p. 337.
[5] *Cf.* Lake: *ibid.*, pp. 337f.
[6] *Op. cit.*, p. 27.
[7] *Cf.* Lake: *op. cit.*, pp. 338f.
[8] *Op. cit.*, p. 315.

words of Sanday and Headlam: "There is nothing in the next thirteen verses [15:1–13] which unfits them for general circulation. They are in fact more suitable for an encyclical letter than is chap. xiv. It is to us inconceivable that St. Paul should have himself mutilated his own argument by cutting off the conclusion of it."[9]

In view of the unity of 14:1–23 and 15:1–13 more reasonable would be the hypothesis that the shorter recension, ending at 14:23 and omitting reference to Rome in 1:7, 15, was the original in the form of a general epistle. When the other two chapters were added and the whole addressed to the church at Rome, the insertion of "Rome" at 1:7, 15 could be readily understood and 15:1–13 could be regarded as a necessary and fitting expansion of the theme dealt with in 14:1–23, especially of 14:13–23.[10] To this hypothesis also there is the decided objection that the elimination of reference to Rome in 1:7, 15 does not remove the definiteness of destination involved in 1:8–15. A circular or general epistle would include churches that Paul had visited and it is apparent that these verses have in view a community that he had not yet visited. The fact is simply that the omission of Rome at 1:7, 15 does not remove the notices in 1:8–15 which militate against the hypothesis of a circular Pauline recension.[11]

Since the evidence indicates that a text ending at 14:23 existed in the third century, how are we to explain this abridged edition of the epistle? For the reasons given above and in T. W. Manson's words, "It cannot be the work of the author".[12] Surely no hypothesis has more in its support than that the circulation in this mutilated form was due to the work of Marcion. We have Origen's word for it that Marcion cut out everything after 14:23.[13] There is no reason to doubt that Marcion's excised text could have exercised sufficient influence to explain the form in which the epistle was in circulation in certain areas. This may have been the text in the hands of Tertullian. But it is not inconceivable that Tertullian was acquainted with the longer text and yet

---

[9] *Op. cit.*, p. xcv; *cf.* also F. J. A. Hort's detailed analysis of Lightfoot's theory in *Biblical Essays*, as cited above, pp. 321–351.

[10] *Cf.* Lake: *op. cit.*, pp. 362–365.

[11] *Cf.* Hort: *op. cit.*, pp. 347–350 for his summation of the argument against two Pauline recensions.

[12] *Op. cit.*, p. 233.

[13] *Cf.* Bruce: *op. cit.*, p. 27; Manson: *op. cit.*, p. 233; and, for fuller defence, Sanday and Headlam: *op. cit.*, pp. xcvi–xcviii.

refrained from appeal to chapters 15 and 16 in his books against Marcion for the reason that Marcion did not include these chapters in the *corpus* of Paul's epistles.

There is still another hypothesis respecting the last two chapters of Romans, particularly as it concerns the doxology and chapter 16. For more than a hundred years it has been contended that 16:1–23 was not addressed to the church at Rome but to the church at Ephesus. This was the thesis of E. Renan. But the contention was not original with him.[14] The discovery of the papyrus manuscript P46 has given new impetus to the hypothesis for, as noted, P46 adds the doxology of 16:25–27 at the end of chapter 15 and in this respect is the sole witness to this location. On this basis T. W. Manson concludes that "we should regard P46 as offering in chapters i–xv the form in which the epistle was received at Rome; and, what is perhaps more important, its text should be taken as descended from the pre-Marcionite Roman text of the letter".[15] But as Sir Frederic Kenyon says, "it would be dangerous to adopt this conjecture without confirmation, and it is possible that the variable position (*i.e.* of the doxology) is due to its being treated like a doxology to a hymn, and being read at the end of xiv. or xv., when xvi., which is mainly a string of names, was omitted".[16]

It is necessary now to pay some attention to the supposition that chapter 16:1–23 is a letter or part of a letter to Ephesus. Various arguments have been pleaded in support of the Ephesian destination. These have been well summed up most recently by F. F. Bruce, though not himself defending the hypothesis.[17] J. B. Lightfoot subjected the thesis of E. Renan to thorough analysis and has probably presented the case for the Roman destination more fully and competently than any other.[18] For succinctness and

---

[14] *Cf.* Manson: *op. cit.*, pp. 231, 234 for the references to R. Schumacher and David Schulz.

[15] *Op. cit.*, p. 236. On this view it would be only chapter 15 that Marcion struck from his text of the epistle and the references to Rome in 1:7, 15. Leaving Marcion out of account, then the main question would be to explain the two types of text, the Roman of fifteen chapters and what Manson calls the Egyptian of sixteen (*cf. ibid.*, p. 237).

[16] *Our Bible and the Ancient Manuscripts*, Revised by A. W. Adams, London, 1958, p. 189.

[17] *Op. cit.*, pp. 266f.

[18] *Op. cit.*, pp. 294–306; *cf.* also Lightfoot's *St. Paul's Epistle to the Philippians*, London, 1908, pp. 171–178. Though Lake deems the case for the Roman

persuasiveness no statement of the case for Rome surpasses that of F. F. Bruce.[19]

The most plausible argument for Ephesus is that concerned with the mention of Prisca and Aquila and the church in their house (16:3, 5). Paul first met Prisca and Aquila at Corinth. They had recently come from Rome because of Claudius' edict (Acts 18:2). When Paul departed from Corinth after eighteen months (Acts 18:11) or possibly longer (Acts 18:18), he was accompanied by Prisca and Aquila and when he came to Ephesus he left them there (Acts 18:18, 19). When Paul wrote I Corinthians from Ephesus (I Cor. 16:8) Prisca and Aquila were still there and Paul again refers to the church in their house (I Cor. 16:19). By the time II Timothy was written they were again in Ephesus (II Tim. 4:19); at least they were not in Rome. The argument for residence in Ephesus, when Romans 16:3, 5 was penned, rests on the relatively brief interval between the date of I Corinthians and that of Romans. On certain calculations it is possible that the time elapsing was too brief to allow for a journey back to Rome and the establishment of the kind of residence there that Romans 16:3, 5 presupposes. But it is compatible with the known facts to interpose a period of approximately a year and on other reckonings more than a year. Aquila belonged to Pontus. Prisca and Aquila came from Rome after the edict of Claudius. They left Corinth with Paul and stayed in Ephesus. These migrations are of themselves indicative of the mobility of this couple and there is no reason to suppose that they had not returned to Rome. In view of their having come from Rome and their occupation as tentmakers it would have been easy to set up residence and business there again. In fact, a branch business in Rome may have required their return. In F. F. Bruce's words, "Tradespeople like Priscilla and Aquila led very mobile lives in those days, and there is nothing improbable or unnatural about

---

hypothesis comparatively weak, except for the tradition, yet he adds: "Still, the fact always remains that Rom. xvi. 1–23 is an integral part of all MSS. of the Epistle which we now possess. Thus the earliest tradition which we have connects it with Rome, not with Ephesus. This is not everything, but it is a great deal. Probably it is enough to prevent the Ephesian hypothesis from ever being unanimously accepted, and rightly so, for it can never be proven fully" (*op. cit.*, p. 334).

[19] *Op. cit.*, pp. 267–270.

their moving back and forth in this way between Rome, Corinth and Ephesus".[20]

The case for the integrity of the epistle as that addressed by Paul to the church at Rome may be summed up in the following observations.

1. The evidence clearly supports the Pauline authorship of chapters 15 and 16, including the doxology of 16:25–27.

2. The Pauline authorship of the doxology would not be in question even if it were placed after 15:33. It would be a fitting conclusion at this point. In that event chapter 16 would be an appendix largely devoted to greetings.

3. The only authority favouring this location for the doxology is P[46]. This is not enough to pit against the preponderant evidence for 16:25–27. Besides, it is contrary to Paul's uniform pattern to close an epistle without a benediction. Since there is not sufficient support for the benediction of 16:24, it would be a complete departure from Paul's custom to end an epistle with 16:23. The doxology is, indeed, a departure from pattern in that it is doxology and not a benediction. But its consonance as to content with the epistle as a whole, the distinctive character of the epistle itself, the analogy of 11:33–36 as the conclusion to a well-defined segment of the epistle, and the occurrence of benedictions at 15:13; 15:33 and 16:20 are considerations which combine to show the appropriateness of such a lengthy doxology at the end rather than the customary brief benediction.

4. If the doxology were placed after 15:33, this would constitute an additional argument for the genuineness of 16:24 and would remove the anomaly of an ending without a benediction. But the evidence for the doxology at an earlier point is not sufficient.

5. There is no good reason for positing Ephesus as the destination of 16:1–23. Thus we may conclude that the traditional position as supported by the preponderant evidence must continue to be accepted.

---

[20] *Ibid.*, p. 268.

INDEX OF CHIEF SUBJECTS

INDEX OF PERSONS AND PLACES

271

INDEX OF AUTHORS

INDEX OF SCRIPTURE REFERENCES
OLD TESTAMENT

INDEX OF SCRIPTURE REFERENCES
NEW TESTAMENT